Good Reasons with Contemporary Arguments

Reading, Designing, and Writing Effective Arguments

Second Edition

Lester Faigley
University of Texas at Austin

Jack Selzer
The Pennsylvania State University

PEARSON
Longman

New York San Francisco Boston
London Toronto Sydney Tokyo Singapore Madrid
Mexico City Munich Paris Cape Town Hong Kong Montreal

In memory of our teacher and friend,
James L. Kinneavy (1920–1999)

Senior Vice President and Publisher: Joseph Opiela
Vice President and Publisher: Eben W. Ludlow
Media Supplement Edition: Nancy García
Senior Supplements Editor: Donna Campion
Executive Marketing Manager: Ann Stypuloski
Senior Production Manager: Bob Ginsberg
Project Coordination, Text Design, and Electronic Page Makeup: Pre-Press Company, Inc.
Cover Design Manager: Nancy Danahy
Cover Designer: Keithley and Associates, Inc.
Cover Image: © Getty Images/Photodisc, Inc.
Manufacturing Buyer: Lucy Hebard
Printer and Binder: Courier Corporation Westford
Cover Printer: Phoenix Color Corporation

For permission to use copyrighted textual material, grateful acknowledgment is made to the copyright holders on pages 732–736, which are hereby made part of this copyright page.

Library of Congress Cataloging-in-Publication Data
Faigley, Lester, 1947–
   Good reasons with contemporary arguments: reading, designing, and
writing effective arguments / Lester Faigley, Jack Selzer.-- 2nd ed.
      p. cm.
Includes index.
   ISBN 0-321-17277-9
   1. English language--Rhetoric. 2. Persuasion (Rhetoric) 3. Report
writing. I. Selzer, Jack. II. Title.
   PE1431 .F35 2004
   808' .042--dc21   2003044607

Please visit our Web site at http://www.ablongman.com/faigley

ISBN 0-321-17277-9
1 2 3 4 5 6 7 8 9 10—CRW—06 05 04 03

PEARSON
Longman

Contents

On Censorship   599

Affirmative Action   660

Alternate Table of Contents: Types of Arguments

Evaluation Arguments

Narrative Arguments

Rebuttal Arguments

Preface

Like many other college writing teachers, we have come to believe that a course focusing on argument is an essential part of a college writing curriculum. Most students come to college with very little experience in reading and writing extended arguments. Because so much writing in college concerns arguments in the disciplines, a basic course in writing arguments is foundational for an undergraduate education. You will find that college courses frequently require you to analyze the structure of arguments, to identify competing claims, to weigh the evidence offered, to recognize assumptions, to locate contradictions, and to anticipate opposing views. The ability to write cogent arguments is also highly valued in most occupations that require college degrees. Just as important, you need to be able to read arguments critically and write arguments skillfully if you are to participate in public life after you leave college. The long-term issues that will affect your life after your college years—education, the environment, social justice, and the quality of life, to name a few—have many diverse stakeholders and long, complex histories. They cannot be reduced to slogans and sound bites. If you are to help make your views prevail in your communities, you must be able to participate in sustained give-and-take on a range of civic issues.

We find that other argument textbooks spend too much time on complicated schemes and terminology for analyzing arguments and too little time thinking about helping students produce real arguments that work. This book begins by considering why people take the time to write arguments in the first place. People write arguments because they want things to change. They want to change attitudes and beliefs about particular issues, and they want things done about problems they identify. We start out by making you examine exactly why you might want to write an argument and how what you write can lead to extended discussion and long-term results. We then provide you with practical means to find good reasons that support convincingly the positions you want to advocate. *Good Reasons* is also distinctive in its attention to the delivery and presentation of arguments—to the visual aspects of argument, in other words—and to arguments in electronic media. It encourages you to formulate arguments in different genres and different media.

Several textbooks on writing arguments have appeared in recent years that use Stephen Toulmin's method of analyzing arguments. We take a simpler approach. Toulmin's method provides useful analytic tools, but we do not find it a necessary one to teach the practical art of making arguments. In fact, our experience is that Toulmin's terminology is often more confusing than helpful. The key to the Toulmin method is understanding how warrants work. *Warrants*, in the Toulmin scheme, are the assumptions, knowledge, and beliefs that allow an audience to connect evidence with a claim. We feel that you will understand this concept better if you focus not on "Toulminizing" an argument but on conceptualizing the rhetorical situation—examining what assumptions, knowledge, and beliefs a particular audience might have about a specific issue. The only technical terms this book uses are the general classical concepts of *pathos, ethos,* and *logos:* sources of good reasons that emerge from the audience's most passionately held values, from the speaker's expertise and credibility, or from reasonable, commonsense thinking.

Likewise, you will not find explicit discussions of syllogisms or enthymemes in *Good Reasons.* We have avoided introducing these terms because, like the Toulmin terminology, they too often hinder rather than help. The crux of teaching argument, in our view, is to get you to appreciate its rhetorical nature. What makes a good reason *good* in public debate is not that it follows logically from a set of truth claims arranged in syllogisms but that the audience accepts the writer or speaker as credible and accepts the assumptions, knowledge, and beliefs on which the argument is based—and thus accepts the reasons given as *good reasons.*

Another difference is that our book does not make a sharp distinction between what some people think of as rational and irrational arguments. Rationality is a socially constructed concept. Until the twentieth century, it was rational to believe that women should not participate in politics. To question the absolute nature of rationality is not to say that rationality does not exist. Driving on the right side of the road is rational in North, South, and Central America and most of western Europe, just as driving on the left side is rational in Great Britain, Ireland, India, and Japan. But insisting on a dichotomy between rational and irrational has some unfortunate consequences, including a sharp division between argument and persuasion. Advertisements are often held up as typifying persuasion that plays to emotion rather than reason. Other pieces of writing, however, are not so easy to classify as either argument or persuasion. For example, personal and fictional narratives often include arguments or have an argumentative aim. Personal narratives are critical in many essays because they supply cultural knowledge of other perspectives and group experiences, which in turn enables the writer to advance good reasons in support of an argumentative purpose. We treat narratives in *Good Reasons* as an important aspect of argument. We also pay attention to ads and other genres of persuasion that are usually not represented in textbooks on argument. In short, you will find examples in the readings that illustrate the wide range of argument.

The dichotomy between rational and irrational also leads to an almost total neglect of the visual nature of writing. Visual thinking remains excluded from the mainstream literacy curriculum in the schools, and it is taught only in specialized courses in college in disciplines such as architecture and art history. This exclusion might be justified (though we would argue otherwise) if writing courses were still bound by the technology of the typewriter, but the great majority of college students today prepare their work on personal computers. Commonly used word processing programs and Web page editors now allow you to include pictures, icons, charts, and graphs, making design an important part of an argument. While we still believe that the heart of an argument course should be the critical reading and critical writing of prose, we also believe that the basics of visual persuasion should be included as well. In Part 3, therefore, you will find an extensive discussion of visual design and how good design can support good reasons in both written and oral arguments.

If our goal is to help you become an active citizen in a participatory democracy, then it would be counterproductive for us to ignore that most of the writing you will do in your future public and private life will be electronically mediated. Most students now have access to the most powerful publishing technology ever invented—the World Wide Web. Until very recently, students who published on the Web had to learn HTML and had to manipulate cumbersome file transfer programs. But current word processing programs and WYSIWYG ("what you see is what you get") editors now bypass the step of coding HTML, and the process of putting a Web page on a server has become almost as simple as opening a file on a PC. The Web has become a vast arena of argument, with nearly every interest group maintaining a Web presence. Chapter 13 provides an introduction to arguments on the Web.

The popularity of argument courses is not an accident. Even though we hear frequently that people have become cynical about politics, they are producing self-sponsored writing in quantities never before seen. It's almost as if people have rediscovered writing. While writing personal letters is perhaps becoming a lost art, participating in online discussion groups, putting up Web sites, and sending email have become commonplace. Citizen participation in local and national government forums, in a multitude of issue-related online discussions, and in other forms such as online magazines is increasing daily. You already have many opportunities to speak in the electronic polis. We want you to recognize and value the breadth of information available on the Internet and to evaluate, analyze, and synthesize that information. And we want to prepare you for the changing demands of the professions and public citizenship in your future.

Those goals govern our selection of example arguments included in Part 4: Contemporary Arguments. So that you can see how argument is a social act—that is, how arguments develop out of and respond to other arguments—we have grouped selections around interesting current issues: the environment, sexual difference, immigration, the body, controlling substances, censorship, affirmative action, and Title IX. We also include visual arguments on child labor. In each section, we represent a range of viewpoints so that you can see how arguers develop their points in response to the perspectives of others—and so that you might develop your own arguments (in some cases) around those various points of view. So that you can observe the range of argumentative styles and approaches that we discuss in the book, you will notice an unusual diversity in the samples provided: You will encounter not only a diversity of opinions and genres (including ads, cartoons, and photos as well as point arguments) but also a diversity of writers and writing styles. You will see arguments that originally appeared on the Internet and others from magazines and newspapers. You will encounter well-known citizens such as Richard Rodriguez, Alice Walker, Henry Louis Gates, Jr., bell hooks, Jesse Jackson, Anna Quindlen, and N. Scott Momaday as well as ordinary citizens who make extraordinary cases. And you will find examples of the kinds of arguments that we discuss throughout Parts 1 through 3: definitions, evaluations, causal arguments, narratives, refutations, and proposals.

Our goal in writing this text has been to offer in one book everything that you will need to become a more effective arguer and a more sophisticated reader of the arguments you encounter each day.

Companion Website and Instructor's Manual

The Companion Website to accompany *Good Reasons with Contemporary Arguments*, Second Edition (http://www.ablongman.com/faigley), written by Katherine Grubbs, offers a wealth of resources for both students and instructors. Students can access detailed chapter summaries and objectives, writing exercises, chapter review quizzes, and links to additional Web resources for further study. Instructors will find sample syllabi, Web resources, and the Instructor's Manual available for download.

The Instructor's Manual that accompanies this text was revised by Eric Lupfer and Victoria Davis and is designed to be useful for new and experienced instructors alike. The Instructor's Manual briefly discusses the ins and outs of teaching the material in each chapter. Also provided are in-class exercises, homework assignments, discussion questions for each reading selection, and model paper assignments and syllabi. This revised Instructor's Manual will make your work as a teacher a bit easier. Teaching argumentation and composition becomes a process that has genuine—and often surprising—rewards.

Acknowledgments

We are much indebted to the work of many outstanding scholars of argument and to our colleagues who teach argument at Texas and at Penn State. In particular, we thank the following reviewers for sharing their expertise: William A. Covino, Florida Atlantic University; Caley O'Dwyer Feagin, University of California, Irvine; Richard Fulkerson, Texas A&M University–Commerce; David Harvey, Central Arkansas University; Peggy Jolly, University of Alabama-Birmingham; Joe Law, Wright State University; Elizabeth Losh, University of California, Irvine; Bea Opengart, University of Cincinnati; Rise A. Quay, Heartland Community College; Gardner Rogers, University of Illinois at Urbana-Champaign; Jeffrey Walker, Emory University; Maria W. Warren, The University of West Florida; Patricia J. Webb, Maysville Community College; and Stephen Wilhoit, University of Dayton. We are especially grateful to our students, who have given us opportunities to test these materials in class and who have taught us a great deal about the nature of argument. The segment on Rick Reilly and Jenny Thompson was suggested by Jessica Horn. Andrew Alexander assisted us in finding selections and researching information for headnotes in Part 4. And several people suggested particular items or assisted us in obtaining permissions: Robert Burkholder and Anne Hoag of Penn State; Blake Scott, University of Central Florida; H. Lewis Ulman of Ohio State University; Timothy Crusius of Southern Methodist University; Deborah Anderson of Photosearch, Inc.; and Mike Kendall of Longman Publishers.

Our editor, Eben Ludlow, convinced us we should write this book and gave us wise guidance throughout. Elsa van Bergen and Katy Faria at Pre-Press, Bob Ginsberg and Bill Russo at Longman, and our copy editors, Carol Noble and Margery Niblock, all did splendid work in preparing our book for publication. Finally we thank our families, who make it all possible.

LESTER FAIGLEY
JACK SELZER

PART 1

Persuading with Good Reasons

What Do We Mean by Argument?

For over thirty years, the debate over legalized abortion has raged in the United States. The following scene is a familiar one: Outside an abortion clinic, a crowd of pro-life activists has gathered to try to stop women from entering the clinic. They carry signs that read "ABORTION = MURDER" and "A BABY'S LIFE IS A HUMAN LIFE." Pro-choice supporters are also present in a counterdemonstration. Their signs read "KEEP YOUR LAWS OFF MY BODY" and "WOMEN HAVE THE RIGHT TO CONTROL THEIR BODIES." Police keep the two sides apart, but they do not stop the shouts of "Murderer!" from the pro-life side and "If you're anti-abortion, don't have one!" from the pro-choice side.

When you imagine an argument, you might think of two people engaged in a heated exchange or two groups of people with different views, shouting back and forth at each other like the pro-choice and pro-life demonstrators. Or you might think of the arguing that occurs in the courthouse, where district attorneys and defense lawyers debate strenuously. Written arguments can resemble these oral arguments in being heated and one sided. For example, the signs that the pro-choice and pro-life demonstrators carry might be considered written arguments.

But in college courses, in public life, and in professional careers, written arguments are not thought of as slogans. Bumper stickers require no supporting evidence or reasons. Many other kinds of writing do not offer reasons either. An instruction manual, for example, does not try to persuade you. It assumes that you want to do whatever the manual tells you how to do; indeed, most people are willing to follow the advice, or else they would not be consulting the manual. Likewise, an article written by someone who is totally committed to a particular cause or belief often assumes that everyone should think the same way. These writers can count on certain phrases and words to produce predictable responses.

Effective arguments do not make the assumption that everyone should think the same way or hold the same beliefs. They attempt to change people's minds by convincing them of the validity of new ideas or that a particular course of action is the best one to take. Written arguments not only offer evidence and reasons but also often examine the assumptions on which they are based, think through opposing arguments, and anticipate objections. They explore positions thoroughly and take opposing views into account.

Extended written arguments make more demands on their readers than most other kinds of writing. Like bumper stickers, they often appeal to our emotions. But they typically do much more. They expand our knowledge with the depth of their analysis and lead us through a complex set of claims by providing networks of logical relations and appropriate evidence. They explicitly build on what has been written before by offering trails of sources, which also demonstrates that they can be trusted because the writers have done their homework. They cause us to reflect on what we read, in a process that we will shortly describe as critical reading.

Our culture is a competitive culture, and often the goal is to win. If you are a professional athlete, a top trial lawyer, or a candidate for president of the United States, it really is win big or lose. But most of us live in a world in which the opponents don't go away when the game is over. Even professional athletes have to play the team they beat in the championship game the next year.

In real life, most of us have to deal with the people who disagree with us at times but with whom we have to continue to work and live in the same communities. The idea of winning in such situations can only be temporary. Other situations will come up soon enough in which we will need the support of those who were on the other side of the current issue. Probably you can think of times when friendly arguments ended up with everyone involved coming to a better understanding of the others' views. And probably you can think of other times when someone was so concerned with winning an argument that even though the person might have been technically right, hard feelings were created that lasted for years.

Usually, listeners and readers are more willing to consider your argument seriously if you cast yourself as a respectful partner rather than as a competitor and put forth your arguments in the spirit of mutual support and negotiation—in the interest of finding the *best* way, not "my way." How can you be the person that your reader will want to cooperate with rather than resist? Here are a few suggestions, both for your writing and for discussing controversial issues in class:

- **Try to think of yourself as engaged not so much in winning over your audience as in courting your audience's cooperation.** It is important to argue vigorously, but you don't want to argue so vigorously that opposing views are vanquished or silenced. Remember that your goal is to invite a response that creates a dialog.

- **Show that you understand and genuinely respect your listener's or reader's position even if you think the position is ultimately wrong.** Often, that amounts to remembering to argue against an opponent's position, not against the opponent himself or herself. It often means representing your opponent's position in terms that your opponent would accept. Look for ground that you already share with your reader, and search for even more. See yourself as a mediator. Consider that neither you nor the other person has arrived at a best solution, and carry on in the hope that dialog will lead to an even better course of action than the one you now recommend. Expect and assume the best of your listener or reader, and deliver your own best yourself.

■ **Cultivate a sense of humor and a distinctive voice.** Many textbooks on argument emphasize using a reasonable voice. But a reasonable voice doesn't have to be a dull one. Humor is a legitimate tool of argument. Although playing an issue strictly for laughs risks not having the reader take it seriously, nothing creates a sense of goodwill quite so much as good humor. You will be seen as open to new possibilities and to cooperation if you occasionally show a sense of humor. And a sense of humor can sometimes be especially welcome when the stakes are high, the sides have been chosen, and tempers are flaring.

Consider that your argument might be just one move in a larger process that might end up helping *you*. Most times we argue because we think we have something to offer. But in the process of developing and presenting your views, realize also that you might learn something in the course of your research or from an argument that answers your own. Holding onto that attitude will keep you from becoming too overbearing and dogmatic.

CHAPTER 1

What to Argue About

A Book That Changed the World

In 1958, Rachel Carson received a copy of a letter that her friend Olga Huckens had sent to the *Boston Herald*. The letter described what had happened during the previous summer when Duxbury, Massachusetts, a small town just north of Cape Cod where Huckens lived, was sprayed several times from an airplane with the chemical pesticide DDT to kill mosquitoes. The mosquitoes came back as hungry as ever, but the songbirds, bees, and other insects vanished except for a few dead birds that Huckens had to pick up out of her yard. Huckens asked Carson if she knew anyone in Washington who could help to stop the spraying.

Rachel Carson

The letter from Olga Huckens struck a nerve with Rachel Carson. Carson was a marine biologist who had worked for many years for the U.S. Fish and Wildlife Service and who had written three highly acclaimed books about the sea and wetlands. In 1944, she published an article on how bats use radarlike echoes to find insects, which was reprinted in *Reader's Digest* in 1945. The editors at *Reader's Digest* asked whether she could write something else for them, and Carson replied in a letter that she wanted to write about experiments using DDT. DDT was being hyped as the solution for controlling insect pests, but Carson knew in 1945 that fish, waterfowl, and other animals would also be poisoned by widespread spraying and that eventually people could die too. *Reader's Digest* was not interested in Carson's proposed article, so she dropped the idea and went on to write about other things.

Huckens's letter brought Carson back to the subject of chemical spraying. In the late 1940s and 1950s, pesticides—especially the chlorinated hydrocarbons DDT, aldrin, and dieldrin—were sprayed on a massive scale throughout the United States and were hailed as a panacea for world hunger and famine. In 1957, much of the greater New York City area, including Long Island, was sprayed with DDT to kill gypsy moths. But there were noticeable side effects. Many people complained about not only birds, fish, and useful insects being killed but also their plants, shrubs, and pets. Other scientists had written about the dangers of massive spraying of pesticides, but they had not convinced the public of the hazards of pesticides and of the urgency for change.

Rachel Carson decided that she needed to write a magazine article about the facts of DDT. When she contacted *Reader's Digest* and other magazines, she found that they still would not consider publishing on the subject. Carson then concluded that she should write a short book. She knew that her job was not going to be an easy one because people in the United States still trusted science to solve all problems. Science had brought the "green revolution" that greatly increased crop yields through the use of chemical fertilizers and chemical pesticides. Carson's subject matter was also technical and difficult to communicate to the general public. The public did not think much at that time about air and water pollution, and most people were unaware that pesticides could poison humans as well as insects. And she was sure to face opposition from the pesticide industry, which had become a multimillion-dollar business. Carson knew the pesticide industry would do everything it could to stop her from publishing and to discredit her if she did.

Rachel Carson nonetheless wrote her book, *Silent Spring*. It sounded the alarm about the dangers caused by the overuse of pesticides, and the controversy it raised has still not ended. No book has had a greater impact on our thinking about the environment. *Silent Spring* was first published in installments in *The New Yorker* in the summer of 1962, and it created an immediate furor. Chemical companies threatened to sue Carson, and the trade associations that they sponsored launched full-scale attacks against the book in pamphlets and magazine articles. The chemical companies treated *Silent Spring* as a public relations problem; they hired scientists whose only job was to ridicule the book and to dismiss Carson as a "hysterical woman." Some even accused *Silent Spring* of being part of a communist plot to ruin U.S. agriculture.

But the public controversy over *Silent Spring* had another effect. It helped to make the book a success shortly after it published in September 1962. A half million hardcover copies of *Silent Spring* were sold, keeping it on the best-seller list for thirty-one weeks. President John F. Kennedy read *Silent Spring* and met with Carson and other scientists to discuss the pesticide problem. Kennedy requested that the President's Scientific Advisory Committee study the effects of pesticides and make a report.

> **That we still talk so much about the environment is testimony to the lasting power of *Silent Spring*.**

This report found evidence around the world of high levels of pesticides in the environment, including the tissues of humans. The report confirmed what Carson had described in *Silent Spring*.

In the words of a news commentator at the time, *Silent Spring* "lit a fire" under the government. Many congressional hearings were held on the effects of pesticides and other pollutants on the environment. In 1967, the Environmental Defense Fund was formed; it developed the guidelines under which DDT was eventually banned. Three years later, President Richard Nixon became convinced that only an independent agency within the executive branch could operate with enough independence to enforce environmental regulations. Nixon created the Environmental Protection Agency (EPA) in December 1970, and he named William Ruckelshaus as its first head. One of the missions of the EPA, according to Ruckelshaus, was to develop an environmental ethic.

The United States was not the only country to respond to *Silent Spring*. The book was widely translated and inspired legislation on the environment in nearly all industrialized nations. Moreover, it changed the way we think about the environment. Carson pointed out that the nerve gases that were developed for use on our enemies in World War II were being used as pesticides after the war. She criticized the view of the environment as a battlefield where people make war on those natural forces that they believe impede their progress. Instead, she advocated living in coexistence with the environment because we are part of it. She was not totally opposed to pesticides, but she wanted to make people more aware of the environment as a whole and how changing one part would affect other parts. Her message was to try to live in balance with nature. That we still talk so much about the environment is testimony to the lasting power of *Silent Spring*. In 1980, Rachel Carson was posthumously awarded the highest civilian decoration in the nation, the Presidential Medal of Freedom. The citation accompanying the award expresses the way she is remembered:

> Never silent herself in the face of destructive trends, Rachel Carson fed a spring of awareness across America and beyond. A biologist with a gentle, clear voice, she welcomed her audiences to her love of the sea, while with an equally clear voice she warned Americans of the dangers human beings themselves pose for their own environment. Always concerned, always eloquent, she created a tide of environmental consciousness that has not ebbed.

Why *Silent Spring* Became a Classic

A book that covered much of the same ground as *Silent Spring*, titled *Our Synthetic Environment*, had been published six months earlier. The author, Murray Bookchin, writing under the pen name Lewis Herber, also wrote about the pollution of the natural world and the effects on people. Bookchin was as committed to warning people about the hazards of pesticides as Carson, but *Our Synthetic Environment* was read only by a small community of scientists. Why, then, did Carson succeed in reaching a larger audience?

Rachel Carson had far more impact than Murray Bookchin not simply because she was a more talented writer or because she was a scientist while Bookchin was not. She also thought a great deal about who she was writing for—her **audience.** If she was going to stop the widespread spraying of dangerous pesticides, she knew she would have to connect with the values of a wide audience, an audience that included a large segment of the public as well as other scientists.

The opening chapter in *Silent Spring* begins not by announcing Carson's thesis or giving a list of facts. Instead, the book starts out with a short fable about a small town located in the middle of prosperous farmland, where wildflowers bloomed much of the year, trout swam in the streams, and wildlife was abundant. Suddenly, a strange blight came on the town, as if an evil spell had been cast upon it. The chickens, sheep, and cattle on the farms grew sick and died. The families of the townspeople and farmers alike developed mysterious illnesses. Most of the birds disappeared, and the few that remained could neither sing nor fly. The apple trees bloomed, but there were no bees to pollinate the trees, and so they bore no fruit. The wildflowers withered as if they had been burned. Fishermen quit going to the streams because the fish had all died.

But it wasn't witchcraft that caused everything to grow sick and die. Carson writes that "the people had done it to themselves." She continues, "I know of no community that has experienced all the misfortunes I describe. Yet every one of these disasters has actually happened somewhere, and many real communities have already suffered a substantial number of them. A grim specter has crept upon us almost unnoticed, and this imagined tragedy may easily become a stark reality." Carson's fable did happen several times after the book was published. In July 1976, a chemical reaction went out of control at a plant near Seveso, Italy, and a cloud of powdery white crystals of almost pure dioxin fell on the town. The children ran out to play in the powder because it looked like snow. Within four days, plants, birds, and animals began dying, and the next week, people started getting sick. Most of the people had to go to the hospital, and everyone had to move out of the town. An even worse disaster happened in December 1982, when a storage tank in a pesticide plant exploded near Bhopal, India, showering the town. Two thousand people died quickly, and another fifty thousand became sick for the rest of their lives.

Perhaps if Rachel Carson were alive today and writing a book about the dangers of pesticides, she might begin differently. But remember that at the time she was writing, people trusted pesticides and believed that DDT was a miracle solution for all sorts of insect pests. She first had to make people aware that DDT could be harmful to them. In the second chapter of *Silent Spring* (reprinted at the end of this chapter), Carson continued appealing to the emotions of her audience. People in 1962 knew about the dangers of radiation even if they were ignorant about pesticides. They knew that the atomic bombs that had been dropped on Hiroshima and Nagasaki at the end of World War II were still killing Japanese people through the effects of radiation many years later, and they feared the fallout from nuclear bombs that were still being tested and stockpiled in the United States and Soviet Union.

Getting people's attention by exposing the threat of pesticides wasn't enough by itself. There are always people writing about various kinds of threats, and most aren't taken seriously except by those who already believe that the threats exist. Carson wanted to reach people who didn't think that pesticides were a threat but might be persuaded to take this view. To convince these people, she had to explain why pesticides are potentially dangerous, and she had to make readers believe that she could be trusted.

Rachel Carson was an expert marine biologist. To write *Silent Spring*, she had to read widely in sciences that she had not studied, including research about insects, toxic chemicals, cell physiology, biochemistry, plant and soil science, and public health. Then she had to explain complex scientific processes to people who had very little or no background in science. It was a very difficult and frustrating task. While writing *Silent Spring*, Carson confided in a letter to a friend the problems she was having: "How to reveal

Tactics of *Silent Spring*

Chapter 1 of *Silent Spring* tells a parable of a rural town where the birds, fish, flowers, and plants die and people become sick after a white powder is sprayed on the town. At the beginning of Chapter 2, Rachel Carson begins her argument against the mass aerial spraying of pesticides. Most of her readers were not aware of the dangers of pesticides, but they were well aware of the harmful effects of radiation. Let's look at her tactics:

The history of life on earth has been a history of interaction between living things and their surroundings. To a large extent, the physical form and the habits of earth's vegetation and its animal life have been molded by the environment. Considering the whole span of earthly time, the opposite effect, in which life actually modifies its surroundings, has been relatively slight. Only within the moment of time represented by the present century has one species—man—acquired significant power to alter the nature of his world.

The interrelationship of people and the environment provides the basis for Carson's argument.

During the past quarter century this power has not only increased to one of disturbing magnitude but it has changed in character. The most alarming of all man's assaults upon the environment is the contamination of air, earth, rivers, and sea with dangerous and even lethal materials. This pollution is for the most part irrecoverable; the chain of life it initiates not only in the world that must support life but in living tissues is for the most part irreversible. In this now universal contamination of the environment, chemicals are the sinister and little-recognized partners of radiation in changing the very nature of the world—the very nature of its life. Strontium 90, released through nuclear explosions into the air, comes to earth in rain or drifts down as fallout, lodges in the soil, enters into the grass or corn or wheat grown there, and in time takes its abode in the

Carson shifts her language to a metaphor of war against the environment rather than interaction with the natural world.

In 1963 the first treaty was signed by the United States and the Soviet Union that banned the testing of nuclear weapons above ground, under water, and in space.

(continued)

Tactics of *Silent Spring* (continued)

bones of a human being, there to remain until his death. Similarly, chemicals sprayed on croplands or forests or gardens lie long in soil, entering into living

The key move: Carson associates the dangers of chemical pesticides with those of radiation.

organisms, passing from one to another in a chain of poisoning and death. Or they pass mysteriously by underground streams until they emerge and, through the alchemy of air and sunlight, combine into new forms that kill vegetation, sicken cattle, and work unknown harm on those who drink from once-pure wells. As Albert Schweitzer has said, "Man can hardly even recognize the devils of his own creation."

Albert Schweitzer (1875–1965) was a concert musician, philosopher, and doctor who spent most of his life as a medical missionary in Africa.

---

enough to give understanding of the most serious effects of the chemicals without being technical, how to simplify without error—these have been problems of rather monumental proportions."

To make people understand the bad effects of pesticides required explaining what is not common sense: why very tiny amounts of pesticides can be so harmful. The reason lies in how pesticides are absorbed by the body. DDT is fat-soluble and gets stored in organs such as the adrenals, thyroid, liver, and kidneys. Carson explains how pesticides build up in the body:

> This storage of DDT begins with the smallest conceivable intake of the chemical (which is present as residues on most foodstuffs) and continues until quite high levels are reached. The fatty storage deposits act as biological magnifiers, so that an intake of as little as $\frac{1}{10}$ of 1 part per million in the diet results in storage of about 10 to 15 parts per million, an increase of one hundredfold or more. These terms of reference, so commonplace to the chemist or the pharmacologist, are unfamiliar to most of us. One part in a million sounds like a very small amount—and so it is. But such substances are so potent that a minute quantity can bring about vast changes in the body. In animal experiments, 3 parts per million has been found to inhibit an essential enzyme in the heart muscle; only 5 parts per million has brought about necrosis or disintegration of liver cells.

Throughout the book, Carson succeeds in translating scientific facts into language that, to use her words, "most of us" can understand. Of course Carson was a scientist and quite capable of reading scientific articles. She establishes her credibility as a scientist by using technical terms such as *necrosis*. But at the same time she identifies herself with people who are not scientists and gains our trust by taking our point of view.

To accompany these facts, Carson tells about places that have been affected by pesticides. One of the more memorable stories is about Clear Lake, California, in the mountainous country north of San Francisco. Clear Lake is popular for fishing, but it is also an ideal habitat for a species of gnat. In the late 1940s the state of California began spraying the lake with DDD, a close relative of DDT. Spraying had to be repeated because the gnats kept coming back. The western grebes that lived on the lake began to die, and when scientists examined their bodies, the grebes were loaded with extraordinary levels of DDD. Microscopic plants and animals filtered the lake water for nutrients and concentrated the pesticides at 20 times their level in the lake water. Small fish ate these tiny plants and animals and again concentrated the DDD at levels 10 to 100 times that of their microscopic food. The grebes that ate the fish suffered the effects of this huge magnification.

Although DDT is still used in parts of the developing world, the influence of *Silent Spring* led to the banning of it and most other similar pesticides in the United States and Canada. Rachel Carson's book eventually led people to stop relying only on pesticides and to look instead to other methods of controlling pests, such as planting crops that are resistant to insects and disease. When pesticides are used today, they typically are applied much more selectively and in lower amounts than was common when Carson was writing.

Rachel Carson's more lasting legacy is our awareness of our environment. She urges us to be aware that we share this planet with other creatures and that "we are dealing with life—with living populations and all their pressures and counterpressures, their surges and recessions." She warns against dismissing the balance of nature. She writes:

> The balance of nature is not the same today as in Pleistocene times, but it is still there: a complex, precise, and highly integrated system of relationships between living things which cannot safely be ignored any more than the law of gravity can be defied with impunity by a man perched on the edge of a cliff. The balance of nature is not a *status quo*; it is fluid, ever shifting, in a constant state of adjustment.

Since the publication of *Silent Spring*, we have grown much more conscious of large-scale effects on ecosystems caused by global warming, acid rain, and the depleted ozone layer in addition to the local effects of pesticides described in Carson's book. The cooperation of nations today in attempting to control air and water pollution, in encouraging more efficient use of energy and natural resources, and in promoting sustainable patterns of consumption is due in no small part to the long-term influence of *Silent Spring*.

Analyzing Arguments: Pathos, Ethos, and Logos

When the modern concept of democracy was developed in Greece in the fifth century B.C.E., the study of rhetoric also began. It's not a coincidence that the teaching of rhetoric was closely tied to the rise of democracy. In the Greek city-states, all citizens had the right to speak and vote at the popular assembly and in the committees of the assembly that functioned as the criminal courts. Citizens took turns serving as the officials of government. Because the citizens of Athens and other city-states took their responsibilities quite seriously, they highly valued the ability to speak effectively in public. Teachers of rhetoric were held in great esteem.

In the next century, the most important teacher of rhetoric in ancient Greece, Aristotle (384–323 B.C.E.), made the study of rhetoric systematic. He defined *rhetoric* as the art of finding the best available means of persuasion in any situation. Aristotle set out three primary tactics of argument: appeals to the emotions and deepest-held values of the audience (*pathos*), appeals based on the trustworthiness of the speaker (*ethos*), and appeals to good reasons (*logos*).

Carson makes these appeals with great skill in *Silent Spring*. Very simply, her purpose is to stop pesticide pollution. She first appeals to *pathos*, engaging her readers in her subject. She gives many specific examples of how pesticides have accumulated in the bodies of animals and people. But she also engages her readers through her skill as a writer, making us care about nature as well as be concerned about our own safety. She uses the fate of robins to symbolize her crusade. Robins were the victims of spraying for Dutch elm disease. Robins feed on earthworms, which in turn process fallen elm leaves. The earthworms act as magnifiers of the pesticide, which either kills the robins outright or renders them sterile. Thus when no robins sang, it was indeed a silent spring.

Carson is also successful in creating a credible *ethos*. We believe her not just because she establishes her expertise. She convinces us also because she establishes her ethos as a person with her audience's best interests at heart. She anticipates possible objections, demonstrating that she has thought about opposing positions. She takes time to explain concepts that most people do not understand fully, and she discusses how everyone can benefit if we take a different attitude toward nature. She shows that she has done her homework on the topic. By creating a credible ethos,

(continued)

Analyzing Arguments: Pathos, Ethos, and Logos *(continued)*

Carson makes an effective moral argument that humans as a species have a responsibility not to destroy the world they live in.

Finally, Carson supports her argument with good reasons, what Aristotle called *logos*. She offers "because clauses" to support her main claims. She describes webs of relationships among the earth, plants, animals, and humans, and she explains how changing one part will affect the others. Her point is not that we should never disturb these relationships but that we should be as aware as possible of the consequences.

Reading Arguments

If you have ever been coached in a sport or have been taught an art such as dancing or playing a musical instrument, you likely have viewed a game or a performance in two ways. You might enjoy the game or performance like everyone else, but at the same time, you might be especially aware of something that you know from your experience is difficult to do and therefore appreciated the skill and the practice necessary to develop it. A similar distinction can be made about two kinds of reading. For the sake of convenience, the first can be called *ordinary reading*, although we don't really think there is a single kind of ordinary reading. In ordinary reading, on the first time through, the reader forms a sense of content and gets an initial impression: whether it's interesting, whether the author has something important to say, whether you agree or disagree.

For most of what you read, one time through is enough. When you read for the second or third time, you start to use different strategies because you have some reason to do so. You are no longer reading to form a sense of the overall content. Often, you are looking for something in particular. If you reread a textbook chapter, you might want to make sure you understand how a key concept is being used. When you reread your apartment contract, you might want to know what is required to get your deposit back. This second kind of reading can be called *critical reading*. Critical reading does not mean criticizing what the writer has to say (although that's certainly possible). Critical reading begins with questions and specific goals.

Writers of arguments engage in critical reading even on the first time through. They know that they will have to acknowledge what else has been written about a particular issue. If the issue is new (and few are), then the writer will need to establish its significance by comparing it to other issues on

Become a Critical Reader

The best way to read arguments is with a pencil—not a pen or high-lighter. Pens don't erase, and highlighters are distracting. Much of the time, you don't know what is important the first time through an argument, and highlighters don't tell you why something is important. Use a pencil instead, and write in the margins.

If you are reading on a computer screen, open a new window in your word processing program so that you can write while you read. Reading on a computer has the advantage of letting you copy parts of what you read to your file. You just have to be careful to distinguish what you copy from what you write. Always remember to include the information about where it came from. (Your Web browser allows you to copy text and paste it in a new file. Look in the Edit menu on Netscape or Internet Explorer.)

Before you start reading, find out when the argument was written, where it first appeared, and who wrote it. Arguments don't appear in vacuums. They most often occur in response to something else that has been written or some event that has happened. In this book, you'll find this information in the headnotes. You also have a title, which suggests what the argument might be about. This information will help you to form an initial impression about why the writer wrote this particular argument, who the writer imagined as the readers, and what purposes the writer might have had in mind. Then pick up your pencil and start reading.

Ask Questions

On the first time through, you need to understand what's in the argument. So circle the words and references that you don't know and look them up. If a statement part of the argument isn't clear, note that section in the margin. You might figure out what the writer is arguing later, or you might have to work through it slowly a second time through.

Analyze

On your second reading, you should start analyzing the structure of the argument. Here's how to do it:

- Identify the writer's main claim or claims. You should be able to para-phrase it if it doesn't appear explicitly.

(continued)

Become a Critical Reader *(continued)*

- What are the reasons that support the claim? List them by number in the margins. There might be only one reason, or there could be several (and some reasons could be supported by others).

- Where is the evidence? Does it really support the reasons? Can you think of contradictory evidence?

- Does the writer refer to expert opinion or research about this subject? Do other experts see this issue differently?

- Does the writer acknowledge opposing views? Does the writer deal fairly with opposing views?

Respond

Write your thoughts as you read. Often you will find that something you read reminds you of something else. Jot that down. It might be something to think about later, and it might give you ideas for writing. Think also about what else you should read if you want to write about this topic. Or you might want to write down whether you are persuaded by the argument and why.

which much has been written. Writers of argument, therefore, begin reading with **questions.** They want to know *why* a particular argument was written. They want to know *what* the writer's basic assumptions are. They want to know *who* the writer had in mind when the argument was written. Critical readers most often read with pen or pencil in hand or with a window open on their computer in which they can write. They write their questions in the margins or in the file.

Critical readers do more than just question what they read. They **analyze** how the argument works. Critical readers look at how an argument is laid out. They identify key terms and examine how the writer is using them. They consider how the writer appeals to our emotions, represents himself or herself, and uses good reasons. They analyze the structure of an argument—the organization—and the way in which it is written—the style.

Finally, critical readers often **respond** as they read. They don't just take in what they read in a passive way. They jot down notes to themselves in the margins or on the blank pages at the front and back of a book. They use these notes later when they start writing. Reading is often the best way to get started writing.

Finding Arguments

Rachel Carson did not so much find the subject for *Silent Spring* as the subject found her. She wrote about a subject that she had cared about for many years. Subjects that we argue about often find us. There are enough of them in daily life. We're late for work because the traffic is bad or the bus doesn't run on time. We can't find a place to park when we get to school or work. We have to negotiate through various bureaucracies for almost anything we do—making an appointment to see a doctor, getting a course added or dropped, or correcting a mistake on a bill. Most of the time, we grumble and let it go at that.

But sometimes, like Rachel Carson, we stick with a subject. Neighborhood groups in cities and towns have been especially effective in getting things done by writing about them—from stopping a new road from being built to getting better police and fire protection to having a vacant lot turned into a park. Most jobs that require college degrees sooner or later demand the ability to write extended arguments. Usually, it is sooner; the primary cause of new employees being fired during their first year at *Fortune* 500 companies is poor communications skills. If your writing skills are not up to speed, you may pay heavily down the road.

Being either inspired or required to write an argument is only the beginning. Once Rachel Carson decided that she wanted to write a book about the hazards of pesticides, she did her homework before she started writing. She used these questions as guides to her research:

- How do pesticides work?
- Why are pesticides used?
- Who and what benefits from the use of pesticides?
- Who or what is harmed by the use of pesticides?
- Who creates pesticides?
- Who supports the use of pesticides?
- When can pesticides be used beneficially? When is their use harmful?
- What alternatives to pesticides are feasible?

Position and Proposal Arguments

In *Silent Spring*, Rachel Carson made an effective argument against the massive use of synthetic pesticides. Arguing against the indiscriminate use of pesticides, however, did not solve the problem of what to do about harmful insects that destroy crops and spread disease. Carson also did the harder job of offering solutions. In her final chapter, "The Other Road," Carson gives alternatives to the massive use of pesticides. She describes how a pest organism's natural enemies can be used against it instead.

These two kinds of arguments can be characterized as **position** and **proposal** arguments.

Position Arguments

In a position argument, the writer makes a claim about a controversial issue.

- **The writer first has to define the issue.** Carson had to explain what synthetic pesticides are in chemical terms and how they work, and she had to give a history of their increasing use after World War II before she could begin arguing against pesticides.

- **The writer should take a clear position.** Carson wasted no time setting out her position by describing the threat that high levels of pesticides pose to people worldwide.

- **The writer should make a convincing argument and acknowledge opposing views.** Carson used a variety of strategies in support of her position, including research studies, quotes from authorities, and her own analyses and observations. She took into account opposing views by acknowledging that harmful insects needed to be controlled and conceded that selective spraying is necessary and desirable.

Proposal Arguments

In a proposal argument, the writer proposes a course of action in response to a recognizable problem situation. The proposal says what can be done to improve the situation or change it altogether.

- **The writer first has to define the problem.** The problem Carson had to define was complex. Not only was the overuse of pesticides

(continued)

Position and Proposal Arguments *(continued)*

killing helpful insects, plants, and animals and threatening people, but the harmful insects the pesticides were intended to eliminate were becoming increasingly resistant. More spraying and more frequent spraying produced pesticide-resistant "superbugs." Mass spraying resulted in actually helping bad bugs such as fire ants by killing off their competition.

- **The writer has to propose a solution or solutions.** Carson did not hold out for one particular approach to controlling insects, but she did advocate biological solutions. She proposed biological alternatives to pesticides, such as sterilizing and releasing large numbers of male insects and introducing predators of pest insects. Above all, she urged that we work with nature rather than being at war with it.

- **The solution or solutions must work, and they must be feasible.** The projected consequences should be set out, arguing that good things will happen, bad things will be avoided, or both. Carson discussed research studies that indicated her solutions would work, and she argued that they would be less expensive than massive spraying. Today, we can look at Carson's book with the benefit of hindsight. Not everything Carson proposed ended up working, but her primary solution—learn to live with nature—has been a powerful one. Mass spraying of pesticides has stopped in the United States, and species that were threatened by the excessive use of pesticides, including falcons, eagles, and brown pelicans, have made remarkable comebacks.

In much the same way, you can explore a topic by asking questions.

Carson also kept in mind what had been written before about the environment. She was trained as a scientist, and she could have written only for other scientists. But she wanted to reach a much wider audience, and she wanted people to think about more than just the hazards of pesticides. She wanted to create a revolution in the way we think about the environment. Carson's respect for the integrity and interconnectedness of life contributed a great deal to the power of her argument. Her goal was not so much to make chemical companies into the Evil Ones as it was to promote a different way of thinking that would reconnect people with the world around them. She alludes to Robert Frost's poem "The Road Not Taken" for her concluding chapter, "The Other Road." "We stand now where two roads diverge," she says, the one "a smooth superhighway on which we progress with great speed" but on which disaster lies at the end, the other the road "less-traveled" but on which is our chance to preserve the earth. The greatest legacy of *Silent Spring* is that we are still concerned with and actively discussing the issues she raised.

RACHEL CARSON

The Obligation to Endure

Rachel Carson (1907–1964) was born and grew up in Springdale, Pennsylvania, eighteen miles up the Allegheny River from Pittsburgh. When Carson was in elementary school, her mother was fearful of infectious diseases that were sweeping through the nation and often kept young Rachel out of school. In her wandering on the family farm, Rachel developed the love of nature that she maintained throughout her life. At twenty-two she began her career as a marine biologist at Woods Hole, Massachusetts, and she later went to graduate school at Johns Hopkins University in Baltimore. She began working for the U.S. government in 1936 in the agency that later became the Fish and Wildlife Service, and she was soon recognized as a talented writer as well as a meticulous scientist. She wrote three highly praised books about the sea and wetlands: Under the Sea Wind *(1941),* The Sea around Us *(1951), and* The Edge of the Sea *(1954).*

Carson's decision to write Silent Spring *marked a great change in her life. For the first time, she became an environmental activist rather than an inspired and enthusiastic writer about nature. She had written about the interconnectedness of life in her previous three books, but with* Silent Spring *she had to convince people that hazards lie in what had seemed familiar and harmless. Although many people think of birds when they hear Rachel Carson's name, she was the first scientist to make a comprehensive argument that links cancer to environmental causes. Earlier in this chapter, you saw how Carson associated pesticides with the dangers of radiation from nuclear weapons. Notice how else she gets her readers to think differently about pesticides in this selection, which begins Chapter 2 of* Silent Spring.

1 THE history of life on earth has been a history of interaction between living things and their surroundings. To a large extent, the physical form and the habits of the earth's vegetation and its animal life have been molded by the environment. Considering the whole span of earthly time, the opposite effect, in which life actually modifies its surroundings, has been relatively slight. Only within the moment of time represented by the present century has one species—man—acquired significant power to alter the nature of his world.

2 During the past quarter century this power has not only increased to one of disturbing magnitude but it has changed in character. The most alarming of all man's assaults upon the environment is the contamination of air, earth, rivers, and sea with dangerous and even lethal materials. This pollution is for the most part irrecoverable; the chain of evil it initiates not only in the world that must support life but in living tissues is for the most part irreversible. In this now universal contamination of the environment, chemicals are the sinister and little recognized partners of radiation in changing the very nature of the world—the very nature of its life. Strontium 90, released through nuclear explosions into the air, comes to earth in rain or drifts down as fallout, lodges in soil, enters into the grass or corn or wheat grown there, and in time takes up its abode in the bones of a human being, there to remain until his death. Similarly, chemicals sprayed on croplands or forests or gardens lie long in soil, entering into living organisms, passing from one to another in a chain of poisoning and death. Or they pass mysteriously by underground streams until they emerge and, through the alchemy of air and sunlight, combine into new forms that kill vegetation, sicken cattle, and work unknown harm on those who drink from once-pure wells. As Albert Schweitzer has said, "Man can hardly even recognize the devils of his own creation."

3 It took hundreds of millions of years to produce the life that now inhabits the earth—eons of time in which that developing and evolving and diversifying life reached a state of adjustment and balance with its surroundings. The environment, rigorously shaping and directing the life it supported, contained elements that were hostile as well as supporting. Certain rocks gave out dangerous radiation; even within the light of the sun, from which all life draws its energy, there were short-wave radiations with power to injure. Given time—time not in years but in millennia—life adjusts, and a balance has been reached. For time is the essential ingredient; but in the modern world there is no time.

4   The rapidity of change and the speed with which new situations are created follow the impetuous and heedless pace of man rather than the deliberate pace of nature. Radiation is no longer merely the background radiation of rocks, the bombardment of cosmic rays, the ultraviolet of the sun that have existed before there was any life on earth; radiation is now the unnatural creation of man's tampering with the atom. The chemicals to which life is asked to make its adjustment are no longer merely the calcium and silica and copper and all the rest of the minerals washed out of the rocks and carried in rivers to the sea; they are the synthetic creations of man's inventive mind, brewed in his laboratories, and having no counterparts in nature.

5   To adjust to these chemicals would require time on the scale that is nature's; it would require not merely the years of a man's life but the life of generations. And even this, were it by some miracle possible, would be futile, for the new chemicals come from our laboratories in an endless stream; almost five hundred annually find their way into actual use in the United States alone. The figure is staggering and its implications are not easily grasped—500 new chemicals to which the bodies of men and animals are required somehow to adapt each year, chemicals totally outside the limits of biologic experience.

6   Among them are many that are used in man's war against nature. Since the mid-1940s over 200 basic chemicals have been created for use in killing insects, weeds, rodents, and other organisms described in the modern vernacular as "pests"; and they are sold under several thousand different brand names.

7   These sprays, dusts, and aerosols are now applied almost universally to farms, gardens, forests, and homes—nonselective chemicals that have the power to kill every insect, the "good" and the "bad," to still the song of birds and the leaping of fish in the streams, to coat the leaves with a deadly film, and to linger on in soil—all this though the intended target may be only few weeds or insects. Can anyone believe it is possible to lay down such a barrage of poisons on the surface of the earth without making it unfit for all life? They should not be called "insecticides," but "biocides."

8   The whole process of spraying seems caught up in an endless spiral. Since DDT was released for civilian use, a process of escalation has been going on in which ever more toxic materials must be found. This has happened because insects, in a triumphant vindication of Darwin's principle of the survival of the fittest, have evolved super races immune to the par-

ticular insecticide used, hence a deadlier one has always to be developed—and then a deadlier one than that. It has happened also because, for reasons to be described later, destructive insects often undergo a "flareback," or resurgence, after spraying, in numbers greater than before. Thus the chemical war is never won, and all life is caught in its violent crossfire.

9   Along with the possibility of the extinction of mankind by nuclear war, the central problem of our age has therefore become the contamination of man's total environment with such substances of incredible potential for harm—substances that accumulate in the tissues of plants and animals and even penetrate the germ cells to shatter or alter the very material of heredity upon which the shape of the future depends.

10   Some would-be architects of our future look toward a time when it will be possible to alter the human germ plasm by design. But we may easily be doing so now by inadvertence, for many chemicals, like radiation, bring about gene mutations. It is ironic to think that man might determine his own future by something so seemingly trivial as the choice of an insect spray.

11   All this has been risked—for what? Future historians may well be amazed by our distorted sense of proportion. How could intelligent beings seek to control a few unwanted species by a method that contaminated the entire environment and brought the threat of disease and death even to their own kind? Yet this is precisely what we have done. We have done it, moreover, for reasons that collapse the moment we examine them. We are told that the enormous and expanding use of pesticides is necessary to maintain farm production. Yet is our real problem not one of *overproduc-tion?* Our farms, despite measures to remove acreages from production and to pay farmers *not* to produce, have yielded such a staggering excess of crops that the American taxpayer in 1962 is paying out more than one billion dollars a year as the total carrying cost of the surplus-food storage program. And is the situation helped when one branch of the Agriculture Department tries to reduce production while another states, as it did in 1958, "It is believed generally that reduction of crop acreages under provisions of the Soil Bank will stimulate interest in use of chemicals to obtain maximum production on the land retained in crops."

12   All this is not to say there is no insect problem and no need of control. I am saying, rather, that control must be geared to realities, not to mythical situations, and that the methods employed must be such that they do not destroy us along with the insects.

Getting Started: Listing and Analyzing Issues

A good way to get started is to list possible issues to write about. Make a list of questions that can be answered "YES because . . ." or "NO because . . ." (Following is a list to get you started.) These questions all ask whether we should do something, and therefore they are all phrased as arguments of policy. You'll find out that often before you can make recommendations of policy, you first have to analyze exactly what is meant by a phrase like *censorship of the Internet*. Does it mean censorship of the World Wide Web or of everything that goes over the Internet, including private email? To be convincing, you'll have to argue that one thing causes another, for good or bad.

Think about issues that affect your campus, the place where you live, the nation, and the world. Which ones interest you? In which could you make a contribution to the larger discussion?

Campus

- Should students be required to pay fees for access to computers on campus?
- Should smoking be banned on campus?
- Should varsity athletes get paid for playing sports that bring in revenue?
- Should admissions decisions be based exclusively on academic achievement?
- Should knowledge of a foreign language be required for all degree plans?
- Should your college or university have a computer literacy requirement?
- Should fraternities be banned from campuses if they are caught encouraging alcohol abuse?

Community

- Should people who ride bicycles and motorcycles be required to wear helmets?
- Should high schools be allowed to search students for drugs at any time?
- Should high schools distribute condoms?
- Should bilingual education programs be eliminated?
- Should the public schools be privatized?
- Should bike lanes be built throughout your community to encourage more people to ride bicycles?
- Should more tax dollars be shifted from building highways to public transportation?

Nation/World

- Should advertising be banned on television shows aimed at preschool children?
- Should capital punishment be abolished?
- Should the Internet be censored?
- Should the government be allowed to monitor all phone calls and all email to combat terrorism?
- Should handguns be outlawed?
- Should beef and poultry be free of growth hormones?
- Should a law be passed requiring that the parents of teenagers who have abortions be informed?
- Should people who are terminally ill be allowed to end their lives?
- Should it be made illegal to kill animals for their fur?
- Should the United States punish nations with poor human rights records?

After You Make a List

1. Put a check beside the issues that look most interesting to write about or the ones that mean the most to you.
2. Put a question mark beside the issues that you don't know very much about. If you choose one of these issues, you will probably have to do in-depth research—by talking to people, by using the Internet, or by going to the library.
3. Select the two or three issues that look most promising. For each issue, make another list:
   - Who is most interested in this issue?
   - Whom or what does this issue affect?
   - What are the pros and cons of this issue? Make two columns. At the top of the left one, write "YES because." At the top of the right one, write "NO because."
   - What has been written about this issue? How can you find out what has been written?

Getting Started: Making an Idea Map

When you identify an issue that looks promising and interests you, the next step is to discover how much you know about it and how many different aspects of it you can think of. One way to take this inventory is to make an *idea map* that describes visually how the many aspects of a particular issue relate to each other. Idea maps are useful because you can see everything at once and make connections among the different aspects of an issue—definitions, causes, effects, proposed solutions, and your personal experience.

A good way to get started is to write down ideas on sticky notes. Then you can move the sticky notes around until you figure out which ideas fit together.

As an example, let's say you pick binge drinking among college students. Several stories have been in your campus newspaper this year about binge drinking. You read an article recently that reported the results of an annual study of student drinking behavior done by Harvard University's School of Public Health. From this article you have a few statistics and facts to go with your knowledge of binge drinking. Figure 1.1 shows what your idea map might look like after you assemble your notes.

Harvard survey released March 2000
- 44% of 14,000 students surveyed at 119 schools reported that they had binged at least once in the preceding 2 weeks
- 23% are frequent bingers
- Little change in drinking patterns since 1994
- Increase in drinking deliberately to get drunk, and in alcohol-related problems—including injuries, drunk driving, violence, and academic difficulties

Causes of binge drinking
- Binge drinking is a part of college culture
- Alumni and students binge at tailgate parties at sporting events
- Many bars and liquor stores close to campus
- Many alcohol promotions such as 2-for-1 happy hours and free nights for women
- Administrators condone drinking
- No exams on Friday allow students to binge Thursday through Sunday

Experience with binge drinking
- Three students on my dorm floor are regular binge drinkers and become obnoxious
- Not enough alcohol-free alternatives at my school
- Legal drinking age of 21 leads to more drinking rather than less because it gives alcohol a mystique
- Students under much pressure and look for a release

Definition of binge drinking
- More than 5 drinks a night for men
- More than 4 drinks a night for women

Binge Drinking

Fraternities and sororities
- Harvard study reports 4 of 5 residents in fraternities and sororities binge
- Most recent alcohol-related deaths of college students involved fraternity parties
- High school seniors often go to fraternity parties
- Administrators hesitant to regulate fraternities for fear of angering alumni donors

Effects of binge drinking
- Rise in alcohol-related deaths on campus
- Colleges are being sued by families of students injured by excessive drinking
- Rise in alcohol-related problems including drunk driving and academic difficulties
- Binge drinkers harm nonbingers, interrupting sleep, committing violent acts, driving drunk

Proposed solutions to binge drinking
- Education campaigns about risks of binge drinking
- Ban alcohol in residence halls and in fraternities and sororities
- Ban alcohol and alcohol ads at sporting events
- Punish disruptive behavior
- Notify parents when students binge
- Provide alcohol-free alternatives

Figure 1.1   Idea Map on Binge Drinking

CHAPTER 2

Finding Good Reasons

The Basics of Arguments

Many people think of the term *argument* as a synonym for *debate*. College courses and professional careers, however, require a different kind of argument—one that, most of the time, is cooler in emotion and much more elaborate in detail than oral debate. At first glance an **argument** in writing doesn't seem to have much in common with debate. But the basic elements and ways of reasoning used in written arguments are similar to those we use in everyday conversations. Let's look at an example of an informal debate:

> **JEFF:** I think students should not have to pay tuition to go to state colleges and universities.
>
> **MARIA:** Cool idea, but why should students not have to pay?
>
> **JEFF:** Because you don't have to pay to go to high school.
>
> **MARIA:** Yeah, but that's different. The law says that everyone has to go to high school, at least to age 16. Everyone doesn't have to go to college.
>
> **JEFF:** Well, in some other countries like the United Kingdom, students don't have to pay tuition.

MARIA: The whole system of education is different in Britain from the United States. Plus you're wrong. Students started paying tuition at British universities in fall 1998.

JEFF: OK, maybe the United Kingdom isn't a good example. But students should have a right to go to college, just like they have the right to drive on the highway.

MARIA: Jeff, you pay for driving through taxes. Everyone who buys gas and has a driver's license helps pay for the highways. Going to college isn't necessary, and not everyone does it. Only people who go to college should pay. Why should everyone have to pay taxes for some people to go to college?

JEFF: Because our nation would be better if everyone had the opportunity to go to college free of charge.

MARIA: Why? What evidence do you have that things would be better if everyone went to college? It would put an enormous drain on the economy. People would have to pay a lot more in taxes.

JEFF: The way to help poor people is to provide them with a good education. That's what's wrong now: Poor people don't get a good education and can't afford to go to college.

In this discussion, Jeff starts out by making a **claim** that students should not have to pay tuition. Maria immediately asks him why students should not have to pay tuition. She wants a **good reason** to accept his claim. A reason is typically offered in a **because clause** that begins with the

> **A good reason works because it includes a link to your claim that your readers will find valid.**

word *because* and then provides a supporting reason for the claim. Jeff's first attempt is to argue that students shouldn't have to pay to go to college *because* they don't have to pay to go to high school.

The word *because* signals a **link** between the reason and the claim. When Jeff tells Maria that students don't have to pay to go to public high schools, Maria does not accept the link. Maria asks **"So what?"** every time Jeff presents a new reason. She will accept Jeff's evidence only if she accepts that his reason supports his claim.

In this small discussion, we find the basics of arguments. Jeff makes a claim for which he offers a reason.

CLAIM ⬅━━ REASON

Every argument that is more than a shouting match or a simple assertion has to be supported by one or more reasons. That reason in turn has to be linked to the claim if it is to become a *good reason*.

CLAIM ◄━━ *LINK (because)* ◄━━ REASON

Jeff's problem in convincing Maria is that he can't convince her to link his reasons to his claim. Maria challenges Jeff's links and keeps asking "So what?" For her, Jeff's reasons are not good reasons.

CLAIM ◄━━ *LINK (because)* ◄━━ REASON
↑
CHALLENGES (So what?)

By the end of this short discussion, Jeff has begun to build an argument. He has had to come up with another claim to support his main claim, and if he is to convince Maria, he will probably have to provide a **series of claims** that she will accept as linked to his primary claim. He will also need to find evidence to support these claims.

CLAIM ◄━━ *LINK (because)* ◄━━ REASON ◄━━ EVIDENCE
↑
CHALLENGES (So what?)

Benjamin Franklin observed that "so convenient a thing it is to be a rational creature, since it enables us to find or make a reason for every thing one has a mind to do." It is not hard to think of reasons. What is difficult is to convince your audience that your reasons are *good reasons*. In a conversation, you get immediate feedback that tells you whether your listener agrees or disagrees. When you are writing, you usually don't have someone reading who can question you immediately unless you are writing on a computer connected to other computers. Consequently, you have to be more specific about what you are claiming, you have to connect with the values you hold in common with your readers, and you have to anticipate what questions and objections your readers might have if you are going to convince someone who doesn't agree with you or know what you know already.

When you write an argument, imagine a reader like Maria who is going to listen carefully to what you have to say but is not going to agree with you automatically. When you present a reason, she will ask, "So what?" You will have to have evidence, and you will have to link it to your claim in ways she will accept if she is to agree that your reason is a good one.

To begin, you must make a claim. If that claim is very general, it is often hard to argue. For example, Jeff's assertion that our nation would be better off if everyone went to college is almost like saying our nation would be better if everyone obeyed traffic laws. Jeff's claim seems unrealistic because it doesn't

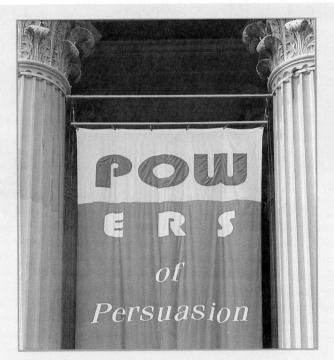

National Archives building, Washington, D.C.

take into account what it would take to accomplish the goal or why things would be better as a result. He makes a more specific claim in response to Maria that education is the route out of poverty, but that claim too is very broad.

Your claim should be specific, and it should be contestable. If you claim that you like sour cream on a baked potato, your claim is specific but not contestable. Someone could tell you that a baked potato is less fattening without sour cream, but it still doesn't change the fact that you like sour cream. Besides, you might want to gain weight.

What Is Not Arguable

Just about everything is arguable, but much of the time certain types of argument are not advanced. Statements of **facts** are usually not considered arguable. Jeff's claim that students at universities in the United Kingdom do

(continued)

What Is Not Arguable *(continued)*

not pay tuition is a statement of fact that turned out not to be true. Most facts can be verified by doing research. But even simple facts can sometimes be argued. For example, Mount Everest is usually acknowledged to be the highest mountain in the world at 29,028 feet above sea level. But if the total height of a mountain from base to summit is the measure, then the volcano Mauna Loa in Hawaii is the highest mountain in the world. Although the top of Mauna Loa is 13,667 feet above sea level, the summit is 31,784 above the ocean floor. Thus the "fact" that Mount Everest is the highest mountain on the earth depends on a definition of *highest* being the point farthest above sea level. You could argue for this definition.

Another category of claims that are not arguable are those of **personal taste.** Your favorite food and your favorite color are examples of personal taste. If you hate fresh tomatoes, no one can convince you that you actually like them. But many claims of personal taste turn out to be value judgments using arguable criteria. For example, if you think that *Alien* is the best science fiction movie ever made, you can argue that claim using evaluative criteria that other people can consider as good reasons (see Chapter 7). Indeed, you might not even like science fiction and still argue that *Alien* is the best science fiction movie ever.

Finally, many claims rest on **beliefs** or **faith**. If someone accepts a claim as a matter of religious belief, then for that person, the claim is true and cannot be refuted. Of course, people still make arguments about the existence of God and which religion reflects the will of God. Any time an audience will not consider an idea, it's possible but very difficult to construct an argument. Many people claim to have evidence that UFOs exist, but most people refuse to acknowledge that evidence as even being possibly factual.

The Basics of Reasoning

You decide to pick up a new pair of prescription sunglasses at the mall on your way to class. The company promises that it can make your glasses in an hour, but what you hadn't counted on was how long it would take you to park and how long you would have to wait in line at the counter. You jog into the mall, drop off your prescription, and go out of the store to wait. There's a booth nearby where volunteers are checking blood pressure. You don't have anything better to do, so you have your blood pressure checked.

After the volunteer takes the blood pressure cuff off your arm, he asks how old you are. He asks you whether you smoke, and you say no. He tells you that your reading is 150 over 100. He says that's high for a person your age and that you ought to have it checked again. "This is all I need," you think. "I have a test coming up tomorrow, a term paper due Friday, and if I don't make it to class, I won't get my homework turned in on time. And now something bad is wrong with me."

When you get your blood pressure checked again at the student health center after your test the next day, it turns out to be 120/80, which the nurse says is normal. When you think about it, you realize that you probably had a high reading because of stress and jogging into the mall.

Your blood pressure is one of the most important indicators of your health. When the volunteer checking your blood pressure tells you that you might have a serious health problem because your blood pressure is too high, he is relying on his knowledge of how the human body works. If your blood pressure is too high, it eventually damages your arteries and puts a strain on your entire body. But he used the word *might* because your blood pressure is not the same all the time. It can go up when you are under stress or even when you eat too much salt. And blood pressure varies from person to person and even in different parts of your body. For example, your blood pressure is higher in your legs than in your arms.

Doctors use blood pressure and other information to make diagnoses. Diagnoses are claims based on evidence. But as the blood pressure example shows, often the link is not clear, at least from a single reading. A doctor will collect several blood pressure readings over many weeks or even years before concluding that a patient has a condition of high blood pressure called *hypertension*. These readings will be compared to readings from thousands of other patients in making a diagnosis. Doctors are trained to rely on **generalizations** from thousands of past observations in medical science and to make diagnoses based on **probability.** In everyday life, you learn to make similar generalizations from which you make decisions based on probability. If you are in a hurry in the grocery store, you likely will go to the line that looks the shortest. You pick the shortest line because you think it will probably be the fastest.

Sometimes we don't have past experience to rely on, and we have to reason in other ways. When we claim that one thing is like something else, we make a link by **analogy.** Jeff's attempt to argue that American colleges and universities should be tuition free because British universities are tuition free is an argument by analogy. Analogies work only if the resemblances are more convincing than the dissimilarities. Maria pointed out that Jeff simply didn't know the facts.

Another way we reason is by using **cultural assumptions,** which we often think of as common sense. For example, you walk down the street and see a 280Z speed around a car that is double-parked, cross the double line, and sideswipe a truck coming the other way. A police officer arrives shortly, and you tell her that the 280Z is at fault. Maybe you've seen many accidents before, but the reason you think the 280Z is at fault is because in the United States, drivers are supposed to stay on the right side of two-way roads. It is part of our culture that you take for granted—that is, until you try to drive in Japan, Great Britain, or India, where people drive on the left. Driving on the left will seem unnatural to you, but it's natural for the people in those countries.

Driving on the right or left side of a street is a cultural assumption. Many assumptions are formally written down as laws. Others are simply part of cultural knowledge. There is no law that people who are waiting should stand in a line or that people who are first in line should receive attention first, but we think someone is rude who cuts in front of us when we stand in a line. In some other cultures, people don't stand in line when they wait. Crowding up to the counter, which seems rude to us, is the norm for them. Other cultures sometimes find the informality of Americans rude. For example, in some cultures, calling people by their first name when you first meet them is considered rude instead of friendly.

Particular cultural assumptions can be hard to challenge because you often have to take on an entire system of belief. The metric system is much easier to use to calculate distances than the English system of miles, feet, and inches. Nonetheless, people in the United States have strongly resisted efforts to convert to metric measures. When cultural assumptions become common sense, people accept them as true even though they often can be questioned. It seems like common sense to say that salad is good for you, but in reality it depends on what's in the salad. A salad consisting of lettuce and a mayonnaise-based dressing has little nutritional value and much fat.

Finding Good Reasons

A good reason works because it includes a link to your claim that your readers will find valid. Your readers are almost like a jury that passes judgment on your good reasons. If they accept them and cannot think of other, more compelling good reasons that oppose your position, you will convince them.

Most good reasons derive from mulling things over "reasonably," or, to use the technical term, from logos. *Logos* refers to the logic of what you communicate; in fact, logos is the root of our modern word *logic*. Good reasons

are thus commonly associated with logical appeals. Over the years, professional rhetoricians have devised a number of informal methods, known as *heuristics*, to help speakers and writers find good reasons to support their arguments. (The word *heuristics* comes from the same root as the Greek word *eureka*, which means "I have found it!") In the rest of this section, you will find a set of heuristics for developing good reasons for your arguments. Think of them as a series of questions that can help you to develop persuasive arguments.

These questions will equip you to communicate more effectively when you are speaking before a group as well as writing an argument. But do not expect every question to be productive in every case. Sometimes, a certain question won't get you very far; and often, the questions will develop so many good reasons and strategies that you will not be able to use them all. You will ultimately have to select from among the best of your good reasons to find the ones that are most likely to work in a given case.

If a certain question does not seem to work for you at first, do not give up on it the next time. Get in the habit of asking these questions in the course of developing your arguments. If you ask them systematically, you will probably have more good reasons than you need for your arguments.

CAN YOU ARGUE BY DEFINITION?

Probably the most powerful kind of good reason is an **argument from definition.** You can think of a definition as a simple statement: _____ *is a* _____. You use these statements all the time. When you need a course to fulfill your social science requirement, you look at the list of courses that are defined as social science courses. You find out that the anthropology class you want to take is one of them. It's just as important when _____ *is not a* _____. Suppose you are taking College Algebra this semester, which is a math course taught by the math department, yet it doesn't count for the math requirement. The reason it doesn't count is because College Algebra is not defined as a college-level math class. So you have to enroll next semester in Calculus I.

Many definitions are not nearly as clear cut as the math requirement. If you want to argue that figure skaters are athletes, you will need to define what an athlete is. You start thinking. An athlete competes in an activity, but that definition alone is too broad, since many competitions do not require physical activity. Thus, an athlete must participate in a competitive physical activity and must train for it. But that definition is still not quite narrow enough, since soldiers train for competitive physical activity. You decide to add that the activity must be a sport and that it must require special competence and precision. Your because clause turns out as follows: *Figure skaters are athletes because true athletes train for and compete in physical sporting competitions that require special competence and precision.*

If you can get your audiences to accept your definitions of things, you've gone a long way toward convincing them of the validity of your claim. That is why the most controversial issues in our culture—abortion, affirmative action, gay rights, pornography, women's rights, gun control, the death penalty—are argued from definition. Is abortion a crime or a medical procedure? Is pornography protected by the First Amendment, or is it a violation of women's rights? Is the death penalty just or cruel and inhuman? You can see from these examples that definitions often rely on cultural assumptions for their links.

Because cultural assumptions about controversial issues are strongly held, people usually don't care about the practical consequences. Arguing that it is much cheaper to execute prisoners who have been convicted of first-degree murder than to keep them in prison for life does not convince those who believe that it is morally wrong to kill anyone, no matter what they have done.

CAN YOU ARGUE FROM VALUE?

A special kind of argument from definition, one that often implies consequences, is the **argument from value.** You can support your claim with a because clause (or several of them) that includes a sense of evaluation.

Arguments from value follow from claims like _____ *is a good* _____ or _____ *is not a good* _____.

You make arguments from value every day. Your old TV set breaks, so you go to your local discount store to buy a new one. When you get there, you find too many choices. You have to decide which one to buy. You have only $230 to spend, but there are still a lot of choices. Which is the best TV for $230 or less? The more you look, the more confusing it gets. There are several 19-inch TVs in your price range. All have remote control. Some have features such as front surround sound, multilingual on-screen display, and A/V inputs. But you realize that there is one test that will determine the best TV for you: the picture quality. You buy the one with the best picture.

Evaluative arguments usually proceed from the presentation of certain criteria. These criteria come from the definitions of good and bad, of poor and not so poor, that prevail in a given case. A really good 19-inch TV fulfills certain criteria; so does an outstanding movie, an excellent class, or, if you work in an office, an effective telephone system. Sometimes the criteria are straightforward, as in the TV example. The TV that you select has to be under a certain cost, equipped with a remote, and ready to hook up to your cable. After those criteria are met, the big ones are picture and sound quality. But if your boss asks you to recommend a new telephone system, then it's not quite so straightforward. You are presented with many options, and you have to decide which of them are worth paying for. You have to decide how the phone system is going to be used, examine which features will be important for your office, and then rate the systems according to the criteria you have set out. The key to evaluation arguments is identifying and arguing for the right criteria. If you can convince your readers that you have the right criteria and that your assessments are correct, then you will be convincing.

CAN YOU COMPARE OR CONTRAST?

Evaluative arguments can generate comparisons often enough. But even if they don't generate comparisons, your argument might profit if you get in the habit of thinking in comparative terms—in terms of what things are like or unlike the topic you are discussing. **Claims of comparisons** take the form _____ *is like* _____ or _____ *is not like* _____. If you are having trouble coming up with good reasons, think of comparisons that help your readers agree with you. If you want to argue that figure skaters are athletes, you might think about how their training and competitions resemble those of other athletes. Making comparisons is an effective way of building common ground.

A particular kind of comparison is an analogy. An **analogy** is an extended comparison—one that is developed over several sentences or paragraphs for explanatory or persuasive purposes. Analogies take different forms. A **historical analogy** compares something that is going on now with a similar case in the past. One of the most frequent historical analogies is to compare a current situation in which one country attacks or threatens another with Germany's seizing of Czechoslovakia in 1938 and then invading Poland in 1939, starting World War II. The difficulty with this analogy is that circumstances today are not the same as those in 1939, and it is easy to point out how the analogy fails.

Other analogies make literal comparisons. A **literal analogy** is a comparison between current situations, in which you argue what is true or works in one situation should be true or work in another. Most advanced nations provide basic health care to all their citizens either free or at minimal charge. All citizens of Canada are covered by the same comprehensive health care system, which is free for both rich and poor. Canadians go to the doctor more frequently than citizens of the United States do, and they receive what is generally regarded as better care than their southern neighbors, who pay the most expensive health care bills on the planet.

The Canadian analogy has failed to convince members of the U.S. Congress to vote for a similar system in the United States. Opponents of adopting the Canadian system argue that health care costs are also high in Canada, but Canadians pay the costs in different ways. They pay high taxes, and the Canadian national debt has increased since the universal health system was approved. These opponents of adopting the Canadian system for the United States believe that the best care can be obtained for the lowest cost if health care is treated like any other service and consumers decide what they are willing to pay. Comparisons can always work both ways.

Analogies are especially valuable when you are trying to explain a concept to a willing listener or reader, but analogies are far from foolproof if the reader does not agree with you from the outset. Using an analogy can be risky if the entire argument depends on the reader's accepting it.

CAN YOU ARGUE FROM CONSEQUENCE?

Another powerful source of good reasons comes from considering the possible consequences of your position: Can you sketch out the good things that will follow from your position? Can you establish that certain bad things will be avoided if your position is adopted? If so, you will have other good reasons to use.

Arguments from consequence take the basic form of _____ causes _____ (or _____ *does not cause* _____). Very often, arguments from consequence are more complicated, taking the form _____ causes _____ *which, in turn, causes* _____ and so on. In Chapter 1 we describe how *Silent Spring* makes powerful arguments from consequence. Rachel Carson's primary claim is that *DDT should not be sprayed on a massive scale because it will poison animals and people.* The key to her argument is the causal chain that explains how animals and people are poisoned. Carson describes how nothing exists alone in nature. When a potato field is sprayed with chemical poison such as DDT, some of that poison is absorbed by the skin of the potatoes and some washes into the groundwater, where it contaminates drinking water. Other poisonous residue is absorbed into streams, where it is ingested by insect larvae, which in turn are eaten by fish. Fish are eaten by other fish, which are then eaten by waterfowl and people. At each stage, the poisons become more concentrated. Carson shows why people are in danger from drinking contaminated water and eating contaminated vegetables and fish. Even today, over thirty years after DDT stopped being used in the United States, dangerous levels exist in the sediment at the bottom of many lakes and bays.

Proposal arguments are future-oriented arguments from consequence. In a proposal argument, you cannot stop with naming good reasons; you also have to show that these consequences would follow from the idea or course of action that you are arguing. As an example, let's say you want to argue that all high school graduates in your state should be computer literate. You want a computer requirement more substantial than the one computer literacy course you had in the eighth grade. You want all high school graduates to be familiar with basic computer concepts and terminology, to be able to use a word processing application and at least two other applications, and to understand issues of ethics and privacy raised by new electronic technologies.

Your strongest good reason is that high school graduates should be competent in the use of computers, the tool that they will most certainly use for most writing tasks and many other activities during their lifetime. Even if your readers accept that good reason, you still have to prove that the requirement will actually give students the competency they require. Many students pass language requirements without being able to speak, read, or write the language they have studied.

Furthermore, you have to consider the feasibility of any proposal that you make. A good idea has to be a practical one. If you want to impose a computer literacy requirement, you have to argue for increased funding for expensive technology. High school students in poor communities cannot become computer literate unless they have access to computers. More teachers might also need to be hired. And you will need to figure out how to fit the computer requirement into an already crowded curriculum. Sometimes, feasibility is not a major issue (for example, if you're proposing that the starting time for basketball games be changed by thirty minutes); but if it is, you must address it.

CAN YOU COUNTER OBJECTIONS TO YOUR POSITION?

Another good way to find convincing good reasons is to think about possible objections to your position. If you can imagine how your audience might counter or respond to your argument, you will probably include in your argument precisely the points that will address your readers' particular needs and objections. If you are successful, your readers will be convinced that you are right. You've no doubt had the experience yourself of mentally saying to a writer in the course of your reading, "Yeah, but what about this other idea?"—only to have the writer address precisely this objection.

You can impress your readers that you've thought about why anyone would oppose your position and exactly how that opposition would be expressed. If you are writing a proposal argument for a computer literacy requirement for all high school graduates, you might think about why anyone would object, since computers are becoming increasingly important to our jobs and lives. What will the practical objections be? What philosophical ones? Why hasn't such a requirement been put in place already? By asking such questions in your own arguments, you are likely to develop robust because clauses that may be the ones that most affect your readers.

Sometimes, writers actually create an objector by posing rhetorical questions such as "You might say, 'But won't that make my taxes go up to pay for computers for all students?'" Stating objections explicitly can be effective if you make the objections as those of a reasonable person with an alternative point of view. But if the objections you state are ridiculous ones, then you risk being accused of setting up a *straw man*, that is, making the position opposing your own so simplistic that no one would likely identify with it.

Supporting Good Reasons

Good reasons are essential ingredients of good arguments, but they don't do the job alone. You must support or verify good reasons with evidence. Evidence consists of hard data or examples or narratives or episodes or tabulations of

Questions for Finding Good Reasons

1. **Can you argue by definition—from "the nature of the thing"?**

   ■ Can you argue that while many (most) people think X is a Y, X is better thought of as a Z?

   Example: Most people do not think of humans as an endangered species, but small farmers have been successful in comparing their way of life to an endangered species and thus have extended the definition of an endangered species to include themselves.

   ■ Can you argue that while X is a Y, X differs from other Ys and might be thought of as a Z?

   Example: Colleges and universities are similar to public schools in having education as their primary mission, but unlike public schools, colleges and universities receive only part of their operating costs from tax revenues and therefore, like a business, must generate much of their own revenue.

2. **Can you argue from value?**

   ■ Can you grade a few examples of the kind of thing you are evaluating as good, better, and best (or bad and worse)?

   Example: There have been lots of great actors in detective films, but none can compare to Humphrey Bogart.

   ■ Can you list the features you use to determine whether something is good or bad and then show why one is most important?

   Example: Coach Powers taught me a great deal about the skills and strategy of playing tennis, but most of all, she taught me that the game is fun.

3. **Can you compare or contrast?**

   ■ Can you think of items, events, or situations that are similar or dissimilar to the one you are writing about?

   Example: We should require a foreign language for all students at our college because our main competitor does not have such a requirement.

   ■ Can you distinguish why your subject is different than one usually thought of as similar?

(continued)

Questions for Finding Good Reasons *(continued)*

Example: While poor people are often lumped in with the un-employed and those on welfare, the majority of poor people do work in low-paying jobs.

4. **Can you argue from consequence?**

   ■ Can you argue that good things will happen if a certain course of action is followed or that bad things will be avoided?

   Example: Eliminating all income tax deductions would save every taxpayer many hours and would create a system of taxation that does not reward people for cheating.

   ■ Can you argue that while there were obvious causes of Y, Y would not have occurred had it not been for X?

   Example: A seventeen-year-old driver is killed when her car skids across the grass median of an interstate highway and collides with a pickup truck going the other direction. Even though a slick road and excessive speed were the immediate causes, the driver would be alive today if the median had had a concrete barrier.

   ■ Can you argue for an alternative cause rather than the one many people assume?

   Example: Politicians take credit for reducing the violent crime rate because of "get-tough" police policies, but in fact, the rate of violent crime is decreasing because more people are working.

5. **Can you counter objections to your position?**

   ■ Can you think of the most likely objections to your claim and turn them into your own good reasons?

   Example: High school administrators might object to requiring computer literacy because of cost, but schools can now lease computers and put them on a statewide system at a cost less than they now pay for textbooks.

   ■ Can the *reverse* or opposite of an opposing claim be argued?

   Example: A proposed expressway through a city is claimed to help traffic, but it also could make traffic worse by encouraging more people to drive to the city.

episodes (known as *statistics*) that are seen as relevant to the good reasons that you are putting forward. To put it another way, a writer of arguments puts forward not only claims and good reasons but also evidence that those good reasons are true. And that evidence consists of examples, personal experiences, comparisons, statistics, calculations, quotations, and other kinds of data that a reader will find relevant and compelling.

How much supporting evidence should you supply? How much evidence is enough? That is difficult to generalize about; as is usual in the case of rhetoric, the best answer is to say, "It depends." If a reader is likely to find one of your good reasons hard to believe, then you should be aggressive in offering support. You should present detailed evidence in a patient and painstaking way. As one presenting an argument, you have a responsibility not just to *state* a case but to *make* a case with evidence. Arguments that are unsuccessful tend to fail not because of a shortage of good reasons; more often, they fail because the reader doesn't agree that there is enough evidence to support the good reason that is being presented.

If your good reason isn't especially controversial, you probably should not belabor it. Think of your own experiences as a reader. How often do you recall saying to yourself, as you read a passage or listened to a speaker, "OK! OK! I get the point! Don't keep piling up all of this evidence for me because I don't want it or need it." However, such a reaction is rare, isn't it? By contrast, how often do you recall muttering under your breath, "How can you say that? What evidence do you have to back it up?" When in doubt, err on the side of offering too much evidence. It's an error that is seldom made and not often criticized.

When a writer doesn't provide satisfactory evidence for a because clause, readers might feel that there has been a failure in the reasoning process. In fact, in your previous courses in writing and speaking, you may have learned about various fallacies associated with faulty arguments (which are listed at the end of this section).

Strictly speaking, there is nothing false about these so-called logical fallacies. The fallacies most often refer to failures in providing evidence; when you don't provide enough good evidence to convince your audience, you might be accused of committing a fallacy in reasoning. You will usually avoid such accusations if the evidence that you cite is both *relevant* and *sufficient*.

Relevance refers to the appropriateness of the evidence to the case at hand. Some kinds of evidence are seen as more relevant than others for particular audiences. For example, in science and industry, personal testimony is seen as having limited relevance, while experimental procedures and controlled observations have far more credibility. Compare someone who defends the use of a particular piece of computer software because "it worked for me" with someone who defends it because "according to a journal article published last month, 84 percent of the users of the software were satisfied or very satisfied with it." On the other hand, in writing to the general public on controversial issues such as gun control, personal experience is often considered more relevant than other kinds of data. The so-called Brady Bill, which requires a mandatory waiting period for the purchase of handguns, was named for President Ronald Reagan's press secretary, James Brady, who was permanently disabled when John W. Hinckley, Jr., made an assassination attempt on the president in 1981. James Brady's wife, Sarah, effectively told the story of her husband's suffering in lobbying for the bill.

Sufficiency refers to the amount of evidence cited. Sometimes a single piece of evidence, a single instance, will carry the day if it is especially compelling in some way—if it represents the situation well or makes a point that isn't particularly controversial. More often, people expect more than one piece of evidence if they are to be convinced of something. Convincing readers that they should approve a statewide computer literacy requirement for all high school graduates will require much more evidence than the story of a single graduate who succeeded with her computer skills. You will likely need statistical evidence for such a broad proposal.

If you anticipate that your audience might not accept your evidence, face the situation squarely. First, think carefully about the argument you are presenting. If you cannot cite adequate evidence for your assertions, perhaps those assertions must be modified or qualified in some way. If you remain convinced of your assertions, then think about doing more research to come up with additional evidence. If you anticipate that your audience might suspect you have overlooked or minimized important information, reassure them that you have not and deal explicitly with conflicting arguments. Another strategy is to acknowledge explicitly the limitations of your evidence. Acknowledging limitations doesn't shrink the limitations, but it does build your credibility and convinces your audience that alternatives have indeed been explored fully and responsibly. If you are thinking of your reader as a partner rather than as an adversary, it is usually easy to acknowledge limitations because you are looking not for victory and the end of debate but for a mutually satisfactory situation that might emerge as a result of the communication process that you are part of.

Fallacies in Arguments

Reasoning in arguments depends less on *proving* a claim than it does on finding evidence for the claim that readers will accept as valid. Logical fallacies in argument reflect a failure to provide adequate evidence for the

(continued)

Fallacies in Arguments (continued)

claim that is being made. Among the most common fallacies are the following.

- **Bandwagon appeals.** *It doesn't matter if I cheat on a test because everyone else does.* This argument suggests that everyone is doing it, so why shouldn't you? Close examination may reveal that in fact everyone really isn't doing it—and in any case, it may not be the right thing to do.

- **Begging the question.** *People should be able to use land any way they want to because using land is an individual right.* The fallacy of begging the question occurs when the claim is restated and passed off as evidence.

- **Either-or.** *Either we build a new freeway crossing downtown or else there will be perpetual gridlock.* The either-or fallacy suggests that there are only two choices in a complex situation. This is rarely, if ever, the case. (In this example, the writer ignores other transportation options besides freeways.)

- **False analogies.** *The Serbian seizure of Bosnian territory was like Hitler's takeover of Czechoslovakia in 1938, and having learned the hard way what happens when they give in to dictators, Western nations stood up to Serbian aggression.* Analogies always depend on the degree of resemblance of one situation to another. In this case, the analogy fails to recognize that Serbia in 1993 was hardly like Nazi Germany in 1938.

- **Hasty generalization.** *We had three days this summer when the temperature reached an all-time high; that's a sure sign of global warming.* A hasty generalization is a broad claim made on the basis of a few occurrences. The debate over global warming takes into account climate data for centuries. Individual climate events such as record hot days do not confirm trends.

- **Name calling.** Name calling is as frequent in political argument as on the playground. Candidates are "accused" of being tax-and-spend liberals, ultraconservatives, radical feminists, and so on. Rarely are these terms defined; hence they are meaningless.

(continued)

Fallacies in Arguments *(continued)*

- **Non sequitur.** *A university that can afford to build a new football stadium should not have to raise tuition.* A non sequitur (a Latin term meaning "it does not follow") ties together two unrelated ideas. In this case, the argument fails to recognize that the money for new stadiums is often donated for that purpose and is not part of a university's general revenue.

- **Oversimplification.** *No one would run stop signs if we had a mandatory death penalty for doing it.* This claim may be true, but the argument would be unacceptable to most citizens. More complex, if less definitive, solutions are called for.

- **Polarization.** *Feminists are all man haters.* Polarization, like name calling, exaggerates positions and groups by representing them as extreme and divisive.

- **Post hoc fallacy.** *I ate a hamburger last night and got deathly sick—must have been food poisoning.* The post hoc fallacy (from the Latin *post hoc ergo hoc,* "after this, therefore this") assumes that things that follow in time have a causal relationship. In this example, you may have simply started coming down with the flu—as would be obvious two days later.

- **Rationalization.** *I could have done better on the test if I thought the course mattered to my major.* People frequently come up with excuses and weak explanations for their own and others' behavior that avoid actual causes.

- **Slippery slope.** *We shouldn't grant amnesty to illegal immigrants now living in the United States because it will mean opening our borders to a flood of people from around the world who want to move here.* The slippery slope fallacy assumes that if the first step is taken, other steps necessarily follow.

- **Straw man.** *Environmentalists won't be satisfied until not a single human being is allowed to enter a national park.* A straw man argument is a diversionary tactic that sets up another's position in a way that can be easily rejected. In fact, only a small percentage of environmentalists would make an argument even close to this one.

Deciding Which Good Reasons to Use

Asking a series of questions can generate a list of because clauses, but even if you have plenty, you still have to decide which ones to use. How can you decide which points are likely to be most persuasive? In choosing which good reasons to use in your arguments, consider your readers' attitudes and values and the values that are especially sanctioned by your community.

When people communicate, they tend to present their own thinking— to rely on the lines of thought that have led them to believe as they do. That's natural enough, since it is reasonable to present to others the reasons that make us believe what we are advocating in writing or speech. People have much in common, and it is natural to think that the evidence and patterns of thought that have guided your thinking to a certain point will also guide others to the same conclusions.

But people are also different, and what convinces you might not always convince others. When you are deciding what because clauses to present to others, therefore, try not so much to recapitulate your own thinking process as to influence the thinking of others. Ask yourself not just why you think as you do but also what you need to convince others to see things your way. Don't pick the because clauses that seem compelling to you; pick those that will seem compelling to your audience.

LANI GUINIER

The Tyranny of the Majority

During her college years at Harvard and the Yale Law School, Lani Guinier (1950–) became intensely committed to voting rights, one of the long-standing initiatives of the civil rights movement. She grew up in an interracial family—with an African-American father and a white, Jewish mother—and as a young attorney gained a reputation as a coalition builder. In 1988 she became the first African-American woman tenured professor in the Harvard Law School.

This excerpt, taken from her 1994 book The Tyranny of the Majority, *was inspired by the work of one of the founders of the United States, James Madison, who later became the fourth president. Madison believed that the "tyranny of the majority" represented the biggest threat to the system of democracy proposed for the new nation because the majority could become as despotic in its rule as a king. Guinier explores*

*ways in which a majority can work with rather than tyrannize a minority
in a diverse society.*

1   I have always wanted to be a civil rights lawyer. This lifelong ambition is
based on a deep-seated commitment to democratic fair play—to playing by
the rules as long as the rules are fair. When the rules seem unfair, I have
worked to change them, not subvert them. When I was eight years old, I was
a Brownie. I was especially proud of my uniform, which represented a commitment to good citizenship and good deeds. But one day, when my Brownie
group staged a hatmaking contest, I realized that uniforms are only as honorable as the people who wear them. The contest was rigged. The winner was
assisted by her milliner mother, who actually made the winning entry in full
view of all the participants. At the time, I was too young to be able to change
the rules, but I was old enough to resign, which I promptly did.

2   To me, fair play means that the rules encourage everyone to play. They
should reward those who win, but they must be acceptable to those who
lose. The central theme of my academic writing is that not all rules lead to
elemental fair play. Some even commonplace rules work against it.

3   The professional milliner competing with amateur Brownies stands
as an example of rules that are patently rigged or patently subverted. Yet,
sometimes, even when rules are perfectly fair in form, they serve in practice to exclude particular groups from meaningful participation. When
they do not encourage everyone to play, or when, over the long haul, they
do not make the losers feel as good about the outcomes as the winners,
they can seem as unfair as the milliner who makes the winning hat for her
daughter.

4   Sometimes, too, we construct rules that force us to be divided into winners and losers when we might have otherwise joined together. This idea was
cogently expressed by my son, Nikolas, when he was four years old, far exceeding the thoughtfulness of his mother when she was an eight-year-old Brownie.
While I was writing one of my law journal articles, Nikolas and I had a conversation about voting prompted by a *Sesame Street Magazine* exercise. The magazine pictured six children: four children had raised their hands because they
wanted to play tag; two had their hands down because they wanted to play
hide-and-seek. The magazine asked its readers to count the number of children
whose hands were raised and then decide what game the children would play.

5   Nikolas quite realistically replied, "They will play both. First they will
play tag. Then they will play hide-and-seek." Despite the magazine's "rules,"

he was right. To children, it is natural to take turns. The winner may get to play first or more often, but even the "loser" gets something. His was a positive-sum solution that many adult rule-makers ignore.

6   The traditional answer to the magazine's problem would have been a zero-sum solution. "The children—all the children—will play tag, and only tag." As a zero-sum solution, everything is seen in terms of "I win; you lose." The conventional answer relies on winner-take-all majority rule, in which the tag players, as the majority, win the right to decide for all the children what game to play. The hide-and-seek preference becomes irrelevant. The numerically more powerful majority choice simply subsumes minority preferences.

7   In the conventional case, the majority that rules gains all the power and the minority that loses gets none. For example, two years ago Brother Rice High School in Chicago held two senior proms. It was not planned that way. The prom committee at Brother Rice, a boys' Catholic high school, expected just one prom when it hired a disc jockey, picked a rock band, and selected music for the prom by consulting student preferences. Each senior was asked to list his three favorite songs, and the band would play the songs that appeared most frequently on the lists.

8   Seems attractively democratic. But Brother Rice is predominantly white, and the prom committee was all white. That's how they got two proms. The black seniors at Brother Rice felt so shut out by the "democratic process" that they organized their own prom. As one black student put it: "For every vote we had, there were eight votes for what they wanted. . . . [W]ith us being in the minority we're always outvoted. It's as if we don't count."

9   Some embittered white seniors saw things differently. They complained that the black students should have gone along with the majority: "The majority makes a decision. That's the way it works."

10   In a way, both groups were right. From the white students' perspective, this was ordinary decision making. To the black students, majority rule sent the message: "we don't count" is the "way it works" for minorities. In a racially divided society, majority rule may be perceived as majority tyranny.

11   That is a large claim, and I do not rest my case for it solely on the actions of the prom committee in one Chicago high school. To expand the range of the argument, I first consider the ideal of majority rule itself, particularly as reflected in the writings of James Madison and other founding members of our Republic. These early democrats explored the relationship between majority rule and democracy. James Madison warned, "If a majority be united by a common interest, the rights of the minority will be insecure."

The tyranny of the majority, according to Madison, requires safeguards to protect "one part of the society against the injustice of the other part."

12　　For Madison, majority tyranny represented the great danger to our early constitutional democracy. Although the American revolution was fought against the tyranny of the British monarch, it soon became clear that there was another tyranny to be avoided. The accumulations of all powers in the same hands, Madison warned, "whether of one, a few, or many, and whether hereditary, self-appointed, or elective, may justly be pronounced the very definition of tyranny."

13　　As another colonist suggested in papers published in Philadelphia, "We have been so long habituated to a jealousy of tyranny from monarchy and aristocracy, that we have yet to learn the dangers of it from democracy." Despotism had to be opposed "whether it came from Kings, Lords or the people."

14　　The debate about majority tyranny reflected Madison's concern that the majority may not represent the whole. In a homogeneous society, the interest of the majority would likely be that of the minority also. But in a heterogeneous community, the majority may not represent all competing interests. The majority is likely to be self-interested and ignorant or indifferent to the concerns of the minority. In such case, Madison observed, the assumption that the majority represents the minority is "altogether fictitious."

15　　Yet even a self-interested majority can govern fairly if it cooperates with the minority. One reason for such cooperation is that the self-interested majority values the principle of reciprocity. The self-interested majority worries that the minority may attract defectors from the majority and become the next governing majority. The Golden Rule principle of reciprocity functions to check the tendency of a self-interested majority to act tyrannically.

16　　So the argument for the majority principle connects it with the value of reciprocity: You cooperate when you lose in part because members of the current majority will cooperate when they lose. The conventional case for the fairness of majority rule is that it is not really the rule of a fixed group— The Majority—on all issues; instead it is the rule of shifting majorities, as the losers at one time or on one issue join with others and become part of the governing coalition at another time or on another issue. The result will be a fair system of mutually beneficial cooperation. I call a majority that rules but does not dominate a Madisonian Majority.

17　　The problem of majority tyranny arises, however, when the self-interested majority does not need to worry about defections. When the majority is fixed and permanent, there are no checks on its ability to be overbearing. A majority that does not worry about defectors is a majority with total power.

18   In such a case, Madison's concern about majority tyranny arises. In a heterogeneous community, any faction with total power might subject "the minority to the caprice and arbitrary decisions of the majority, who instead of consulting the interest of the whole community collectively, attend sometimes to partial and local advantages."

19   "What remedy can be found in a republican Government, where the majority must ultimately decide," argued Madison, but to ensure "that no one common interest or passion will be likely to unite a majority of the whole number in an unjust pursuit." The answer was to disaggregate the majority to ensure checks and balances or fluid, rotating interests. The minority needed protection against an overbearing majority, so that "a common sentiment is less likely to be felt, and the requisite concert less likely to be formed, by a majority of the whole."

20   Political struggles would not be simply a contest between rulers and people; the political struggles would be among the people themselves. The work of government was not to transcend different interests but to reconcile them. In an ideal democracy, the people would rule, but the minorities would also be protected against the power of majorities. Again, where the rules of decision making protect the minority, the Madisonian Majority rules without dominating.

21   But if a group is unfairly treated, for example, when it forms a racial minority, *and* if the problems of unfairness are not cured by conventional assumptions about majority rule, then what is to be done? The answer is that we may need an *alternative* to winner-take-all majoritarianism. In this book, a collection of my law review articles, I describe the alternative, which, with Nikolas's help, I now call the "principle of taking turns." In a racially divided society, this principle does better than simple majority rule if it accommodates the values of self-government, fairness, deliberation, compromise, and consensus that lie at the heart of the democratic ideal.

22   In my legal writing, I follow the caveat of James Madison and other early American democrats. I explore decision-making rules that might work in a multiracial society to ensure that majority rule does not become majority tyranny. I pursue voting systems that might disaggregate The Majority so that it does not exercise power unfairly or tyrannically. I aspire to a more cooperative political style of decision making to enable all of the students at Brother Rice to feel comfortable attending the same prom. In looking to create Madisonian Majorities, I pursue a positive-sum, taking-turns solution.

23   Structuring decision making to allow the minority "a turn" may be necessary to restore the reciprocity ideal when a fixed majority refuses to cooperate with the minority. If the fixed majority loses its incentive to follow the Golden Rule principle of shifting majorities, the minority never gets to take a turn. Giving the minority a turn does not mean the minority gets to rule; what it does mean is that the minority gets to influence decision making and the majority rules more legitimately.

24   Instead of automatically rewarding the preferences of the monolithic majority, a taking-turns approach anticipates that the majority rules, but is not overbearing. Because those with 51 percent of the votes are not assured 100 percent of the power, the majority cooperates with, or at least does not tyrannize, the minority.

25   The sports analogy of "I win; you lose" competition within a political hierarchy makes sense when only one team can win; Nikolas's intuition that it is often possible to take turns suggests an alternative approach. Take family decision making, for example. It utilizes a taking-turns approach. When parents sit around the kitchen table deciding on a vacation destination or activities for a rainy day, often they do not simply rely on a show of hands, especially if that means that the older children always prevail or if affinity groups among the children (those who prefer movies to video games, or those who prefer baseball to playing cards) never get to play their activity of choice. Instead of allowing the majority simply to rule, the parents may propose that everyone take turns, going to the movies one night and playing video games the next. Or as Nikolas proposes, they might do both on a given night.

26   Taking turns attempts to build consensus while recognizing political or social differences, and it encourages everyone to play. The taking-turns approach gives those with the most support more turns, but it also legitimates the outcome from each individual's perspective, including those whose views are shared only by a minority.

27   In the end, I do not believe that democracy should encourage rule by the powerful—even a powerful majority. Instead, the idea of democracy promises a fair discussion among self-defined equals about how to achieve our common aspirations. To redeem that promise, we need to put the idea of taking turns and disaggregating the majority at the center of our conception of representation. Particularly as we move into the twenty-first century as a more highly diversified citizenry, it is essential that we consider the ways in which voting and representational systems succeed or fail at encouraging Madisonian Majorities.

28   To use Nikolas's terminology, "it is no fair" if a fixed, tyrannical majority excludes or alienates the minority. It is no fair if a fixed, tyrannical majority monopolizes all the power all the time. It is no fair if we engage in the periodic ritual of elections, but only the permanent majority gets to choose who is elected. Where we have tyranny by The Majority, we do not have genuine democracy.

Getting Started on Your Draft

Before You Start Writing Your Draft

1. Pick one of the issues from the list you made in Chapter 1 as a possible candidate. Then write in one sentence your position on this issue. You can change the statement later if you need to, but at this point, you need to know whether you can write a paper using this statement as your thesis.
2. Use the questions on pp. 42–43 to help you think of as many reasons as you can. List your reasons as because clauses after your claim—for example, "Smoking should be banned on campus *because* nonsmokers are endangered by secondhand smoke."
3. When you finish listing your reasons, put checks beside the strongest ones.
4. What evidence do you have to support your strongest reasons? Do you have any facts, statistics, testimony from authority, or personal observations to back up the reasons? Make notes beside your reasons.
5. List as many reasons as you can against your claim. For example, "Smoking should not be banned on campus *because* the risk of secondhand smoke is minimal if smokers go outside and *because* it would discourage or even prevent smokers from working or going to school on campus." Think about how you are going to answer the arguments against your position.
6. Think about who is going to read your argument. How much will they know about the issues involved? Where are they likely to stand on these issues? Will they define the issues the same way you do? On what are they most likely to agree and disagree with you?

Writing Your Draft

Some people write best from detailed outlines; others write from notes. Try making some notes about your beginning, middle, and end to get you started and to give you a sense of where you're headed.

1. **The beginning.** How much do you need to explain the issue before making your claim? How can you get off to a fast start? What can you do to convince your reader to keep reading? Do you need to establish that there's a problem that your paper will address? Are you answering a specific argument by someone else?

2. **The middle.** If you have more than one reason, which reason do you want to put first? Most of the time, you want your strongest reason to be up front or else at the end. Group similar arguments together. Weaker arguments might go in the middle. Next, you have to think about how you are going to bring in the evidence that you have. If you have only one reason, the evidence will make or break your argument. Finally, you need to think about where you are going to acknowledge opposing viewpoints and how much space you need to give to countering those viewpoints. If most of your readers are likely to think differently than you, then you need to spend time anticipating and refuting objections to your claim.

3. **The ending.** Endings are always tricky. Simply stating your claim again isn't the best way to finish. The worst endings say something like "In my essay, I've said this." Is there a summarizing point you can make? Some implication you can draw? Another example you can include that will sum up your position? If you are writing a proposal, your ending might be a call for action.

CHAPTER 3

Thinking More about Your Audience

What Exactly Is an Audience?

The audience is the most important concern in any kind of persuasion—from advertising to the kind of extended written arguments that you write in college. Thinking in advance about your audience pays off when you write. But what exactly is an audience?

Often, the answer is easy to supply. In those cases, *audience* refers to the person or people who actually hear an oral communication or who actually read a written one. Audience denotes the real consumers of communications. The idea of a *real audience* is usually a concrete reality for people who are speaking, because those audiences are actually, visibly present at the scene. When real audiences are present in the flesh, they are hard to ignore. In fact, you do so at your own risk, for audiences who are lost or confused by an oral presentation can make their discomfort known by body language ("If this speech doesn't end soon, I'm going to scream!" their bodies say) or by their verbal responses ("Excuse me, but I'm really confused by what you just said"). Sometimes, the audiences for written communications can be almost as real (and just as responsive) as the ones who take in a verbal performance, especially if you are writing to people whom you know well or who work closely with you. The real audience for this book is certainly immediate to the people who are writing it. The authors are aware of you—the flesh-and-blood student with a real name, a real presence, a student like the ones we work with every semester. And the authors know that you are likely to respond in real ways to what you read.

> *Audience* **is a concrete and useful concept even if you do not know who eventually will read what you write.**

When the term *audience* is used in this book, then, it most often refers to the real audience. But there is also another way of thinking about audience, another way in which you are the audience for this book: The authors had to imagine you reading while they were composing the chapters. In this sense, an audience can be an imaginary concept in the mind of the writer, not just a real, flesh-and-blood presence. You have this sense of audience whenever you think about someone later reading what you are writing as you write. In fact, from the point of view of the writer, it does not even matter whether the person you imagine reading eventually does read what you write. What is important is that this imaginary reader helps you to think about the reasons and supporting evidence you need to write your argument. When you have very little sense of who will eventually read what you write, this imaginary reader becomes especially important.

The goal of this chapter is to help you make the audience in your mind a concrete, useful concept, whether or not you know the real people who will ultimately read what you write. Real audiences exist, and you can think about them in productive ways. But even if your real audience doesn't have a concrete presence for you, you can make *audience* a creative concept in your mind as you write. Whether the audience is a real presence or something in the mind of the writer finally might not make much difference.

To imagine an audience for what you write, think about what readers actually do when they read. Most people are not very aware of how they read because reading is almost like breathing. They have done it so often for so long that they are hardly conscious of how they do it. Think for a moment about the following examples:

▨ A third grader brings his mother a flower he has picked from the yard and a note that says "I love you Mom." Earlier in the day, he was bouncing a ball against the hearth in the living room and broke a lamp. His mother reads the note and realizes that he is trying to gain her forgiveness. She thanks him politely and, even though she is still mad about the lamp, hugs him.

 A psychologist finds a reference to an article in a scholarly journal that pertains to her area of research. When she looks up the article in the library, she quickly scans the introduction to learn exactly what question is being investigated. Because she has read many similar articles, she knows where to find what she is looking for. She flips to the "Discussion" section to find out what conclusions the author has drawn and then turns back to the "Methods" and "Results" sections. She decides that the experiment being reported does not test what it claims to test. Later, when she writes a review of research in her field, she criticizes the experiment.

A developer of desert land decides to use the contest gimmick to attract customers. Later, a college student, among many others on a mailing list, receives a card telling him that he will win a new car just for visiting El Rancho Estates. The student has a friend who responded to a similar notice, only to find out that the new car was a toy. He throws the card in the trash.

A financial analyst who works for a large New York holding company reads the annual financial statement of a small bank in Vermont. Her company may be interested in acquiring the bank. She notices a particularly high amount of deposits in comparison to outstanding loans. She turns to the list of depositors to learn more about why so much money is deposited in the rural bank. On the basis of her review of bank documents, she decides that the bank has the potential for increased profits, and she writes a report recommending that the bank be purchased.

These examples suggest that we rely on a great deal more than what is on the page when we read. The mother understood that the note "I love you Mom" really meant something like "Don't be mad at me anymore." In the same way, the college student determined that the announcement that he had just won a contest was a gimmick to get him to visit the real estate development. We don't read just by decoding the words on the page. We read by connecting what's on the page with what we know about the world. The numbers that the financial analyst looked at were meaningless by themselves. They became meaningful when she connected them with what she knew about banks.

Reading is often represented as if people were machines that decode characters on the page. But people don't function like machines when they read. They are more like artists who turn a sketch into a painting. They transform a plan into a particular form by filling in gaps and imagining a background. They are not passive receivers. They infer motives, make judgments, debate points, and sometimes write responses.

Who Will Read Your Argument?

Many times, you know exactly who you are writing for. If you write a letter to a close friend, you know that only your friend will read it. You and your friend know the same people, so you don't have to explain who they are. In the workplace, you sometimes write memos making arguments to people you know almost as well as close friends. You don't have to fill them in on the background of the issue because you know they are familiar with the subject. Such audiences are called **simple audiences.**

Other times, your real audience might consist of many individuals, but you can conceive of them as a simple audience because their knowledge is very similar. If you write an article for a journal in your field, you can assume that your readers are familiar with the terms and concepts in that field. Although the people who are reading the journal are different individuals, they are similar in their interest in and knowledge about a particular field.

In other situations, the issue of audience is much more complicated. Take as an example the financial statement from the small bank in Vermont that was mentioned in the previous section. Many different people might read that statement for different reasons—officers of the bank, other employees, shareholders, government regulatory officials, financial analysts, and potential investors in the bank. This kind of complex audience—a group of people who read for different reasons—is a **multiple audience.** Multiple audiences are often very difficult to write for.

In writing arguments to multiple audiences, you will have to take into account differing levels of knowledge about your subject among your potential readers and differing attitudes about that subject. Before you begin writing, think carefully about all the people who might read your argument and then analyze what they know and don't know about your subject and what their attitudes toward your subject and you are likely to be.

WHAT DOES YOUR AUDIENCE ALREADY KNOW— AND NOT KNOW?

Critical to your argument is your audience's knowledge of your subject. If they are not familiar with the background information, they probably won't understand your argument fully. If you know that your readers will be unfamiliar with your subject, you will have to supply background information before attempting to convince them of your position. A good tactic is to tie your new information with what your readers already know. Comparisons and analogies can very helpful in linking old and new information.

Another critical factor is your audience's level of expertise. How much technical language can you use? For example, if you are writing a proposal to put high-speed Internet connections into all dormitory rooms, will your readers know the difference between a T1 line and a T3 line? The director of the computation center should know the difference, but the vice president for student affairs might not. If you are unsure of your readers' knowledge level, it's better to include background information and explain technical terms. Few readers will be insulted, and they can skip over this information quickly if they are familiar with your subject.

WHAT ARE YOUR AUDIENCE'S ATTITUDES TOWARD YOU?

Does your audience know you at all, either by reputation or from previous work? Are you considered your reader's equal, superior, or subordinate? How your audience regards you will affect the tone and presentation of your message. Does your audience respect you and trust you? What can you include in your presentation to build trust? In many cases, your audience will know little about you. Especially in those circumstances, you can build trust in your reader by following the advice on ethos, discussed in Chapter 4.

WHAT ARE YOUR AUDIENCE'S ATTITUDES TOWARD YOUR SUBJECT?

People have prior attitudes about controversial issues that you must take into consideration as you write or speak. Imagine, for instance, that you are preparing an argument for a guest editorial in your college newspaper advocating that your state government provide parents with choices among public and private schools. You will argue that the tax dollars that now automatically go to public schools should go to private schools if the parents so choose. You have evidence that the sophomore-to-senior dropout rate in private schools is less than half the rate of public schools. Furthermore, students from private schools attend college at nearly twice the rate of public school graduates. You intend to argue that one of the reasons private schools are more successful is that they spend more money on instruction and less on administration. And you believe that school choice speaks to the American desire for personal freedom.

Not everyone on your campus will agree with your stand. How might the faculty at your college or university feel about this issue? The administrators? The staff? Other students? Interested people in the community who read the student newspaper? What attitudes toward public funding of private schools will they have before they start reading what you have to say? How are you going to deal with the objection that because many students in private schools come from more affluent families, it is not surprising that they do better?

Even when you write about a much less controversial subject, you must think carefully about your audience's attitudes toward what you have to say or write. Sometimes, your audience may share your attitudes; other times, your audience may be neutral; at still other times, your audience will have attitudes that differ sharply from your own. If possible, you should anticipate these various attitudes and act accordingly. You should show awareness of the attitudes of your audience, and if those attitudes are very different from yours, you will have to work hard to counter them without insulting your audience. It's not just a particular attitude that you have to address but also a set of assumptions that follow from that attitude. The next section will include more about identifying assumptions that follow from attitudes.

An even more difficult situation is when your audience is indifferent to what you write. You feel very strongly that your college or university should have a varsity gymnastics team, but most people on campus are indifferent to the issue. The first task, then, is to get your readers engaged in your subject. Sometimes, you can begin by using a particularly striking example to get your readers interested. Another tactic is to add visuals—illustrations, charts, or tables—to catch your readers' attention.

Why People Reach Different Conclusions from the Same Evidence

Some people think that if the facts of an issue are accurately described, then all reasonable people should come to similar conclusions about what course of action should be followed. As you get older, however, you discover that your friends and other people whom you respect often don't agree with your conclusions even when you all agree on the facts. Arguments would be easy to write if reasonable people considered the same facts and came to the same conclusions. But often they don't. Why do reasonable people look at the same facts and come to different conclusions? Let's look at an example.

One set of facts that has caused great concern is the spread of AIDS among young people. A fifth of the people now living with AIDS are in their twenties. Because the incubation period for the disease can be as long as ten years, many contracted AIDS when they were teenagers. Because of the AIDS epidemic, many parents, politicians, clergy, and school board officials have debated whether condoms should be given out to high school students without fees and without parents' consent. In some high schools, condoms are being distributed in school clinics if parents give their consent. In other cities and communities, school boards have voted down proposals to distribute condoms.

The AIDS epidemic is of particular concern in New York City, which has just 3 percent of the nation's thirteen- to twenty-one-year-old population but 20 percent of the nation's AIDS cases for that age group. On November 26, 1991, after almost two years of public controversy, New York City became the first city in the country to make condoms available to students in its 120 high schools.

Let's take a look at how different viewpoints were argued in the condom debate in New York City. The first article, "Clinic Visit" by Anna Quindlen, appeared on the editorial page of the *New York Times*. The second article, "Condom Sense," was first printed as an unsigned editorial in *Commonweal*, a magazine that has a largely Catholic readership. The author's knowledge of the religious and moral values that the Catholic community holds in common shapes the rhetorical strategy. For example, the author does not define morality because he or she can assume an agreed-upon definition.

Quindlen, Anna. "Clinic Visit." *The New York Times* 21 Feb. 1991, sec A: 19.

There are two examining rooms, a nurse practitioner and the three pediatricians who alternate days. There is a social worker and a health educator. The psychiatrist comes on Fridays.

Welcome to the clinic at Martin Luther King Jr. High School. You can check your old notions of the school nurse and the kid with the phony stomachache at the door. Most of the students have no family physician and no insurance coverage. Here they can get treatment for their asthma, their acne or their depression. Dr. Alwyn T. Cohall, who runs 3 of the city's 17 school-based clinics, says they've taken care of everything from a splinter to a stab wound. The happiest thing they ever do is a physical for a kid going to college.

There's a questionnaire for patients, and to read it is both a delight, because it was clearly written by someone who knows adolescents, and a sorrow, because it was written by someone who knows what it's like to be young in 1991. Questions range from "If you were alone on an island, who would you want to visit you?" to "Have you ever been in any trouble with the police?" and "Did you ever try to kill yourself?" There's a poignancy to finding the section on thumb-sucking just after the one on sex. Adolescence is that point in life when, like some mythological creature, we are half one thing, half another. Teenagers think of themselves as adults; parents think of them as kids.

Which brings us to condoms.

Ah, condoms, this year's gnashing-of-teeth issue. Put the idea of teenagers and sex together, and you have two things: reality and controversy. The Chancellor proposes providing condoms to New York City high school students, and he is accused of promoting promiscuity and usurping the essential role of parents. I believe in the essential role. Parents should give their children accurate information about sex. They should discuss their own standards of morality, their ideas of right and wrong. They should let their kids know that they are always available to talk and, more important, to listen.

It's just that they don't. Some great wall rises between parents and children on this issue, a wall that is only scaled by the stalwart. Partly this is because while parents are saying "no, no," adolescent hormones are saying "yes, yes." And partly it is that parents only want to listen to what they want to hear.

The doctors at the clinic deal with what is: adolescents who need no permission from the Chancellor, the doctor or anyone else to begin sleeping together. The girl who got the notice that she was positive for the AIDS virus before she got her diploma. The girl who spent three weeks in the hospital being treated for kidney failure caused by secondary syphilis. AIDS has gotten most of the publicity in the condom debate. But one in four sexually active teenagers will get a sexually transmitted disease before high school graduation, and reducing that figure is one reason Dr. Cohall would like to dispense condoms to his patients.

The staff at the clinic have lots of problems as compelling as this one. They have to keep in touch with the kids who are depressed and the ones with drug problems. They need to send pregnant young women to good prenatal care

Adult authority often is missing.

Teens are sexually active regardless.

Condoms reduce AIDS and STDs.

programs. They'd like to be able to prescribe contraceptives for those girls who want them, but for now they refer them to a hospital clinic and hope that they go. Despite abstinence counseling and family planning services, they have a hard time keeping pregnancy tests in stock.

The school clinic requires a parental consent form, and the form allows parents to cross out any services that they don't want their child to receive. Only about 5 percent of the parents do. Dr. Cohall says this is the refrain: "I wish my kid wasn't having sex, but . . ." *Teens have rights to their bodies.*

His work is the "but." But keep him alive. Keep her from getting pregnant. Keep them all from getting sterile because of some disease. The staff at the clinic do what parents should do: They listen, and they inform, and they try to make the kids hear themselves, hear what they're really saying about how they feel. They deal with what is.

What is is that young men and women are getting sick, even dying, because of unprotected sex. And we can help prevent that. Abstinence, if you can sell it. A condom, if you cannot. To doom the young before they've even shed the chrysalis of adolescence because you disapprove of their behavior is the triumph of pride over charity and self-righteousness over sense. *The community is responsible for teens' bodies.*

Body integrity is prior to moral integrity. In this clinic, where the staff greet their patients with a hug, where the problems are so enormous, it seems both mean-spirited and shortsighted.

"Condom Sense." *Commonweal* 13 Sept. 1991: 499.

"You can play with them," reads a New York subway ad picturing teenagers gleefully playing volleyball with an inflated condom.

"Don't play around without them. Use a condom," it clinches its point. The clever word play delivers a message about preventing AIDS, but not the one that New York teenagers need to hear. Instead, the merry punsters at New York City's Health Department seem to encourage premature—and possibly lethal—sexual activity among the young while disinviting serious thinking about the dangers AIDS actually presents. The Health Department is not alone.

This past winter New York Schools Chancellor Joseph A. Fernandez pushed a condom distribution plan through the school board with the help of Mayor David Dinkins as part of a utilitarian approach to combating the spread of AIDS among sexually active adolescents. To insure the program's effectiveness, neither parental consent nor notification will be required. According to the experts, parents only scare students away. Nor will the schools require counseling as part of its condom distribution program. Presumably that too might scare students away. Condoms will be available in New York City high schools later this fall.

As the subway poster and the school board's decision demonstrate, something vital has been lost in the city's approach. That vital something is morality, and "moral" questions about sexual behavior. This is a policy that deethicizes sexual behavior precisely where sexual responsibility is most needed. What, after all, is the likely result of trying to modify sexual behavior without reference to concepts of moral responsibility? Volleyball seems to be the answer.

It's hard to believe the chancellor and his advisors have asked themselves how dispensing condoms along with textbooks can possibly shape the most intimate of human relations. Would they expect students to make themselves accountable if similar minimal expectations were applied to school work? Or to obtaining a driver's license? Could a high school field a sports team if students were simply issued uniforms and told to play the games as they saw fit? It is as if Mr. Fernandez reasons that survival during a drought depended on providing each individual with his or her own well-digging equipment. Survival in such desperate circumstances depends on more compelling forms of cooperation. Thus excluding parents from the school condom program has to be among the most self-defeating aspects of the policy. And there are others.

Mr. Fernandez argues that counseling or guidance is unnecessary: "People at any age have ready access to condoms at supermarkets and drugstores without the benefit of an educational or counseling component." (Let us leave aside the questions about why contraceptive services are being added to an overburdened school system if condoms are so readily available—as they are, and often for free.) More important, if someone is too thoughtless to buy condoms at a drugstore, what chance is there that he will bother to obtain a condom at school? Or that he or she would have the resolve to actually use a condom at the crucial moment? Indeed, the logic of Mr. Fernandez's argument suggests that the more responsible plan would have been to introduce supervised sex into the school system. If the children are going to have sex whether we think it proper or not, shouldn't we provide as safe an environment as possible? The city's unwillingness to go that far (we hope) demonstrates how the seemingly straightforward logic of the chancellor's argument conceals, rather than illuminates, the social and moral questions at stake.

The condom policy implicitly reduces sexual relations to a mechanical and nearly uncontrollable biological urge. It is this absence of a sense of human dignity—something adolescents, especially those who are poor, feel intensely in a society that already marginalizes them in countless ways—that lies at the root of this moral and sexual agnosticism. In an effort to make condom distribution matter-of-fact and therefore palatable, proponents present its case in a way that empties sex of meaning and moral consequence. Condoms and sexual information of all kinds are easily available, yet the tragic consequences of AIDS and other sexually transmitted diseases, of teen-age childbearing, and of sexual crime are increasingly with us, suggesting that sexual behavior is not so amenable to "common sense" and rationalized expectations as those with a penchant for social engineering would have us believe.

Condoms don't reduce AIDS and STDs.

But the problem goes still deeper. The condom plan's illusory practicality is symptomatic; a policy that medicalizes the social and moral question of adolescent sex is a way of avoiding more troubling realities. For example, it encourages us to continue to ignore the poverty and family breakdown that lie at the heart of destructive sexual behavior among many adolescents. AIDS is increasingly a disease of the urban poor, especially intravenous drug users and their sexual partners. Preventing the spread of AIDS among these adolescents is a question of influencing complex behavior and of understanding human motivation and the wellsprings of moral accountability. In subordinating sexual morality to the technology of contraception, the condom-distribution plan naively hopes to address human sexual life with the cause-and-effect logic of a vaccination procedure. Sex doesn't work that way. Indeed, in this context, the medicalization of sexual life dehumanizes it by removing it from the context of family life and the necessary ballast afforded the young by tradition and community values.

Teens are sexually active because adults do not teach moral behavior.

Authority figures can influence teens.

Protecting and promoting, rather than undermining, the authority of the family is essential in fostering the kind of moral responsibility that will keep young people alive in these circumstances. Adolescent sexual behavior is not a blind force

Parents are responsible for teens' bodies.

of nature. It is shaped and driven by many different cultural values—and at this time many of them are frankly exploitative. The school board's condom plan subtly absolves children of moral responsibility exactly where it should insist upon it. It establishes a premature adolescent autonomy and choice without examining what is being chosen. Self-reliance and self-discipline are essential qualities of maturity. Giving condoms to teen-agers because we have despaired of influencing their sexual decision making announces the board's enormous failure of moral and psychological imagination and tragically undermines the dignity of those it hopes to protect. Adolescents desperately want more, not less, expected of them.

Moral integrity is prior to bodily integrity.

"Clinic Visit" and "Condom Sense" agree about the facts: Many high school students are sexually active, and teenage AIDS cases rose at an alarming rate in the 1990s. From these facts, however, the articles move in different directions. The author of "Condom Sense" argues that providing condoms will aggravate the problem; the author of "Clinic Visit" argues that providing condoms will alleviate the problems.

The reason that the articles move in different directions is because the authors have different attitudes and different assumptions. These assumptions provide the links between evidence and claim. It takes some close analysis to identify these assumptions, but once they are laid out, it becomes clear how two very different positions can be constructed from the same evidence.

How Different Assumptions Produce Different Claims from the Same Evidence

Evidence: Many high school students are sexually active and at risk of contracting AIDS.

Claim 1: Providing condoms will help to alleviate the problem.

Claim 2: Providing condoms will make the problem worse.

First Assumption

Claim 1: Adult authority figures might not exist or might not have influence.

Claim 2: Authority figures do exist in teens' lives and can influence behavior.

(continued)

How Different Assumptions Produce Different Claims from the Same Evidence *(continued)*

Second Assumption

Claim 1: Teens are sexually active regardless.

Claim 2: Teens are sexually active because adults do not teach moral behavior.

Third Assumption

Claim 1: Using condoms reduces AIDS and STDs because they make sex safe.

Claim 2: Using condoms increases the risk of AIDS and STDs because they promote sexual activity and aren't 100 percent effective.

Fourth Assumption

Claim 1: Teens have the right to control their own bodies.

Claim 2: Parents have the right to control teens' bodies.

Fifth Assumption

Claim 1: The community is responsible for teens' bodies.

Claim 2: The parents or family are responsible for teens' bodies.

Sixth Assumption

Claim 1: Body integrity is prior to moral integrity.

Claim 2: Moral integrity is prior to bodily integrity.

Creating Your Readers

So far in this chapter on audience, you have been encouraged to think about your real audiences—the actual individuals who will read your arguments. But at the beginning of the chapter, you were also told that another kind of audience would be discussed before the chapter ends: the audience not *of* the argument but *in* the argument—the audience in the text.

What is the audience in the text? This is a rather difficult but important concept. First, consider an example—a short poem called "Spring and Fall: To a Young Child," written around 1880 by Gerard Manley Hopkins, a Jesuit priest who died in Dublin in 1889. The speaker in the poem is addressing a young child, "Margaret," who is crying in a sense of loss at the sight of "Goldengrove unleaving"—the sight of beautiful autumn leaves falling off the trees in front of her and turning into melancholy late November "leafmeal" (bits of leaves):

> Margaret, are you grieving
> Over Goldengrove unleaving?
> Leaves, like the things of man, you
> With your fresh thoughts care for, can you?
> Ah! As the heart grows older
> It will come to such sights colder
> By and by, nor spare a sigh
> Though worlds of wanwood leafmeal lie;
> And yet you weep and know why.
> Now no matter, child, the name:
> Sorrow's springs are the same.
> Nor mouth had, no nor mind, expressed
> What heart heard of, ghost guessed:
> It is the blight man was born for,
> It is Margaret you mourn for.

Who is the audience of this poem? Despite its title and the presence of "Margaret" in the poem, "Spring and Fall" wasn't really written for a young child at all. Children cannot understand poetry this complicated (indeed, it might be hard for you to understand parts of it). The theme of the poem— mutability (the idea that humans will all turn into leafmeal one day and had best remember that!)—isn't exactly an idea that young children are ready for. The real audience is adults who have grown older, adults whom Hopkins wants to remind that what is truly important in life is the certainty of death. "Margaret" serves as the **audience in the text**—a fictional character created by the author to aid him in making his rhetorical point. Think of it this way: Hopkins creates in his poem a sort of miniature drama, complete with characters (Margaret and the speaker) and action (the leaves falling, the tears, the speaker's sermon). The real readers eavesdrop on and observe this created drama for the author to achieve his rhetorical purpose: to remind readers, in a sort of sermon, about their ultimate end.

What does all this have to do with argument? All writing, believe it or not, can be seen as a sort of verbal drama akin to "Spring and Fall." It has fictional speakers just as this poem has a speaker; it has fictional listeners just as this poem has its Margaret; and it has verbal action. Sometimes the fictional listeners are overtly present, like young Margaret. An open letter that is published in a newspaper is one such example; the letter is addressed to a particular person but is really intended for all the readers of the paper. Martin Luther King, Jr.'s famous "Letter from Birmingham Jail" begins "To My Fellow Clergymen" and then seems to address those clergymen as "you" throughout the course of the letter. But the letter wasn't really addressed to the clergymen, or King would not have published it in several public places. The clergymen served as the audience in the text, but the real audience was the general public whose support King sought for the civil rights movement.

You can make these strategies work for you. When you write an argument, it's important first to think about what you want your readers to do. If you want to change their attitude, you will have to work hard to influence them with good reasons. But if you want them to take some action, you should give some thought to the kind of role you imply for your reader. You might want to say specifically to your readers that if they share your beliefs about a certain subject—for example, the importance of clean water in the streams and lakes of your city or town—then they should be willing to vote for strict zoning and pollution laws and to pay for the cost of enforcing them.

RICK REILLY

Bare in Mind

Rick Reilly (1958–) is a senior writer for Sports Illustrated. *His "Life of Reilly" column, which runs weekly on the last page of* SI, *both delights and infuriates many readers. The topics of his columns have ranged from following ice skater Katarina Witt behind the Iron Curtain to hanging out with actor Jack Nicholson in the front row of Los Angeles Lakers games to playing golf with Bill Clinton and with O.J. Simpson. He is the author of two novels,* Missing Links *and* Slo-Mo: My Untrue Story, *and a collection of his columns,* Life of Reilly, *and he is coauthor of biographies of Brian Bosworth, Wayne Gretzky, Charles Barkley, and Marv Albert.*

Jenny Thompson, winner of eight
Olympic gold medals.

In "Bare in Mind," Reilly writes in response to columns and letters to the editor by outraged readers of Sports Illustrated *that criticized the publication of a partly nude photo of Olympic swimmer Jenny Thompson. The letters and the controversial photo are reproduced here. Typical of his column, Reilly uses provocative language, calling critics of his magazine "hypocrites" and "prudes." Why do you think Reilly takes this mocking tone? What responses does he anticipate from the readers of* Sports Illustrated? *Ultimately, who do you agree with, Reilly or one of the letter writers—and why?*

Letters to the Editor, *Sports Illustrated*, September 4, 2000
Leave the toplessness in your swimsuit issue where the bimbos belong and put Jenny Thompson in the same place of respect that you put other top athletes.

Kim Baer, Broken Arrow, Okla.

After seeing the pose of Thompson, I turned every page of your magazine. Funny, the male athletes were fully clothed. Not one had his pants off with his hands covering his anatomy.

Elizabeth Vidmar, Gobles, Mich.

1   **WOW**, Jenny Thompson has a nice pair, doesn't she? Massive. Firm. Perfectly shaped.

2   Her thighs, I mean.

3   At least that's what blew *me* away when I saw the five-time Olympic gold-medalist swimmer topless, hands over her breasts, in these pages re-

cently. Killer thighs that could crush anvils. Calves sharp enough to slice tomato. Biceps that ought to be on a box of baking soda.

4   So why do some women have their girdles all in a wad? Why is the Women's Sports Foundation (WSF) so upset? Why did former WSF president Donna de Varona say of Thompson and other women athletes who have posed nude, "I want them to keep their clothes on." Why did *USA Today* columnist Christine Brennan go all Aunt Bea, complaining that the Thompson picture "sends [girls] the insecure message that an old stereotype still lives and thrives. If you doubt this, look at the picture and notice where your eye goes first . . . right to her chest."

5   What a load of hypocrites. When Dennis Rodman posed nude on a motorcycle, I don't recall Brennan complaining about where women's eyes went. Lance Armstrong, Dan O'Brien and Ricky Williams have all posed nude, and I don't remember de Varona rushing around trying to get them to put on a towel.

6   "I don't get this," WSF executive director Donna Lopiano told *The Orlando Sentinel.* "When you've spent half your life looking down at the line at the bottom of the pool—and you've given up everything—it's incongruent to take that body you worked so hard to build and use it for sex."

7   I agree, Ms. Lopiano. You *don't* get it. Thompson took her clothes off *because* she spent her whole life looking at the bottom of swimming pools. If she had to miss a lifetime of proms and parties and triple fudge cake, at least she should be able to show the world what she was building in the gym six hours a day. "I'm proud of my body," Thompson says, "and the work it's taken to get it where it is."

8   Retired Olympic swimmer Anita Nall told ESPN's *Outside the Lines* that the picture gives young girls the message that "women achieve empowerment through sexuality." But I don't see sex in that picture. Thompson isn't half in heat. She's not pouring a pitcher of milk on herself. She's not biting her knuckles. She's just standing there, staring right at us, confident, strong, with a look that says, *C'mon, let's wrestle. You'll lose.*

9   I mean, *look* at that picture! That picture tells you more about the kind of dedication it takes to be an Olympian than could be said in an entire issue of *Women's Sports and Fitness.* Maybe that's why *Women's Sports and Fitness* just ran nude shots of Thompson along with sister swimmers Dara Torres, Amy Van Dyken and Angel Martino.

10   And it's not just them. The Australian women's soccer team and Katarina Witt and Brandi Chastain and 12 women U.S. track and field athletes, including middle-distance runner Nnenna Lynch and high jumpers Amy

Acuff and Tisha Waller, and plenty others have also posed in the buff. There's no old stereotype here. These women aren't hung up about getting liberated. They *are* liberated, were born that way. They're coming from a whole new place in feminism—rugged, gorgeous, prideful athleticism—free of the old butch, male-hater stereotype women jocks used to fight.

11   That's what's really insulting about this prude uproar. These aren't 18-year-old girls having to strip at the Baby Doll Club to pay their rent. These are intelligent, grown women. Thompson is heading for medical school. Lynch is a Rhodes scholar. Waller is a churchgoing former elementary school teacher. It's kind of like the Herminator holding up his Atomics or Richard Petty standing next to his Plymouth. *Hey, you wanna see under the hood?* Aren't these grumpy women pro choice?

12   Bad messages? Here are women with *real* bodies, *fit* bodies, *attainable* bodies—not bodies you can only get through the Lucky Gene Club or plastic surgery or throwing up your lunch every day. You want a bad message? Set up Elle Macpherson as the ideal feminine role model. Trying to be 5' 11", 103 pounds with a 22-inch waist and a 38-inch bust sends a bad message.

13   Thompson sends young girls a terrific message: Fit is sexy. Muscles are sexy. Sport is sexy. Give it a try sometime.

14   And will somebody please remind de Varona that ancient Olympians competed in the nude in the first place?

Ad for "Got Milk?" with Stone Cold Steve Austin

Men's bodies, like women's bodies, are used to sell products. The "Got Milk?" series of ads display people with great bodies along with the claim that drinking milk helps to build those bodies.

Former World Wrestling Federation champion Steve Austin exemplifies a new ideal in men's bodies made possible by diet and weightlifting—bodies that expand muscles and reduce body fat to a degree never before possible. From what we know through works of art from classical times, no man's body in ancient Greece or Rome resembled Steve Austin's. The Roman copy of the Greek sculpture Dying Gaul *represents the ideal man's body of classical times, but the body appears as a boy's in comparison to Steve Austin's body. Bodies today, however, are not created just with diet and exercise; steroids assist men and women today in increasing muscle mass, though often with dangerous side effects.*

Getting Started: Writing for Particular Audiences

1. Write a letter to the editor of your campus newspaper arguing that your college or university (A) should emphasize computer education OR (B) has placed too much emphasis on technology and should encourage more face-to-face education.

If you choose A, here are some points you might think about:

- Technology will be increasingly involved in how we create, communicate, store, and use knowledge.
- Computers offer access to vast amounts of information and to people around the world.
- Nearly every occupation that requires a college education requires extensive use of computers.

If you choose B, here are some other points you might think about:

- Technology is a means to an end, not an end in itself; therefore, emphasizing technology neglects what is at the heart of education.
- Computers are expensive and divert money from other programs.
- Occupations in the future will require people who can adapt quickly to change, not people who are trained in the use of specific technologies.

2. Rewrite your letter for junior high school students, persuading them that (A) gaining expertise in using computers will be essential for their later education OR (B) gaining a solid general education is more important than learning how to use computers.

3. Rewrite your letter for the governor of your state, urging him or her to take leadership. If you don't know your governor's views on education, assume for the moment that he or she is very much in favor of students going to school over the Internet and doesn't believe in building more campuses or hiring more faculty.

4. Analyze the changes you made when you rewrote the letters. Did you change any reasons? Did you provide different background? How did you adjust the style? What other changes did you make?

CHAPTER 4

The Rhetoric of Arguments

Facts Alone Do Not Persuade

Chapter 1 explains how *Silent Spring* became an influential book that shaped thinking about the environment in the United States. Rachel Carson was not the first person to warn against the excessive use of pesticides, nor was she the first to urge that people think of the environment as a unified system in which changing one part means affecting the others. But she engaged her readers as no scientific writer on the environment had done before. She had good reasons to support her claims, but the way she wrote also stirred her readers into action.

Part of the brilliance of *Silent Spring* is that Carson didn't let the facts speak for themselves. In the following two paragraphs, she makes a simple point that insect populations are held in check by nature. Notice how she illustrates this broad principle with a personal example:

> No one knows how many species of insects inhabit the earth because there are so many yet to be identified. But more than 700,000 have already been described. This means that in terms of the number of species, 70 to 80 percent of the earth's creatures are insects. The vast majority of

these insects are held in check by natural forces, without any intervention by man. If this were not so, it is doubtful that any conceivable volume of chemicals—or any other methods—could possibly keep down their population.

The trouble is that we are seldom aware of the protection afforded by natural enemies until it fails. Most of us walk unseeing through the world, unaware of its beauties, its wonders, and the strange and sometimes terrible intensity of the lives that are being lived about us. So it is that the activities of insect predators and parasites are known to few. Perhaps we many have noticed an oddly shaped insect of ferocious mien on a bush in the garden and been dimly aware that the praying mantis lives at the expense of other insects. But we see with understanding eye only if we have walked in the garden at night and here and there with a flashlight have glimpsed the mantis stealthily creeping upon her prey. Then we sense something of the drama of the hunter and the hunted. Then we begin to feel something of that relentlessly pressing force by which nature controls her own.

Your success in arguing depends on how you represent yourself and how you connect with your audience's values.

Carson turned a dull point into a fascinating observation. She was keenly aware that the facts by themselves are not persuasive. She knew that she had to appeal to the heart as well as the mind. Her task wasn't simply to get people to feel sorry for animals that were killed by pesticides. She wanted people to think about nature differently. She wanted people to think of themselves as part of the natural world, and she wanted her readers to share her own great curiosity about nature. Convincing her readers that massive poisoning of insects meant also poisoning ourselves was a way to get people to think about ecology.

Let's take a look at a more recent book that also makes an argument that goes against the grain of popular thinking: *Eat Fat* by Richard Klein. Klein is a professor of comparative literature at Cornell University who grew tired of writing just for other professors and decided to write for a broad audience on a topic that was close to his heart: being overweight. *Eat Fat* became a brilliant success, enjoying rave reviews and selling many copies. Klein begins by observing that no nation is more obsessed with being thin than the United States. Consumers spend $33 billion a year on weight loss. But the results of all this money and self-denial are largely negative. People in the United States are the fattest people on the earth, at least among developed nations. Fashion models keep getting thinner to the point of looking like victims of starvation, but nearly half of U.S. women wear size 14 or larger, and about 32 percent wear size 16 or larger. Americans continue to gain weight at an astounding rate, adding 10 percent to their bulk on the average from 1984 to 1996, a time when health consciousness was never higher and when Americans dieted more and exercised more than they ever had in their history. But almost all their good efforts were doomed to failure. Out of 100 people who went on diets, 96 were even fatter three or four years later.

Richard Klein takes a position contrary to what most of us believe. He thinks that maybe the fact that Americans are getting fatter isn't really failure, that there may be good reasons why so many people are getting fatter. Furthermore, he argues that maybe this is a good thing rather than a bad thing. He begins by analyzing our hatred of fat. He says that there are three primary motives for people's desire to be thin. First, they believe that fat is ugly. Although this attitude is less than a hundred years old, it is constantly reinforced by the images of beautiful people that pervade the media. Second, people believe that fat is unhealthy. The medical, diet, and insurance industries have all promoted the idea that being thin is healthier and that thin people live longer. Third, people believe that fat weighs them down. Thinner people are seen as sexier, faster, and more agile—better suited for the fast-paced lifestyle of Western nations.

For each of these beliefs, Klein offers good reasons to think otherwise. Fat has not always seemed so disgusting to Americans. Indeed, a hundred years ago, fat signified health and well-being. People wanted to gain weight, and books were written telling them how to become plump. The turn of the century brought the so-called Banquet Years, marked by feasts on every occasion. One of the biggest eaters was President William H. Taft, who weighed over 300 pounds at his inauguration in 1908.

To question the attitude that fat is unhealthy, Klein notes that the spread of dieting has often led to less-healthy people, causing eating disorders in children as young as nine years of age, not to mention thousands of teenagers and adults. Furthermore, dieting has exactly the opposite effect of its purpose; it makes people fatter after a few years. Apparently, when the body is deprived of something it wants, it finds ingenious methods of satisfying those cravings. Evidence from research studies suggests that the human body has a certain level of fat that it tries to maintain. When someone cuts down on fat, the body may overreact and make fat more efficiently, thus causing the person to blow up rather than slim down. And contrary to the belief that thin people are sexier, Klein cites several studies showing that fat people are more sexually active.

Nevertheless, Klein is well aware that he is not going to convince many people with good reasons that appeal to the intellect. The problem (and opportunity) that Klein faces in defending fat is people's attitude toward it.

Nearly everyone in the United States believes down deep that being fat is bad. Klein writes, "It's easy in our society to love thin, but hard to achieve it. It's easy to be fat today, but hard to love it." Klein's task of arguing a position that people should not only accept fat but come to believe that fat is beautiful seems too ridiculous even to consider. After all, Americans have been taught all their lives to loathe fat.

So what do you do when you are in a very difficult rhetorical situation like the one into which Klein puts himself? Klein has an ingenious strategy, and he's honest about what he is attempting. He writes:

> My fundamental purpose, the whole aim of this book, summed up in its title, is not to convince but to charm you. By that I don't only mean to please you or seduce you into accepting my arguments, in the common sense of charm; I mean as well something more literal, more concrete: this book aims to work like a charm, to cast a spell by conjuring a spirit— a compelling voice, repetitive, monotonous, as if from another world, that says over and over EAT
>
> FAT.

Klein aims to persuade not through appealing to the reader's intellect but through the power of his voice. His voice makes the reader want to keep reading. And a reader who keeps reading at least grants the possibility that there are other attitudes toward fat besides the one that dominates in U.S. culture. Maybe the reader even admits that people in the United States would be a little happier if they weren't so obsessed with fat. If this happens, Klein has been successful.

In Chapter 1, we discuss how Aristotle recognized that good reasons that appeal to the intellect (logos) is only one strategy for effective arguments. He maintained that an audience has to view a speaker as trustworthy and reliable if they are to consider seriously the speaker's argument. Thus, an effective speaker has to seem credible to the audience through the effects of what Aristotle called ethos. Aristotle also recognized that appeals to emotions, values, and beliefs play important roles in effective arguments. He classified these appeals as pathos. Appeals to emotions, values, and beliefs often get downplayed in college writing courses, especially in the sciences and social sciences. But Rachel Carson knew that dry scientific argument would not move the government to ban DDT. And Richard Klein understood from the beginning that he would have to use alternative appeals; that is, he would have to win his readers by his witty style, his knowledge of history, and his shrewd observations about modern culture. Much can be learned from their tactics.

Ethos: Creating an Effective Persona

You have probably noticed that many times in the course of reading, you get a very real sense of the kind of person who is doing the writing. Even if you have never read this person's writing before, even if you really know nothing about the actual person behind the message, you still often get a sense of the character and personality of the writer just by reading. How you respond to the message to some extent depends on how you respond to the person who delivers it. The term *ethos* refers to the persuasive value associated with this person that is created in the text. People sometimes use the term *persona* to distinguish the narrator—the voice in the text—from the real author. You have encountered a great number of created personas in your reading. Sometimes it is obvious that the narrator is not the author; for example, Huckleberry Finn is a created persona to be distinguished from the real author, Mark Twain. Mark Twain, the pen name used by Samuel Clemens, is also a kind of persona. Clemens did public lecture tours adopting the Mark Twain personality, performing the equivalent of today's stand-up comedy. But in fact, every piece of writing is delivered by a created character, a persona, who may or may not have much in common with the real author.

In March 1997, scientists at the Oregon Regional Primate Research Center held a press conference to announce that they had successfully cloned two rhesus monkeys from early stage embryos. They had taken a set of chromosomes from cells in a primitive monkey embryo and inserted them into egg cells from which the original DNA had been removed. These embryos were then implanted in the wombs of host mothers using in vitro fertilization techniques. The monkeys were born normally and were expected to live as long as twenty years. Donald Wolf, a senior scientist at the center, called the cloning a major breakthrough, since it would remove some of the uncertainties in animal research that might have been attributed to genetic differences among animals.

Other people were greatly alarmed by the cloning of the monkeys that followed closely the announcement of the successful cloning of sheep. President Bill Clinton called the research "troubling" and immediately banned any federal funding for experiments that might lead to the cloning of human beings. The U.S. Congress organized hearings that began in March 1997 to examine the implications of cloning research.

Following are two examples of letters sent to the House Science Subcommittee on Technology following the hearings. What persona did the writer of each of the following letters create?

Rep. Connie Morella, Chairperson
House Science Subcommittee on Technology
2319 Rayburn House Office Building
Washington, DC 20515

Dear Representative Morella:

I am pleased to see among members of Congress great concern that humans
should not be cloned. What perplexes me is the lack of protest against cloning
animals. "Repulsive," "repugnant," "offensive"—scientists and politicians alike
have used these words to describe human cloning experiments, but these adjec-
tives should also be invoked to describe cloning experiments on animals.

There are both ethical and scientific reasons to oppose the cloning of animals.
Animals are simply not commodities with whose genetic material we can tam-
per in pursuit of human ends. M. Susan Smith, director of the Oregon Primate
Research Center, where Rhesus monkeys were cloned from embryo cells, says
that we should be glad that scientists will now need to use "only" 3 or 4 animals
instead of 20 or 30. But Smith and other proponents of animal experimentation
really just don't get it. What about the 3 or 4 beings who will suffer and die in
experiments? We don't bargain with lives—3 or 40—it's their use in experiments
that's wrong.

Smith and other scientists justify their work by stating that genetically identical
monkeys will help research into AIDS, alcoholism, depression and other illnesses.
Scientists can clone a million monkeys, but they still won't be good models for
human disease. It is not genetic variability that limits the effectiveness of animal
experimentation—it's that the physiology of animal species differs. Animals are
not "little humans," and there's no way that researchers can clone themselves
around that reality.

At the recent Congressional hearings on the ethics of cloning, testimony was
heard from the following: the director of National Institutes of Health, the largest
funding agency of animal experimentation in the country; the head of Genzyme
Transgenics Corporation, a company that seeks to profit from genetically manipulated animals; a representative from the U.S. Department of Agriculture, which
is interested in the potential of cloning animals for food; Smith of Oregon Primate
Research Center; and an ethicist who declared (and numerous exposés of animal
experiments refute) that we do not permit research that is cruel to animals in our
society.

There was a voice missing from this panel biased in favor of animal cloning: someone to represent the animals, whose lives and interests are so readily dismissed.
We all need to speak up for them now and demand legislation to ban all cloning
experiments.

Sincerely,
Helen Barnes

Rep. Connie Morella, Chairperson
House Science Subcommittee on Technology
2319 Rayburn House Office Building
Washington, DC 20515

Dear Representative Morella:

I cannot believe you actually pretended to have a hearing on animal cloning and only invited people in favor of cloning. Why didn't you invite someone to speak for the animals? What a waste of our tax dollars! You should be passing laws against cloning instead of trying to justify it.

Don't you understand that the monkeys are being cloned to be killed? Thousands of monkeys have died in research on cancer and AIDS, and we're still no closer to finding cures. Don't you see that such research is useless? It's not that difficult to figure out. Monkeys are not people. It doesn't matter if they have identical genes or not.

We see what's happening. This is another example of government protecting big business over the interests of the people. The only people who will benefit from cloning animals are the big executives of the high-tech companies and a few scientists who will make big profits.

Haven't you read the polls and noticed that the great majority of Americans are opposed to cloning? You'll find out how we feel when you have to run for reelection!

                              Sincerely,
                              Ed Younger

Both letters contain the same major points, and both are passionate in demanding legislation to end cloning of animals. Both assert that cloning monkeys for research purposes is wrong because it lacks scientific and ethical justification. But they stand apart in the ethos of the writer.

The writer of the first letter, Helen Barnes, attempts to establish common ground by noting that nearly everybody is opposed to the cloning of humans. Barnes makes a bridge to her issue by noting that the terms used for human cloning—*repulsive, repugnant, offensive*—should also be used for the cloning of animals. She urges Representative Morella to look at monkeys as beings rather than genetic material for the use of researchers. She points out the absence of any voices opposed to the use of monkeys for experiments at the hearings on cloning. She takes a strong stand at the end, but she uses "we," inviting Representative Morella to join her.

The writer of the second letter, by contrast, is confrontational from the outset. Ed Younger accuses Representative Morella of stacking the deck by inviting only proponents of cloning to the hearing. He insinuates that she is stupid if she doesn't realize the cloned monkeys will be killed and that the use of animals for testing has not produced cures for diseases such as cancer and AIDS. He suggests that she is a dupe of high-tech companies by taking their side. He ends with a threat to vote her out of office. His persona is clearly that of angry citizen.

Representatives often receive more than a thousand letters, faxes, and emails each day, and they have to deal with letters from angry people all the time. Usually, staff members answer the mail and simply tally up who is for and against a particular issue. Often, the reply is a form letter thanking the writer for his or her concern and stating the representative's position. But sometimes, representatives personally write detailed answers to letters from their constituents. Imagine that you are Representative Morella and you have to answer these two letters. Ed Younger's persona makes it difficult to say more than "I appreciate hearing your opinion on this issue." Helen Barnes's persona leaves open the possibility of an exchange of ideas.

People make judgments about you that are based on how you represent yourself when you write. Sometimes the angry voice is the one to present if you believe that your readers need a wake-up call. However, most people don't like to be yelled at. Just as you can change your voice orally when the situation calls for it—just as you can speak in a friendly way, in an excited way, or in a stern way in different circumstances—so too you should be able to modulate your voice in writing, depending on what is called for. Some important factors are the following:

- Your relationship with your audience (your voice can be less formal when you know someone well or when you are communicating with people in the same circumstances than when you are communicating with a relative stranger or with someone above or below you in an organization)

- Your audience's personality (different people respond sympathetically to different voices)
- Your argument (some arguments are more difficult to make than others)
- Your purpose (you may take a more urgent tone if you want your readers to act immediately)
- Your genre (arguments in formal proposals usually have a different voice from arguments in newspaper sports and opinion columns)

Argue Responsibly

In Washington, D.C., cars with diplomatic license plates often park illegally. Their drivers know they will not be towed or have to pay a ticket. For people who abuse the diplomatic privilege, the license plate says in effect, "I'm not playing by the rules."

In a similar way, you announce you are not playing by the rules when you begin an argument by saying "in my opinion." First, a reader assumes that if you make a claim in writing, you believe that claim. More important, it is rarely *only* your opinion. Most beliefs and assumptions are shared by many people. If it is only your opinion, it can be easily dismissed. But if your position is likely to be held by at least a few other members of your community, then a responsible reader must consider your position seriously.

Choosing an Appropriate Voice

Arguments that are totally predictable quickly lose their effectiveness. If you use the same strategy all the time—introduce your points, make your points, and summarize your points—you will get the job done, but you might not convince anyone who doesn't think the same way you do already. People who write about complex issues don't expect to convert everyone to their way of thinking with a few paragraphs. It's enough to both register a point of view and get their readers to think a little bit differently. Often they can have some fun along the way too.

In the September 24, 1987, issue of *Rolling Stone,* P. J. O'Rourke published "LSD: Let the Sixties Die" in response to a Sixties revival that was going on at the time. (A similar revival occurred in 1997–1998, and we'll no doubt see the Sixties return again in 2007–2008.) O'Rourke wasted no time letting his readers know how he felt about the revival:

> There's a stench of patchouli oil in the air. The overrated old Grateful Dead have a hit record. Hemlines are headed up. Beatle bangs are growing out. People are saddling their children with goofy names. The peace symbol—footprint of the American chicken—is giving the spray-paint industry a bad name again. Oh, God! The Sixties are coming back.
>
> Well, speaking strictly for this retired hippie and former pinko beatnik, if the Sixties head my way, they won't get past the porch steps. I've got a twelve-gauge, double-barreled duck gun chambered for three-inch Magnum shells. Any Sixties come around here, they'll be history. Which, for chrissakes, is what they're supposed to be.

O'Rourke goes on to make fun of the excesses of the Sixties, using the language of the Sixties. Slang that was popular in the Sixties—"can you dig it?," "the whole riff," "pick up on the heavy vibes," "if you know where I'm coming from"—now sounds silly. Other phrases, such as "Wow, man, which way to the bummer tent?" remind us that all wasn't peace and love at the big rock concerts.

Through the first half of his argument, O'Rourke uses satire to point out that many Sixties fads were ridiculous, much of its music was bad, and the acceptance of widespread drug use harmed many young people. But he didn't stop there. He next says, "Even if we wanted to, we couldn't recreate the Sixties now. We just don't have what it takes any more. First of all, there aren't any politicians left worth killing." The focus of his satire shifts subtly from the Sixties to the Eighties. Of young people, he writes, "And too many of today's college students are majoring in Comparative Greed and Advanced Studies in Real-Estate Arts." He also jabs his own generation, which used to shun possessions.

Near the end, O'Rourke gives his piece one more twist: "There was another bad thing about the Sixties, all those loopy beliefs—Karma, Krishna, Helter Skelter, participatory democracy, and all that." It's startling to find "participatory democracy" in that list of dismissed fads, but that's exactly O'Rourke's point. Thus, it's not until the end that O'Rourke chooses to make his implicit claim: that Sixties revivals are bad not just because they celebrate vacuous fads such as bell-bottom pants and psychedelic music but also because they reduce what is worth recovering from the Sixties to fad status.

Being aware of your options in creating a voice when you write is one of the secrets of arguing successfully. Before those options are described for a specific argument, a little background for the case in point will be useful. In June 1989, the Supreme Court ruled in *Texas* v. *Johnson* to uphold the First Amendment right to burn the U.S. flag as symbolic political speech. An outraged Congress approved the Flag Protection Act of 1989, but the Senate voted down an amendment to the Constitution. After the Flag Protection Act became law, there were many protests against it. Some protesters were arrested, but the courts ruled that the Flag Protection Act was unconstitutional. Pressure built to get a flag protection amendment

Demonstration in Washington, D.C., May 1970

into the Constitution, and legislation was introduced for such an amendment in the 1995, 1997, 1999, and 2001 sessions of Congress.

Imagine that you have decided to write an argument arguing that flag burning should be protected as free speech. You think that people could find better ways to protest than by burning the flag, but nonetheless, they still should have that right. When you start researching the issue and look at the text of laws that have been passed against flag burning, you discover that the laws are vague about defining what a flag is. You realize that people could be arrested and put in prison for cutting a cake with an image of the flag in the icing at a Fourth of July picnic.

You decide that examining definitions of the U.S. flag is a great way to begin your paper because if the flag cannot be defined, then you have a good argument that attempts to ban burning of the flag are doomed to failure. Congress cannot pass an amendment against something that it cannot accurately define. You look up the U.S. Code about the flag that was federal law from 1968 to 1989, when it was overturned in the Supreme Court case of *Texas* v. *Johnson*. It reads:

Whoever knowingly casts contempt upon any flag of the United States by publicly mutilating, defacing, defiling, burning, or trampling upon it shall be fined not more than $1,000 or imprisoned for not more than one year, or both.

The term "flag of the United States" as used in this section, shall include any flag, standard colors, ensign, or any picture or representation of either, or of any part or parts of either, made of any substance or represented on any substance, of any size evidently purporting to be either of said flag, standard, color, or ensign of the United States of America, or a picture or a representation of either, upon which shall be shown the colors, the stars and the stripes, in any number of either thereof, or of any part or parts of either, by which the average person seeing the same without deliberation may believe the same to represent the flag, standards, colors, or ensign of the United States of America.

You think the definition in the second paragraph is ridiculous. It could apply to red and white striped pants or almost anything that has stars and is red, white, and blue. But the question is how to make the point effectively in your analysis. Here are three versions of an analysis paragraph that would come after you quote the above law:

Version 1 (Distant, balanced)
The language of the 1968 law, passed in the midst of the protest over the Vietnam War, demonstrates the futility of passing laws against flag burning. Congress realized that protesters could burn objects that resembled the American flag and evade prosecution so they extended the law to apply to anything "the average person" believed to represent the flag. The great irony was that the major violators of this law were the most patriotic people in America, who put flags on their cars and bought things with images of flags. When they threw away their flag napkins, they desecrated the flag and violated the law.

Version 2 (Involved, angry)
The 1968 law against flag burning is yet another example of why the Washington bureaucrats who love big government always get it wrong. They see on TV something they don't like—protesters burning a flag. So they say, "Let's pass a law against it." But for the law to have teeth, they realize that it has to be far reaching, including every imagined possibility. So they make the law as broad as possible so the police can bust the heads of anyone they want to. The attempt to ban flag burning shows how people with good intentions take away your liberties.

Version 3 (Comedic)
"Wait a second!" you're probably saying to yourself. "Any number of stars? Any part or parts of either? On any substance? Or a picture or representa-

tion?" You bet. Burning a photo of a drawing of a three-starred red, white, and blue four-striped flag would land you in jail for a year. I'm not making this up. Do you still trust them to define what a flag is? I don't.

You can hear the differences in voices of these paragraphs. The first is the modulated voice of a radio or television commentator, appearing to give a distanced and balanced perspective. The second is the voice of an angry libertarian, asserting that the government that governs best is the one that governs least. The third is the voice of Comedy Central or the alternative press, laughing at what government tries to do. Once again, the point is not which one is most effective, because each could be effective for different audiences. The point is to be aware that you can take on different voices when you write and to learn how to control these voices.

TIPS

Strong Beginnings

Stephen Covey begins his international best-seller, *The Seven Habits of Highly Effective People,* with this sentence: "In more than 25 years of working with people in business, university, and marriage and family settings, I have come in contact with many individuals who have achieved an incredible degree of outward success, but have found themselves struggling with an inner hunger, a deep need for personal congruency and effectiveness and for healthy, growing relationships with other people." The first sentence tells you a great deal about why the book became a best-seller. In one sentence, Covey establishes his own credentials and sets out the central issues that the book addresses. He also accomplishes the two things you have to do before you can get anyone to consider your claims and good reasons. You first have to convince your readers that what you want to talk about is worth their time to read. Next, you have to convince them that you know enough to be worthy of their attention.

By starting out with "25 years of working with people in business, university, and marriage and family settings," Covey establishes his ethos as the voice of experience. In the main part of the sentence, Covey poses in a subtle way the problem the book addresses: "I have come in contact with many individuals who have achieved an incredible degree of outward success, but have found themselves struggling with an inner hunger." He could have said something like "Many people who are well off are still unhappy," but that's not quite his point. He sets out the problem as a

(continued)

Strong Beginnings *(continued)*

contrast: Many people who have achieved outward success struggle with an inner hunger. But what does *inner hunger* mean? Covey finishes the sentence by defining *inner hunger*—"a deep need for personal congruency and effectiveness and for healthy, growing relationships with other people"—in a grammatical construction called an **appositive.** You've heard appositives frequently on newscasts. Broadcasters use appositives to sum up or describe the significance of an event in sentences such as "Today, the prime ministers of India and Pakistan signed a treaty concerning disputed territory in Kashmir, an agreement that will help to ease building tensions between the two countries."

So far so good. But what exactly does Covey mean by "a deep need for personal congruency and effectiveness" and "healthy, growing relationships"? Those concepts are abstract, and if Covey is going to keep his potential readers, he must make those concepts relate to those readers. The primary readers for *The Seven Habits of Highly Effective People* presumably are people who already work for corporations and organizations. Therefore, Covey follows with a series of examples his clients have related to him:

> I've set and met my career goals and I'm having tremendous professional success. But it's cost me my personal and family life. I'm not even sure I know myself and what's really important to me. I've had to ask myself—is it worth it?
>
> I've started a new diet—for the fifth time this year. I know I'm overweight, and I really want to change. I read all the new information, I set goals, I get myself all psyched up with a positive mental attitude and tell myself I can do it. But I don't. After a few weeks, I fizzle. I just can't seem to keep a promise I make to myself.
>
> I'm busy—really busy. But sometimes I wonder if what I'm doing will make any difference in the long run. I'd really like to think there was meaning in my life, that somehow things were different because I was here.

Evidently readers recognized themselves in these examples. The sales of *The Seven Habits of Highly Effective People* remain strong years after it was first published.

Covey offers a lesson about strong beginnings. Even if you don't have twenty-five years of experience on a particular subject, you can still get off to a fast start. Establish your subject, your voice, and what's at stake for your readers right away, and there's a good chance your readers will stick with you.

Pathos: Appealing to Your Reader's Values

Chapter 3 on audience discusses how to take into account your audience's attitude toward you and your argument as you develop your content. *Pathos* also is audience-oriented and attitude-oriented; it refers to appeals to your audience's most basic, heartfelt attitudes and values.

Sometimes, pathos is defined (and dismissed) simply as an unsubtle appeal to your audience's barely controllable emotional side. You know that your reader fears something, loves something, or despises something, and you somehow tie your argument to those feelings. Critics of television advertising contend that advertisers depend on purely emotional arguments when they connect driving a particular automobile with achieving success or depict drinking a brand of beer as part of a happy social life. Because in Western culture the emotions are often associated with the instinctive and irrational and subconscious—with the so-called animal side of human beings—pathos seldom gets much respectful attention in argument. Most people in academic disciplines and the professions, especially the sciences and engineering, never want to be accused of making bald-faced emotional arguments like the ones you see on television. Therefore, it is not surprising that arguments in most academic writing are presented as sober and reasonable, avoiding overt appeals to an audience's subconscious instincts and emotions.

Then again, there is nothing necessarily irrational about the emotions. As many of the old *Star Trek* episodes with Mr. Spock show, emotions make people human just as much as reason does. There's nothing irrational or unreasonable about an argument that "Our city should attend to its solid waste problems because we want our children to live in safe, healthy, and attractive communities," even if there are emotional values latent in that argument. As that statement also illustrates, there is also probably no such thing as a purely emotional argument—an argument that totally bypasses reason. Even a beer ad on television that depicts men as beach bums and women as bikini-clad bodies has an implicit argument with a claim: "If you drink our beer, you'll have more fun."

Appealing to emotions is not necessarily a bad strategy, but pathos is a broader concept than simply appealing to emotions. The example claim, "Our city should attend to its solid waste problems because we want our children to live in safe, healthy, and attractive communities," illustrates that there is another way to think about pathos. Think of pathos as an appeal to the most basic values held by your audience. Pathos carries emotional values because it refers to the values that people hold so dearly that they don't think about them very much and don't question them very often—values such as the importance of safety and security, freedom and personal liberty, loyalty and friendship, equal opportunity and fairness. If your claim is "Interstate highways in urban areas should have concrete dividers placed in the median to prevent vehicles from skidding across the median into oncoming traffic," you have made a logical, matter-of-fact statement. But this argument carries pathetic overtones because safety is one of most basic values. Indeed, it might be a good strategy to begin with an example of a tragic head-on collision that might have been prevented if all urban interstate highways had concrete dividers on their median strips.

Pathos fails in argument when the linkage isn't clear. The linkage in TV ads is often absent. Many ads imply that the user of the product will be attractive to the opposite sex, younger, or happier, but how these changes are supposed to happen is never made clear. Using pathos is not a shortcut to making an effective argument.

Strong Endings

Endings are often the toughest part of a work to write. The easy way out is to repeat what you have said earlier. If you're writing a PhD dissertation, summarizing your conclusions is a good way to end. But if your argument is relatively short—the equivalent of three or four double-spaced pages—then you should hope that your readers have not forgotten your main points by the time they get to the end. Instead, think of a way to end that will be emphatic rather than sleep inducing. Here is how Anne Marie O'Keefe concluded an argument against the use of drug testing by employers ("The Case against Drug Testing," *Psychology Today* [June 1987]: 36–38):

> Civil libertarians claim that as long as employees do their work well, inquiries into their off-duty drug use are no more legitimate than inquiries into their sex lives. Then why has drug testing become so popular? Perhaps because it is simple and "objective"—a litmus test. It is not easily challenged because, like the use of lie detectors, it relies on technology that few understand. It is quicker and cheaper than serious and sustained efforts to reduce illegal drug use, such as the mass educational efforts that have successfully reduced cigarette smoking. And finally, while drug testing may do little to address the real problem of drug use in our society, it reinforces the employer's illusion of doing something.
>
> Apparently some employers would rather test their employees for drugs than build a relationship with them based on confidence and loyalty. Fortunately,

(continued)

Strong Endings *(continued)*

there are employers, such as Drexelbrook Engineering Company in Pennsylvania, who have decided against drug testing because of its human costs. As Drexelbrook's vice president put it, a relationship "doesn't just come from a paycheck. When you say to an employee, 'you're doing a great job; just the same, I want you to pee in this jar and I'm sending someone to watch you,' you've undermined that trust."

O'Keefe's next-to-last paragraph answers the question, If drug testing is so bad, then why do so many employers require it? Her last paragraph concludes her article with a positive example rather than restating what she has said before. An example, an additional point, a quotation, or a call to action is a good alternative to a bland summary in the final paragraph.

The Language of Arguments

So far, this chapter has focused on language as a means of creating a voice when you write, but voice is just one way to discuss style in arguments. Just as a personal style reflects all that a person does—the way she dresses, the way she talks, her personality—so too does style in argument. At the most fundamental level, style in argument begins with language—the words and sentences that the writer selects and assembles. Paying close attention to the words you use and how you put sentences together can pay big dividends for you as a writer.

Advertisers have long understood the critical role that words play in persuading people. The writers of advertising copy are well aware that the average American is exposed to over three thousand ads a day and that such oversaturation has made people cynical about ads. Advertisers have to be clever to get our attention, so ads often use the tactics of poets and comedians. Words in ads often use puns and metaphors to draw our attention to the products they promote. A watch ad runs with the banner "Every second counts." An ad for a coffeemaker asks, "Who better to handle his ugly mug in the morning?" A plastic wrap ad shows two chicken legs under the headline "Stop our legs from drying out." A used-car ad appears under the words "Born again."

But it is not just clever plays on words that do the work in the language of advertising. We often find words in ads that do not make much sense at first reading. For example, a Nikon camera ad displays in big bold letters, "It's a stealth bomber with fuzzy dice." Calling a camera a "stealth bomber with fuzzy dice" is an example of metaphor. **Metaphor** is a Greek term that means "carry over," which describes what happens when you encounter a metaphor. You carry over the meaning from one word to another. Metaphor is but one kind of **figurative language.** Also common in advertising are **synecdoche,** in which the part is used to represent the whole (a hood ornament represents a car), and **metonymy,** in which something stands for something else with which it is closely associated (using flowers to represent a product's fresh scent).

There are other kinds of figurative language, but all involve the transfer of meaning from one word or phrase to another. How this transfer works is more complicated. If we encounter an unfamiliar metaphor such as the stealth bomber example, we do our best to make sense of what the writer means. Most metaphors, however, are much more familiar and don't force us to put forth much mental effort. Think of all the clichés you hear daily: Clichés are the spice of life, the bread and butter of any conversation, the greatest things since sliced bread, the . . . well, you get the picture. Time flies when you're having fun, and we could keep writing clichés like there's no to-morrow, but there's no use flogging a dead horse. Clichés at some point in their past were original metaphors, but through repeated use, their attention-grabbing power has worn out.

Shakespeare used his knowledge of how figurative language works to great effect in his sonnets, in which, again and again, he sets up a cliché, such as comparing his love to a summer day in *Sonnet 18,* only to subvert that cliché by carrying over other meanings. He says that his love is more temper-ate and more lovely than a summer's day, but more important, a summer day is closely followed by autumn and winter: "A summer's lease hath all too short a date." If beauty lasts for only a day, then it's not desirable. Shakespeare turns the cliché of comparing one's lover to a summer's day inside out.

What meanings, then, is the reader supposed to carry over from "stealth bomber with fuzzy dice" to a Nikon camera? Cameras don't have wings, wheels, jet engines, or bomb bays, nor are they covered with fake fur. The ad-vertisers didn't want the reader to work too hard, so they put in fine print at the bottom their interpretation of the metaphor: "The technology of a seri-ous camera. The spontaneity of a point-and-shoot. Now you don't have to choose between the two."

Metaphors are but one way in which advertisers exploit the associations many words carry in addition to their literal meanings. Many ads are sexually suggestive. A moisturizing cream ad announces: "Shed your inhibitions." An ad for an online shopping service tells us to "Go naked to the mall." A whiskey ad in an outdoor magazine states: "Get in touch with your masculine side." Nowhere are the associative meanings of words more carefully consid-ered than in the discourse of politics. Politicians sprinkle their speeches with positive words referring to themselves and their party, words such as these:

*change, opportunity, truth, moral, courage, reform, prosperity, crusade, chil-
dren, family, debate, candid, humane, pristine, liberty, commitment, principle,
unique, duty, precious, care, tough, listen, learn, help, lead, vision, success,
empower(ment), citizen, activist, mobilize, dream, freedom, peace, rights, pioneer, proud/pride, building, preserve, flag, environment, reform, strength,
choice/choose, fair, protect, confident, incentive, hard work, initiative, common
sense, passionate*

In referring to their opponents, they use words such as these:

*decay, failure, crisis, destructive, destroy, sick, pathetic, lie, bureaucracy, betray,
shallow, endanger, coercion, hypocrisy, radical, threaten, waste, corruption,
incompetent, impose, self-serving, greed, ideological, insecure, pessimistic,
excuses, intolerant, stagnation, corrupt, selfish, insensitive, status quo, shame,
disgrace, punish, cynicism, cheat, steal, abuse of power*

Saying good things about yourself and bad things about your opponents is
characteristic of all politicians. The key to winning most elections is to get
the positive associations linked to the candidate you are supporting and the
negative associations linked to the opponent.

Some people denounce the language of advertising and politics as being
corrupted with bias. Although it is unfortunate that much advertising and
political discourse does involve outright deception, to expect such language
to be completely objective and free of bias is unrealistic. With the exception
of purely functional words such as *the*, *to*, and *for*, all words carry various
meanings and associations that they have picked up in the larger culture and
individual experience. The word "Mom," for example, brings associations of
your own mother and how motherhood is understood in your culture.

Rhetorical Analysis

To the general public the term *rhetoric* most commonly seems to denote
highly ornamental or deceptive or even manipulative speech or writing:
"That politician is just using a bunch of rhetoric" or "the rhetoric of that advertisement is highly deceptive" you hear people say. But the term *rhetoric* is
also commonly used as a synonym for speaking or writing in general or for any
other kind of communication: "*Silent Spring* is one of the most influential
pieces of environmental rhetoric ever written," someone might say. As a college subject, rhetoric is often associated with how to produce effective pieces
of communication following Aristotle's classic definition of rhetoric as "the

art of finding in any given case the available means of persuasion." But in recent years rhetoric has also taken on an interpretive function; it has come to be used not just as a means of producing effective communications but also as a way of understanding communication. In short, rhetoric can be understood as both a productive and interpretive enterprise: "the study of language—and the study of how to use it."

Aristotle's emphasis on persuasion has been influential in the history of rhetoric. And so it is now common to understand rhetoric as fundamentally involved in the study of persuasion. But "persuasion" as used here must be persuasion very broadly construed, because recently the realm of rhetoric has come to include a great deal of territory—written and oral language used to persuade, to be sure, but also a great many other kinds of communication that have general designs on people's values and actions, attitudes, and beliefs. Rhetorical analysis can be interpreted as *an effort to understand how people within specific social situations attempt to influence others through language.* But not just through language: Rhetoricians today attempt to understand every kind of important symbolic action—not only speeches and articles, but also architecture (isn't it clear that the U.S. Capitol building in Washington makes an argument?), movies and television shows (doesn't *Ally McBeal* offer an implicit argument about the appropriate conduct of young professional women? doesn't *Friends* have designs on viewers' values and attitudes?), memorials (don't the AIDS quilt and the Vietnam Veterans Memorial make arguments about AIDS and about our national understanding of the Vietnam War?), as well as visual art, Web sites, advertisements, photos and other images, dance, popular songs, and so forth.

Rhetorical analysis is applicable to all these persuasive uses of symbolic words and acts (in Part 3 we discuss visual rhetoric). Through rhetorical analysis, people strive to understand particular pieces of writing and other types of communication. Rhetorical analysis is a kind of critical reading, which we describe in Chapter 1 as opposed to ordinary reading. Today we study the words of Abraham Lincoln at Gettysburg or Martin Luther King's 1963 "I Have a Dream" speech or Abigail Adams's famous letters to her husband—rhetorical performances never intended for a twenty-first-century audience. As a rhetorical analyst your job is to understand them better, to appreciate the *rhetorical situation* (i.e., the circumstances of subject, audience, occasion, and purpose) that Lincoln, King, and Adams found themselves in and how they made choices to further their aims. Rhetorical analysis is an effort to read interpretively, with an eye toward understanding an act of communication from different perspectives and how that act is crafted to earn a particular response. All the chapters in this book give you tools for rhetorical analysis, and in the reading selection for this chapter, we show you a few ways they can be applied.

E. B. WHITE

Education

E. B. White (1899–1985) is best known today as the author of Charlotte's Web *(1952). He contributed many essays to* The New Yorker *and other publications over his long career. "Education" was published first in* Harper's *in 1939 and later collected in* One Man's Meat. *White wrote the essay over a half century ago, but you may find it interesting and readable still, in part at least because it concerns a perennial American question: What should our schools be like? Is education better carried out in large, fully equipped, but relatively impersonal settings, or in smaller but intensely personal, teacher-dominated schools? At first it might seem that the author takes no sides, that he simply wishes to describe objectively the two alternatives, to record his son's experiences in each circumstance, and to celebrate each as an expression of national values. He gives equal time to each school, he spends the same amount of space on concrete details about each, and he seems in firm control of his personal biases ("I have always rather favored public schools"). Through his light and comic tone White implies that all will be well for his son—and our children—in either circumstance, that the two schools each are to be neither favored nor feared by us. "All one can say is that the situation is different" (paragraph 4), not better, in the two places.*

Or is it? Perhaps "Education" is less an objective, neutral appraisal than it is a calculated argument that subtly favors the country school.

1   I have an increasing admiration for the teacher in the country school where we have a third-grade scholar in attendance. She not only undertakes to instruct her charges in all the subjects of the first three grades, but she manages to function quietly and effectively as a guardian of their health, their clothes, their habits, their mothers, and their snowball engagements. She has been doing this sort of Augean task for twenty years, and is both kind and wise. She cooks for the children on the stove that heats the room, and she can cool their passions or warm their soup with equal competence. She conceives their costumes, cleans up their messes, and shares their confidences. My boy already regards his

The teacher who presides over the country school appeals to the reader's emotions as the "ideal mother" stereotype.

Cleaning the Augean stables was one of the labors of Hercules.

teacher as his great friend, and I think tells her a great deal more than he tells us.

2   The shift from city school to country school was something we worried about quietly all last summer. I have always rather favored public school over private school, if only because in public school you meet a greater variety of children. This bias of mine, I suspect, is partly an attempt to justify my own past (I never knew anything but public schools) and partly an involuntary defense against getting kicked in the shins by a young ceramist on his way to the kiln. My wife was unacquainted with public schools, never having been exposed (in her early life) to anything more public than the washroom of Miss Winsor's. Regardless of our backgrounds, we both knew that the change in schools was something that concerned not us but the scholar himself. We hoped it would work out all right. In New York our son went to a medium-priced private institution with semi-progressive ideas of education, and modern plumbing. He learned fast, kept well, and we were satisfied. It was an electric, colorful, regimented existence with moments of pleasurable pause and giddy incident. The day the Christmas angel fainted and had to be carried out by one of the Wise Men was educational in the highest sense of the term. Our scholar gave imitations of it around the house for weeks afterward, and I doubt if it ever goes completely out of his mind.

White establishes his ethos in this paragraph. By disclosing his bias and by poking gentle humor at just about everything— his son "the scholar"; his wife the prim graduate of Miss Winsor's private school; himself; and, of course, both schools—White makes himself seem enormously sympathetic and trustworthy: fair-minded and unflappable, balanced and detached.

3   His days were rich in formal experience. Wearing overalls and an old sweater (the accepted uniform of the private seminary), he sallied forth at morn accompanied by a nurse or a parent and walked (or was pulled) two blocks to a corner where the school bus made a flag stop. This flashy vehicle was as punctual as death: seeing us waiting at the cold curb, it would sweep to a halt, open its mouth, suck the boy in, and spring away with an angry growl. It was a good deal like a train picking up a bag of mail. At school the scholar was worked on

White's son has to be "pulled" to the bus stop for the city school.

The metaphor for the school bus is a monster that sucks up children.

Students are not taught but "worked on" by a team of professionals.

for six or seven hours by half a dozen teachers and a nurse, and was revived on orange juice in mid-morning. In a cinder court he played games supervised by an athletic instructor, and in a cafeteria he ate lunch worked out by a dietitian. He soon learned to read with gratifying facility and discernment and to make Indian weapons of a semi-deadly nature. Whenever one of his classmates fell low of a fever the news was put on the wires and there were breathless phone calls to physicians, discussing periods of incubation and allied magic.

4   In the country all one can say is that the situation is different and somehow more casual. Dressed in corduroys, sweatshirt, and short rubber boots, and carrying a tin dinner pail, our scholar departs at the crack of dawn for the village school, two and a half miles down the road, next to the cemetery. When the road is open and the car will start, he makes the journey by motor, courtesy of his old man. When the snow is deep or the motor is dead or both, he makes it on the hoof. In the afternoons he walks or hitches all or part of the way home in fair weather, gets transported in foul. The schoolhouse is a two-room frame building, bungalow type, shingles stained a burnt brown with weather-resistant stain. It has a chemical toilet in the basement and two teachers above the stairs. One takes the first three grades, the other the fourth, fifth, and sixth. They have little or no time for individual instruction, and no time at all for the esoteric. They teach what they know themselves, just as fast and as hard as they can manage. The pupils sit still at their desks in class, and do their milling around outdoors during recess.

5   There is no supervised play. They play cops and robbers (only they call it "Jail") and throw things at one another—snowballs in the winter, rose hips in fall. It seems to satisfy them. They also construct darts, pinwheels, and "pick-up-sticks" (jackstraws), and the school itself does a brisk

The experience of the city school makes children sick.

The image of the one-room or two-room schoolhouse appeals to the American love of the frontier and small town (associated with values of self-reliance, decency, and innocence).

Facilities and staff are minimal at the country school.

Instruction in the country school is about the basics, but students learn fast and well.

Play at the country school is organized by the students, not by the school staff. It is spontaneous and fresh.

White's language describing the country school emphasizes activity as opposed to the regimentation of the city school.

trade in penny candy, which is for sale right in the classroom and which contains "surprises." The most highly prized surprise is a fake cigarette, made of cardboard, fiendishly lifelike.

6   The memory of how apprehensive we were at the beginning is still strong. The boy was nervous about the change too. The tension, on that first fair morning in September when we drove him to school, almost blew the windows out of the sedan. And when later we picked him up on the road, wandering along with his little blue lunch-pail, and got his laconic report "All right" in answer to our inquiry about how the day had gone, our relief was vast. Now, after almost a year of it, the only difference we can discover in the two school experiences is that in the country he sleeps better at night—and *that* probably is more the air than the education. When grilled on the subject of school-in-country vs. school-in-city, he replied that the chief difference is that the day seems to go so much quicker in the country. "Just like lightning," he reported.

White is quite subtle in his conclusion, but of course the bottom line is that his son likes to go to the country school. Although he never states his claim explicitly, clearly White finds a personalized, unstructured school environment superior to a structured, supervised curriculum.

The first and last paragraphs are the positions of emphasis. White gives both to the country school while placing the city school in a less prominent position in the middle.

Steps in Writing a Rhetorical Analysis

1. **Find an argument that you either strongly agree with or strongly disagree with.** You can find arguments on the editorial pages of newspapers; in opinion features in magazines such as *Time*, *Newsweek*, and *U.S. News and World Report*, in magazines that take political positions such as *National Review*, *Mother Jones*, *New Republic*, *Nation*, and the online journal *Slate*; and the Web sites of activist organizations (for a list of these organizations, see www.yahoo.com/Society_and_Culture/ Issues_and_Causes/). Letters to the editor and online newsgroup postings probably won't work for this assignment unless they are long and detailed.

2. **Analyze the structure of the argument.** First, number the paragraphs, then on a separate page write a sentence summarizing each of the paragraphs. Where is the main claim located? Underline it. What are the rea-

sons offered in support of the claim? Put stars beside those. Are any opposing positions considered? If so, put an "O" beside those.

3. **Analyze the language and style of the argument.** Make a list of the key words in the argument. Which are controversial? Are the key terms adequately defined? Are any metaphors or other figurative language used in the argument? Does the writer use "I" or "we" or does he or she speak from a distanced viewpoint? How would you characterize the writer's style? Is it formal or informal? Is it serious, humorous, or satirical?

4. **Analyze the ethos.** How does the writer represent himself or herself? Does the writer have any credentials to be an authority on the topic? Do you trust the writer? Why or why not?

5. **Analyze the logos.** Where do you find facts and evidence in the argument? What kinds of facts and evidence does the writer present: Direct observation? Statistics? Interviews? Surveys? Secondhand sources such as published research? Quotes from authorities?

6. **Analyze the pathos.** Who do you think the argument was written for? Are there any places where the writer attempts to invoke an emotional response? Where do you find appeals to shared values with the audience? You are a member of that audience, so what values do you hold in common with the writer? What values do you not hold in common?

7. **Write a draft.**

   Introduction:
   - Describe briefly the argument you are analyzing, including where it was published, how long it is, and who wrote it. If the argument is on an issue unfamiliar to your readers, you may have to supply some background.

   Body:
   - Analyze the language and structure of the argument, using steps 2 through 6. Remember that you don't want to present your analysis as a list. Instead you might wish to focus on a particular aspect. For example, if you are analyzing E. B. White's "Education," a possible thesis is "White builds his ethos in several ways in 'Education.'"

   Conclusion:
   - Do more than simply summarize what you have said. You might, for instance, end with an example that typifies the argument. You don't have to end by either agreeing or disagreeing with the writer. Your task in this assignment is to analyze the strategies the writer uses.

8. **Revise, revise, revise. See Chapter 11 for detailed instructions.**

   Stage 1. Read your analysis aloud.
   Do no more in this stage than put checks in the margins that you can return to later. Think in particular about these things:

- **Your claim.** When you finish reading, summarize in one sentence what you claim in your analysis.
- **Your representation of yourself.** Forget for a moment that you wrote what you are reading. What impression do you have of you, the writer?
- **Your consideration of your readers.** Do you give enough background if your readers are unfamiliar with the issue?

Stage 2. Analyze your argument in detail.

- **Examine your organization.** What are the topics of each paragraph? Is the relationship of one paragraph to another clearly signaled?
- **Examine your evidence.** Are your claims supported by evidence in your analysis?
- **Consider your title and introduction.** Be as specific as you can in your title and, if possible, suggest your stance. Does your introduction get off to a fast start and convince your reader to keep reading?
- **Consider your conclusion.** Think about whether there is a summarizing point you can make, an implication you can draw, or another example you can include that sums up your position.
- **Analyze the visual aspects of your text.** Do the font and layout you selected look attractive? Would headings and subheadings help to identify key sections of your argument? Would the addition of graphics augment key points?

Stage 3. Focus on your style and proofread carefully.

- **Check the connections between sentences.** Notice how your sentences are connected. If you need to signal the relationship from one sentence to the next, use a transitional word or phrase.
- **Check your sentences for emphasis.** Elements at the beginning and the end of sentences tend to stand out more than things in the middle.
- **Eliminate wordiness.** See how many words you can take out without losing the meaning.
- **Use active verbs.** Anytime you can use a verb besides a form of *be* (*is, are, was, were*), take advantage of the opportunity to make your style more lively.
- **Proofread your spelling carefully.** Your spelling checker will miss many mistakes.
- **Use your handbook to check items of mechanics and usage.** Look up any item you are unsure of.

PART 2

Putting Good Reasons into Action

Options for Arguments

Imagine that you bought a new car in June and you take some of your friends to your favorite lake over the Fourth of July weekend. You have a great time until, as you are heading home, a drunk driver—a repeat offender—swerves into your lane and totals your new car. You and your friends are lucky not to be hurt, but you're outraged because you believe that repeat offenders should be prevented from driving, even if that means putting them in jail. You also remember going to another state that had sobriety checkpoints on holiday weekends. If such a checkpoint had been at the lake, you would still be driving your new car. You live in a town that encourages citizens to contribute to the local newspaper, and you think you could get a guest editorial published. The question is, how do you want to write the editorial?

You could tell your story about how a repeat drunk driver endangered the lives of you and your friends. You could argue for a stricter definition of driving while intoxicated (DWI) and for standard testing procedures. You could compare the treatment of drunk drivers in your state with the treatment of drunk drivers in another state. You could cite statistics that drunk drivers killed 15,786 people in 1999, a figure that was down from previous years but still represented too many needless deaths. You could evaluate the present enforcement of drunk driving laws as unsuccessful or less than totally successful. You could propose taking vehicles away from repeat drunk drivers and forcing them to serve mandatory sentences. You could argue that your community should have sobriety checkpoints at times when drunk drivers are likely to be on the road.

You're not going to have much space in the newspaper, so you decide to argue for sobriety checkpoints. You know that they are controversial. One of your friends in the car with you said that they are unconstitutional because they involve search without cause. However, after doing some research to find out whether they are defined as legal or illegal, you learn that on June 14, 1990, the U.S. Supreme Court upheld the constitutionality of using checkpoints as a deterrent and enforcement tool against drunk drivers. But you still want to know whether most people would agree with your friend that sobriety checkpoints are an invasion of privacy. You find opinion polls and surveys going back to the 1980s that show 70 to 80 percent of those polled support sobriety checkpoints. You also realize that you can argue by analogy that security checkpoints for alcohol are similar in many ways to airport security checkpoints that protect the passengers. You decide you will finish by making an argument from consequence. If people who go to the lake with plans to drink a lot know in advance that there will be checkpoints, they will find a designated driver or some other means of safe transportation, and everyone else will also be a little safer.

The point of this example is that people very rarely set out to define something in an argument for the sake of definition, compare for the sake of comparison, or adopt any of the other ways of structuring an argument. Instead, they have a purpose in mind, and they use the kinds of arguments that are discussed in Part 2—most often in combination—as means to an end. Most arguments use multiple kinds of approaches and multiple sources of good reasons. Proposal arguments in particular often analyze a present situation with definition, causal, and evaluative arguments before advancing a course of future action. The advantage of thinking explicitly about the structure of arguments is that you often find other ways to argue. Sometimes you just need a way to get started writing about complex issues.

An even greater advantage of thinking explicitly about specific kinds of arguments is that they can often give you a sequence for constructing arguments. Take affirmative action policies for granting admission to college as an example. No issue has been more controversial on college campuses during the last ten years. But what exactly does *affirmative action* mean? You know that it is a policy that attempts to address the reality of contemporary inequality based on past injustice. But injustice to whom and by whom? Do all members of minorities, all women, and all people with disabilities have equal claims for redress of past injustices? If not, how do you distinguish among them? And what exactly does affirmative action entail? Do all students who are admitted by affirmative action criteria automatically receive scholarships? Clearly, you need to define affirmative action first before proposing any changes in the policy.

Since affirmative action policies have been around for a few years, next you might investigate how well they have worked. If you view affirmative action as a cause, then what have been its effects? You might find, for example, that the percentage of African Americans graduating from college dropped from 1991 through 2001 in many states. Furthermore, affirmative action policies have created a backlash attitude among many whites who believe, rightly or wrongly, that they are victims of reverse racism. But you might find that enrollment of minorities at your university has increased substantially since affirmative action policies were instituted. And you might come across a book by the then-presidents of Princeton and Harvard, William G. Bowen and Derek Bok, entitled *The Shape of the River: Long-Term Consequences of Considering Race in College and University Admissions*, which examines the effects of affirmative action policies at twenty-eight of the nation's most select universities. They found that African-American graduates of elite schools were more likely than their white counterparts to earn graduate degrees and to take on civic responsibilities after graduation.

With a definition established and evidence collected, you can move to evaluation. Is the goal of achieving diversity through affirmative action admissions policies a worthy one because white people enjoyed preferential treatment until the last few decades? Or are affirmative action admissions policies bad because they continue the historically bad practice of giving preference to people of certain races and because they cast into the role of victims the people they are trying to help? When you have a definition with evidence and have made an evaluation, you have the groundwork for making a recommendation in the form of a proposal. A proposal argues what "should" or "must" be done in the future.

Even though types of argument are distinguished in Part 2, they are closely linked parts of a whole. Though each type of argument can stand alone, they always involve multiple aspects. If you are clear in your purpose for your argument and have a good sense of the knowledge and attitudes of the people your argument is aimed toward, then the types of arguments you want to use will often be evident to you.

CHAPTER 5

Definition Arguments

In early 2000 Chrysler began selling its PT Cruiser, which quickly became one of its best-selling products. But what exactly is the PT Cruiser—a car or a truck? It is built on the chassis of a Dodge Neon, which is a car. The press referred to it as a station wagon. Chrysler, however, argued that the PT Cruiser is a truck because it has a flat cargo area when the rear seats are folded down. The definition of the PT Cruiser as a truck or as a car did not matter much to the people who bought the vehicle, but the definition mattered a great deal to Chrysler.

The National Highway Traffic and Safety Administration sets the standards for fuel economy for passenger cars and trucks, called Corporate Average Fuel Economy (CAFE). The CAFE standards for 2001 require that a manufacturer's cars average 27.5 miles per gallon and that its trucks average 20.7 miles per gallon.

> **Definition arguments are the most powerful arguments.**

Chrysler had no difficulty meeting the car standard because it produces no cars with V-8 engines. Chrysler, however, sells many trucks and jeeps with V-8 and V-10 engines that get poor gas mileage, making it difficult to meet the CAFE standard for trucks. Exceeding the CAFE standard costs the manufacturer a huge chunk of money in penalties—$5.50 for each truck for each tenth of a mile over the limit. By lumping the PT Cruiser, which gets high gas

Chrysler's PT Cruiser

mileage, in with the trucks, Chrysler can sell many more V-8 and V-10 trucks and jeeps that would otherwise be assessed the penalty for poor gas mileage.

The PT Cruiser example illustrates why definitions often matter more than we might think at first. It also illustrates three very important principles that operate when definitions are used in arguments.

First, people make definitions that benefit their interests. You learned very early in life the importance of defining actions as "accidents." Windows can be broken from being careless, especially when you are tossing a ball against the side of the house, but if it's an accident, well, accidents just happen (and don't require punishment).

Second, most of the time when you are arguing a definition, your audience may either have a different definition in mind or be unsure of the definition. Your mother or father probably didn't think breaking the window was an accident, so you had to convince Mom or Dad that you were really being careful, but the ball just slipped out of your hand. It's your job to get them to accept your definition.

Third, if you can get your audience to accept your definition, then usually you succeed. For this reason definition arguments are the most powerful arguments.

Kinds of Definitions

Rarely do you get far into an argument without having to define something. Imagine that you are writing an argument about the United States's decades-old and largely ineffective "war on drugs." We all know that the war on drugs is being waged against drugs that are illegal, like cocaine and marijuana, and not against the legal drugs produced by the multibillion-dollar drug industry. Our society classifies drugs into two categories: "good" drugs, which are legal, and "bad" drugs, which are illegal.

How exactly does our society arrive at these definitions? Drugs would be relatively easy to define as good or bad if the difference could be defined at the molecular level. Bad drugs would contain certain molecules that define them as bad. The history of drug use in the United States, however, tells us that it is not so simple. In the last century alcohol was on the list of illegal drugs for over a decade, while opium was considered a good drug and distributed in many patent medicines by pharmaceutical companies. Similarly, LSD and MDMA (ecstasy) were developed by the pharmaceutical industry but later placed in the illegal category. In a few states marijuana is now crossing over to the legal category for medicinal use.

If drugs cannot be classified as good or bad by their molecular structure, then perhaps society classifies them by effects. In might be reasonable to assume that drugs that are addictive are illegal, but that's not the case. Nicotine is highly addictive and is a legal drug; so too are many prescription medicines. Neither are drugs taken for the purpose of offering pleasure necessarily illegal (think of alcohol and Viagra), nor are drugs that alter consciousness or change personality (Prozac).

How a drug is defined as legal or illegal apparently is determined by example. The nationwide effort in the United States to stop people from drinking alcohol during the first decades of the twentieth century led to the passage of the Eighteenth Amendment and the ban on sales of alcohol from 1920 to 1933, known as Prohibition. Those who argued for Prohibition used examples of drunkenness, especially among the poor, to show how alcohol broke up families and left mothers and children penniless in the street. Those who opposed Prohibition initially pointed to the consumption of beer and wine in many ethnic traditions. Later they raised examples of the bad effects of Prohibition—the rise of organized crime, the increase in alcohol abuse, and the general disregard for laws.

When you make a definitional argument, it's important to think about what kind of definition you will use.

FORMAL DEFINITIONS

Formal definitions typically categorize an item into the next higher classification and give distinguishing criteria from other items within that classification. Most dictionary definitions are formal definitions. For example, fish are cold-blooded aquatic vertebrates that have jaws, fins, and scales and are distinguished from other cold-blooded aquatic vertebrates (such as sea snakes) by the presence of gills. If you can construct a formal definition with specific criteria that your audience will accept, then likely you will have a strong argument. The key is to get your audience to agree to your criteria.

OPERATIONAL DEFINITIONS

Many concepts cannot be easily defined by formal definitions. Researchers in the natural and social sciences must construct operational definitions that they use for their research. For example, in the idea map in Chapter 1, we discuss a study of binge drinking among college students that defines a binge as five or more drinks in one sitting for a man, and four or more drinks for a woman. Some people think this standard is too low and should be raised to six to eight drinks to distinguish true problem drinkers from the general college population. No matter what the number, researchers must argue that the particular definition is one that suits the concept.

DEFINITIONS FROM EXAMPLE

Many human qualities such as honesty, courage, creativity, deceit, and love must be defined by examples that the audience accepts as representative of the concept. Few would not call the firemen who entered the World Trade Center on September 11, 2001, courageous. Most people would describe someone with a diagnosis of terminal cancer who refuses to feel self-pity as courageous. But what about a student who declines to go to a concert with her friends so she can study for an exam? Her behavior might be admirable, but most people would hesitate to call it courageous. The key to arguing a definition from examples is that the examples must strike the audience as in some way typical of the concept, even if the situation is unusual.

Building a Definitional Argument

Because definition arguments are the most powerful arguments, they are often at the center of the most important debates in American history. The major arguments of the civil rights movement were definition arguments, none more eloquent than Martin Luther King, Jr.'s "Letter from Birmingham Jail." From 1957 until his assassination in April 1968, King served as president of the Southern

Martin Luther King, Jr.

Christian Leadership Conference, an organization of primarily African-American clergymen dedicated to bringing about social change. King, who was a Baptist minister, tried to put into practice Mahatma Gandhi's principles of nonviolence in demonstrations, sit-ins, and marches throughout the South. During Holy Week in 1963, King led demonstrations and a boycott of downtown merchants in Birmingham, Alabama, to end racial segregation at lunch counters and discriminatory hiring practices.

On Wednesday, April 10, the city obtained an injunction directing the demonstrations to cease until their legality could be argued in court. But after meditation, King decided, against the advice of his associates, to defy the court order and proceed with the march planned for Good Friday morning. On Friday morning, April 12, King and fifty followers were arrested. King was held in solitary confinement until the end of the weekend, allowed neither to see his attorneys nor to call his wife. On the day of his arrest, King read in the newspaper a statement objecting to the demonstrations signed by eight white Birmingham clergymen of Protestant, Catholic, and Jewish faiths, urging that the protests stop and that grievances be settled in the courts.

On Saturday morning, King started writing an eloquent response that addresses the criticisms of the white clergymen, who are one primary audience of his response. But King intended his response to the ministers for widespread publication, and he clearly had in mind a larger readership. The clergymen gave him the occasion to address moderate white leaders in the South as well as religious and educated people across the nation and supporters of the civil rights movement. King begins "Letter from Birmingham Jail" by addressing the ministers as "My Dear Fellow Clergymen," adopting a conciliatory and tactful tone from the outset but at the same time offering strong arguments for the necessity of acting now rather than waiting for change. A critical part of King's argument is justifying not obeying certain laws. The eight white clergymen ask that laws be obeyed until they are changed. Here's how King responds:

> You express a great deal of anxiety over our willingness to break laws. This
> is certainly a legitimate concern. Since we so diligently urge people to obey

the Supreme Court's decision of 1954 outlawing segregation in the public schools, at first glance it may seem rather paradoxical for us consciously to break laws. One may well ask: "How can you advocate breaking some laws and obeying others?" The answer lies in the fact that there are two types of laws: just and unjust. I would be the first to advocate obeying just laws. One has not only a legal but a moral responsibility to obey just laws. Conversely, one has a moral responsibility to disobey unjust laws. I would agree with St. Augustine that "an unjust law is no law at all."

Now, what is the difference between the two? How does one determine whether a law is just or unjust? A just law is a man-made code that squares with the moral law or the law of God. An unjust law is a code that is out of harmony with the moral law. To put it in the terms of St. Thomas Aquinas: An unjust law is a human law that is not rooted in eternal law and natural law. Any law that uplifts human personality is just. Any law that degrades human personality is unjust. All segregation statutes are unjust because segregation distorts the soul and damages the personality. It gives the segregator a false sense of superiority and the segregated a false sense of inferiority. Segregation, to use the terminology of the Jewish philosopher Martin Buber, substitutes an "I-it" relationship and ends up relegating persons to the status of things. Hence segregation is not only politically, economically and sociologically unsound, it is morally wrong and sinful. Paul Tillich has said that sin is separation. Is not segregation an existential expression of man's tragic separation, his awful estrangement, his terrible sinfulness? Thus it is that I can urge men to obey the 1954 decision of the Supreme Court, for it is morally right; and I can urge them to disobey segregation ordinances, for they are morally wrong.

Martin Luther King's analysis of just and unjust laws is a classic definitional argument. Definitional arguments take this form: *X is a Y if X possesses certain criteria that differentiate it from other similar things in its general class.* According to King, a **just law** possesses the criteria of being consistent with moral law and uplifting human personality. Just as important, King sets out the criteria of **unjust law,** when X is not a Y. Unjust laws have the criteria of being out of harmony with moral law and damaging human personality. The criteria are set out in because clauses: *X is a Y because it has criteria A and B.* The criteria provide the link between X and Y:

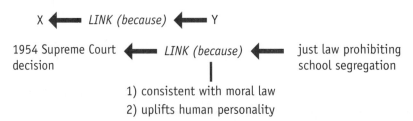

The negative can be argued in the same way:

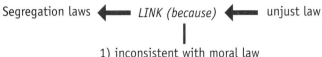

Segregation laws ◄■■■ *LINK (because)* ◄■■■ unjust law

1) inconsistent with moral law
2) degrades human personality

An extended definition like King's is a two-step process. First you have to determine the criteria of Y. Then you have to argue that X has these criteria. If you want to argue that housing prisoners in unheated and non-air-conditioned tents is cruel and unusual punishment, then you have to make exposing prisoners to hot and cold extremes one of the criteria of cruel and unusual punishment. The keys to a definitional argument are getting your audience to accept your criteria and getting your audience to accept that the case in point meets those criteria. King's primary audience was the eight white clergymen; therefore, he used religious criteria and cited Protestant, Catholic, and Jewish theologians as his authority. His second criterion about just laws uplifting the human personality was a less familiar concept than the idea of moral law. King therefore offered a more detailed explanation drawing on the work of Martin Buber.

But King was smart enough to know that not all of his potential readers would put quite so much stock in religious authorities. Therefore, he follows the religious criteria with two other criteria that appeal to definitions of democracy:

> Let us consider a more concrete example of just and unjust laws. An unjust law is a code that a numerical or power majority group compels a minority group to obey but does not make binding on itself. This is *difference* made legal. By the same token, a just law is a code that a majority compels a minority to follow and that it is willing to follow itself. This is *sameness* made legal.
>
> Let me give another explanation. A law is unjust if it is inflicted on the minority that, as a result of being denied the right to vote, has no part in enacting or devising the law. Who can say that the legislature of Alabama which set up that state's segregation laws was democratically elected? Throughout Alabama all sorts of devious methods are used to prevent Negroes from becoming registered voters, and there are some counties in which, even though Negroes constitute a majority of the population, not a single Negro is registered. Can any law enacted under such circumstances be considered democratically structured?

King expands his criteria for just and unjust laws to include four major criteria, and he defines both by classifying and by giving examples.

Segregation laws ◄──── *LINK (because)* ◄──── unjust law

1) inconsistent with moral law
2) damages human personality
3) applies to minority group but not majority group that made the law
4) made by a body that was not democratically elected

King's "Letter from Birmingham Jail" draws much of its rhetorical power from its reliance on a variety of arguments that are suited for different readers. An atheist could reject the notion of laws made by God but could still be convinced by the criteria that segregation laws are undemocratic and therefore unjust.

To make definitional arguments work, often you must put much effort into identifying and explaining your criteria. You must convince your readers that your criteria are the best ones for what you are defining and that they apply to the case your are arguing. King backs up his assertion that Alabama's segregation laws in 1963 were unjust because the Alabama legislature was not democratically elected by pointing to counties that had African-American majorities but no African-American voters.

SCOTT MCCLOUD

Setting the Record Straight

Scott McCloud is the pseudonym of Scott Willard McLeod, who was born in Boston in 1960 and graduated from Syracuse University in 1982. After a short stint in the production department at DC Comics, he quickly became a highly regarded writer and illustrator of comics. His works include the ten-issue series Zot! *(1984–1985),* Destroy!! *(1986), and the nonfiction* Understanding Comics: The Invisible Art *(Northampton, MA: Tundra, 1993), from which this selection is taken.*

Understanding Comics is a brilliant explanation of how comics combine words and pictures to achieve effects that neither words nor pictures can do alone. At the beginning of the book, McCloud finds it necessary to define what comics are and are not before he can begin to analyze the magic of comics. Notice how he has to refine his criteria several times before he has an adequate definition.

IN LESS THAN A *YEAR,* I BECAME *TOTALLY OBSESSED* WITH COMICS! I DECIDED TO BECOME A *COMICS ARTIST* IN 10th *GRADE* AND BEGAN TO *PRACTICE, PRACTICE, PRACTICE!*

I FELT THAT THERE WAS SOMETHING *LURKING* IN COMICS... SOMETHING THAT HAD *NEVER BEEN DONE.*

SOME KIND OF *HIDDEN POWER!*

BUT WHENEVER I TRIED TO *EXPLAIN* MY FEELING, I FAILED *MISERABLY.*

COMIC BOOKS?! HA! HA! HA!

BUT IT-- BUT IT'S-- BUH...

SURE, I REALIZED THAT COMIC BOOKS WERE USUALLY *CRUDE, POORLY-DRAWN, SEMILITERATE, CHEAP, DISPOSABLE KIDDIE FARE--*

--*BUT*--

THEY DON'T *HAVE* TO BE!

THE *PROBLEM* WAS THAT FOR *MOST PEOPLE,* THAT WAS WHAT *"COMIC BOOK"* MEANT!

DON'T GIMME THAT *COMIC BOOK* TALK, BARNEY!

IF PEOPLE FAILED TO *UNDERSTAND* COMICS, IT WAS BECAUSE THEY DEFINED WHAT COMICS COULD BE *TOO NARROWLY!*

A *PROPER DEFINITION,* IF WE COULD *FIND* ONE, MIGHT GIVE *LIE* TO THE STEREOTYPES--

--AND SHOW THAT THE *POTENTIAL* OF COMICS IS *LIMITLESS* AND *EXCITING!*

THIS IS WHERE OUR JOURNEY *BEGINS.*

[Scott McCloud observes that the problem is finding a definition that is broad enough to cover the many different kinds of comics but not so broad as to include anything that is not comics. A comic book is a physical object, but what exactly is comics*?]*

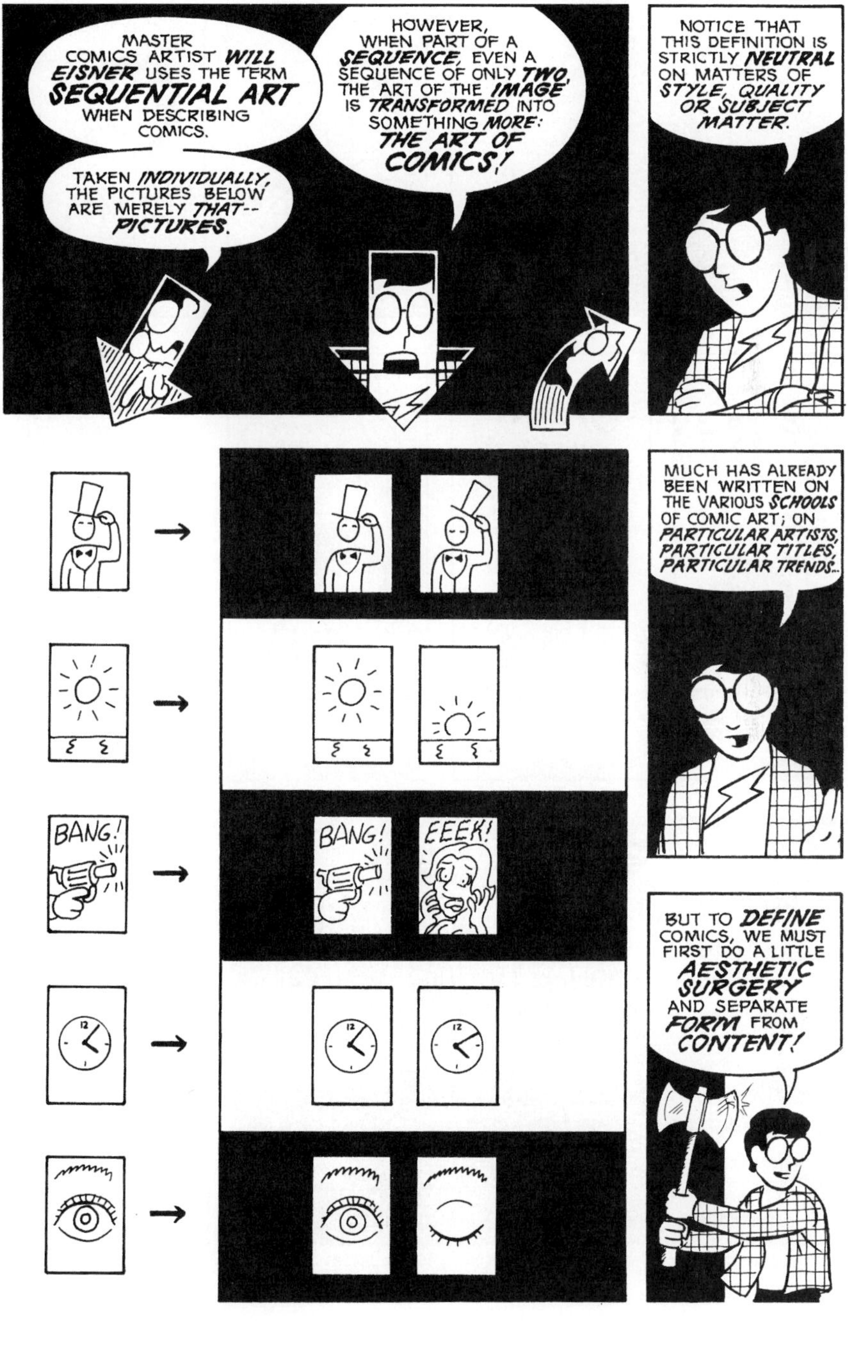

* EISNER'S OWN *COMICS AND SEQUENTIAL ART* BEING A HAPPY EXCEPTION.

*JUXTAPOSED= ADJACENT, SIDE-BY-SIDE.
GREAT ART SCHOOL WORD.

MEGHANN O'CONNOR

Cheerleading Is a Competitive Sport

Meghann O'Connor cheered for four years on both the varsity basketball squad and the competitive squad at Lewisburg (Pennsylvania) Area High School. Her letter is addressed to the Lewisburg Athletic Director, Jim Cotner, who is in charge of funding and practice times and spaces for the sports teams.

November 11, 1998

Dear Mr. Cotner,

1   Imagine individuals propelling their bodies to flip, twist, and turn in ways one did not know was humanly possible. Picture these individuals being hurled into the air, reaching unfathomable heights, and then being safely caught by their own teammates. Feel the excitement in your own being as you watch strength and skill come together to create an awesome display of athleticism. Realize that these individuals are cheerleaders; their sport, cheerleading.

2   Sport? Cheerleading? Many feel that these two words have no business being grouped in the same sentence together. It is a popular stereotype to consider cheerleaders to be a group of screaming girls in short skirts. Because there is no equipment involved, and there are not any playoffs for the cheerleading squads, many support the opinion that cheerleading is far from a competitive sport. However, in the following paragraphs I will explain why cheerleading should be weighed as a competitive sport and be granted the same rights and respect that other athletic teams receive.

3   There is a myriad of rationale as to why cheerleading should be defined as a competitive sport instead of only an activity. One of the most important reasons is because of the fact that cheerleaders do, in fact, compete. The New Merriam Webster Dictionary defines competition as a **contest, match;** *also:* **one's competitors.** Cheerleaders from all over the world compete at various levels in many different kinds of competitions. Who do they compete against? They oppose their competitors, of course. How is it, then, that both schools and organizations claim that cheerleading is not a competitive sport? There are local, state, regional, and national competitions for cheerleading squads of all different levels including, Midget, Junior High, Jayvee, Varsity, Coed, All-Star, and Collegiate. A qualified panel of judges

rate the cheerleading squads based on a point system and that determines the winners of these competitions. The squad that finishes with the highest total of points will then be declared the winner. There are many different areas that the judges focus on, including the levels of difficulty, creativity, and athletic ability. This type of judging is similar to the panels of judges found in the Olympic Games, such as figure skating and gymnastics. Both of these activities are viewed as competitive sports, so why can cheerleading not be viewed in the same way? When dealing with the issue of pragmatics, it is only sensible to agree with the fact that cheerleading is a competitive sport. To say that competition is not a huge aspect of cheerleading would be incorrect and inaccurate.

4   Just as other sporting teams practice and prepare for upcoming contests, so do cheerleaders. Football teams sweat on the field. Basketball players run up and down the court. Swimmers race in the pool. Each of these teams practice day in and day out, making sure that their skills are where they should be and that they are prepared for their upcoming competition. Cheerleaders do the same! They practice, sweat, and strive to be the best they can be, just as other teams do. It would be unfair to discredit the time and energy cheerleaders spend preparing for their upcoming contest. Ethically, it is unjust and discriminatory to not give cheerleaders credit where credit is due. Ultimately, they put an equal amount of time into practicing and getting ready for their "games" as the other sporting teams do.

5   Cheerleaders are talented athletes who work hard. If one has ever taken the time to pause on ESPN long enough to watch a National Cheerleading Competition, one would see the great acts of athleticism that are displayed by squads from all different areas and of all different age groups. Coordination and timing are crucial in synchronizing motions and dance movements. Strength is required for the amazing stunts that are built within the routine. Power and grace are necessities in tumbling from one end of the floor to the other. If these aspects are not considered characteristics of an athlete, then what are the components that make up this type of individual? All athletes compete; therefore, since cheerleaders accomplish athletic feats, it is only evenhanded to consider them competitors.

6   Schools who falter in considering cheerleading a competitive game will lag behind what the rest of society is doing. By failing to label cheerleading as a competitive sport, an example of regressiveness is being exhibited. For instance, many high schools, colleges, and universities around the country already group cheerleading in the same category as all other sports. The University of Michigan and Ohio State University provide scholarships for the

cheerleaders that attend their universities. If these prestigious institutions of higher education are able to view cheerleading as the competitive sport it truly is, then why cannot all school districts and colleges do the same? Just because it has traditionally been thought that cheerleading is not a sport doesn't mean that this line of thinking has to continue. It will one day be out of date and against the norm to not classify cheerleading as a competitive sport, so it is imperative to make the crucial change now.

7   Several arguments have been made against cheerleading as a competitive sport. One of them is the fact that in cheerleading, a team can not win anything such as a district championship. This argument is entirely false because cheerleaders are always up for awards in their competitions. Not only can they win first, second, or third place, at many different levels, but also they can place in other categories as well such as jumping ability, tumbling ability, and how difficult their stunting is.

8   Another unsupported claim against the sport of cheerleading is the statement made by Dr. Shaft, who claims that, "Real athletes don't wear skirts." This assertion is absolutely ridiculous. It should not matter at all what the uniforms of the athletes look like. That is a frivolous and unnecessary aspect of competition and should have nothing to do with the subject at hand. The fact that Dr. Shaft is drawing attention to the cheerleaders' skirts could also be grounds for sexual discrimination. A skirt is a form of clothing for women, and when Dr. Shaft proclaims cheerleading an invalid sport due to the fact that a skirt is worn, it seems as though he is discrediting women's sports in general.

9   Another justification Dr. Shaft has of why cheerleading should not be a sport is because he feels that there are no coaches involved. This is entirely inaccurate. At every level of cheerleading there are coaches who put in just as much time, effort and energy as any other coach of any other sport. These coaches are paid for their hard work and deserve the respect the coaches of other sporting teams receive.

10   My support of the idea that cheerleading should be a competitive sport remains even after hearing the points made by those who oppose me. Cheerleaders compete and spend just as much time practicing as any other team, they display great feats of athletic talent, and by not considering cheerleading a competitive sport, one is ultimately primitive and tardy in their beliefs, due to the increasing number of organizations that are in accordance with my thoughts. How would one feel if he or she spent endless hours planning and preparing for upcoming competitions to only then be told that they do not even participate in a "real" sport? This individual may become extremely discouraged and confused, which are the last emotions

any school wants for its active students. By acknowledging the cheerleading squad as competitors, a great deal of self-esteem could rise from each individual member. This cheerleader would feel that they are equal with the other athletes in their school and feel as if they were finally treated on the same level. This "happiness" could become contagious. First, it may spread throughout the squad, causing them to have a sense of belonging to their school. Their renewed spirit would radiate at matches, games, and competitions, which would benefit those who the cheerleaders were supporting. The added confidence felt when the squad performs would not only be beneficial to them but to their organization and all of its members as well. On the subject of aesthetics, their renewed sense of ease and comfort would shine through during practices and competitions, bringing nothing but positive consequences to considering cheerleaders competitive athletes.

11   Our society has made a great deal of progress when dealing with the issues of equality and fairness. To continue on with this tradition, it would only be fair to view cheerleading as a competitive sport.

Steps in Writing a Definition Argument

If your instructor asks for a topic proposal, use steps 1–4 to guide you in writing the proposal.

1. **Make a definitional claim on a controversial issue that focuses on a key term.** Use this formula: *X is (or is not) a Y because it has (or does not have) features A, B, and C (or more).*

   Examples:
   - Hate speech (or pornography, literature, films, and so on) is (or is not) free speech protected by the First Amendment because it has (does not have) these features.
   - Hunting (or using animals for cosmetics testing, keeping animals in zoos, wearing furs, and so on) is (or is not) cruelty to animals because it has (or does not have) these features.
   - Doctors should be (should not be) allowed to assist patients to die if they are terminally ill and suffering.
   - Displaying pinup calendars (or jokes, innuendo, rap lyrics, and so on) is (is not) an example of sexual harrassment.

2. **What's at stake in your claim?** If nearly everybody would agree with you, then your claim probably isn't interesting or important. If you can

think of people who would disagree, then something is at stake. Who argues the opposite of your claim? Why do they benefit from a different definition?

3. **Make your list of criteria.** Write as many criteria as you can think of. Which criteria are necessary for X to be a Y? Which are not necessary? Which are the most important? Does your case in point meet all the criteria?

4. **Analyze your potential readers.** Who are your readers? How does the definitional claim you are making affect them? How familiar will they be with the issue, concept, or controversy that you're writing about? What are they likely to know and not know? Which criteria are they most likely to accept with little explanation and which will they disagree with? Which criteria will you have to argue for?

5. **Write a draft.**

   Introduction:
   - Set out the issue, concept, or controversy.
   - Explain why the definition is important.
   - Give the background that your intended readers will need.

   Body:
   - Set out your criteria and argue for the appropriateness of the criteria.
   - Determine whether the criteria apply to the case in point.
   - Anticipate where readers might question either your criteria or how they apply to your subject.
   - Address opposing points of view by acknowledging how their definitions might differ and by showing why your definition is better.

   Conclusion:
   - Do more than simply summarize what you have said. You can, for example, go into more detail about what is at stake or the implications of your definition.

6. **Revise, revise, revise. See Chapter 11 for detailed instructions.**

   Stage 1. Read your argument aloud.
   Do no more in this stage than put checks in the margins that you can return to later. Think in particular about these things:
   - **Your claim.** When you finish reading, summarize in one sentence what you are arguing. What's at stake in your claim?
   - **Your criteria.** How many criteria do you offer? Where are they located? Are they clearly connected to your claim?
   - **Your representation of yourself.** Forget for a moment that you wrote what you are reading. What impression do you have of you, the writer?

- **Your consideration of your readers.** Do you give enough background if your readers are unfamiliar with the issue? Do you acknowledge opposing views that they might have? Do you appeal to common values that you share with them?

Stage 2. Analyze your argument in detail.

- **Examine your organization.** What are the topics of each of the paragraphs? Is the relationship of one paragraph to another clearly signaled? If any paragraphs appear out of order, think of another way to arrange them.
- **Examine your evidence.** If you noted places where you could use more evidence when you read through the first time, now is the time to determine what kinds of additional evidence you need.
- **Consider your title and introduction.** Be as specific as you can in your title, and if possible, suggest your stance. Does your introduction get off to a fast start and convince your reader to keep reading?
- **Consider your conclusion.** Think about whether there is a summarizing point you can make, an implication you can draw, or another example you can include that sums up your position.
- **Analyze the visual aspects of your text.** Do the font and layout you selected look attractive? Would headings and subheadings help to identify key sections of your argument? Would the addition of graphics augment key points?

Stage 3. Focus on your style and proofread carefully.

- **Check the connections between sentences.** Notice how your sentences are connected. If you need to signal the relationship from one sentence to the next, use a transitional word or phrase.
- **Check your sentences for emphasis.** Elements at the beginning and the end of sentences tend to stand out more than things in the middle.
- **Eliminate wordiness.** See how many words you can take out without losing the meaning.
- **Use active verbs.** Anytime you can use a verb besides a form of *be* (*is, are, was, were*), take advantage of the opportunity to make your style more lively.
- **Proofread your spelling carefully.** Your spelling checker will miss many mistakes.
- **Use your handbook to check items of mechanics and usage.** Look up any item you are unsure of.

CHAPTER 6

Causal Arguments

Why has binge drinking greatly increased among college students over the last fifteen years while the overall percentage of students who drink has remained about the same? Why do some countries have long histories of people of different religious and ethnic backgrounds living together in peace while in other countries

> **Effective causal arguments move beyond the obvious to get at underlying causes.**

people regularly kill each other because of religious and ethnic differences? Why do owners of professional sports teams complain about losing money and then offer multimillion-dollar salaries not only to stars but even to mediocre players? Why is the United States the only major industrialized country not to have a system of national health care? Why do universities in the United States have general education requirements while universities in most of the rest of the world do not, allowing students to take courses only in their major and minor fields? Why have the death rates for some kinds of cancer gone way up in this country (for example, deaths from lung cancer in women increased 438 percent from 1962 to 1992) while the rates for other kinds of cancer went down (deaths from cancer of the cervix dropped 67 percent during the same period)? If meteorologists now have massive amounts of satellite data and supercomputers to crunch the numbers for long-range weather forecasting, why haven't they become much more reliable than the *Farmer's Almanac*?

Besides big questions like the ones above, you also are confronted with little questions of causation in your everyday life. Why did the driver who passed you on a blind curve risk his life to get one car ahead at the next traffic light? Why is it hard to recognize people you know when you run into them unexpectedly in an unfamiliar setting? Why do nearly all kids want the same toy each Christmas, forcing their parents to stand in line for hours to buy them? Why does your mother or father spend an extra hour plus the extra gas driving to a grocery store across town just to save a few pennies on one or two items on sale? Why do some people get upset about animals that are killed for medical research but still eat meat and wear leather clothing? Why do some of your friends keep going to horror films when they can hardly sit through them and have nightmares afterward?

Life is full of big and little mysteries, and people spend a lot of time speculating about the causes. Most of the time, however, they don't take the time to analyze in depth what causes a controversial trend, event, or phenomenon. But before and after you graduate, you likely will have to write causal arguments that require in-depth analysis. In a professional career you will have to make many detailed causal analyses: Why did a retail business fail when it seemed to have an ideal location? What causes cost overruns in the development of a new product? What causes people in some circumstances to prefer public transportation over driving? What causes unnecessary slowdowns in a local computer network? Answering any of these questions requires making a causal argument, which takes a classic form: X *causes (or does not cause) Y*. The causal claim is at the center of a causal argument. Therefore, to get started on a causal argument, you need to propose one or more causes.

Methods of Finding Causes

The big problem with causal arguments is that any topic worth writing about is likely to be complex. Identifying causes usually isn't easy. The philosopher John Stuart Mill recognized this problem long ago and devised four methods for finding causes:

1. **The Common Factor Method.** When the cause-and-effect relationship occurs more than once, look for something in common in the events and circumstances of each effect; any common factor could be the cause. Scientists

have used this method to explain how seemingly different phenomena are associated. There were a variety of explanations of fire until, in the 1700s, Joseph Priestley in England and Antoine Lavoisier in France discovered that oxygen was a separate element and that burning was caused by oxidation.

2. *The Single Difference Method.* This method works only when there are at least two similar situations, one that leads to an effect and one that does not. Look for something that was missing in one case and present in another—the single difference. The writer assumes that if everything is substantially alike in both cases, then the single difference is the (or a) cause. At the Battle of Midway in 1942, the major naval battle of World War II in the Pacific, the Japanese Navy had a four-to-one advantage over the U.S. Navy. Both fleets were commanded by competent, experienced leaders. But the U.S. commander, Admiral Nimitz, had a superior advantage in intelligence, which proved to be decisive.

3. *Concomitant Variation.* This tongue twister is another favorite method of scientists. If an investigator finds that a possible cause and a possible effect have a similar pattern of variation, then one can suspect that a relationship exists. For example, scientists noticed that peaks in the eleven-year sunspot cycle have predictable effects on high-frequency radio transmission on the earth.

4. *Process of Elimination.* Many possible causes can be proposed for most trends and events. If you are a careful investigator, you have to consider all that you can think of and eliminate the ones that cannot be causes.

For an example of how these methods might work for you, suppose you want to research the causes of the increase in legalized lotteries in the United States. You might discover that lotteries go back to colonial times. Harvard and Yale have been longtime rivals in football, but the schools' rivalry goes back much further. Both ran lotteries before the Revolutionary War! In 1747, the Connecticut legislature voted to allow Yale to conduct a lottery to raise money to build dormitories, and in 1765, the Massachusetts legislature gave Harvard permission for a lottery. Lotteries were common before and after the American Revolution, but they eventually ran into trouble because they were run by private companies that occasionally took off with the money without paying off the winners. After 1840, laws against lotteries were passed, but they came back after the Civil War in the South. The defeated states of the Confederacy needed money to rebuild the bridges, buildings, and schools that had been destroyed in the Civil War, and they turned to selling lottery tickets throughout the nation, tickets which, perhaps ironically, were very popular in the North. Once again, the lotteries were run by private companies, and scandals eventually led to their banning.

In 1964, the voters in New Hampshire approved a lottery as a means of funding education in preference to an income tax or sales tax. Soon other northeastern states followed this lead, establishing lotteries with the reasoning that if people are going to gamble, the money should remain at home. During the 1980s, other states approved not only lotteries but also other forms of state-run gambling such as keno and video poker. By 1993, only Hawaii and Utah had no legalized gambling of any kind.

If you are analyzing the causes of the spread of legalized gambling, you might use the **common factor method** to investigate what current lotteries have in common with earlier lotteries. That factor is easy to identify: It's economic. The early colonies and later the states have turned again and again to lotteries as a way of raising money that avoids unpopular tax increases. But why have lotteries spread so quickly and seemingly become so permanent since 1964, when before that, they were used only sporadically and were eventually banned? The **single difference method** points us to the major difference between the lotteries of today and those of previous eras: Lotteries in the past were run by private companies, and inevitably someone took off with the money instead of paying it out. Today's lotteries are owned and operated by state agencies or else contracted under state control, and while they are not immune to scandals, they are much more closely monitored than lotteries were in the past.

The controversies over legal gambling now focus on casinos. In 1988, Congress passed the Indian Gaming Regulatory Act, which started a new era of casino gambling in the United States. The Foxwoods Casino in Connecticut, owned by the Mashantucket Pequot Tribe, became a huge moneymaker—with over $1 billion wagered in 2000—and its revenues exceeded those of the Connecticut lottery. Other tribes and other states were quick to cash in on casino gambling. Iowa legalized riverboat gambling in 1989, followed shortly by Louisiana, Illinois, Indiana, Mississippi, and Missouri. As with lotteries, the primary justification for approving casino gambling has been economic. States have been forced to fund various programs that the federal government used to pay for. Especially in states where lottery revenues had begun to sag, legislatures and voters turned to casinos to make up the difference.

Casinos, however, have been harder to sell to voters than lotteries. For many voters, casinos are a NIMBY ("not in my back yard") issue. They may believe that people should have the right to gamble, but they don't want a casino in their town. Casino proponents have tried to overcome these objections by arguing that casinos bring added tourist dollars, benefiting the community as a whole. Opponents argue the opposite: that people who go to casinos spend their money on gambling and not on tourist attractions. The cause-and-effect benefit of casinos to community businesses can be examined by **concomitant variation.** Casino supporters argue that people who come to gamble spend a lot of money elsewhere. Opponents of casinos claim that people who come for gambling don't want to spend money elsewhere. Furthermore, they point out that gambling represents another entertainment option for people within easy driving distance and can hurt area businesses such as restaurants, amusement parks, and bowling alleys. So far, the record has been mixed, some businesses being helped and others being hurt when casinos are built nearby.

Many trends don't have causes as obvious as the spread of legalized gambling. One such trend is the redistribution of wealth in the United States since 1973. From 1950 to 1973, businesses in the United States grew by 90 percent, and the resulting wealth benefited all income classes. Since 1973, however, almost all the growth in wealth has gone to people at the top of the economic ladder. During the 1980s, the incomes of the richest 1 percent of the population grew by 62.9 percent, and the incomes of the bottom 60 percent actually declined. According to U.S. News & World Report, in 1996, the richest 1 percent of Americans, with minimum assets of $2.3 million per family, hold 42 percent of all marketable assets, exerting unprecedented influence on the economy. Often-cited statistics are those for the pay of top executives. Business Week reports that the average CEO of a major corporation made 42 times the average hourly worker's pay in 1980, 85 times in 1990, and an incredible 531 times in 2000.

The increasing divide between the rich and the rest of the people in the United States is well documented, but economists don't agree about the reasons why the U.S. middle class has been increasingly divided into those who are very well off and those who are struggling to keep their heads above water. The explanations that have been given include the tax cuts of 1986, the decline of labor unions, the downsizing of corporations, the increase in corporate mergers, automation, competition from low-wage nations, and simple greed. Although each of these may be a contributing cause, there must be other causes too.

The **process of elimination** method can be a useful tool when several possible causes are involved. The shift in income to the wealthy started before the tax cuts of 1986, so the tax cuts cannot be the only cause. Low-wage nations now produce cheap exports, but the sectors of the U.S. economy that compete directly with low-wage nations make up a small slice of the total pie (about 2 percent). And it's hard to explain why people might be greedier now than in earlier decades; greed has always been a human trait.

In a book published in 1995 entitled The Winner-Take-All Society, Robert H. Frank and Phillip J. Cook argue that changes in attitudes help to account for the shifts in wealth since 1973. In an article summarizing their book, published in Across the Board (33:5 [May 1996]: 4), they describe what they mean by the winner-take-all society:

Our claim is that growing income inequality stems from the growing importance of what we call "winner-take-all markets"—markets in which small differences in performance give rise to enormous differences in economic reward. Long familiar in entertainment, sports, and the arts, these markets have increasingly permeated law, journalism, consulting, medicine, investment banking, corporate management, publishing, design, fashion, even the hallowed halls of academe.

An economist under the influence of the human-capital metaphor might ask: Why not save money by hiring two mediocre people to fill an important position instead of paying the exorbitant salary required to attract the best? Although that sort of substitution might work with physical capital, it does not necessarily work with human capital. Two average surgeons or CEOs or novelists or quarterbacks are often a poor substitute for a single gifted one.

The result is that for positions for which additional talent has great value to the employer or the marketplace, there is no reason to expect that the market will compensate individuals in proportion to their human capital. For these positions—ones that confer the greatest leverage or "amplification" of human talent—small increments of talent have great value and may be greatly rewarded as a result of the normal competitive market process. This insight lies at the core of our alternative explanation of growing inequality.

A winner-take-all market is one in which reward depends on relative, not absolute, performance. Whereas a farmer's pay depends on the absolute amount of wheat he produces and not on how that compares with the amounts produced by other farmers, a software developer's pay depends largely on her performance ranking. In the market for personal income-tax software, for instance, the market reaches quick consensus on which among the scores or even hundreds of competing programs is the most comprehensive and user-friendly. And although the best program may be only slightly better than its nearest rival, their developers' incomes may differ a thousandfold.

Frank and Cook find that technology has accelerated the trend toward heaping rewards on those who are judged best in a particular arena. In the 1800s, for example, a top tenor in a major city such as London might have commanded a salary many times above that of other singers, but the impact of the tenor was limited by the fact that only those who could hear him live could appreciate his talent. Today, every tenor in the world competes with Luciano Pavarotti because opera fans everywhere can buy Pavarotti's CDs. This worldwide fan base translates into big money. In another example, it might not surprise you that in 1992, Michael Jordan reportedly received $20 million for promoting Nike shoes, an amount that was greater than the combined annual payrolls for all six factories in Indonesia that made the shoes.

What is new is how other professions have become more like sports and entertainment.

The Winner-Take-All Society is a model of causal analysis that uses the **process of elimination** method. The authors

 ▪ Describe and document a trend

 ▪ Set out the causes that have been previously offered and show why together they are inadequate to explain the trend, and then

 ▪ Present a new cause, explaining how the new cause works in concert with those that have been identified

But it's not enough just to identify causes. They must be connected to effects. For trends in progress, such as the growing divide between the rich and the rest in the United States, the effects must be carefully explored to learn about what might lie ahead. Frank and Cook believe that the winner-take-all attitude is detrimental for the nation's future because, like high school basketball players who expect to become the next Michael Jordan, many people entering college or graduate school grossly overestimate their prospects for huge success and select their future careers accordingly:

> The lure of the top prizes in winner-take-all markets has also steered many of our most able graduates toward career choices that make little sense for them as individuals and still less sense for the nation as a whole. In increasing numbers, our best and brightest graduates pursue top positions in law, finance, consulting, and other overcrowded arenas, in the process forsaking careers in engineering, manufacturing, civil service, teaching, and other occupations in which an infusion of additional talent would yield greater benefit to society.
>
> One study estimated, for example, that whereas a doubling of enrollments in engineering would cause the growth rate of the GDP to rise by half a percentage point, a doubling of enrollments in law would actually cause a decline of three-tenths of a point. Yet the number of new lawyers admitted to the bar each year more than doubled between 1970 and 1990, a period during which the average standardized test scores of new public-school teachers fell dramatically.
>
> One might hope that such imbalances would fade as wages are bid up in underserved markets and driven down in overcrowded ones, and indeed there have been recent indications of a decline in the number of law-school applicants. For two reasons, however, such adjustments are destined to fall short.
>
> The first is an informational problem. An intelligent decision about whether to pit one's own skills against a largely unknown field of adversaries obviously requires a well-informed estimate of the odds of

winning. Yet people's assessments about these odds are notoriously inaccurate. Survey evidence shows, for example, that some 80 percent of us think we are better-than-average drivers and that more than 90 percent of workers consider themselves more productive than their average colleague. Psychologists call this the "Lake Wobegon Effect," and its importance for present purposes is that it leads people to overestimate their odds of landing a superstar position. Indeed, overconfidence is likely to be especially strong in the realm of career choice, because the biggest winners are so conspicuous. The seven-figure NBA stars appear on television several times each week, whereas the many thousands who fail to make the league attract little notice.

The second reason for persistent overcrowding in winner-take-all markets is a structural problem that economists call "the tragedy of the commons." This same problem helps explain why we see too many prospectors for gold. In the initial stages of exploiting a newly discovered field of gold, the presence of additional prospectors may significantly increase the total amount of gold that is found. Beyond some point, however, additional prospectors contribute very little. Thus, the gold found by a newcomer to a crowded gold field is largely gold that would have been found by others.

This short example illustrates why causal arguments for any significant trend that involves people almost necessarily have to be complex. Most people don't quit their day job expecting to hit it big in the movies, the record business, or professional athletics, yet people do select fields such as law that have become in many ways like entertainment, with a few big winners and the rest just getting by. Frank and Cook point to the "Lake Wobegon Effect" (named for Garrison Keillor's fictional town where "all children are above average") to give an explanation of why people are realistic about their chances in some situations and not in others.

BUILDING A CAUSAL ARGUMENT

Effective causal arguments move beyond the obvious to get at underlying causes. The immediate cause of the growing income inequality in the United States is that people at the top make a lot more now than they did thirty years ago while people in the middle make the same and people at the bottom make less. Those causes are obvious to anyone who has looked at the numbers. What isn't obvious is why those changes occurred.

Insightful causal analyses of major trends and events avoid oversimplification by not relying on only one direct cause but instead showing how that cause arises from another cause or works in combination with other causes. Indeed, Frank and Cook have been criticized for placing too much emphasis on the winner-take-all hypothesis.

The great causal mystery today is global warming. Scientists generally agree that the average surface temperature on earth has gone up by 0.3 to 0.6 degrees Celsius over the last hundred years and that the amount of carbon dioxide has increased by 25 percent. But the causes of those facts are much disputed. Some people believe that the rise in temperature is a naturally occurring climate variation and that the increase in carbon dioxide is only minimally the cause or not related at all. Others argue that the burning of fossil fuels and the cutting of tropical forests have led to the increase in carbon dioxide, which in turn traps heat, thus increasing the temperature of the earth. The major problem for all participants in the global warming debate is that the causation is not a simple, direct one.

Scientists use powerful computer models to understand the causes and effects of climate change. These models predict that global warming will affect arctic and subarctic regions more dramatically than elsewhere. In Iceland, average summer temperatures have risen by 0.5 to 1.0 degrees Celsius since the early 1980s. All of Iceland's glaciers except a few that surge and ebb independent of weather are now in rapid retreat, a pattern observed throughout regions in the far north. Arctic sea ice shrank by 6 percent from 1978 to 1998, and Greenland's massive ice sheet has been thinning by more than three feet a year. Environmentalists today point to the melting of the glaciers and sea ice as proof that human-caused global warming is taking place.

Scientists, however, are not so certain. Their difficulty is to sort human causes from naturally recurring climate cycles. Much of the detailed data about the Great Melt in the north goes back only to the early 1990s—not long enough to rule out short-term climate cycles. If we are in a

Glaciers in retreat

regular, short-term warming cycle, then the question becomes how does greenhouse warming interact with that cycle? Computer models suggest there is a very low probability that such rapid change could occur naturally. But the definitive answers to the causes of the Great Melt are probably still a long way off.

Another pitfall common in causal arguments using statistics is mistaking correlation for causation. For example, the FBI reported that criminal victimization rates in the United States in 1995 dropped 13 percent for personal crimes and 12.4 percent for property crimes, the largest decreases ever. During that same year, the nation's prison and jail populations reached a record high of 1,085,000 and 507,000 inmates, respectively. The easy inference is that putting more people behind bars lowers the crime rate, but there are plenty of examples to the contrary. The drop in crime rates in the 1990s remains quite difficult to explain. Others have argued that the decline in SAT verbal scores during the late 1960s and 1970s reflected a decline in literacy caused by an increase in television viewing. But the fact that the number of people who took the SAT during the 1970s greatly increased suggests that there was not an actual decline in literacy, only a great expansion in the population who wanted to go to college.

EDWARD R. TUFTE

The Cholera Epidemic in London, 1854

Edward R. Tufte (1942–) is a leading thinker on the construction and presentation of visual information. Tufte's ideas on visual design are set out in three influential books: The Visual Display of Quantitative Information *(1983),* Envisioning Information *(1990), and* Visual Explanations: Images and Quantities, Evidence and Narrative *(1997). He urges that visual information be presented truthfully, with a minimum of unnecessary noise and with full respect for the complexity of what is being represented. Educated at Stanford and Yale Universities, Tufte has been a professor of political economy and graphic design at Yale since 1977.*

In "The Cholera Epidemic in London, 1854," taken from Envisioning Information, *Tufte demonstrates his belief that effective graphics can extend our powers of reasoning. He also shows how the presentation of data is critical in reaching conclusions based on visual evidence.*

The Cholera Epidemic in London, 1854

In a classic of medical detective work, *On the Mode of Communication of Cholera,*[1] John Snow described—with an eloquent and precise language of evidence, number, comparison—the severe epidemic:

> The most terrible outbreak of cholera which ever occurred in this kingdom, is probably that which took place in Broad Street, Golden Square, and adjoining streets, a few weeks ago. Within two hundred and fifty years of the spot where Cambridge Street joins Broad Street, there were upwards of five hundred fatal attacks of cholera in ten days. The mortality in this limited area probably equals any that was ever caused in this country, even by the plague; and it was much more sudden, as the greater number of cases terminated in a few hours. The mortality would undoubtedly have been much greater had it not been for the flight of the population. Persons in furnished lodgings left first, then other lodgers went away, leaving their furniture to be sent for. . . . Many houses were closed altogether owing to the death of the proprietors; and, in a great number of instances, the tradesmen who remained had sent away their families; so that in less than six days from the commencement of the outbreak, the most afflicted streets were deserted by more than three-quarters of their inhabitants.[2]

Cholera broke out in the Broad Street area of central London on the evening of August 31, 1854. John Snow, who had investigated earlier epidemics, suspected that the water from a community pump-well at Broad and Cambridge Streets was contaminated. Testing the water from the well on the evening of September 3, Snow saw no suspicious impurities, and thus he hesitated to come to a conclusion. This absence of evidence, however, was not evidence of absence:

> Further inquiry . . . showed me that there was no other circumstance or agent common to the circumscribed locality in which this sudden increase of cholera occurred, and not extending

---

[1]John Snow, *On the Mode of Communication of Cholera* (London, 1855). An acute disease of the small intestine, with severe watery diarrhea, vomiting, and rapid dehydration, cholera has a fatality rate of 50 percent or more when untreated. With the rehydration therapy developed in the 1960s, mortality can be reduced to less than 1 percent. Epidemics still occur in poor countries, as the bacterium *Vibrio cholerae* is distributed mainly by water and food contaminated with sewage.
[2]Snow, *Cholera*, p. 38.

beyond it, except the water of the above mentioned pump. I found, moreover, that the water varied, during the next two days, in the amount of organic impurity, visible to the naked eye, on close inspection, in the form of small white, flocculent [loosely clustered] particles. . . .[3]

From the General Register Office, Snow obtained a list of 83 deaths from cholera. When plotted on a map, these data showed a close link between cholera and the Broad Street pump. Persistent house-by-house, case-by-case detective work had yielded quite detailed evidence about a possible cause-effect relationship, as Snow made a kind of streetcorner correlation:

> On proceeding to the spot, I found that nearly all of the deaths had taken place within a short distance of the pump. There were only ten deaths in houses situated decidedly nearer to another street pump. In five of these cases the families of the deceased persons informed me that they always sent to the pump in Broad Street, as they preferred the water to that of the pump which was nearer. In three other cases, the deceased were children who went to school near the pump in Broad Street. Two of them were known to drink the water; and the parents of the third think it probable that it did so. The other two deaths, beyond the district which this pump supplies, represent only the amount of mortality from cholera that was occurring before the irruption took place.
>
> With regard to the deaths occurring in the locality belonging to the pump, there were sixty-one instances in which I was informed that the deceased persons used to drink the pump-water from Broad Street, either constantly or occasionally. In six instances I could get no information, owing to the death or departure of every one connected with the deceased individuals; and in six cases I was informed that the deceased persons did not drink the pump-water before their illness.[4]

Thus the theory implicating the particular pump was confirmed by the observed covariation: in this area of London, there were few occurrences of cholera exceeding the normal low level, except among those people who drank water from the Broad Street pump. It was now time to act; after all, the reason we seek causal explanations is in order to *intervene*, to govern

[3]Snow, *Cholera*, p. 39.
[4]Snow, *Cholera*, pp. 39–40.

the cause so as to govern the effect: "Policy-thinking is and must be causality-thinking."[5] Snow described his findings to the authorities responsible for the community water supply, the Board of Guardians of St. James's Parish, on the evening of September 7, 1854. The Board ordered that the pump-handle on the Broad Street well be removed immediately. The epidemic soon ended.

Moreover, the result of this intervention (a before/after experiment of sorts) was consistent with the idea that cholera was transmitted by impure water. Snow's explanation replaced previously held beliefs that cholera spread through the air or by some other means. In those times many years before the discovery of bacteria, one fantastic theory speculated that cholera vaporously rose out of the burying grounds of plague victims from two centuries earlier.[6] In 1886 the discovery of the bacterium *Vibrio cholerae* confirmed Snow's theory. He is still celebrated for establishing the mode of cholera transmission *and* consequently the method of prevention: keep drinking water, food, and hands clear of infected sewage. Today at the old site of the Broad Street pump there stands a public house (a bar) named after John Snow, where one can presumably drink more safely than 140 years ago.

Why was the centuries-old mystery of cholera finally solved? Most importantly, Snow had a *good idea*—a causal theory about how the disease spread—that guided the gathering and assessment of evidence. This theory developed from medical analysis and empirical observation; by mapping earlier epidemics, Snow detected a link between different water supplies and varying rates of cholera (to the consternation of private water companies who anonymously denounced Snow's work). By the 1854 epidemic, then, the intellectual framework was in place, and the problem of how cholera spread was ripe for solution.

Along with a good idea and a timely problem, there was a *good method*. Snow's scientific detective work exhibits a shrewd intelligence about evidence, a clear logic of data display and analysis:

1. *Placing the data in an appropriate context for assessing cause and effect.* The original data listed the victims' names and described their circumstances, all in order by date of death. Such a stack of death certificates naturally lends itself to time-series displays, chronologies of the epidemic (see Figures 6.1 and 6.2). *But descriptive narration is not*

---

[5]Robert A. Dahl, "Cause and Effect in the Study of Politics," in Daniel Lerner, ed., *Cause and Effect* (New York, 1965), p. 88.
[6]H. Harold Scott, *Some Notable Epidemics* (London, 1934), pp. 3–4.

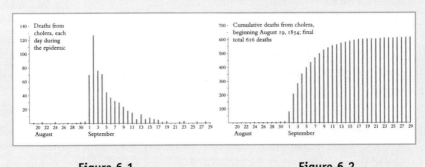

Figure 6.1   **Figure 6.2**

causal explanation; the passage of time is a poor explanatory variable, practically useless in discovering a strategy of how to intervene and stop the epidemic.

Instead of plotting a time-series, which would simply report each day's bad news, Snow constructed a graphical display that provided direct and powerful testimony about a possible cause-effect relationship. Recasting the original data from their one-dimensional temporal ordering into a two-dimensional spatial comparison, Snow marked deaths from cholera (Figure 6.3) on this map, along with locations of the area's 11 community water pump-wells (●). The notorious well is located amid an intense cluster of deaths, near the D in BROAD STREET. This map reveals a strong association between cholera and proximity to the Broad Street pump, in a context of simultaneous comparison with other local water sources and the surrounding neighborhoods without cholera.

2. *Making quantitative comparisons.* The deep, fundamental question in statistical analysis is *Compared with what?* Therefore, investigating the experiences of the victims of cholera is only part of the search for credible evidence; to understand fully the cause of the epidemic also requires an analysis of those who *escaped* the disease. With great clarity, the map presented several intriguing clues for comparisons between the living and the dead, clues strikingly visible at a brewery and a workhouse. Snow wrote in his report:

> There is a brewery in Broad Street, near to the pump, and on perceiving that no brewer's men were registered as having died of cholera, I called on Mr. Huggins, the proprietor. He informed me that there were above seventy workmen

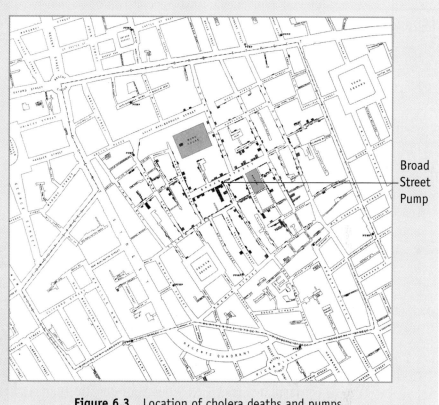

Figure 6.3 Location of cholera deaths and pumps.

employed in the brewery, and that none of them had suffered from cholera—at least in severe form—only two having been indisposed, and that not seriously, at the time the disease prevailed. The men are allowed a certain quantity of malt liquor, and Mr. Huggins believes they do not drink water at all; and he is quite certain that the workmen never obtained water from the pump in the street. There is a deep well in the brewery, in addition to the New River water. (p. 42)

Saved by the beer! And at a nearby workhouse, the circumstances of non-victims of the epidemic provided important and credible evidence about the cause of the disease, as well as a quantitative calculation of an expected rate of cholera compared with the actual observed rate:

> The Workhouse in Poland Street is more than three-fourths surrounded by houses in which deaths from cholera occurred, yet out of five-hundred-thirty-five inmates only five died of cholera, the other deaths which took place being those of persons admitted after they were attacked. The workhouse has a pump-well on the premises, in addition to the supply from the Grand Junction Water Works, and the inmates never sent to Broad Street for water. If the mortality in the workhouse had been equal to that in the streets immediately surrounding it on three sides, upwards of one hundred persons would have died. (p. 42)

3. *Considering alternative explanations and contrary cases.* Sometimes it can be difficult for researchers—who both report *and* advocate their findings—to face up to threats to their conclusions, such as alternative explanations and contrary cases. Nonetheless, the credibility of a report is enhanced by a careful assessment of *all* relevant evidence, not just the evidence overtly consistent with explanations advanced by the report. The point is to get it right, not to win the case, not to sweep under the rug all the assorted puzzles and inconsistencies that frequently occur in collections of data.

   Both Snow's map and the time-sequence of deaths show several apparently contradictory instances, a number of deaths from cholera with no obvious link to the Broad Street pump. And yet . . .

   > In some of the instances, where the deaths are scattered a little further from the rest on the map, the malady was probably contracted at a nearer point to the pump. A cabinet-maker who resided on Noel Street [some distance from Broad Street] worked in Broad Street. . . . A little girl, who died in Ham Yard, and another who died in Angel Court, Great Windmill Street, went to the school in Dufour's Place, Broad Street, and were in the habit of drinking the pump-water. . . .[7]

   In a particularly unfortunate episode, one London resident made a special effort to obtain Broad Street well-water, a delicacy of taste with a side-effect that unwittingly cost two lives. Snow's report is one of careful description and precise logic:

[7]Snow, *Cholera*, p. 47.

Dr. Fraser also first called my attention to the following circumstances, which are perhaps the most conclusive of all in
proving the connexion between the Broad Street pump and
the outbreak of cholera. In the 'Weekly Return of Births and
Deaths' of September 9th, the following death is recorded:
'At West End, on 2nd September, the widow of a percussion-
cap maker, aged 59 years, diarrhea two hours, *cholera epi-
demica* sixteen hours.' I was informed by this lady's son that
she had not been in the neighbourhood of Broad Street for
many months. A cart went from Broad Street to West End
every day, and it was the custom to take out a large bottle
of the water from the pump in Broad Street, as she preferred
it. The water was taken on Thursday, 31st August, and she
drank of it in the evening, and also on Friday. She was seized
with cholera on the evening of the latter day, and died on
Saturday. . . . A niece, who was on a visit to this lady, also
drank of the water; she returned to her residence, in a high
and healthy part of Islington, was attacked with cholera,
and died also. There was no cholera at the time, either at
West End or in the neighbourhood where the niece died.[8]

Although at first glance these deaths appear unrelated to the Broad
Street pump, they are, upon examination, strong evidence pointing to
that well. There is here a clarity and undeniability to the link between
cholera and the Broad Street pump; only such a link can account for what
would otherwise be a mystery, this seemingly random and unusual occurrence of cholera. And the saintly Snow, unlike some researchers, gives full
credit to the person, Dr. Fraser, who actually found this crucial case.

Ironically, the most famous aspect of Snow's work is also the most
uncertain part of his evidence: it is not at all clear that the removal of
the handle of the Broad Street pump had much to do with ending the
epidemic. As shown by this time-series (see Figure 6.4), the epidemic
was already in rapid decline by the time the handle was removed. Yet,
in many retellings of the story of the epidemic, the pump-handle removal is *the* decisive event, the unmistakable symbol of Snow's contribution. Here is the dramatic account of Benjamin Ward Richardson:

On the evening of Thursday, September 7th, the vestrymen
of St. James's were sitting in solemn consultation on the

[8]Snow, *Cholera*, pp. 44–45.

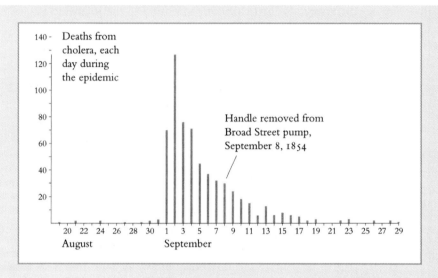

Figure 6.4 Plotted from the table in Snow, *Cholera*, p. 49.

causes of the [cholera epidemic]. They might well be solemn, for such a panic possibly never existed in London since the days of the great plague. People fled from their homes as from instant death, leaving behind them, in their haste, all the mere matter which before they valued most. While, then, the vestrymen were in solemn deliberation, they were called to consider a new suggestion. A stranger had asked, in modest speech, for a brief hearing. Dr. Snow, the stranger in question, was admitted and in few words explained his view of the 'head and front of the offending.' He had fixed his attention on the Broad Street pump as the source and center of the calamity. He advised removal of the pump-handle as the grand prescription. The vestry was incredulous, but had the good sense to carry out the advice. The pump-handle was removed, and the plague was stayed.[9]

Note the final sentence, a declaration of cause and effect. Modern epidemiologists, however, are distinctly skeptical about the evidence that links this intervention to the epidemic's end:

---

[9]Benjamin W. Richardson, "The Life of John Snow, M.D.," foreword to John Snow, *On Chloroform and Other Anaesthetics: Their Action and Administration* (London, 1858), pp. XX–XXI.

John Snow, in the seminal act of modern public health epidemiology, performed an intervention that was non-randomized, that was appraised with historical controls, and that had major ambiguities in the equivocal time relationship between his removal of the handle of the Broad Street pump and the end of the associated epidemic of cholera—but he correctly demonstrated that the disease was transmitted through water, not air.[10]

At a minimum, removing the pump-handle prevented a recurrence of cholera. Snow recognized several difficulties in evaluating the effect of his intervention; since most people living in central London had fled, the disease ran out of possible victims—which happened simultaneously with shutting down the infected water supply. The case against the Broad Street pump, however, was based on a diversity of additional evidence: the cholera map, studies of unusual instances, comparisons of the living and dead with their consumption of well-water, and an idea about a mechanism of contamination (a nearby underground sewer had probably leaked into the infected well). Also, the finding that cholera was carried by water—a life-saving scientific discovery that showed how to intervene and prevent the spread of cholera—derived not only from study of the Broad Street epidemic but also from Snow's mappings of several other cholera outbreaks in relation to the purity of community water supplies.

4. *Assessment of possible errors in the numbers reported in graphics.* Snow's analysis attends to the sources and consequences of errors in gathering the data. In particular, the credibility of the cholera map grows out of supplemental details in the text—as image, word, and number combine to present the evidence and make the argument. Detailed comments on possible errors annotate both the map and the table, reassuring readers about the care and integrity of the statistical detective work that produced the data graphics:

> The deaths which occurred during this fatal outbreak of cholera are indicated in the accompanying map, as far as I could ascertain them. There are necessarily some deficiencies, for in a few of the instances of persons who died in the hospitals after their removal from the neighbourhood of

---

[10]Alvan R. Feinstein, *Clinical Epidemiology: The Architecture of Clinical Research* (Philadelphia, 1985), pp. 409–410.

Broad Street, the number of the house from which they had been removed was not registered. The address of those who died after their removal to St. James's Workhouse was not registered; and I was only able to obtain it, in a part of the cases, on application at the Master's Office, for many of the persons were too ill, when admitted, to give any account of themselves. In the case also of some of the workpeople and others who contracted the cholera in this neighbourhood, and died in different parts of London, the precise house from which they had removed is not stated in the return of deaths. I have heard of some persons who died in the country shortly after removing from the neighbourhood of Broad Street; and there must, no doubt, be several cases of this kind that I have not heard of. Indeed, the full extent of the calamity will probably never be known. The deficiencies I have mentioned, however, probably do not detract from the correctness of the map as a diagram of the topography of the outbreak; for, if the locality of the few additional cases could be ascertained, they would probably be distributed over the district of the outbreak in the same proportion as the large number which are known.[11]

The deaths in the above table [the time-series of daily deaths] are compiled from the sources mentioned above in describing the map; but some deaths which were omitted from the map on account of the number of the house not being known, are included in the table. . . .[12]

Snow drew a *dot map*, marking each individual death. This design has statistical costs and benefits: death *rates* are not shown, and such maps may become cluttered with excessive detail; on the other hand, the sometimes deceptive effects of aggregation are avoided. And of course dot maps aid in the identification and analysis of individual cases, evidence essential to Snow's argument.

The big problem is that dot maps fail to take into account the number of people living in an area and at risk to get a disease: "an area of the map may be free of cases merely because it is not populated."[13]

[11]Snow, *Cholera*, pp. 45–46.
[12]Snow, *Cholera*, p. 50.
[13]Brian MacMahon and Thomas F. Pugh, *Epidemiology: Principles and Methods* (Boston, 1970), p. 150.

Snow's map does not fully answer the question *Compared with what?* For example, if the population as a whole in central London had been distributed just as the deaths were, then the cholera map would have merely repeated the unimportant fact that more people lived near the Broad Street pump than elsewhere. This was not the case; the entire area shown on the map—with and without cholera—was thickly populated. Still, Snow's dot map does not assess varying densities of population in the area around the pump. Ideally, the cholera data should be displayed on both a dot and a rate map, with population-based rates calculated for rather small and homogeneous geographic units. In the text of his report, however, Snow did present rates for a few different areas surrounding the pump.

Even in the face of issues raised by a modern statistical critique, it remains wonderfully true that John Snow did, after all, show exactly how cholera was transmitted and therefore prevented. In 1955, the *Proceedings of the Royal Society of Medicine* commemorated Snow's discovery. A renowned epidemiologist, Bradford Hill, wrote: "For close upon 100 years we have been free in this country from epidemic cholera, and it is a freedom which, basically, we owe to the logical thinking, acute observations and simple sums of Dr. John Snow."[14]

 Steps in Writing a Causal Argument

If your instructor asks for a topic proposal, use steps 1–4 to guide you in writing the proposal.

1. **Make a causal claim on a controversial trend, event, or phenomenon.** Use this formula: X *causes (or does not cause)* Y *or* X *causes* Y, *which in turn causes* Z.

   Examples:
   - One-parent families (or television violence, bad diet, and so on) is (or is not) the cause of emotional and behavioral problems in children.

- Firearms control laws (or right-to-carry-handgun laws) reduce (or increase) violent crimes.
- The trend toward home schooling (or private schools) is (or is not) improving the quality of education.
- The length of U.S. presidential campaigns forces candidates to become too much influenced by big-dollar contributors (or prepares them for the constant media scrutiny that they will endure as president).
- Putting grade school children into competitive sports teaches them how to succeed in later life (or puts undue emphasis on winning and teaches many who are slower to mature to have a negative self-image).

2. **What's at stake in your claim?** If the cause is obvious to everyone, then it probably isn't worth writing about. Sex is the cause of STDs among college students, of course, but why do some students engage in unprotected sex when they know they are at risk?

3. **Make a diagram of causes.** Write as many causes as you can think of. Then make a fishbone diagram in which you show the causes.

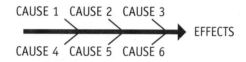

Which are the immediate causes? Which are the background causes? Which are the hidden causes? Which are the causes that most people have not recognized?

4. **Analyze your potential readers.** Who are your readers? How familiar are they with the trend, event, or phenomenon that you're writing about? What are they likely to know and not know? How does it affect them? How likely are they to accept your causal explanation? What alternative explanation might they argue for?

5. **Write a draft.**

Introduction:
- Describe the controversial trend, event, or phenomenon.
- Give the background necessary for your intended readers.

Body:
- For a trend, event, or phenomenon that is unfamiliar to your readers, you can explain the cause or chain of causation. Remember that providing facts is not the same thing as estab-

lishing causes, although facts can help to support your causal analysis.

■ Another way of organizing the body is to set out the causes that have been offered and reject them one by one. Then you can present the cause that you think is most important.

■ A third way is to treat a series of causes one by one, analyzing the importance of each.

Conclusion:

■ Do more than simply summarize what you have said. You might consider additional effects beyond those that have been previously noted.

6. **Revise, revise, revise. See Chapter 11 for detailed instructions.**

Stage 1. Read your argument aloud.

Do no more in this stage than put checks in the margins that you can return to later. Think in particular about these things:

■ **Your claim.** When you finish reading, summarize in one sentence what you are arguing. What's at stake in your claim?

■ **Your good reasons.** What are the good reasons for your claim? Would a reader have any trouble identifying them?

■ **Your representation of yourself.** Forget for a moment that you wrote what you are reading. What impression do you have of you, the writer?

■ **Your consideration of your readers.** Do you give enough background if your readers are unfamiliar with the issue? Do you acknowledge opposing views that they might have? Do you appeal to common values that you share with them?

Stage 2. Analyze your argument in detail.

■ **Examine your organization.** What are the topics of each of the paragraphs? Is the relationship of one paragraph to another clearly signaled? If any paragraphs appear out of order, think of another way to arrange them.

■ **Examine your evidence.** If you noted places where you could use more evidence when you read through the first time, now is the time to determine what kinds of additional evidence you need.

■ **Consider your title and introduction.** Be as specific as you can in your title, and if possible, suggest your stance. Does your introduction get off to a fast start and convince your reader to keep reading?

- **Consider your conclusion.** Think about whether there is a summarizing point you can make, an implication you can draw, or another example you can include that sums up your position.
- **Analyze the visual aspects of your text.** Do the font and layout you selected look attractive? Would headings and subheadings help to identify key sections of your argument? Would the addition of graphics augment key points?

Stage 3. Focus on your style and proofread carefully.

- **Check the connections between sentences.** Notice how your sentences are connected. If you need to signal the relationship from one sentence to the next, use a transitional word or phrase.
- **Check your sentences for emphasis.** Elements at the beginning and the end of sentences tend to stand out more than things in the middle.
- **Eliminate wordiness.** See how many words you can take out without losing the meaning.
- **Use active verbs.** Anytime you can use a verb besides a form of *be* (*is, are, was, were*), take advantage of the opportunity to make your style more lively.
- **Proofread your spelling carefully.** Your spelling checker will miss many mistakes.
- **Use your handbook to check items of mechanics and usage.** Look up any item you are unsure of.

CHAPTER 7

Evaluation Arguments

People make evaluations all the time. Newspapers and magazines have picked up on this love of evaluation by running "best of" polls. They ask their readers what's the best Mexican, Italian, or Chinese restaurant; the best pizza; the best local band; the best coffeehouse; the best dance club; the best neighborhood park; the best swimming hole; the best bike ride (scenic and challenging); the best volleyball court; the best place to get married; and so on. If you ask one of your friends who voted in a "best" poll why she picked a particular restaurant as the best of its kind, she might respond by saying simply, "I like it." But if you ask her why she likes it, she might start offering good reasons such as these: The food is good, the service prompt, the prices fair, and the atmosphere comfortable. It's really not a mystery why these polls are often quite predictable and why the same restaurants tend to win year after year. Many people think that evaluations are matters of personal taste, but when we begin probing the reasons, we often discover that the criteria that different people use to make evaluations have a lot in common.

> **Evaluation arguments depend on the criteria you select.**

If you simply want to announce that you like or don't like something, then all you have to do is say so, but if you want to convince other people that your judgment is sound, then you have to appeal to criteria that they will agree with and, if necessary, argue for the validity of additional criteria that you think your readers should also consider. Once you have established the criteria you will use for your evaluation, then you can apply those criteria to whatever you are evaluating to see how well it measures up. You make judgments of good or bad, best or worst, on the basis of the match with the criteria. For some items the criteria are relatively easy to establish, and the judgment is easy to make. If you accidentally knock your clock radio off your nightstand, break it, and have to replace it, you might do a little comparison shopping. Setting the alarm on your old clock was more difficult than it should have been, so you want an alarm that is easy to set. You need to see the clock at night, so you want a luminous display. You sometimes listen to the radio while you're waking up, so the radio needs to sound good enough to get your day off to a pleasant start. And you don't want to pay much. So you decide to test several brands that all cost about $20, and you buy the one that is easiest to use with the best sound and display.

Kinds of Evaluations

Arguments of evaluation are structured much like arguments of definition. Recall that the criteria in arguments of definition are set out in because clauses: *X is a Y because it has criteria A and B*. In arguments of evaluation the claim takes the form *X is a good (bad, the best, the worst) Y if measured by criteria A, B, and C*.

X ⬅— LINK (because) ⬅— good (bad, best, worst) Y

X is ⬅— LINK (because) ⬅— the best clock radio for under $20

      A) it has the best display
      B) it has the best sounding radio
      C) it is easy to use

The key move in writing most evaluative arguments is first deciding what kind of criteria to use and then finding appropriate criteria.

    Imagine that the oldest commercial building in your city is about to be torn down. Your goal is to get the old store converted to a museum, which is a proposal argument. First you will need to make an evaluative argument that will form the basis of your proposal. You might argue that the stonework in the building is of excellent quality and deserves preservation. You might argue that a downtown museum would be much better than more office space because it would draw more visitors. Or you might argue that it is only fair that the oldest commercial building be preserved because the oldest house and other historic buildings have been saved.

Each of these arguments uses different criteria. An argument that the old building is beautiful and that beautiful things should be preserved uses **aesthetic** criteria. An argument that a museum is better than an office building because it would bring more visitors to the downtown area is based on **practical** criteria. An argument that the oldest store building deserves the same treatment as the oldest house is based on fairness, a concept that relies on **moral** criteria.

Building an Evaluation Argument

Most people have a lot of practice making consumer evaluations, and when they have enough time to do their homework, they usually make an informed decision. But sometimes, criteria for evaluations are not so obvious, and evaluations are much more difficult to make. Sometimes, one set of criteria favors one choice while another set of criteria favors another. You might have encountered this problem when you chose a college. If you were able to leave home to go to school, you had a potential choice of over 1,400 accredited colleges and universities. Until twenty years ago, there wasn't much information about choosing a college other than what colleges said about themselves. You could find out the price of tuition and what courses were offered, but it was hard to compare one college with another.

In 1983, the magazine *U.S. News & World Report* began ranking U.S. colleges and universities from a consumer's perspective. Those rankings have remained highly controversial ever since. Many college officials have attacked the criteria that *U.S. News* uses to make its evaluations. In an August 1998 *U.S. News* article, Gerhard Casper, the president of Stanford University (which is consistently near the top of the rankings), says, "Much about these rankings—particularly their specious formulas and spurious precision—is utterly misleading." Casper argues that using graduation rates as a criterion of quality rewards easy schools. Other college presidents have called for a national boycott of the *U.S. News* rankings (without much success).

U.S. News replies in its defense that colleges and universities themselves do a lot of ranking, beginning with ranking students for admissions, using their SAT or ACT scores, high school GPA, ranking in high school class, quality of high school, and other factors, and then grading the students and ranking them against each other when they are enrolled in college. Furthermore, schools also evaluate faculty members and take great interest in the national ranking of their departments. They care very much about where they stand in relation to each other. Why, then, *U.S. News* argues, shouldn't people be able to evaluate colleges and universities, since colleges and universities are so much in the business of evaluating people?

Arguing for the right to evaluate colleges and universities is one thing; actually doing comprehensive and reliable evaluations is quite another. *U.S. News* uses a formula in which 25 percent of a school's ranking is based on a survey of reputation in which the president, provost, and dean of admissions at each college rate the quality of schools in the same category, and the remaining 75 percent is based on statistical criteria of quality. These statistical criteria fall into six major categories: retention of students, faculty resources, student selectivity, financial resources, alumni giving, and (for national universities and liberal arts colleges only) "graduation rate performance," the difference between the proportion of students who are expected to graduate and the proportion that actually do. These major categories are made up of factors that are weighted for their importance. For example, the faculty resources category is determined by the size of classes (the proportion of classes with fewer than twenty students and the proportion of classes with fifty or more students), the average faculty pay weighted by the cost of living in different regions of the country, the percentage of professors with the highest degree in their field, the overall student-faculty ratio, and the percentage of faculty who are full time.

Those who have challenged the *U.S. News* rankings argue that the magazine should use different criteria or weight the criteria differently. *U.S. News* answers those charges on its Web site (http://www.usnews.com/usnews/edu/college/corank.htm) by claiming that it has followed a trend toward emphasizing outcomes such as graduation rates. If you are curious about where your school ranks, take a look at the *U.S. News* Web site.

Reviews are a common type of evaluative argument that uses aesthetic criteria. When you read movie reviews, concert reviews, or other reviews, notice how the writer identifies criteria. Sometimes, these criteria are not obvious, and you will notice that the writer makes an argument about what criteria make a truly excellent horror film or a superior rock concert. You might have to argue for your criteria too. For example, suppose you want to argue that the 1955 film *Rebel without a Cause*, starring James Dean, Natalie Wood, and Sal Mineo, is a classic of teen drama films. The obvious definitional criteria are that *Rebel without a Cause* is a film, is a drama, and is about teens. But if you want to argue that *Rebel without a Cause* is exemplary of the genre and has qualities that make it timeless, then you have to define qualities that make a film a classic in this genre.

You mention your idea to your roommate, and she says, "That's total nonsense. Have you seen it recently? The dialog is awful, and the plot is even worse with that sappy ending. If James Dean hadn't gotten killed in a car wreck at age twenty-four, believe me, nobody would ever watch it now." You realize that she has a point about the tragic deaths of the main characters. Not only did James Dean die in the most famous car crash in history before Princess Diana, but also Natalie Wood later drowned mysteriously in a boating accident off Catalina, and Sal Mineo was murdered near his West Hollywood apartment. And she's right that the dialog hasn't aged well and that the ending, in which the James Dean character reconciles with his father, doesn't fit with the rest of the film. But there's still something about *Rebel without a Cause* that makes it a classic, and that's what you want to convince her of.

James Dean

First, you realize that even though there have been a lot of bad films about teens since *Rebel without a Cause*, there really were none before it. So you argue that *Rebel without a Cause* is a classic because it pioneered much of what was to come later. It was the first film to portray teens in a somewhat realistic fashion (though the stars did overact). The main character, Jim Stark (played by James Dean), is both vulnerable and defiant. His friend Plato (the Sal Mineo character) is about as gay as a film character could be in the 1950s, when direct portrayal of homosexuality was banned by the censors. Jim's eventual girlfriend, Judy (Natalie Wood), who snubs him at the beginning, is confused and rejected by her parents. And the parents in the film are totally ineffectual. Jim has a weak father (played by Jim Backus, the voice of Mr. Magoo) who won't stand up against his domineering wife. Judy also lacks parental support, and Plato's parents have abandoned him. So even if *Rebel without a Cause* is a little cheesy, it's honest about teen problems.

You decide to argue that another criterion that makes *Rebel without a Cause* a classic is its implicit critique of U.S. culture. It was released in 1955 at the peak of U.S. self-confidence and at the high-water mark of what later came to be called family values. These were supposed to be the years of the family ideal—of *Father Knows Best*, *Leave It to Beaver*, and *Donna Reed*—yet the film depicted an entire generation of young men and women who were struggling to find an identity. The film was the first to ask why U.S. teenagers were so troubled if everything was supposed to be so good. It exposed a big flaw in the portrait of the United States as the ideal society and accused the parents of being responsible for the alienation of the teenagers.

Finally, you won't concede that the fame of the film is strictly because of James Dean's early death. It's no accident, you argue, that boys in the 1950s spent hours trying to comb their hair into pompadours to look like James Dean. He has a terrific screen presence, and he conveys many conflicting emotions. But above all, he's always lonely, always groping for love from a family and society he finds unresponsive. Dean's role is the blueprint for the alienated teen. He's still a rebel after all these years.

ERIC GABLE AND RICHARD HANDLER

In Colonial Williamsburg, the New History Meets the Old

Eric Gable is an assistant professor of sociology and anthropology at Mary Washington College. Richard Handler is a professor of anthropology at the University of Virginia. They are the authors of The New History in an Old Museum: Creating the Past at Colonial Williamsburg *(Duke University Press, 1997).*

Some evaluations are obviously evaluations from the moment you glance at them. Reviews fall into this category. But other evaluations can be more subtle. "In Colonial Williamsburg, the New History Meets the Old," originally published in the Chronicle of Higher Education, *takes a long time giving background before the authors begin to make evaluative judgments. Notice how they define the criteria for a good museum. Do you agree with these criteria?*

1    $\mathbf{IN}$ recent years, the way in which museums and other public displays have presented history often has generated vituperative debate among scholars

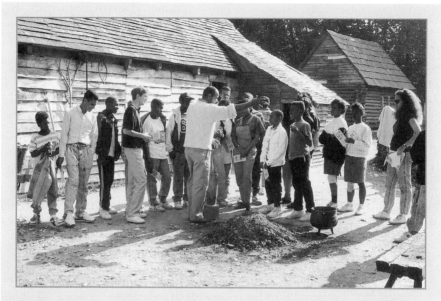

An interpreter explains eighteeth-century life at the reconstructed slave quarters of Colonial Williamsburg.

and the public at large. The popular media have portrayed public history as an ideological struggle—left-wing professors shattering (desecrating) popular assumptions. In the most common media treatment, "tenured radicals" view the previous generation's scholarly work as little more than ruling-class propaganda papering over the negative aspects of American history. In reaction, today's historians promulgate a more pessimistic version of America's past—one that destroys Americans' grounds for taking pride in their country.

2   We stepped into the middle of these often contentious appraisals of public history a few years ago, when we conducted an ethnographic study of Colonial Williamsburg, arguably America's premier public-history site. Colonial Williamsburg is a replica of the capital of Revolutionary-era Virginia. The reconstruction of this entire town, begun in 1926, was initially underwritten by John D. Rockefeller's largesse, but it is now financed by public donations, ticket sales, hotel and restaurant revenues, the marketing of Colonial-era reproductions, and revenue from an endowment established by Rockefeller.

3   For much of its history, the replica was widely criticized by historians and knowledgeable laypeople as little more than an airbrushed, consumer-oriented, patriotic shrine celebrating an upscale idyll loosely based on the life styles of Virginia's Colonial elite. But beginning in the 1970s, a new group of

historians was hired as researchers and curators to refashion the site. They were trained in the "new social history," which emerged out of the social turmoil of the 1960s and which focused on groups and individuals neglected by older, traditional scholars. The top administrators prompted this change in part to keep Colonial Williamsburg at the cutting edge of scholarship, and in part because historians have argued convincingly that a new version of the past will be more popular, accurate, and inclusive than the entrenched story.

4   As a result of this shift, we wanted to see how public history was being made "on the ground." We focused on the way it was managed, as historians attempted to use the materials at this particular site to create their vision of the past; as middle-level managers trained front-line staff members (dressed in reproduction costumes as craftworkers, farmers, and other residents of the town) to deliver historical stories to the public; as these front-line employees resisted or opposed new interpretations; and as visitors digested what they heard and saw.

5   We found that, during the past decade, Colonial Williamsburg has changed in significant ways the history that it presents to the public. Most notable is the greater prominence of African Americans—those the museum calls "the other half"—in its narrative of nationhood. A small but active unit devoted to African-American history has created dozens of special programs and tours to illuminate the lives of slaves and free black people in colonial Virginia. For example, you can now tour a reconstructed slave quarter and meet a costumed African-American guide who will tell you about the daily life of the enslaved. Or you can stroll Williamsburg's back alleys with such characters as the entrepreneurial Chicken Hattie, who sells eggs to the town's white inhabitants.

6   Some programs do not dodge the horror of slavery: an enactment of a slave auction, a video about a runaway slave, a tour with graphic discussions of the Middle Passage on slave ships, and discussions of the breakup of African-American families.

7   Yet the more widely disseminated story still is an upbeat one, in which slaves, like other immigrants, establish themselves in a new land and work hard to improve their lot. Moreover, black history remains secondary at Williamsburg. It is still easy for visitors to tour the entire site without hearing anything about African Americans other than how much they cost their owners, and how many lived and worked in a particular white person's residence.

8   At Colonial Williamsburg, then, the influence of social historians has apparently been less than media depictions of "tenured radicals" might lead one to expect. There has been no all-out ideological struggle, and the bulk of the history told here is not so different from that told 30 years ago. We asked ourselves why.

9   It seems to us that Colonial Williamsburg and sites like it remain stages for the retelling of such conventional American narratives as the Horatio Alger story. In this scenario, individuals or ethnic groups are depicted as pulling themselves up by their bootstraps. This narrative is applied as readily to African slaves such as Chicken Hattie as to a European-immigrant-turned-entrepreneurial-businessman such as Mr. Benjamin Powell, whose house you can visit. What this narrative does not do is challenge visitors to rethink their notions of America's past, or its present.

10   Like many other museums, Colonial Williamsburg is a tourist attraction as well as an educational institution, and the ideas of hospitality and courtesy are deeply ingrained in its corporate culture. Management repeats ceaselessly that visitors—customers—will not return unless they enjoy their visits. The assumption is that stories depicting the harshness of slavery—and, more generally, histories critical of America's shortcomings—will pain, embarrass, and ultimately turn away tourists.

11   Moreover, on the front line, where employees meet visitors—and behind the scenes, where managers of competing programs at the site wage institutional turf wars—facts are weapons more readily wielded than are the complicated arguments that social historians favor about the ideological underpinnings of history. Thus, for example, at one point we observed African-American guides and white guides at a particular re-created house debate how to discuss miscegenation: The general issue of the entanglement of sexual practices and racial politics was displaced by an unresolvable factual dispute: whether a particular slaveholder had fathered a particular child by a particular slave.

12   Time and again, we watched as seemingly productive debates deteriorated into narrowly construed arguments about fact. Even staff historians were prone to lose sight of the big picture as they chased after stray details. This "just the facts, please" tendency was exacerbated because the market niche of history museums depends on their claim to possess "real" history, embodied in their buildings and objects, in contrast to what the museums see as the "fakery" of their major competitors—theme parks such as those of Disney.

13   Thus, despite some changes, the new social history has not transformed this particular old museum and its decades-old culture of patriotic realism. The Fife and Drum Corps continues to play patriotic songs as it marches down the main street—the high point of a tourist's day. More significantly, the corps continues to be the central icon in the photographs, brochures, and commercials that the museum produces to attract visitors and convince people that donating to the site's continuing work is an act of patriotism. Other such icons are the coach and coachmen (usually black) in

livery. Visitors continue to pay extra for the privilege of a short coach ride through town, perhaps to identify themselves with the masters.

14   Because of the efforts of historians who have worked at Williamsburg, the site is now demographically more diverse than it used to be. It has more African-American employees in positions other than menial ones, and African Americans are often included in the stories that guides tell about America's Revolutionary past. But, by and large, these changes are just additional pieces in a narrative framework that continues to celebrate America while playing down inequalities.

15   In the end, then, Colonial Williamsburg continues to be a patriotic shrine that fosters tourists' fantasies. Despite media portrayals of ideological revolutions in the nation's museums, the new social historians at this site have not subverted the old story. It is not so much that they have been muzzled—or have backed down—as that their efforts have not overcome a wider cultural tendency, in which older cultural images persist and continue to frame the site as a whole. Williamsburg thus provides a fractured puzzle of the past—and continues to play down historic and current inequalities.

NATASCHA POCEK

The Diet Zone: A Dangerous Place

In 1997 Natascha Pocek wrote the following essay as a response to an assignment in her first-year writing course at Penn State.

1   DIET Coke, diet Pepsi, diet Cherry Coke, diet pills, diet shakes, no-fat diet, vegetable diet, carbohydrate diet, diet, diet, diet—enough! We are assaulted by the word "diet" every time we go into a supermarket, turn on the television, listen to the radio, or read an advertisement. We are not only surrounded by the word "diet" everywhere we look and listen, but we as "Americans" are also linked with "diet" in general; Americans are automatically associated with the stereotypical image of either extreme thinness or obesity. We have so easily been lured by the promise and potential of diet products, which include everything from pills to foods, that we have stopped thinking about what diet products are doing to us. Diet products, in fact, promote the "easy way out," a most elemental form of deception. It is imperative that we realize that diet products adversely affect not only our

weight, but also our values of dedication and persistence. We are paying for products that harm us, physically and psychologically. Therefore, we must stop purchasing diet products without recognizing the harm we are doing to ourselves. We must realize that in purchasing diet products we are effectively purchasing physical problems and psychological decay in a commercial package. The time has come for us to accept the fact that solutions don't come in bottles or from miracle no-calorie chemicals; solutions come from the mind, and diet products are promoting the wrong solution.

2   As a teenager, I learned the hard way that losing weight with diet products as an aid only results in a vicious cycle of failure. Statistically overweight from the age of 15 to 18, I was unhappy and sought a solution, a way to lose the extra pounds that I carried around on my frame. No bottle, pill, powder, or shake took off my excess weight; I earned the body that I now live in by watching what I ate. Period. As a typical teenager, I admit, I tried many fad diets. I attempted an advertised vegetable diet which reduced me to the meal plan of a rabbit, and a drink-as-much-water-as-you-can-so-you're-not-hungry diet. I also tried to lose weight by using diet pills and diet food products. The diet pills were, without a doubt, one of my biggest mistakes. The pills were only a temporary solution because while taking the pills my eating habits didn't change. I had not learned how to eat healthily and moderately. I had learned how to quickly lose a few pounds with no effort. The pills shifted my focus from the most important aspect, the food, and placed it on watching the clock to see when I needed to swallow the next pill. The pills circumvented the real issue of my unhealthy eating habits; I didn't even consider my eating habits since I had not taken any foods out of my daily food intake. Consequently, as soon as I stopped popping the miracle pills, the few pounds I had lost returned, along with a few more unexpected ones. Success had obviously eluded me.

3   The consumption of "diet-food" products was *the* single biggest mistake that I made in attempting to lose weight. I allowed myself to fall into a very relaxed mind set in which I did not really have to think about what I ate; my brain was dormant while my stomach was active. The diet foods and drinks that I consumed became my excuse for the chocolate cake at dinner, the extra helping of pasta, and the late-night cup of hot chocolate. It was acceptable to allow myself these treats because I had "saved calories" elsewhere. Needless to say, although I lost weight, it didn't stay off for long. Once again, I had not trained myself to acquire a taste for healthier foods. My eating habits stayed bad from the first Diet Coke I drank, to the last Low-Fat Granola Bar I ate. Diet foods, just like the diet pills, had been a huge failure which resulted from my lack of thought.

4   The mistake that I—and countless other Americans—made in using diet products carries much greater significance than not losing weight for the long run: diet products significantly weaken us psychologically. On one level, we are not allowing our brains to acknowledge that our weight problems lie not in actually losing the weight, but in controlling the consumption of fatty, high-caloric, unhealthy foods. Diet products allow us to skip the thinking stage completely and instead go straight for the scale. Dr. James Ferguson, a nationally prominent clinician who specializes in treating eating disorders and teaching weight control, says that "self-observation [is the] prime method of assessing eating behaviors" (65). Precisely. Diet products only allow us to ignore the crucial issue of eating habits altogether: They bypass the real problem. In reality, we aren't the ones contributing to the loss of our pounds; the diet products are responsible for shedding the pounds from our bodies. All we have to be able to do is swallow or recognize the word "diet" in food labels. The effort we put into losing weight is zero, no effort, non-existent. Consequently, when we stop consuming diet products, our bodies lose the dictators that worked to control the unruly pounds and our eating habits fall into chaos again.

5   On another level, the psychological effects of diet products have much greater ramifications. Every time we swallow a pill or drink a zero-calorie beverage, we are unconsciously telling ourselves that we don't have to work to get results, that we can select the "easy way out," the quick way out. I see Americans eating sweet foods endlessly because they are pacified by the low-fat label; they don't just eat the cakes and candies and cookies, they inhale them in huge amounts, and their excuse is that "they're low-fat, so it's okay." Diet products are subconsciously instilling in Americans the idea that gain comes without pain, that life can be devoid of resistance and struggle. The diet industry is not only making it easy to ignore the principle of not always getting what you want—it is, in fact, promoting its disappearance. People *can* eat whatever they want because most "bad foods" are now diet, light, or reduced fat. The diet pills and potions become important at the end of the vicious diet cycle when we say, "Oops, I ate twice as many cookies because they were low-fat and I gained weight." The diet pills become the dust pan and brush that clean up the mess we made with the diet products. The cycle of diet products is a virus that affects us psychologically and doesn't enforce any values of determination, perseverance, hard work, or self-discipline.

6   The danger of diet products lies not only in the psychological effects they have on us, but also in the immediate physical danger that they present. Death is unfortunately a possible side-effect of using diet products. In 1994, the drug Ephedrine, which is found in diet pills, was "linked to the

deaths of two people and severe reactions in several others" (Rosencrans). Cellulose fiber diet pills were identified as a "cause of esophageal obstruction" (Jones) and in 1992, 26 cases were reported to the Food and Drug Administration in which diet pills were the cause of "esophageal and small bowel obstruction" (Lewis 1424). Clearly, diet pills pose health threats. Diet foods become dangerous when used in place of other foods because they contain a minimal amount of nutrients. The next time you go to the supermarket and have the urge to buy a diet beverage, read the label. For example, the nutrition label of a Crystal Light bottle reads: Total Fat, 0 grams; Total Carb, 0 grams; Protein, 0 grams; Calories, 5. Wouldn't it be more appropriate to name the label the "malnutrition" label? When we drink a Crystal Light, we are swallowing a lot of precisely what, if there are 0 grams of everything in it? The answer is nothing—besides chemicals. As you continue reading the label on the bottle, you will come to the ingredient list, which includes sodium benzoate, artificial flavor, potassium sorbate, potassium citrate (controls acidity), BHA (preserves freshness) and so on. The ingredient and nutrition label illustrates the fact that diet foods can indirectly harm our bodies because consuming them instead of healthy foods means we are depriving our bodies of essential nutrients. Beyond an indirect harm, diet products can actually cause direct harm as well. Packets of Sweet n' Low and Care-Free gum carry warning labels which read, the "use of this product may be hazardous to your health. This product contains saccharin, which has been determined to cause cancer in laboratory animals." Would you like to take the chance that saccharin might give *you* cancer? The point is that diet foods and diet pills are only zero-caloric because the diet industry has created chemicals that can be manipulated to produce these miracle products. There is no insurance that a diet product is nutritional, and the chemicals that go into diet products are potentially dangerous.

7   As we walk down the aisle of the supermarket tomorrow, we will once again be bombarded by "diet" food labels that call to us from left and right. We will also see all the promising diet pills that make losing weight seem so easy. After demonstrating the harmful physical and psychological effects that diet products have on us, our instinct should be to turn and walk away. Now that we are more knowledgeable on the subject of diet products and can no longer claim ignorance about the harms that diet products have, it is time to seriously contemplate our purchase of diet products. Losing weight lies in the power of our minds, not in the power of chemicals. Once we realize this, we will be much better able to resist diet products, and thereby resist the psychological deterioration and physical deprivation that comes from using diet products.

Works Cited

Ferguson, James M. *Habits Not Diets: The Secret to Lifetime Weight Control.* Palo Alto, CA: Bull Publishing, 1988.

Jones, K. R. "Cellulose Fiber Diet Pills, A New Cause of Esophageal Obstruction." *Archives of Otolaryngology—Head and Neck Surgery* 116 (1990): 1091.

Lewis, J. H. "Esophageal and Small Bowel Obstruction from Guar Gum-Containing 'Diet Pills.'" *American Journal of Gastroenterology* 87 (1992): 1424–28.

Rosencrans, Kendra. "Diet Pills Suspected in Deaths." *Healthy Weight Journal* 8:4 (1994): 68.

 # Steps in Writing an Evaluation Argument

If your instructor asks for a topic proposal, use steps 1–4 to guide you in writing the proposal.

1. **Make an evaluative claim based on criteria.** Use this formula: X *is a good (bad, the best, the worst)* Y *if measured by certain criteria (aesthetic, practical, or moral).*

   Examples:
   - Write a book review or a movie review.
   - Write a defense of a particular kind of music or art.
   - Evaluate a controversial aspect of sports (e.g., the current system of determining who is champion in Division I college football by a system of bowls and polls) or evaluate a sports event (e.g., this year's WNBA playoffs) or a team.
   - Evaluate the effectiveness of an educational program (such as your high school honors program or your college's core curriculum requirement) or some other aspect of your campus.
   - Evaluate the effectiveness of a social policy or law such as legislating 21 as the legal drinking age, current gun control laws, or environmental regulation.

2. **What's at stake in your claim?** If nearly everybody would agree with you, then your evaluative claim probably isn't interesting or important. If you can think of people who would disagree, then something is at stake. Who argues the opposite of your claim? Why do they make a different evaluation?

3. **Make a list of criteria (aesthetic, practical, moral).** Which criteria make something a good Y? Which are the most important?

Which are fairly obvious and which will you have to argue for? Or what are all the effects of what you are evaluating? Which are the most important? Which are fairly obvious and which will you have to argue for?

4. **Analyze your potential readers.** Who are your primary and secondary readers? How familiar will they be with the person, group, institution, event, or thing that you are evaluating? What are they likely to know and not know? Which criteria are most important to them?

5. **Write a draft.**

Introduction:
- Introduce the person, group, institution, event, or object that you are going to evaluate. You might want to announce your stance at this point or wait until the concluding section.
- Give the background necessary for your intended readers.
- If there are opposing views, briefly describe them.

Body:
- If you are making an evaluation by criteria, describe each criterion and then analyze how well what you are evaluating meets that criterion.
- If you are making an evaluation according to the effects someone or something produces, describe each effect in detail.

Conclusion:
- If you have not yet announced your stance, then you can conclude that, on the basis of the criteria you set out or the effects you have analyzed, X is a good (bad, best, worst) Y. If you have made your stance clear from the beginning, then you can end with a compelling example or analogy.

6. **Revise, revise, revise. See Chapter 11 for detailed instructions.**

Stage 1. Read your argument aloud.
Do no more in this stage than put checks in the margins that you can return to later. Think in particular about these things:

- **Your claim.** When you finish reading, summarize in one sentence what you are arguing. What's at stake in your claim?
- **Your criteria.** How many criteria do you offer? Where are they located? Are they clearly connected to your claim?
- **Your representation of yourself.** Forget for a moment that you wrote what you are reading. What impression do you have of you, the writer?

- **Your consideration of your readers.** Do you give enough background, if your readers are unfamiliar with the issue? Do you acknowledge opposing views that they might have? Do you appeal to common values that you share with them?

Stage 2. Analyze your argument in detail.

- **Examine your organization.** What are the topics of each of the paragraphs? Is the relationship of one paragraph to another clearly signaled? If any paragraphs appear out of order, think of another way to arrange them.
- **Examine your evidence.** If you noted places where you could use more evidence when you read through the first time, now is the time to determine what kinds of additional evidence you need.
- **Consider your title and introduction.** Be as specific as you can in your title, and if possible, suggest your stance. Does your introduction get off to a fast start and convince your reader to keep reading?
- **Consider your conclusion.** Think about whether there is a summarizing point you can make, an implication you can draw, or another example you can include that sums up your position.
- **Analyze the visual aspects of your text.** Do the font and layout you selected look attractive? Would headings and subheadings help to identify key sections of your argument? Would the addition of graphics augment key points?

Stage 3. Focus on your style and proofread carefully.

- **Check the connections between sentences.** Notice how your sentences are connected. If you need to signal the relationship from one sentence to the next, use a transitional word or phrase.
- **Check your sentences for emphasis.** Elements at the beginning and the end of sentences tend to stand out more than things in the middle.
- **Eliminate wordiness.** See how many words you can take out without losing the meaning.
- **Use active verbs.** Anytime you can use a verb besides a form of *be* (*is, are, was, were*), take advantage of the opportunity to make your style more lively.
- **Proofread your spelling carefully.** Your spelling checker will miss many mistakes.
- **Use your handbook to check items of mechanics and usage.** Look up any item you are unsure of.

CHAPTER 8

Narrative Arguments

In 1980, 53,172 people were killed in traffic accidents in the United States, and over half the deaths involved alcohol. Americans had become accustomed to losing around 25,000 to 30,000 people every year to drunk drivers. But it was the tragic death in 1980 of Cari Lightner, a thirteen-year-old California girl who was killed by a hit-and-run drunk driver while walking along a city street, that made people start asking whether this carnage could be prevented. The driver had been out on bail only two days for another hit-and-run drunk driving crash, and he had three previous drunk driving arrests. He was allowed to plea bargain for killing Cari and avoided going to prison. Cari's mother, Candy Lightner, was outraged that so little was being done to prevent needless deaths and injuries. She and a small group of other women founded Mothers Against Drunk Driving (MADD) with the goals of getting tougher laws against drunk driving, stiffer penalties for those who kill and injure while driving drunk, and greater public awareness of the seriousness of driving drunk.

> Narrative arguments often do not make a specific claim but rely on the reader to infer the writer's position.

Cari Lightner's story aroused to action other people who had been injured themselves or lost loved ones to drunk drivers. Chapters of MADD spread quickly across the country, and it has become one of the most effective citizen groups ever formed, succeeding in getting much new legislation against drunk driving on the books. These laws and changing attitudes about drunk driving have had a significant impact. The National Highway Traffic Safety Administration reported that in 2000, 16,653 people were killed in alcohol-related traffic accidents in the United States compared to 24,045 in 1986, a 30 percent reduction.

The success of MADD points to why arguing by narrating succeeds sometimes when other kinds of arguments have little effect. The story of Cari Lightner appealed to shared community values in ways that statistics did not. The story vividly illustrated that something was very wrong with the criminal justice system if a repeat drunk driver was allowed to run down and kill a child on a sidewalk only two days after committing a similar crime.

Martin Luther King, Jr., was another master of using narratives to make his points. In "Letter from Birmingham Jail," he relates in one sentence the disappointment of his six-year-old daughter when he had to explain to her why, because of the color of her skin, she could not go to an amusement park in Atlanta advertised on television. This tiny story vividly illustrates the pettiness of segregation laws and their effect on children.

Kinds of Narrative Arguments

Using narratives for advocating change is nothing new. As far back as we have records, we find people telling stories and singing songs about their own lives that argue for change. Folk songs have always given voice to political protest and have celebrated marginalized people. When workers in the United States began to organize in the 1880s, they adapted melodies that soldiers had sung in the Civil War. In the 1930s, performers and songwriters such as Paul Robeson, Woody Guthrie, Huddie Ledbetter (Leadbelly), and Aunt Molly Jackson relied on traditions of hymns, folk songs, and African-American blues to protest social conditions. In the midst of the politically quiet 1950s, folk songs told stories that critiqued social conformity and the dangers of nuclear war. In the 1960s, the civil rights movement and the movement against the Vietnam War brought a strong resurgence of folk music. The history of folk music is a continuous recycling of old tunes, verses, and narratives to engage new political situations. What can be said for folk songs is also true for any popular narrative genre, be it the short story, novel, drama, movies, or even rap music.

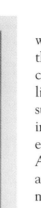

Folk singer/songwriter Shawn Colvin is one of many contemporary folk and blues singers who continue the tradition of making narrative arguments in their songs.

Narrative arguments work in a different way from those that spell out their criteria and argue for explicit links. A narrative argument succeeds if the experience being described invokes the life experiences of the readers. Anyone who has ever been around children knows that most kids love amusement parks. Martin Luther King, Jr., did not have to explain to his readers why going to an amusement park advertised on television was so important for his daughter. Likewise, the story of Cari Lightner was effective because even if you have not known someone who was killed by a drunk driver, most people have known someone who died tragically and perhaps needlessly. Furthermore, you often read about and see on television many people who die in traffic accidents. Narrative arguments allow readers to fill in the conclusion. In the cases of King's arguments against segregation laws and MADD's campaign against drunk drivers, that's exactly what happened. Public outcry led to changes in laws and public opinion.

Narrative arguments can be representative anecdotes, as we have seen with the examples from MADD and Martin Luther King, Jr., or they can be longer accounts of particular events that express larger ideas. One such story is George Orwell's account of a hanging in Burma (the country that is now known as Myanmar) while he was a colonial administrator in the late 1920s. In "A Hanging," first published in 1931, Orwell narrates an execution of a nameless prisoner who was convicted of a nameless crime. Everyone quietly and dispassionately performs their jobs—the prison guards, the hangman, the superintendent, and even the prisoner, who offers no resistance when he is bound and led to the gallows. All is totally routine until a very small incident makes Orwell aware of what is happening:

> It was about forty yards to the gallows. I watched the bare brown back of the prisoner marching in front of me. He walked clumsily with his bound arms, but quite steadily, with that bobbing gait of the Indian who never

straightens his knees. At each step his muscles slid neatly into place, the lock of hair on his scalp danced up and down, his feet printed themselves on the wet gravel. And once, in spite of the men who gripped him by each shoulder, he stepped lightly aside to avoid a puddle on the path.

It is curious; but till that moment I had never realized what it means to destroy a healthy, conscious man. When I saw the prisoner step aside to avoid the puddle, I saw the mystery, the unspeakable wrongness, of cutting a life short when it is in full tide. This man was not dying, he was alive just as we are alive. All the organs of his body were working—bowels digesting food, skin renewing itself, nails growing, tissues forming—all toiling away in solemn foolery. His nails would still be growing when he stood on the drop, when he was falling through the air with a tenth-of-a-second to live. His eyes saw the yellow gravel and gray walls, and his brain still remembered, foresaw, reasoned—even about puddles. He and we were a party of men walking together, seeing, hearing, feeling, understanding the same world; and in two minutes, with a sudden snap, one of us would be gone—one mind less, one world less.

Orwell's narrative leads a dramatic moment of recognition, which gives this story its lasting power.

Building a Narrative Argument

The biggest problem with narrative arguments is that anyone can tell a story. On the one hand, there are compelling stories that argue against capital punishment. For example, a mentally retarded man who was executed in Arkansas had refused a piece of pie at his last meal, telling the guards that he wanted to save the pie for later. On the other hand, there are also many stories about the victims of murder and other crimes. Many families have Web sites on which they call for killing those responsible for murdering their loved ones. They too have compelling stories to tell.

Violent deaths of all kinds make for especially vivid narrative arguments. In the late 1990s, there were several incidents in which schoolchildren used guns taken from the family home to kill other students. Stories of these tragedies provided strong arguments for gun control. Gun rights organizations, including the National Rifle Association (NRA), attempted to counter these stories by claiming that they are not truly representative. The NRA claims that between sixty million and sixty-five million Americans own guns and thirty million to thirty-five million own handguns. They argue that more than 99.8 percent of all guns and 99.6 percent of handguns will not be used to commit crimes in any given year. Thus, the NRA argues that narratives of tragic gun deaths are either not representative or the result of allowing too many criminals to avoid prison or execution.

There are two keys to making effective narrative arguments: establishing credibility and establishing representativeness. It's easy enough to make up stories that suit the point you want to make. Writing from personal experience can give you a great deal of impact, but that impact vanishes if your readers doubt that you are telling the truth. Second, the story you tell may be true enough, but the question remains how representative the incident is. We don't ban bananas because someone once slipped on a banana peel. Narratives are often useful for illustrating how people are affected by particular issues or events, but narrative arguments are more effective if you have more evidence than just one incident. The death of Cari Lightner was a tragedy, but the deaths of over 25,000 people a year caused by drunk drivers made Cari Lightner's death representative of a national tragedy, a slaughter that could be prevented. Cari Lightner's tragic story had power because people understood it to be representative of a much larger problem.

LESLIE MARMON SILKO

The Border Patrol State

Leslie Marmon Silko (1948–   ) was born in Albuquerque and graduated from the University of New Mexico. She now teaches at the University of Arizona. She has received much critical acclaim for her writings about Native Americans. Her first novel, Ceremony *(1977), describes the struggles of a veteran returning home after World War II to civilian life on a New Mexico reservation. Her incorporation of Indian storytelling techniques in* Ceremony *drew strong praise. One critic called her "the most accomplished Indian writer of her generation." She has since published two more novels,* Almanac of the Dead *(1991) and* Gardens in the Dunes *(1999); a collection of essays,* Yellow Woman and a Beauty of the Spirit: Essays on Native American Life Today *(1996); two volumes of poems and stories; and many shorter works. Silko's talents as a storyteller are evident in this essay, which first appeared in the magazine* Nation *in 1994.*

1   I used to travel the highways of New Mexico and Arizona with a wonderful sensation of absolute freedom as I cruised down the open road and across the vast desert plateaus. On the Laguna Pueblo reservation, where I

was raised, the people were patriotic despite the way the U.S. government had treated Native Americans. As proud citizens, we grew up believing the freedom to travel was our inalienable right, a right that some Native Americans had been denied in the early twentieth century. Our cousin, old Bill Pratt, used to ride his horse 300 miles overland from Laguna, New Mexico, to Prescott, Arizona, every summer to work as a fire lookout.

2   In school in the 1950s, we were taught that our right to travel from state to state without special papers or threat of detainment was a right that citizens under communist and totalitarian governments did not possess. That wide open highway told us we were U.S. citizens; we were free. . . .

3   Not so long ago, my companion Gus and I were driving south from Albuquerque, returning to Tucson after a book promotion for the paperback edition of my novel *Almanac of the Dead*. I had settled back and gone to sleep while Gus drove, but I was awakened when I felt the car slowing to a stop. It was nearly midnight on New Mexico State Road 26, a dark, lonely stretch of two-lane highway between Hatch and Deming. When I sat up, I saw the headlights and emergency flashers of six vehicles—Border Patrol cars and a van were blocking both lanes of the highway. Gus stopped the car and rolled down the window to ask what was wrong. But the closest Border Patrolman and his companion did not reply; instead, the first agent ordered us to "step out of the car." Gus asked why, but his question seemed to set them off. Two more Border Patrol agents immediately approached our car, and one of them snapped, "Are you looking for trouble?" as if he would relish it.

4   I will never forget that night beside the highway. There was an awful feeling of menace and violence straining to break loose. It was clear that the uniformed men would be only too happy to drag us out of the car if we did not speedily comply with their request (asking a question is tantamount to resistance, it seems). So we stepped out of the car and they motioned for us to stand on the shoulder of the road. The night was very dark, and no other traffic had come down the road since we had been stopped. All I could think about was a book I had read—*Nunca Mas*—the official report of a human rights commission that investigated and certified more than 12,000 "disappearances" during Argentina's "dirty war" in the late 1970s.

5   The weird anger of these Border Patrolmen made me think about descriptions in the report of Argentine police and military officers who became addicted to interrogation, torture and the murder that followed. When the military and police ran out of political suspects to torture and kill, they resorted to the random abduction of citizens off the streets. I thought how easy it would be for the Border Patrol to shoot us and leave our bodies and

car beside the highway, like so many bodies found in these parts and ascribed to "drug runners."

6   Two other Border Patrolmen stood by the white van. The one who had
asked if we were looking for trouble ordered his partner to "get the dog,"
and from the back of the van another patrolman brought a small female
German shepherd on a leash. The dog apparently did not heel well enough
to suit him, and the handler jerked the leash. They opened the doors of our
car and pulled the dog's head into it, but I saw immediately from the expression in her eyes that the dog hated them, and that she would not serve
them. When she showed no interest in the inside of the car, they brought
her around back to the trunk, near where we were standing. They half-
dragged her up into the trunk, but still she did not indicate any stowed-
away human beings or illegal drugs.

7   The mood got uglier; the officers seemed outraged that the dog could
not find any contraband, and they dragged her over to us and commanded
her to sniff our legs and feet. To my relief, the strange violence the Border
Patrol agents had focused on us now seemed shifted to the dog. I no longer
felt so strongly that we would be murdered. We exchanged looks—the dog
and I. She was afraid of what they might do, just as I was. The dog's handler
jerked the leash sharply as she sniffed us, as if to make her perform better,
but the dog refused to accuse us: She had an innate dignity that did not
permit her to serve the murderous impulses of those men. I can't forget the
expression in the dog's eyes; it was as if she were embarrassed to be associated with them. I had a small amount of medicinal marijuana in my purse
that night, but she refused to expose me. I am not partial to dogs, but I will
always remember the small German shepherd that night.

8   Unfortunately, what happened to me is an everyday occurrence here
now. Since the 1980s, on top of greatly expanding border checkpoints, the
Immigration and Naturalization Service and the Border Patrol have implemented policies that interfere with the rights of U.S. citizens to travel freely
within our borders. I.N.S. agents now patrol all interstate highways and roads
that lead to or from the U.S.-Mexico border in Texas, New Mexico, Arizona
and California. Now, when you drive east from Tucson on Interstate 10 toward El Paso, you encounter an I.N.S. check station outside Las Cruces, New
Mexico. When you drive north from Las Cruces up Interstate 25, two miles
north of the town of Truth or Consequences, the highway is blocked with
orange emergency barriers, and all traffic is diverted into a two-lane Border
Patrol checkpoint—ninety-five miles north of the U.S.-Mexico border.

9   I was detained once at Truth or Consequences, despite my and my companion's Arizona driver's licenses. Two men, both Chicanos, were detained at

the same time, despite the fact that they too presented ID and spoke English without the thick Texas accents of the Border Patrol agents. While we were stopped, we watched as other vehicles—whose occupants were white—were waved through the checkpoint. White people traveling with brown people, however, can expect to be stopped on suspicion they work with the sanctuary movement, which shelters refugees. White people who appear to be clergy, those who wear ethnic clothing or jewelry and women with very long hair or very short hair (they could be nuns) are also frequently detained; white men with beards or men with long hair are likely to be detained, too, because Border Patrol agents have "profiles" of "those sorts" of white people who may help political refugees. (Most of the political refugees from Guatemala and El Salvador are Native American or mestizo because the indigenous people of the Americas have continued to resist efforts by invaders to displace them from their ancestral lands.) Alleged increases in illegal immigration by people of Asian ancestry mean that the Border Patrol now routinely detains anyone who appears to be Asian or part Asian, as well.

10   Once your car is diverted from the Interstate Highway into the checkpoint area, you are under the control of the Border Patrol, which in practical terms exercises a power that no highway patrol or city patrolman possesses: They are willing to detain anyone, for no apparent reason. Other law-enforcement officers need a shred of probable cause in order to detain someone. On the books, so does the Border Patrol; but on the road, it's another matter. They'll order you to stop your car and step out; then they'll ask you to open the trunk. If you ask why or request a search warrant, you'll be told that they'll have to have a dog sniff the car before they can request a search warrant, and the dog might not get there for two or three hours. The search warrant might require an hour or two past that. They make it clear that if you force them to obtain a search warrant for the car, they will make you submit to a strip search as well.

11   Traveling in the open, though, the sense of violation can be even worse. Never mind high-profile cases like that of former Border Patrol agent Michael Elmer, acquitted of murder by claiming self-defense, despite admitting that as an officer he shot an "illegal" immigrant in the back and then hid the body, which remained undiscovered until another Border Patrolman reported the event. (Last month, Elmer was convicted of reckless endangerment in a separate incident, for shooting at least ten rounds from his M-16 too close to a group of immigrants as they were crossing illegally into Nogales in March 1992.) Or that in El Paso a high school football coach driving a vanload of players in full uniform was pulled over on the freeway and a

Border Patrol agent put a cocked revolver to his head. (The football coach was Mexican-American, as were most of the players in his van; the incident eventually caused a federal judge to issue a restraining order against the Border Patrol.) We've a mountain of personal experiences like that which never make the newspapers. A history professor at U.C.L.A. told me she had been traveling by train from Los Angeles to Albuquerque twice a month doing research. On each of her trips, she had noticed that the Border Patrol agents were at the station in Albuquerque scrutinizing the passengers. Since she is six feet tall and of Irish and German ancestry, she was not particularly concerned. Then one day when she stepped off the train in Albuquerque, two Border Patrolmen accosted her, wanting to know what she was doing, and why she was traveling between Los Angeles and Albuquerque twice a month. She presented identification and an explanation deemed "suitable" by the agents, and was allowed to go about her business.

12   Just the other day, I mentioned to a friend that I was writing this article and he told me about his 73-year-old father, who is half Chinese and who had set out alone by car from Tucson to Albuquerque the week before. His father had become confused by road construction and missed a turnoff from Interstate 10 to Interstate 25; when he turned around and circled back, he missed the turnoff a second time. But when he looped back for yet another try, Border Patrol agents stopped him and forced him to open his trunk. After they satisfied themselves that he was not smuggling Chinese immigrants, they sent him on his way. He was so rattled by the event that he had to be driven home by his daughter.

13   This is the police state that has developed in the southwestern United States since the 1980s. No person, no citizen, is free to travel without the scrutiny of the Border Patrol. In the city of South Tucson, where 80 percent of the respondents were Chicano or Mexicano, a joint research project by the University of Wisconsin and the University of Arizona recently concluded that one out of every five people there had been detained, mistreated verbally or nonverbally, or questioned by I.N.S. agents in the past two years.

14   Manifest Destiny may lack its old grandeur of theft and blood—"lock the door" is what it means now, with racism a trump card to be played again and again, shamelessly, by both major political parties. "Immigration," like "street crime" and "welfare fraud," is a political euphemism that refers to people of color. Politicians and media people talk about "illegal aliens" to dehumanize and demonize undocumented immigrants, who are for the most part people of color. Even in the days of Spanish and Mexican rule, no attempts were made to interfere with the flow of people and goods from south to north and north

to south. It is the U.S. government that has continually attempted to sever contact between the tribal people north of the border and those to the south.[1]

15   Now that the "Iron Curtain" is gone, it is ironic that the U.S. government and its Border Patrol are constructing a steel wall ten feet high to span sections of the border with Mexico. While politicians and multinational corporations extol the virtues of NAFTA and "free trade" (in goods, not flesh), the ominous curtain is already up in a six-mile section at the border crossing at Mexicali; two miles are being erected but are not yet finished at Naco; and at Nogales, sixty miles south of Tucson, the steel wall has been all rubber-stamped and awaits construction likely to begin in March. Like the pathetic multimillion-dollar "antidrug" border surveillance balloons that were continually deflated by high winds and made only a couple of meager interceptions before they blew away, the fence along the border is a theatrical prop, a bit of pork for contractors. Border entrepreneurs have already used blowtorches to cut passageways through the fence to collect "tolls," and are doing a brisk business. Back in Washington, the I.N.S. announces a $300 million computer contract to modernize its record-keeping and Congress passes a crime bill that shunts $255 million to the I.N.S. for 1995, $181 million earmarked for border control, which is to include 700 new partners for the men who stopped Gus and me in our travels, and the history professor, and my friend's father, and as many as they could from South Tucson.

16   It is no use; borders haven't worked, and they won't work, not now, as the indigenous people of the Americas reassert their kinship and solidarity with one another. A mass migration is already under way; its roots are not simply economic. The Uto-Aztecan languages are spoken as far north as Taos Pueblo near the Colorado border, all the way south to Mexico City. Before the arrival of the Europeans, the indigenous communities throughout this region not only conducted commerce, the people shared cosmologies, and oral narratives about the Maize Mothers, the Twin Brothers and their Grandmother, Spider Woman, as well as Quetzalcoatl the benevolent snake. The great human migration within the Americas cannot be stopped; human beings are natural forces of the Earth, just as rivers and winds are natural forces.

17   Deep down the issue is simple: The so-called "Indian Wars" from the days of Sitting Bull and Red Cloud have never really ended in the Americas.

---

[1]The Treaty of Guadalupe Hidalgo, signed in 1848, recognizes the right of Tohano O'Odom (Papago) people to move freely across the U.S.-Mexico border without documents. A treaty with Canada guarantees similar rights to those of the Iroquois nation in traversing the U.S.-Canada border. [Author's note]

The Indian people of southern Mexico, of Guatemala and those left in El Salvador, too, are still fighting for their lives and for their land against the "cavalry" patrols sent out by the governments of those lands. The Americas are Indian country, and the "Indian problem" is not about to go away.

18   One evening at sundown, we were stopped in traffic at a railroad crossing in downtown Tucson while a freight train passed us, slowly gaining speed as it headed north to Phoenix. In the twilight I saw the most amazing sight: Dozens of human beings, mostly young men, were riding the train; everywhere, on flat cars, inside open boxcars, perched on top of boxcars, hanging off ladders on tank cars and between boxcars. I couldn't count fast enough, but I saw fifty or sixty people headed north. They were dark young men, Indian and mestizo; they were smiling and a few of them waved at us in our cars. I was reminded of the ancient story of Aztlán, told by the Aztecs but known in other Uto-Aztecan communities as well. Aztlán is the beautiful land to the north, the origin place of the Aztec people. I don't remember how or why the people left Aztlán to journey farther south, but the old story says that one day, they will return.

 ## Steps in Writing a Narrative Argument

If your instructor asks for a topic proposal, use steps 1–4 to guide you in writing the proposal.

1. **Identify an experience that you had that makes an implicit argument.** Think about experiences that made you realize that something is wrong or that things need to be changed. The experience does not have to be one that leads to a moral lesson at the end, but it should be one that makes your readers think.

    Examples:

    - Being arrested and hauled to jail for carrying a glass soft drink bottle in a glass-free zone made you realize how inefficiently your police force is being used.

    - After going through a complicated system of getting referrals for a serious medical condition and then having the treatment your physician recommends denied by your HMO, you want to tell your story to show just how flawed the HMO system really is.

- When you moved from a well-financed suburban school to a much poorer rural school, you came to realize what huge differences exist among school systems in your state.

- If you have ever experienced being stereotyped in any way, narrate that experience and describe how it affected you.

2. **List all the details you can remember about the experience.** When did it happen? How old were you? Why were you there? Who else was there? Where did it happen? If the place is important, describe what it looked like. Then go through your list of details and put a check beside the ones that are important to your story.

3. **Examine the significance of the event for you.** Take a few minutes to write about how you felt about the experience at the time. How did it affect you then? What was your immediate reaction? Next, take a few minutes to write about how you feel about the experience now. How do you see it differently now?

4. **Analyze your potential readers.** How much would your readers know about the background of the experience you are describing? Are they familiar with the place where it happened? Would anything similar ever likely have happened to them? How likely are they to agree with your feelings about the experience?

5. **Write a draft.**

- You might need to give some background first, but if you have a compelling story, often it's best to launch right in.

- You might want to tell the story as it happened (chronological order) or you might want to begin with a striking incident and then go back to tell how it happened (flashback).

- You might want to reflect on your experience at the end, but you want your story to do most of the work. Your readers should share your feelings if you tell your story well.

6. **Revise, revise, revise. See Chapter 11 for detailed instructions.**

   Stage 1. Read your argument aloud.

   Do no more in this stage than put checks in the margins that you can return to later. Think in particular about these things:

   - **Your story.** Narratives must be well told to be effective. Note any places where a break or rough spot occurs.

■ **Your representation of yourself.** Forget for a moment that you wrote what you are reading. What impression do you have of you, the writer?

■ **Your consideration of your readers.** Do you give enough background if your readers are unfamiliar with what you describe? How are they likely to judge what you describe?

Stage 2. Analyze your argument in detail.

■ **Examine your organization.** Many narratives do not follow strict chronological order. Look at the sequence of events you set out and ask yourself whether that sequence works best.

■ **Check for details.** Key details often make a narrative come alive. Look for places where you might add details that contribute to your reader's understanding.

■ **Consider your title and introduction.** Be as specific as you can in your title and, if possible, suggest your stance. In the introduction, get off to a fast start and convince your reader to keep reading.

■ **Consider your conclusion.** Sometimes you may announce what you consider to be the significance of your narrative, but in many cases, you want a more subtle conclusion. Leave your reader thinking about what you have written.

Stage 3. Focus on your style and proofread carefully.

■ **Check the connections between sentences.** Notice how your sentences are connected. If you need to signal the relationship from one sentence to the next, use a transitional word or phrase.

■ **Check your sentences for emphasis.** Elements at the beginning and the end of sentences tend to stand out more than things in the middle.

■ **Eliminate wordiness.** See how many words you can take out without losing the meaning.

■ **Use active verbs.** Anytime you can use a verb besides a form of *be* (*is, are, was, were*), take advantage of the opportunity to make your style more lively.

■ **Proofread your spelling carefully.** Your spelling checker will miss many mistakes.

■ **Use your handbook to check items of mechanics and usage.** Look up any item you are unsure of.

CHAPTER 9

Rebuttal Arguments

When you hear the word **rebuttal,** you might think of a debate team or the part of a trial when the attorney for the defense answers the plaintiff's accusations. Although **rebuttal** has those definitions, arguments of rebuttal can be thought of in much larger terms. Indeed, much of what people know about the world today is the result of centuries of arguments of rebuttal.

In high school and college, you no doubt have taken many courses that required the memorization of knowledge and evidence, which you demonstrated by repeating these facts on tests. You probably didn't think much about how the knowledge came about. Once in a while, though, something happens that makes people think consciously about a piece of knowledge that they have learned. For example, in elementary school, you learned that the earth rotates on its axis once a day. Maybe you didn't think about it much at the time, but once, years later, you were out on a clear night and noticed the Big Dipper in one part of the sky, and then you looked for it later and found it in another part of the sky. Perhaps you became interested enough that you watched the stars for a few hours. If you've ever spent a clear night out stargazing, you

> **Effective rebuttal arguments depend on critical thinking.**

have observed that the North Star, called Polaris, stays in the same place. The stars near Polaris appear to move in a circle around Polaris, and the stars farther away move from east to west until they disappear below the horizon.

If you are lucky enough to live in a place where the night sky is often clear, you can see the same pattern repeated night after night. And if you stop to think about why you see the stars circling around Polaris, you remember what you were taught long ago—that you live on a rotating ball, so the stars appear to move across the sky, but in fact, stars are so distant from the earth that their actual movement is not visible to humans over a short term.

An alternative explanation for these facts not only is possible but is the one that people believed from ancient times until about five hundred years ago. People assumed that their position on the earth was fixed and that the entire sky rotated on an axis connecting Polaris and the earth. The flaw in this theory for people in ancient times is the movement of the planets. If you watch the path of Mars over several nights, you will observe that it also moves across the sky from east to west, but it makes an anomalous backward movement during its journey and then goes forward again. The other planets also seem to wander back and forth as they cross the night sky. The ancient Greeks developed an explanation of the strange wanderings of the planets by theorizing that the planets move in small circles imposed on larger orbits. By graphing little circles on top of circles, the course of planets could be plotted and predicted. This theory culminated in the work of Ptolemy, who lived in Alexandria in the second century A.D. Ptolemy proposed displaced centers for the small circles called *epicycles*, which gave a better fit for predicting the path of planets.

Because Ptolemy's model of the universe was numerically accurate in its predictions, educated people for centuries assumed its validity, even though there was evidence to the contrary. For example, Aristarchus of Samos, who lived in the fourth century B.C.E., used the size of the earth's shadow cast on the moon during a lunar eclipse to compute the sizes of the moon and sun and their distances from the earth. Even though his calculations were inaccurate, Aristarchus recognized that the sun is much bigger than the earth, and he advanced the heliocentric hypothesis: that the earth orbits the sun.

Many centuries passed, however, before educated people believed that the sun, not the earth, was the center of the solar system. In the early sixteenth century, the Polish astronomer Nicolaus Copernicus recognized that Ptolemy's model could be greatly simplified if the sun was at the center of the solar system. He kept his theory a secret for much of his life and saw the published account of his work only a few hours before his death in 1543. Even though Copernicus made a major breakthrough, he was not able to take full advantage of the heliocentric hypothesis because he followed the tradition that orbits are perfect circles; thus, he still needed circles on top of circles to explain the motion of the planets but far fewer than did Ptolemy.

The definitive rebuttal of Ptolemy came a century later with the work of the German astronomer Johannes Kepler. Kepler performed many tedious calculations, which were complicated by the fact that he had to first assume an orbit for the earth before he could compute orbits for the planets. Finally he made a stunning discovery: All the orbits of the planets could be described as an ellipse with the sun at the center. The dominance of the Ptolemaic model of the universe was finally over.

Critical Thinking

The relationship of facts and theories lies at the heart of the scientific method. Both Ptolemy's theory and Kepler's theory explain why the stars appear to move around Polaris at night. Kepler made a convincing argument by rebuttal to the Ptolemaic model because he could give a much simpler analysis. The history of astronomy is a history of arguments of rebuttal. Modern astronomy was made possible because Copernicus challenged the established relationship of theory and evidence in astronomy. This awareness of the relationship of factual and theoretical claims in science is one definition of **critical thinking** in the sciences. What is true for the history of astronomy is true for the sciences; critical thinking in the sciences relies on arguments of rebuttal.

Similar kinds of arguments of rebuttal are presented today in the debate over global warming. One of the main sources of data for arguments of rebuttal against global warming is the twenty-year record of temperature readings from NASA weather satellites orbiting the earth at the North and South poles. These satellites use microwave sensors to measure temperature variation in the atmosphere from the surface to about six miles above the earth. Computer models predict a gradual warming in the earth's lower atmosphere along with the surface because of the buildup of carbon dioxide and other greenhouse gases, the gases produced from burning fossil fuels. But while temperatures measured on the earth's surface have gradually increased, the corresponding rises in the atmosphere as recorded by satellites didn't appear to happen. In August 1998, however, two scientists discovered a flaw in the satellites that was making them lose altitude and therefore misreport temperature data. When adjusted, the satellite data confirm what thermometers on the ground tell us: The earth is getting warmer.

In some cases, particular disciplines have specialized training to assess the relationship of theory and evidence. But more often, people must engage in **general critical thinking** to assess the validity of claims based on evidence. Often, one has to weigh competing claims of people who have excellent qualifications. One group of nutritional experts says that people should take calcium supplements to strengthen their bones. Another group warns that people are in danger of suffering from kidney stones if they take too much calcium. Critical thinking is involved in all the kinds of arguments that are discussed in this book, but it is especially important in arguments of rebuttal.

Building a Rebuttal Argument

If you think back to the basic model of how arguments work, you can see that there are two primary strategies for rebuttal arguments:

CLAIM ◀━━ LINK (because) ◀━━ REASON ◀━━ EVIDENCE

CHALLENGES (So What?)

First, you can challenge the assumptions on which the claim is based. Copernicus did not question Ptolemy's data concerning how the stars and planets appear in the sky to an observer on the earth. Instead, he questioned Ptolemy's central assumption that the earth is the center of the solar system. Second, you can question the evidence. Sometimes, the evidence presented is simply wrong, as was the case for the satellites that lost altitude and reported faulty temperature data. Sometimes, the evidence is incomplete or unrepresentative, and sometimes, counterevidence can be found.

The great majority of issues that involve people cannot be decided with the certainty of the statement that the earth indeed orbits the sun. Even when the facts are generally agreed upon, there is often disagreement over the causes. Violent crime rates decreased from 1980 to 1992, and some politicians credited tougher sentencing that put more people in prison. But others pointed out that the drop could be attributed to the fact that older people, who commit fewer violent crimes, became a much larger segment of the overall population. The crime rates for the youngest age groups actually rose during this time. Those who disputed that putting more people in prison reduced violent crime argued that the drop was a reflection of the aging population of the United States.

Arguments over controversial issues lasting for many years often become primarily arguments of rebuttal. One such issue that has been debated throughout the twentieth century is drug policy in the United States. Today, almost everyone who writes about illegal drugs in the United States says that the current policy is bad. Even though U.S. jails and prisons are bursting with people who have been convicted and sentenced for drug offenses, millions of people still use illegal drugs. The social, political, and economic costs of illegal drugs are staggering, and the debate continues over what to do about these substances. On one side are those who want more police, more drug users in jail, and military forces sent to other countries to stop the drug traffic. On the other are those who compare current efforts to stop the flow of drugs to those of failed efforts under Prohibition (1919–1933) to halt the sale of alcohol. They want most illegal drugs to be legalized or decriminalized.

On September 7, 1989, Nobel prize–winning economist Milton Friedman published in the *Wall Street Journal* an open letter to William Bennett, then the drug czar (director of the Office of National Drug Policy) under President Bush. Friedman wrote:

Dear Bill:

In Oliver Cromwell's eloquent words, "I beseech you, in the bowels of Christ, think it possible you may be mistaken" about the course you and President Bush urge us to adopt to fight drugs. The path you propose of more police, more jails, use of the military in foreign countries, harsh penalties for drug users, and a whole panoply of repressive measures can only make a bad situation worse. The drug war cannot be won by those tactics without undermining the human liberty and individual freedom that you and I cherish.

You are not mistaken in believing that drugs are a scourge that is devastating our society. You are not mistaken in believing that drugs are tearing asunder our social fabric, ruining the lives of many young people, and imposing heavy costs on some of the most disadvantaged among us. You are not mistaken in believing that the majority of the public share your concerns. In short, you are not mistaken in the end you seek to achieve.

Your mistake is failing to recognize that the very measures you favor are a major source of the evils you deplore. Of course the problem is demand, but it is not only demand, it is demand that must operate through repressed and illegal channels. Illegality creates obscene profits that finance the murderous tactics of the drug lords; illegality leads to the corruption of law enforcement officials; illegality monopolizes the efforts of honest law forces so they are starved for resources to fight the simpler crimes of robbery, theft and assault.

Drugs are a tragedy for addicts. But criminalizing their use converts that tragedy into a disaster for society, for users and non-users alike. Our experience with the prohibition of drugs is a replay of our experience with the prohibition of alcoholic beverages. . . .

Had drugs been decriminalized 17 years ago [when Friedman first made an appeal that drugs be decriminalized], "crack" would never have been invented (it was invented because the high cost of illegal drugs made it profitable to provide a cheaper version) and there would today be far fewer addicts. The lives of thousands, perhaps hundreds of thousands of innocent victims would have been saved, and not only in the U.S. The ghettos of our major cities would not be drug-and-crime-infested no-man's lands. Fewer people would be in jails, and fewer jails would have been built.

Colombia, Bolivia, and Peru would not be suffering from narco-terror, and we would not be distorting our foreign policy because of narco-terror. Hell would not, in the words with which Billy Sunday welcomed Prohibition, "be forever for rent," but it would be a lot emptier.

In the first two paragraphs, Friedman carefully identifies the common ground he shares with Bennett. Both are political conservatives, as Friedman reminds Bennett when he mentions the "human liberty and individual free-dom that you and I cherish." Friedman also agrees with Bennett about the severity of the drug problem, noting that it is "tearing asunder our social fab-ric, ruining the lives of many young people, and imposing heavy costs on some of the most disadvantaged among us."

Where Friedman differs from Bennett is in Bennett's central assump-tion: If drugs are now illegal and still being used, then the solution is to make them even more illegal, increasing penalties and extending law enforcement beyond U.S. borders. Friedman calls attention to the centrality of this as-sumption when he quotes Oliver Cromwell's famous words: "I beseech you, in the bowels of Christ, think it possible you may be mistaken." If, in fact, this central assumption is flawed, then the reason to spend millions of dol-lars, to violate civil liberties, and to antagonize other nations is suddenly taken away.

William Bennett responded to Friedman quickly. On September 19, 1989, the *Wall Street Journal* published an open letter of reply from Bennett to Friedman. Here is part of Bennett's response, which has a much more strident tone than Friedman's letter:

Dear Milton:

There was little, if anything, new in your open letter to me calling for the legalization of drugs. As your 1972 article made clear, the legalization argument is an old and familiar one, which has recently been revived by a small number of journalists and academics who insist that the only solution to the drug problem is no solution at all. What surprises me is that you would continue to advocate so unrealistic a proposal without pausing to consider seriously its consequences.

If the argument for drug legalization has one virtue it is its sheer simplicity. Eliminate laws against drugs, and street crime will disappear.

Take the profit out of the black market through decriminalization and regulation, and poor neighborhoods will no longer be victimized by drug dealers. Cut back on drug enforcement, and use the money to wage a public health campaign against drugs, as we do with tobacco and alcohol.

The basic premise of all these propositions is that using our nation's laws to fight drugs is too costly. To be sure, our attempts to reduce drug use do carry with them enormous costs. But the question that must be asked—and which is totally ignored by the legalization advocates—is, what are the costs of *not* enforcing laws against drugs?

In my judgment, and in the judgment of virtually every serious scholar in this field, the potential costs of legalizing drugs would be so large as to make it a public policy disaster.

Of course, no one, including you, can say with certainty what would happen in the U.S. if drugs were suddenly to become a readily purchased product. We do know, however, that wherever drugs have become cheaper and more easily obtained, drug use—and addiction—has skyrocketed. In opium and cocaine producing countries, addiction is rampant among the peasants involved in drug production.

Professor James Q. Wilson tells us that during the years in which heroin could be legally prescribed by doctors in Britain, the number of addicts increased forty-fold. And after the repeal of Prohibition—an analogy favored but misunderstood by legalization advocates—consumption of alcohol soared by 350%.

Could we afford such dramatic increases in drug use? I doubt it. Already the toll of drug use on American society—measured in lost productivity, in rising health insurance costs, in hospitals flooded with drug overdose emergencies, in drug caused accidents, and in premature death—is surely more than we would like to bear.

You seem to believe that by spending just a little more money on treatment and rehabilitation, the costs of increased addiction can be avoided. That hope betrays a basic misunderstanding of the problems facing drug treatment. Most addicts don't suddenly decide to get help. They remain addicts either because treatment isn't available or because they don't seek it out. . . .

As for the connection between drugs and crime, your unswerving commitment to a legalization solution prevents you from appreciating the complexity of the drug market. Contrary to your claim, most addicts do not turn to crime to support their habit. Research shows that many of them were involved in criminal activity before they turned to drugs. Many former addicts who have received treatment continue to commit crimes during their recovery. And even if drugs were legal, what evidence do you have that the habitual drug user wouldn't continue to rob and steal to get money for clothes, food or shelter? Drug addicts always want more drugs than they can afford, and no legalization scheme has yet come up with a way of satisfying that appetite.

Bennett goes on to maintain that "A true friend of freedom understands that government has a responsibility to craft and uphold laws that help educate citizens about right and wrong. That, at any rate, was the Founders' view of our system of government." He ends by describing Friedman's proposal as "irresponsible and reckless public policy."

Friedman was not content to let Bennett have the last word, so he in turn wrote a reply that appeared on September 29, 1989, in the *Wall Street Journal*. At this point, Friedman drops the open letter strategy and writes instead a more conventional response, referring to Bennett as *he* instead of *you*:

> William Bennett is entirely right (editorial page, Sept. 19) that "there was little, if anything, new in" my open letter to him—just as there is little, if anything, new in his proposed program to rid this nation of the scourge of drugs. That is why I am so disturbed by that program. It flies in the face of decades of experience. More police, more jails, more-stringent penalties, increased efforts at interception, increased publicity about the evils of drugs—all this has been accompanied by more, not fewer, drug addicts; more, not fewer, crimes and murders; more, not less, corruption; more, not fewer, innocent victims.
>
> Like Mr. Bennett, his predecessors were "committed to fighting the problem on several fronts through imaginative policies and hard work over a long period of time." What evidence convinces him that the same policies on a larger scale will end the drug scourge? He offers none in his response to me, only assertion and the conjecture that legalizing drugs would produce "a public policy disaster"—as if that is not exactly what we already have.

Friedman then claims that "legalizing drugs is not equivalent to surrender" but rather the precondition for an effective fight against drug use. He allows that the number of addicts might increase, but he argues that it is certain that the number of innocent victims would drop drastically. He adds that another category of victims are foreign nations when we base our foreign policy on drug control.

Friedman's sharpest criticism of Bennett comes over Bennett's claim to represent the tradition of the Founders of the United States. Friedman completely rejects Bennett's assertion that the Founders wanted government to educate citizens about what is right and what is wrong. Friedman says "that is a totalitarian view utterly unacceptable to the Founders. I do not believe, and neither did they, that it is the responsibility of government to tell free citizens what is right and wrong."

LANCE ARMSTRONG

A Defense of the Open Road

Lance Armstrong (1971–   ) grew up in Plano, Texas, as the child of a single mother. He won his first triathlon at age 13 and became a professional triathlete at 16. By the time he finished high school, swimming and running gave way to his passion for cycling. By age 25 he had become one of the top professional bicycle racers in the world. But in 1996, he found himself in a battle for his life with advanced testicular cancer, and his doctors gave him less than a 50 percent chance of survival. Armstrong's chemotherapy treatments were successful, and within a year he was training again. Few expected him to attain the level he achieved before his illness, but Armstrong returned a stronger and more determined rider. He won the most prestigious race in cycling—the three-week-long Tour de France—in 1999, in 2000, in 2001, and in 2002.

"A Defense of the Open Road," published in the Austin American Statesman *in February 2001, was written in response to bills introduced into the Texas legislature banning bicycle teams from training in the state. Imagine being in Lance Armstrong's shoes, training hard to defend his Tour de France title, only to discover that instead of being supported, a few members of the Texas legislature were attempting to stop him from training. It is a good example of why people sometimes have to write rebuttal arguments to expose incredible stupidity. The public outrage in response to Armstrong's rebuttal led to an early death of the bike-banning bills.*

1   I learned to love Texas as a teenager cycling on a long, flat road past the plains of Plano to the ranch land and cotton fields, past the wildflowers and mesquite.

2   Sometimes I'd ride alone and sometimes with friends, racing or pulling each other as a team—working together against the dry, dusty wind. Drafting behind a friend, and then pulling ahead to pull your friends, is part of the camaraderie and teamwork of cycling.

3   That's why I'm so disappointed that two Hill Country legislators want to keep cyclists from riding the best roads in Texas. One legislator wants to ban riding with more than one friend on many rural roads, and another wants to ban all riding on certain rural roads.

4   Going further, Senate Bill 238, in a face-slap of an insult, would make all cyclists—children, adults, amateurs, and pros—ride single file on every road, with a "Slow Moving Vehicle" triangle hanging off our rear ends. This is the anti-sport, nanny-like equivalent of requiring golfers to use a putter off the tee to prevent a hook into the next fairway.

5   Although banning groups might be slightly more convenient for cars, it's vastly more dangerous for cyclists. Riding as a peloton, or group, is safer (not to mention more practical and efficient). Would you prefer your son or daughter to ride with a group or have to ride almost alone?

6   For example, when the U.S. Postal team holds training camp in Austin, we ride double pace lines through the Hill Country. The single-file rule and no-peloton rule would outlaw such team training rides. Plus, a single-file rule would make it illegal for riders to even pass each other.

7   The rules also would outlaw families riding together, Saturday-morning rides with friends, organized rides and races, charity rides and fund raisers and bicycle tours of Texas roads. From the forests of East Texas to the rugged mountains of West Texas, there is nothing like seeing Texas from a bike. These rules would make it an impossibility.

8   The current law—stay to the right, ride no more than two abreast and don't impede the reasonable flow of traffic—is based on common sense and thus easy to follow. The examples cited as reasons for the proposed laws seem to be based on a few cyclists disobeying the current law.

9   But a few bad acts shouldn't be the basis for passing a bad bill. Imposing new limits—potholed with exceptions for certain events, situations, speeds or roads—would be a nightmare to follow and to enforce. The more complex a rule, and the more distant it is from common sense, the less likely it can be followed.

10   Shoulders appear and disappear, and maps don't designate "roads with shoulders" and "roads without." Maps don't designate "high-traffic roads" and "low-traffic roads." Time of day, growth and other factors make this a moving target anyway. Often the road less traveled leads to the road more trafficked, which leads to another road less traveled. Restricting access to some roads is just not practical.

11   I am proud to be a Texan, and I want Texas to continue to attract riders with the beauty of our long, open roads. The rules of the road should be rules of reason and rules of respect, unencumbered by unworkable, excessive government regulation.

Steps in Writing a Rebuttal Argument

If your instructor asks for a topic proposal, use steps 1–5 to guide you in writing the proposal.

1. **Identify an argument that you want to argue against.** Use this formula: It is wrong (or misguided or irresponsible) to claim X. You might consider using the open letter genre, addressing your rebuttal to a specific person but with the goal of having others read it too.

    Examples:
    - Requiring fine arts students to take math courses (or engineering students to take foreign language courses, or the like) is a bad idea.
    - Using tax dollars to pay for new stadiums for professional sports teams (or providing grants to artists and theater companies) is a misuse of public funds.
    - Requiring riders of bicycles and motorcycles to wear helmets is an unnecessary restriction of individual freedom.

2. **Identify the main claim(s) of the argument that you reject.** What exactly are you arguing against? If you are taking on affirmative action admissions policies for colleges and universities, then what do those policies involve and whom do they affect? Are there secondary claims attached to the main claim? A fair summary of your opponent's position should be in your finished argument.

3. **Examine the facts on which the claim is based.** Are the facts accurate? Are the facts a truly representative sample? Are the facts

current? Is there another body of facts that you can present as coun-terevidence? If the author uses statistics, is evidence for the validity of those statistics presented? Can the statistics be interpreted differently? If the author quotes from sources, how reliable are those sources? Are the sources treated fairly, or are quotations taken out of context? If the author cites outside authority, how much trust can you place in that authority?

4. **Examine the assumptions on which the claim is based.** What is the primary assumption of the claim you are rejecting? What other assump-tions support that claim? How are those assumptions flawed? If you are arguing against a specific piece of writing, then how does the author fall short? Does the author resort to name calling? Use faulty reasoning? Ignore key facts?

5. **Analyze your potential readers.** To what extent do your potential readers support the claim that you are rejecting? If they strongly support that claim, then how might you appeal to them to change their minds? What common assumptions and beliefs do you share with them?

6. **Write a draft.**

   Identify the issue and the argument you are rejecting:
   - If the issue is not familiar to most of your readers, you might need to provide some background. Even if it is familiar, it might be helpful to give a quick summary of the competing positions. Remember that of-fering a fair and accurate summary is a good way to build credibility with your audience.

   Take on the argument that you are rejecting:
   - You might want to question the evidence that is used to support the argument. You can challenge the facts, present counterevidence and countertestimony, cast doubt on the representativeness of the sam-ple, cast doubt on the currency and relevance of the examples, chal-lenge the credibility of any authorities cited, question the way in which statistical evidence is presented and interpreted, and argue that quotations are taken out of context.
   - In most cases, you will want to question the assumptions and poten-tial outcomes.

   Conclude with emphasis:
   - You should have a strong argument in your conclusion that under-scores your objections. You might wish to close with a counterargu-ment or counterproposal.

7. **Revise, revise, revise. See Chapter 11 for detailed instructions.**

   Stage 1. Read your argument aloud.

   Do no more in this stage than put checks in the margins that you can return to later. Think in particular about these things:

   - **Your claim.** When you finish reading, summarize in one sentence what you are arguing and why the primary assumption in the claim you are rejecting is faulty.

   - **Your good reasons.** What are the good reasons for your claim? Would a reader have any trouble identifying them?

   - **Your representation of yourself.** Forget for a moment that you wrote what you are reading. What impression do you have of you, the writer?

   - **Your consideration of your readers.** Do you give enough background if your readers are unfamiliar with the issue? Do you acknowledge opposing views that they might have? Do you appeal to common values that you share with them?

   Stage 2. Analyze your argument in detail.

   - **Examine your organization.** What are the topics of each of the paragraphs? Is the relationship of one paragraph to another clearly signaled? If any paragraphs appear out of order, think of another way to arrange them.

   - **Examine your evidence.** If you noted places where you could use more evidence when you read through the first time, now is the time to determine what kinds of additional evidence you need.

   - **Consider your title and introduction.** Be as specific as you can in your title and, if possible, suggest your stance. Does your introduction get off to a fast start and convince your reader to keep reading?

   - **Consider your conclusion.** Think about whether there is a summarizing point you can make, an implication you can draw, or another example you can include that sums up your position.

   - **Analyze the visual aspects of your text.** Do the font and layout you selected look attractive? Would headings and subheadings help to identify key sections of your argument? Would the addition of graphics augment key points?

   Stage 3. Focus on your style and proofread carefully.

   - **Check the connections between sentences.** Notice how your sentences are connected. If you need to signal the relationship from one sentence to the next, use a transitional word or phrase.

- **Check your sentences for emphasis.** Elements at the beginning and the end of sentences tend to stand out more than things in the middle.

- **Eliminate wordiness.** See how many words you can take out without losing the meaning.

- **Use active verbs.** Anytime you can use a verb besides a form of *be* (*is*, *are*, *was*, *were*), take advantage of the opportunity to make your style more lively.

- **Proofread your spelling carefully.** Your spelling checker will miss many mistakes.

- **Use your handbook to check items of mechanics and usage.** Look up any item you are unsure of.

CHAPTER 10

Proposal Arguments

You no doubt have at least one friend who loves to argue. If you say you love a movie, your friend will trash it. If you mention that knowingly breaking the rules in a game is wrong, your friend will reply that it's fine as long as the referee doesn't catch you. These kinds of face-to-face arguments can become the basis for extended written arguments. But when

> **Proposal arguments often include definition, causal, evaluation, narrative, and rebuttal arguments.**

someone finally gets motivated enough to write an extended argument, most often it is because she or he wants something to be changed or wants to stop something from being changed. These kinds of arguments are called **proposal arguments,** and they take the classic form: *We should (or should not) do X.*

At this moment, you might not think that you have anything you feel strongly enough about to write a proposal argument. But if you make a list of things that make you mad or at least a little annoyed, then you have a start toward writing a proposal argument. Some things on your list are not going to produce proposal arguments that many people would want to read. If your roommate or partner is a slob, you might be able to write a proposal for that person to start cleaning up more, but it is hard to imagine that anyone else would be interested. Similarly, it might be annoying to you that it stays too hot for too long in the summer where you live or too cold for too long in the winter, but unless you have a direct line to God, it is hard to imagine a serious proposal to change the climate where you live. (Cutting down on air pollution, of course, is something that people can change.) Short of those extremes, however, are a lot of things that you might think, "Why hasn't someone done something about this?" If you believe that others have something to gain if this problem is solved or at least made a little better, then you might be able to develop a good proposal argument.

For instance, suppose you are living off campus, and you buy a student parking sticker when you register for courses so that you can park in the student lot. However, you quickly find out that there are too many cars and trucks for the number of available spaces, and unless you get to campus by 8:00 A.M., you aren't going to find a place to park in your assigned lot. The situation makes you angry because you believe that if you pay for a sticker, you should have a reasonable chance of finding a space to park. You see that there are unfilled lots that are reserved for faculty and staff next to the student parking lot, and you wonder why more spaces aren't allotted to students. You decide to write to the president of your college. You want her to direct parking and traffic services to give more spaces to students or else build a parking garage that will accommodate more vehicles.

But when you start talking to other students on campus, you begin to realize that the problem may be more complex than your first view of it. Your college has taken the position that the fewer students who drive to campus, the less traffic there will be on and around your campus. The administration wants more students to ride shuttle buses, form car pools, or bicycle to campus instead of driving alone. You also find out that faculty and staff members pay ten times as much as students for their parking permits, so they pay a very high premium for a guaranteed space—much too high for most students. If the president of your college is your primary audience, you first have to argue that a problem really exists. You have to convince the president that many students have no choice but to drive if they are to attend classes. You, for example, are willing to ride the shuttle buses, but they don't run often enough for you to make your classes, get back to your car that you left at home, and then drive to your job.

Next, you have to argue that your solution will solve the problem. An eight-story parking garage might be adequate to park all the cars of students who want to drive, but parking garages are very expensive to build. Even if a parking garage is the best solution, the question remains: Who is going to pay for it? Many problems in life could be solved if you had access to unlimited resources, but very few people have such resources at their command. It's not enough to have a solution that can resolve the problem. You have to be able to argue for the feasibility of your solution. If you want to argue that a parking garage is the solution to the parking problem on your campus, then you must also propose how the garage will be financed.

Components of Proposals

Proposal arguments are often complex and involve the kinds of arguments that are discussed in Chapters 5 through 9. Successful proposals have four major components:

1. ***Identifying the problem.*** Sometimes, problems are evident to your in-tended readers. If your city is constantly tearing up the streets and then leaving them for months without doing anything to repair them, then you shouldn't have much trouble convincing the citizens of your city that streets should be repaired more quickly. But if you raise a problem that will be unfamiliar to most of your readers, you will first have to argue that the problem exists. As we saw in Chapter 1, Rachel Carson in *Silent Spring* had to use several kinds of arguments to make people aware of the dangers of pesticides, including narrative arguments, definition arguments, evaluation arguments, and arguments of comparison. Often, you will have to do simi-lar work to establish exactly what problem you are attempting to solve. You will have to define the scope of the problem. Some of the bad roads in your city might be the responsibility of the state, not city government.

2. ***Stating your proposed solution.*** You need to have a clear, definite state-ment of exactly what you are proposing. You might want to place this statement near the beginning of your argument, or later, after you have considered and rejected other possible solutions.

3. ***Convincing your readers with good reasons that your proposed solution is fair and will work.*** When your readers agree that a problem exists and a solution should be found, your next task is to convince them that your solution is the best one to resolve the problem. If you're writing about the problem your city has in getting streets repaired promptly, then you need to analyze carefully the process that is involved in repairing streets. Sometimes there are mandatory delays so that competing bids can be so-licited and unexpected delays when tax revenue falls short of expectations. You should be able to put your finger on the problem in a detailed causal

analysis. You should be able to make an evaluation argument that your solution is fair to all concerned. You should also be prepared to make arguments of rebuttal against other possible solutions.

4. *Demonstrating that your solution is feasible.* Your solution not only has to work; it must be feasible to implement. Malaysia effectively ended its drug problem by imposing mandatory death sentences for anyone caught selling even small amounts of drugs. Foreign nationals, teenagers, and grandmothers have all been hanged under this law. Malaysia came up with a good solution for its purposes, but this solution probably would not work in most countries because the punishment seems too extreme. If you want a parking garage built on your campus and you learn that no other funds can be used to construct it, then you have to be able to argue that the potential users of the garage will be willing to pay greatly increased fees for the convenience of parking on campus.

Building a Proposal Argument

Proposal arguments don't just fall out of the sky. For any problem of major significance—gun control, poverty, teenage pregnancy, abortion, capital punishment, drug legalization—you will find long histories of debate. An issue with a much shorter history can also quickly pile up mountains of arguments if it gains wide public attention. In 1972, for example, President Richard Nixon signed into law the Education Amendments Act, including Title IX, which prohibits sex discrimination at colleges that receive federal aid. Few people at the time might have guessed that Title IX would have such far-reaching consequences. When Title IX was first passed, 31,000 women participated in intercollegiate athletics. In the academic year 2000–2001, more than 163,000 women athletes participated in varsity college sports. Even more striking is the increase in girls' participation in high school sports. The number of boy athletes remains close to same as the figure for 1971 (approximately 3.6 million), while the number of girl athletes grew from 294,000 in 1971 to 2.7 million in 2001.

Proponents of Title IX are justifiably proud of the increased level of participation of women in varsity athletics. But for all the good that Title IX has done to increase athletic opportunities for women, critics blame Title IX for decreasing athletic opportunities for college men. According to the U.S. General Accounting Office (GAO), more than three hundred men's teams have been eliminated in college athletics since 1993. In 2000, the University of Miami dropped its men's swimming team, which had produced many

Girls' sports leagues were a rarity in many communities just thirty years ago.

Olympians, including Greg Louganis, who won gold medals in both platform and springboard diving in two consecutive Olympics. In 2001 the University of Nebraska also discontinued its men's swimming team, which had been in place since 1922, and the University of Kansas dropped men's swimming and tennis. Wrestling teams have been especially hard hit, dropping from 363 in 1981 to 192 in 1999. The effects were noticeable at the 2000 Olympics in Australia, where U.S. freestyle wrestlers failed to win any gold medals for the first time since 1968.

College and university administrators claim that they have no choice but to drop men's teams if more women's teams are added. Their belief comes not from the original Title IX legislation, which does not mention athletics, but from a 1979 clarification by the Office of Civil Rights (OCR), the agency that enforces Title IX. OCR set out three options for schools to comply with Title IX:

1. Bring the proportion of women in varsity athletics roughly equal to the percentage of women students.

2. Prove a "history and continuing practice" of creating new opportunities for women.

3. Prove that the school has done everything to "effectively accommodate" the athletic interests of women students.

University administrators have argued that the first option, known as *proportionality*, is the only one that can be argued successfully in a courtroom if the school is sued.

Proportionality is difficult to achieve at schools with football programs. Universities that play NCAA Division 1-A football offer eighty-five scholarships, the majority of athletic scholarships given to men. Since there is no equivalent sport for women, football throws the gender statistics way out of balance. Defenders of football ask that it be exempted from Title IX because it is the cash cow that pays most of the bills for both men's and women's sports. Only a handful of women's basketball programs make money. All other women's sports are money losers and, like men's "minor" sports, depend on men's football and basketball revenues and student fees to pay their bills. College officials maintain that if they cut the spending for football, football will bring in less revenue, and thus all sports will be harmed.

Those who criticize Title IX argue that it assumes that women's interest in athletics is identical to men's. They point out that male students participate at much higher rates in intramural sports, which have no limitations on who can play. In contrast, women participate at much higher rates in music, dance, theater, and other extracurricular activities, yet Title IX is not being applied to those activities.

Defenders of Title IX argue that women's interest in athletics cannot be determined until they have had equal opportunities to participate. They claim Title IX is being used as a scapegoat for college administrators who do not want to make tough decisions. They point out that in 2001, women made up 53 percent of all college students but only 42 percent of all college athletes. At major colleges and universities, men still received 73 percent of the funds devoted to athletics. Without Title IX, in their view, schools would have no incentive to increase opportunities for women.

The battle over Title IX is not likely to go away soon. In an increasing competition for the revenues produced by football bowl games, the NCAA basketball tournament, television revenue, and increased ticket prices, the schools that play big-time college football and basketball are now engaged in an "athletics arms race." Football coaches who win championships are paid over two million dollars a year, and some assistant coaches make more than their university's president. Men's athletics directors believe that they have to keep spending to stay competitive.

Defenders of Title IX reject this argument and maintain that a simple solution is available: If revenues do not increase, reduce the budgets of all sports by the same proportion rather than dropping some sports. They argue

that football budgets are out of control, with luxuries such as staying in a hotel the night before home games and lavish spending on travel to away games
now considered routine. One of the most powerful voices in this debate is
Donna Lopiano's. In the essay that follows, Lopiano uses the analogy of a
family to propose solutions for equality in college athletics. (For additional
arguments on the issue of Title IX and college sports, see pages xx–xx.)

DONNA LOPIANO

Don't Blame Title IX

*Donna Lopiano (1947–   ) is the former director of women's athletics at
the University of Texas at Austin and is the current executive director of
the Women's Sports Foundation, founded in 1974 by the tennis star Billie
Jean King. As an athlete, Lopiano participated in twenty-six national
championships in four sports and was an All-American in softball in four
different positions at Southern Connecticut State University. She has
also coached men's and women's volleyball, and women's basketball,
field hockey, and softball at the collegiate level. Lopiano is a member of
the National Sports Hall of Fame and earned a Ph.D. from the University
of Southern California.*

*Lopiano has been a tireless crusader for the rights of girls and
women to have equal opportunities in athletics. She is proud to point
out that in the early 1970s, one out of every twenty-seven high school
girls played varsity sports. Today, that figure is better than one in three.
But because one in two boys participates in sports, Lopiano believes one
in three isn't good enough. She frequently attacks the argument that
college football pays the bills for both women's and men's sports, using
the NCAA's own statistics to point out that fewer than half of the major
college football programs (Division 1-A) actually make a profit.*

*"Don't Blame Title IX" was published in 2001 on the Women's
Sports Foundation Web site (www.womenssportsfoundation.org).*

1   **I'M** often asked, "Is it fair to eliminate sports opportunities for men as a
method of complying with Title IX of the Education Amendments of 1972,
the federal law prohibiting sex discrimination in educational programs or
activities at schools and colleges that receive federal funds?" Schools often
cite insufficient finances to add more sports opportunities for women, cut a
men's non-revenue sport and use these funds to start a new women's team.

When alumni and students complain about the decision, the institution blames the law (Title IX requires no such reduction in opportunities for men) and female athletes.

2   The real problem can be simply described. Your first two children are boys. You give them everything. Their rooms are palaces of athletics privilege—full of every sport gift imaginable—gloves, balls, bats, hockey sticks, football helmets, etc. They go to two or three sport camps every summer. They play Little League baseball, soccer, and Pop Warner football. One becomes an outstanding football player and the other excels in tennis. Then, you have another child, a girl, and your income doesn't change. She comes to you one day and says, "Mom, Dad—I want to play sports." What are your options?

3   Option A: Kill your last born son (i.e., drop the men's tennis team) so you still have only two children to provide for.

4   Option B: Tell your daughter she can't have the same privileges as her brothers. If she wants a glove she has to go to work and save up to buy it. Tell her she can't go to a summer sports camp unless she earns her own money and pays for it herself. Suggest that she sell cookies or get together with her girlfriends to have a bake sale (this is the way it was before Title IX) to scrape up enough money for equipment to play.

5   Option C: You gather the family around the kitchen table and explain to your children that your daughter is just as important as your sons and you don't have the dollars to provide the same privileges for your daughter as you did for your sons but that you are going to try your best to give all of your children every opportunity to participate in sports. You tell your sons that it is important to share their equipment and all you have provided for them. You probably come up with a system where each child gets to choose one summer sports camp instead of each attending several. The family gives up spring vacation in Disney World and tightens its belt. Everyone sacrifices and each child makes do with a smaller piece of the pie because now there are three (the Title IX situation).

6   The solution is Option C. Institutions that are dropping men's teams are choosing Option A not because of Title IX, but because they are being terrible parents (educational leaders). The answer to Title IX is very simple: If revenues don't increase, then everyone must make do with a smaller piece of the budget pie. The NCAA and its athletic conferences are simply refusing to legislate lower costs and a lower standard of living for men's sports in order to free up money for new women's teams.

7   Men's revenue sports are issuing threats regarding their own demise if their budgets are reduced in any way. First, tightening a sport's budget will

not cause this sport business to fail. Commercial entities initiate such cost cuts every day to eliminate fat, increase profit margins, and satisfy stockholders.

8   Second, and more important, there can never be an economic justification for discrimination. No one should ever be permitted to say that I can't comply with the law because I can't afford it. It is the same as saying, "I should be allowed to practice racism (or sexism) if I can't afford to initiate a change in the way I live or do business."

9   Using an employment discrimination example, the analogy would be that reducing the salaries of all employees is the preferred method of generating funds in an effort to increase salaries for the group that has historically experienced discrimination. This never happens. Rather, the salaries of the disadvantaged gender or individuals are always raised to the level of the advantaged group. As in the area of salary discrimination, the goal should be to bring the treatment of the group experiencing discrimination up to the level of the group that has received fair treatment, not to bring male athletes in minor sports down to the level of female athletes who simply were not provided with opportunities to play.

10   Even worse, when an institution eliminates a men's team in the name of Title IX, such action usually results in the development of destructive acrimony, pitting the men's non-revenue sports against women's sports. Alumni of the dropped men's sport get upset. An unnecessary domino effect results in the development of attitudes antithetical to solving discrimination in the long run. Gains for the underrepresented group come grudgingly and at a high cost to the previously advantaged group.

11   The last alternative should be cutting opportunities for students to participate in an educational activity. Other solutions, in order of preference, that should be considered are

12   1.   **Raising new revenues.** Gender equity can be used as an opportunity to raise new funds in much the same way as the need for a new building is used to initiate a capital campaign. However, it is essential that there be a positive spin on alumni solicitations for this purpose like adding one or two dollars to the current price of all sport tickets "so our daughters will have an equal chance to play" and other similarly creative revenue solutions. "Providing an equal opportunity for women to participate in varsity athletics" is also an excellent theme for an annual giving campaign targeted to female alumnae and supporters.

13   The demographic shift in higher education toward increasing percentages of women in undergraduate and graduate schools must also be noted. These are future generations of alumnae. Any position which antagonizes a group of future donors to the institution is short-sighted.

14   Presidential or school principal leadership is essential. The institution has the choice of "taking the high ground" and calling upon alumni and supporters of men's sports to "dig deeper" so our daughters are given the same chances to play as our sons, or pitting the have-nots against the have-nots by cutting men's sports teams. At many institutions, the resentment against Title IX has prevented athletic directors from "seeing the forest for the trees." The result has been the adoption of less than exemplary solutions to a very difficult problem.

15   2. **Reducing excess expenditures on the most expensive men's sports and using the savings to expand opportunities and treatment for the underrepresented gender.** There are many expenditures in the budgets of well-funded sports which can be eliminated without having a negative impact on either competitiveness vis-a-vis other institutions or the quality of the athletics experience. Such reductions include: provision of hotel rooms the night before home contests, ordering new uniforms less frequently, reducing the distance traveled for non-conference competition by selecting others as competitive opponents in closer geographic proximity.

16   3. **Athletic conference cost-saving.** The conference can adopt across-the-board mandated cost reductions that will assist all schools in saving funds while ensuring that the competitive playing field remains level (i.e., travel squad limits, adding the same sports for the underrepresented gender at the same time in order to ensure competition within a reasonable geographic area, etc.).

17   4. **Internal across-the-board budget reductions.** All sports can be asked to cut their budgets by a fixed percentage, thereby allowing each sport to choose the way it might least be affected, to free up funds for expanded opportunities for women. This method is preferred in that it does not have a disproportionate impact on low-budget sports.

18   5. **Moving to a lower competitive division.** At the college level, Division I programs can move to Division IAA or Division II competition, thereby reducing scholarship and other expenses.

19   6. **Using tuition waiver savings to fund gender equity.** States can initiate legislation which provides for waiver of higher education tuition for athletic scholarships to members of the underrepresented gender, similar to the law adopted by the State of Washington. This legislation mandates the use of these scholarship savings to expand opportunities for the underrepresented gender. Such initiatives recognize that correcting gender inequities is an institutional obligation, not just an athletic department issue. There are other precedents for states to enact laws which confer

financial relief in an effort to remedy widespread discrimination. The states of Washington, Florida and Minnesota have all enacted state laws to provide funding to achieve gender equity in athletics.

20   Unfortunately, at most institutions, it is easier for a college president to cut wrestling or men's gymnastics than to deal with the politics of reducing the football or men's basketball budgets. Simply put, educational leaders need more guts to step up and do the right thing.

 # Steps in Writing a Proposal Argument

If your instructor asks for a topic proposal, use steps 1–6 to guide you in writing the proposal.

1. **Make a proposal claim advocating a specific change or course of action.** Use this formula: *We should (or should not) do* X. In an essay of five or fewer pages, it's difficult to propose solutions to big problems such as continuing poverty. Proposals that address local problems are not only more manageable; sometimes, they get actual results.

   Examples:
   - The process of registering for courses (getting appointments at the health center, getting email accounts) should be made more efficient.
   - Your community should create bicycle lanes to make bicycling safer and to reduce traffic (build a pedestrian overpass over a dangerous street; make it easier to recycle newspapers, bottles, and cans).

2. **Identify the problem.** What exactly is the problem? Who is most affected by the problem? What causes the problem? Has anyone tried to do anything about it? If so, why haven't they succeeded? What is likely to happen in the future if the problem isn't solved?

3. **Propose your solution.** State your solution as specifically as you can. What exactly do you want to achieve? How exactly will your solution work? Can it be accomplished quickly, or will it have to be phased in over a few years? Has anything like it been tried elsewhere? Who will be involved? Can you think of any reasons why your solution might not work? How will you address those arguments? Can you think of any ways of strengthening your proposed solution in light of those possible criticisms?

4. **Consider other solutions.** What other solutions have been or might be proposed for this problem, including doing nothing? What are the advantages and disadvantages of those solutions? Why is your solution better?

5. **Examine the feasibility of your solution.** How easy is your solution to implement? Will the people who will be most affected be willing to go along with it? (For example, lots of things can be accomplished if enough people volunteer, but groups often have difficulty getting enough volunteers to work without pay.) If it costs money, how do you propose paying for it? Who is most likely to reject your proposal because it is not practical enough? How can you convince your readers that your proposal can be achieved?

6. **Analyze your potential readers.** Who are you writing for? You might be writing a letter addressed to a specific person. You might be writing a guest editorial to appear in your campus newspaper or in your club's or organization's newsletter. You might be creating a Web site. How interested will your readers be in this problem? How much does this problem affect them? How would your solution benefit them directly and indirectly?

7. **Write a draft.**

   Define the problem:
   - Set out the issue or problem. You might begin by telling about your experience or the experience of someone you know. You might need to argue for the seriousness of the problem, and you might have to give some background on how it came about.

   Present your solution:
   - You might want to set out your solution first and explain how it will work, then consider other possible solutions and argue that yours is better; or you might want to set out other possible solutions first, argue that they don't solve the problem or are not feasible, and then present your solution.
   - Make clear the goals of your solution. Many solutions cannot solve problems completely. If you are proposing a solution for juvenile crime in your neighborhood, for example, you cannot expect to eliminate all juvenile crime.
   - Describe in detail the steps in implementing your solution and how they will solve the problem you have identified. You can impress your readers by the care with which you have thought through this problem.

■ Explain the positive consequences that will follow from your proposal. What good things will happen and what bad things will be avoided if your advice is taken?

Argue that your proposal is feasible:

■ Your proposal for solving the problem is a truly good idea only if it can be put into practice. If people have to change the ways they are doing things now, explain why they would want to change. If your proposal costs money, you need to identify exactly where the money would come from.

Conclude with a call for action:

■ Your conclusion should be a call for action. You should put your readers in a position such that if they agree with you, they will take action. You might restate and emphasize what exactly they need to do.

8. **Revise, revise, revise. See Chapter 11 for detailed instructions.**

Stage 1. Read your argument aloud.

Do no more in this stage than put checks in the margins that you can return to later. Think in particular about these things:

■ **Your good reasons.** What are the good reasons for your proposal? Would a reader have any trouble identifying them?

■ **Your representation of yourself.** Forget for a moment that you wrote what you are reading. What impression do you have of you, the writer?

■ **Your consideration of your readers.** Do you give enough background if your readers are unfamiliar with the issue? Do you acknowledge opposing views that they might have? Do you appeal to common values that you share with them?

Stage 2. Analyze your argument in detail.

■ **Review step 7.** Find where you define the problem and ask yourself whether you need to provide more evidence. Look at your solution, especially where you argue that good consequences can be achieved and negative consequences avoided and where you argue that the proposal is feasible.

■ **Examine your evidence.** If you noted places where you could use more evidence when you read through the first time, now is the time to determine what kinds of additional evidence you need.

■ **Consider your title and introduction.** Be as specific as you can in your title and, if possible, suggest your stance. In the introduction get off to a fast start and convince your reader to keep reading.

▧ **Consider your conclusion.** Think about whether there is a summarizing point you can make, an implication you can draw, or another example you can include that sums up your position.

▧ **Analyze the visual aspects of your text.** Do the font and layout you selected look attractive? Would headings and subheadings help to identify key sections of your argument? Would the addition of graphics augment key points?

Stage 3. Focus on your style and proofread carefully.

▧ **Check the connections between sentences.** Notice how your sentences are connected. If you need to signal the relationship from one sentence to the next, use a transitional word or phrase.

▧ **Check your sentences for emphasis.** Elements at the beginning and the end of sentences tend to stand out more than things in the middle.

▧ **Eliminate wordiness.** See how many words you can take out without losing the meaning.

▧ **Use active verbs.** Anytime you can use a verb besides a form of *be* (*is, are, was, were*), take advantage of the opportunity to make your style more lively.

▧ **Proofread your spelling carefully.** Your spelling checker will miss many mistakes.

▧ **Use your handbook to check items of mechanics and usage.** Look up any item you are unsure of.

CHAPTER 11

Revision: Putting It All Together

Skilled writers know that one secret to writing well is rethinking and rewriting. Even the best writers often have to reconsider their aims and methods in the course of writing and to revise several times to get the result they want. If you want to become a better writer, therefore, take three words of advice: revise, revise, revise.

The biggest trap you can fall into is seeking a fast resolution and skipping revision. The quality of an argument varies in direct proportion to the amount of time devoted to it. You cannot revise a paper effectively if you finish it at the last minute. You have to allow your ideas to develop, and you have to allow what you write to sit for a while before you go back through it. So try your best to write your arguments over a period of several days. Be patient. Test your ideas against your reading and the informal advice of trusted friends and advisors. And once you are satisfied with what you have written, allow at least a day to let what you write cool off. With a little time you gain enough distance to "resee" it, which, after all, is what revision means. To be able to revise effectively, you have to plan your time.

Most of all, keep your eyes focused on the big picture, especially early in the process of making your argument. Don't sweat the small stuff at the

Revise, revise, revise.

beginning. If you see a word that's wrong or if you are unsure about a punctuation mark, you may be tempted to drop everything and fix the errors first. Don't do that: If you start searching for the errors early in the process, then it's hard to get back to the larger concerns that ultimately make your argument successful or unsuccessful.

Over time you have to develop effective strategies for revising if you're going to be successful. These strategies include the following:

1. Keep your goals in mind—but stay flexible about them.
2. Read as you write.
3. Switch your thinking from you and your argument to your reader.
4. Focus on your argument.
5. Attend to your style and proofread carefully.

In addition, plan to get responses to what you write in time for you to revise your work based on those responses.

Keep Your Goals in Mind— But Stay Flexible

People who argue effectively know what they want to achieve. They understand their readers' needs, know what they want to accomplish, and keep their goals in mind as they write and revise. But they also know that writing about a subject likely will change how they think about it, often in productive ways. Thus they remain flexible enough to modify their goals as they write. You may begin writing an argument because you have strong feeling about an issue; in fact, a rush of strong feelings can often motivate you to compose a strong statement at one sitting. That's good. But at some point before you commit what you write to a final version, give yourself a chance to rethink your goals. It may be that you can make a better argument in the end if you leave yourself open to adjustments in what you are arguing and to whom you are arguing it.

Consider, for example, the case of a student at a northeastern university, Nate Bouton (not his real name), who arrived on his campus in the midst of a controversy in 2000 over the raising of the Confederate Battle Flag over the South Carolina state capitol building. You probably recall the controversy: In 1999 the NAACP, in the conviction that the Confederate flag was a symbol of racism, called on citizens to boycott South Carolina tourist venues until the flag no longer was displayed over the state capitol building. After contentious debate and considerable thought, legislators decided to remove the flag. On July 1, 2000, it was taken down and displayed instead in a nearby memorial to Confederate soldiers. But public opinion within and outside South Carolina remained divided: Some citizens continued to ask that the flag be restored to the capitol, while others demanded that it be removed from the Confederate memorial as well.

As a native of South Carolina, Nate felt that students at his university were coming to uninformed, premature conclusions, which stemmed from faulty assumptions about the flag issue in particular and South Carolinians in general. When the players on the baseball team at Nate's university decided not to play previously scheduled games in South Carolina, he was ready to join the argument. He decided to write about the flag issue, in his words, "in order to straighten people out. People in the northeast just didn't know the facts and that ticked me off. I wanted to write an argument supporting what was being done in South Carolina."

Nate's interest and enthusiasm for his topic generated a series of notes and several draft paragraphs, and he was able to explain his goals forcefully in class. Here is what he wrote when his teacher asked for an account of what he planned to do in his essay: "I would like to evaluate the decision to remove the Confederate Battle Flag from the statehouse dome in Columbia, South Carolina. I do not believe it was handled properly and I do not think the valiant soldiers that fought in the war between the states and defended their way of life should be dishonored by a bunch of politicians who use people's feelings to their disadvantage. Now that politicians have won a battle, many more are springing up all over the South wanting to destroy a way of life and turn it into a politically correct zombie. I want to show that the flag is about pride, not prejudice."

But as Nate wrote a first draft, his goals gradually changed. In the course of discussing his ideas with his classmates and with his friends, he discovered that they had a number of what he considered to be misperceptions. They did not know much about the South and its traditions, and their conclusions on the flag issue, he was convinced, followed from their lack of knowledge. Nate also learned that several of his friends and classmates had different notions of what the Confederate flag stood for. African Americans in his dorm explained that when they stopped at a restaurant and saw the Confederate flag in the window, they understand from experience that it meant, "We don't want black people eating here."

Nate decided that one of his goals would be to educate people about the thinking of many South Carolinians and that the Confederate flag was not necessarily a symbol of racism. He would defend the decision of the South Carolina legislature, which had attempted to find some middle ground on the issue. Rather than calling for the return of the flag to the capitol, he would support the legislature's decision to raise the flag only at the monument to Confederate soldiers.

Read as You Write

Nate's conversations with his friends indicated to him that he had to become more knowledgeable before he could complete his argument. He continued reading in the library as he developed his points, using many of the search strategies we discuss in Chapter 15. Nate's decision reflects an important fact about effective arguments: They usually emerge from substantial knowledge. If you have not explored your topic fully, then you must read widely about the subject before going further. Not only will your reading alert you to arguments that you can cite in support of your own points, but it will also clarify for you the thinking of those who disagree with you so that you can take into account their points of view. Finally, reading will allow you to take seriously what we advise early in this book: that arguing is often more a contribution to a continuing conversation than a final resolution of all doubts, and that you can sometimes do far more good by persuading people to cooperate with you than by fervently opposing them.

Nate's reading gave him a number of insights into the flag issue. He learned about the original design of the flag, which was related to the crosses of St. Andrew and St. George. He also learned about the history of the flag's display at the capitol—including the fact that the flag was first raised there in 1962, in the midst of the civil rights movement. He also found that George Wallace began displaying the Battle Flag in Alabama shortly after his confrontations with Robert Kennedy over the issue of segregation. Nate read about the NAACP and the reasons for its opposition to the flag. He sampled Web sites that supported the flag's display over the capitol (including one that quoted the famous historian Shelby Foote), and he considered others that opposed that position. After several hours of note taking, Nate was ready to assemble a serious draft.

Switch from Writer to Reader

In most first drafts, it makes sense to get your ideas on paper without thinking about readers. Such a practice makes positive use of strong feelings and gets the skeleton of an argument out. (Nate's first draft expressed ideas that he had been formulating for some time.) The first draft, however, is only the beginning. You need to take time to think about how your argument will come across to your readers.

First, pretend you are someone who is either uninformed about your subject or informed but holding an opposing viewpoint. If possible think of an actual person and pretend to be that person. (Nate could easily imagine a person holding an opposing view because he knew people in his dorm who disagreed with him on this issue.) Then read your argument aloud all the way through. When you read aloud, you often hear clunky phrases and catch errors, but do no more in this stage than put checks in the margins that you can return to later. Once again, you don't want to get bogged down with the little stuff. Rather, what you are after in this stage is getting an overall sense of how well you accomplished what you set out to do. Think in particular about these things:

1. **Your claim.** When you finish reading, can you summarize in one sentence what you are arguing? If you cannot, then you need to focus your claim. Then ask yourself what's at stake in your claim. Who benefits by what you are arguing? Who doesn't? How will readers react to what you are arguing? If what you are arguing is obvious to everyone and if all or nearly all would agree with you, then you need to identify an aspect on which people would disagree and restate your claim.

2. **Your good reasons**. What are the good reasons for your claim? Would a reader have any trouble identifying them? Will those readers be likely to accept your reasons? What evidence is offered to support these good reasons and how is the evidence relevant to the claim (the "so what?" question in Chapter 2)? Note any places where you might add evidence and any places where you need to explain why the evidence is relevant.

3. **Your representation of yourself.** To the extent you can, forget for a moment that you wrote what you are reading. What impression do you have of you, the writer? Is the writer believable? Trustworthy? Has the writer done his or her homework on the issue? Does the writer take an appropriate tone? Note any places where you can strengthen your credibility as a writer.

4. **Your consideration of your readers.** Do you give enough background if your readers are unfamiliar with the issue? Do you acknowledge opposing views that they might have? Do you appeal to common values that you share with them? Note any places where you might do more to address the concerns of your readers.

Here is a sample paragraph from a first draft of Nate's essay on the Confederate flag:

The Confederate Battle Flag is not a racist sign; it is the most powerful and widely recognized symbol of Southern valor and independence. The flag honors the Confederate dead, who fought for their way of life and defended their homes from Northern aggression in the War Between the States. People today owe it to the men and women who fought for their belief in liberty and states' rights, a sacrifice rarely seen today. People ought to honor the memories of the Confederate fallen just as they remember people involved in every other war. While people are making monuments to war dead in Washington, including monuments to those who died in Vietnam and Korea, there are those who are trying to dishonor Confederate dead by taking the Battle Flag from the Confederate monument in Columbia.

When Nate put himself in the shoes of his readers, he quickly saw the need for substantial changes in that paragraph. He still felt strongly about his belief in the symbolism of the flag, but he also realized that people who disagreed with him—the people he was trying to persuade—would not appreciate his use of the term "War Between the States" because they would suspect him of thinking that the war was not fought over the issue of slavery and accuse him of resisting any racist notions associated with the flag. "States' rights" is a phrase that is honorable, but not when one of the rights is the right to own slaves. Here is how he revised his paragraph:

The Confederate Battle Flag is not a racist sign; it is the most powerful and widely recognized symbol of Southern valor and independence. It is true, unfortunately, that many racists today display the Confederate flag. But that unfortunate truth should not permit us to discontinue to honor the flag, any more than the use of the cross by the Ku Klux Klan should permit us to discontinue honoring the cross in our churches. It is also true that the Civil War was conducted in large part because of the issue of slavery, that many people therefore associate the Confederate flag with white supremacy, and that many whites during the Civil Rights era flew the flag as a sign of resistance to the end of segregation. But the Civil War was also fought for other reasons in the South by many people who neither owned slaves nor who had any use for slavery. The flag honors the Confederate dead who fought for their way of life and who believed they were defending their homes from Northern aggression. People today owe it to those who fought for their belief in liberty (our nation's most basic belief) to permit their monuments to include the flag they fought under. The Confederate flag needs to be restored to its original symbolism, and that can only take place if it continues to be displayed in honorable places. To change the Confederate monument in Columbia by taking away the Confederate flag would be to dishonor those who died under it. People ought to honor the memories of the Confederate fallen just as they remember people involved in every other war. Shelby Foote, the well known Southern historian and author of a three-volume history of the Civil War, said it best: "Many among the finest people this country ever produced died [under the Confederate flag]. To take it as a symbol of evil is a misrepresentation" (www.southerninitiative.com, April 30, 2001).

Do you think Nate's revisions were successful in answering his reader's objections and in creating a more effective ethos? How will his quotation from the Southern historian go over with his Northern readers?

Focus on Your Argument

Now it's time to go through your argument in detail.

1. Find your main claim.

What kind of claim is it? Are you writing a proposal, an evaluation, a rebuttal, a narrative, or what? What things follow from that? (All arguments, as we have emphasized in Chapters 5 through 10, tend to develop in certain ways, depending on their kind.) Nate's argument that the Confederate flag ought to be permitted to remain on the Confederate monument (but not over the state capitol building) is a proposal argument. Identifying the type of claim helps you to think about how it might be developed further. We offer guidelines for proposal arguments in Chapter 10.

2. How will you support your claim?

What good reasons will you use? Will you use definitions, an evaluation, a causal argument, a list of consequences, a comparison or contrast, or a combination of these? Nate's paragraph, one segment of his overall proposal, offers a definition: "The Confederate Battle Flag is not a racist sign; it is the most powerful and widely recognized symbol of Southern valor and independence." If Nate can get his readers to accept that definition, that "good reason" for agreeing to his overall thesis, he will have gone a long way toward achieving his goals. It may take him several paragraphs to argue for the definition, but eventually it will be worth the effort. Nate might also use other good reasons to support his overall position on the flag issue: the good consequences that will follow if his advice is heeded (e.g., goodwill; an end to polarization in the community), the bad consequences that might be avoided (e.g., continued controversy and divisiveness in South Carolina), the useful comparisons or contrasts that can be cited as support (e.g., the comparison between the Klan's use of the cross and racists' use of the Confederate flag), and so forth. Altogether, those good reasons will make up a complete and satisfactory argument.

3. Analyze your organization.

Turn to one of the Steps in Writing guides at the end of Chapters 5 though 10 that best fits your argument (or Chapter 4 if you are doing an analysis). The guides will help you determine what kind of overall organization you need. For example, if you have a definition argument, go to the Steps in Writing guide at the end of Chapter 5. You should be able to identify the criteria for your definition. How many criteria do you offer? Where are they located? Are they clearly connected to your claim? In what order should they be offered?

In addition, think about other effective ordering principles. Since readers often remember things that come first or last, do you want to put your strongest good reasons early and repeat them toward the end? Or do you want to build toward a climactic effect by ordering your reasons from least important to most important? Can you group similar ideas? Should you move from least controversial to most controversial? Or from most familiar to least familiar?

4. Examine your evidence.

If you noted places where you could use more evidence when you first read through your draft, now is the time to determine what kinds of additional evidence you need. Evidence can come in the shape of examples, personal experiences, comparisons, statistics, calculations, quotations, and other kinds of data that a reader will find relevant and compelling. Decide what you need and put it in.

5. Consider your title and introduction.

Many students don't think much about titles, but titles are important: A good title makes the reader want to discover what you have to say. Be as specific as you can in your title and, if possible, suggest your stance. In the introduction get off to a fast start and convince your reader to keep reading. You may need to establish right away that a problem exists. You may have to give some background. You many need to discuss an argument by someone else that you are addressing. But above all, you want to convince your reader to keep reading.

6. Consider your conclusion.

Restating your claim usually isn't the best way to finish. The worst endings say something like "in my paper I've said this." Think about whether there is a summarizing point you can make, an implication you can draw, or another example you can include that sums up your position. If you are writing a proposal, your ending might be a call for action or a challenge. If you have a telling quotation from an authority, sometimes that can make an effective clincher.

7. Analyze the visual aspects of your text.

Do the font and layout you selected look attractive? Do you use the same font throughout? If you use more than one font, have you done so consistently? Would headings and subheadings help to identify key sections of your argument? If you include statistical data, would charts be effective? Would illustrations help to establish key points? For example, a map could be very useful if you are arguing about the location of a proposed new highway.

Focus on Your Style and Proofread Carefully

In our advice about revision, we have ignored so far issues of style and correctness. We did that not because we think style and correctness are unimportant but because some people forget that revision can involve much more than those things. In your final pass through your text, you should definitely concentrate on the style of your argument and eliminate as many errors as you can. Here are some suggestions that may help.

1. Check the connections between sentences.

Notice how your sentences are connected. If you need to signal the relationship from one sentence to the next, use a transitional word or phrase. For example, compare the following:

Silent Spring was widely translated and inspired legislation on the environment in nearly all industrialized nations. *Silent Spring* changed the way we think about the environment. →

Silent Spring was widely translated and inspired legislation on the environment in nearly all industrialized nations. **Moreover,** the book changed the way we think about the environment.

2. Check your sentences for emphasis.

When most people talk, they emphasize points by speaking louder, using gestures, and repeating themselves. You should know that it is possible to emphasize ideas in writing too.

- **Things in main clauses tend to stand out more than things in subordinate clauses.** Compare these two sentences: "Kroger, who studied printing in Germany, later organized a counterfeiting ring"; and "Before he organized a counterfeiting ring, Kroger studied printing in Germany." These two sentences contain exactly the same information, but they emphasize different things. The first sentence emphasizes that Kroger organized a counterfeiting ring. The second sentence emphasizes that Kroger studied printing. Signal what you want to emphasize by putting it into main clauses, and put less important information in subordinate clauses or in modifying phrases. (If two things are equally important, signal that by using coordination: "Kroger studied printing in Germany; he later organized a counterfeiting ring.")

- **Things at the beginning and at the end of sentences tend to stand out more than things in the middle.** Compare these three sentences: "After he studied printing in Germany, Kroger organized a counterfeiting ring"; "Kroger, after he studied printing in Germany, organized a counterfeiting ring"; and "Kroger organized a counterfeiting ring after he studied printing in Germany." All three sentences contain the exact same words and use the same main clause and subordinate clause, but they emphasize different things, depending on which items are placed in the beginning, middle, and end.

- **Use punctuation for emphasis.** Dashes add emphasis; parentheses de-emphasize. Compare these two sentences: "Kroger (who studied printing in Germany) organized a counterfeiting ring"; and "Kroger—who studied printing in Germany—organized a counterfeiting ring."

3. Eliminate wordiness.

Drafts often contain unnecessary words. When you revise, often you can find long expressions that can easily be shortened ("at this point in time" → "now"). Sometimes you become repetitive, saying about the same thing you said a sentence or two before. See how many words you can take out without losing the meaning.

4. Use active verbs.

Anytime you can use a verb besides a form of *be* (*is, are, was, were*), take advantage of the opportunity to make your style more lively. Sentences that begin with "There is (are)" and "It is" often have better alternatives:

> "It is true that exercising a high degree of quality control in the manufacture of our products will be an incentive for increasing our market share."
> → "If we pay attention to quality when we make our products, more people will buy them".

Notice too that active verbs often cut down on wordiness.

5. Know what your spelling checker can and can't do.

Spelling checkers are the greatest invention since peanut butter. They turn up many typos and misspellings that are hard to catch. But spelling checkers do not catch wrong words (e.g. "to much" should be "too much"), incorrect word endings ("three dog"), and other, similar errors. You still have to proofread carefully to eliminate misspellings and word choice errors.

6. Use your handbook to check items of mechanics and usage.

Nothing hurts your credibility more than leaving mechanics and usage errors in what you write. A handbook will help you identify the most common errors and answer questions of usage. Readers probably shouldn't make such harsh judgments when they find errors, but in real life they do. We've seen job application letters tossed in the rejected pile because an applicant made a single, glaring error. The conventions of punctuation, mechanics, and usage aren't that difficult to master, and you'll become a lot more confident when you know the rules or at least know how to look up the rules. You should also trust your ear: If you noticed that a sentence was hard to read aloud or that it doesn't sound right, think about how you might rephrase it. If a sentence seems too long, then you might break it into two or more sentences. If you notice a string of short sentences that sound choppy, then you might combine them. If you notice any run-on sentences or sentence fragments, fix them.

Get Help on Your Draft

Don't trust your own ears (and eyes) exclusively. Most good writers let someone else—a trusted advisor or several of them—read what they write before they share it with their audience. You too need to develop a way of getting advice that you can use to shape your revisions. Be sure to leave enough time for someone else to review your work and for you to make revisions.

A good reviewer is one who is willing to give you time and an honest opinion, and who knows enough about the subject of your paper to make useful suggestions. A roommate or close friend can serve, but often such a friend will be reluctant to give negative evaluations. Perhaps you can develop a relationship with people with whom you can share drafts—you read theirs; they read yours. Whomever you choose, give that person time to read your work carefully and sympathetically. You need not take every piece of advice you get, but you do need to consider suggestions with an open mind.

Making Effective Arguments

Designing, Presenting, and Documenting

Advances in digital technology have made it possible for almost anyone to publish color images along with text, both on paper and on the World Wide Web. Programs such as PowerPoint make it easy to prepare visuals for oral presentations. Furthermore, many students now routinely publish animations, audio, and video clips along with images on Web sites. What is now possible using relatively common and inexpensive computers and software is staggering in comparison to what could be done just a decade ago.

But if new technologies for writing have given us a great deal of potential power, they have also presented us with a variety of challenges. Designing a piece of writing wasn't much of an issue with a typewriter. You could either single or double space, and increase or decrease the margins. But today with a word processing program you can change the typeface, typestyle, and type size, insert illustrations, create and insert tables and other graphics, and print in color. If you are publishing on the Web, you can introduce sound, animation, and video. Sometimes it seems like there are too many choices.

Likewise when you do research on the Web, you often find too much rather than too little. Much of what you find is of little value for a serious argument. And if the physical act of making changes to what you write is easier with a computer, the mental part is still hard work. Even experienced writers struggle with getting what they write into the shape they want it. In the chapters in Part 3, we offer you strategies for creating effective arguments using both new and old technologies.

CHAPTER 12

Effective Visual Design

Understanding Visual Arguments

The average American is exposed to over 3,000 arguments each day, the great majority of which come in the form of advertisements. Many rely on images in addition to text. A typical example is a magazine ad for a leading department store that includes only a picture of a handsome professional woman dressed in a black suit looking at herself in a mirror, the name of the store, and the caption "Somehow you just know." Because the effects of such ads are difficult to explain, some people have called them irrational and even deceptive. But they are anything but irrational. We don't need to be told that being well dressed is important for a professional image.

Products such as clothing, detergent, deodorant, cigarettes, and soft drinks rely heavily on images to sell their products. Nonetheless, as was discussed in the previous chapters, writers also offer images of themselves in order to be convincing. The key difference, of course, is that we are presented with visual images when we encounter advertising, while we have to construct our image of a writer from the voice in the text. Yet it isn't quite that

Figure 12.1 Advertisement for Harrison K-9 Security Services

simple. Some ads include a fair amount of text, and increasingly, writers incorporate graphics in what they write.

Let's take a look at an ad that has both text and images. The text of the ad for Harrison K-9 Security Services in Figure 12.1 is framed by a header across the top: the word "VIGILANCE" imposed over an image of a woman, a child, and a dog and a proportionally much larger image of a German shepherd positioned in the left third of the frame. We can describe three main elements of this ad: the text, the images, and the graphic design.

TEXT

The text fills the center right of the frame. The first paragraph gives the argument of the ad:

> When you're away from home, you need to know that your family is safe. There is no substitute for the vigilant eyes and ears of Harrison K-9 Security Services European German Shepherd protectors.

The second paragraph describes the training the dogs receive and who has bought them: "families, business executives, entertainers, and professional athletes." The third paragraph describes training for the purchasers of the dogs, and finally, the logo of the company is followed by its address and phone number.

IMAGES

The image of the German shepherd on the left of the frame is shot from a low angle, making the dog appear quite large. Its coat is thick, and its ears point up toward the word "VIGILANCE" at the top. The smaller second image shows a woman seated on a carpet, a young child kneeling beside her, and a dog resting nearby. The woman and child are looking at something in the child's hand. They are dressed casually in jeans, and the viewer assumes that they are a mother and daughter at home. The dog looks both relaxed and alert, its gaze fixed on the viewer.

This small image is consistent with the text in several ways. First, since there is no man in the frame, the father is presumably absent. The text says that people who have bought dogs include "families, business executives, entertainers, and professional athletes." The image thus suggests that the buyer of the dog will likely be a man who travels, leaving his wife and children at home, rather than a woman who is employed as a business executive, entertainer, or professional athlete. But the image can also be viewed from the perspective of the "intruder" mentioned in the text. The dog is between the intruder and the woman and child. To get to them requires getting past the dog.

GRAPHIC DESIGN

Graphic designers consider the relationship of the elements when they design an ad. The images and text support each other in this ad, but through good graphic design, these relationships can be enhanced. When you page through the magazine where the ad appeared, your eyes are first drawn to the image of the dog. The background color of the ad is maroon, which enhances the rich, light brown tones of the dog's coat. The dog's ears direct attention to the word "VIGILANCE," printed in a color very similar to that of the dog's coat. "VIGILANCE" is superimposed over the image of the woman, child, and dog; thus, even a quick glance at the ad takes in the two images and the word. If you continue looking at the ad, you next move clockwise to the text, which is set in a sans serif typeface (we'll explain typefaces shortly) in white letters against the dark maroon background. The typeface and background color set the text of the ad apart from the text of the magazine, which uses black serif type against a white background.

This ad demonstrates how a graphic designer coordinates images with the message of an ad. A designer organizes words and images to achieve a desired effect for a particular audience and purpose. These principles of graphic design are not so very different from the rhetorical principles that were discussed in the previous chapters. It all has to do with understanding how particular effects can be achieved for particular readers in particular situations. Best of all, you too can use graphic design to your own advantage.

Print Is a Visual Medium

Perhaps the most important thing to know about design is that there are very few hard-and-fast rules. As for all arguments, everything depends on the rhetorical situation. All your decisions hinge on your purpose, your subject, and the type of document you are writing, your intended audience(s), and how you want your reader(s) to perceive you. Sometimes, you succeed by breaking the rules.

Let's start with how your readers perceive you. You see an ad for a part-time position designing Web sites, brochures, and newsletters for a copy shop that pays good money, and since you have the necessary skills, you decide to apply. You write your letter of application:

Jennifer Barnes

308 Bruffee Street
Minneapolis, MN 55423

January 5, 2002

Andrew J. Johnson, Vice President
Copy Mart
742 Church Street S.E.
Minneapolis, MN 55454

Dear Mr. Johnson:

I wish to apply for the design position that you advertised in the
Minneapolis Tribune on January 3, 2002.

I am a communications major at the University of Minnesota, and I have
three years experience designing brochures, newsletters, and Web pages
for businesses and nonprofit organizations in the Twin Cities. I am skilled
in using JavaScript, Adobe PageMaker, Photoshop, and Illustrator, and
Macromedia Director, Dreamweaver, and Flash. My résumé is enclosed,
complete with a list of Web sites that I have designed and the names,
addresses, and phone numbers of people who have employed me.

You may reach me by email or at my home phone, (612) 634-5789,
on most afternoons. I look forward to hearing from you.

Sincerely,

Jennifer Barnes

The letter is fine, but it looks a little bland. You are, after all, applying for a design position. So you decide to change your letterhead using the WordArt feature of your word processing program and use a different font for the body to make it more snappy. After a little while, you come up with this:

Jennifer Barnes

308 Bruffee Street
Minneapolis, MN 55423

January 5, 2002

Andrew J. Johnson, Vice President
Copy Mart
742 Church Street S.E.
Minneapolis, MN 55454

Dear Mr. Johnson:

I wish to apply for the design position that you advertised in the *Minneapolis Tribune* on January 3, 2002.

I am a communications major at the University of Minnesota, and I have three years experience designing brochures, newsletters, and Web pages for businesses and nonprofit organizations in the Twin Cities. I am skilled in using JavaScript, Adobe PageMaker, Photoshop, and Illustrator, and Macromedia Director, Dreamweaver, and Flash. My résumé is enclosed, complete with a list of Web sites that I have designed and the names, addresses, and phone numbers of people who have employed me.

You may reach me by email or at my home phone, (612) 634-5789, on most afternoons. I look forward to hearing from you.

Sincerely,

Jennifer Barnes

This is better, you think, but maybe still not professional enough. You try one more time, simply using shading and a different font for the letterhead:

 308 Bruffee Street
Minneapolis, MN 55423

January 5, 2002

Andrew J. Johnson, Vice President
Copy Mart
742 Church Street S.E.
Minneapolis, MN 55454

Dear Mr. Johnson:

I wish to apply for the design position that you advertised in the *Minneapolis Tribune* on January 3, 2002.

I am a communications major at the University of Minnesota, and I have three years experience designing brochures, newsletters, and Web pages for businesses and nonprofit organizations in the Twin Cities. I am skilled in using JavaScript, Adobe PageMaker, Photoshop, and Illustrator, and Macromedia Director, Dreamweaver, and Flash. My résumé is enclosed, complete with a list of Web sites that I have designed and the names, addresses, and phone numbers of people who have employed me.

You may reach me by email or at my home phone, (612) 634-5789, on most afternoons. I look forward to hearing from you.

Sincerely,

Jennifer Barnes

That's the professional look you want. You send the letter, and you get the job.

Your first newsletter assignment comes from a local group, Stop Stadium Welfare (SSW), which is opposed to using taxpayer dollars to pay for a new stadium. Like most people, the members of SSW want their newsletter in a hurry, and what they bring you is a visual mess. They hand you several short articles and no model to follow, since this is the group's first newsletter.

You start reading what they hand you. The first article has the title "Do Stadiums Really Bring in Jobs and New Businesses?" It begins:

> Stadium boosters like to claim fabulous economic impacts from building new stadiums with taxpayers' dollars. But the record suggests just the opposite. Most sports stadiums lose money. Stadiums built in the 1970s and 1980s, including the Superdome in New Orleans, the Silverdome in suburban Detroit, and the Meadowlands in New Jersey, are now considered obsolete, and each loses over a million government dollars a year. They are drains on the local economy, not economic multipliers.

There are four other, shorter articles, so there's plenty of material for a four-page newsletter. But how will you put it together?

You start out by making a header and then type in the stories one after the other (see Figure 12.2). You quickly realize that putting the stories in 1, 2, 3 order is not the solution. Your newsletter looks like a term paper with long stretches of unbroken text. It has little visual interest, and it's not easy to read. You remember that a professor once said that lines with more than twelve to fourteen words become hard to read. So the first thing you do is to divide the page into two columns. That's simple to do using the columns command in your word processing program. But you still haven't solved the problem of the long article that you started out with. You then decide to make the columns into text boxes so that you can carry over some text to later pages. That allows you to get three stories on the first page.

Next you change the typeface from Times Roman to Arial, which allows you to use smaller type to get more on the page and gives your newsletter a clean, simple look. You decide that a photo would be nice, and you quickly find a shot of the Metrodome in your office's photo file. Since the

Stop Stadium Welfare

Volume 1, Issue 1   2002

Do Stadiums Really Bring in Jobs and New Businesses?
By Reginald Alexander

Stadium boosters like to claim fabulous economic impacts from building new stadiums with taxpayers' dollars. But the record suggests just the opposite. Most sports stadiums lose money. Stadiums built in the 1970s and 1980s, including the Superdome in New Orleans, the Silverdome in suburban Detroit, and the Meadowlands in New Jersey, are now obsolete, and each lose over a million government dollars a year. They are drains on the local economy, not multipliers.

Before the Metrodome, we had Metropolitan Stadium, south of Minneapolis in the suburb of Bloomington. It was built with local business support in an open field. The old Met virtually made the Hwy 494 "strip," a belt of restaurants, clubs, hotels and stores. It was an outdoor stadium, like the ones the owners want built now. The controversial government-built successor, the Metrodome, has not had the same impact on downtown Minneapolis. Downtown Minneapolis has continued to decline.

What is most amazing is that the same arguments used to justify the Metrodome are being made for a new stadium. If the Metrodome failed to revive downtown, why would another stadium be different? The Metrodome's primary economic spinoffs appear to be a few $5 parking lots.

A study by the Brookings Institution published in 1997 examined sports facilities from a variety of economic perspectives. The authors conclude that the economic impact of a new sports facility is very small at best and often negative. In no case do the effects justify the enormous investment in a new stadium. Probably the most successful new stadium has been Oriole Park in Baltimore, which brings in many people from outside the area. Nevertheless, the net gain for Baltimore's economy in terms of tax revenues and jobs created is only $3 million a year—a minimal return on a $200 million investment.

Meanwhile, local politicians talk about giving the Twins an even bigger subsidy to help reduce their losses. These losses are not documented, or at least the figures not shown to the public. And the owner of the Twins, Carl Pohlad, is a billionaire. Even if the Twins are losing money, why would Mr. Pohlad expect taxpayers to cover his baseball losses any more than they would bail out another venture?

North Carolina Voters Just Say No to Stadium Tax
By Arlene Smith

North Carolina voters rejected the use of taxes to help build a new stadium so theTwins could move to North Carolina. Referendum results show Forsythe County 41-59% against, Guilford County 33-67% against. Commisioner of Baseball Bud Selig made the following statement: "There's no other way to say it: The people in the Twin Cities have to deal with it. They still have to deal with the stadium issue."

Figure 12.2   Version 1 of Stop Stadium Welfare Newsletter

Metrodome has become a symbol of Minneapolis, it works well to point out that people want to tear it down only twenty years after it was built. You add some headings and subheadings to break up the text and give emphasis. Finally, you put in a table of contents so that people will know what else is in the newsletter besides what is on the front page. You're pleased with the result (see Figure 12.3), and it took nothing more than using the commands on your word processing program. Good design doesn't necessarily require fancy tools.

Stop Stadium Welfare

Volume 1, Issue 1   2002

North Carolina Voters Just Say No to Stadium Tax

Arlene Smith

North Carolina voters rejected the use of taxes to help build a new stadium so the Twins could move to North Carolina. Referendum results show Forsythe County 41-59% against, Guilford County 33-67% against. Commissioner of Baseball Bud Selig made the following statement: "There's no other way to say it: The people in the Twin Cities have to deal with it. They still have to deal with the stadium issue."

Deal with what, Bud? Do you think we are too stupid to know what is in our best interest? We're tired of paying for sweetheart deals that benefit only the rich owners and overpaid players. We're tired of giving welfare payments to rich owners who then complain they need even more money out of our pockets.

Entertainment for the Elite

Sports stadiums used to bring people together. The rich people had the best seats, but they were only a few rows in front of where ordinary people sat. Now the wealthy want to sit in luxury boxes, separated from the crowd. What's wrong with most older stadiums is not that they are obsolete but that they lack dozens of luxury boxes.

continued on page 2

INSIDE THIS ISSUE

Do Stadiums Really Bring in Jobs and New Businesses?

Reginald Alexander

Stadium boosters like to claim fabulous economic impacts from building new stadiums with taxpayers' dollars. But the record suggests just the opposite. Most sports stadiums lose money. Stadiums built in the 1970s and 1980s, including the Superdome in New Orleans, the Silverdome in suburban Detroit, and the Meadowlands in New Jersey, are now obsolete, and each lose over a million government dollars a year. They are drains on the local economy, not multipliers.

The Metrodome Hasn't Delivered on the Promise to Revive Downtown

Before the Metrodome, we had Metropolitan Stadium, south of Minneapolis in the suburb of Bloomington. It was built with local business support in an open field. The old Met virtually made the Hwy 494 "strip," a belt of restaurants, clubs, hotels and stores. It was an outdoor stadium, like the ones the owners want built now. The controversial government-built successor, the Metrodome, has not had the same impact on downtown Minneapolis. Downtown Minneapolis has continued to decline.

The Metrodome was opened in 1982 and remains one of the newer baseball stadiums.

What is most amazing is that the same arguments used to justify the Metrodome are being made for a new stadium. If the Metrodome failed to revive downtown, why would another stadium be different? The Metrodome's primary economic spinoffs appear to be a few $5 parking lots.

continued on page 3

Figure 12.3   Version 2 of Stop Stadium Welfare Newsletter

▨ Design Basics

Before a discussion of principles of graphic design, it is important to know, in the most basic terms, how language and visual design work. Language is extremely well adapted for describing things that fall into a linear order. Because humans perceive time as linear, language allows them from a very young age to tell stories. It's also possible to tell stories with images; indeed, images have become the preferred medium with the invention of movies and later television in the twentieth century. But it's not so easy to put together a video story, say of your last vacation, no matter how easy the editing features are on your camcorder. Telling someone the story of your vacation, however, is easy. You just have to remember where you went and what you did.

Even if you are describing a place, you still have to decide what to tell about first. Suppose someone asks you how your house is laid out. You might begin by saying that inside the front door, there is an entryway that goes to the living room. The dining room is on the right, and the kitchen is adjacent. On the left is a hallway, which connects to two bedrooms on the right, one on the left, and a bathroom at the end. But if you draw a floor plan, you can show at once how the house is arranged. That's the basic difference between describing with spoken language and describing with visual images. Spoken language forces you to put things in a *sequence;* visual design forces you to arrange things in *space.* Written language—especially writing on a computer—permits you to do both: to use sequence and space simultaneously. Some of the same principles apply for both language and design when you write. Three of the most important groups of design principles are arrangement, consistency, and contrast.

ARRANGEMENT

Place every item on a page in a visual relationship with the other items.

Many people get through high school by mastering the five-paragraph theme. When they get the assignment, they first have to figure out exactly three points about the topic. Then they write an introduction announcing that they have three points, write a paragraph on each of the three points, and conclude with a paragraph that repeats the three points. It is amazing how far that formula can carry one. The basic structure of announcing the subject, developing it sequentially, and concluding with a summary works well enough in a great many circumstances—from business letters to short reports. Even many PhD dissertations are five-paragraph themes on a larger scale.

But if you translate the five-paragraph formula to space, it's not so simple. Think about putting it on a business card. How would you do it?

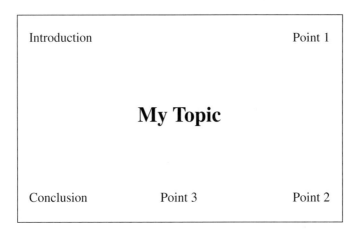

Your eyes naturally go to the center, where the topic is boldfaced. But where do they go after that? It's not a given that a reader will start in the upper left-hand corner and go clockwise around the card.

Let's switch to an example business card.

(919) 684-2741	23 Maple Street Durham, NC 27703
Todd Smith	
Westin Associates	Management Consulting

Again, the name in the middle is where you go first, but where do your eyes go after that? The problem is that nothing on the card has any obvious visual relationship with anything else.

The way beginning designers often solve this problem is to put everything in the center. This strategy forces you to think about what is most important, and you usually put that at the top. On the following card, the information is grouped so that the relationship of the elements is clear. One of the most important design tools—white space—separates the main elements.

Todd Smith

Westin Associates

Management Consulting

23 Maple Street
Durham, NC 27703
(919) 684-2741

But centering everything isn't the only solution for showing the relationship of elements. Another way is by **alignment.** In the next example, the elements are aligned on the right margin and connected by an invisible line. This alignment is often called **flush right.**

Todd Smith

Westin Associates

Management Consulting

23 Maple Street
Durham, NC 27703
(919) 684-2741

If you are in the habit of centering title pages and other elements, try using the flush left and flush right commands along with grouping similar elements. You'll be surprised what a difference it makes and how much more professional and persuasive your work will appear. Turn back to the revised Stop Stadium Welfare newsletter on page 234 to see how the strong flush left alignment of text, headings, and the picture produces a professional look.

CONSISTENCY

> Make what is similar look similar.

You learned the principle of consistency in elementary school when your teacher told you to write on the lines, make the margins even, and indent your paragraphs. When you write using a computer, these things are done for you by your word processing program. However, too many people stop there when they use a computer to write. You can do a whole lot more.

Sometime during your college years, you likely will write a report or paper that uses headings. Readers increasingly expect you to divide what you write into chunks and label those chunks with headings. It's easy enough to simply center every heading so that your report looks like this:

```
                              Title
     Xxxxxxxx xxxxxxxx xxxxxxx xxxxxxx xxxxxxxx xxxxxxxx
     xxxxxxx xxxxxxx xxxxxxxx xxxxxxx xxxxxxx xxxxxxxx
     xxxxxxx xxxxxxx xxxxxxx xxxxxxx xxxxxxx xxxxxxx xxxxx
     xxxxxxx xxxxxxx xxxxxxx xxxxxxx xxxxxxx xxxxxxx
     xxxxxxx xxxxxxx

                            Heading 1
     Xxxxxxxx xxxxxxxx xxxxxxx xxxxxxx xxxxxxxx xxxxxxxx
     xxxxxxx xxxxxxx xxxxxxxx xxxxxxx xxxxxxx xxxxxxxx
     xxxxxxx xxxxxxx xxxxxxx xxxxxxx xxxxxxx xxxxxxx xxxxx
     xxxxxxx xxxxxxx xxxxxxx xxxxxxx xxxxxxx xxxxxxx
     xxxxxxx xxxxxxx xxxxxxx xxxxxxxx xxxxxxxxx xxxxxxx
     xxxxxxxx xxxxxxx

                            Heading 2
     Xxxxxxxx xxxxxxxx xxxxxxx xxxxxxx xxxxxxxx xxxxxxxx
     xxxxxxx xxxxxxx xxxxxxxx xxxxxxx xxxxxxx xxxxxxxx
     xxxxxxx xxxxxxx xxxxxxx xxxxxxx xxxxxxx xxxxxxx xxxxx
     xxxxxxx xxxxxxx xxxxxxx xxxxxxx xxxxxxx xxxxxxx
     xxxxxxx xxxxxxx
```

If you write a report that looks like this one, you can make it much more visually appealing by devising a system of consistent headings that indicate the overall organization. You first have to determine the level of importance of each heading by making an outline to see what fits under what. Then you make the headings conform to the different levels so that what is equal in importance will have the same level of heading.

Title

Xxxxxxxx xxxxxxxx xxxxxxx xxxxxxx xxxxxxxx xxxxxxxx
xxxxxx xxxxxxx xxxxxxxx xxxxxxx xxxxxxx xxxxxxxx
xxxxxx xxxxxxx xxxxxxx xxxxxxx xxxxxxx xxxxxxx
xxxxxx xxxxxxx xxxxxxx xxxxxxx xxxxxxx xxxxxxx
xxxxxx xxxxxxx

Major Heading

Xxxxxxxx xxxxxxxx xxxxxxx xxxxxxx xxxxxxxx xxxxxxxx
xxxxxx xxxxxxx xxxxxxxx xxxxxxx xxxxxxx xxxxxxxx
xxxxxx xxxxxxx xxxxxxx xxxxxxx xxxxxxx xxxxxxx
xxxxxx xxxxxxx xxxxxxx xxxxxxxx xxxxxxxx xxxxxxx
xxxxxxxx xxxxxxx

Level 2 Heading   Xxxxxxxx xxxxxxxx xxxxxxx xxxxxxx
xxxxxxxx xxxxxxxx xxxxxxx xxxxxxx xxxxxxxx xxxxxxx
xxxxxx xxxxxxxx xxxxxxx xxxxxxx xxxxxxx xxxxxxx
xxxxxx xxxxxxx xxxxxxx xxxxxxx

Other useful tools that word processing programs offer are ways of making lists. Bulleted lists are used frequently to present good reasons for claims and proposals. For example:

The proposed new major in Technology, Literacy, and Culture will:

- Prepare our students for the changing demands of the professions and public citizenship.
- Help students to move beyond technical skills and strategies to understand the historical, economic, political, and scientific impacts of new technologies.
- Allow students to practice new literacies that mix text, graphics, sound, video, animation, hypermedia, and real-time communication.
- Help to ensure that wise decisions are made about the collection, organization, storage, and distribution of and access to information via new technologies.
- Provide students with a deeper, richer, and more profound understanding of the dynamic relationships among technology, culture, and the individual.

A bulleted list is an effective way of presenting a series of items or giving an overview of what is to come. However, bulleted lists can be ineffective if the items in the list are not similar.

CONTRAST

Make what is different look different.

We tend to follow the principle of consistency because that's what we've been taught and that's what writing technologies—from typewriters to computers—do for us. But the principle of contrast takes some conscious effort on our part to implement. Take a simple résumé as an example:

Roberto Salazar

Address: 3819 East Jefferson Avenue, Escondido, CA 92027

Send email to: salazar@capaccess.org

Job Title: Financial Consultant, Credit Reviewer, Financial Analyst

Relocation: Yes—particular interest in Latin America.

Experience

1997-present. Credit Services Group, Carpenter & Tokaz LLP, 3000 Wilshire Boulevard, Los Angeles, California 90017

CONSULTING: Presented Directorate with report findings, conclusions, and recommendations for operation improvements. Coordinated a process improvement engagement for a large finance company, which resulted in the consolidation of credit operations.

SUPERVISION: Supervised, trained, and assessed the work of staff (1–4) involved in audit assists. Reviewed real estate investments, other real estate owned, and loan portfolios for documentation, structure, credit analysis, risk identification, and credit scoring.

Education

1997 San Diego State University, San Diego, California, Bachelor of Business Administration

Languages

Fluent in English and Spanish. Experience in tutoring students with Spanish lessons at San Diego State University, San Diego, California

Computers

Proficient with Microsoft Word and Excel, Lotus Notes, AmiPro, Lotus 1-2-3, WordPerfect, and Sendero SV simulation modeling software. Familiarity with several online information retrieval methods.

References Available On Request.

The résumé has consistency but there is no contrast between what is more important and what is less important. The overall impression is that the person is dull, dull, dull.

Your résumé, along with your letter of application, might be the most important piece of persuasive writing you'll do in your life. It's worth taking some extra time to distinguish yourself. Your ability to write a convincing letter and produce a handsome résumé is a good reason for an employer to hire you. Remember why you are paying attention to graphic design. You want your readers to focus on certain elements, and you want to create the right ethos. Use of contrast can emphasize the key features of the résumé and contribute to a much more forceful and dynamic image.

Roberto Salazar

3819 East Jefferson Avenue
Escondido, CA 92027
salazar@capaccess.org

Position Titles Sought

Financial Consulting
Credit Reviewer
Financial Analyst
(Willing to relocate, especially to Latin America)

Education

1997	**Bachelor of Business Administration.** San Diego State University.

Experience

1997-present	**Credit Services Group, Carpenter & Tokaz, LLP.** 3000 Wilshire Boulevard Los Angeles, California 90017

Consulting: Presented Directorate with report findings, conclusions, and recommendations for operation improvements. Coordinated a process improvement engagement for a large finance company, which resulted in the consolidation of credit operations.

Supervision: Supervised, trained, and assessed the work of four staff involved in audit assists. Reviewed real estate investments, other real estate owned, and loan portfolios for documentation, structure, credit analysis, risk identification, and credit scoring.

Languages

Fluent in English and Spanish. Experience as a Spanish Tutor at SDSU.

Computer Skills

Proficient with Microsoft Word & Excel, Lotus Notes, AmiPro, Lotus 1-2-3, WordPerfect, and Sendero SV simulation modeling software. Familiarity with several online information retrieval methods.

References

Available on request.

Notice that arrangement and consistency are also important to the revised résumé. Good design requires that all elements be brought into play to produce the desired results.

The Rhetoric of Type

Until computers and word processing software came along, most writers had little or no control over the type style they used. If they typed, they likely used Courier, a fact that many typists didn't even know. Furthermore, the typewriter gave no choice about type size. Writers worked with either 10-point type or 12-point type. (A point is a printer's measure. One inch equals 72 points.) You had no way to include italics. The convention was to underline the word so that the printer would later set the word in italics. Boldfacing could be accomplished only by typing the word over again, making it darker.

Even if the general public knew little about type styles and other aspects of printing before computers came along, printers had five hundred years' experience learning about which type styles were easiest to read and what effects different styles produced. Type styles are grouped into families of **typefaces.** When you open the pull-down font menu of your word processing program, you see a small part of that five-hundred-year tradition of developing typefaces. At first, many of the typefaces will look about the same to you, but after you get some practice with using various typefaces, you will begin to notice how they differ.

The two most important categories of typefaces are **serif** and **sans serif.** Serif (rhymes with "sheriff") type was developed first, imitating the strokes of an ink pen. Serifs are the little wedge-shaped ends on letter forms, which scribes produced with wedge-tipped pens. Serif type also has thick and thin transitions on the curved strokes. Five of the most common serif typefaces are the following:

Times

Palatino

Bookman

Garamond

New Century Schoolbook

If these typefaces look almost alike to you, it's not an accident. Serif typefaces were designed to be easy to read. They don't call attention to themselves. Therefore, they are well suited for long stretches of text and are used frequently.

Sans serif type (*sans* is French for "without") doesn't have the little wedge-shaped ends on letters, and the thickness of the letters is the same. Popular sans serif typefaces include the following:

Helvetica

Avant Garde

Arial

Sans serif typefaces work well for headings and short stretches of text. They give the text a crisp, modern look. And some sans serif typefaces are easy to read on a computer screen.

Finally, there are many script and decorative typefaces. These typefaces tend to draw attention to themselves. They are harder to read, but sometimes they can be used for good effects. Some script and decorative typefaces include the following:

Zapf Chancery

STENCIL

Mistral

Tekton

Changing typefaces will draw attention. It is usually better to be consistent in using typefaces within a text unless you want to signal something.

It's easy to change the size of type when you compose on a computer. A specific size of a typeface is called a **font.** The font size displays on the menu bar. For long stretches of text, you probably should use at least 10-point or 12-point type. For headings, you can use larger type.

type	8 point
type	10 point
type	12 point
type	14 point
type	18 point
type	24 point
type	36 point

type

48 point

type

72 point

Fonts also have different weights. **Weight** refers to the thickness of the strokes. Take a look at the fonts on your font menu. You probably have some fonts that offer options ranging from light to bold, such as Arial Condensed Light, Arial, Arial Rounded MT Bold, and Arial Black. Here's what each of these looks like as a heading:

1. *Arial Condensed Light*

Position Titles Sought

Financial Consultant
Credit Reviewer
Financial Analyst
(Willing to relocate, especially to Latin America)

2. *Arial*

Position Titles Sought

Financial Consultant
Credit Reviewer
Financial Analyst
(Willing to relocate, especially to Latin America)

3. *Arial Rounded MT Bold*

Position Titles Sought

Financial Consultant
Credit Reviewer
Financial Analyst
(Willing to relocate, especially to Latin America)

4. *Arial Black*

Position Titles Sought

Financial Consultant
Credit Reviewer
Financial Analyst
(Willing to relocate, especially to Latin America)

You can get strong contrasts by using heavier weights of black type for headings and using white space to accent what is different.

Finally, most word processing programs have some special effects that you can employ. The three most common are **boldface,** *italics*, and <u>underlining</u>. All three are used for emphasis, but underlining should be avoided because it makes text harder to read.

Graphic Presentation of Information

TABLES AND CHARTS

Word processing software gives you the capability of creating tables, graphs, and charts in one software program and then importing those graphics into a text file. For example, tables and charts created with Microsoft Excel can easily be imported into Microsoft Word files. Many arguments can be made more effective with the visual presentation of important information. If you have statistical information to support your argument, you should consider whether to present that information in words, as a table, or as a graphic—or in some combination of these.

Let's take as an example the ongoing debate between gun rights advocates and gun control advocates. Gun rights advocates typically rely on definitional arguments. Their foremost argument is based on their interpretation of the Second Amendment to the U.S. Constitution, which reads "A well regulated Militia, being necessary to the security of a free State, the right of the people to keep and bear Arms, shall not be infringed." What exactly the Second Amendment means today is much disputed. Gun control advocates interpret the Second Amendment in its historical context, in which the newly formed states of the United States required local armies to battle against Native Americans. The Supreme Court reached the same conclusion in a 1939 case (*U.S. v. Miller*, 307 U.S. 174), finding that possession of a firearm is not protected by the Second Amendment unless it has some reasonable relationship to the preservation or efficiency of a well-regulated militia. No gun control law ever brought before the Supreme Court or other federal courts has ever been overturned on Second Amendment grounds. Nevertheless, the National Rifle Association and other gun rights advocates continue to argue that ownership of guns is protected by the Bill of Rights.

Those who wish to regulate firearms, however, often bypass the constitutional argument in favor of arguments of consequence. Gun control advocates point to comparisons between the United States and other advanced nations of the world, all of which have much stricter gun laws than the United States and much lower rates of deaths by firearms. The rate of firearm deaths in the United States is three times higher than Canada's, four times higher than Australia's, nine times higher than Germany's, twenty-four times higher than the United Kingdom's (even including Northern Ireland), and almost two hundred times higher than Japan's.

The problem when you start giving a lot of statistics in words is that your readers shortly lose track of your numbers. If you want to argue effectively using statistics, you have to put the numbers in formats that permit your readers to take them in. Tables are quite useful for presenting much numerical data at one glance. If you have the numbers, you can make the table quickly and easily with a program like Microsoft Excel.

Table 12.1 shows a tabular comparison of the death rates due to firearms in the United States and other advanced nations.

	Total Firearm Deaths		Firearm Homicides		Firearm Suicides		Fatal Firearm Accidents	
	Rate	Number	Rate	Number	Rate	Number	Rate	Number
United States (1995)	13.7	35,957	6	15,835	7	18,503	0.5	1,225
Australia (1994)	3.05	536	0.56	96	2.38	420	0.11	20
Canada (1994)	4.08	1,189	0.6	176	3.35	975	0.13	38
Germany (1995)	1.47	1,197	0.21	168	1.23	1,004	0.03	20
Japan (1995)	0.07	93	0.03	34	0.04	49	0.01	10
Sweden (1992)	2.31	200	0.31	27	1.95	169	0.05	4
Spain (1994)	1.01	396	0.19	76	0.55	219	0.26	101
United Kingdom (1994)	0.57	277	0.13	72	0.33	193	0.02	12

(rates are per 100,000 people)
Source: United Nations, *United Nations International Study on Firearms Regulation* (Vienna, Austria: United Nations Crime Prevention and Criminal Justice Division, 1997) 109.

Table 12.1 Firearm Deaths by Country

Although tables can present an array of numbers at once, they lack the dramatic impact of charts. Charts visually represent the magnitude and proportion of data. The differences in death rates due to firearms is striking when presented as a chart. One of the easiest charts to make is a simple bar chart (Figure 12.4).

The tools available in a software program such as Microsoft Excel allow you a number of options. For example, you can represent the bars in three dimensions (Figure 12.5). Be aware, though, that three-dimensional bars can distort the data and make it more difficult to compare the heights of the columns.

Alternatively, you can make a horizontal bar chart instead of a vertical bar chart (Figure 12.6).

The options available to you involve rhetorical decisions. You can manipulate the length of the axes on a bar chart, either exaggerating or minimizing differences. Or in the case of firearm deaths, you can use the total numbers instead of the rate. Notice how much more exaggerated the number of firearm deaths in the United States appears when the total number is used instead of the rate per 100,000 people (compare Figures 12.7 and 12.8). As always it's important to keep your rhetorical goals in mind when you make a chart.

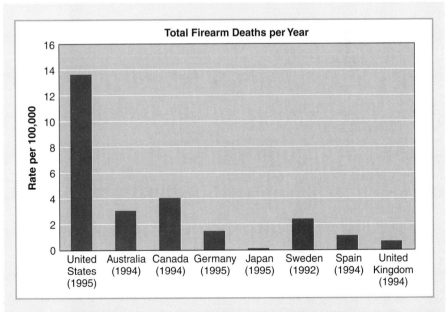

Figure 12.4 Bar Chart of Firearm Deaths by Country

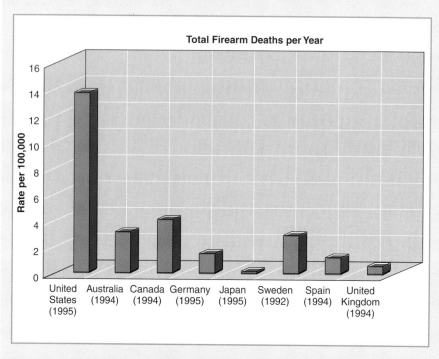

Figure 12.5 3-D Bar Chart of Firearm Deaths by Country

Another family of charts that are very easy to create are pie charts. As the name suggests, **pie charts** illustrate how the pie is divided. They are especially useful for representing percentages, but they work only if the percentages of the parts add up to 100 percent. Gun control advocates frequently cite a study done in Seattle that identified all gunshot deaths over a six-year period (A. L. Kellermann and D. L. Reay, "Protection or Peril: An Analysis of Firearm-Related Deaths in the Home," *New England Journal of Medicine* 314 (1986): 1557–1560). Of the 733 deaths by firearms, a majority (398) occurred in the home in which the firearm involved was kept. Of those 398 deaths, 333 (83.6 percent) were suicides, 41 (10.3 percent) were criminal homicides, 12 (3.0 percent) were accidental, 7 (1.7 percent) were justifiable self-defense, and only 2 (0.5 percent) involved an intruder shot during an attempted entry (see Figure 12.9). Gun control advocates use this study to question the advisability of keeping firearms in the home for protection. Gun rights advocates, however, fault the study because there is no evidence on how many attempts to enter the home were prevented because intruders feared that the owner was armed.

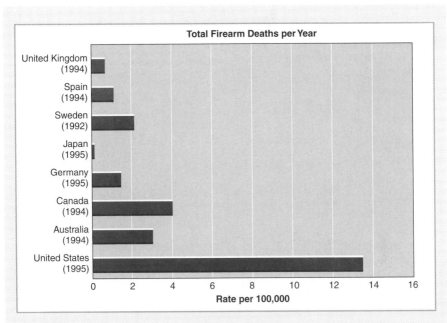

Figure 12.6 Horizontal Bar Chart of Firearm Deaths by Country

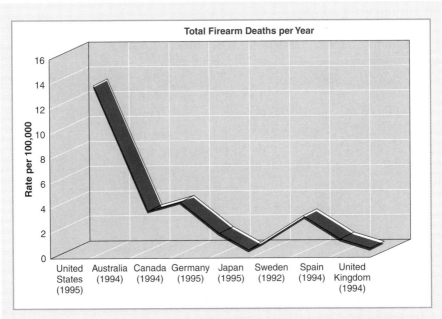

Figure 12.7 3-D Line Chart of Firearm Deaths by Rate per 100,000

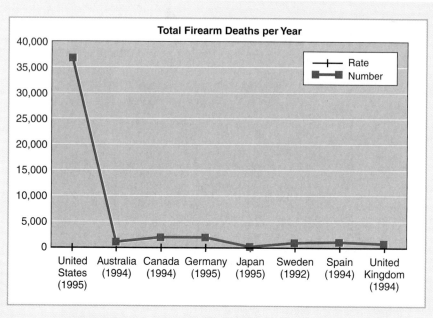

Figure 12.8 Line Chart of Firearm Deaths by Number

MISLEADING CHARTS

Charts can be misleading as well as informative. Line graphs are useful for representing changes over time, and from Table 12.2, you can make a line chart of energy consumption from 1970 to 1995. The line chart would appear to rise significantly from 1970 to 1995, from 66.4 to 90.6 quadrillion British thermal units, indicating a 36 percent increase. If plotted on a line chart, the increase would appear steep. But if the growth in population in the United States is taken into consideration, the increase is not nearly as great, from 327 to 345, only a 5.5 percent increase. A line chart would appear relatively flat.

OTHER GRAPHICS

Other graphics, such as maps and pictures, can also be useful in arguments. If you want to argue for the preservation of old-growth forests, for example, including maps of the surviving old-growth forests are a good tactic because so little of this type of forest survives. The problem is that good maps and images take a long time to create. You can find maps and images on the Web that may

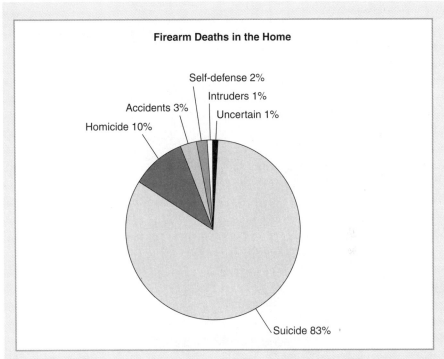

Figure 12.9 Pie Chart of Firearm Deaths in the Home

Year	Energy Consumption in Quadrillion British Thermal Units	Energy Consumption per Capita in BTUs
1970	66.4	327
1975	70.6	327
1980	76	334
1985	74	311
1990	84.2	337
1995	90.6	345

Source: Bureau of the Census. *Statistical Abstract of the United States, 1997* (Washington, D.C.: U.S. Department of Commerce, 1997) 592.

Table 12.2 Table of Energy Consumption in the United States, 1970–1995

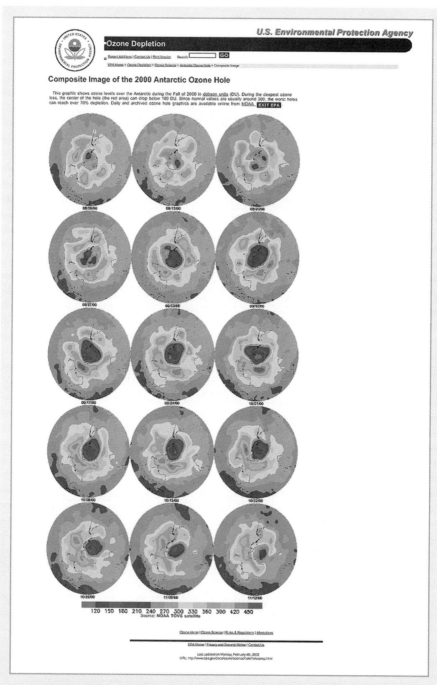

Figure 12.10 Composite Image of the Antarctic Ozone Hole in 2000 (http://www.epa.gov/docs/ozone/science/hole/holecomp.html)

be useful. For example, if you are writing about the depletion of the ozone layer over the earth, you can find this composite image of the Antarctic ozone hole on the Environmental Protection Agency's Web site (Figure 12.10).

If you download maps and images from the Web, you might have to change their format. Images on the Web are usually in JPEG or GIF format, and if your word processing program does not do the conversion for you, you might have to convert the file yourself with a program such as Graphic Converter or Adobe Photoshop.

The main thing you want to avoid is using images strictly for decoration. Readers quickly get tired of pictures and other graphics that don't contribute to the content. Think of pictures, charts, and graphics as alternative means of presenting information. Good use of graphics contributes to your overall argument.

CHAPTER 13

Effective Web Design

Arguments on the Web

Because the Web is a grassroots medium with millions of people putting up Web sites, it's no surprise that the Web has turned out to be a vast forum for arguments. Many organizations and individuals have taken advantage of the low cost of using the Web to publicize their stands on issues. To get a sense of the range of interest groups that use the Web to publicize their views, go to Yahoo! (www.yahoo.com), where you'll find under the "Society and Culture" heading, the subheading "Issues and Causes." As you can see from the list (see Figure 13.1), the issues extend from abortion, affirmative action, and animal rights to weight and nutrition, welfare reform, and xenotransplantation.

It seems that if anyone has an opinion about anything, there's a Web site representing that position. If you have strong feelings about any broad issue, you can find on the Web people who think like you do.

The problem with many argument sites on the Web is that they don't provide much depth. Their links, if any, take you to similar sites, with no context for making the link. It's up to you to figure out the relevance of the link. This strategy works for people who are already convinced of the position

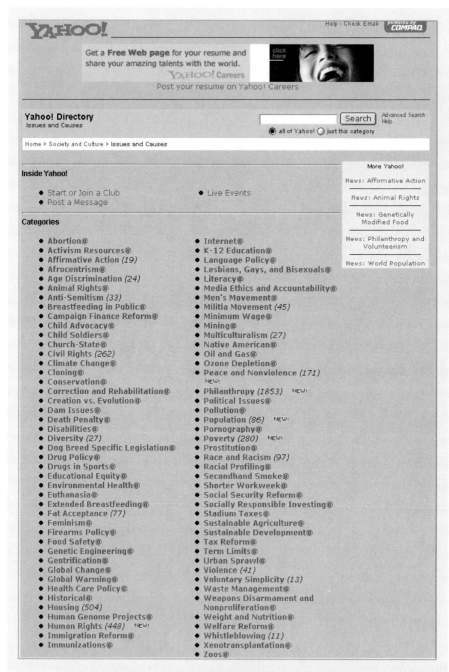

Figure 13.1 Yahoo's Issues and Causes Index

http://www.yahoo.com/Society_and_Culture/Issues_and_Causes/

being advocated, but it's not a strategy that works well with people who haven't made up their mind. When you create a Web site that advocates a position, the ease of linking on the Web doesn't make your work any easier. Good arguments still require much thinking on your part and careful planning. You cannot expect your readers to do your work for you. You still have to supply good reasons.

Creating a Web Site

Creating a Web site used to be a chore because the files for the site had to be hand-coded in Hypertext Markup Language (HTML). HTML works in the same way early word processing programs worked. If you wanted boldface type, you had to insert a switch to turn on the boldfacing and another to turn off the boldfacing. HTML uses switches called tags. If you want to boldface a word, you have to insert <b> before the word and </b> after the word so it looks like this:

<div align="center"><b>**boldface**</b></div>

As word processing programs improved and computer memory expanded, you no longer had to insert tags in the text. Word processing programs displayed on the screen what gets printed on the page—known as WYSIWYG ("what you see is what you get").

Until recently, you had to know how to write HTML code to make Web pages. Now, you don't have to know any HTML to make Web pages. Web authoring software makes it very easy to compose Web pages. Most of them work much like word processing programs. When you want to make a heading or a link, you simply highlight that text with your mouse and then click to get what you want—bigger or smaller text, boldface, italics, centering, links, and so on. The most popular Web authoring programs are

- Netscape Composer (free as part of Netscape Communicator)
- Adobe PageMill
- Claris Home Page
- Microsoft FrontPage

One of the most popular Web authoring software programs for professional Web designers is Macromedia Dreamweaver. You may want to learn to use a professional software package if you intend to create extensive Web sites.

Tutorials and other guides show you how to put text on the Web, but they don't tell you how reading is different on the Web. In most printed books, magazines, and newspapers, the text is continuous. Printed text isn't necessarily linear—witness the boxes and sidebars in this book. While it's possible to go back and forth in print, the basic movement in print is linear and the basic unit is the paragraph. By contrast the basic movement on the Web is nonlinear and the basic unit is the screen. Perhaps the most important fact to remember is that fewer than 10 percent of people who click on a Web site ever scroll down the page. Their eyes stop at the bottom of the screen. And those who do scroll down usually don't scroll down very far.

THE FIRST SCREEN IS THE MOST IMPORTANT

People who browse Web sites don't stay long if they aren't interested or if it takes too long to find out what's on the Web site. That's why the first screen is critical. If you have something to tell your visitors, tell them right away. They probably aren't going to click through a bunch of screens or scroll though long stretches to find out where you stand on an issue. You have to let your readers know on the first screen what your site is about.

The first screen is also the front door to your site, and when visitors enter your front door, they need to know where to go next. Supplying navigation tools on the first page is critical. These can take the form of menu bars, buttons, or clickable images. Whatever form you choose, the labels should indicate what the visitor will find on the next screen.

The Web page in Figure 13.2 was created by Grace Bernhardt for a class project on the conflict surrounding the Balcones Canyonlands Preserve (BCP), a nature reserve located within the city limits of Austin, Texas, and the habitat for six endangered species. The text on the first page describes the place and the various stakeholders in the Balcones Canyonlands Preserve. It also provides a menu to the main areas of the site.

DIVIDE YOUR TEXT INTO CHUNKS

Long stretches of text on the Web tend not to get read. Part of the problem is that most people do not have large-screen monitors. For those people, reading text on the Web is like trying to read a newspaper through a three-inch-square hole. It's possible to do but not much fun. Newspapers grew to their present size because our eyes can take in a large expanse of information when we scan the page. Perhaps in the next few years, large-screen monitors will

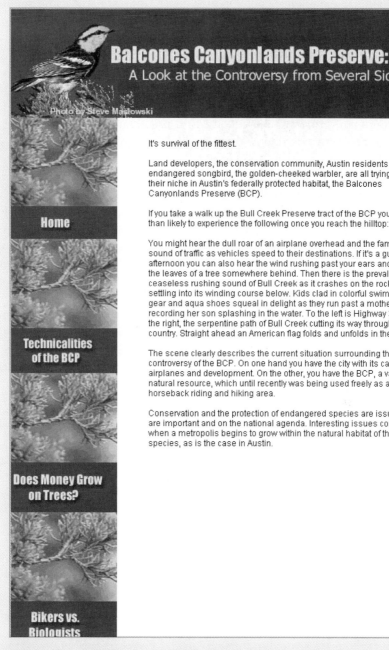

It's survival of the fittest.

Land developers, the conservation community, Austin residents and the endangered songbird, the golden-cheeked warbler, are all trying to find their niche in Austin's federally protected habitat, the Balcones Canyonlands Preserve (BCP).

If you take a walk up the Bull Creek Preserve tract of the BCP you're more than likely to experience the following once you reach the hilltop:

You might hear the dull roar of an airplane overhead and the familiar sound of traffic as vehicles speed to their destinations. If it's a gusty afternoon you can also hear the wind rushing past your ears and rustling the leaves of a tree somewhere behind. Then there is the prevalent, ceaseless rushing sound of Bull Creek as it crashes on the rocks before settling into its winding course below. Kids clad in colorful swimming gear and aqua shoes squeal in delight as they run past a mother recording her son splashing in the water. To the left is Highway 360, to the right, the serpentine path of Bull Creek cutting its way through the hill country. Straight ahead an American flag folds and unfolds in the wind.

The scene clearly describes the current situation surrounding the controversy of the BCP. On one hand you have the city with its cars, airplanes and development. On the other, you have the BCP, a valuable natural resource, which until recently was being used freely as a biking, horseback riding and hiking area.

Conservation and the protection of endangered species are issues that are important and on the national agenda. Interesting issues come up when a metropolis begins to grow within the natural habitat of these species, as is the case in Austin.

Figure 13.2   Balcones Canyonlands Preserve: A Look at the Controversy from Several Sides
http://www.tlc.utexas.edu/courses/2001s_321/bcp/p4d.htm

give us a similar experience, but for now, most of us are still using small-screen monitors.

Given the limitations of the monitors that most people now use, many Web designers try to divide text into chunks whenever possible. For example, when they present a list of facts, they often put space between items or use a bulleted list rather than a long paragraph. The page in Figure 13.3 is from a student Web site designed by Chungpei Hu on safety issues for Sixth Street, the entertainment district in Austin, Texas. It uses a bulleted list to enumerate frequent fire code violations in bars and clubs along Sixth Street.

You can put a great deal of background information on a Web site connected by links to the main argument. Thus you can offer a short summary on the main page with links to other pages that give background and evidence. One advantage of this strategy is that you design a single site both for those who know a great deal about the subject and want to skip the background information, and for those who know little and need to know the background. You can include additional evidence that would be hard to work into a paper otherwise. Furthermore, the act of clicking on particular words can make readers aware of the links in an argument.

But because text on the Web is usually truncated and readers skim quickly and jump from one page to another, it's more difficult to place a detailed, sustained argument on a Web site. Some people don't even try. They simply place a long text on the Web and assume those who are really inter-

Figure 13.3 Sixth Street Safety & Awareness
http://www.tlc.utexas.edu/courses/2001s_321/sixth_street/gateway.htm

ested will download that text, print it, and read it. Making that assumption, however, means risking losing all but the most interested readers on a particular subject. Readers increasingly expect arguments on the Web to be designed for the Web.

MAKE THE TEXT READABLE

Above all, make your text readable. Remember that other people's monitors may be smaller than yours; thus what appears as small type on your monitor may require a magnifying glass for others. Also, dark backgrounds make for tough reading. If you use a dark background and want people to read what you write, be sure to increase the font size, make sure the contrast between text and background is adequate, and avoid using all caps and italics.

TEXT IN ALL CAPS IS HARD TO READ ON A BLACK BACKGROUND,

ESPECIALLY IF THE TEXT IS IN ITALICS.

Stay Organized

When you decide to put up a Web site, it's critical that you do some planning in advance.

1. **Make an outline of your site.** You should draw on paper how you want your site organized.

2. **Collect all the source materials for your site.** These materials may include text and images. Keep the materials together in a manila folder. When you have this material in digital form, put it in a folder, labeled "Sources" or the name of your project, on your hard drive and on a backup disk.

3. **Use a system for naming files.** Use only lowercase letters because later you may forget which letters you capitalized. Don't use punctuation marks like semicolons, which have specific meanings

(continued)

you may not intend, because they may cause you problems down the road. All Web pages have to end in .htm (on PCs) or .html (on Macs). Label image files by their type, such as .gif (for GIF files) or .jpg (for JPEG files).

4. **Put your files in a folder.** You're going to put the files on your Web site server in a folder just like you do on your computer. The simplest way is to put the whole folder on the server when you are ready. You probably will need only one folder, but if you are creating a site that may become bigger down the road, you might think about using more than one folder.

5. **Save, save, save.** It always is a good idea to make backup copies. You should make copies on a diskette or even better, on a Zip disk, which can store large files.

Principles of Web Design

When you design your Web site, you have many tools available that you don't have with ordinary text. You can add graphics and create links to your own pages and pages made by others. When you become more advanced, you can even add animations and audio and video clips. Pictures and other multimedia elements can make your Web site appealing and give your content visual impact. But pictures that do not contribute to your content can also be confusing, distracting readers from the substance of your argument. Furthermore, pictures and graphics also have a great deal to do with the performance of your site—how long it takes for pages to load on the screen.

DETERMINE THE VISUAL THEME OF YOUR SITE

Most Web sites contain more than one page, and because it is so easy to move from one page to another on the Web, it's important to make your site as unified as possible. Using common design elements, such as color, icons, typeface, and layout, contributes to the unity of the site. The Balcones Canyonlands Preserves site shown in Figure 13.2 repeats the image of its most famous resident—the endangered golden-cheeked warbler—on each page, along with images of foliage. Even without the text, the images on the site make it evident that the site deals with environmental issues.

DIRECT THE VIEWER'S EYES

The design principles we discuss in Chapter 12 also apply to Web design, with one important addition. The top of a Web page is even more critical than the top of a printed page because, as discussed earlier, many people have monitors that do not display an entire Web page. And because many people never scroll down, you have to pay special attention to the top of the page.

Many Web pages use jarring colors for striking effects—hot pinks and fluorescent greens on black backgrounds. Many others have visually intense backgrounds that distract from the text or make the text hard to read. If you want people to read your text, you have to use lighter tones for backgrounds and supporting images. Reserve the bright colors for points you most wish to emphasize or avoid bright colors altogether, as they may overwhelm the rest of the text on your site.

KEEP THE VISUALS SIMPLE

The students who produced the Web sites in this chapter could have included many large pictures if they had chosen to. But they deliberately kept the visual design simple. A less complicated site is not only more friendly because it loads faster, but if it is well designed, it can be elegant. Simple elements are also easier to repeat. Too many icons, bullets, horizontal rules, and other embellishments give a page a cluttered appearance. A simple, consistent design is always effective for pages that contain text.

Finally, keep in mind that although good graphic design provides visual impact and can help the visitor navigate a Web site, it has little value if it is not supported by substance. People still expect to come away from a Web site with substantial information. Good visual design makes your Web site more appealing, but it does not do the work of argument for you.

NAVIGATIONAL DESIGN

People don't read Web sites the same way they read a book. They scan quickly and move around a lot. They don't necessarily read from top to bottom. If you are trying to make an argument on the Web, you have to think differently about how the reader is going to encounter your argument. If you

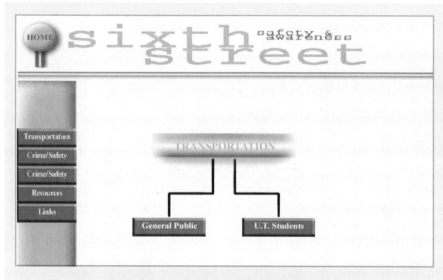

Figure 13.4   Sixth Street Safety & Awareness
*http://www.tlc.utexas.edu/courses/2001s_321/sixth_street/html/transportation/
transportation.htm*

put the argument on more than one page, you have to plan the site so that readers can navigate easily.

Designing navigational tools for your Web site is a three-step process. First, you should decide on the overall structure of your Web site, assuming you plan to include more than one page. Web sites that have a main page should have clear navigation tools. For example, the transportation section of Sixth Street Safety & Awareness (Figure 13.4) offers sections for both the general public and University of Texas students. The navigation icons make the possibilities obvious.

Audience Considerations on the Web

A Web site can potentially reach millions of people, which is its greatest benefit but at the same time can present a major difficulty in planning your site. The concept of audience becomes more complicated on the Web. Not only do you not know who will click on your Web site, but you also don't know exactly how each visitor will see or hear what you put up. Some people will have the latest Web browsers, powerful computers, big-screen monitors, and very fast ethernet, DSL, or cable modem connections. Others may be connecting to your Web site by slow dial-up modem connections and may have older, less-powerful computers that cannot run the latest versions of Web browsers. You can include sound, image, and even movie files, but not everyone can download these files. If you want all your visitors to see everything on your Web site without waiting minutes for your pages to load, you have to think about them when you are designing your site. The Sixth Street Safety & Awareness site (Figures 13.3 and 13.4) is posted in two versions, allowing those with fast and slow connections to experience the site.

A famous architect, Ludwig Mies van der Rohe, once said "less is more." He was talking about a general principle for the design of buildings: Simple is better. This principle is a good one to keep in mind when you are designing your Web site. "Less is more" means using fewer, simpler typefaces, fewer colors, and fewer potentially distracting elements. On the Web, less size also means more speed. So we might change van der Rohe's aphorism to "less is faster." Pay attention to size when you put images on the Web. Smaller images not only load faster but they also look better.

Evaluating a Web Site

You can use the following criteria to evaluate Web sites you have designed or those designed by others.

1. **Audience:** How does the site identify its intended audience? How does it indicate what else is on the site?

2. **Content:** How informative is the content? Where might more content be added? What do you want to know more about? Are there any mechanical, grammar, or style problems?

3. **Readability:** Is there sufficient contrast between the text and the background to make it legible? Are the margins wide enough? Are there any paragraphs that go on too long and need to be divided? Are headings inserted in the right places, and if headings are used for more than one level, are these levels indicated consistently? Is text in boldface and all caps kept short?

4. **Visual Design:** Does the site have a consistent visual theme? Where is the focal point on each page? Do the images contribute to the visual appeal or do they detract from it?

5. **Navigation:** How easy or difficult is it to move from one page to another on the site? Are there any broken links?

CHAPTER 14

Effective Oral Presentations

Becoming effective in oral communication is just as important as in written communication. You may be asked to give oral presentations in your later life and perhaps in your college career. Oral presentations can be developed from written assignments and supported by visual elements such as slides, overheads, film clips, and other media.

Planning an Oral Presentation

GETTING STARTED

Successful oral presentations, like written arguments, require careful planning. You first step is to find out what kind of oral presentation you are being asked to give. Kinds of oral presentations include the following:

- **Persuasive speeches** attempt to change the audience's attitudes and beliefs or convince them that a particular course of action is best.

- **Informative speeches** explain a subject or demonstrate a process.
- **Entertaining speeches** keep the audience's attention with stories and jokes.
- **Debates** directly confront an opposing viewpoint.
- **Group presentations** involve team members who present aspects of a subject individually.

Look closely at your assignment. If the kind of presentation is not stated explicitly, words such as *argue for*, *report*, and *propose* are important clues about what is expected.

Another important consideration is length. How much time you have to give a speech determines the depth you can go into. Speakers who ignore this simple principle often announce near the end of their time that they will have to omit major points and rush to finish. Their presentations end abruptly and leave the audience confused about what the speaker had to say.

You also should consider early on where you will be giving the speech. If you want to use visual elements to support your presentation, you need to make sure the room has the equipment you need. If you know the room is large or has poor acoustics, you will need to bring audio equipment. If you know the visual equipment available is inadequate or the lighting is difficult to control you may choose not to use presentation software or overheads. You often can adjust for room conditions if you plan in advance.

SELECTING YOUR TOPIC

Choosing and researching a topic for an oral presentation is similar to choosing and researching a topic for a written assignment. If you have a broad choice of topics, make a list of subjects that interest you. Then go through your list and ask yourself these questions:

- Will you enjoy speaking on this topic?
- Will your audience be interested in this topic?
- Does the topic fit the situation for your presentation?
- Do you know enough to speak on this topic?
- If you do not know enough, are you willing to do research to learn more about the topic?

Remember that enthusiasm is contagious, so if you are excited about a topic, chances are your audience will become interested too.

Research for an oral presentation is similar to the research you must do for a written argument. You will find guidelines in Chapter 15 for planning your research. Remember that you will need to develop a bibliography for an oral presentation that requires research just as you would for a written argument. You will need to document the sources of your information and provide those sources in your talk.

Thinking About Your Audience

Unlike writing, when you give a speech, you have your audience directly before you. They will give you concrete feedback during your presentation by smiling or frowning, by paying attention or losing interest, by asking questions or sitting passively.

When planning your presentation, you should think about the general characteristics of your audience.

- What is the age range of your audience?
- What occupations are represented?
- What is the likely mix of men and women?
- What is the educational background?
- What is the ethnic and cultural background?

You should also think about your audience in relation to your topic.

- Will your audience be interested in your topic?
- Are there ways you can get them more interested?
- What is your audience likely to know or believe about your topic?
- What does your audience probably not know about your topic?
- What key terms will you have to define or explain?
- What assumptions do you hold in common with your audience (such as political or religious beliefs, or business philosophy)?
- Where is your audience most likely to disagree with you?
- What questions are they likely to ask?

Supporting Your Presentation

The steps for writing listed in Part 2 can be used to organize an oral presentation. When you have organized your main points, you need to decide how to support those points. Look at your research notes and think about how best to incorporate the information you found. Consider using one or more of these strategies:

- **Facts.** Speakers who know their facts build credibility.

- **Statistics.** Good use of statistics gives the impression that the speaker has done his or her homework. Statistics also can indicate that a particular example is representative. One tragic car accident doesn't mean a road is dangerous, but an especially high accident rate relative to other nearby roads does make the case.

- **Statements by authorities.** Quotations from credible experts are another common way of supporting key points.

- **Narratives.** Narratives are small stories that can illustrate key points. Narratives are a good way of keeping the attention of the audience. Keep them short so they don't distract from your major points.

- **Humor.** In most situations audiences appreciate humor. Humor is a good way to convince an audience that you have common beliefs and experiences, and that your argument may be one they can agree with.

Planning Your Introduction

No part of your speech is more critical than the introduction. You have to get the audience's attention, introduce your topic, convince the audience that it is important to them, present your thesis, and give your audience either an overview of your presentation or a sense of your direction. Accomplishing all this in a short time is a tall order, but if you lose your audience in the first two minutes, you won't recover their attention. You might begin with a compelling example or anecdote that both introduces your topic and indicates your stance.

Planning Your Conclusion

The next most important part of your speech is your conclusion. You want to end on a strong note. First, you need to signal that you are entering the conclusion. You can announce that you are concluding, but you also can give signals in other ways. Touching on your main points again will help your audience to remember them. But simply summarizing is a dull way to close. Think of an example or an idea that captures the gist of your speech, something that your audience can take away with them.

Delivering an Oral Presentation

THE IMPORTANCE OF PRACTICE

There is no substitute for rehearsing your speech several times in advance. You will become more confident and have more control over the content. The best way to overcome nervousness about speaking in front of others is to be well prepared. When you know what you are going to say, you can pay more attention to your audience, making eye contact and watching body language for signals about how well you are making your points. When you rehearse you can also become comfortable with any visual elements you will be using. Finally, rehearsing your speech is the only reliable way to find out how long it will take to deliver.

Practice your speech in front of others. If possible, go to the room where you will be speaking and ask a friend to sit in the back so you can learn how well you can be heard. You can also learn a great deal by videotaping your rehearsal and watching yourself as an audience member.

SPEAKING EFFECTIVELY

Talking is so much a part of our daily lives that we rarely think about our voices as instruments of communication unless we have some training in acting or public speaking. You can become better at speaking by becoming more aware of your delivery. Pay attention to your breathing as you practice your speech. When you breathe at your normal rate, you will not rush your speech. Plan where you will pause during your speech. Pauses allow you to take a sip of water and give your audience a chance to sum up mentally what you have said. And don't be afraid to repeat key points. Repetition is one of the easiest strategies for achieving emphasis.

Most of the time nervousness is invisible. You can feel nervous and still impress your audience as being calm and confident. If you make mistakes while speaking, know that the audience understands and will be forgiving.

Stage fright is normal; sometimes it can be helpful in raising the energy level of a presentation.

NONVERBAL COMMUNICATION

While you are speaking, you are also communicating with your presence. Stand up unless you are required to sit. Move around instead of standing behind the podium. Use gestures to emphasize main points, and only main points; if you gesture continually, you may appear nervous.

Maintaining eye contact is crucial. Begin your speech by looking at the people directly in front of you and then move your eyes around the room, looking to both sides. Attempting to look at each person during a speech may seem unnatural, but it is the best way to convince all the members of your audience that you are speaking directly to them.

For Effective Speeches

Usually more effective	Usually less effective
Practice in advance	Don't practice
Talk	Read
Stand	Sit
Make eye contact	Look down
Move around	Stand still
Speak loudly	Mumble
Use visual elements	Lack visual elements
Focus on main points	Get lost in details
Give an overview of what you are going to say in the introduction	Start your talk without indicating where you are headed
Give a conclusion that summarizes your main points and ends with a key idea or example	Stop abruptly
Finish on time	Run overtime

HANDLING QUESTIONS

Your presentation doesn't end when you finish. Speakers are usually expected to answer questions afterward. How you handle questions is also critical to your success. Speakers who are evasive or fail to acknowledge questions sometimes lose all the credibility they have built in their speech. But speakers who listen carefully to questions and answer them honestly build their credibility further.

Keep in mind a few principles about handling questions:

- Repeat the question so that the entire audience can hear it and to confirm you understood it.
- Take a minute to reflect on the question. If you do not understand the question, ask the questioner to restate it.
- Some people will make a small speech instead of asking a question. Acknowledge their point of view but avoid getting into a debate.
- If you cannot answer a question, don't bluff and don't apologize. You can offer to research the question or you can ask the audience if they know the answer.
- If you are asked a question during your speech, answer it if it is a short, factual question or one of clarification. Postpone questions that require long answers until the end to avoid losing the momentum of your speech.

Multimedia Presentations

VISUAL ELEMENTS

Visual elements can both support and reinforce your major points. They give you another means of reaching your audience and keeping them stimulated. Visual elements range from simple transparencies and handouts to elaborate multimedia presentations. Some of the easier visual elements to create are

- Outlines
- Text
- Statistical charts
- Flow charts

- Photographs
- Models
- Maps

At the very minimum, you should consider putting an outline of your talk on an overhead transparency. Some speakers think that they will kill interest in their talk if they show the audience what they are going to say in advance. Just the opposite is the case. An outline allows an audience to keep track of where you are in your talk. Outlines also help you to make transitions to your next point.

Most printers can make transparencies from blank transparency sheets fed through the paper feeder. Charts, maps, photographs, and other graphics in digital format can thus be printed onto transparencies. Many photocopiers can also make transparencies.

Keep the amount of text short. You don't want your audience straining to read long passages on the screen and neglecting what you have to say. Except for quotations, use single words and short phrases—not sentences—on transparencies and slides.

Readable Transparencies and Slides

If you put text on transparencies or slides, make sure that the audience can read the text from more than 10 feet away. You may depend on your transparencies and slides to convey important information, but if your audience cannot read the slides, not only will the information be lost but the audience will become frustrated.

Use these type sizes for transparencies and slides.

	Transparencies	Slides
Title:	36 pt	24 pt
Subtitles:	24 pt	18 pt
Other text:	18 pt	14 pt

Preview your transparencies and slides from a distance equal to the rear of the room where you will be speaking. If you cannot read them, increase the type size.

One major difficulty with visual elements is that they tempt you to look at the screen instead of at your audience. You have to face your audience while your audience is looking at the screen. Needless to say, you have to practice to feel comfortable.

PRESENTATION SOFTWARE

You likely have seen many presentations that use Microsoft PowerPoint because it has become a favorite of faculty who lecture. If you have Microsoft Word on your computer, you likely have PowerPoint since they are often bundled together. PowerPoint is straightforward to use, which is one of the reasons it has become so popular. You can quickly get an outline of your presentation onto slides, and if projection equipment is available in the room where you are speaking, the slides are easily displayed.

PowerPoint offers a choice of many backgrounds, which is a potential pitfall. Light text on a dark background is hard to read. It forces you to close every window and turn off all the lights in order for your audience to see the text. Darkened rooms create problems. You may have difficulty reading your notes in a dark room, and your audience may fall asleep. Instead, always use dark text on a white or light-colored background. Usually your audience can read your slides with a light background in a room with the shades up or lights on.

Usually you can leave a slide on the screen for about one to two minutes, which allows your audience time to read and connect the slide to what you are saying. You will need to practice to know when to display a new slide. Without adequate practice, you can easily get too far ahead or behind in your slide show and then be forced to interrupt yourself to get your slides back in synch with your speech. You also need to know how to darken the screen if you want the audience to focus on you during parts of your presentation.

Another pitfall of PowerPoint is getting carried away with all the special effects possible such as fade-ins, fade-outs, and sound effects. Presentations heavy on the special effects often come off as heavy on style and light on substance. They also can be time-consuming to produce.

CHAPTER 15

Effective Research

Research: Knowing What Information You Need

The writing that you do in school sometimes seems isolated from the real world. After all, when you write for a class, your real audience is usually the teacher. For the same reason, the research associated with writing for school tends to get isolated from real-world problems. Instead of asking questions such as how compounds that mimic estrogen might be causing reproductive abnormalities in certain animal species, students ask questions such as "What do I need to know to write this paper?" This approach tends to separate research from writing. If you've ever said to yourself, "I'll go to the library to do the research tonight, and then tomorrow afternoon I'll start writing the paper," you might be making some assumptions about the nature of research and writing that will actually make your task harder instead of easier. So for now, set aside what you already know about how to do research and think instead in terms of gathering information to solve problems and answer questions.

Effective research depends on two things: knowing what kind of information you are looking for and knowing where to get it. What you already know about writing arguments will help you to make some decisions about what kind of information you should be looking for. For instance, if you have decided to write a proposal for solving the problem of HMOs limiting sub-scribers' health care options, you already know that you will need to find sta-tistics (to help your readers understand the urgency and scope of the prob-lem) and several different analyses of the situation by writers from different camps (to help you make sure your own understanding of the situation is ac-curate, complete, and fair to all participants). But if you keep thinking about the demands of the proposal as a type of argument, you might also decide that you need to look at how this problem has been solved in the British or Canadian health system or how programs like Medicare and Medicaid are dealing with it.

Even if you don't yet know enough about your subject to know what type of argument you will want to write, there are still some basic questions you can use to plan your research. To make a thoughtful and mature contri-bution to any debate in the realm of public discourse, you will need to know the background of the issue. As you begin your research, then, you can use the following questions as a guide.

1. Who are the speakers on this issue and what are they saying?

Subdividing the group of everyone who has something to say on this issue and everything that is being said into narrower categories will help you to gain a better understanding of what the debate looks like. For example, you might make the following divisions:

- Who are the experts on this issue? What do the experts say?
- Who else is talking about it? What do they say?
- Are the people whose interests are most at stake participating in the debate? What are they saying?

In addition to the categories of experts, nonexpert speakers, and those whose interests are at stake, there are other general categories you can begin from, such as supporters and opponents of a position, liberals and conservatives, and so on.

Also remember that any given debate will have its own specific set of opponents. In a debate about constructing a storage facility for nuclear waste in Nevada, for instance, conservationists and proponents of growth in the state of Nevada are lining up against the federal government. On another significant issue—water usage—proponents of growth stand in opposition to conservationists, who object to the demands Las Vegas makes on the waters of the Colorado River. On yet other issues, conservationists depend on the federal government to use its power to protect land, water, and other re-sources that are vulnerable to the activities of businesses and individuals.

2. What is at stake?

Political debates often boil down to arguments about control of, or access to, resources or power. Therefore, resources and power are good places to start looking for what is at stake in any given debate. Depending on the nature of the debate, you might also look at what is at stake in terms of ethical and moral issues. For example, as a country and as a human community, what does this nation stand to lose if a whole generation of African-American urban young people grows up alienated from other people in the United States? To help narrow down your search, you might rephrase this question in several different ways:

- How or why does this issue matter: to the world, to the citizens of this country, to the people whose interests are at stake, to me?
- What stands to be gained or lost for any of these stakeholders?
- Who is likely to be helped and hurt the most?

3. What kinds of arguments are being made about this issue?

Just as it is helpful to subdivide the whole field of speakers on your issue into narrower groups that line up according to sides, it is also helpful to subdivide the whole field of what is being said according to types or categories of arguments. It might help to set up a chart of speakers and their primary arguments to see how they line up.

- What are the main claims being offered?
- What reasons are offered in support of these claims?
- What are the primary sources of evidence?
- Is some significant aspect of this issue being ignored or displaced in favor of others?
- If so, why?

4. Who are the audiences for this debate?

Sometimes, the audience for a debate is every responsible member of society, everyone living in a certain region, or everyone who cares about the fate of the human species on this planet. More often, however, arguments are made to specific types of audiences, and knowing something about those audiences can help you to understand the choices that the writers make. Even more important, knowing who is already part of the audience for a debate can help you to plan your own strategies.

- Do you want to write to one of the existing audiences to try to change its mind or make it take action?
- Or do you want to try to persuade a new, as-yet-uninvolved audience to get involved in the debate?
- How much do they know about the issues involved?
- Where do they likely stand on these issues?
- Will they define the issues the same way you do?

5. What is your role?

At some point, as you continue to research the issue and plan your writing strategies, you will need to decide what your role should be in this debate. Ask yourself:

- What do I think about it?
- What do I think should be done about it?
- What kind of argument should I write, and to whom?

What Makes a Good Subject for Research

- **Find a subject that you are interested in.** Research can be enjoyable if you are finding out new things rather than just confirming what you already know. The most exciting part of doing research is making small discoveries.

(continued)

What Makes a Good Subject for Research *(continued)*

- **Make sure that you can do a thorough job of research.** If you select a topic that is too broad, such as proposing how to end poverty, you will not be able to do an adequate job.

- **Develop a strategy for your research early on.** If you are researching a campus issue such as a parking problem, then you probably will rely most on interviews, observations, and possibly a survey. But if you find out that one of the earliest baseball stadiums, Lakefront Park in Chicago (built in 1883), had the equivalent of today's luxury boxes and you want to make an argument that the trend toward building stadiums with luxury boxes is not a new development, then you will have to do library research.

- **Give yourself enough time to do a thorough job.** You should expect to find a few dead ends, and you should expect to better focus your subject as you proceed. If you are going to do research in the field, by survey, or in the library, remember the first principle of doing research: *Things take longer than you think they will.*

Use these questions to take inventory of how much you already know about the issue and what you need to find out more about. When you have worked through these questions, you are ready to make a claim that will guide your research efforts. See the Steps in Writing exercises at the end of Chapters 5 through 10 to get started.

Planning Your Research

Once you have a general idea about the kind of information you need to make your argument, the next step is to decide where to look for it. People who write on the job—lawyers preparing briefs, journalists covering news stories, policy analysts preparing reports, engineers describing a manufacturing process, members of Congress reporting to committees, and a host of others—have general research strategies available to them. The first is to gather the information themselves, which is called **primary** or **firsthand evidence.** We can distinguish two basic kinds of primary research.

Experiential research involves all the information you gather just through observing and taking note of events as they occur in the real world. You meet with clients, interview a candidate, go to a committee meeting, talk to coworkers, read a report from a colleague, observe a manufacturing process, witness an event, or examine a patient. In all these ways, you are adding to your store of knowledge about a problem or issue. In many cases, however, the knowledge that is gained through experience is not enough to answer all the questions or solve all the problems. In that case, writers supplement experiential research with empirical research and research in the library.

Empirical research is a way of gathering specific and narrowly defined data by developing a test situation and then observing and recording events as they occur in the test situation. Analysis of tissue samples and cell cultures in a laboratory, for instance, can add important information to what a doctor can learn by examining a patient. Crash tests of cars help automakers and materials engineers understand why crumpling is an important part of a car's ability to protect its passengers in a crash. Surveys of adult children of divorced parents make it possible for psychologists to identify the long-term effects of divorce on family members. Many people believe that this kind of research is what adds new information to the store of human knowledge; so for many audiences, reporting the results of empirical research is an important part of making a strong argument. (Therefore, writers often use statistics and reports of research done by experts in the field to support their claims.)

For the most part, however, debates about public issues occur outside the fairly narrow intellectual spaces occupied by the true experts in any given field. Experts do, of course, participate in public debates, but so do all other interested citizens and policymakers. The majority of speakers on an issue rely on the work of others as sources of information—what is known as **secondary** or **secondhand evidence.** Many people think of library research as secondary research—the process of gathering information by reading what other people have written on a subject. In the past, library research was based almost exclusively on collections of printed materials housed in libraries; in addition to public and university libraries, organizations of all kinds had their own collections of reference materials specific to their work. Today, the Internet has brought significant changes in the way people record, store, view, distribute, and gain access to documents. For most issues, searching the Internet will be an important part of your library research.

Interviews, Observations, and Surveys

Interviews

■ Decide first why one or more interviews could be important for your argument. Knowing the goals of your interview will help you to determine whom you need to interview and to structure the questions in the interview. You might, for example, learn more about the history of a campus issue than you were able to find out in the campus newspaper archives.

■ Schedule each interview in advance, preferably by email or letter. Let the person know why you are conducting the interview. Then follow up with a phone call to find out whether the person is willing and what he or she might be able to tell you.

■ Plan your questions. You should have a few questions in mind as well as written down. Listen carefully so that you can follow up on key points.

■ Come prepared with at least a notebook and pencil. If you use a tape recorder, be sure to get the person's permission in advance and be sure that the equipment is working.

Observations

■ Make detailed observations that you can link to your claim. For example, if you believe that the long lines in your student services building are caused by inefficient use of staff, you could observe how many staff members are on duty at peak and slack times.

■ Choose a place where you can observe without intrusion. Public places work best because you can sit for a long time without people wondering what you are doing.

■ Carry a notebook and write extensive notes whenever you can. Write down as much as you can. Be sure to record where you were, the date, exactly when you arrived and left, and important details such as the number of people present.

(continued)

Interviews, Observations, and Surveys *(continued)*

Surveys

- Like interview questions, questions on surveys should relate directly to the issue of your argument. Take some time to decide what exactly you want to know first.

- Write a few specific, unambiguous questions. The people you contact should be able to fill out your survey quickly, and they should not have to guess what a question means. It's always a good idea to test the questions on a few people to find out whether they are clear before you conduct the survey.

- You might include one or two open-ended questions, such as "What do you like about X?" or "What don't you like about X?" Answers to these questions can be difficult to interpret, but sometimes they provide insights.

- Decide whom you want to participate in your survey and how you will contact them. If you are going to use your survey results to claim that the people surveyed represent the views of undergraduates at your school, then you should match the gender, ethnic, and racial balance to the proportions at your school.

- If you are going to mail or email your survey, include a statement about what the survey is for and how the results will be used.

- Interpreting your results should be straightforward if your questions require definite responses. Multiple-choice formats make data easy to tabulate, but they often miss key information. If you included one or more open-ended questions, you need to figure out a way to analyze responses.

Finding What You Are Looking for in Print Sources

Large libraries can be intimidating, even to experienced researchers when they begin working on a new subject. You can save time and frustration if you have some idea of how you want to proceed when you enter the library.

Libraries have two major kinds of sources: books and periodicals. Periodicals include a range of items from daily newspapers to scholarly journals that are bound and put on the shelves like books.

Most books are shelved according to the Library of Congress Classification System, which uses a combination of letters and numbers to give you the book's unique location in the library. The Library of Congress call number begins with a letter or letters that represent the broad subject area into which the book is classified. The Library of Congress system has the advantage of shelving books on the same subject together, so you can sometimes find additional books by browsing in the stacks. You can use the *Library of Congress Subject Headings*, available in print in your library's reference area or on the Web (http://lcweb.loc.gov), to help you find out how your subject might be indexed.

If you want to do research on cloning, you might type "cloning" in the subject index of your online card catalog, which would yield something like the following results:

1 Cloning—23 item(s)

2 Cloning—Bibliography.—1 item(s)

3 Cloning—Congresses.—2 item(s)

4 Cloning—Fiction.—6 item(s)

5 Cloning—Government policy—United States.—2 item(s)

6 Cloning—History.—1 item(s)

7 Cloning, Molecular—36 item(s) Indexed as: MOLECULAR CLONING

8 Cloning—Moral and ethical aspects.—13 item(s)

9 Cloning—Moral and ethical aspects—Government policy—United States.—1 item(s)

10 Cloning—Moral and ethical aspects—United States.—2 item(s)

11 Cloning—Religious aspects—Christianity.—2 item(s)

12 Cloning—Research—History.—1 item(s)

13 Cloning—Research—Law and legislation—United States.—1 item(s)

14 Cloning—Research—United States—Finance.—1 item(s)

15 Cloning—Social aspects.—1 item(s)

16 Cloning—United States—Religious aspects.—1 item(s)

This initial search helps you to identify more precisely what you are looking for. If you are most interested in the ethical aspects of cloning, then the books listed under number 8 would be most useful to you.

Finding articles in periodicals works much the same way. To find relevant newspaper and magazine articles, use a periodical index. These indexes are located in the reference area of your library. They may be in print form, on CD-ROM, or sometimes available on your library's Web site. General indexes that list citations to articles on popular and current topics include

> *ArticleFirst* (electronic)
>
> *CARL Uncover* (electronic)
>
> *Expanded Academic ASAP* (electronic)
>
> *InfoTrac* (electronic)
>
> *Lexis/Nexis* (electronic)
>
> *Readers' Guide to Periodical Literature* (print)
>
> *Periodical Abstracts* (electronic)
>
> *ProQuest* (electronic)

Some of these indexes contain the full text of articles, which you can print out. Others will give you a reference, which you then have to find in your library. In addition to these general periodical indexes, there are many specialized indexes that list citations to journal articles in various fields. Deciding which kind of articles you want to look for—scholarly, trade, or popular—will help you to select the right index.

Follow these steps to find articles:

1. Select an index that is appropriate to your subject.
2. Search the index using the relevant subject heading(s).
3. Print or copy the complete citation to the article(s).
4. Check the periodicals holdings to see whether your library has the journal.

Scholarly, Trade, and Popular Journals

Some indexes give citations for only one kind of journal. Others include more than one type. Although the difference between types of journals is not always obvious, you should be able to judge whether a journal is scholarly, trade, or popular by its characteristics.

Characteristics of Scholarly Journals

- Articles are long with few illustrations.
- Articles are written by scholars in the field, usually affiliated with a university or research center.
- Articles have footnotes or a works-cited list at the end.
- Articles usually report original research.
- Authors write in the language of their discipline, and readers are assumed to know a great deal about the field.
- Scholarly journals contain relatively few advertisements.

Examples: *American Journal of Mathematics, College English, JAMA: Journal of the American Medical Association, Plasma Physics*

Characteristics of Trade Journals

- Articles are frequently related to practical job concerns.
- Articles usually do not report original research.
- Articles usually do not have footnotes or have relatively few footnotes.

(continued)

Scholarly, Trade, and Popular Journals (continued)

- Items of interest to people in particular professions and job listings are typical features.

- Advertisements are aimed at people in the specific field.

Examples: *Advertising Age, Industry Week, Macworld, Teacher Magazine*

Characteristics of Popular Journals

- Articles are short and often illustrated with color photographs.

- Articles seldom have footnotes or acknowledge where their information came from.

- Authors are usually staff writers for the magazine or freelance writers.

- Advertisements are aimed at the general public.

- Copies can be bought at newsstands.

Examples: *Cosmopolitan, Newsweek, Sports Illustrated, GQ, People*

Finding What You Are Looking for in Electronic Sources

If you are familiar with searchable electronic databases like your library's catalog, you might want to think of the Internet as just another database. However, there are two significant differences between the Internet and your library's catalog and other indexes you might have used in the library. The first difference, obviously, is that while catalogs and indexes of print material give you information *about* books, articles, and other resources, they don't usually contain the documents themselves. An Internet search, on the other hand, can give you direct access to sources that are available all over the world. In the early days of public access to the Internet, when Internet resources were very limited and not as useful as readily available print resources, the Internet was not very helpful in most areas of research. But as the Internet grows up, it is becoming accepted as a legitimate—and even essential—part of our ability to record and share knowledge.

The other significant difference between the Internet and other research databases is that while only "authorized personnel" can add entries to or delete them from a traditional database, anyone who has access to a server can create a Web site (add an entry), and anyone who has a Web site can shut it down (delete an entry) or move it to a different location. There are literally millions of Web sites (entries) in the Internet's giant database, and sites are being added, moved, and deleted every day. To navigate this global library, we have search engines, programs that are so fast and sophisticated that they can sort through the wealth of available material and return a list of sites that match your search request (called *hits*) within seconds if you have a fast connection.

KINDS OF SEARCH ENGINES

A search engine is a set of programs that sort through millions of items with incredible speed. There are four basic kinds of search engines.

1. **Keyword search engines** (e.g., AltaVista, Google, Hotbot, Lycos). Keyword search engines use both a **robot**, which moves through the Web capturing information about Web sites, and an **indexer**, which organizes the information found by the robot. Each keyword search engine gives different results because each assigns different weights to the information it finds. These search engines often use words in the title of a Web site or words in a meta tag to order the results they report.

2. **Web directories** (e.g., Britannica, Galaxy, LookSmart, WebCrawler, Yahoo!). Web directories classify Web sites into categories and are the closest equivalent to the cataloging system used by libraries. On most directories professional editors decide how to index a particular Web site. Web directories also allow keyword searches.

3. **Metasearch agents** (e.g., Dogpile, Mamma, Metacrawler, ProFusion, SavvySearch). Metasearch agents allow you to use several search engines simultaneously. While the concept is sound, metasearch agents are limited by the number of hits they can return and their inability to handle advanced searches.

4. **Natural language search engines** (e.g., Ask Jeeves). Natural or real language search engines allow you to search by asking questions such as "Where can I find a recipe for pound cake?" Natural language search engines are still in their infancy, and no doubt they will become much more powerful in the future.

Search Engines

If you don't have much experience with search engines, try out a few different ones until you find one or two favorites, then learn how to use them well. Keyword search engines can be frustrating because they turn up so much, but you become better at using them with practice.

- To start your search, open your browser and select "Search." You may be offered a selection of Web navigators and search engines.

- To use a keyword search, enter a word, name, or phrase. Some search engines require quotation marks to indicate a phrase or full name. If you type Gwyneth Paltrow without quotation marks, you will get hits for all instances of Gwyneth and all instances of Paltrow.

(continued)

Search Engines *(continued)*

- When you want the search to retrieve any form of a word, for example both child and children, you can use "child*" to get both terms. The asterisk is sometimes referred to as a wild card.

- Most search engines will retrieve only exact matches to the terms you use in your search request. Try all the variations you can think of if you want to do a thorough search.

- Some search engines use a plus sign (+) to indicate that a term is required (as in "+ADHD +children") and a minus sign (–) to indicate that sites containing that term should not be included. For example, "+ADHD –children" will exclude sites on ADHD that mention children. Other search engines use AND, OR, and NOT in capital letters. The pluses, minuses, ANDs, ORs, and NOTs, are called Boolean operators.

- Use the search tips or help button on a search engine for particular advice.

Evaluating Sources

Not only is the volume of information on the Web overwhelming, but the quality varies a great deal too. No one polices the Web; therefore a great deal of misinformation is posted.

The reliability and relevance of sources are not new problems with the Web. Print sources also contain their share of biased, inaccurate, and misleading information. Other print sources may be accurate but not suited to the purpose of your project. A critical review can help you to sort through the sources you have gathered. Even though print and Internet sources differ in many ways, some basic principles of evaluation can be applied to both.

Traditional Criteria for Evaluating Print Sources

Over the years librarians have developed criteria for evaluating print sources.

1. *Source.* Who printed the book or article? Scholarly books that are published by university presses and articles in scholarly journals are assessed by

experts in the field before they are published. Because of this strict review process, they contain generally reliable information. But since the review process takes time, scholarly books and articles are not the most current sources. For people outside the field, they also have the disadvantage of being written for other experts. Serious trade books and journals are also generally reliable, though magazines devoted to politics often have an obvious bias. Popular magazines and books vary in quality. Often, they are purchased for their entertainment value, and they tend to emphasize what is sensational or entertaining at the expense of accuracy and comprehensiveness. Many magazines and books are published to represent the viewpoint of a particular group or company, so that bias should be taken into account. Newspapers also vary in quality. National newspapers, such as the *New York Times*, *Washington Post*, and *Los Angeles Times*, employ fact checkers and do a thorough editorial review and thus tend to be more reliable than newspapers that lack such resources.

2. **Author.** Who wrote the book or article? Is the author's name mentioned? Are the author's qualifications listed?

3. **Timeliness.** How current is the source? Obviously, if you are researching a fast-developing subject such as cloning, then currency is very important. But if you are interested in an issue that happened years ago, then currency might not be as important.

4. **Evidence.** How adequate is the evidence to support the author's claims? Where does the evidence come from—interviews, observations, surveys, experiments, expert testimony, or counterarguments? Does the author acknowledge any other ways in which the evidence might be interpreted?

5. **Biases.** Can you detect particular biases of the author? Is the author forthright about his or her biases? How do the author's biases affect the interpretation that is offered?

6. **Advertising.** Is the advertising prominent in the journal or newspaper? Is there any way that ads might affect what gets printed? For example, some magazines that ran many tobacco ads refused to run stories about the dangers of smoking.

Traditional print criteria can be helpful in evaluating some Internet sources. For example, if you evaluate messages sent to a Usenet newsgroup, most do not list the qualifications of the author or offer any support for the validity of evidence. Sources on the Web, however, present other difficulties. Some of these are inherent in the structure of the Web, with its capability for linking to other pages. When you are at a site that contains many links, you often find that some links go to pages on the same site but others take you off the site. You have to pay attention to the URLs to know where you are in re-lation to where you started. Furthermore, when you find a Web page using a search engine, often you go deep into a complex site without having any sense of the context of that page. You might have to spend thirty minutes or more just to get some idea of what is on the overall site. Another difficulty of doing research on the Web is that you are limited by the equipment you are using and the speed of your connection.

ADDITIONAL CRITERIA FOR EVALUATING WEB SOURCES

Traditional criteria for evaluating print sources remain useful for evaluat-ing sources on the Web, but you should keep in mind how the Web can be different.

1. *Source.* If a Web site indicates what organization or individual is responsi-ble for the information found on it, then you can apply the traditional cri-teria for evaluating print sources. For example, most major newspapers maintain Web sites where you can read some of the articles that appear in print. If a Web site doesn't indicate ownership, then you have to make judgments about who put it up and why. Documents are easy to copy and put up on the Web, but they are also very easily quoted out of context or al-tered. For example, you might find something that is represented as an "of-ficial" government document that is in fact a fabrication.

2. *Author.* Often, it is difficult to know who put up a particular Web site. Even when an author's name is present, in most cases the author's qualifica-tions are not listed.

3. *Timeliness.* Many Web pages do not list when they were last updated; therefore, you do not know how current they are. Furthermore, there are thousands of ghost sites on the Web—sites that the owners have aban-doned but have not bothered to remove. You can stumble onto these old sites and not realize that the organization might have a more current site elsewhere. Also, many Web site maintainers do not update their links, and when you start clicking, you get many error messages.

4. *Evidence.* The accuracy of any evidence found on the Web is often hard to verify. There are no editors or fact checkers guarding against mistakes or misinformation. The most reliable information on the Web stands up to the tests of print evaluation, with clear indication of an edited source, credentials of the author, references for works cited, and dates of publication.

5. **Biases.** Many Web sites are little more than virtual soapboxes. Someone who has an ax to grind can potentially tell millions of people why he or she is angry. Other sites are equally biased but conceal their attitude with a reasonable tone and seemingly factual evidence such as statistics.

6. **Advertising.** Many Web sites are "infomercials" of one sort or another. While they can provide useful information about specific products or services, the reason the information was placed on the Web is to get you to buy the product or service. Advertising on the Web costs a fraction of broadcast ads, so it's no wonder that advertisers have flocked to the Web.

Taking Notes

Before personal computers became widely available, most library research projects involved taking notes on notecards. This method was cumbersome, but it had some big advantages. You could spread out the notecards on a table or pin them to a bulletin board and get an overview of how the information that you gathered might be connected. Today, many people make notes in computer files. If you make notes in a computer file, then you don't have to retype when you write your paper. For example, if you copy a direct quote and decide to use it, you can cut and paste it. It is, of course, possible to print all your notes from your computer and then spread them out, or you can even paste your notes on cards, which will let you enjoy the best of both systems. Whatever way works best for you, there are a few things to keep in mind.

Make sure you get the full bibliographic information when you make notes. For books, you should get the author's name, title of the book, place of publication, publisher, and date of publication. This information is on the front and back of the title page. For journals, you need the author's name, title of the article, title of the journal, issue of the journal, date of the issue, and page numbers. For Web sites, you need the name of the page, the author if listed, the sponsoring organization if listed, the date the site was posted, the date you visited, and the complete URL.

Make photocopies of sources you plan to use in your paper. Photocopies save you the time of copying and lessen the chances you'll make mistakes. If you do take notes, be sure to indicate which words are the author's and which words are yours. It's easy to forget later. If you're using electronic sources, then print the sources you plan to use. Attach the bibliographic information to photocopies and printouts so that you won't get mixed up about where the source came from.

Finally, know when to say you have enough information. Many topics can be researched for a lifetime. It's not just the quantity of sources that counts. You should have enough diversity that you are confident you know the major points of view on a particular issue. When you reach a possible stopping point, group your notes and see whether a tentative organization for your paper becomes evident. People who like to work with notecards some-times write comment cards to attach to each card, indicating how that piece of information fits. People who work with computer files sometimes type in caps how they see their notes fitting together. The method doesn't matter as much as the result. You should have a sketch outline by the time you finish the information-gathering stage.

CHAPTER 16

MLA Documentation

Intellectual Property and Scholastic Honesty

Hasbro had the hit toy of the holidays in 1998 with Furby, but if Furby reminded you of Gizmo, the cuddly creature in the Warner Bros. movies *Gremlins* and *Gremlins 2: The New Batch*, you weren't alone. The executives at Warner Bros. also noticed the similarities, and reportedly, Hasbro paid Warner Bros. a large out-of-court settlement for recasting the image of Gizmo. The flap over Furby is but one of many instances of the complex issues surrounding the concept of intellectual property. Copyright laws were established in the 1700s to protect the financial interests of publishers and authors, but over the last century, the domain of intellectual property has spread to music scores and lyrics, recordings, photographs, films, radio and television broadcasts, computer software, and, as the Furby example illustrates, all sorts of other likenesses. During the past decade, the legal battles over intellectual property rights have involved the Internet, which eventually will have major consequences for how much information will be freely available on the World Wide Web.

However, intellectual property rights are not the main reason that college writing requires strict standards of documentation. Writing at the college level follows a long tradition of scholarly writing that insists on accuracy in referencing other work so that a reader can consult a writer's sources. Often, scholarly arguments build on the work of others, and experiments almost always identify an area that other researchers have addressed. Sometimes, other pieces of writing are the primary data, as when a historian uses letters and public documents to construct what happened in the past. It is important for other historians to be able to review the same documents to confirm or reject a particular interpretation.

There is also a basic issue of fairness in recognizing the work of others. If you find an idea in someone else's work that you want to use, it seems only fair to give that person proper credit. In Chapter 6, we discuss Robert H. Frank and Phillip J. Cook's controversial argument that changes in attitudes help to account for the increasing divide between rich and poor people since 1973, a shift that they summarize as the winner-take-all society. The phrase "winner-take-all society" has become common enough that you might hear it in news features describing the contemporary United States, but certainly any extended treatment of the concept should acknowledge Frank and Cook for coming up with the idea. Many students now acknowledge the work of other students if they feel that their classmates have made an important contribution to their work. And why not? It's only fair.

In our culture in general and in the professions in particular, work that people claim is their own is expected to be their own. Imagine that you are the director of marketing at a company that paid a consulting firm to conduct a survey, only to find out that the work the firm presented to you had been copied from another survey. Wouldn't you be on the phone right away to your company's attorneys? Even though the unethical copying of the survey might have been the failure of only one employee, surely the reputation of the consulting firm would be damaged, if not ruined. Many noteworthy people in political and public life have been greatly embarrassed by instances of plagiarism; in some cases, people have lost their positions as a result. Short of committing a felony, plagiarism is one of the few things that can get you expelled from your college or university if the case is serious enough. So it's worth it to you to know what plagiarism is and isn't.

AVOIDING PLAGIARISM

Stated most simply, you plagiarize when you use the words or ideas of someone else without acknowledging the source. That definition seems easy enough, but when you think about it, how many new ideas are there? And how could you possibly acknowledge where all your ideas came from? In practical terms, you are not expected to acknowledge everything. You do not have to acknowledge what is considered general knowledge, such as facts that you could find in a variety of reference books. For example, if you wanted to assert that Lyndon Johnson's victory over Barry Goldwater in the 1964 presidential election remains the largest popular vote percentage (61 percent) in presidential election history, you would not have to acknowledge the source. This information should be available in encyclopedias, almanacs, and other general sources.

But if you cite a more obscure fact that wouldn't be as readily verifiable, you should let your readers know where you found it. Likewise, you should acknowledge the sources of any arguable statements, claims, or judgments. The sources of statistics, research findings, examples, graphs, charts, and illustrations also should be acknowledged. People are especially skeptical about statistics and research findings if the source is not mentioned. For example, if you argue that the Internet has led to even greater marginalization of the rural poor in the United States, you might include statistics that in 1995, the households of rural poor (incomes less than $10,000) had the lowest levels of computer penetration—only 4.5 percent—of any population group. By contrast, 7.6 percent of households of the poor in central cities had computers. Failing to give the source of these statistics could undercut your argument, but since these statistics are from the U.S. Department of Commerce ("Falling through the Net: A Survey of the 'Have Nots' in Rural and Urban America," Washington, DC: U.S. Department of Commerce, July 1995), the source adds credibility.

Where most people get into plagiarism trouble is when they take words directly and use them without quotation marks or else change a few words and pass them off as their own words. It is easiest to illustrate where the line is drawn with an example. Suppose you are writing an argument about attempts to censor the Internet, and you want to examine how successful other nations have been. You find the following paragraph about China:

> China is encouraging Net use for business, but not what it considers seditious or pornographic traffic and "spiritual pollution." So the state is building its communications infrastructure like a mammoth corporate system—robust within the country, but with three gateways to the world, in Beijing, Shanghai, and Shenzhen. International exchanges can then be monitored and foreign content "filtered" at each information chokepoint, courtesy of the Public Security Bureau.
>
> —Jim Erickson. "WWW.POLITICS.COM." *Asiaweek* 2 Oct. 1998: 42.

You want to mention the point about the gateways in your paper. You have two basic options: to paraphrase the source and to quote it directly.

If you quote directly, you must include all words you take from the original inside quotation marks:

> According to one observer, "China is encouraging Net use for business,
> but not what it considers seditious or pornographic traffic and 'spiritual
> pollution'" (Erickson 42).

This example is typical of MLA style. The citation goes outside the quotation marks but before the period. The reference is to the author's last name, which refers you to the full citation in the works-cited list at the end. Following the author's name is the page number where the quotation can be located. Notice also that if you quote material that contains quotation marks, then the double quotation marks change to the single quotation mark. If you include the author's name, then you need to cite only the page number:

> According to Jim Erickson, "China is encouraging Net use for business,
> but not what it considers seditious or pornographic traffic and 'spiritual
> pollution'" (42).

If an article appears on one page only, you do not need to include the page number:

> According to Jim Erickson, "China is encouraging Net use for business, but
> not what it considers seditious or pornographic traffic and 'spiritual
> pollution.'"

If the newspaper article did not include the author's name, you would include the first word or two of the title. The logic of this system is to enable you to find the reference in the works-cited list.

The alternative to quoting directly is to paraphrase. When you paraphrase, you change the words without changing the meaning. Here are two examples:

Plagiarized

China wants its citizens to use the Internet for business, but not for
circulating views it doesn't like, pornography, and "spiritual pollution."
So China is building its communications infrastructure like a mammoth
corporate system—well linked internally but with only three ports to the
outside world. The Public Security Bureau will monitor the foreign traffic
at each information choke-point (Erickson).

This version is unacceptable. Too many of the words in the original are used directly here, including much of one sentence: "is building its communications infrastructure like a mammoth corporate system." If an entire string of words is lifted from a source and inserted without using quotation marks, then the passage is plagiarized. The first sentence is also too close in structure and wording to the original. Changing a few words in a sentence is not a paraphrase. Compare the following example:

> **Acceptable paraphrase**
>
> The Chinese government wants its citizens to take advantage of the Internet
> for commerce while not allowing foreign political ideas and foreign values to
> challenge its authority. Consequently, the Chinese Internet will have only
> three ports to the outside world. Traffic through these ports will be
> monitored and censored by the Public Security Bureau (Erickson).

There are a few words from the original in this paraphrase, such as *foreign* and *monitored*, but these sentences are original in structure and wording while accurately conveying the meaning of the original.

USING SOURCES EFFECTIVELY

The purpose of using sources is to *support* your argument, not to make your argument for you. Next to plagiarism, the worst mistake you can make with sources is stringing them together without building an argument of your own. Your sources help to show that you've done your homework and that you've thought in depth about the issue.

One choice you have to make when using sources is when to quote and when to paraphrase. Consider the following example about expressways:

> Urban planners of the 1960s saw superhighways as the means to prevent
> inner cities from continuing to decay. Inner-city blight was recognized as
> early as the 1930s, and the problem was understood for four decades as
> one of circulation (hence expressways were called "arterials"). The
> planners argued that those who had moved to the suburbs would return
> to the city on expressways. By the end of the 1960s, the engineers were
> tearing down thousands of units of urban housing and small businesses to
> build expressways with a logic that was similar to the logic of mass

bombing in Vietnam—to destroy the city was to save it (Patton 102). Shortly the effects were all too evident. Old neighborhoods were ripped apart, the flight to the suburbs continued, and the decline of inner cities accelerated rather than abated.

Not everyone in the 1950s and 1960s saw expressways as the answer to urban dilapidation. Lewis Mumford in 1958 challenged the circulation metaphor. He wrote: "Highway planners have yet to realize that these arteries must not be thrust into the delicate tissue of our cities; the blood they circulate must rather enter through an elaborate network of minor blood vessels and capillaries" (236). Mumford saw that new expressways produced more congestion and aggravated the problem they were designed to overcome, thus creating demand for still more expressways. If road building through cities were allowed to continue, he predicted the result would be "a tomb of concrete roads and ramps covering the dead corpse of a city" (238).

Notice that two sources are cited: Phil Patton, *Open Road: A Celebration of the American Highway*. New York: Simon & Schuster, 1986; and Lewis Mumford, "The Highway and the City," *The Highway and the City*. New York: Harcourt, Brace, 1963. 234-46.

The writer decided that the point from Patton about tearing down thousands of units of urban housing and small businesses to build expressways in the 1960s should be paraphrased but Mumford's remarks should be quoted directly. In both direct quotations from Mumford, the original wording is important. Mumford rejects the metaphor of arteries for expressways and foresees the future of cities as paved-over tombs in vivid language. As a general rule, you should use direct quotations only when the original language is important. Otherwise, you should paraphrase.

If a direct quotation runs more than four lines, then it should be indented one inch and double-spaced. But you still should integrate long quotations into the text of your paper. Long quotations should be attributed; that is, you should say where the quotation comes from in your text as well as in the reference. And it is a good idea to include at least a sentence or two after the quotation to describe its significance for your argument. The original wording in the long quotation in the following paragraph is important because it gives a sense of the language of the Port Huron Statement. The sentences following the quotation explain why many faculty members in the

1960s looked on the Port Huron Statement as a positive sign (of course, college administrators were horrified). You might think of this strategy as putting an extended quotation in an envelope with your words before and after:

> Critiques of the staleness and conformity of American education made the first expressions of student radicalism in the 1960s such as the "Port Huron Statement" from the Students for a Democratic Society (SDS) in 1962 appear as a breath of fresh air. The SDS wrote:
>
> > Almost no students value activity as a citizen. Passive in public, they are hardly more idealistic in arranging their private lives; Gallup concludes they will settle for "low success, and won't risk high failure." There is not much willingness to take risks (not even in business), no setting of dangerous goals, no real conception of personal identity except one manufactured in the image of others, no real urge for personal fulfillment except to be almost as successful as the very successful people. Attention is being paid to social status (the quality of shirt collars, meeting people, getting wives or husbands, making solid contacts for later on); much, too, is paid to academic status (grades, honors, the med-school rat race). But neglected generally is real intellectual status, the personal cultivation of mind. (238)
>
> Many professors shared the SDS disdain for the political quietism on college campuses. When large-scale ferment erupted among students during the years of the Vietnam War, some faculty welcomed it as a sign of finally emerging from the intellectual stagnation of the Eisenhower years. For some it was a sign that the promise of John F. Kennedy's administration could be fulfilled, that young people could create a new national identity.

Note three points about form in the long quotation. First, there are no quotation marks around the extended quotation. Readers know that the material is quoted because it is blocked off. Second, words quoted in the original retain the double quotation marks. Third, the page number appears after the period at the end of the quotation.

Whether long or short, make all quotations part of the fabric of your paper while being careful to indicate which words belong to the original. A reader should be able to move through the body of your paper without having to stop and ask: Why did the writer include this quotation? or Which words are the writer's and which are being quoted?

MLA Works-Cited List

Different disciplines use different styles for documentation. The two styles that are used most frequently are the APA style and the MLA style. APA stands for American Psychological Association, which publishes a style manual used widely in the social sciences (see Chapter 17). MLA stands for the Modern Language Association, and its style is the norm for humanities disciplines, including English and rhetoric and composition.

Both MLA and APA styles use a works-cited list placed at the end of a paper. Here is an example of an MLA works-cited list:

Center "Works Cited."

Double-space all entries. Indent all but the first line five spaces.

Alphabetize entries by last name of authors or by title if no author is listed.

Underline the titles of books and periodicals.

Works Cited

Bingham, Janet. "Kids Become Masters of Electronic Universe: School Internet Activity Abounds." Denver Post 3 Sept. 1996: A13.

Dyrli, Odvard Egil, and Daniel E. Kinnaman. "Telecommunications: Gaining Access to the World." Technology and Learning 16.3 (Nov. 1995): 79-84.

Ellsworth, Jill H. Education on the Internet: A Hands-On Book of Ideas, Resources, Projects, and Advice. Indianapolis: Sams, 1994.

Engardio, Pete. "Microsoft's Long March." Business Week 24 June 1996: 52-54.

National Center for Education Statistics. "Internet Access in Public Education." Feb. 1998. NCES. 4 Jan. 1999 <http://nces.ed.gov/pubs98/98021.html>.

"UK: A Battle for Young Hearts and Minds." Computer Weekly 4 Apr. 1996: 20.

The works-cited list eliminates the need for footnotes. If you have your sources listed on notecards, then all you have to do when you finish your paper is to find the cards for all the sources that you cite, alphabetize the cards, and type your works-cited list. For works with no author listed, alphabetize by the first content word in the title (ignore *a*, *an*, and *the*).

Some of the more common citation formats in MLA style are listed in the following section. If you have questions that these examples do not address, you should consult the *MLA Handbook for Writers of Research Papers* (6th edition, 2003) and the *MLA Style Manual and Guide to Scholarly Publishing* (2nd edition, 1998).

CITING BOOKS

The basic format for listing books in the works-cited list is the author's name (last name first), the title (underlined), the place of publication, the short name of publisher, and the date of publication. You will find the exact title on the title page (not on the cover), the publisher, and the city (use the first city if several are listed). The date of publication is included in the copyright notice on the back of the title page.

Book by One Author

Ellsworth, Jill H. Education on the Internet: A Hands-On Book of
    Ideas, Resources, Projects, and Advice. Indianapolis: Sams,
    1994.

Book by Two or More Authors

Sturken, Marita, and Lisa Cartwright. Practices of Looking: An Introduction
    to Visual Culture. New York: Oxford UP, 2001.

Two or More Books by the Same Author

Berger, John. About Looking. New York: Pantheon, 1980.
- - - . Ways of Seeing. New York: Viking, 1973.

Translation

Martin, Henri-Jean. The History and Power of Writing. Trans. Lydia G.
    Cochrane. Chicago: U of Chicago P, 1994.

Edited Book

Bizzell, Patricia, and Bruce Herzberg, eds. The Rhetorical Tradition:
    Readings from Classical Times to the Present. Boston: Bedford,
    1990.

One Volume of a Multivolume Work

Habermas, Jürgen. Lifeworld and System: A Critique of Functionalist
    Reason. Trans. Thomas McCarthy. Boston: Beacon, 1987. Vol. 2 of
    The Theory of Communicative Action. 2 vols. 1984-87.

Selection in an Anthology or Chapter in an Edited Collection

Merritt, Russell. "Nickelodeon Theaters, 1905-1914: Building an Audience
    for the Movies." The American Film Industry. Rev. ed. Ed. Tino Balio.
    Madison: U of Wisconsin P, 1985. 83-102.

Government Document

Malveaux, Julianne. "Changes in the Labor Market Status of Black Women."
    A Report of the Study Group on Affirmative Action to the Committee
    on Education and Labor. U.S. 100th Cong., 1st sess. H. Rept. 100-L.
    Washington: GPO, 1987. 213-55.

Bible

Holy Bible. Revised Standard Version Containing the Old and New
    Testaments. New York: Collins, 1973. [Note that "Bible" is not
    underlined.]

CITING PERIODICALS

When citing periodicals, the necessary items to include are author's name
(last name first), the title of the article inside quotation marks, the title of the
journal or magazine (underlined), the volume number (for scholarly journals), the date, and page numbers. Many scholarly journals are printed to be
bound as one volume, usually by year, and the pagination is continuous for
that year. If, say, a scholarly journal is printed in four issues and the first issue
ends on page 278, then the second issue will begin with page 279. For jour-

nals that are continuously paginated, you do not need to include the issue number. Some scholarly journals, however, are paginated like magazines with each issue beginning on page 1. For journals paginated by issue, you should list the issue number along with the volume (e.g., for the first issue of volume 11, you would put "11.1" in the entry after the title of the journal).

Article in a Scholarly Journal—Continuous Pagination

Berlin, James A. "Rhetoric and Ideology in the Writing Class." College English
    50 (1988): 477-94.

Article in a Scholarly Journal—Pagination by Issue

Kolby, Jerry. "The Top-Heavy Economy: Managerial Greed and Unproductive
    Labor." Critical Sociology 15.3 (1988): 53-69.

Review

Chomsky, Noam. Rev. of Verbal Behavior, by B. F. Skinner. Language 35
    (1959): 26-58.

Magazine Article

Engardio, Pete. "Microsoft's Long March." Business Week 24 June 1996:
    52-54.

Newspaper Article

Bingham, Janet. "Kids Become Masters of Electronic Universe: School
    Internet Activity Abounds." Denver Post 3 Sept. 1996: A13.

Letter to the Editor

Luker, Ralph E. Letter. Chronicle of Higher Education 18 Dec. 1998: B9.

Editorial

"An Open Process." Editorial. Wall Street Journal 30 Dec. 1998: A10.

CITING ONLINE SOURCES

Online sources pose special difficulties for systems of citing sources. Many on-line sources change frequently. Sometimes you discover to your frustration that what you had found on a Web site the previous day has been altered or in some cases no longer exists. Furthermore, basic information such as who put up a Web site and when it was last changed are often absent. Many print sources have also been put on the Web, which raises another set of difficulties. The basic format for citing a generic Web site is author's name (last name first), the title of the document (in quotation marks), the title of the complete work or name of the journal (underlined), the date of Web publication or last update, the sponsoring organization, the date you visited, and the URL (enclosed in angle brackets).

Web Site

Ayres, Edward L., Anne Sarh Rubin, and William G. Thomas, III. "A
    Walking Tour." The Valley of the Shadow: Two Communities in the
    American Civil War. 2001. U of Virginia. 10 Dec. 2002.
    <http://www.iath.virginia.edu/vshadow2/cwtour2.html>.

Book on the Web

Rheingold, Howard. Tools for Thought: The People and Ideas of the
    Next Computer Revolution. New York, 1985. 1996. The Well.
    4 Jan. 1999 <http://www.well.com/user/hlr/texts/
    tftindex.html>.

Article in a Scholarly Journal on the Web

Browning, Tonya. "Embedded Visuals: Student Design in Web Spaces."
    Kairos. 2.1 (1997). 4 Jan. 1999 <http://www.as.ttu.edu/kairos/2.1/
    features/browning/index.html>.

Article in a Magazine on the Web

"Happy New Euro." Time Daily 30 Dec. 1998. 4 Jan. 1999
    <http://cgi.pathfinder.com/time/daily/
    0,2960,17455-101990101,00.html>.

Personal Web Site

Vitanza, Victor. Victor's Uncanny Web Site. 4 Jan. 1999
    <http://www.uta.edu/english/V/Victor_.html>.

CD-ROM

Boyer, Paul, et al. The Enduring Vision, Interactive Edition. CD-ROM.

    1993 ed. Lexington, MA: Heath, 1993.

CITING OTHER SOURCES

Interview

Williams, Errick Lynn. Telephone interview. 4 Jan. 1999.

Unpublished Dissertation

Rouzie, Albert. "At Play in the Fields of Writing: Play and Digital Literacy in

    a College-Level Computers and Writing Course." Diss. U of Texas at

    Austin, 1997.

Film

Saving Private Ryan. Dir. Stephen Spielberg. Perf. Tom Hanks, Matt Damon,

    Tom Sizemore. Paramount, 1998.

Television Program

"The Attitude." Ally McBeal. Dir. Allan Arkush, Daniel Attias, et al. Writ.

    David E. Kelley. Perf. Calista Flockhart, Courtney Thorne-Smith.

    3 Nov. 1997.

Recording

Glass, Phillip. "Low" Symphony. Point Music, 1973.

Speech

Khrushchev, Sergei. "Russia, Putin, and the War on Terrorism." National

    Press Club, Wasington. 6 Dec. 2001.

Sample Argument Paper Using Sources

The paper that follows, by Chris Thomas, is an example of a student argument that uses sources well and that documents those sources appropriately.

Chris Thomas

Professor Selzer

Eng. 15 Sect. 20

24 October 1998

Should Race Be a Qualification to Attend College?

An Examination of Affirmative Action

Imagine that you are an African American student like me and that
it is your first day of classes at a prestigious university. As you make your
rounds on campus, you become increasingly aware of the swift glances
that you are receiving from some of your predominately white
classmates. You assume that the looks are generated because you are
among the few African American students around, but you soon learn
that your assumptions were too shallow. A student that you begin to
have a conversation with asks what you received on your SATs. You
initially believe that this inquiry is just a piece of general freshman
curiosity, but your classmate's line of questioning ends with the
question, "Do you think that you got into school because of your race
and affirmative action?" That leads you to feel resented by the classmate
because of your presence in this university.

Believe it or not, thousands of African American students
experience similar scenarios every year. These predicaments force
African Americans to question their merit and sense of belonging and
draw attention to the controversial issue of affirmative action and its
relevance to college admissions. Let me explore both sides of the issue
by clearly defining the policy, looking at its causes, assessing the facts,
evaluating the policy, and examining conflicting ideas on what should
be done in the future about affirmative action.

This page follows MLA recommendations for a student research paper that does not use a title
page. If you have a title page, you need only your name and title on the first page.

Thomas   2

With reference to college admission, the definition of affirmative action is relatively simple. In his book <u>Preferential Policies: An International Perspective</u>, Thomas Sowell states, "What is called 'affirmative action' in the United States is . . . [a] government-mandated preferential policy toward government-designated groups" (13). There is general understanding that affirmative action is a program that aims to overcome the effects of past discrimination by giving preferential treatment to ethnic minorities and women. Barbara R. Bergmann's <u>In Defense of Affirmative Action</u> confirms that "Affirmative Action planning and acting [are designed] to end the absence of certain kinds of people—those who belong to groups that have been subordinated or left out from certain jobs and schools. The term is usually applied to those plans that set forth goals, required since the early 1970s, for government contractors and universities receiving public funds" (7). The Equal Opportunities Act of 1972 set up a right to act on such plans. Bergmann goes on to state, "[affirmative action] is an insurance company taking steps to break its tradition of promoting only white men to executive positions." The program is also seen as a means to producing a diverse learning and working environment.

In the case of African Americans, affirmative action was created to compensate for a history of slavery and systemic racial discrimination. The program was initiated because American society had produced an atmosphere that was strictly conducive to white men's success and dominance. Affirmative action programs arose out of governmental and judicial decisions requiring efforts to remedy continuing discrimination based on sex and race (Ponterotto et al. 6). This program is an effort to "level the playing field" and to try to make it possible for African Americans to have an equal, fair, and just opportunity to succeed. One aim of the program is to help curb the negative stereotypes and stigmas that American society has bestowed upon African Americans. The ultimate goal of such programs is to enable these individuals, through educational and vocational achievement, to have greater access to socioeconomic opportunity and stability (Ponterotto et al. 6). (For a full account of the history and intent of affirmative action, I recommend Affirmative Action on Campus by Joseph G. Ponterotto et al.)

How does affirmative action work with reference to college admission? It is understood that preferential treatment in some respects is given to African American applicants. On college campuses, affirmative action's ideals are translated into combating sexism and racism and social acceptance of minority-group members (Ponterotto et al. 6). In Ending Affirmative Action, Terry Eastland notes, "[Supreme Court] Justice Powell said in his Bakke opinion [referring to the University of California v. Bakke affirmative action case], that a university has the First Amendment freedom to make judgments about its educational mission. This freedom includes the latitude to select a student body [which] can help promote the educational environment most conducive to 'speculation, experiment, and creation' in which all students, minorities and non-minorities alike, benefit" (77).

If it is understood that affirmative action is implemented to compensate for past discriminations of African Americans, then what's the problem? The debate lies not in the definition, causes, or goals of affirmative action in the college admission process, but in the contradictory evaluation policies that develop out of the process. Is affirmative action a good, bad, or fair program that should be used to assist African Americans in the college admission process? There are opposing arguments on this issue; there are those who believe that it is a just and necessary program and those who strongly oppose the issue. The components of the issue that have caused the greatest controversy are the qualifications of the African American applicants, the aims of the program, and the progression of the program.

Thomas   4

Shouldn't the most qualified applicants to a university receive top priority in admissions? "The answers to such a question require a critical examination of just what is meant by 'best qualified,'" states Norman Matloff in "Toward Sensible Affirmative Action Policies." Consider the question of admissions policy for any famous university, with many more applicants than open slots. Let us ask whether, say, applicants with higher SAT scores should get automatic priority in admissions over those with lower scores (Matloff 1). It goes without saying that "test scores alone [are] not the way to determine admission," according to John Furedy, professor of psychology at the University of Toronto (qtd. in Saha 1); standardized test scores are not perfect measurement tools, and thus they should not be overapplied in admissions decisions. Yet for most students, test scores will at least reliably predict whether the student's academic skills are "in the league with" those of typical students at the given school. In "Why Not a Lottery to Get into UC?" Norman Matloff affirms that "first one must keep in mind that neither SAT scores nor any other numeric measure will be a very accurate predictor of future grades. It thus makes no sense to admit one applicant over another simply because the first applicant had higher test scores." Even the staunchest supporters of standardized tests seem to agree "that the scores reflect only a small part of the factors that predict freshman grades, and far less of what it takes to graduate from college" (Lederman A36).

Supporters of affirmative action believe that an overemphasis shouldn't be placed solely on SAT scores. They believe that "you need to understand the degree to which race, gender, and religion affect that person. You need to look at that person as a whole," notes Earl Lewis, interim dean of the graduate school at the University of Michigan (qtd. in Saha 2), and family and collegiate background of the applicant should be taken into consideration. Supporters agree that academic strength should be the most important component of college admissions, but they

Thomas   5

also believe that an applicant's family background also influences the probability that a person will succeed in college. It is widely understood that students with parents or family members that attended college have a better chance at college success than those without such a history. Supporters of affirmative action also argue that past societal limitations have restricted African American students from colleges, thus producing a situation in which relatively few African Americans have a history of attending college to pass on to their children. Moreover, past discrimination has created a college environment for African Americans that isn't as conducive to college pursuits as white applicants. Supporters argue that affirmative action will help to gradually increase the number of African American family members that attend college. Supporters also believe that admissions should look at the well-roundedness of the applicant. They should look at situations such as the applicant's involvement in school, his or her living environment, and possible required work experiences which would account for not so stellar grades.

On the other hand, opponents of affirmative action say that the preferential aspects of the program overlook academically qualified white students. Opponents believe that preferential treatment should be given to those of strong academic caliber, not to those of a particular race, and they see admissions decisions as central to maintaining high institutional standards. "The students who are denied at Berkeley will move down one notch," says David Murray; "we must not throw out the thermometer [of test scores] because we don't like the temperature it's taking" (qtd. in Lederman A37). As this quotation indicates, critics of affirmative action have a high regard for test scores: "Much of the discussion presumes that the tests are a very profound measure of academic preparation, and can really predict how well people do in college," notes Claude Steele, a psychology professor at Stanford University (qtd. in Lederman A37).

Thomas   6

Another element of debate is the actual goals of affirmative action in college admissions. Supporters contend that the main goal of the program is to "level the playing field" in all aspects of society by giving qualified African American applicants the opportunity to attend college. The supporters argue that giving this preferential treatment to African Americans will provide minorities the opportunity "to defy the pernicious stereotypes and stigmas cast upon them by others"—for example, that African Americans are lazy, unsuccessful, and are strictly drug and sex driven (Lewis 2). Upholders of affirmative action argue that "the whole point of employing racial preferences in admissions is to change the composition of the student body—to bring more members of 'favored' groups into the institution," thus diversifying the college atmosphere (Thernstrom 36).

While opponents of affirmative action in college admission often concede that the program has been needed as an aid to stop past discrimination, they strongly believe that now "a dual system of criteria, based solely on race, strikes most Americans of all races as offensive" (Maguire 52). They vehemently argue that affirmative action is "reverse discrimination." They believe that affirmative action is "the 'ignorant' way of fighting discrimination. There is one simple rule to fight discrimination: do not discriminate," notes Furedy (qtd. in Saha 2). They affirm that one cannot fight discrimination with reverse discrimination targeted toward white Americans.

Opponents also claim that the supposed beneficiaries of the program, African Americans, in fact get hurt the most by negative effects of affirmative action. Clint Bolick, for instance, in The Affirmative Action Fraud, states that "preference policies may do their beneficiaries more harm than good. Race-based diminution of admissions standards inevitably causes a mismatch between students' abilities and the demands of the school" (79). Eastland too concedes that "being treated differently in order to be treated equally—a 'benign' act, according to advocates of affirmative action—has had its costs" (72), which can be described as a general idea that African Americans' degrees will have a low value. Furedy observes that this degree-devaluing of African Americans is possible because "people who are accepted [to college with the help of affirmative action] have a smear attached to them; it will be assumed that they were accepted not for their merit, but for their race" (qtd. in Saha 1), that they were able to obtain it because of their race, not because of their academic abilities. It will also lead African American students to question their sense of belonging. Opponents state that if standards for admission are lowered when considering the admission of African American students, then these programs will "distort what is now a level playing field and bestow preferential treatment on undeserving minorities because of their skin" (Lewis 1).

There is, then, much debate over the evaluation of affirmative action and its link to college admission of African Americans. Both supporters and opponents have strong arguments on the issue. Both sides state why the program is good or bad and have an arguable and justifiable argument for their beliefs. Where, then, should we go from here?

Supporters believe that affirmative action in college admission of African Americans should continue to be practiced. Syndicated columnist William Raspberry states that he has thoroughly interviewed "two eminent American educators [who] have taken a good hard look at affirmative action in college admissions, and their conclusion is that by virtually any reasonable measure, affirmative action works." Advocates believe that affirmative action is still needed because "without the deconstruction of white power and privilege, how can we legitimately claim that the playing field is level" (Lewis 22), even if African Americans

Thomas 8

are no longer discriminated against and suppressed to quite the extent that they once were. In the words of Kerry Colligan, "you need to talk about the debt this country has to pay. You cannot negate 300 years of slavery and 100 years of oppression" (2).

On the other hand, opponents believe that the affirmative action policies college admissions follow should be curbed because it is an unfair act of "reverse discrimination" that causes racial tension from resentful white Americans. Opponents believe that "[g]roups seen as newly favored because of their race or ethnicity may become targets of the majority's animosity, or they may be seen as needing special treatment because of their supposed inferiority" (Ponterotto et al. 6). They suggest that the program be made unconstitutional because it violates both the 14th Amendment, which guarantees equal protection under the law, and Title VI of the 1964 Civil Rights Act, which forbids discrimination in programs receiving federal financial aid (Colligan 1). Realizing that discrimination is still a problem, some opponents suggest that "the focus should be on education in the K-12 sector in order to prepare everyone equally well . . . for entrance exams" (Doyle 1).

Exactly where does this leave us? The critics that attack affirmative action are correct when they say that affirmative action corrupts the purity of the process. Extreme care must be taken in determining if affirmative action in the admission of African Americans to college should be practiced, for how long, and to what degree. While the policies of affirmative action are not perfect and they do raise some legitimate concerns, they take us away from a system that is inherently unfair to some groups. "The active deconstruction of the white privilege that grew out of virulent American racism affords African Americans a greater chance at equal opportunity and will have the side effect of forcing us to re-evaluate a society that unfairly disadvantages minorities" (Lewis 4).

Thomas   9

The issue is more confusing if you consider that "affirmative action prefers individuals on the basis of their group membership, [not considering that] those minorities with academic credentials competitive with regularly admitted students may nonetheless be regarded with skepticism as affirmative action admittees" (Eastland 90). Therefore, further research on and evaluation of the issue is definitely needed to see if the progression or regression of the program's aims will uphold the aims of the respective arguing sides of the issue.

Thomas   10

Works Cited

Barr, Margaret J., et al. Affirmative Action on Campus. San Francisco:

    Jossey-Bass, 1990.

Bergmann, Barbara R. In Defense of Affirmative Action. New York: Basic,

    1996.

Bolick, Clint. The Affirmative Action Fraud. Washington: Cato Institute,

    1996.

Colligan, Kerry. "Panelists Discuss History of Affirmative Action, Lawsuit."

    The University Record 26 Nov. 1997. 14 Dec. 1998 <http://www.

    umich.edu/~newinfo/U_Record/Issues97/Nov/afhist.htm>.

Doyle, Rebecca A. "Students Express Views on Racism, Discrimination."

    The University Record 26 Nov. 1997. 14 Dec. 1998

    <http://www.umich.edu/~newinfo/U_Record/Issues97/Nov/

    afhist.htm>.

Eastland, Terry. Ending Affirmative Action: The Case for Colorblind

    Justice. New York: Basic, 1996.

Kahlenberg, Richard D. The Remedy. New York: Basic, 1996.

Lederman, Douglas. "Persistent Racial Gap in SAT Scores Fuels

    Affirmative Action Debate." The Chronicle of Higher Education 30

    Oct. 1998: A36-38.

Lewis, Brian C. "An Ethical and Practical Defense of Affirmative Action."

    1996. 18 Dec. 1998 <http://www.princeton.edu/~bclewis/action>.

Maguire, Timothy. "My Bout with Affirmative Action." Commentary 93

    (April 1992): 50-52.

Matloff, Norman. "Why Not a Lottery to Get into UC?" Los Angeles Times

    24 Jan. 1995: B7.

---. "Toward Sensible Affirmative Action Policies." King Hall (UC Davis)

    Law School Advocate Nov. 1994. 18 Dec. 1998

    <http://www.heather.cs.ucdavis.edu/pub/AffirmativeAction/

    Advocate>.

Thomas   11

McWhirter, Darien A. The End of Affirmative Action. New York: Birch
    Lane, 1996.

Ponterotto, Joseph G., et al. Affirmative Action on Campus. San Francisco:
    Jossey-Bass, 1990.

Raspberry, William. "Despite the Myths, Affirmative Action Works."
    Centre Daily Times 4 Oct. 1998: 9A.

Saha, Paula. "Panel Presents Perspectives on Diversity in Higher
    Education." The University Record 26 Nov. 1997. 18 Dec. 1998
    <http://www.umich.edu/~newinfo/U_Record/Issues97/Nov/
    affac.htm>.

Sowell, Thomas. Preferential Policies: An International Perspective. New
    York: Morrow, 1990.

Thernstrom, Stephan. "Farewell to Preferences." Public Interest 130
    (1998): 34-49.

Zelnick, Bob. Backfire: A Reporter's Look at Affirmative Action.
    Washington: Regner, 1996.

CHAPTER 17

APA Documentation

Disciplines in the social sciences (anthropology, government, linguistics, psychology, sociology) and in education most frequently use the APA (American Psychological Association) documentation style. This chapter offers a brief overview of the APA style. For a detailed treatment you should consult the *Publication Manual of the American Psychological Association*, fifth edition (2001).

The APA style has many similarities to the MLA style described in Chapter 16. Both styles use parenthetical references in the body of the text with complete bibliographical citations in the reference list at the end. The most important difference is the emphasis on the date of publication in the APA style. When you cite an author's name in the body of your paper with APA style, you always include the date of publication and the page number:

> By the end of the 1960s, the engineers were tearing down thousands of units of urban housing and small businesses to build expressways with a logic that was similar to the logic of mass bombing in Vietnam—to destroy the city was to save it (Patton, 1986, p. 102). Shortly the effects were all too evident. Old neighborhoods were ripped apart, the flight to the suburbs continued, and the decline of inner cities accelerated rather than abated.

Not everyone in the 1950s and 1960s saw expressways as the answer to urban dilapidation. Mumford (1958) challenged the circulation metaphor: "Highway planners have yet to realize that these arteries must not be thrust into the delicate tissue of our cites; the blood they circulate must rather enter through an elaborate network of minor blood vessels and capillaries" (p. 236).

Notice that unlike MLA, a comma is placed after the author's name and the abbreviation for page is included (Patton, 1986, p. 102).

▌ APA Reference List

The APA list of works cited is titled *References*:

Center "References"

Double-space all entries. Indent all but first line five spaces.

Alphabetize entries by last name of authors or by title if no author is listed.

Notice that author's initials are listed rather than first names.

Notice that only the first words and proper nouns are capitalized in titles of articles and books.

Notice that article titles are not placed inside quotation marks.

Italicize the titles of books and periodicals.

When there are two authors, alphabetize by the last name of the first author. Use an ampersand (&) before the second author's name.

References

Bingham, J. (1996, September 3). Kids become masters of electronic universe: School Internet activity abounds. *Denver Post*, p. A13.

Dyrli, O. E., & Kinnaman, D. E.. (1995). Telecommunications: Gaining access to the world. *Technology and Learning, 16*(3), 79-84.

Engardio, P. (1996, June 24). Microsoft's long march. *Business Week*, 52-54.

The future just happened. (2001, July 29). *BBC Online*. Retrieved August 29, 2001, from http://news.bbc.co.uk/hi/english/static/in_depth/programmes/2001/future/tv_series_1.stm

Lewis, M. (1989). *Liar's poker: Rising through the wreckage on Wall Street*. New York: Norton.

Lewis, M. (2000). *The next new thing: A Silicon Valley story*. New York: Norton.

Lewis, M. (2001). Next: *The future just happened*. New York: Norton.

National Center for Education Statistics. (1998, February). Internet Access in Public Education. Retrieved May 21, 1998, from http://nces.ed.gov/pubs98/98021.html

UK: A battle for young hearts and minds. (1996, April 4). *Computer Weekly*, 20.

When there are three or more authors, alphabetize by the last name of the first author. Use commas to separate the names and an ampersand (&) before the final name.

If an author has more than one entry, put the earliest publication first.

The reference list eliminates the need for footnotes. If you have your sources listed on notecards, all you have to do when you finish your paper is find the cards for all the sources that you cite, alphabetize the cards, and type your reference list. For works with no author listed, alphabetize by the first significant word in the title (ignore *a*, *an*, and *the*).

CITING BOOKS

The basic format for listing books in the reference list is

1. Author's name (last name first, initials)
2. Year of publication (in parentheses)
3. Title (in italics)
4. Place of publication
5. Name of publisher

Use the abbreviation for pages (pp.) for chapters in a book.

Book by One Author

Ellsworth, J. H. (1994). *Education on the Internet: A hands-on book of ideas, resources, projects, and advice.* Indianapolis, IN: Sams.

Book by Two or More Authors

Scribner, S., & Cole, M. (1981). *The psychology of literacy.* Cambridge, MA: Harvard University Press.

Translation

Martin, H.-J. (1994). *The history and power of writing* (L. G. Cochrane, Trans.). Chicago: University of Chicago Press.

Edited Book

Bizzell, P., & Herzberg, B. (Eds.). (1990). *The rhetorical tradition: Readings from classical times to the present.* Boston: Bedford.

One Volume of a Multivolume Work

de Selincourt, E., & Darbishire, H. (Eds.). (1958). *The poetical works of William Wordsworth* (Vol. 5). Oxford, England: Oxford University Press.

Selection in an Anthology or Chapter in an Edited Collection

Merritt, R. (1985). Nickelodeon theaters, 1905–1914: Building an audience for the movies. In T. Balio (Ed.), *The American film industry* (Rev. ed., pp. 83–102). Madison: University of Wisconsin Press.

Unpublished Dissertation

Rouzie, A. (1997). *At play in the fields of writing: Play and digital literacy in a college-level computers and writing course.* Unpublished doctoral dissertation, University of Texas at Austin.

CITING PERIODICALS

When citing periodicals, the necessary items to include are

1. Author's name (last name first, initials)
2. Date of publication (in parentheses). For scholarly journals, give the year. For newspapers and weekly magazines, give the year followed by the month and day (2001, December 13)
3. Title of the article
4. Title of the journal or magazine (in italics)
5. Volume number (in italics)
6. Page numbers

For articles in newspapers, use the abbreviation for pages (p. or pp.).

Many scholarly journals are printed to be bound as one volume, usually by year, and the pagination is continuous for that year. If, say, a scholarly journal is printed in four issues and the first issue ends on page 278, then the second issue will begin with page 279. For journals that are continuously paginated, you do not need to include the issue number. Some scholarly journals, however, are paginated like magazines with each issue beginning on page 1. For journals paginated by issue, you should list the issue number along with the volume (e.g., for the first issue of volume 11, you would put *11*(1) in the entry after the title of the journal).

Article in a Scholarly Journal—Continuous Pagination

Berlin, J. A. (1988). Rhetoric and ideology in the writing class. *College*

  English, 50, 477-94.

Article in a Scholarly Journal—Pagination by Issue

Kolby, J. (1988). The top-heavy economy: Managerial greed and

  unproductive labor. *Critical Sociology, 15*(3), 53-69.

Review

Chomsky, N. (1959). [Review of the book *Verbal behavior*]. *Language, 35,* 26-58.

Magazine Article

Engardio, P. (1996, June 24). Microsoft's long march. *Business Week,* 52-54.

Magazine Article—No Author Listed

UK: A battle for young hearts and minds. (1996, April 4). *Computer Weekly,* 20.

Newspaper Article

Bingham, J. (1996, September 3). Kids become masters of electronic

  universe: School Internet activity abounds. *Denver Post,* p. A13.

CITING ONLINE SOURCES

The *Publication Manual of the American Psychological Association* specifies that those citing Web sources should direct readers to the exact source page if possible, not to menu or home pages. URLs have to be typed with complete accuracy to identify a Web site. If you type an uppercase letter for a lowercase letter, a browser will not find the site. To avoid typos in URLs, load the page in your browser, highlight the URL, and copy it (Control C on Windows or Command C on a Mac), then paste it into the reference. You may have to change the font to match your text, but you will have the accurate URL.

The basic format for citing online sources is as follows:

1. Author's last name, initials
2. Date of document or last revision in parentheses
3. Title of document. Capitalize only the first word and any proper nouns.
4. Title of periodical (if applicable). Use italics and capitalize only the first word and any proper nouns.
5. Date of retrieval
6. URL or access path. Notice that there is no period after a URL.

Article in a Scholarly Journal on the Web

Agre, P. (1998). The Internet and public discourse. *First Monday, 3*(3). Retrieved July 10, 2001, from http://www.firstmonday.dk/ issues/issue3_3/agre/

Electronic Copy of an Article Retrieved from a Database

Schott, G., & Selwyn, N. (2001). Examining the "male, antisocial" stereotype of high computer users. *Journal of Educational Computing Research, 23,* 291–303. Retrieved from PsychINFO database.

Electronic Copy of an Abstract Retrieved from a Database

Putsis, W. P., & Bayus, B. L. (2001). An empirical analysis of firms' product line decisions. *Journal of Marketing Research, 37*(8), 110–118. Abstract obtained from PsychINFO database.

Article in a Newspaper on the Web

Mendels, P. (1999, May 26). Nontraditional teachers more likely to use the Net. *New York Times on the Web.* Retrieved September 19, 2001, from http://www.nytimes.com/library/tech/99/05/cyber/education/ 26education.html

Article from an Online News Service

Rao, M. (1999, February 10). WorldTel in $100 M community initiative for Indian state. *Asia InternetNews.* Retrieved April 15, 2001, from http://asia.internet.com/1999/2/1003-india.html

Article in a Magazine on the Web

Happy new Euro. (1998, December 30). *Time Daily*. Retrieved May 10, 2000,
    from http://www.time.com/time/nation/article/0,8599,17455,00.html

Online Encyclopedia

Semiconductor. (1999). *Encyclopaedia Britannica Online*. Retrieved November
    30, 2000, from http://search.eb.com/bol/topic?eu=68433&sctn=1#s_top

Document on a Web Site

Kaplan, N. (1997, December 17). E-literacies: Politexts, hypertexts and
    other cultural formations in the late age of print. Retrieved July 2,
    2001, from http://raven.ubalt.edu/staff/kaplan/lit/

Document on a Web Site of an Organization

National Audubon Society. (2001). Cowbirds and conservation. Retrieved
    August 15, 2001, from http://www.audubon.org/bird/research/

Electronic Version of a U.S. Government Report

U.S. Public Health Service. Office of the Surgeon General. (2001, January 11).
    Clean Indoor Air Regulations Fact Sheet. Retrieved February 12, 2001,
    from http://www.cdc.gov/tobacco/sgr/sgr_2000/factsheets/
    factsheet_clean.htm

Graphic, Audio, or Video Files

East Timor awaits referendum. (1999, August 31). *NPR Online*. Retrieved
    August 31, 1999, from http://www.audubon.org/bird/research/
    http://www.npr.org/ramfiles/atc/19990830.atc.10.ram

Electronic Mailing List Posting

Selzer, J. (1998, July 4). Ed Corbett. Message posted to WPA-L@lists.asu.edu

Newsgroup Posting

Brody, P. (1999, May 9). Chamax. Message posted to news: sci.archaeology.
    mesoamerican

Personal Email

APA omits personal email from the list of references. Personal communi-
    cation can be cited in parenthetical references in the

text. Provide a date if possible.

S. Wilson (personal communication, April 6, 2002)

CITING OTHER SOURCES

Government Report

U.S. Environmental Protection Agency. (1992). *Respiratory health effects of passive smoking: Lung cancer and other disorders.* (EPA Publication No. 600/6-90/006 F). Washington, DC: Author.

Film

Spielberg, S. (Director). (1998). *Saving Private Ryan* [Motion picture]. United States: Paramount Pictures.

Television Broadcast

Burns, K. (Writer). (1992, January 29). *Empire of the air: The men who made radio* [Television broadcast]. Walpole, NH: Florentine Films.

Television Series

Connelly, J. (Producer). (1957). *Leave it to Beaver* [Television series]. New York: CBS Television.

Music Recording

Glass, P. (1973). *"Low" symphony* [CD]. New York: Point Music.

PART 4

Contemporary
Arguments

Negotiating the Environment

As noted in the first chapter, Rachel Carson's *Silent Spring* in 1962 stimulated the environmental movement in the United States. Carson's book explicitly indicted pesticides commonly used in the agriculture industry, particularly DDT, but implicitly she was arguing for something broader—for a new sense of our relation to our environment, for the conviction that we should be living in balance with nature, not in domination over it. Thus, Carson's book ultimately influenced not just agricultural practice but also efforts to protect endangered species, to regulate population growth, and to clean up our air and water resources. When President Richard Nixon created the Environmental Protection Agency in 1973, environmental concern became institutionalized in the United States; most states created

> We are the most dangerous species of life on the planet, and every other species, even the earth itself, has cause to fear our power to exterminate. But we are also the only species which, when it chooses to do so, will go to great effort to save what it might destroy.
>
> —*Wallace Stegner*

Thomas Cole's American Lake Scene (1844)
Source: *American Lake Scene,* 1844 by Thomas Cole, gift of Douglas R. Roby, photograph ©1986 The Detroit Institute of the Arts.

their own departments of natural resources or environmental protection soon after.

In part, Rachel Carson was successful because her appeals struck a chord deep within many Americans. For in a very real sense environmentalism is ingrained within the American character. It derives from a respect for the land—the American Eden—that is evident in the legend of Rip Van Winkle, in the work of Hudson River painters such as Thomas Cole, in the landscape architecture of Frederick Law Olmsted, in Henry David Thoreau's *Walden* and in Ralph Waldo Emerson's Transcendentalist writings in the 1850s, in John Muir's testimonials about Yosemite, and in Theodore Roosevelt's withdrawals into the Badlands and his campaign to begin a system of national parks. Of course, the exploitation of the American green world for profit is also ingrained in our national character: Even as some Americans were reverencing the land as a special landscape that sustained them physically and spiritually, pioneers moving westward were subduing it for their own purposes, in the process spoiling rivers and air and virgin forests—and native peoples—in the name of development.

And so the tension between the uses of nature and its protection is persistent. This tension helps to explain why arguments about environmental issues are so prevalent in public discourse today. Are science and technology friends or foes of the environment? What is the proper relationship between people and the natural environment? What is a suitable balance between resource development and resource protection—resources including everything from timber and coal to streams and animals? How serious a problem is global warming, and what should be done about it? To what extent should we invest scarce resources in the protection of little-known species or lands whose benefit to people has not been demonstrated? How can poorer nations develop economically without global environmental repercussions? Is it already too late to avoid such repercussions? Such questions are debated each day in every kind of media, especially as organized environmental groups are legion, ranging from the activist Earth First! (whose ten thousand members sometimes advocate direct action in support of environmental aims) to more mainstream groups such as the Sierra Club or the Nature Conservancy, which has created a membership of nearly one million in an explicit effort to create partnerships between scientists and businesspersons in the interests of environmental reform. On the other hand, conservatives such as Ronald Reagan and Rush Limbaugh have often ridiculed the efforts of environmentalists in the interest of a relatively unbridled developmentalism that is in the optimistic tradition of nineteenth-century free enterprise.

Debates about environmental issues, in other words, are part and parcel of American culture. What follows is a sampling of several arguments on which our future depends.

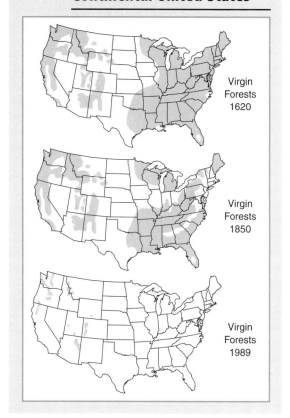

How Forests Have Diminished in the Continental United States

Virgin Forests 1620

Virgin Forests 1850

Virgin Forests 1989

The Land Ethic

Aldo Leopold (1887–1948), a professional forester by trade who worked at the University of Wisconsin, was one of the most influential nature writers of the twentieth century and one of the founders of modern ecology. He revised the following essay (first published in 1933) shortly before he died while fighting a brushfire in a neighbor's field; it appeared in Leopold's posthumously published Sand County Almanac *(1949). Like much of Leopold's work—an effort to create a new ecological conscience—"The Land Ethic" offers a new way of understanding our relationship with the environment, a conception that has powerfully influenced environmental policy debates in the United States.*

1   When god-like Odysseus returned from the wars in Troy, he hanged all on one rope a dozen slave-girls of his household whom he suspected of misbehavior during his absence.

2   This hanging involved no question of propriety. The girls were property. The disposal of property was then, as now, a matter of expediency, not of right and wrong.

3   Concepts of right and wrong were not lacking from Odysseus' Greece: witness the fidelity of his wife through the long years before at last his black-prowed galleys clove the wine-dark seas for home. The ethical structure of that day covered wives, but had not yet been extended to human chattels. During the three thousand years which have since elapsed, ethical criteria have been extended to many fields of conduct, with corresponding shrinkages in those judged by expediency only.

The Ethical Sequence

4   This extension of ethics, so far studied only by philosophers, is actually a process in ecological evolution. Its sequences may be described in ecological as well as in philosophical terms. An ethic, ecologically, is a limitation on freedom of action in the struggle for existence. An ethic, philosophically, is a differentiation of social from anti-social conduct. These are two definitions of one thing. The thing has its origin in the tendency of interdependent individuals or groups to evolve modes of co-operation. The ecologist calls these symbioses. Politics and economics are advanced symbioses in

which the original free-for-all competition has been replaced, in part, by co-operative mechanisms with an ethical content.

5   The complexity of co-operative mechanisms has increased with population density, and with the efficiency of tools. It was simpler, for example, to define the anti-social uses of sticks and stones in the days of the mastodons than of bullets and billboards in the age of motors.

6   The first ethics dealt with the relation between individuals; the Mosaic Decalogue is an example. Later accretions dealt with the relation between the individual and society. The Golden Rule tries to integrate the individual to society; democracy to integrate social organization to the individual.

7   There is as yet no ethic dealing with man's relation to land and to the animals and plants which grow upon it. Land, like Odysseus' slave-girls, is still property. The land-relation is still strictly economic, entailing privileges but not obligations.

8   The extension of ethics to this third element in human environment is, if I read the evidence correctly, an evolutionary possibility and an ecological necessity. It is the third step in a sequence. The first two have already been taken. Individual thinkers since the days of Ezekiel and Isaiah have asserted that the despoliation of land is not only inexpedient but wrong. Society, however, has not yet affirmed their belief. I regard the present conservation movement as the embryo of such an affirmation.

9   An ethic may be regarded as a mode of guidance for meeting ecological situations so new or intricate, or involving such deferred reactions, that the path of social expediency is not discernible to the average individual. Animal instincts are modes of guidance for the individual in meeting such situations. Ethics are possibly a kind of community instinct in-the-making.

The Community Concept

10   All ethics so far evolved rest upon a single premise: that the individual is a member of a community of interdependent parts. His instincts prompt him to compete for his place in that community, but his ethics prompt him also to co-operate (perhaps in order that there may be a place to compete for).

11   The land ethic simply enlarges the boundaries of the community to include soils, waters, plants, and animals, or collectively: the land.

12   This sounds simple: do we not already sing our love for and obligation to the land of the free and the home of the brave? Yes, but just what and whom do we love? Certainly not the soil, which we are sending helter-skelter downriver. Certainly not the waters, which we assume have no function except to turn turbines, float barges, and carry off sewage. Certainly not the plants, of which we exterminate whole communities without

batting an eye. Certainly not the animals, of which we have already extirpated many of the largest and most beautiful species. A land ethic of course cannot prevent the alteration, management, and use of these "resources," but it does affirm their right to continued existence, and, at least in spots, their continued existence in a natural state.

13   In short, a land ethic changes the role of *Homo sapiens* from conqueror of the land-community to plain member and citizen of it. It implies respect for his fellow-members, and also respect for the community as such.

14   In human history, we have learned (I hope) that the conqueror role is eventually self-defeating. Why? Because it is implicit in such a role that the conqueror knows, *ex cathedra,* just what makes the community clock tick, and just what and who is valuable, and what and who is worthless, in community life. It always turns out that he knows neither, and this is why his conquests eventually defeat themselves.

15   In the biotic community, a parallel situation exists. Abraham knew exactly what the land was for: it was to drip milk and honey into Abraham's mouth. At the present moment, the assurance with which we regard this assumption is inverse to the degree of our education.

16   The ordinary citizen today assumes that science knows what makes the community clock tick; the scientist is equally sure that he does not. He knows that the biotic mechanism is so complex that its workings may never be fully understood.

17   That man is, in fact, only a member of a biotic team is shown by an ecological interpretation of history. Many historical events, hitherto explained solely in terms of human enterprise, were actually biotic interactions between people and land. The characteristics of the land determined the facts quite as potently as the characteristics of the men who lived on it.

18   Consider, for example, the settlement of the Mississippi valley. In the years following the Revolution, three groups were contending for its control: the native Indian, the French and English traders, and the American settlers. Historians wonder what would have happened if the English at Detroit had thrown a little more weight into the Indian side of those tipsy scales which decided the outcome of the colonial migration into the cane-lands of Kentucky. It is time now to ponder the fact that the cane-lands, when subjected to the particular mixture of forces represented by the cow, plow, fire, and axe of the pioneer, became bluegrass. What if the plant succession inherent in this dark and bloody ground had, under the impact of these forces, given us some worthless sedge, shrub, or weed? Would Boone and Kenton have held out? Would there have been any overflow into Ohio, Indiana, Illi-

nois, and Missouri? Any Louisiana Purchase? Any transcontinental union of new states? Any Civil War?

19 Kentucky was one sentence in the drama of history. We are commonly told what the human actors in this drama tried to do, but we are seldom told that their success, or the lack of it, hung in large degree on the reaction of particular soils to the impact of the particular forces exerted by their occupancy. In the case of Kentucky, we do not even know where the bluegrass came from—whether it is a native species, or a stowaway from Europe.

20 Contrast the cane-lands with what hindsight tells us about the Southwest, where the pioneers were equally brave, resourceful, and persevering. The impact of occupancy here brought no bluegrass, or other plant fitted to withstand the bumps and buffetings of hard use. This region, when grazed by livestock, reverted through a series of more and more worthless grasses, shrubs, and weeds to a condition of unstable equilibrium. Each recession of plant types bred erosion; each increment to erosion bred a further recession of plants. The result today is a progressive and mutual deterioration, not only of plants and soils, but of the animal community subsisting thereon. The early settlers did not expect this: on the *ciénagas* of New Mexico some even cut ditches to hasten it. So subtle has been its progress that few residents of the region are aware of it. It is quite invisible to the tourist who finds this wrecked landscape colorful and charming (as indeed it is, but it bears scant resemblance to what it was in 1848).

21 This same landscape was "developed" once before, but with quite different results. The Pueblo Indians settled the Southwest in pre-Columbian times, but they happened *not* to be equipped with range livestock. Their civilization expired, but not because their land expired.

22 In India, regions devoid of any sod-forming grass have been settled, apparently without wrecking the land, by the simple expedient of carrying the grass to the cow, rather than vice versa. (Was this the result of some deep wisdom, or was it just good luck? I do not know.)

23 In short, the plant succession steered the course of history; the pioneer simply demonstrated, for good or ill, what successions inhered in the land. Is history taught in this spirit? It will be, once the concept of land as a community really penetrates our intellectual life.

The Ecological Conscience

24 Conservation is a state of harmony between humans and land. Despite nearly a century of propaganda, conservation still proceeds at a snail's pace; progress still consists largely of letterhead pieties and convention

oratory. On the back forty we still slip two steps backward for each forward stride.

25   The usual answer to this dilemma is "more conservation education." No one will debate this, but is it certain that only the *volume* of education needs stepping up? Is something lacking in the *content* as well?

26   It is difficult to give a fair summary of its content in brief form, but, as I understand it, the content is substantially this: obey the law, vote right, join some organizations, and practice what conservation is profitable on your own land; the government will do the rest.

27   Is not this formula too easy to accomplish anything worthwhile? It defines no right or wrong, assigns no obligation, calls for no sacrifice, implies no change in the current philosophy of values. In respect of land-use, it urges only enlightened self-interest. Just how far will such education take us? An example will perhaps yield a partial answer.

28   By 1930 it had become clear to all except the ecologically blind that southwestern Wisconsin's topsoil was slipping seaward. In 1933 the farmers were told that if they would adopt certain remedial practices for five years, the public would donate CCC labor to install them, plus the necessary machinery and materials. The offer was widely accepted, but the practices were widely forgotten when the five-year contract period was up. The farmers continued only those practices that yielded an immediate and visible economic gain for themselves.

29   This led to the idea that maybe farmers would learn more quickly if they themselves wrote the rules. Accordingly the Wisconsin Legislature in 1937 passed the Soil Conservation District Law. This said to farmers, in effect: *We, the public, will furnish you free technical service and loan you specialized machinery, if you will write your own rules for land-use. Each county may write its own rules and these will have the force of law.* Nearly all the counties promptly organized to accept the proffered help, but after a decade of operation, *no county has yet written a single rule.* There has been visible progress in such practices as strip-cropping, pasture renovation, and soil liming, but none in fencing woodlots against grazing, and none in excluding plow and cow from steep slopes. The farmers, in short, have selected those remedial practices which were profitable anyhow, and ignored those which were profitable to the community, but not clearly profitable to themselves.

30   When one asks why no rules have been written, one is told that the community is not yet ready to support them; education must precede rules. But the education actually in progress makes no mention of obligations to land over and above those dictated by self-interest. The net result is that we

have more education but less soil, fewer healthy woods, and as many floods as in 1937.

31   The puzzling aspect of such situations is that the existence of obligations over and above self-interest is taken for granted in such rural community enterprises as the betterment of roads, schools, churches, and baseball teams. Their existence is not taken for granted, nor as yet seriously discussed, in bettering the behavior of the water that falls on the land, or in the preserving of the beauty or diversity of the farm landscape. Land-use ethics are still governed wholly by economic self-interest, just as social ethics were a century ago.

32   To sum up: we asked the farmer to do what he conveniently could to save his soil, and he has done just that, and only that. The farmer who clears the woods off a 75 per cent slope, turns his cows into the clearing, and dumps its rainfall, rocks, and soil into the community creek, is still (if otherwise decent) a respected member of society. If he puts lime on his fields and plants his crops on contour, he is still entitled to all the privileges and emoluments of his Soil Conservation District. The District is a beautiful piece of social machinery, but it is coughing along on two cylinders because we have been too timid, and too anxious for quick success, to tell the farmer the true magnitude of his obligations. Obligations have no meaning without conscience, and the problem we face is the extension of the social conscience from people to land.

33   No important change in ethics was ever accomplished without an internal change in our intellectual emphasis, loyalties, affections, and convictions. The proof that conservation has not yet touched these foundations of conduct lies in the fact that philosophy and religion have not yet heard of it. In our attempt to make conservation easy, we have made it trivial.

Substitutes for a Land Ethic

34   When the logic of history hungers for bread and we hand out a stone, we are at pains to explain how much the stone resembles bread. I now describe some of the stones which serve in lieu of a land ethic.

35   One basic weakness in a conservation system based wholly on economic motives is that most members of the land community have no economic value. Wildflowers and songbirds are examples. Of the 22,000 higher plants and animals native to Wisconsin, it is doubtful whether more than 5 per cent can be sold, fed, eaten, or otherwise put to economic use. Yet these creatures are members of the biotic community, and if (as I believe) its stability depends on its integrity, they are entitled to continuance.

36   When one of these non-economic categories is threatened, and if we happen to love it, we invent subterfuges to give it economic importance. At the beginning of the century songbirds were supposed to be disappearing. Ornithologists jumped to the rescue with some distinctly shaky evidence to the effect that insects would eat us up if birds failed to control them. The evidence had to be economic in order to be valid.

37   It is painful to read these circumlocutions today. We have no land ethic yet, but we have at least drawn nearer the point of admitting that birds should continue as a matter of biotic right, regardless of the presence or absence of economic advantage to us.

38   A parallel situation exists in respect of predatory mammals, raptorial birds, and fish-eating birds. Time was when biologists somewhat overworked the evidence that these creatures preserve the health of game by killing weaklings, or that they control rodents for the farmer, or that they prey only on "worthless" species. Here again, the evidence had to be economic in order to be valid. It is only in recent years that we hear the more honest argument that predators are members of the community, and that no special interest has the right to exterminate them for the sake of a benefit, real or fancied, to itself. Unfortunately this enlightened view is still in the talk stage. In the field the extermination of predators goes merrily on: witness the impending erasure of the timber wolf by fiat of Congress, the Conservation Bureaus, and many state legislatures.

39   Some species of trees have been "read out of the party" by economics-minded foresters because they grow too slowly, or have too low a sale value to pay as timber crops: white cedar, tamarack, cypress, beech, and hemlock are examples. In Europe, where forestry is ecologically more advanced, the non-commercial tree species are recognized as members of the native forest community, to be preserved as such, within reason. Moreover some (like beech) have been found to have a valuable function in building up soil fertility. The interdependence of the forest and its constituent tree species, ground flora, and fauna is taken for granted.

40   Lack of economic value is sometimes a character not only of species or groups, but of entire biotic communities: marshes, bogs, dunes, and "deserts" are examples. Our formula in such cases is to relegate their conservation to government as refuges, monuments, or parks. The difficulty is that these communities are usually interspersed with more valuable private lands; the government cannot possibly own or control such scattered parcels. The net effect is that we have relegated some of them to ultimate extinction over large areas. If the private owner were ecologically minded,

he would be proud to be the custodian of a reasonable proportion of such areas, which add diversity and beauty to his farm and to his community.

41   In some instances, the assumed lack of profit in these "waste" areas has proved to be wrong, but only after most of them had been done away with. The present scramble to reflood muskrat marshes is a case in point.

42   There is a clear tendency in American conservation to relegate to government all necessary jobs that private landowners fail to perform. Government ownership, operation, subsidy, or regulation is now widely prevalent in forestry, range management, soil and watershed management, park and wilderness conservation, fisheries management, and migratory bird management, with more to come. Most of this growth in governmental conservation is proper and logical, some of it is inevitable. That I imply no disapproval of it is implicit in the fact that I have spent most of my life working for it. Nevertheless the question arises: What is the ultimate magnitude of the enterprise? Will the tax base carry its eventual ramifications? At what point will governmental conservation, like the mastodon, become handicapped by its own dimensions? The answer, if there is any, seems to be in a land ethic, or some other force which assigns more obligation to the private landowner.

43   Industrial landowners and users, especially lumbermen and stockmen, are inclined to wail long and loudly about the extension of government ownership and regulation to land, but (with notable exceptions) they show little disposition to develop the only visible alternative: the voluntary practice of conservation on their own lands.

44   When the private landowner is asked to perform some unprofitable act for the good of the community, he today assents only with outstretched palm. If the act costs him cash this is fair and proper, but when it costs only forethought, open-mindeness, or time, the issue is at least debatable. The overwhelming growth of land-use subsidies in recent years must be ascribed, in large part, to the government's own agencies for conservation education: the land bureaus, the agricultural colleges, and the extension services. As far as I can detect, no ethical obligation toward land is taught in these institutions.

45   To sum up: a system of conservation based solely on economic self-interest is hopelessly lopsided. It tends to ignore, and thus eventually to eliminate, many elements in the land community that lack commercial value, but that are (as far as we know) essential to its healthy functioning. It assumes, falsely, I think, that the economic parts of the biotic clock will function without the uneconomic parts. It tends to relegate to government many functions eventually too large, too complex, or too widely dispersed to be performed by government.

46   An ethical obligation on the part of the private owner is the only visible remedy for these situations.

The Land Pyramid

47   An ethic to supplement and guide the economic relation to land presupposes the existence of some mental image of land as a biotic mechanism. We can be ethical only in relation to something we can see, feel, understand, love, or otherwise have faith in.

48   The image commonly employed in conservation education is "the balance of nature." For reasons too lengthy to detail here, this figure of speech fails to describe accurately what little we know about the land mechanism. A much truer image is the one employed in ecology: the biotic pyramid. I shall first sketch the pyramid as a symbol of land, and later develop some of its implications in terms of land-use.

49   Plants absorb energy from the sun. This energy flows through a circuit called the biota, which may be represented by a pyramid consisting of layers. The bottom layer is the soil. A plant layer rests on the soil, an insect layer on the plants, a bird and rodent layer on the insects, and so on up through various animal groups to the apex layer, which consists of the larger carnivores.

50   The species of a layer are alike not in where they came from, or in what they look like, but rather in what they eat. Each successive layer depends on those below it for food and often for other services, and each in turn furnishes food and services to those above. Proceeding upward, each successive layer decreases in numerical abundance. Thus, for every carnivore there are hundreds of his prey, thousands of their prey, millions of insects, uncountable plants. The pyramidal form of the system reflects this numerical progression from apex to base. Man shares an intermediate layer with the bears, raccoons, and squirrels which eat both meat and vegetables.

51   The lines of dependency for food and other services are called food chains. Thus soil-oak-deer-Indian is a chain that has now been largely converted to soil-corn-cow-farmer. Each species, including ourselves, is a link in many chains. The deer eats a hundred plants other than oak, and the cow a hundred plants other than corn. Both, then, are links in a hundred chains. The pyramid is a tangle of chains so complex as to seem disorderly, yet the stability of the system proves it to be a highly organized structure. Its functioning depends on the co-operation and competition of its diverse parts.

52   In the beginning, the pyramid of life was low and squat; the food chains short and simple. Evolution has added layer after layer, link after link. Man is one of thousands of accretions to the height and complexity of the

pyramid. Science has given us many doubts, but it has given us at least one certainty: the trend of evolution is to elaborate and diversify the biota.

53   Land, then, is not merely soil; it is a fountain of energy flowing through a circuit of soils, plants, and animals. Food chains are the living channels which conduct energy upward; death and decay return it to the soil. The circuit is not closed; some energy is dissipated in decay, some is added by absorption from the air, some is stored in soils, peats, and long-lived forests; but it is a sustained circuit, like a slowly augmented revolving fund of life. There is always a net loss by downhill wash, but this is normally small and offset by the decay of rocks. It is deposited in the ocean and, in the course of geological time, raised to form new lands and new pyramids.

54   The velocity and character of the upward flow of energy depend on the complex structure of the plant and animal community, much as the upward flow of sap in a tree depends on its complex cellular organization. Without this complexity, normal circulation would presumably not occur. Structure means the characteristic numbers, as well as the characteristic kinds and functions, of the component species. This interdependence between the complex structure of the land and its smooth functioning as an energy unit is one of its basic attributes.

55   When a change occurs in one part of the circuit, many other parts must adjust themselves to it. Change does not necessarily obstruct or divert the flow of energy; evolution is a long series of self-induced changes, the net result of which has been to elaborate the flow mechanism and to lengthen the circuit. Evolutionary changes, however, are usually slow and local. Man's invention of tools has enabled him to make changes of unprecedented violence, rapidity, and scope.

56   One change is in the composition of floras and faunas. The larger predators are lopped off the apex of the pyramid; food chains, for the first time in history, become shorter rather than longer. Domesticated species from other lands are substituted for wild ones, and wild ones are moved to new habitats. In this world-wide pooling of faunas and floras, some species get out of bounds as pests and diseases, others are extinguished. Such effects are seldom intended or foreseen; they represent unpredicted and often untraceable readjustments in the structure. Agricultural science is largely a race between the emergence of new pests and the emergence of new techniques for their control.

57   Another change touches the flow of energy through plants and animals and its return to the soil. Fertility is the ability of soil to receive, store, and release energy. Agriculture, by overdrafts on the soil, or by too radical a substitution of domestic for native species in the superstructure, may

derange the channels of flow or deplete storage. Soils depleted of their storage, or of the organic matter which anchors it, wash away faster than they form. This is erosion.

58   Waters, like soil, are part of the energy circuit. Industry, by polluting waters or obstructing them with dams, may exclude the plants and animals necessary to keep energy in circulation.

59   Transportation brings about another basic change: the plants or animals grown in one region are now consumed and returned to the soil in another. Transportation taps the energy stored in rocks, and in the air, and uses it elsewhere; thus we fertilize the garden with nitrogen gleaned by the guano of birds and from the fishes of seas on the other side of the equator. Thus the formerly localized and self-contained circuits are pooled on a world-wide scale.

60   The process of altering the pyramid for human occupation releases stored energy, and this often gives rise, during the pioneering period, to a deceptive exuberance of plant and animal life, both wild and tame. These releases of biotic capital tend to becloud or postpone the penalties of violence.

61   This thumbnail sketch of land as an energy circuit conveys three basic ideas:
1. That land is not merely soil.
2. That the native plants and animals kept the energy circuit open; others may or may not.
3. That man-made changes are of a different order than evolutionary changes, and have effects more comprehensive than is intended or foreseen.

62   These ideas, collectively, raise two basic issues: Can the land adjust itself to the new order? Can the desired alterations be accomplished with less violence?

63   Biotas seem to differ in their capacity to sustain violent conversion. Western Europe, for example, carries a far different pyramid than Caesar found there. Some large animals are lost; swampy forests have become meadows or plowland; many new plants and animals are introduced, some of which escape as pests; the remaining natives are greatly changed in distribution and abundance. Yet the soil is still there and, with the help of imported nutrients, still fertile; the waters flow normally; the new structure seems to function and to persist. There is no visible stoppage or derangement of the circuit.

64   Western Europe, then, has a resistant biota. Its inner processes are tough, elastic, resistant to strain. No matter how violent the alterations, the

pyramid, so far, has developed some new *modus vivendi* which preserves its habitability for man, and for most of the other natives.

65   Japan seems to present another instance of radical conversion without disorganization.

66   Most other civilized regions, and some as yet barely touched by civilization, display various stages of disorganization, varying from initial symptoms to advanced wastage. In Asia Minor and North Africa diagnosis is confused by climatic changes, which may have been either the cause or the effect of advanced wastage. In the United States the degree of disorganization varies locally; it is worst in the Southwest, the Ozarks, and parts of the South, and least in New England and the Northwest. Better land-uses may still arrest it in the less advanced regions. In parts of Mexico, South America, South Africa, and Australia a violent and accelerating wastage is in progress, but I cannot assess the prospects.

67   This almost world-wide display of disorganization in the land seems to be similar to disease in an animal, except that it never culminates in complete disorganization or death. The land recovers, but at some reduced level of complexity, and with a reduced carrying capacity for people, plants, and animals. Many biotas currently regarded as "lands of opportunity" are in fact already subsisting on exploitative agriculture, i.e., they have already exceeded their sustained carrying capacity. Most of South America is overpopulated in this sense.

68   In arid regions we attempt to offset the process of wastage by reclamation, but it is only too evident that the prospective longevity of reclamation projects is often short. In our own West, the best of them may not last a century.

69   The combined evidence of history and ecology seems to support one general deduction: the less violent the man-made changes, the greater the probability of successful readjustment in the pyramid. Violence, in turn, varies with human population density; a dense population requires a more violent conversion. In this respect, North America has a better chance for permanence than Europe, if she can contrive to limit her density.

70   This deduction runs counter to our current philosophy, which assumes that because a small increase in density enriched human life, that an indefinite increase will enrich it indefinitely. Ecology knows of no density relationship that holds for indefinitely wide limits. All gains from density are subject to a law of diminishing returns.

71   Whatever may be the equation for humans and land, it is improbable that we as yet know all its terms. Recent discoveries in mineral and vitamin nutrition reveal unsuspected dependencies in the up-circuit: incredibly

minute quantities of certain substances determine the value of soils to plants, of plants to animals. What of the down-circuit? What of the vanishing species, the preservation of which we now regard as an esthetic luxury? They helped build the soil; in what unsuspected ways may they be essential to its maintenance? Professor Weaver proposes that we use prairie flowers to reflocculate the wasting soils of the dust bowl; who knows for what purpose cranes and condors, otters and grizzlies may some day be used?

Land Health and the A–B Cleavage

72   A land ethic, then, reflects the existence of an ecological conscience, and this in turn reflects a conviction of individual responsibility for the health of the land. Health is the capacity of the land for self-renewal. Conservation is our effort to understand and preserve this capacity.

73   Conservationists are notorious for their dissensions. Superficially these seem to add up to mere confusion, but a more careful scrutiny reveals a single plane of cleavage common to many specialized fields. In each field one group (A) regards the land as soil, and its function as commodity-production; another group (B) regards the land as a biota, and its function as something broader. How much broader is admittedly in a state of doubt and confusion.

74   In my own field, forestry, group A is quite content to grow trees like cabbages, with cellulose as the basic forest commodity. It feels no inhibition against violence; its ideology is agronomic. Group B, on the other hand, sees forestry as fundamentally different from agronomy because it employs natural species, and manages a natural environment rather than creating an artificial one. Group B prefers natural reproduction on principle. It worries on biotic as well as economic grounds about the loss of species like chestnut, and the threatened loss of the white pines. It worries about a whole series of secondary forest functions: wildlife, recreation, watersheds, wilderness areas. To my mind, Group B feels the stirrings of an ecological conscience.

75   In the wildlife field, a parallel cleavage exists. For Group A the basic commodities are sport and meat; the yardsticks of production are ciphers of take in pheasants and trout. Artificial propagation is acceptable as a permanent as well as a temporary recourse—if its unit costs permit. Group B, on the other hand, worries about a whole series of biotic side-issues. What is the cost in predators of producing a game crop? Should we have further recourse to exotics? How can management restore the shrinking species, like prairie grouse, already hopeless as shootable game? How can management restore the threatened rarities, like trumpeter swan and whooping crane? Can management principles be extended to wildflowers? Here again it is clear to me that we have the same A–B cleavage as in forestry.

76   In the larger field of agriculture I am less competent to speak, but there seem to be somewhat parallel cleavages. Scientific agriculture was actively developing before ecology was born, hence a slower penetration of ecological concepts might be expected. Moreover the farmer, by the very nature of his techniques, must modify the biota more radically than the forester or the wildlife manager. Nevertheless, there are many discontents in agriculture which seem to add up to a new vision of "biotic farming."

77   Perhaps the most important of these is the new evidence that poundage or tonnage is no measure of the food-value of farm crops; the products of fertile soil may be qualitatively as well as quantitatively superior. We can bolster poundage from depleted soils by pouring on imported fertility, but we are not necessarily bolstering food-value. The possible ultimate ramifications of this idea are so immense that I must leave their exposition to abler pens.

78   The discontent that labels itself "organic farming," while bearing some of the earmarks of a cult, is nevertheless biotic in its direction, particularly in its insistence on the importance of soil flora and fauna.

79   The ecological fundamentals of agriculture are just as poorly known to the public as in other fields of land-use. For example, few educated people realize that the marvelous advances in technique made during recent decades are improvements in the pump, rather than the well. Acre for acre, they have barely sufficed to offset the sinking level of fertility.

80   In all of these cleavages, we see repeated the same basic paradoxes: man the conqueror *versus* man the biotic citizen; science the sharpener of his sword *versus* science the searchlight on his universe; land the slave and servant *versus* land the collective organism. Robinson's injunction to Tristram may well be applied, at this juncture, to *Homo sapiens* as a species in geological time:

> Whether you will or not
> You are a King, Tristram, for you are one
> Of the time-tested few that leave the world,
> When they are gone, not the same place it was.
> Mark what you leave.

The Outlook

81   It is inconceivable to me that an ethical relation to land can exist without love, respect, and admiration for land, and a high regard for its value. By value, I of course mean something far broader than mere economic value; I mean value in the philosophical sense.

82   Perhaps the most serious obstacle impeding the evolution of a land ethic is the fact that our educational and economic system is headed away from, rather than toward, an intense consciousness of land. Your true modern is separated from the land by many middlemen, and by innumerable physical gadgets. He has no vital relation to it; to him it is the space between cities on which crops grow. Turn him loose for a day on the land, and if the spot does not happen to be a golf links or a "scenic" area, he is bored stiff. If crops could be raised by hydroponics instead of farming, it would suit him very well. Synthetic substitutes for wood, leather, wool, and other natural land products suit him better than the originals. In short, land is something he has "outgrown."

83   Almost equally serious as an obstacle to a land ethic is the attitude of the farmer for whom the land is still an adversary, or a taskmaster that keeps him in slavery. Theoretically, the mechanization of farming ought to cut the farmer's chains, but whether it really does is debatable.

84   One of the requisites for an ecological comprehension of land is an understanding of ecology, and this is by no means co-extensive with "education"; in fact, much higher education seems deliberately to avoid ecological concepts. An understanding of ecology does not necessarily originate in courses bearing ecological labels; it is quite as likely to be labeled geography, botany, agronomy, history, or economics. This is as it should be, but whatever the label, ecological training is scarce.

85   The case for a land ethic would appear hopeless but for the minority which is in obvious revolt against these "modern" trends.

86   The "key-log" which must be moved to release the evolutionary process for an ethic is simply this: quit thinking about decent land-use as solely an economic problem. Examine each question in terms of what is ethically and esthetically right, as well as what is economically expedient. A thing is right when it tends to preserve the integrity, stability, and beauty of the biotic community. It is wrong when it tends otherwise.

87   It of course goes without saying that economic feasibility limits the tether of what can or cannot be done for land. It always has and it always will. The fallacy the economic determinists have tied around our collective neck, and which we now need to cast off, is the belief that economics determines *all* land-use. This is simply not true. An innumerable host of actions and attitudes, comprising perhaps the bulk of all land relations, is determined by the land-user's tastes and predilections, rather than by his purse. The bulk of all land relations hinges on investments of time, forethought, skill, and faith rather than on investments of cash. As a land-user thinketh, so is he.

88   I have purposely presented the land ethic as a product of social evolution because nothing so important as an ethic is ever "written." Only the most superficial student of history supposes that Moses "wrote" the Decalogue; it evolved in the minds of a thinking community, and Moses wrote a tentative summary of it for a "seminar." I say tentative because evolution never stops.

89   The evolution of a land ethic is an intellectual as well as emotional process. Conservation is paved with good intentions which prove to be futile, or even dangerous, because they are devoid of critical understanding either of the land, or of economic land-use. I think it is a truism that as the ethical frontier advances from the individual to the community, its intellectual content increases.

90   The mechanism of operation is the same for any ethic: social approbation for right actions: social disapproval for wrong actions.

91   By and large, our present problem is one of attitudes and implements. We are remodeling the Alhambra with a steamshovel, and we are proud of our yardage. We shall hardly relinquish the shovel, which after all has many good points, but we are in need of gentler and more objective criteria for its successful use.

RONALD BAILEY

Seven Doomsday Myths about the Environment

Ronald Bailey (1933–) has been a science writer for Forbes *magazine. His* Eco-Scam: The False Prophets of Ecological Apocalypse *(1993) attempts a refutation of many tenets of the environmental movement; the quasi-apocalyptic rhetoric associated with some elements of the environmental movement has left it vulnerable to this kind of rebuttal. The following essay appeared in the January–February 1994 issue of* The Futurist, *a nonpartisan publication that offers forecasts, trends, and commentaries about the future.*

1   As the author of *Eco-Scam: The False Prophets of Ecological Apocalypse,* I know by surprising experience that what I am about to say is going to make many people angry. But here goes.

2   THE END IS NOT NIGH! That's right—the Apocalypse has been postponed for the foreseeable future, despite the gloomy prognostications by the likes of Paul Ehrlich, Lester Brown, Al Gore, Stephen Schneider, and Carl Sagan. There is no scientific evidence to support the often heard claim that there is a global ecological crisis threatening humanity and life on the entire Planet Earth.

3   There are local environmental problems, of course, but no global threats. Instead, there is a record of enormous environmental progress and much to be optimistic about. As far as the global environment is concerned, there is a brilliant future for humanity and Planet Earth.

4   Of course, millions of people believe that we have only a few more years before the end, and no doubt some such doomsters are among the readers of this article. But I would like to remind them of seven false doomsday predictions—many of which are still being peddled by unscrupulous activists—and take a hard look at what actually happened.

False Doomsday Prediction No. 1

5   GLOBAL FAMINE   "The battle to feed all of humanity is over. In the 1970s the world will undergo famines—hundreds of millions of people are going to starve to death in spite of any crash programs embarked upon now," predicted population alarmist Paul Ehrlich in his book *The Population Bomb* (1968).

6   Two years later Ehrlich upped the ante by also painting a gruesome scenario in the Earth Day 1970 issue of *The Progressive,* in which *65 million* Americans would die of famine and a total of *4 billion* people worldwide would perish in "the Great Die-Off" between the years 1980 and 1989.

7   **WHAT REALLY HAPPENED?**   While the world's population *doubled* since World War II, food production *tripled.* The real price of wheat and corn dropped by 60%, while the price of rice was cut in half. Worldwide life expectancy rose from 47.5 years in 1950 to 63.9 years in 1990, while the world infant mortality rate dropped from 155 to 70 per 1,000 live births. Even in the poorest countries, those with per capita incomes under $400, average life expectancy rose spectacularly from 35 years in 1960 to 60 years in 1990.

8   And there's even more good news—for the last decade, grain output rose 5% per year in the developing world, while population growth has slowed from 2.3% to 1.9% and continues to fall. These figures strongly bolster University of Chicago agricultural economist Gale Johnson when he claims, "The scourge of famine due to natural causes has been almost conquered and could be entirely eliminated by the end of the century."

False Doomsday Prediction No. 2

9   **EXHAUSTION OF NONRENEWABLE RESOURCES**   In 1972, the Club of Rome's notorious report, *The Limits to Growth,* predicted that at exponential growth rates the world would run out of raw materials—gold by 1981, mercury by 1985, tin by 1987, zinc by 1990, oil by 1992, and copper, lead, and natural gas by 1993.

10   **WHAT REALLY HAPPENED?**   Humanity hasn't come close to running out of any mineral resource. Even the World Resources Institute estimates that the average price of all metals and minerals *fell* by more than 40% between 1970 and 1988. As we all know, falling prices mean that goods are becoming more abundant, not more scarce. The U.S. Bureau of Mines estimates that, at 1990 production rates, world reserves of gold will last 24 years, mercury 40 years, tin 28 years, zinc 40 years, copper 65 years, and lead 35 years. Proven reserves of petroleum will last 44 years and natural gas 63 years.

11   Now don't worry about the number of years left for any of these reserves. Just as a family replenishes its larder when it begins to empty, so, too, does humanity look for new mineral reserves only when supplies begin to run low. Even the alarmist Worldwatch Institute admits that "recent trends in price and availability suggest that for most minerals we are a long way from running out."

False Doomsday Prediction No. 3

12   SKYROCKETING POLLUTION   In 1972, *The Limits to Growth* also predicted that pollution would skyrocket as population and industry increased: "Virtually every pollutant that has been measured as a function of time appears to be increasing exponentially."

13   In 1969, Paul Ehrlich outlined a future "eco-catastrophe" in which he prophesied that 200,000 people would die in 1973 in "smog disasters" in New York and Los Angeles.

14   WHAT REALLY HAPPENED?   Since the publication of *The Limits to Growth*, the U.S. population has risen 22% and the economy has grown by more than 58%. Yet, instead of increasing as predicted, air pollutants have dramatically declined.

15   Sulfur-dioxide emissions are down 25% and carbon monoxide down 41%. Volatile organic compounds—chief contributors to smog formation—have been reduced by 31%, and total particulates like smoke, soot, and dust have fallen by 59%. Smog dropped by 50% in Los Angeles over the last decade.

16   Water quality deteriorated until the 1960s; now, water pollution is abating. Experts estimate that up to 95% of America's rivers, 92% of its lakes, and 86% of its estuaries are fishable and swimmable. These favorable pollution trends are being mirrored in both western Europe and Japan.

17   But what about the developing countries and former communist countries? It is true that industrial pollution continues to rise in some poorer countries. But a recent study by two Princeton University economists, Gene Grossman and Alan Krueger, using World Health Organization data, concluded that air pollution typically increases in a city until the average per capita income of its citizens reaches $4,000–$5,000, at which point pollution levels begin to fall. This is what happened in the developed nations and will happen as developing nations cross that threshold. In other words, economic growth leads to less pollution—not more, as asserted by the doomsters.

False Doomsday Prediction No. 4

18   THE COMING ICE AGE   The public has forgotten that the chief climatological threat being hyped by the eco-doomsters in the 1970s was the beginning of a new ice age. The new ice age was allegedly the result of mankind's polluting haze, which was blocking sunlight. "The threat of a new ice age must now stand alongside nuclear war as a likely source of wholesale death and misery for mankind," declared Nigel Calder, former editor of *New Scientist,* in 1975.

19   WHAT REALLY HAPPENED?   Global temperatures, after declining for 40 years, rebounded in the late 1970s, averting the feared new ice age. But was

this cause for rejoicing? NO! Now we are supposed to fear global warming. Freeze or fry, the problem is always viewed as industrial capitalism, and the solution, international socialism.

False Doomsday Prediction No. 5

20   THE ANTARCTIC OZONE HOLE   There have been widespread fears that the hole in the ozone layer of the earth's atmosphere will wipe out life all over the world. John Lynch, program manager of polar aeronomy at the National Science Foundation, declared in 1989, "It's terrifying. If these ozone holes keep growing like this, they'll eventually eat the world."

21   WHAT REALLY HAPPENED?   In 1985, British scientists detected reduced levels of stratospheric ozone over Antarctica. Could the Antarctic ozone hole "eventually eat the world"? No. "It is a purely localized phenomenon," according to Guy Brasseur at the National Center for Atmospheric Research. It is thought that the "ozone hole" results from catalytic reactions of some chlorine-based chemicals, which can take place only in high, very cold (below –80° C, or –176° F) clouds in the presence of sunlight. It is a transitory phenomenon enduring only a bit more than a month in the austral spring. The polar vortex—that is, the constant winds that swirl around the margins of the ice continent—tightly confine the hole over Antarctica.

22   What about the southern ecosystems? Isn't the increased ultraviolet light threatening plants and animals there? U.S. Vice President Albert Gore credulously reports in his book that hunters are finding rabbits and fish blinded by ultraviolet light in Patagonia.

23   This is sheer nonsense. Scientists have found not one example of animals being blinded by excess ultraviolet light in the Southern Hemisphere.

24   What about the phytoplankton in the seas around Antarctica? Osmond Holm-Hansen, a marine ecologist at Scripps Institute of Oceanography, has been studying the effects of ultraviolet light on Antarctica's ecosystems since 1988. He found that the extra ultraviolet-B light reduces phytoplankton by less than 4%–5%, which is well within the natural variations for the region. Holm-Hansen concludes, "Unlike the scare stories you hear some scientists spreading, the Antarctic ecosystem is absolutely not on the verge of collapse due to increased ultraviolet light."

False Doomsday Prediction No. 6

25   OZONE HOLE OVER AMERICA   In 1992, NASA spooked Americans by declaring that an ozone hole like the one over Antarctica could open up over the United States. *Time* magazine showcased the story on its front cover

(February 16, 1992), warning that "danger is shining through the sky. . . . No longer is the threat just to our future; the threat is here and now." Then-Senator Albert Gore thundered in Congress: "We have to tell our children that they must redefine their relationship to the sky, and they must begin to think of the sky as a threatening part of their environment."

26 WHAT REALLY HAPPENED?   On April 30, 1992, NASA sheepishly admitted that no ozone hole had opened up over the United States. *Time*, far from trumpeting the news on its cover, buried the admission in four lines of text in its May 11 issue. It's no wonder the American public is frightened.

27   But let's stipulate that there have been minor reductions in ozone over the United States due to chlorofluorocarbons in the stratosphere. So what?

28   Reduced stratospheric ozone over the United States was never going to be a disaster or a catastrophe. At most, it might have become an environmental nuisance in the next century.

29   But doesn't reduced stratospheric ozone severely injure crops and natural ecosystems? The answer is no. Ultraviolet levels vary naturally by as much as 50% over the United States. The farther south you go, the higher the ultraviolet exposure a person or plant receives. For example, an average 5% reduction in the ozone layer over the United States would increase ultraviolet exposure by about as much as moving a mere 60 miles south—the distance from Palm Beach to Miami. How many people worry about getting skin cancer as a result of moving 60 miles? Not many, I bet.

30   Alan Teramura, who is perhaps the world's leading expert on the effects of ultraviolet light on plants, says, "There is no question that terrestrial life is adapted to ultraviolet." His experiments have shown that many varieties of crops would be unaffected by reductions in the ozone layer. In fact, corn, wheat, rice, and oats all grow in a wide variety of ultraviolet environments now.

False Doomsday Prediction No. 7

31 GLOBAL WARMING   Global warming is "the Mother of all environmental scares," according to the late political scientist Aaron Wildavsky. Based on climate computer models, eco-doomsters predict that the earth's average temperature will increase by 4°–9°F over the next century due to the "greenhouse effect": Burning fossil fuels boosts atmospheric carbon dioxide, which traps the sun's heat.

32 WHAT IS REALLY HAPPENING?   The earth's average temperature has apparently increased by less than a degree (0.9) Fahrenheit in the last century. Un-

fortunately for the global-warming alarmists, most of that temperature rise occurred before World War II, when greenhouse gases had not yet accumulated to any great extent in the atmosphere.

33 And here's more bad news for doomsters: Fifteen years of very precise satellite data show that the planet has actually cooled by 0.13° C. Some years are warmer while others are cooler, according to NASA space scientist Roy Spencer, but the global temperature trend has been slightly downward. The satellites can measure temperature differences as small as 0.01° C. By contrast, the computer models of the doomsters predict that temperatures should have risen by an easily detectable 0.3° C per decade. They have not.

34 Even more bad news for the global-warming doomsters: One of the more robust predictions of the climate computer models is that global warming should be strongest and start first in the Arctic. Indeed, Albert Gore says in his book: "Global warming is expected to push temperatures up much more rapidly in the polar regions than in the rest of the world."

35 However, scientists did a recent comprehensive analysis of 40 years of arctic temperature data from the United States and the former Soviet Union. In an article in the prestigious scientific journal *Nature,* the scientists reported, "We do not observe the large surface warming trends predicted by the models; indeed, we detect significant surface cooling trends over the western Arctic Ocean during the winter and autumn." This is the exact opposite of what the doomsters are predicting is happening; the Arctic is becoming *cooler.*

36 Climate doomsters also predict that the ice caps of Antarctica and Greenland will melt, drastically raising sea levels and inundating New York, London, Bangladesh, and Washington, D.C. Recent scientific evidence shows that in fact the glaciers in both Antarctica and Greenland are accumulating ice, which means that sea levels will drop, not rise. Another false apocalypse averted.

37 Furthermore, over the past 100 years, winters in the Northern Hemisphere have become warmer. Why? Because the world is becoming cloudier. Cloud blankets warm long winter nights while long summer days are shaded by their cloud shields. This means longer growing seasons and fewer droughts for crops. This is decidedly not a recipe for a climate disaster.

38 Given the dismal record of the environmental doomsayers, why do so many people think the world is coming to an end? I think it's pretty clear. People are afraid because so many interest groups have a stake in making them afraid. "Global emergencies" and "worldwide crises" keep hundreds of millions of dollars in donations flowing into the coffers of environmental organizations. As environmental writer Bill McKibben admitted in *The End of*

Nature, "The ecological movement has always had its greatest success in convincing people that we are threatened by some looming problem." That success is now measured at the cash register for many leading environmental groups. For example, in 1990, the 10 largest environmental organizations raised $400 million from donors. That pays for a lot of trips to international environmental conferences, furnishes some nice headquarters, and buys a lot of influence on Capitol Hill.

39   Crises also advance the careers of certain politicians and bureaucrats, attract funds to scientists' laboratories, and sell newspapers and TV air time. The approach of inevitable doom is now the conventional wisdom of the late twentieth century.

40   But despite the relentless drumbeat of environmental doomsaying, people have to want to believe that the end is nigh. How do we account for the acquiescence of such a large part of the public to a gloomy view of the future?

41   I conclude that the psychological attraction of the apocalyptic imagination is strong. Eric Zencey, a self-described survivor of apocalyptic environmentalism, wrote about his experience in the *North American Review* (June 1988): "There is a seduction in apocalyptic thinking. If one lives in the Last Days, one's actions, one's very life, take on historical meaning and no small measure of poignance. . . . Apocalypticism fulfills a desire to escape the flow of real and ordinary time, to fix the flow of history into a single moment of overwhelming importance."

42   To counteract the seduction of the apocalypse, scientists, policymakers, intellectuals, and businessmen must work to restore people's faith in themselves and in the fact of human progress. History clearly shows that our energy and creativity will surmount whatever difficulties we encounter. Life and progress will always be a struggle and humanity will never lack for new challenges, but as the last 50 years of solid achievement show, there is nothing out there that we cannot handle.

43   So what's the moral of the story? Please don't listen to the doomsters' urgent siren calls to drastically reorganize society and radically transform the world's economy to counter imaginary ecological apocalypses. The relevant motto is not "He who hesitates is lost," but rather, "Look before you leap."

BILL McKIBBEN

Power Play Endangers Hawaii's Rain Forest

Currently a freelance writer and environmentalist who lives in the Adirondack Mountains of upstate New York, Bill McKibben (1951–   ) was a staff writer at The New Yorker *magazine from 1982 to 1987. His first book,* The End of Nature *(1989), offered a groundbreaking account of global environmental problems, especially global warming, which, he says, has had the effect of making everything on earth "artificial" (in the sense of "made by people"). McKibben frequently contributes to* Rolling Stone, *which carried the following essay on May 31, 1990.*

1   Consider, as you read this story, two images:

2   The first is the Hyatt Regency Waikoloa, a hotel that opened in 1988 on the Kona coast of the Big Island of Hawaii. Arriving guests at this $360 million pleasure dome have, in one visitor's words, "all sorts of ways to get their bags to their room—electric boats, electric monorail. Walking is not an option." The Hyatt Regency Waikoloa has been described as "the most spectacular resort on earth." It also draws four percent of the island's peak-load electricity. One hotel—four percent.

3   The second is of a gracious dinner out on a breezy porch. As the sun sets, someone flips on a light—a light powered by a twelve-volt solar panel on the roof. The television runs off the

A scene from a rain forest, similar to the one in Hawaii

same panels; the sun also heats the water, so it's only lukewarm this week. But not bad.

4   On the Puna side of the big island, the Kilauea volcano slopes down to the ocean. It is the nation's youngest and most active volcano; at the moment it is pouring lava from one vent into the ocean, adding as much as an acre a week to the size of the island. Not far from where the lava pours into the hissing, steaming sea, there is a rain forest—the largest lowland rain forest left in the fifty states.

5   In some ways the Wao Kele o Puna rain forest resembles the great ones of South America and Indonesia: Dominant trees, in this case *ohias*, shade a dense understory filled with layer upon layer of lush, almost obscene greenery. But there is one reason that this rain forest is unique, and that is that it sits on the side of an active volcano. It does not lie undisturbed for eons; al-

ROSA EHRENREICH

I Hate Trees

Rosa Ehrenreich (1969–) has published many essays since her graduation from Harvard in 1991. She has written about her experiences as an undergraduate, as a law student in South Africa, and as a Marshall scholar in England in A Garden of Paper Flowers: An American in Oxford *(1994). She recently joined the U.S. State Department's Bureau of Human Rights. The following short piece appeared in* Mademoiselle *magazine in February 1995.*

1   Yes, it's true. I detest, loathe and despise trees. Here's why: Yesterday, I went out to buy stationery, and every kind I found was not only made of recycled paper but had something printed on it, like "earth friendly!" in childlike writing.

2   I went into a fit of rage so uncontrollable that I had to leave the store before I flipped out and flung my newspaper into the trash can instead of the recycling bin. After all, what have trees ever done for us? They don't work on assembly lines. They don't write poems. And when was the last time you saw a tree rush into a burning building to save a child or air-drop food into a famine-ridden country?

most continuously, patches of it are inundated by molten lava, which destroys all plant life and leaves behind a layer of black rock.

6   As a result, the trees don't grow to the same heights that they do in some rain forests. On the other hand, the forest has learned to replace itself quite quickly after a major disaster. "A lot of people look at the trees here and think they're kind of scruffy—they think it couldn't mean much, but it does," says Hampton Carson, a biologist at the University of Hawaii, in Honolulu. "This forest is unique—it's one of the few places on earth where you can tell where life is coming from."

7   But the location that makes the forest special may also be its undoing. For, with state cooperation, developers have now started drilling through the forest floor to the hot steam below. They plan to produce power from

3   Trees have every right to hang out unmolested. But recall Dr. Seuss's Lorax, who spoke for the trees, "for the trees have no tongues." This isn't true today—every tree has a tongue. In fact, they have protectors running around in natural cotton T-shirts. A recent *Times Mirror* poll showed that 56 percent of Americans believe that improving the global environment should be a top priority for the nation. The U.S. has spent $2 trillion on environmental protection. Hell, trees have recycling laws; they even have Rainforest Crunch ice cream.

4   But what about people? You know, all 5.3 billion of us. What about the 15.7 million American children who live below the poverty line? Or the 1.5 million Sudanese who were killed in the recent civil war? Or the 5 million African children who die each year from treatable or preventable illnesses? Who speaks for them? Who has even heard of them?

5   You don't see 56 percent of Americans campaigning for human rights. Nah, we're too busy sipping cappuccino from our refillable plastic mugs. That's the danger of environmentalism. For many of us, it's an easy way to feel good: "Look at me, I'm recycling!"

6   There's nothing wrong with recycling. I recycle (so I lied about hating it; shoot me). And it's okay to buy Rainforest Crunch. Just don't let caring about trees become a substitute for what's harder—caring about people.

7   The next time you buy earth-friendly paper, use it to write to your senator, or write a letter for Amnesty International. Use a recycled envelope to send a check to a cause you care about. Speak for the trees—but speak for people, too.

geothermal steam—perhaps as much as 500 megawatts from dozens of wells scattered throughout the forest.

8　　　　And they are doing it, so they say, in the name of the environment: They will generate electricity from Wao Kele o Puna without burning fossil fuels that give off carbon dioxide and add to the greenhouse effect. A lot of products, large and small, will be sold in the next few years with the label "environmentally friendly." Some of them will be good and solid—and some of them will be shoddy junk.

9　　　　To figure out which category this project falls into, one could begin at any number of places. The most obvious is probably the biological. The state of Hawaii is aware that the United States is pleading with poor nations around the tropics not to cut down their rain forests, and aware that rain forests have been described as the most precious planetary treasure, and aware that most tourists would probably just as soon think of Hawaii as Eden—so it has taken great pains to say that this is not a "good" rain forest. The governor recently labeled it class C forest; University of Hawaii botanist Charles Lamoureux, who is paid by the developers to do surveys of the land, refers to it as A-2 forest, less pristine than nearby groves of A-1.

10　　　　"There are a lot of *ohia* trees," says Lamoureux, "but the understory is heavily infested with guava," an exotic that threatens to crowd out other species. This may be true. On the other hand, the state itself declared the land as one of its first chunks of Natural Area Reserve in the 1970s—a designation discarded a decade later when the geothermal drilling was proposed.

11　　　　And if the forest is so worthless, it's unclear why the state is enforcing what it calls the "strictest" regulations designed to "mitigate" any environmental damage from the drilling. Before any road clearing takes place, for instance, Lamoureux and some assistants go in with the surveyors and try to route them around anything of special significance. "We had them move the drill pad 300 feet to avoid a forest where there were some birds," Lamoureux says. (Unfortunately, when they went to clear the land for that very first site, surely aware that everyone was keeping a close eye on their work, the developers wiped out eight acres instead of the allotted five. They've since closed the drill site to outsiders, including reporters; cops wait near the gates and write down your license plate number if you drive up.)

12　　　　And the state argues that the developers are only going to clear about 300 acres of 30,000. "It's only about one percent—that's so little," says Lamoureux. Unfortunately, much of that acreage will be spread out in the form of roads—and these roads, and the men, animals and trucks that traverse them, may well be perfect avenues for precisely the sort of weed species the state claims are currently degrading the forest. "You'll end up with a honeycomb of roads, corridors and steam pipes, and they'll allow the weeds right into the heart of the forest, where the plants aren't used to foreign competition," says Russell Ruderman of the Big Island Rainforest Action Group. It's like arguing that your veins and arteries only take up one percent of your body so it really shouldn't do much damage to eat nine or ten sticks of butter a day.

13   Class C or A-2 or whatever you want to call it, this is gorgeous, dense forest, undercut with cracks and rifts from the lava flows. I saw it in the company of Michael LaPlante, who lived on the edge of the rain forest until the geothermal plans drove him away. A burly man, he is given to saying things like "that just irks the snot out of me." (He once attended a hearing on the project wearing a shirt he had drenched in hydrogen sulfide, a rank gas that is a byproduct of geothermal drilling. "I found it in a joke store—it was called Morning Breeze Perfume," LaPlante says. "As soon as I sat down, the lady who was supposed to be taking notes for the meeting said, 'I can't do my job under these conditions.' 'Exactly my point,' I said. 'I can't *live* under these conditions.'") Anyway, LaPlante knows his way around this forest. "This is a friendly jungle—no snakes here, nothing to bite your butt," he says. "Look at that *ohia* over there—it probably dates from before Columbus."

14   There are other ways to look at all this—Palikapu Dedman's way, for instance. A native Hawaiian, he tends to get angry at public hearings and shout. "Our religion *is* a healthy environment," he says. "That's our life, our customs, our medicine." Dedman helped start the Pele Defense Fund named for the volcano god, one of the important deities of the Hawaiian pantheon. I have been places before where it is a little difficult to understand why the native people worshiped a *particular* mountain or hillock or lake—but on Hawaii that is not a problem. As far as the natives who lived there knew, the Hawaiian islands, the most remote spot on the planet, were the entire extent of the earth. On one of the islands, Hawaii, there were volcanoes erupting regularly, and in between eruptions, there were often lakes of fiery lava rippling in the craters and always thousands of vents of steam working their way up to the surface; these eruptions were obviously building up the island as the native people watched. It would have been curious if they had *not* venerated the volcano.

15   When the Pele Defense Fund tried to raise this point with the courts, however, they were told that they needed a "site-specific" religious practice in order to protect the land from intrusion. "But Pele religion doesn't work that way," says Tom Luebben, one of the PDF counsels. "You may go here one day and there the next, depending on what's happening, where the steam is."

16   If all this strikes you as too mushy, perhaps some hard economic arguments are in order. A consulting firm hired by the Pele Defense Fund estimates that the total cost of the project, including a cable run at a previously untried depth to the island of Oahu, may run upward of $4 billion. That's between two and three times what the state originally estimated. (The Hawaii Electric Company currently has bids in hand from consortia of giant companies but won't reveal the dollar totals.) "When you make a commitment to costly, risky technology, you're also making a commitment to pay it off," says Robert McKusick, a natural-resources consultant.

17   There are also technical questions about how long the steam will last. One key scientist at the Hawaiian Volcano Observatory says it may be quickly depleted, forcing the developers to pay for their expensive undersea cable by continually expanding their drilling operations into new corners of the forest. Some doctors insist that the hydrogen sulfide that is vented from the wells during initial drilling—and in the event of an accident—will do great damage: Two or three times the neighborhood around a test plant has been evacuated due to hydrogen sulfide emissions.

18   State and company officials answer these sorts of charges by stressing that they have new technology that will control emissions and that other parts of the world have sustained geothermal drilling for decades. But their argument for the geothermal development eventually comes back to a single point. "We don't find any other alternative source of electricity large enough to put a dent in Hawaii's consumption," says Roger Ulveling, the state's director of business and economic development. Hawaii depends heavily on imported oil for electricity generation. Its leaders say they would like to lessen that dependence. And so they want to mine one of their most plentiful resources—the heat of the volcanoes.

19   At first blush, this is a compelling argument. Oil is not such sweet stuff—quite aside from the Joseph Hazelwood factor, oil contributes huge clouds of carbon dioxide to the atmosphere, which may well be raising its temperature. If the choice were between oil and geothermal, it would be a much closer call.

20   But listen to Robert Mowris for a while. He is an energy-efficiency expert from the University of California at Berkeley, who was traveling through Hawaii last month [April 1990] carrying his report on the proposed geothermal complex and a suitcase full of lightbulbs. These lightbulbs, which he would pull out at the slightest provocation, screw into sockets for incandescent bulbs. But they use electricity like fluorescent bulbs, which is to say, slowly. Mowris also had panels of special glass that would greatly reduce the need for air conditioning in Waikiki's hotels. Mowris had gadget

upon gadget, all simple, all available. All together, he said, they could cut the island's energy use forty to sixty percent and at a cost per kilowatt-hour five to seven times less than building the new supply.

21   Say Mowris is only half right—that's still a lot of power you wouldn't need to cut up a rain forest to generate. Traditionally, though, utilities have made their money in the same way that every other business does—by selling product. Under current rate setups, Hawaii Electric can no more make money selling power to people with thrifty lightbulbs than *Rolling Stone* can make money not selling magazines.

22   Something else worth considering: Hawaii has another asset besides lava, and that's sunshine. If there was ever any place where people could take advantage of solar power to heat their homes, it's Hawaii. And some do. LaPlante has had solar panels on his house for fifteen years. Jim Albertini, a farmer and activist in the rain-soaked Puna area, runs his spread off the power that hits his roof. Quite a few people live "off the grid"—relying on the sun or the steady trade winds for their electricity.

23   Even in Hawaii, though, where solar energy should work if it works any place on earth, most people get their power from the same sources as you and I. Ulveling and other officials boast endlessly about the number of solar-heat pumps and water-heating systems in Hawaii (more than most places, which seems natural). But the data published by the Department of Business and Economic Development itself shows that after a surge of conservation following the OPEC embargoes, per capita electricity use has resumed climbing quickly in the islands. And the percentage of housing units with solar water-heating systems—just over ten and a half percent—has not increased [as of 1990] since 1985.

24   Why is this? The reason, I think, is that having a solar collector on your roof is not quite as "nice" as having a line running into your house from some power plant. The water in your shower may not be quite as hot. You can't run your lightbulbs and your appliances as many hours a day if it's cloudy out. It's not as utterly and overwhelmingly convenient. When I was talking with Lamoureux, the botanist who works for the geothermal development, he said something almost as an aside that struck me. "I'm not out beating the drum for geothermal," he said. "Left to my own devices, I'd probably say, 'Leave the forest alone, and turn off your lights.' But that's not going to happen. I could live more uncomfortably than my neighbors, but I'm not sure that's what I want."

25   Which made me think of something W. S. Merwin had said a day or two before when we were sitting in the semidark of evening in his living room, which is lit in the day by the sun and at night, if light is needed, by

the sixteen solar panels on his roof. Merwin, who lives on Maui, actively opposes developing the rain forest. He's also a Pulitzer Prize–winning poet and a man who seems able to sum up the issues of energy, forestry and personal responsibility that lie at the center of this, and most other, environmental arguments.

26   When he moved to Maui, his land was scrub. On it he cultivated rare species of palms from around the world, some of them extinct in their proper habitats. "This tree is from Isle de Reunion," Merwin says. "This is a Guinean oil palm. This has the largest leaf in the vegetable kingdom, fifteen feet across." It is a daily labor of love. "I've grown up all my life seeing what people do to the earth, and it makes me sick," says Merwin. "This was a chance to see, if I had a piece of land, how I would treat it." With little money and a good set of hand tools, he has built a reasonable set for whoever wants to turn Genesis into a movie. But he recognizes that it is a garden. "Only a forest makes a forest," he says.

27   "What's the purpose of a rain forest?" Merwin asks. "The first answer is, There is no purpose. Life doesn't exist because it has a purpose, it exists because it exists. But the second answer is, *Any* species is valuable beyond any way we can assess it. When we look at the world around us in a particular way, that's what we are. If we look at it as something to exploit, that's what we become—exploiters. If we look at it the other way, it's a sort of endless relationship."

28   In Brazil they cut down rain forests for cattle ranching; in Hawaii they "bisect" them so you can ride the electric monorail to your hotel room. The question is, How much forest will be left when we finally come to our senses?

N. SCOTT MOMADAY

The Way to Rainy Mountain

N. Scott Momaday (1934–   ) tells us something about himself in the following introductory chapter from his 1969 book The Way to Rainy Mountain, *an account of his homeland in the Wichita Mountains of Oklahoma. Momaday's father was a Kiowa and his mother was a descendant of white pioneers, and hence a concern with the uneasy relations between American subcultures has always permeated his work. In addition to essays and fiction, Momaday has created paintings, memoirs, and plays. He is now Regents Professor of English at the University of Arizona.*

1   A single knoll rises out of the plain in Oklahoma, north and west of the Wichita Range. For many people, the Kiowas, it is an old landmark, and they gave it the name Rainy Mountain. The hardest weather in the world is there. Winter brings blizzards, hot tornadic winds arise in the spring, and in summer the prairie is an anvil's edge. The grass turns brittle and brown, and it cracks beneath your feet. There are green belts along the rivers and creeks, linear groves of hickory and pecan, willow and witch hazel. At a distance in July or August the steaming foliage seems almost to writhe in fire. Great green and yellow grasshoppers are everywhere in the tall grass, popping up like corn to sting the flesh, and tortoises crawl about on the red earth, going nowhere in the plenty of time. Loneliness is an aspect of the land. All things in the plain are isolate; there is no confusion of objects in the eye, but *one* hill or *one* tree or *one* man. To look upon that landscape in the early morning, with the sun at your back, is to lose the sense of proportion. Your imagination comes to life, and this, you think, is where Creation was begun.

2   I returned to Rainy Mountain in July. My grandmother had died in the spring, and I wanted to be at her grave. She had lived to be very old and at last infirm. Her only living daughter was with her when she died, and I was told that in death her face was that of a child.

3   I like to think of her as a child. When she was born, the Kiowas were living that last great moment of their history. For more than a hundred years they had controlled the open range from the Smoky Hill River to the Red, from the headwaters of the Canadian to the fork of the Arkansas and Cimarron. In alliance with the Comanches, they had ruled the whole of the southern plains. War was their sacred business, and they were among the

finest horsemen the world has ever known. But warfare for the Kiowas was preeminently a matter of disposition rather than of survival, and they never understood the grim, unrelenting advance of the U.S. Cavalry. When at last, divided and ill-provisioned, they were driven onto the Staked Plains in the cold rains of autumn, they fell into panic. In Palo Duro Canyon they abandoned their crucial stores to pillage and had nothing then but their lives. In order to save themselves, they surrendered to the soldiers at Fort Sill and were imprisoned in the old stone corral that now stands as a military museum. My grandmother was spared the humiliation of those high gray walls by eight or ten years, but she must have known from birth the affliction of defeat, the dark brooding of old warriors.

4   Her name was Aho, and she belonged to the last culture to evolve in North America. Her forebears came down from the high country in western Montana nearly three centuries ago. They were a mountain people, a mysterious tribe of hunters whose language has never been positively classified in any major group. In the late seventeenth century they began a long migration to the south and east. It was a journey toward the dawn, and it led to a golden age. Along the way the Kiowas were befriended by the Crows, who gave them the culture and religion of the Plains. They acquired horses, and their ancient nomadic spirit was suddenly free of the ground. They acquired Tai-me, the sacred Sun Dance doll, from that moment the object and symbol of their worship, and so shared in the divinity of the sun. Not least, they acquired the sense of destiny, therefore courage and pride. When they entered upon the southern Plains they had been transformed. No longer were they slaves to the simple necessity of survival; they were a lordly and dangerous society of fighters and thieves, hunters and priests of the sun. According to their origin myth, they entered the world through a hollow log. From one point of view, their migration was the fruit of an old prophecy, for indeed they emerged from a sunless world.

5   Although my grandmother lived out her long life in the shadow of Rainy Mountain, the immense landscape of the continental interior lay like memory in her blood. She could tell of the Crows, whom she had never seen, and of the Black Hills, where she had never been. I wanted to see in reality what she had seen more perfectly in the mind's eye, and traveled fifteen hundred miles to begin my pilgrimage.

6   Yellowstone, it seemed to me, was the top of the world, a region of deep lakes and dark timber, canyons and waterfalls. But, beautiful as it is, one might have the sense of confinement there. The skyline in all directions is close at hand, the high wall of the woods and deep cleavages of shade. There is a perfect freedom in the mountains, but it belongs to the

eagle and the elk, the badger and the bear. The Kiowas reckoned their stature by the distance they could see, and they were bent and blind in the wilderness.

7   Descending eastward, the highland meadows are a stairway to the plain. In July the inland slope of the Rockies is luxuriant with flax and buckwheat, stonecrop and larkspur. The earth unfolds and the limit of the land recedes. Clusters of trees, and animals grazing far in the distance, cause the vision to reach away and wonder to build upon the mind. The sun follows a longer course in the day, and the sky is immense beyond all comparison. The great billowing clouds that sail upon it are shadows that move upon the grain like water, dividing light. Farther down, in the land of the Crows and Blackfeet, the plain is yellow. Sweet clover takes hold of the hills and bends upon itself to cover and seat the soil. There the Kiowas paused on their way; they had come to the place where they must change their lives. The sun is at home on the plains. Precisely there does it have the certain character of a god. When the Kiowas came to the land of the Crows, they could see the dark lees of the hills at dawn across the Bighorn River, the profusion of light on the grain shelves, the oldest deity ranging after the solstices. Not yet would they veer southward to the caldron of the land that lay below; they must wean their blood from the northern winter and hold the mountains a while longer in their view. They bore Tai-me in procession to the east.

8   A dark mist lay over the Black Hills, and the land was like iron. At the top of a ridge I caught sight of Devil's Tower upthrust against the gray sky as if in the birth of time the core of the earth had broken through its crust and the motion of the world was begun. There are things in nature that engender an awful quiet in the heart of man; Devil's Tower is one of them. Two centuries ago, because they could not do otherwise, the Kiowas made a legend at the base of the rock. My grandmother said:

> Eight children were there at play, seven sisters and their brother. Suddenly the boy was struck dumb; he trembled and began to run upon his hands and feet. His fingers became claws, and his body was covered with fur. Directly there was a bear where the boy had been. The sisters were terrified; they ran, and the bear after them. They came to the stump of a great tree, and the tree spoke to them. It bade them climb upon it, and as they did so it began to rise into the air. The bear came to kill them, but they were just beyond its reach. It reared against the tree and scored the bark all around with its claws. The seven sisters were borne into the sky, and they became the stars of the Big Dipper.

From that moment, and so long as the legend lives, the Kiowas have kins-men in the night sky. Whatever they were in the mountains, they could be no more. However tenuous their well-being, however much they had suf-fered and would suffer again, they had found a way out of the wilderness.

9   My grandmother had a reverence for the sun, a holy regard that now is all but gone out of mankind. There was a wariness in her, and an ancient awe. She was a Christian in her later years, but she had come a long way about, and she never forgot her birthright. As a child she had been to the Sun Dances; she had taken part in those annual rites, and by them she had learned the restoration of her people in the presence of Tai-me. She was about seven when the last Kiowa Sun Dance was held in 1887 on the Washita River above Rainy Mountain Creek. The buffalo were gone. In order to consummate the ancient sacrifice—to impale the head of a buffalo bull upon the medicine tree—a delegation of old men journeyed into Texas, there to beg and barter for an animal from the Goodnight herd. She was ten when the Kiowas came together for the last time as a living Sun Dance culture. They could find no buffalo; they had to hang an old hide from the sacred tree. Before the dance could begin, a company of soldiers rode out from Fort Sill under orders to disperse the tribe. Forbidden without cause the essential act of their faith, having seen the wild herds slaughtered and left to rot upon the ground, the Kiowas backed away forever from the medicine tree. That was July 20, 1890, at the great bend of the Washita. My grandmother was there. Without bitterness, and for as long as she lived, she bore a vision of decide.

10   Now that I can have her only in memory, I see my grandmother in the several postures that were peculiar to her: standing at the wood stove on a winter morning and turning meat in a great iron skillet; sitting at the south window, bent above her beadwork, and afterwards, when her vision failed, looking down for a long time into the fold of her hands; going out upon a cane, very slowly as she did when the weight of age came upon her; pray-ing. I remember her most often at prayer. She made long, rambling prayers out of suffering and hope, having seen many things. I was never sure that I had the right to hear, so exclusive were they of all mere custom and com-pany. The last time I saw her she prayed standing by the side of her bed at night, naked to the waist, the light of a kerosene lamp moving upon her dark skin. Her long, black hair, always drawn and braided in the day, lay upon her shoulders and against her breasts like a shawl. I do not speak Kiowa, and I never understood her prayers, but there was something inher-ently sad in the sound, some merest hesitation upon the syllables of sorrow. She began in a high and descending pitch, exhausting her breath to silence;

then again and again—and always the same intensity of effort, of something that is, and is not, like urgency in the human voice. Transported so in the dancing light among the shadows of her room, she seemed beyond the reach of time. But that was illusion; I think I knew then that I should not see her again.

11   Houses are like sentinels in the plain, old keepers of the weather watch. There, in a very little while, wood takes on the appearance of great age. All colors wear soon away in the wind and rain, and then the wood is burned gray and the grain appears and the nails turn red with rust. The windowpanes are black and opaque; you imagine there is nothing within, and indeed there are many ghosts, bones given up to the land. They stand here and there against the sky, and you approach them for a longer time than you expect. They belong in the distance; it is their domain.

12   Once there was a lot of sound in my grandmother's house, a lot of coming and going, feasting and talk. The summers there were full of excitement and reunion. The Kiowas are a summer people; they abide the cold and keep to themselves, but when the season turns and the land becomes warm and vital they cannot hold still; an old love of going returns upon them. The aged visitors who came to my grandmother's house when I was a child were made of lean and leather, and they bore themselves upright. They wore great black hats and bright ample shirts that shook in the wind. They rubbed fat upon their hair and wound their braids with strips of colored cloth. Some of them painted their faces and carried the scars of old and cherished enmities. They were an old council of warlords, come to remind and be reminded of who they were. Their wives and daughters served them well. The women might indulge themselves; gossip was at once the mark and compensation of their servitude. They made loud and elaborate talk among themselves, full of jest and gesture, fright and false alarm. They went abroad in fringed and flowered shawls, bright beadwork and German silver. They were at home in the kitchen, and they prepared meals that were banquets.

13   There were frequent prayer meetings, and great nocturnal feasts. When I was a child I played with my cousins outside, where the lamplight fell upon the ground and the singing of the old people rose up around us and carried away into the darkness. There were a lot of good things to eat, a lot of laughter and surprise. And afterwards, when the quiet returned, I lay down with my grandmother and could hear the frogs away by the river and feel the motion of the air.

14   Now there is a funeral silence in the rooms, the endless wake of some final word. The walls have closed in upon my grandmother's house. When I returned to it in mourning, I saw for the first time in my life how small it

was. It was late at night, and there was a white moon, nearly full. I sat for a long time on the stone steps by the kitchen door. From there I could see out across the land; I could see the long row of trees by the creek, the low light upon the rolling plains, and the stars of the Big Dipper. Once I looked at the moon and caught sight of a strange thing. A cricket had perched upon the handrail, only a few inches away from me. My line of vision was such that the creature filled the moon like a fossil. It had gone there, I thought, to live and die, for there, of all places, was its small definition made whole and eternal. A warm wind rose up and purled like the longing within me.

15   The next morning I awoke at dawn and went out on the dirt road to Rainy Mountain. It was already hot, and the grasshoppers began to fill the air. Still, it was early in the morning, and the birds sang out of the shadows. The long yellow grass on the mountain shone in the bright light, and a scissortail hied above the land. There, where it ought to be, at the end of a long and legendary way, was my grandmother's grave. Here and there on the dark stones were ancestral names. Looking back once, I saw the mountain and came away.

ALICE WALKER

Am I Blue?

Alice Walker (1944–) is best known for her award-winning 1982 novel
The Color Purple, *which was made into a movie by Steven Spielberg. But
Walker has also written a great deal of other material—poems, essays,
short stories, other novels—in the past three decades, material that
is a reflection of her upbringing in rural Georgia and a product of her
commitments to social justice and women's issues. Walker included "Am
I Blue?" in her 1988 collection of essays called* Living by the Word, *which
meditates on the insidious effects of power in our relationships with
animals.*

1   For about three years my companion and I rented a small house in the
country that stood on the edge of a large meadow that appeared to run
from the end of our deck straight into the mountains. The mountains, however, were quite far away, and between us and them there was, in fact, a
town. It was one of the many pleasant aspects of the house that you never
really were aware of this.

2   It was a house of many windows, low, wide, nearly floor to ceiling in
the living room, which faced the meadow, and it was from one of these that
I first saw our closest neighbor, a large white horse, cropping grass, flipping
its mane, and ambling about—not over the entire meadow, which stretched
well out of sight of the house, but over the five or so fenced-in acres that
were next to the twenty-odd that we had rented. I soon learned that the
horse, whose name was Blue, belonged to a man who lived in another town,
but was boarded by our neighbors next door. Occasionally, one of the children, usually a stocky teenager, but sometimes a much younger girl or boy,
could be seen riding Blue. They would appear in the meadow, climb up on
his back, ride furiously for ten or fifteen minutes, then get off, slap Blue on
the flanks, and not be seen again for a month or more.

3   There were many apple trees in our yard, and one by the fence that
Blue could almost reach. We were soon in the habit of feeding him apples,
which he relished, especially because by the middle of summer the meadow
grasses—so green and succulent since January—had dried out from lack of
rain, and Blue stumbled about munching the dried stalks half-heartedly.
Sometimes he would stand very still just by the apple tree, and when one of
us came out he would whinny, snort loudly, or stamp the ground. This
meant, of course: I want an apple.

4   It was quite wonderful to pick a few apples, or collect those that had fallen to the ground overnight, and patiently hold them, one by one, up to his large, toothy mouth. I remained as thrilled as a child by his flexible dark lips, huge, cubelike teeth that crunched the apples, core and all, with such finality, and his high, broad-breasted *enormity;* beside which, I felt small indeed. When I was a child, I used to ride horses, and was especially friendly with one named Nan until the day I was riding and my brother deliberately spooked her and I was thrown, head first, against the trunk of a tree. When I came to, I was in bed and my mother was bending worriedly over me; we silently agreed that perhaps horseback riding was not the safest sport for me. Since then I have walked, and prefer walking, to horseback riding—but I had forgotten the depth of feeling one could see in horses' eyes.

5   I was therefore unprepared for the expression in Blue's. Blue was lonely. Blue was horribly lonely and bored. I was not shocked that this should be the case; five acres to tramp by yourself, endlessly, even in the most beautiful of meadows—and his was—cannot provide many interesting events, and once rainy season turned to dry that was about it. No, I was shocked that I had forgotten that human animals and nonhuman animals can communicate quite well; if we are brought up around animals as children we take this for granted. By the time we are adults we no longer remember. However, the animals have not changed. They are in fact *completed* creations (at least they seem to be, so much more than we) who are not likely *to* change; it is their nature to express themselves. What else are they going to express? And they do. And, generally speaking, they are ignored.

6   After giving Blue the apples, I would wander back to the house, aware that he was observing me. Were more apples not forthcoming then? Was that to be his sole entertainment for the day? My partner's small son had decided he wanted to learn how to piece a quilt; we worked in silence on our respective squares as I thought. . . .

7   Well, about slavery: about white children, who were raised by black people, who knew their first all-accepting love from black women, and then, when they were twelve or so, were told they must "forget" the deep levels of communication between themselves and "mammy" that they knew. Later they would be able to relate quite calmly, "My old mammy was sold to another good family." "My old mammy was _____ _____." Fill in the blank. Many more years later a white woman would say: "I can't understand these Negroes, these blacks. What do they want? They're so different from us."

8   And about the Indians, considered to be "like animals" by the "settlers" (a very benign euphemism for what they actually were), who did not understand their description as a compliment.

9   And about the thousands of American men who marry Japanese, Korean, Filipina, and other non-English-speaking women and of how happy they report they are, *"blissfully,"* until their brides learn to speak English, at which point the marriages tend to fall apart. What then did the men see, when they looked into the eyes of the women they married, before they could speak English? Apparently only their own reflections.

10   I thought of society's impatience with the young. "Why are they playing the music so loud?" Perhaps the children have listened to much of the music of oppressed people their parents danced to before they were born, with its passionate but soft cries for acceptance and love, and they have wondered why their parents failed to hear.

11   I do not know how long Blue had inhabited his five beautiful, boring acres before we moved into our house; a year after we had arrived—and had also traveled to other valleys, other cities, other worlds—he was still there.

12   But then, in our second year at the house, something happened in Blue's life. One morning, looking out the window at the fog that lay like a ribbon over the meadow, I saw another horse, a brown one, at the other end of Blue's field. Blue appeared to be afraid of it, and for several days made no attempt to go near. We went away for a week. When we returned, Blue had decided to make friends and the two horses ambled or galloped along together, and Blue did not come nearly as often to the fence underneath the apple tree.

13   When he did, bringing his new friend with him, there was a different look in his eyes. A look of independence, of self-possession, of inalienable *horse*ness. His friend eventually became pregnant. For months and months there was, it seemed to me, a mutual feeling between me and the horses of justice, of peace. I fed apples to them both. The look in Blue's eyes was one of unabashed "this is *it*ness."

14   It did not, however, last forever. One day, after a visit to the city, I went out to give Blue some apples. He stood waiting, or so I thought, though not beneath the tree. When I shook the tree and jumped back from the shower of apples, he made no move. I carried some over to him. He managed to half-crunch one. The rest he let fall to the ground. I dreaded looking into his eyes—because I had of course noticed that Brown, his partner, had gone—but I did look. If I had been born into slavery, and my partner had been sold or killed, my eyes would have looked like that. The children next door explained that Blue's partner had been "put with him" (the same expression that old people used, I had noticed, when speaking of an ancestor during slavery who had been impregnated by her owner) so that they could mate

and she conceive. Since that was accomplished, she had been taken back by her owner, who lived somewhere else.

15   Will she be back? I asked.

16   They didn't know.

17   Blue was like a crazed person. Blue *was*, to me, a crazed person. He galloped furiously, as if he were being ridden, around and around his five beautiful acres. He whinnied until he couldn't. He tore at the ground with his hooves. He butted himself against his single shade tree. He looked always and always toward the road down which his partner had gone. And then, occasionally, when he came up for apples, or I took apples to him, he looked at me. It was a look so piercing, so full of grief, a look so *human*, I almost laughed (I felt too sad to cry) to think there are people who do not know that animals suffer. People like me who have forgotten, and daily forget, all that animals try to tell us. "Everything you do to us will happen to you; we are your teachers, as you are ours. We are one lesson" is essentially it, I think. There are those who never once have even considered animals' rights: those who have been taught that animals actually want to be used and abused by us, as small children "love" to be frightened, or women "love" to be mutilated and raped. . . . They are the great-grandchildren of those who honestly thought, because someone taught them this: "Women can't think," and "niggers can't faint." But most disturbing of all, in Blue's large brown eyes was a new look, more painful than the look of despair: the look of disgust with human beings, with life; the look of hatred. And it was odd what the look of hatred did. It gave him, for the first time, the look of a beast. And what that meant was that he had put up a barrier within to protect himself from further violence; all the apples in the world wouldn't change that fact.

18   And so Blue remained, a beautiful part of our landscape, very peaceful to look at from the window, white against the grass. Once a friend came to visit and said, looking out on the soothing view: "And it *would* have to be a *white* horse; the very image of freedom." And I thought, yes, the animals are forced to become for us merely "images" of what they once so beautifully expressed. And we are used to drinking milk from containers showing "contented" cows, whose real lives we want to hear nothing about, eating eggs and drumsticks from "happy" hens, and munching hamburgers advertised by bulls of integrity who seem to command their fate.

19   As we talked of freedom and justice one day for all, we sat down to steaks. I am eating misery, I thought, as I took the first bite. And spit it out.

TERRY TEMPEST WILLIAMS

The Clan of One-Breasted Women

Terry Tempest Williams (1955–   ) has deep roots in the Mormon community in Utah. A university professor and naturalist-in-residence at the Utah Museum of Natural History, she has written children's books that aim to teach children environmental values and a collection of short stories set in Utah called Coyote's Canyon *(1989). Her collections of essays include* Pieces of White Shell: A Journey to Navaholand *(1984) and* Refuge: An Unnatural History of Family and Place *(1991), the collection in which the following essay appeared.*

Epilogue

1   I belong to a Clan of One-Breasted Women. My mother, my grandmothers, and six aunts have all had mastectomies. Seven are dead. The two who survive have just completed rounds of chemotherapy and radiation.

2   I've had my own problems: two biopsies for breast cancer and a small tumor between my ribs diagnosed as a "borderline malignancy."

3   This is my family history.

4   Most statistics tell us breast cancer is genetic, hereditary, with rising percentages attached to fatty diets, childlessness, or becoming pregnant after thirty. What they don't say is living in Utah may be the greatest hazard of all.

5   We are a Mormon family with roots in Utah since 1847. The "word of wisdom" in my family aligned us with good foods—no coffee, no tea, tobacco, or alcohol. For the most part, our women were finished having their babies by the time they were thirty. And only one faced breast cancer prior to 1960. Traditionally, as a group of people, Mormons have a low rate of cancer.

6   Is our family a cultural anomaly? The truth is, we didn't think about it. Those who did, usually the men, simply said, "bad genes." The women's attitude was stoic. Cancer was part of life. On February 16, 1971, the eve of my mother's surgery, I accidently picked up the telephone and overheard her ask my grandmother what she could expect.

7   "Diane, it is one of the most spiritual experiences you will ever encounter."

8   I quietly put down the receiver.

9   Two days later, my father took my brothers and me to the hospital to visit her. She met us in the lobby in a wheelchair. No bandages were visible.

I'll never forget her radiance, the way she held herself in a purple velvet robe, and how she gathered us around her.

10   "Children, I am fine. I want you to know I felt the arms of God around me."

11   We believed her. My father cried. Our mother, his wife, was thirty-eight years old.

12   A little over a year after Mother's death, Dad and I were having dinner together. He had just returned from St. George, where the Tempest Company was completing the gas lines that would service southern Utah. He spoke of his love for the country, the sandstoned landscape, bare-boned and beautiful. He had just finished hiking the Kolob trail in Zion National Park. We got caught up in reminiscing, recalling with fondness our walk up Angel's Landing on his fiftieth birthday and the years our family had vacationed there.

13   Over dessert, I shared a recurring dream of mine. I told my father that for years, as long as I could remember, I saw this flash of light in the night in the desert—that this image had so permeated my being that I could not venture south without seeing it again, on the horizon, illuminating buttes and mesas.

14   "You did see it," he said.

15   "Saw what?"

16   "The bomb. The cloud. We were driving home from Riverside, California. You were sitting on Diane's lap. She was pregnant. In fact, I remember the day, September 7, 1957. We had just gotten out of the Service. We were driving north, past Las Vegas. It was an hour or so before dawn, when this explosion went off. We not only heard it, but felt it. I thought the oil tanker in front of us had blown up. We pulled over and suddenly, rising from the desert floor, we saw it, clearly, this golden-stemmed cloud, the mushroom. The sky seemed to vibrate with an eerie pink glow. Within a few minutes, a light ash was raining on the car."

17   I stared at my father.

18   "I thought you knew that," he said. "It was a common occurrence in the fifties."

19   It was at this moment that I realized the deceit I had been living under. Children growing up in the American Southwest, drinking contaminated milk from contaminated cows, even from the contaminated breasts of their mothers, my mother—members, years later, of the Clan of One-Breasted Women.

20   It is a well-known story in the Desert West, "The Day We Bombed Utah," or more accurately, the years we bombed Utah: above ground atomic testing in Nevada took place from January 27, 1951 through July 11, 1962.

Not only were the winds blowing north covering "low-use segments of the population" with fallout and leaving sheep dead in their tracks, but the climate was right. The United States of the 1950s was red, white, and blue. The Korean War was raging. McCarthyism was rampant. Ike was it, and the cold war was hot. If you were against nuclear testing, you were for a communist regime.

21   Much has been written about this "American nuclear tragedy." Public health was secondary to national security. The Atomic Energy Commissioner, Thomas Murray, said, "Gentlemen, we must not let anything interfere with this series of tests, nothing."

22   Again and again, the American public was told by its government, in spite of burns, blisters, and nausea, "It has been found that the tests may be conducted with adequate assurance of safety under conditions prevailing at the bombing reservations." Assuaging public fears was simply a matter of public relations. "Your best action," an Atomic Energy Commission booklet read, "is not to be worried about fallout." A news release typical of the times stated, "We find no basis for concluding that harm to any individual has resulted from radioactive fallout."

23   On August 30, 1979, during Jimmy Carter's presidency, a suit was filed, *Irene Allen* v. *The United States of America.* Mrs. Allen's case was the first on an alphabetical list of twenty-four test cases, representative of nearly twelve hundred plaintiffs seeking compensation from the United States government for cancers caused by nuclear testing in Nevada.

24   Irene Allen lived in Hurricane, Utah. She was the mother of five children and had been widowed twice. Her first husband, with their two oldest boys, had watched the tests from the roof of the local high school. He died of leukemia in 1956. Her second husband died of pancreatic cancer in 1978.

25   In a town meeting conducted by Utah Senator Orrin Hatch, shortly before the suit was filed, Mrs. Allen said, "I am not blaming the government, I want you to know that, Senator Hatch. But I thought if my testimony could help in any way so this wouldn't happen again to any of the generations coming up after us . . . I am happy to be here this day to bear testimony of this."

26   God-fearing people. This is just one story in an anthology of thousands.

27   On May 10, 1984, Judge Bruce S. Jenkins handed down his opinion. Ten of the plaintiffs were awarded damages. It was the first time a federal court had determined that nuclear tests had been the cause of cancers. For the remaining fourteen test cases, the proof of causation was not sufficient. In spite of the split decision, it was considered a landmark ruling. It was not to remain so for long.

28   In April 1987, the Tenth Circuit Court of Appeals overturned Judge Jenkins's ruling on the ground that the United States was protected from suit by the legal doctrine of sovereign immunity, a centuries-old idea from England in the days of absolute monarchs.

29   In January 1988, the Supreme Court refused to review the Appeals Court decision. To our court system it does not matter whether the United States government was irresponsible, whether it lied to its citizens, or even that citizens died from the fallout of nuclear testing. What matters is that our government is immune: "The King can do no wrong."

30   In Mormon culture, authority is respected, obedience revered, and independent thinking is not. I was taught as a young girl not to "make waves" or "rock the boat."

31   "Just let it go," Mother would say. "You know how you feel, that's what counts."

32   For many years, I have done just that—listened, observed, and quietly formed my own opinions, in a culture that rarely asks questions because it has all the answers. But one by one, I have watched the women in my family die common, heroic deaths. We sat in waiting rooms hoping for good news, but always receiving the bad. I cared for them, bathed their scarred bodies, and kept their secrets. I watched beautiful women become bald as Cytoxan, cisplatin, and Adriamycin were injected into their veins. I held their foreheads as they vomited green-black bile, and I shot them with morphine when the pain became inhuman. In the end, I witnessed their last peaceful breaths, becoming a midwife to the rebirth of their souls.

33   The price of obedience has become too high.

34   The fear and inability to question authority that ultimately killed rural communities in Utah during atmospheric testing of atomic weapons is the same fear I saw in my mother's body. Sheep. Dead sheep. The evidence is buried.

35   I cannot prove that my mother, Diane Dixon Tempest, or my grand-mothers, Lettie Romney Dixon and Kathryn Blackett Tempest, along with my aunts developed cancer from nuclear fallout in Utah. But I can't prove they didn't.

36   My father's memory was correct. The September blast we drove through in 1957 was part of Operation Plumbbob, one of the most intensive series of bomb tests to be initiated. The flash of light in the night in the desert, which I had always thought was a dream, developed into a family nightmare. It took fourteen years, from 1957 to 1971, for cancer to manifest in my mother—the same time, Howard L. Andrews, an authority in radioactive fallout at the National Institutes of Health, says radiation cancer

requires to become evident. The more I learn about what it means to be a "downwinder," the more questions I drown in.

37   What I do know, however, is that as a Mormon woman of the fifth generation of Latter-day Saints, I must question everything, even if it means losing my faith, even if it means becoming a member of a border tribe among my own people. Tolerating blind obedience in the name of patriotism or religion ultimately takes our lives.

38   When the Atomic Energy Commission described the country north of the Nevada Test Site as "virtually uninhabited desert terrain," my family and the birds at Great Salt Lake were some of the "virtual uninhabitants."

39   One night, I dreamed women from all over the world circled a blazing fire in the desert. They spoke of change, how they hold the moon in their bellies and wax and wane with its phases. They mocked the presumption of even-tempered beings and made promises that they would never fear the witch inside themselves. The women danced wildly as sparks broke away from the flames and entered the night sky as stars.

40   And they sang a song given to them by Shoshone grandmothers:

Ah ne nah, nah	*Consider the rabbits*
nin nah nah—	*How gently they walk on the earth—*
ah ne nah, nah	*Consider the rabbits*
nin nah nah—	*How gently they walk on the earth—*
Nyaga mutzi	*We remember them*
oh ne nay—	*We can walk gently also—*
Nyaga mutzi	*We remember them*
oh ne nay—	*We can walk gently also—*

The women danced and drummed and sang for weeks, preparing themselves for what was to come. They would reclaim the desert for the sake of their children, for the sake of the land.

41   A few miles downwind from the fire circle, bombs were being tested. Rabbits felt the tremors. Their soft leather pads on paws and feet recognized the shaking sands, while the roots of mesquite and sage were smoldering. Rocks were hot from the inside out and dust devils hummed unnaturally. And each time there was another nuclear test, ravens watched the desert heave. Stretch marks appeared. The land was losing its muscle.

42   The women couldn't bear it any longer. They were mothers. They had suffered labor pains but always under the promise of birth. The red hot pains beneath the desert promised death only, as each bomb became a stillborn. A contract had been made and broken between human beings and the land. A

new contract was being drawn by the women, who understood the face of the earth as their own.

43   Under the cover of darkness, ten women slipped under a barbed-wire fence and entered the contaminated country. They were trespassing. They walked toward the town of Mercury, in moonlight, taking their cues from coyote, kit fox, antelope squirrel, and quail. They moved quietly and deliberately through the maze of Joshua trees. When a hint of daylight appeared they rested, drinking tea and sharing their rations of food. The women closed their eyes. The time had come to protest with the heart, that to deny one's genealogy with the earth was to commit treason against one's soul.

44   At dawn, the women draped themselves in mylar, wrapping long streamers of silver plastic around their arms to blow in the breeze. They wore clear masks, that became the faces of humanity. And when they arrived at the edge of Mercury, they carried all the butterflies of a summer day in their wombs. They paused to allow their courage to settle.

45   The town that forbids pregnant women and children to enter because of radiation risks was asleep. The women moved through the streets as winged messengers, twirling around each other in slow motion, peeking inside homes and watching the easy sleep of men and women. They were astonished by such stillness and periodically would utter a shrill note or low cry just to verify life.

46   The residents finally awoke to these strange apparitions. Some simply stared. Others called authorities, and in time, the women were apprehended by wary soldiers dressed in desert fatigues. They were taken to a white, square building on the other edge of Mercury. When asked who they were and why they were there, the women replied, "We are mothers and we have come to reclaim the desert for our children."

47   The soldiers arrested them. As the ten women were blind-folded and handcuffed, they began singing:

> You can't forbid us everything
> You can't forbid us to think—
> You can't forbid our tears to flow
> And you can't stop the songs that we sing.

The women continued to sing louder and louder, until they heard the voices of their sisters moving across the mesa:

> Ah ne nah, nah
> nin nah nah—
> Ah ne nah, nah

nin nah nah—
Nyaga mutzi
oh ne nay—
Nyaga mutzi
oh ne nay—

48   "Call for reinforcements," one soldier said.

49   "We have," interrupted one woman, "we have—and you have no idea of our numbers."

50   I crossed the line at the Nevada Test Site and was arrested with nine other Utahns for trespassing on military lands. They are still conducting nuclear tests in the desert. Ours was an act of civil disobedience. But as I walked toward the town of Mercury, it was more than a gesture of peace. It was a gesture on behalf of the Clan of One-Breasted Women.

51   As one officer cinched the handcuffs around my wrists, another frisked my body. She found a pen and a pad of paper tucked inside my left boot.

52   "And these?" she asked sternly.

53   "Weapons," I replied.

54   Our eyes met. I smiled. She pulled the leg of my trousers back over my boot.

55   "Step forward, please," she said as she took my arm.

56   We were booked under an afternoon sun and bused to Tonopah, Nevada. It was a two-hour ride. This was familiar country. The Joshua trees standing their ground had been named by my ancestors, who believed they looked like prophets pointing west to the Promised Land. These were the same trees that bloomed each spring, flowers appearing like white flames in the Mojave. And I recalled a full moon in May, when Mother and I had walked among them, flushing out mourning doves and owls.

57   The bus stopped short of town. We were released.

58   The officials thought it was a cruel joke to leave us stranded in the desert with no way to get home. What they didn't realize was that we were home, soul-centered and strong, women who recognized the sweet smell of sage as fuel for our spirits.

Environmentalism in Advertising

This ad, which appeared in Time *magazine on October 4, 1999, is one of many examples of environmentalism in advertising. Industry, which has been responsible for numerous environmental problems such as the depletion of the ozone layer, is now promoting its "environmentally friendly" practices in an attempt to convince consumers that science and technology are not in conflict with the natural environment. Through this ad, Saturn hopes to connect with the growing number of environmentally aware consumers.*

Child Labor:
Visual Arguments
Then and Now

As a country founded with a very rural and agricultural heritage, and with a reliance on slavery (African American slaves, of course, but also white "indentured servants" and "apprentice laborers"), the United States grew up with the reality of child labor. The autobiographies of Frederick Douglass and Benjamin Franklin document vividly the reality of child labor in the early days of the nation. Yet as early as the 1830s, many states had begun placing restrictions on the employment of young children, particularly in industrial settings. By the late 1800s hundreds of laws were on the books, but often they went unenforced (on the grounds that employment of children was said to help poor families), and often they did not apply to immigrant workers. The Supreme Court ruled several times that child labor laws were unconstitutional on the grounds that the laws abrogated property rights and the rights of parents. (For details on the history of child labor, see <www.historyplace.com/unitedstates/childlabor/about.htm>.)

Activists opposing child labor have resorted to every rhetorical medium available to them—to impassioned essays and books, government reports and election campaign speeches, sermons and committee hearings and leaflets. But argument in those media were not especially successful until they began to be accompanied by photographs of actual children at work. Published in books, magazines, and newspapers once the technology had been perfected enough to permit cost-effective reproductions in print media, photographs began making impassioned and successful pleas for enlightened child labor laws.

We offer a few examples here. The first three photos were taken by Jacob Riis. Born in Denmark in 1849, Riis emigrated to the United States in 1870. After working a variety of menial, temporary jobs that impressed upon him the conditions endured by the exploited poor, he finally landed a job with a newspaper. After a series of promotions, he took a newly created position as a photojournalist for the *New York Evening Sun*. In 1890 he published an account of city life, illustrated with his photographs, under the title *How the Other Half Lives*—a book that documented the unspeakable particulars of tenement life, the shattering living conditions endured by immigrants (Jews, Italians, Germans, Chinese, Irish), and the predicament of child workers, especially in sweatshops. The book was seen by Theodore Roosevelt, then the New York Police Commissioner, who asked Riis to accompany him on his own tours of New York slums, who praised Riis as "the most useful citizen of New York" and "the best American I ever knew," and who committed himself to reforms during his subsequent presidency. Over the next quarter century Riis lectured on the problems of the poor, illustrating his presentations with photos that impressed upon his audiences the need to rectify conditions for the poor, especially children. He traveled outside New York; photographed people at work in all sorts of industries, particularly children; and published several other books, among them *Children of the Poor* (1892), *Children of the Tenements* (1903), and *The Making of an American* (1901), his autobiography. Riis died in 1914, having argued successfully, along with other reformers, for better living conditions for the poor, improved sanitation and water, and laws restricting child labor.

Printed in this section are three of Riis's photographs. The first, "Children Sleeping on Mulberry Street," captures both the innocence and the difficult circumstances of so-called "street Arabs"—children, often homeless, who were employed to sell newspapers and who were able to find warm-enough sleeping quarters by huddling around the vent holes letting out steam from basement printing-press rooms. The second, "In a Sweat Shop," fastens on a twelve-year-old boy hard at work in the garment industry: the child's innocence is emphasized by his facial expression and by his position among his coworkers—the fatherly types gathered behind him. "Little Susy at Her Work," the third photo, depicts a twelve-year-old New Yorker (and her sister) making tin boxes in her family apartment for sixty cents a twelve-hour day. Photos such as these were responsible for convincing lawmakers to do more to protect children. In 1907, the National Child Labor Committee was chartered by Congress to assess the situation and to consider possible measures.

Nevertheless, there were still many violations of laws protecting children from the workplace. Louis W. Hine documented many of them. Born in 1874, Hine studied sociology in college, became a teacher, and then gravitated to photography as a way to provide an outlet for his social activism. In 1908 Hine gave up photographing immigrants and took a job as an investigative photojournalist for the National Child Labor Committee, which hoped to amass documentary evidence about the problem they were attacking. After 1909 he began traveling widely to photograph children working in fields, mills, mines, and sweatshops. Reproduced here are six photos by Hine: a famous picture of a young girl gazing wistfully out the window of her textile mill; a photo of young boys sorting coal in a setting that is a mocking facsimile of the schoolroom where they should be; a picture of two girls sewing with their mother, an ironic turnabout on a scene of domestic bliss; two youngsters, one barefoot, precariously close to dangerous equipment; a servile shoeshine boy; and a "street Arab" joylessly selling newspapers amid impassive adults. Inspired by the work of Hine and his colleagues, activists redoubled their efforts at reform, and many states passed stricter laws and enforced them more vigorously.

In 1938, partly on the basis of photos of migrant workers and child laborers gathered by the Labor Defender Photo Group, the Film and Photo League, and photographers employed by the Farm Security Administration (including Dorothea Lange, Walker Evans, and Ben Shahn), Congress at last passed the Fair Labor Standards Act, a law which prohibited child labor under the age of sixteen, except for limited hours after school and during school vacations, and which restricted children under eighteen from working in hazardous jobs, such as mining.

While child labor laws have sharply reduced (though not eliminated) the practice in the United States, millions of children under twelve are still working full workdays in various nations around the world. According to estimates by the International Labor Office, some 120 million children under the age of fourteen currently work full-time in developing nations, often under hazardous conditions. Jean-Pierre Laffont, a well known photojournalist, has traveled to a dozen nations to capture images of children at work in fields, factories, and sweatshops. In spite of the United Nations Declaration of the Rights of Children, which condemns child labor, Laffont found children under twelve working in a host of jobs, often proudly and just as often with the approval of local authorities. Here is reproduced one of Laffont's photographs, capturing very young children at work in a brick factory. The photo is similar to one appearing on the Web site of Benetton, the well known clothing manufacturing and sales company that has operations in over a hundred countries. You might take a look at the Benetton site—<www.benetton.com>—to see other photographic arguments on matters such as AIDS, racism, and poverty. And you might consider why Benetton associates itself with such images and arguments.

If you would like to see more photos on child labor, you should know that many photographs of child laborers, and of course many other subjects, are available on the Internet. The Library of Congress holdings are massive, for many photographers did their work as employees of the U.S. government: see <http://www.americaslibrary.gov/cgi-bin/page.cgi/aa>. For additional examples of the work of Jacob Riis, see <www.mcny.org/riis.htm> and <www.yale.edu/amstud/inforev/riis/title.htm>.

Photo Essay
by Jacob Riis

Jacob Riis

Children Sleeping on Mulberry Street

In a Sweat Shop

Little Susy at Her Work

Photo Essay
by Louis Hine

Louis Hine

"A moment's glimpse of the outer world. Said she was 11 years old. Been working over a year. Rhodes Manufacturing Company, Lincolnton, North Carolina."—Louis Hine

"View of the Ewen Breaker of the Pennsylvania Coal Company. The dust was so dense at times as to obscure the view. . . . A kind of slave driver sometimes stands over the boys, prodding or kicking them into obedience. S. Pittston, Pennsylvania."—Louis Hine

"Some boys and girls were so small they had to climb up on the spinning frame to mend broken threads and to put back the empty bobbins. Bibb Mill No. 1, Macon, Georgia."—Louis Hine

"Mrs. Battaglia with Tessie, age 12, and Tony, age 7. Mrs. Battaglia works in a garment shop, except on Saturdays, when the children sew with her at home. Get two or three cents a pair finishing men's pants. Said they earn $1 to $1.50 on Saturday. Father disabled.... New York City" —Louis Hine

"A Bowery bootblack in New York"—Louis Hine

"A small newsy downtown on a Saturday afternoon, St. Louis, Missouri" —Louis Hine

Photo on Child Labor by
Jean-Pierre Laffont

Children at work in a brick factory near Bogota, Colombia

Confronting
Sexual Difference

In 1998 University of Wyoming political science major Matthew Shepard was beaten to a pulp and pistol-whipped to death in the town of Laramie, Wyoming. Russell Henderson, twenty-one, and Aaron McKinney, twenty, had lured Shepard from a bar (they knew he was gay), driven him to a deserted area, beaten him as he begged for mercy, and removed his shoes and tied him to a post, like a coyote, to warn off others. Henderson and McKinney took Shepard's wallet, left him to die, and then attacked two Latino men before they were arrested. Matthew Shepard, buried two days later before a crowd of 650 mourners (and a small group of protesters holding signs ridiculing "fags"), became a symbol of growing violence against gays in the United States. His murder and the subsequent trial of the

Matthew Shepard as he looked a year before he was beaten and left to die outside Laramie, Wyoming

perpetrators led many citizens and legislators to advocate a range of measures to protect gay, lesbian, and bisexual citizens, and to expand the rights and responsibilities that those citizens might enjoy.

A year before, in 1997, Ellen DeGeneres, star of the comedy series *Ellen*, made public her character's (and her own) lesbian identity and redirected her show toward an exploration of gay and lesbian identity. Before the series closed two years later, it consistently treated (typically as the material of comedy) the social and cultural tribulations faced by gays and lesbians, and challenged viewers to confront those tribulations in their own communities. Since then, a number of other television series have pursued the same end—most prominently, *Will and Grace*, *Six Feet Under*, and *Queer as Folk*, but also soap operas, documentaries, variety shows (such as *Saturday Night Live*), and "reality" shows such as *Survivor*. Television shows like these, as well as a range of movies, ads, and Web sites, have required American citizens to confront a range of cultural practices involving gay, lesbian, and bisexual people—practices including service in the military, same-sex marriage and other domestic issues, and even the ordination of priests.

The cast of *Queer as Folk*

This section of *Good Reasons* contains a range of arguments related to just those issues. Matthew Shepard's murder and subsequent hate crimes in various communities in recent years have focused great attention on the violence that is often leveled at gays and on the issue of rights and protections for gay, lesbian, and bisexual citizens. The question of passing legislation to protect the rights and property and physical bodies of gays, lesbians, and bisexuals has animated citizens in many communities, and there is even a play about the Shepard case that is being presented in many cities, Moises Kaufman's *The Laramie Project*, in order to raise awareness of hate crime legislation. Thus we present an argument by Carmen Vazquez about the predicament of gay and lesbian citizens in the United States that might have implications for legislation.

At the least, such legislation would prohibit hate speech and violent acts directed toward people on account of their sexual preference. Indeed, a number of states and cities have already moved to discourage hate crimes and to include sexual orientation along with provisions that protect people from discrimination based on race, religion, gender, and disability. While proponents of such legislation feel that criminal conduct based on prejudice not only terrorizes victims and strips them of civil rights but also debilitates entire communities, critics note that law enforcement officials may remain indifferent to violence based on sexual orientation no matter what the law is. Critics also have other objections. Some feel that laws already prohibit violence and excessive harassment, that gay rights legislation is really "special rights" legislation as opposed to "civil rights" legislation. Some regard sexual preferences as social behaviors, not inherent and immutable characteristics like gender or race that require protection (and some even believe that such behaviors can be modified through therapy). Some feel that legal protections somehow might grow into affirmative action for gays, lesbians, and bisexuals. And some even argue (based on passages in the Bible) that certain sexual activities not only do not deserve protection but are in fact immoral enough to deserve prosecution. There are even those who claim that gays, lesbians, and bisexuals prey on the young and constitute a threat to the stability of communities and families (especially in the light of the AIDS epidemic), a threat that hardly deserves protection and sanction. We therefore present here an argument (in two parts) by Jay Budziszewski resisting gay, lesbian, and bisexual rights that is based on many of these assumptions, as well as Peter Gomes's presentation countering them.

At most, so-called gay rights legislation might extend the rights of gays, lesbians, and bisexuals to permit a number of practices: the right to serve in the military, the right to marry, the right to be ordained into the clergy, the right to adopt and raise children (not to mention a host of related "marriage rights" relating to property and child rearing), the right to sexual freedom, and protections against discrimination based on AIDS.

The issue of gays in the military became very public when, just after assuming the presidency in 1993, Bill Clinton moved to discontinue the practice of discharging gays and lesbians from the armed services. Conservatives criticized the move, citing traditional concerns about morale and battle-readiness, and about the culture of military life. Since 1994 the services have pursued a "don't ask, don't tell" compromise policy: those who are openly homosexual are still barred from service, but supervisors are not allowed to ask subordinates about their sexual preferences, and homosexuals are permitted to remain in the service so long as they do not discuss their sexual orientation. "Don't ask, don't tell" also has characterized the position of the Catholic Church on the ordination of priests. But in the wake of child-abuse and cover-up scandals in Boston and other cities, the Catholic hierarchy is also rethinking the wisdom of that policy.

The current controversy over gay marriage derives from years of efforts by gay, lesbian, and bisexual activists to achieve family rights on a piecemeal basis—through pressing for domestic partnership laws, for example, or through lawsuits to permit adoption by single persons. Then in 1993, the Hawaii Supreme Court suddenly ruled in support of the recognition of same-sex marriage. Since marriages in one state are usually recognized in all, the ruling in Hawaii made same-sex marriage into a national issue immediately. A federal law soon was passed—the Defense of Marriage Act—that said that states are not required to recognize Hawaiian marriages, but the issue has remained significant in many states because each must now decide whether to permit or at least recognize same-sex marriage. Supporters of same-sex marriage, such as Andrew Sullivan and Anna Quindlen, point to practical consequences: the recognition of a personal, lasting, loving monogamous

Some Gay Rights Web Sites

www.ngltf.org	The National Gay and Lesbian Task Force
www.glaad.org	Gay and Lesbian Alliance Against Defamation
www.aclu.org/issues/ gay/hmgl.html	American Civil Liberties Union
www.advocate.com	*The Advocate* magazine
www.lambdalegal.org	Lambda Legal Defense and Education Fund
www.theweddingparty.org	Seeks to secure equal marriage rights for same-sex couples.
www.hrc.org	Human Rights Campaign
www.noah.cuny.edu/ providers/gmhc.html	Gay Men's Health Crisis organization
www.glsen.org	Gay, Lesbian, Straight Education Network
www.buddybuddy.com	Partners' Taskforce for Gay and Lesbian Couples
www.actwin.com/cahp	Citizens Against Homophobia
www.planetout.com	Collects news and commentary.

commitment (and the consequent freedom from prosecution for sexual behavior); the enjoyment of pension, insurance, and inheritance benefits; protection from child custody battles; greater tolerance for gay and lesbian citizens. In some ways, the movement to permit same-sex marriage is a conservative move in keeping with conservative times: one that would restrict gay lifestyles to monogamous relationships in the image of heterosexual marriage, and one that is consequently supported by many clergymen, including Peter Gomes in the selection we reprint. Thus, same-sex marriage statutes are often resisted by some gays and lesbians, who regard marriage as a straitjacket that enforces traditional sexual norms. Nevertheless, many staunch conservatives dismiss the idea of same-sex marriage outright, arguing that marriage as it is now constituted should remain a public sanctioning for the traditional family that has stood the test of time. Hadley Arkes's essay articulates that point of view.

We conclude our sampling of arguments by returning to where we began this introduction—with several pieces that discuss media representations. In the first, Erik Meers evaluates depictions of gays and lesbians in current television shows. In the other, Norah Vincent tries to convince prominent gay stars to come out publicly at the Academy Awards show, in the interest of creating a more tolerant American citizenry.

ANDREW SULLIVAN

Here Comes the Groom

Andrew Sullivan, the author of Virtually Normal: An Argument about Homosexuality *(1995),* Love Undetectable: Notes on Friendship, Sex, and Survival *(1999), and many essays, is one of the leading commentators on gay, lesbian, and bisexual issues in the nation. Openly gay himself, devotedly Catholic, critical of certain aspects of the gay community, and outspokenly conservative in many respects, he advocates full integration of gays and lesbians into American life. He regards same-sex marriage as the most basic denial of civil rights in America. In 1996 he disclosed that he was receiving treatment for AIDS, entered graduate school to study government at Harvard, and reduced his editorial commitments to* The New Republic *(which published the following argument in 1989). He subsequently completed his PhD in political science, and he lives and writes now (still for* The New Republic*) in Washington, D.C. To learn more about him and his work, see <www.andrewsullivan.com>.*

1   Last month in New York, a court ruled that a gay lover had the right to stay in his deceased partner's rent-control apartment because the lover qualified as a member of the deceased's family. The ruling deftly annoyed almost everybody. Conservatives saw judicial activism in favor of gay rent control: three reasons to be appalled. Chastened liberals (such as the *New York Times* editorial page), while endorsing the recognition of gay relationships, also worried about the abuse of already stretched entitlements that the ruling threatened. What neither side quite contemplated is that they both might be right, and that the way to tackle the issue of unconventional relationships in conventional society is to try something both more radical and more conservative than putting courts in the business of deciding what is and is not a family. That alternative is the legalization of civil gay marriage.

2   The New York rent-control case did not go anywhere near that far, which is the problem. The rent-control regulations merely stipulated that a "family" member had the right to remain in the apartment. The judge ruled that to all intents and purposes a gay lover is part of his lover's family, inasmuch as a "family" merely means an interwoven social life, emotional commitment, and some level of financial interdependence.

3   It's a principle now well established around the country. Several cities have "domestic partnership" laws, which allow relationships that do not fit

into the category of heterosexual marriage to be registered with the city and qualify for benefits that up till now have been reserved for straight married couples. San Francisco, Berkeley, Madison, and Los Angeles all have legislation, as does the politically correct Washington, D.C., suburb, Takoma Park. In these cities, a variety of interpersonal arrangements qualify for health insurance, bereavement leave, insurance, annuity and pension rights, housing rights (such as rent-control apartments), adoption and inheritance rights. Eventually, according to gay lobby groups, the aim is to include federal income tax and veterans' benefits as well. A recent case even involved the right to use a family member's accumulated frequent-flier points. Gays are not the only beneficiaries; heterosexual "live-togethers" also qualify.

4   There's an argument, of course, that the current legal advantages extended to married people unfairly discriminate against people who've shaped their lives in less conventional arrangements. But it doesn't take a genius to see that enshrining in the law a vague principle like "domestic partnership" [DP] is an invitation to qualify at little personal cost for a vast array of entitlements otherwise kept crudely under control.

5   To be sure, potential DPs have to prove financial interdependence, shared living arrangements, and a commitment to mutual caring. But they don't need to have a sexual relationship or even closely mirror old-style marriage. In principle, an elderly woman and her live-in nurse could qualify. A couple of uneuphemistically confirmed bachelors could be DPs. So could two close college students, a pair of seminarians, or a couple of frat buddies. Left as it is, the concept of domestic partnership could open a Pandora's box of litigation and subjective judicial decision-making about who qualifies. You either are or are not married; it's not a complex question. Whether you are in a "domestic partnership" is not so clear.

6   More important, the concept of domestic partnership chips away at the prestige of traditional relationships and undermines the priority we give them. This priority is not necessarily a product of heterosexism. Consider heterosexual couples. Society has good reason to extend legal advantages to heterosexuals who choose the formal sanction of marriage over simply living together. They make a deeper commitment to one another and to society; in exchange, society extends certain benefits to them. Marriage provides an anchor, if an arbitrary and weak one, in the chaos of sex and relationships to which we are all prone. It provides a mechanism for emotional stability, economic security, and the healthy rearing of the next generation. We rig the law in its favor not because we disparage all forms of relationship other than the nuclear family, but because we recognize that not to promote marriage would be to ask too much of human virtue. In the

Two men exchanging rings during their same-sex wedding ceremony in Honolulu, Hawaii

context of the weakened family's effect upon the poor, it might also invite social disintegration. One of the worst products of the New Right's "family values" campaign is that its extremism and hatred of diversity has disguised this more measured and more convincing case for the importance of the marital bond.

7   The concept of domestic partnership ignores these concerns, indeed directly attacks them. This is a pity, since one of its most important objectives—providing some civil recognition for gay relationships—is a noble cause and one completely compatible with the defense of the family. But the decision to go about it is not to undermine straight marriage; it is to legalize old-style marriage for gays.

8   The gay movement has ducked this issue primarily out of fear of division. Much of the gay leadership clings to notions of gay life as essentially outsider, anti-bourgeois, radical. Marriage, for them, is co-optation into straight society. For the Stonewall generation, it is hard to see how this vision of conflict will ever fundamentally change. But for many other gays—my guess, a majority—while they don't deny the importance of rebellion 20 years ago and are grateful for what was done, there's now the sense of a new opportunity. A need to rebel has quietly ceded to a desire to belong. To be

gay and to be bourgeois no longer seems such an absurd proposition. Certainly, since AIDS, to be gay and to be responsible has become a necessity.

9   Gay marriage squares several circles at the heart of the domestic partnership debate. Unlike domestic partnership, it allows for recognition of gay relationships, while casting no aspersions on traditional marriage. It merely asks that gays be allowed to join in. Unlike domestic partnership, it doesn't open up avenues for heterosexuals to get benefits without the responsibilities of marriage, or a nightmare of definitional litigation. And unlike domestic partnership, it harnesses to an already established social convention the yearnings for stability and acceptance among a fast-maturing gay community.

10   Gay marriage also places more responsibilities upon gays: it says for the first time that gay relationships are not better or worse than straight relationships, and that the same is expected of them. And it's clear and dignified. There's a legal benefit to a clear, common symbol of commitment. There's also a personal benefit. One of the ironies of domestic partnership is that it's not only more complicated than marriage, it's more demanding, requiring an elaborate statement of intent to qualify. It amounts to a substantial invasion of privacy. Why, after all, should gays be required to prove commitment before they get married in a way we would never dream of asking of straights?

11   Legalizing gay marriage would offer homosexuals the same deal society now offers heterosexuals: general social approval and specific legal advantages in exchange for a deeper and harder-to-extract-yourself-from commitment to another human being. Like straight marriage, it would foster social cohesion, emotional security, and economic prudence. Since there's no reason gays should not be allowed to adopt or be foster parents, it could also help nurture children. And its introduction would not be some sort of radical break with social custom. As it has become more acceptable for gay people to acknowledge their loves publicly, more and more have committed themselves to one another for life in full view of their families and their friends. A law institutionalizing gay marriage would merely reinforce a healthy social trend. It would also, in the wake of AIDS, qualify as a genuine public health measure. Those conservatives who deplore promiscuity among some homosexuals should be among the first to support it. Burke could have written a powerful case for it.

12   The argument that gay marriage would subtly undermine the unique legitimacy of straight marriage is based upon a fallacy. For heterosexuals, straight marriage would remain the most significant—and only legal—social bond. Gay marriage could only delegitimize straight marriage if it were a

real alternative to it, and this is clearly not true. To put it bluntly, there's precious little evidence that straights could be persuaded by any law to have sex with—let alone marry—someone of their own sex. The only possible effect of this sort would be to persuade gay men and women who force themselves into heterosexual marriage (often at appalling cost to themselves and their families) to find a focus for their family instincts in a more personally positive environment. But this is clearly a plus, not a minus: gay marriage could both avoid a lot of tortured families and create the possibility for many happier ones. It is not, in short, a denial of family values. It's an extension of them.

13   Of course, some would claim that any legal recognition of homosexuality is a de facto attack upon heterosexuality. But even the most hardened conservatives recognize that gays are a permanent minority and aren't likely to go away. Since persecution is not an option in a civilized society, why not coax gays into traditional values rather than rail incoherently against them?

14   There's a less elaborate argument for gay marriage: it's good for gays. It provides role models for young gay people who, after the exhilaration of coming out, can easily lapse into short-term relationships and insecurity with no tangible goal in sight. My own guess is that most gays would embrace such a goal with as much (if not more) commitment as straights. Even in our society as it is, many lesbian relationships are virtual textbook cases of monogamous commitment. Legal gay marriage could also help bridge the gulf often found between gays and their parents. It could bring the essence of gay life—a gay couple—into the heart of the traditional straight family in a way the family can most understand and the gay offspring can most easily acknowledge. It could do as much to heal the gay-straight rift as any amount of gay rights legislation.

15   If these arguments sound socially conservative, that's no accident. It's one of the richest ironies of our society's blind spot toward gays that essentially conservative social goals should have the appearance of being so radical. But gay marriage is not a radical step. It avoids the mess of domestic partnership; it is humane; it is conservative in the best sense of the word. It's also practical. Given the fact that we already allow legal gay relationships, what possible social goal is advanced by framing the law to encourage those relationships to be unfaithful, undeveloped, and insecure?

HADLEY ARKES

The Closet Straight

Hadley Arkes (1944–   ) is a professor of law at Amherst College. His response to the arguments of Andrew Sullivan appeared in 1993 in the National Review *(which is resolute in publishing conservative viewpoints). Arkes's argument counters not the essay "Here Comes the Groom" but a similar essay that Sullivan published in 1993 titled "The Politics of Homosexuality."*

1   John Courtney Murray once observed that the atheist and the theist essentially agree in their understanding of the problem: The atheist does not mean to reject the existence of God only in Staten Island; he means to reject God universally, as a necessary truth. He accepts the same framework of reference, and he makes the same move to a transcendent standard of judgment. In a thoughtful, extended essay, Andrew Sullivan, the young, gay editor of *The New Republic,* has made a comparable concession for the advocate of "gay rights" ["The Politics of Homosexuality," *New Republic,* May 10]. For Sullivan has put into place, as the very ground and framework of his argument, a structure of understanding that must call into question any claims for the homosexual life as a rival good.

2   "The Politics of Homosexuality" confirms, at length, what anyone who has been with Andrew Sullivan can grasp within five minutes: he regards his erotic life as the center of his being, but he also conveys the most powerful need to seek that erotic fulfillment within a framework of domesticity, of the normal and the *natural.* The most persisting thread of anguish in the essay is the pain of awareness and reconciliation in his own family, with the recurring memory of his father weeping when Andrew declared, as he says, his sexuality. Sullivan reserves some of his most stinging words for the producers of a "queer" politics, aimed at "cultural subversion." That brand of politics would simply confirm the strangeness of homosexuals, and deepen the separation from their families. Ironically, says Sullivan, "queer" politics "broke off dialogue with the heterosexual families whose cooperation is needed in every generation, if gay children are to be accorded a modicum of dignity and hope."

3   The delicacy barely conceals that "cooperation is needed in every generation" precisely because "homosexual families" cannot produce "gay

children." Gay children must come into being through the only kind of family that nature knows. Those who wish to preserve, say, a Jewish people, know that Jews need to reproduce and raise their children as Jews. But what would be the comparable path of obligation for the person who is committed to the preservation of a "gay community"? Sullivan is convinced that there is something in our biology or chemistry that "determines" our sexuality, and in that case, the tendency to gay sex may be passed along to the next generation, as readily as temperament and allergies. The person who wishes to preserve, for the next generation, a gay community may be tempted then to render the ultimate service: For the good of the cause, he may cross the line and enter another domain of sex. But in crossing that line, he makes a decisive concession: implicitly, but unmistakably, he is compelled to acknowledge that homosexuality cannot even pretend to stand on the same plane as the way of life it would displace. We do not really find two kinds of "families" carrying out transactions with one another. But rather, we come to recognize again the primacy of "sexuality" in the strictest sense, the only sexuality that can produce "another generation."

4   It is evidently important to Sullivan to insist that homosexuality is rooted in "nature," that it is determined for many people by something in their makeup quite beyond their control. He would wish to draw to his side a certain strand of natural law to suggest that anything so rooted in nature cannot be wrong. And yet, he falls there into an ancient mistake. As the great expounders of natural law explained, we do not make our way to the "natural" simply by generalizing upon the mixed record of our species: by that reckoning, incest and genocide would be in accord with natural law, since they seem to form an intractable part of the human experience. And even if we could show, say, that some of us carried a gene for "arson," that would not settle the moral question on arson. We might not be as quick to blame the bearers of these genes, but we would expect them to exert more self-control, and we would hardly waive our moral reservations about arson.

5   In a passage of searing candor, Sullivan acknowledges that discrimination has not affected gays with the same kinds of deprivations that have been visited upon blacks. "[Gay] men and lesbians suffer no discernible communal economic deprivations and already operate at the highest levels of society." But when they call to their aid the levers of the law, they cultivate the sense of themselves as vulnerable and weak, in need of protection, and they perpetuate, among gays, the tendencies to self-doubt. They suggest that the things most needful to gays are in the hands of other people to confer. In the sweep of his own conviction, Sullivan would soar past those demands alto-

gether. He would stop demanding laws, which confer, upon straight people, the franchise of confirming, or discounting, the worth of gays.

Love and Marriage

6   Except for one, notable thing. What Andrew Sullivan wants, most of all, is marriage. And he wants it for reasons that could not have been stated more powerfully by any heterosexual who had been raised, as Sullivan was, in the Catholic tradition and schooled in political philosophy. "[T]he apex of emotional life," says Sullivan, "is found in the marital bond." The erotic interest may seek out copulation, but the fulfillment of eros depends on the integrity of a bond woven of sentiment and confirmed by law. Marriage is more than a private contract; it is "the highest public recognition of our personal integrity." Its equivalent will not be supplied by a string of sensual nights, accumulated over many years of "living together." The very existence of marriage "premises the core of our emotional development. It is the architectonic institution that frames our emotional life."

7   No one could doubt for a moment: as much as any of the "guys" in the Damon Runyon stories, the man who wrote those lines is headed, irresistibly, for marriage. What he craves—homosexual marriage—would indeed require the approval conferred by law. It would also require a benediction conferred by straight people, who would have to consent to that vast, new modeling of our laws. That project will not be undertaken readily, and it may not be undertaken at all. Still, there is something, rooted in the nature of Andrew Sullivan, that must need marriage.

8   But as Mona Charen pointed out, in an encounter with Sullivan at the National Review Institute conference this winter [*NR*, March 29], it is not marriage that domesticates men; it is women. Left to themselves, these forked creatures follow a way of life that George Gilder once recounted in its precise, chilling measures: bachelors were 22 times more likely than married men to be committed to hospitals for mental disease (and 10 times more likely to suffer chronic diseases of all kinds). Single men had nearly double the mortality rate of married men and 3 times the mortality rate of single women. Divorced men were 3 times more likely than divorced women to commit suicide or die by murder, and they were 6 times more likely to die of heart disease.

9   We have ample reason by now to doubt that the bipeds described in these figures are likely to be tamed to a sudden civility if they are merely arranged, in sets of two or three, in the same house. I had the chance to see my own younger son, settled with three of his closest friends in a

townhouse in Georgetown during his college years. The labors of the kitchen and the household were divided with a concern for domestic order, and the abrasions of living together were softened by the ties of friendship. And yet, no one, entering that house, could doubt for a moment that he was in a camp occupied for a while by young males, with their hormones flowing.

10   This is not to deny, of course, that men may truly love men, or commit themselves to a life of steady friendship. But many of us have continued to wonder just why any of these relations would be enhanced in any way by adding to them the ingredients of penetration—or marriage. The purpose of this alliance, after all, could not be the generation of children, and a marriage would not be needed then as the stable framework for welcoming and sheltering children. For gays, the ceremony of marriage could have the function of proclaiming to the world an exclusive love, a special dedication, which comes along with a solemn promise to forgo all other, competing loves. In short, it would draw its power from the romance of monogamy. But is that the vision that drives the movement for "gay rights"? An excruciating yearning for monogamy?

11   That may indeed be Andrew Sullivan's own yearning, but his position is already marking him as a curious figure in the camp of gay activists. When Sullivan commends the ideal of marriage for gays, he would seem to be pleading merely for the inclusion of gay "couples" in an institution that is indeed confined to pairs, of *adults,* in monogamous unions. But that is not exactly the vision of gay sex.

12   For many activists and connoisseurs, Sullivan would represent a rather wimpish, constricted view of the world they would open to themselves through sexual liberation. After all, the permissions for this new sexual freedom have been cast to that amorphous formula of "sexual orientation": the demand of gay rights is that we should recede from casting moral judgments on the way that people find their pleasure in engagements they regard as "sexual." In its strange abstraction, "sexual orientation" could take in sex with animals or the steamier versions of sado-masochism. The devotees of S&M were much in evidence during the recent march in Washington, but we may put aside for a moment these interests, to consider others which are even more exotic yet. There is, for example, the North American Man–Boy Love Association, a contingent of gay activists who identify themselves, unashamedly, as pedophiles. They insist that nothing in their "sexual orientation" should disqualify them to work as professional counselors, say, in the schools of New York, and to counsel young boys. And since they respect themselves, they will

not hold back from commending their own way of life to their young charges. If there is to be gay marriage, would it be confined then only to adults? And if men are inclined to a life of multiple partners, why should marriage be confined to two persons? Why indeed should the notion of gay marriage be scaled down to fit the notions held by Andrew Sullivan?

Sullivan's Dilemma

13 The sources of anguish run even deeper here than Sullivan may suspect, for his dilemma may be crystallized in this way: If he would preserve the traditional understanding of marriage and monogamy, he would not speak for much of a constituency among gays. But if the notion of "marriage" were enlarged and redefined—if it could take in a plurality of people and shifting combinations—it could hardly be the kind of marriage that Sullivan devoutly wishes as "the apex of emotional life" and "the highest public recognition of our personal integrity."

14 In traditional marriage, the understanding of monogamy was originally tied to the "natural teleology" of the body—to the recognition that only two people, no more and no fewer, can generate children. To that understanding of a union, or a "marriage," the alliance of two men would offer such an implausible want of resemblance that it would appear almost as a mocking burlesque. It would be rather like confounding, as Lincoln used to say, a "horse chestnut" and a "chestnut horse." The mockery would be avoided if the notion of marriage could be opened, or broadened, to accommodate the varieties of sexual experience. The most notable accommodation would be the acceptance of several partners, and the change could be readily reckoned precisely because it would hardly be novel: the proposal for gay marriage would compel us to look again—to look anew with eyes unclouded by prejudice—to the ancient appeal of polygamy. After all, there would be an Equal Protection problem now: we could scarcely confine this new "marital" arrangement only to members of one gender. But then, once the arrangement is opened simply to "consenting adults," on what ground would we object to the mature couplings of aunts and nephews, or even fathers and daughters—couplings that show a remarkable persistence in our own age, even against the barriers of law and sentiment that have been cast up over centuries? All kinds of questions, once placed in a merciful repose, may reasonably be opened again. They become live issues once we are willing to ponder that simple question, Why should marriage be confined, after all, to couples, and to pairs drawn from different sexes?

15   That question, if it comes to be treated as open and problematic, will not readily be closed, or not at least on the terms that Andrew Sullivan seeks. The melancholy news then is this: We cannot deliver to him what he wants without introducing, into our laws, notions that must surely undercut the rationale and the justification for marriage. The marriage that he wants, he cannot practicably have; but in seeking it, he runs the risk of weakening even further the opinion that sustains marriage as "the architectonic institution that frames our emotional life."

16   But for marriage so understood, Sullivan does not seem to command a large following, or even a substantial interest, among gays. New York City must surely contain one of the largest concentrations of accomplished, successful gay men. Since March, New York has allowed the registering of "domestic partners," and by the first of June, 822 couples had come forth to register. By the unofficial estimate of people in the bureau, those couples have been just about evenly distributed between gays and lesbians. Four hundred gay couples would not be a trivial number, but in a city like New York, it does rather suggest that the craving for this public recognition may not be widely diffused. If all of the couples registered under the new law were collected in Yankee Stadium, they would hardly be noticeable in the crowd. Their numbers would not exactly suggest that there is a strong political constituency out there for gay marriage.

Unintended Consequence

17   In making then his own, heartfelt case for marriage, Andrew Sullivan is swept well past the interests and enthusiasms that mark most other people who now make up the "gay community." And he may earnestly put this question to himself: In the sweep of his own convictions, in the sentiment that draws him, powerfully, to marriage, has he not in fact swept past, and discarded, the rationales that sustain the homosexual life?

18   What comes through the writing, finally, is a man who finds his eros in domesticity, who will find pleasure in driving his own children to their soccer games on Saturday mornings. He will explain again to his friends that we must "cooperate" with heterosexual families; that if we would protect gay children we must raise them, and even produce them. There may be winks all around, and the sense that he is doing something for "the cause." But as Andrew Sullivan appreciates, "queer" politics always seeks to take "shame-abandonment to a thrilling conclusion." And what could be more exquisite and subtle than this reversal upon a reversal?: A man lives a highly visible public life as a ho-

mosexual, but he enters a marriage, which is taken as a kind of charade, and he is content to abet the jest with knowing glances. But the secret that dare not speak its name is that he really is, after all, a domesticated man, settled in his marriage. As a writer and a man, Andrew Sullivan is committed to an understanding of political life that finds its ground in nature. And he takes, as the core of our civic life, marriage and the laws that sustain marriage. For all of that, we here, composed, as we are, of eros and of dust, love him.

Evan's Two Moms

Anna Quindlen (1955–   ) won a Pulitzer prize in 1992 for the weekly column she wrote for the New York Times *and other newspapers. Now she writes an essay for* Newsweek *every other week and works on her fiction as well. Her essays, including the one that follows, have been collected into several books, among them* Thinking Out Loud: On the Personal, the Political, and the Public *(1993). (For another argument by Anna Quindlen, see pages 63–65.)*

1   Evan has two moms. This is no big thing. Evan has always had two moms—in his school file, on his emergency forms, with his friends. "Ooooh, Evan, you're lucky," they sometimes say. "You have two moms." It sounds like a sitcom, but until last week it was emotional truth without legal bulwark. That was when a judge in New York approved the adoption of a six-year-old boy by his biological mother's lesbian partner. Evan. Evan's mom. Evan's other mom. A kid, a psychologist, a pediatrician. A family.

2   The matter of Evan's two moms is one in a series of events over the last year that led to certain conclusions. A Minnesota appeals court granted guardianship of a woman left a quadriplegic in a car accident to her lesbian lover, the culmination of a seven-year battle in which the injured woman's parents did everything possible to negate the partnership between the two. A lawyer in Georgia had her job offer withdrawn after the state attorney general found out that she and her lesbian lover were planning a marriage ceremony; she's brought suit. The computer company Lotus announced that the gay partners of employees would be eligible for the same benefits as spouses.

3   Add to these public events the private struggles, the couples who go from lawyer to lawyer to approximate legal protections their straight counterparts take for granted, the AIDS survivors who find themselves shut out of their partners' dying days by biological family members and shut out of their apartments by leases with a single name on the dotted line, and one solution is obvious.

4   Gay marriage is a radical notion for straight people and a conservative notion for gay ones. After years of being sledge-hammered by society, some gay men and lesbian women are deeply suspicious of participating in an institution that seems to have "straight world" written all over it.

5   But the rads of twenty years ago, straight and gay alike, have other things on their minds today. Family is one, and the linchpin of family has commonly been a loving commitment between two adults. When same-sex couples set out to make that commitment, they discover that they are at a disadvantage: No joint tax returns. No health insurance coverage for an uninsured partner. No survivor's benefits from Social Security. None of the automatic rights, privileges, and responsibilities society attaches to a marriage contract. In Madison, Wisconsin, a couple who applied at the Y with their kids for a family membership were turned down because both were women. It's one of those small things that can make you feel small.

6   Some took marriage statutes that refer to "two persons" at their word and applied for a license. The results were court decisions that quoted the Bible and embraced circular argument: marriage is by definition the union of a man and a woman because that is how we've defined it.

7   No religion should be forced to marry anyone in violation of its tenets, although ironically it is now only in religious ceremonies that gay people can marry, performed by clergy who find the blessing of two who love each other no sin. But there is no secular reason that we should take a patchwork approach of corporate, governmental, and legal steps to guarantee what can be done simply, economically, conclusively, and inclusively with the words "I do."

8   "Fran and I chose to get married for the same reasons that any two people do," said the lawyer who was fired in Georgia. "We fell in love; we wanted to spend our lives together." Pretty simple.

9   Consider the case of *Loving* v. *Virginia*, aptly named. At the time, sixteen states had laws that barred interracial marriage, relying on natural law, that amorphous grab bag for justifying prejudice. Sounding a little like God throwing Adam and Eve out of paradise, the trial judge suspended the one-year sentence of Richard Loving, who was white, and his wife, Mildred, who was black, provided they got out of the State of Virginia.

10   In 1967 the Supreme Court found such laws to be unconstitutional. Only twenty-five years ago and it was a crime for a black woman to marry a white man. Perhaps twenty-five years from now we will find it just as incredible that two people of the same sex were not entitled to legally commit themselves to each other. Love and commitment are rare enough; it seems absurd to thwart them in any guise.

PETER J. GOMES

Homophobic? Read Your Bible

Peter J. Gomes (1942–   ) is an American Baptist minister. Widely regarded as one of the most distinguished preachers in the nation, he has served since 1970 in the Memorial Church at Harvard University. Since 1974 he has been Plummer Professor of Christian Morals at Harvard Divinity School as well. He wrote the following essay for the New York Times *in 1992.*

1   Opposition to gays' civil rights has become one of the most visible symbols of American civic conflict this year, and religion has become the weapon of choice. The army of the discontented, eager for clear villains and simple solutions and ready for a crusade in which political self-interest and social anxiety can be cloaked in morality, has found hatred of homosexuality to be the last respectable prejudice of the century.

2   Ballot initiatives in Oregon and Maine would deny homosexuals the protection of civil rights laws. The Pentagon has steadfastly refused to allow gays into the armed forces. Vice President Dan Quayle is crusading for "traditional family values." And Pat Buchanan, who is scheduled to speak at the Republican National Convention this evening, regards homosexuality as a litmus test of moral purity.

3   Nothing has illuminated this crusade more effectively than a work of fiction, *The Drowning of Stephan Jones*, by Bette Greene. Preparing for her novel, Ms. Greene interviewed more than 400 young men incarcerated for gay-bashing, and scrutinized their case studies. In an interview published in *The Boston Globe* this spring, she said she found that the gay-bashers generally saw nothing wrong in what they did, and, more often than not, said their religious leaders and traditions sanctioned their behavior. One convicted teen-age gay-basher told her that the pastor of his church had said, "Homosexuals represent the devil, Satan," and that the Rev. Jerry Falwell had echoed that charge.

4   Christians opposed to political and social equality for homosexuals nearly always appeal to the moral injunctions of the Bible, claiming that Scripture is very clear on the matter and citing verses that support their opinion. They accuse others of perverting and distorting texts contrary to their "clear" meaning. They do not, however, necessarily see quite as clear a meaning in biblical passages on economic conduct, the burdens of wealth, and the sin of greed.

5   Nine biblical citations are customarily invoked as relating to homosexuality. Four (Deuteronomy 23:17, I Kings 14:24, I Kings 22:46, and II Kings 23:7) simply forbid prostitution, by men and women.

6   Two others (Leviticus 18:19–23 and Leviticus 20:10–16) are part of what biblical scholars call the Holiness Code. The code explicitly bans homosexual acts. But it also prohibits eating raw meat, planting two different kinds of seed in the same field, and wearing garments with two different kinds of yarn. Tattoos, adultery, and sexual intercourse during a woman's menstrual period are similarly outlawed.

7   There is no mention of homosexuality in the four Gospels of the New Testament. The moral teachings of Jesus are not concerned with the subject.

8   Three references from St. Paul are frequently cited (Romans 1:26–2:1, I Corinthians 6:9–11, and I Timothy 1:10). But St. Paul was concerned with homosexuality only because in Greco-Roman culture it represented a secular sensuality that was contrary to his Jewish-Christian spiritual idealism. He was against lust and sensuality in anyone, including heterosexuals. To say that homosexuality is bad because homosexuals are tempted to do morally doubtful things is to say that heterosexuality is bad because heterosexuals are likewise tempted. For St. Paul, anyone who puts his or her interest ahead of God's is condemned, a verdict that falls equally upon everyone.

9   And lest we forget Sodom and Gomorrah, recall that the story is not about sexual perversion and homosexual practice. It is about inhospitality, according to Luke 10:10–13, and failure to care for the poor, according to Ezekiel 16:49–50: "Behold, this was the iniquity of thy sister Sodom, pride, fullness of bread, and abundance of idleness was in her and in her daughters, neither did she strengthen the hand of the poor and needy." To suggest that Sodom and Gomorrah is about homosexual sex is an analysis of about as much worth as suggesting that the story of Jonah and the whale is a treatise on fishing.

10   Part of the problem is a question of interpretation. Fundamentalists and literalists, the storm troopers of the religious right, are terrified that Scripture, "wrongly interpreted," may separate them from their values. That fear stems from their own recognition that their "values" are not derived from Scripture, as they publicly claim.

11   Indeed, it is through the lens of their own prejudices that they "read" Scripture and cloak their own views in its authority. We all interpret Scripture: Make no mistake. And no one truly is a literalist, despite the pious temptation. The questions are, By what principle of interpretation do we proceed, and by what means do we reconcile "what it meant then" to "what it means now"?

12   These matters are far too important to be left to scholars and seminarians alone. Our ability to judge ourselves and others rests on our ability to

interpret Scripture intelligently. The right use of the Bible, an exercise as old as the church itself, means that we confront our prejudices rather than merely confirm them.

13   For Christians, the principle by which Scripture is read is nothing less than an appreciation of the work and will of God as revealed in that of Jesus. To recover a liberating and inclusive Christ is to be freed from the semantic bondage that makes us curators of a dead culture rather than creatures of a new creation.

14   Religious fundamentalism is dangerous because it cannot accept ambiguity and diversity and is therefore inherently intolerant. Such intolerance, in the name of virtue, is ruthless and uses political power to destroy what it cannot convert.

15   It is dangerous, especially in America, because it is antidemocratic and is suspicious of "the other," in whatever form that "other" might appear. To maintain itself, fundamentalism must always define "the other" as deviant.

16   But the chief reason that fundamentalism is dangerous is that, at the hands of the Rev. Pat Robertson, the Rev. Jerry Falwell, and hundreds of lesser-known but equally worrisome clerics, preachers, and pundits, it uses Scripture and the Christian practice to encourage ordinarily good people to act upon their fears rather than their virtues.

17   Fortunately, those who speak for the religious right do not speak for all American Christians, and the Bible is not theirs alone to interpret. The same Bible that the advocates of slavery used to protect their wicked self-interests is the Bible that inspired slaves to revolt and their liberators to action.

18   The same Bible that the predecessors of Mr. Falwell and Mr. Robertson used to keep white churches white is the source of the inspiration of the Rev. Martin Luther King, Jr., and the social reformation of the 1960's.

19   The same Bible that antifeminists use to keep women silent in the churches is the Bible that preaches liberation to captives and says that in Christ there is neither male nor female, slave nor free.

20   And the same Bible that on the basis of an archaic social code of ancient Israel and a tortured reading of Paul is used to condemn all homosexuals and homosexual behavior includes metaphors of redemption, renewal, inclusion, and love—principles that invite homosexuals to accept their freedom and responsibility in Christ and demands that their fellow Christians accept them as well.

21   The political piety of the fundamentalist religious right must not be exercised at the expense of our precious freedoms. And in this summer of our discontent, one of the most precious freedoms for which we must all fight is freedom from this last prejudice.

JAY BUDZISZEWSKI

Jay Budziszewski (pronounced "Boojee-shefski"), who teaches government and philosophy at the University of Texas, Austin, is the author of several books, including True Tolerance. *Having experienced a conversion to Christianity, he now promotes "natural law" principles of ethics and government. In 1998 he offered two arguments—the ones that follow—to* Boundless, *in the format of the same "office hours" conversation that he frequently uses in his regular columns. (Boundless is a webzine designed for college students that offers a conservative Christian perspective on current issues.) The two essays, "Homophobia: An Unfinished Story" and "The Seeker," were written as companion pieces, so the second comments on the first. Both items indirectly rebut other essays in this segment, including the ones by Andrew Sullivan, Anna Quinden, and Peter Gomes.*

Homophobia: An Unfinished Story

1   "Are you Professor Theophilus?"

2   I turned. "That's me. Come in."

3   "My name's Lawrence. I'm gay. I came to complain about your talk about constitutional liberties yesterday. It was bigoted and homophobic. I'm filing a formal protest to the people who run the Student Union speakers series."

4   *At least he's direct, I thought.* I waved him to a seat.

5   "Help me out, Mr. Lawrence. How could—"

6   "Just Lawrence."

7   "Thank you. Now how could my talk have been 'bigoted and homophobic' when it didn't mention homosexuality?"

8   "I didn't actually hear the talk itself. I came in during Q&A."

9   "I see. And what did I say during Q&A?"

10   "You said gays have sex with animals."

11   I'm used to this sort of thing, so I merely observed, "I'm afraid you weren't listening carefully."

12   "I remember distinctly," he declared. "A girl asked your opinion of laws against discrimination on the basis of sexual orientation, and you said gays have sex with animals."

13   "No, what I said was 'sexual orientation' can mean many things. Some people are 'sexually oriented' toward the opposite sex; others toward the same sex; others toward children; others toward animals; others toward cadavers. I said that I wondered where this trend will end."

14   "Then you admit that gays don't have sex with animals?"

15   "You brought that up," I reminded him. "I have no information on the point, I'm only suggesting that not all 'orientations' are morally equivalent."

16   He said nothing, but showed no inclination to leave. "Do *you* think all 'orientations' are morally equivalent?" I queried.

17   "I won't even dignify that question with an answer," he said. "But I know what you think of my orientation. I'm sick of you phony Christians with your filthy hypocrisy about the love of God."

18   "So you've heard that I'm a Christian."

19   "Who hasn't? The holy, the sanctimonious, the Most Excellent Professor Theophilus of Post-Everything State University—what else would he be? The whole school reeks of you, of you and the other so-called Christian so-called professors. That's why I walked in on your Q&A. I wanted to see you spit venom."

20   "My goodness. Have I said anything venomous?"

21   "It's what you're thinking that's venomous."

22   "I see," I smiled. "Why don't you stop being bashful, and tell me what's bothering you?"

23   "You must think you're funny."

24   "I'm serious. Tell your complaints one by one, and I'll answer them."

25   "You couldn't answer them. I have too many."

26   "Try me. I'll give short answers."

27   He cocked his head and peered at me. "You mean it, don't you?"

28   "I wouldn't say it if I didn't."

29   "One at a time?"

30   "One at a time."

31   "All right, here's the first. Christians are hypocrites. You're always running down gays, but what about the other things your Bible condemns, like divorce and remarriage? It's other people's sins that bother you, not your own."

32   I laughed. "If you'd spent any time around me, you'd know that I'm just as hard on the sins of heterosexuals as on those of homosexuals.

33   "Easy divorce is a prime example of how one bad thing leads to another—in our case the loss of the ability to make any distinctions about sexual acts at all."

34   Ignoring the reply, he went on to his next complaint. "You're intolerant. You reject people like me just because we're different than you."

35   "Me reject you?" I said. "Aren't you the one who rejects what is different than yourself? Don't you reject the challenge of the other sex?"

36   "I don't need the other sex. I have a committed relationship with my partner."

37   "Research shows that homosexuals with partners don't stop cruising, they just cruise less. When they don't think straights are listening, gay writers say the same."

38   "So what if it's true? There's nothing wrong with gay love anyway."

39   I spoke quietly. "Tell me what's loving about sex acts that cause bleeding, choking, disease and pain," I suggested. "You might start by explaining the meaning of the medical term 'Gay Bowel Syndrome,' or how people get herpes lesions on their tonsils."

40   "You're—how can you even say that?" he demanded. "How dare you tell me who to love?"

41   "I don't think I am telling you who to love."

42   "Oh, no? Then what are you telling me?"

43   "That there is nothing loving about mutual self-destruction."

44   "You must think my relationship with my partner is just dirt!"

45   "No, I respect friendship wherever I find it—your friendship with your partner included. It's just that sex doesn't make every kind of friendship better."

46   "Why not? Are you anti-sex or something?"

47   "Not at all," I said, "but would you say that sex improves the friendship of a father with his daughter?"

48   Seeing from his face that he didn't, I continued. "You get my point. Nor does sex improve the friendship of two men."

49   "That's where you're wrong. Gay sex is just as natural for some people as straight sex is for other people."

50   "What's 'natural'," I said, "is what unlocks our inbuilt potential instead of thwarting it. One of the purposes of marital sex is to get you outside your Self and its concerns, to achieve intimacy with someone who is Really Other."

51   *Was he listening to any of this?* "I'm sorry, Lawrence—I really am—but having sex with another man can't do that. It's too much like loving your reflection. That's what I meant before about refusing the challenge of the other sex."

52   I was about to go on, but abruptly he changed the subject: "It's attitudes like yours that killed Matthew Shepard."

53   "Surely you don't imagine that the thugs who killed Matthew Shepard were Christians, do you?" I smiled at the absurdity of the thought, but seeing that he misunderstood my smile I made my face serious and tried again.

54   "Lawrence, I deplore the violence that killed Matthew Shepard, and I'm glad those men were caught. But shouldn't we also grieve the urge which caused Matthew Shepard to be sexually attracted to violent strangers?"

55   He said only, "You hate me."

56   I paused to study him. Did he really believe that, or was it a smoke-screen?

57   "I don't hate you," I said, "I love you." I paused. "I'd like to be with you forever, in heaven."

58   Lawrence's face displayed shock, as though he had been hit in the stomach. Then he looked confused. The expression of confusion was instantaneously replaced by an expression of anger.

59   For one split-second, it had looked as if the shutters were open. *"God in heaven,"* I thought, *"I need help."* How could they be pried back up?

60   "My love isn't really the issue for you, is it?" I asked.

61   "What do you mean?"

62   "It's God's. God's love is the issue for you." For a few seconds there was no reaction.

63   Then it came. "You're bleeping right God's love is the issue for me," he said. "*Your* God's love. The lying God who says He loves man, but who hates me for loving men."

64   "Do you think God hates you?"

65   "Doesn't He?"

66   "What makes you say that?"

67   "Doesn't your Bible say that? It calls people like me an abomination."

68   "It calls what you *do* abomination. There's a difference."

69   "There's no difference. I do what I am."

70   I considered his point. "Could it be," I said, "that you want God to love you *less?*"

71   "Less!" he spat.

72   "Yes. Don't you know what love is?"

73   "Acceptance."

74   "Acceptance of what kills you? Consider another view. Love is a commitment of the will to the true good of the other person."

75   "What?"

76   "I said love is a commitment of the will to the true good of the other person."

77   "I don't get what you're saying."

78   "Sure you do. The lover wants what's good for the beloved."

79   He hesitated. "I suppose."

80   "Good. Now think. If that's what love is, then a *perfect* Lover would want the *perfect* good of the Beloved. Do you see what that means? He would loathe and detest whatever destroyed the beloved's good—no matter how much the beloved desired it."

81   I couldn't read the look on his face, so I plowed on. "That's what sin does—it destroys us. Yours destroys you, mine destroys me. And so the Lover doesn't 'accept' it; He hates it with an inexorable hatred. To cut the cancer out of us, He will do whatever it takes—like a surgeon. No, more than like a surgeon. If you let Him, He will even take the cancer upon Himself and die in your place."

82   Still inscrutable, he kept his eyes in front of him, just avoiding my own.

83   I asked "What happens, then, if you refuse to let go of what destroys you? What happens if you say this to the divine and perfect Lover who wants your complete and perfect good—if you say, 'I bind myself to my destruction! Accept me, and my destruction with me! I refuse to enter heaven except in the company of Death!'"

84   Neither of us spoke.

85   Lawrence rose from his chair and walked out the door.

The Seeker

1   "It wasn't easy finding your office," said my visitor as he took a seat. "This building is like a rabbit warren."

2   "Yes," I said, "for the first couple of years I worked here, I had to leave a trail of crumbs each day to find my way back out. We haven't met, have we?"

3   "No, I'm over in Antediluvian Studies—I'm a grad student. My name's Adam, Adam Apollolas."

4   "M.E. Theophilus." We shook hands.

5   "You are the same Theophilus who wrote the 'Homophobia' dialogue for Nounless Webzine, aren't you? I was hoping to talk with you about it."

6   "Busted," I smiled. "What would you like to know about it?"

7   "Was it based on a real conversation?"

8   "Yes and no; it was a composite. A homosexual student really did visit to accuse me of saying that 'gays have sex with animals,' and the rest is from real life too, but not necessarily from the same conversation."

9   "But it can't possibly be true that all of the homosexuals who speak with you are as angry and closed-minded as he was."

10   "No, of course not."

11   "Then why did you portray him that way in the dialogue?"

12   "Would you have me pretend that nobody in the homosexual life is angry and closed-minded? A good many are like that—you should see my letters—and I try to show my readers the dynamics of more than one kind of

conversation. You see, when people have honest questions you try to answer them, but when they only churn out smokescreens, then you blow the smoke away."

13   "So you'd be open to different kinds of conversation."

14   "Of course," I said. I smiled. "Are we, perhaps, having one right now?"

15   His eyebrows lifted. "Am I that obvious?"

16   "It was just a shot in the dark, So what did you really want to talk about?"

17   "I'm not very ideological, but I guess you could call me a Seeker. See, I've been in the gay life for five years, but lately I've been having second thoughts. I'm not asking you to convert me, understand? I thought I'd just hear what you have to say, then go away and think about it."

18   "What have you been having second thoughts about?"

19   He hesitated. "Are you going to use this conversation in one of your dialogues?"

20   "If I did, I'd make sure you couldn't be identified. You can speak freely."

21   "Well—" he hesitated. "One thing is intimacy. I've never had problems finding sex, but it's more or less anonymous. That didn't bother me at first, but now it's getting me down."

22   "Is the sex always anonymous?"

23   "No, the first time I had gay sex was in a steady relationship. I've been in two or three others, too—for a month, two months, a year. But they were never what you'd call faithful, know what I mean? It's as though there had to be other sexual outlets for the relationship to work at all. I'm starting to want—I don't know. Something else."

24   "I follow you."

25   He paused. "Another thing. I want to be a Dad. That doesn't fit the stereotype, does it? Are you surprised to hear me say it?"

26   "Not at all."

27   "In that case you're the only one. My friends don't get it. One said, 'Why don't just get a turkey baster and make an arrangement with a lesbian?' But that's not what I want." Another pause. "I used to say to myself, 'Get used to it. You can't have everything you want.' But that doesn't work for me any more."

28   After a second he spoke again. "There's one more thing."

29   "What's that?"

30   "God."

31   "God? How so?"

32   "Oh, I go to church sometimes. Now that must surprise you."

33   "No. What kind of church?"

34   "Different kinds. I didn't go to any church at first. My family never went to church. Most of my gay friends don't have any use for God. Then I started going to a gay church, and that was okay for awhile. But I think I might want the real stuff, do you know what I mean? Or else nothing."

35   "I think so. You don't have any doubts about what the real stuff is?"

36   "No. I'm not saying I believe in Jesus, but -" He thought for a moment. "The gay church said you can be a Christian and still live a gay life. I don't think I ever really believed that. I read a book that the minister in the gay church recommended -"

37   "Yes?"

38   "The title was something like Sex and Dirt. I'm leaving something out. Hold on, it'll come to me."

39   "Never mind, I know the book."

40   "Oh, good. Then you probably remember how the author argues that when the Bible lays down rules about sex, they're just purity codes - not moral laws—so you don't have to keep them."

41   "Sure."

42   "He had me going for a while—right up to where he said 'that's why even having sex with animals is okay,' or words to that effect. Just what the guy in your dialogue accused you of saying gay people think. I could see that the author's conclusion followed from his premises—but after that, I didn't have any use for his premises, if you see what I mean."

43   "I see exactly what you mean. So where does all this leave you?"

44   "Like I said, I want to hear you out, and then I'll go away and think about it."

45   "That's fine, Adam, but just what is it that you want to hear me out about?"

46   "I think what I'm missing is the Big Picture about sex. If there is a Big Picture about sex."

47   "There is indeed a Big Picture about sex."

48   "Draw it, then. Paint it. Lecture me, even. That is," he added, "if you don't mind."

49   I had to laugh. "You asked me before if I was going to use this conversation in one of my dialogues. If I do, nobody will believe it. They'll call it contrived."

50   "Why?"

51   "Because you've set the stage too well. Your 'second thoughts' anticipate everything I'd like to say. And now you ask for a lecture!"

52   "After seven years of college, I'm used to lectures. You do your professor thing, and I'll listen. If I want to argue—believe me, I know how—I'll come back another day."

53   I collected my thoughts. "All right, Adam. The main point of Christian sexual morality is that human nature is designed. We need to live a certain way because we're designed to live that way."

54   He said, "I can see design in an organ like the heart. Human nature—that's a little too big for me."

55   "Then let's start with the heart. Do you see how every part works together toward its purpose, its function?"

56   "Sure. You've got nerves and valves and pumping chambers, all for moving blood."

57   "Right. If you think about the sexual powers instead of the heart, it's just the same. The key to understanding a design is to recognize its purposes. For the heart, the purpose is pumping blood; for the sexual powers—you tell me."

58   "Pleasure?"

59   "Think about it. Would you say pleasure is the purpose of eating?"

60   "No, I'd say nourishment is the purpose of eating, and pleasure is just the result."

61   "If you thought pleasure were the purpose of eating, what would you do if I offered you pleasant-tasting poison?"

62   "Eat it."

63   "And what would happen?"

64   "I'd get sick."

65   "But if you understood that nourishment were the purpose of eating and pleasure merely the result, then what would you do if I offered you pleasant-tasting poison?"

66   "Refuse it and ask for food instead."

67   "It's the same with the sexual powers. Pleasure is a result of their use, but not the purpose of their use. The purposes can tell you which kinds of sexual activity are good and which aren't; by itself, pleasure can't."

68   "So what are the purposes of the sexual powers?"

69   "You've told me already; you just didn't realize you were doing so."

70   "I have? When?"

71   "When you were telling me your second thoughts about the homosexual life. There were three of them. What was the first one about?"

72   "Intimacy. Bonding."

73   "And the second?"

74   "Having children."

75   "Then you won't be surprised to hear that one inbuilt purpose of the sexual powers is to bond a man with a woman, and another is to have and raise children."

76   "If bonding is good, why not use the sexual powers to bond a man with a man?"

77   "Has that worked in your case, Adam?"

78   "Well, no. That's what I was complaining about."

79   "You see, that's no accident. Bonding man with man is contrary to the design."

80   "You say that, but how do you know?"

81   "There are two reasons. First, man and woman are complementary. They're not just different, they match. There is something in male emotional design to which only the female can give completion, and something in female emotional design to which only the male can give completion. When same mates with same, that can't happen. Instead of balancing each other, they unbalance each other."

82   "What's the other reason?"

83   "The other reason is that the linkage of same with same is sterile. You've complained about that, too."

84   "But sometimes a man can't produce children with a woman, either."

85   "The mating of same with same isn't accidentally sterile, Adam, as the union of a particular man with a particular woman might be; it's inherently sterile. A husband and wife who are unable to have a baby haven't set themselves against their own inbuilt purposes. A man and man who have sex together have."

86   He grinned. "There's always the turkey baster."

87   "But when your friend made that suggestion, you refused, didn't you? What was your reason?"

88   "I'm not sure. I just think a kid needs a Mom and a Dad."

89   "That's exactly right. Male and female complement and complete each other not just in having children but in rearing them. Women are better designed for nurture, men are better designed for protection. Besides, two Dads can't model male-female relationships. Neither can two Moms. Neither can one."

90   Adam was silent as he digested this. "You know," he said finally, "this isn't at all what I expected you to talk about."

91   "What did you expect me to talk about?"

92   "Disease." He paused. "Now that I think about it, you didn't say much about disease in that dialogue I read either."

93   "I should think you already know the deadliness of your way of life."

94   "I suppose so. But it does seem unfair. Why should gay sex be less healthy than any other kind?"

95   "Don't we come right back to the design? Start with the fact that not all orifices are created equal."

96   "Hmmm."

97   "Hmmm?"

98   "I think I'll go do what I said I'd do: Go away and think about it all. In the meantime, Professor, I think you have a problem."

99   "Do I?"

100   "That is, if you do intend to use this chat of ours in one of your dialogues."

101   "And what might this problem be?"

102   "We've talked too long. Your dialogues are all 1500 words. This one is way over."

103   I smiled. "I'll talk to my editor about it."

CARMEN VAZQUEZ

Appearances

Carmen Vazquez (1949–) was born in Puerto Rico and raised in Harlem, a predominantly African American community in New York City. Active in the gay/lesbian movement for years, she has published many essays. The following piece was included in Warren J. Blumenfeld's 1992 book called Homophobia: How We All Pay the Price.

1   North of Market Street and east of Twin Peaks, where you can see the white fog mushroom above San Francisco's hills, is a place called the Castro. Gay men, lesbians, and bisexuals stroll leisurely up and down the bustling streets. They jaywalk with abandon. Night and day they fill the cafés and bars, and on weekends they line up for a double feature of vintage classics at their ornate and beloved Castro theater.

2   The 24 bus line brings people into and out of the Castro. People from all walks of life ride the electric-powered coaches. They come from the opulence of San Francisco's Marina and the squalor of Bayview projects. The very gay Castro is in the middle of its route. Every day, boys in pairs or gangs from either end of the city board the bus for a ride through the Castro and a bit of fun. Sometimes their fun is fulfilled with passionately obscene derision: "Fucking cocksucking faggots." "Dyke cunts." "Diseased butt fuckers." Sometimes, their fun is brutal.

3   Brian boarded the 24 Divisadero and handed his transfer to the driver one late June night. Epithets were fired at him the moment he turned for a seat. He slid his slight frame into an empty seat next to an old woman with silver blue hair who clutched her handbag and stared straight ahead. Brian stuffed his hands into the pockets of his worn brown bomber jacket and stared with her. He heard the flip of a skateboard in the back. The taunting shouts grew louder. "Faggot!" From the corner of his eye, he saw a beer bottle hurtling past the window and crash on the street. A man in his forties, wearing a Giants baseball cap and warmup jacket, yelled at the driver to stop the bus and get the hoodlums off. The bus driver ignored him and pulled out.

4   Brian dug his hands deeper into his pockets and clenched his jaw. It was just five stops to the top of the hill. When he got up to move toward the exit, the skateboard slammed into his gut and one kick followed another

until every boy had got his kick in. Despite the plea of the passengers, the driver never called the police.

5   Brian spent a week in a hospital bed, afraid that he would never walk again. A lawsuit filed by Brian against the city states, "As claimant lay crumpled and bleeding on the floor of the bus, the bus driver tried to force claimant off the bus so that the driver could get off work and go home. Claimant was severely beaten by a gang of young men on the #24 Divisadero Bus who perceived that he was gay."

6   On the south side of Market Street, night brings a chill wind and rough trade. On a brisk November night, men with sculptured torsos and thighs wrapped in leather walked with precision. The clamor of steel on the heels of their boots echoed in the darkness. Young men and women walked by the men in leather, who smiled in silence. They admired the studded bracelets on Mickey's wrists, the shine of his flowing hair, and the rise of his laughter. They were, each of them, eager to be among the safety of like company where they could dance with abandon to the pulse of hard rock, the hypnotism of disco, or the measured steps of country soul. They looked forward to a few drinks, flirting with strangers, finding Mr. or Ms. Right or, maybe, someone to spend the night with.

7   At the end of the street, a lone black street lamp shone through the mist. The men in leather walked under the light and disappeared into the next street. As they reached the corner, Mickey and his friends could hear the raucous sounds of the Garden spill onto the street. They shimmied and rocked down the block and through the doors.

8   The Garden was packed with men and women in sweat-stained shirts. Blue smoke stung the eyes. The sour and sweet smell of beer hung in the air. Strobe lights pulsed over the dancers. Mickey pulled off his wash-faded black denim jacket and wrapped it around his waist. An iridescent blue tank top hung easy on his shoulders. Impatient with the wait for a drink, Mickey steered his girlfriend onto the crowded dance floor.

9   Reeling to the music and immersed in the pleasure of his rhythms, Mickey never saw the ice pick plunge into his neck. It was just a bump with a drunk yelling, "Lame-assed faggot." "Faggot. Faggot. Faggot. Punk faggot." Mickey thought it was a punch to the neck. He ran after the roaring drunk man for seven steps, then lurched and fell on the dance floor, blood gushing everywhere. His girlfriend screamed. The dance floor spun black.

10   Mickey was rushed to San Francisco General Hospital, where thirty-six stitches were used by trauma staff to close the wound on his neck. Doctors said the pick used in the attack against him was millimeters away

from his spinal cord. His assailant, charged with attempted murder, pleaded innocent.

11   Mickey and Brian were unfortunate stand-ins for any gay man. Mickey was thin and wiry, a great dancer clad in black denim, earrings dangling from his ear. Brian was slight of build, wore a leather jacket, and boarded a bus in the Castro. Dress like a homo, dance like a homo, must be a homo. The homophobic fury directed at lesbians, gay men, and bisexuals in America most often finds its target. Ironclad evidence of sexual orientation, however, is not necessary for someone to qualify as a potential victim of deadly fury. Appearances will do.

12   The incidents described above are based on actual events reported to the San Francisco Police and Community United Against Violence (CUAV), an agency serving victims of antilesbian and antigay violence where I worked for four years. The names of the victims have been changed. Both men assaulted were straight.

13   Incidents of antilesbian and antigay violence are not uncommon or limited to San Francisco. A *San Francisco Examiner* survey estimates that over one million hate-motivated physical assaults take place each year against lesbians, gays, and bisexuals. The National Gay and Lesbian Task Force conducted a survey in 1984 that found that 94 percent of all lesbians and gay men surveyed reported being physically assaulted, threatened, or harassed in an antigay incident at one time or another. The great majority of these incidents go unreported.

14   To my knowledge, no agency other than CUAV keeps track of incidents of antigay violence involving heterosexuals as victims. An average of 3 percent of the over three hundred victims seen by CUAV each year identify as heterosexuals. This may or may not be an accurate gauge of the actual prevalence of antigay violence directed at heterosexuals. Most law enforcement agencies, including those in San Francisco, have no way of documenting this form of assault other than under a generic "harassment" code. The actual incidence of violence directed at heterosexuals that is motivated by homophobia is probably much higher than CUAV's six to nine victims a year. Despite the official paucity of data, however, it is a fact that incidents of antigay and antilesbian violence in which straight men and women are victimized do occur. Shelters for battered women are filled with stories of lesbian baiting of staff and of women whose husbands and boyfriends repeatedly called them "dykes" or "whores" as they beat them. I have personally experienced verbal abuse while in the company of a straight friend, who was assumed to be my lover.

15   Why does it happen? I have no definitive answers to that question. Understanding homophobic violence is no less complex than understanding racial violence. The institutional and ideological reinforcements of homophobia are myriad and deeply woven into our culture. I offer one perspective that I hope will contribute to a better understanding of how homophobia works and why it threatens all that we value as humane.

16   At the simplest level, looking or behaving like the stereotypical gay man or lesbian is reason enough to provoke a homophobic assault. Beneath the veneer of the effeminate gay male or the butch dyke, however, is a more basic trigger for homophobic violence. I call it *gender betrayal.*

17   The clearest expression I have heard of this sense of gender betrayal comes from Doug Barr, who was acquitted of murder in an incident of gay bashing in San Francisco that resulted in the death of John O'Connell, a gay man. Barr is currently serving a prison sentence for related assaults on the same night that O'Connell was killed. He was interviewed for a special report on homophobia produced by ABC's *20/20* (10 April 1986). When asked what he and his friends thought of gay men, he said, "We hate homosexuals. They degrade our manhood. We was brought up in a high school where guys are football players, mean and macho. Homosexuals are sissies who wear dresses. I'd rather be seen as a football player."

18   Doug Barr's perspective is one shared by many young men. I have made about three hundred presentations to high school students in San Francisco, to boards of directors and staff of nonprofit organizations, and at conferences and workshops on the topic of homophobia or "being lesbian or gay." Over and over again, I have asked, "Why do gay men and lesbians bother you?" The most popular response to the question is, "Because they act like girls," or, "Because they think they're men." I have even been told, quite explicitly, "I don't care what they do in bed, but they shouldn't act like that."

19   They shouldn't act like that. Women who are not identified by their relationship to a man, who value their female friendships, who like and are knowledgeable about sports, or work as blue-collar laborers and wear what they wish are very likely to be "lesbian baited" at some point in their lives. Men who are not pursuing sexual conquests of women at every available opportunity, who disdain sports, who choose to stay at home and be a househusband, who are employed as hairdressers, designers, or housecleaners, or who dress in any way remotely resembling traditional female attire (an earring will do) are very likely to experience the taunts and sometimes the brutality of "fag bashing."

20   The straitjacket of gender roles suffocates many lesbians, gay men, and bisexuals, forcing them into closets without an exit and threatening our very existence when we tear the closet open. It also, however, threatens all heterosexuals unwilling to be bound by their assigned gender identity. Why, then, does it persist?

21   Suzanne Pharr's examination of homophobia as a phenomenon based in sexism and misogyny offers a succinct and logical explanation for the virulence of homophobia in Western civilization:

> It is not by chance that when children approach puberty and increased sexual awareness they begin to taunt each other by calling these names: "queer," "faggot," "pervert." It is at puberty that the full force of society's pressure to conform to heterosexuality and prepare for marriage is brought to bear. Children know what we have taught them, and we have given clear messages that those who deviate from standard expectations are to be made to get back in line. . . .
>
>   To be named as lesbian threatens all women, not just lesbians, with great loss. And any woman who steps out of role risks being called a lesbian. To understand how this is a threat to all women, one must understand that any woman can be called a lesbian and there is no real way she can defend herself: there is no real way to credential one's sexuality. (*The Children's Hour,* a Lillian Hellman play, makes this point when a student asserts two teachers are lesbians and they have no way to disprove it.) She may be married or divorced, have children, dress in the most feminine manner, have sex with men, be celibate—but there are lesbians who do all these things. *Lesbians look like all women and all women look like lesbians.*[1]

I would add that gay men look like all men and all men look like gay men. There is no guaranteed method for identifying sexual orientation. Those small or outrageous deviations we sometimes take from the idealized mystique of "real men" and "real women" place all of us—lesbians, gay men, bisexuals, and heterosexuals alike—at risk of violence, derision, isolation, and hatred.

22   It is a frightening reality. Dorothy Ehrlich, executive director of the Northern California American Civil Liberties Union (ACLU), was the victim of

---

[1]Pharr, Suzanne. *Homophobia: A Weapon of Sexism* (Inverness, CA: Chardon, 1988), 17–19

a verbal assault in the Castro several years ago. Dorothy lives with her husband, Gary, and her two children, Jill and Paul, in one of those worn and comfortable Victorian homes that grace so many San Francisco neighborhoods. Their home is several blocks from the Castro, but Dorothy recalls the many times she and Gary could hear, from the safety of their bedroom, shouts of "faggot" and men running in the streets.

23   When Jill was an infant, Gary and Dorothy had occasion to experience for themselves how frightening even the threat of homophobic violence can be. One foggy, chilly night they decided to go for a walk in the Castro. Dorothy is a small woman whom some might call petite; she wore her hair short at the time and delights in the comfort of jeans and oversized wool jackets. Gary is very tall and lean, a bespectacled and bearded cross between a professor and a basketball player who wears jean jackets and tweed jackets with the exact same slouch. On this night they were crossing Castro Street, huddled close together with Jill in Dorothy's arms. As they reached the corner, their backs to the street, they heard a truck rev its engine and roar up Castro, the dreaded "faggot" spewing from young men they could not see in the fog. They looked around them for the intended victims, but there was no one else on the corner with them. They were the target that night: Dorothy and Gary and Jill. They were walking on "gay turf," and it was reason enough to make them a target. "It was so frightening," Dorothy said. "So frightening and unreal."

24   But it is real. The *20/20* report on homophobia ends with the story of Tom and Jan Matarrase, who are married, have a child, and lived in Brooklyn, New York, at the time of their encounter with homophobic violence. On camera, Tom and Jan are walking down a street in Brooklyn lined with brown townhouses and black wrought-iron gates. It is snowing, and, with hands entwined, they walk slowly down the street where they were assaulted. Tom is wearing a khaki trenchcoat, slacks, and loafers. Snowflakes melt into the tight dark curls on his head. Jan is almost his height, her short bobbed hair moving softly as she walks. She is wearing a black leather jacket, a red scarf, and burnt orange cords. The broadness of her hips and softness of her face belie the tomboy flavor of her carriage and clothes, and it is hard to believe that she was mistaken for a gay man. But she was.

25   They were walking home, holding hands and engrossed with each other. On the other side of the street, Jan saw a group of boys moving toward them. As the gang approached, Jan heard a distinct taunt meant for her and Tom: "Aw, look at the cute gay couple." Tom and Jan quickened their step but it was too late. Before they could say anything, Tom was being punched in the face and slammed against a car. Jan ran toward Tom and the

car, screaming desperately that Tom was her husband. Fists pummeled her face as well. Outnumbered and in fear for their lives, Tom yelled at Jan to please open her jacket and show their assailants that she was a woman. The beating subsided only when Jan was able to show her breasts.

26   For the *20/20* interview, Jan and Tom sat in the warmth of their living room, their infant son in Jan's lap. The interviewer asked them how they felt when people said they looked like a gay couple. "We used to laugh," they said. "But now we realize how heavy the implications are. Now we know what the gay community goes through. We had no idea how widespread it was. It's on every level."

27   Sadly, it *is* on every level. Enforced heterosexism and the pressure to conform to aggressive masculine and passive feminine roles place fag bash-ers and lesbian baiters in the same psychic prison with their victims, gay or straight. Until all children are free to realize their full potential, until all women and men are free from the stigma, threats, alienation, or violence that come from stepping outside their roles, we are all at risk.

28   The economic and ideological underpinnings of enforced heterosexism and sexism or any other form of systematic oppression are formidable foes and far too complex for the scope of this essay. It is important to remember, however, that bigots are natural allies and that poverty or the fear of it has the power to seduce us all into conformity. In Castro graffiti, *faggot* appears right next to *nigger* and *kike*. Race betrayal or any threat to the sanctimony of light-skinned privilege engenders no less a rage than gender betrayal, most especially when we have a great stake in the elusive privilege of proper gender roles or the right skin color. *Queer lover* and *fag hag* are cut from the same mold that gave us *nigger lover*, a mold forged by fears of change and a loss of privilege.

29   Unfortunately, our sacrifices to conformity rarely guarantee the privi-lege or protection we were promised. Lesbians, gay men, and bisexuals who have tried to pass know that. Heterosexuals who have been perceived to be gay know that. Those of us with a vision of tomorrow that goes beyond tol-erance to a genuine celebration of humanity's diversity have innumerable fronts to fight on. Homophobia is one of them.

30   But how will this front be won? With a lot of help, and not easily. Challenges to homophobia and the rigidity of gender roles must go beyond the visible lesbian and gay movement. Lesbians, gay men, and bisexuals alone cannot defuse the power of stigmatization and the license it gives to frighten, wound, or kill. Literally millions of us are needed on this front, straight and gay alike. We invite any heterosexual unwilling to live with the damage that "real men" or "real women" messages wreck on them, on their

children, and on lesbians, gay men, and bisexuals to join us. We ask that you not let queer jokes go unchallenged at work, at home, in the media, or anywhere. We ask that you foster in your children a genuine respect for themselves and their right to be who and what they wish to be, regardless of their gender. We ask that you embrace your daughter's desire to swing a bat or be a carpenter, that you nurture your son's efforts to express affection and sentiment. We ask that you teach your children how painful and destructive words like *faggot* or *bulldyke* are. We ask that you invite your lesbian, gay, and bisexual friends and relatives into the routine of your lives without demanding silence or discretion from them. We invite you to study our history, read the literature written by our people, patronize our businesses, come into our homes and neighborhoods. We ask that you give us your vote when we need it to protect our privacy or to elect open lesbians, gay men, and bisexuals to office. We ask that you stand with us in public demonstrations to demand our right to live as free people, without fear. We ask that you respect our dignity by acting to end the poison of homophobia.

31   Until individuals are free to choose their roles and be bound only by the limits of their own imagination, *faggot, dyke*, and *pervert* will continue to be playground words and adult weapons that hurt and limit far many more people than their intended victims. Whether we like it or not, the romance of virile men and dainty women, of Mother, Father, Dick, Jane, Sally, and Spot is doomed to extinction and dangerous in a world that can no longer meet the expectations conjured by history. There is much to be won and so little to lose in the realization of a world where the dignity of each person is worthy of celebration and protection. The struggle to end homophobia can and must be won, for all our sakes. Personhood is imminent.

ERIK MEERS

Keeping It Real

Erik Meers, a writer, serves as managing editor of the leading edge magazine Paper, *a monthly publication intended for "culture vultures" who follow film, music, fashion, and social trends. Thus he writes regularly on all sorts of cultural and political issues, and not just for* Paper. *On April 30, 2002, he published the following essay in* The Advocate, *the leading gay and lesbian newsmagazine, one that covers public affairs, cultural developments, and politics.*

1   After several weeks of dating Kurt, a schoolteacher from Minneapolis, Chris Beckman, a strapping 23-year-old artist from Boston, brought him back for a sleepover at the loft apartment in Chicago that he shared with six other castmates on *The Real World.* MTV's camera zoomed in on the duo as they cuddled and kissed on Chris's bed before heading under the sheets. When Kurt sent Chris flowers the next day, Chris's straight roommate Theo groused, "This is a little bit too gay for me," undoubtedly speaking for many young viewers who had never seen two men in a romance before.

2   Regularly rattling viewers with frank gay content has been part of a winning formula for so-called reality TV programs for decades, and it's something *The Real World* has perfected during its decade-long run. In fact, the show is enjoying record audiences this season, thanks in large measure to its two charismatic gay cast members, Beckman and Aneesa (who has declined to reveal her last name).

3   The show's candor about same-sex romance surprised even Beckman. "Those were the [remote-controlled] cameras that were inside the room," he says of his bedroom scene. "I had no idea they could record from those cameras. Even when they weren't there, they could be recording us. Seeing that scene was like, 'Wow! Hi!'"

4   "Wow" is right. Lesbians and gays are everywhere on the tube this spring courtesy of the endless proliferation of reality TV. In addition to *The Real World,* the CBS juggernaut *Survivor: Marquesas* features out castaway John Carroll, a nurse from Omaha, as well as a rumored lesbian yet to be revealed, and *The Amazing Race 2* highlights gay buddies Oswald and Danny from Miami. This fall, *Eco-Challenge Fiji 2002*—a grueling 500-plus-kilometer race to be broadcast on the USA Network—will feature an all-gay team sponsored by Subaru. And this is not to mention the countless openly gay people

who continue to pop up as participants everywhere, including *Who Wants to Be a Millionaire,* the various confront-your-fears shows, and possibly even that heterofest *Temptation Island.*

5   All these vérité programs are breaking fresh ground for gay visibility and defusing a bit of the frustration felt by activists at the timidity of some fictional network shows like *Will & Grace,* "Five seasons ago on *The Real World,* we would not see someone like [Beckman] lying in bed and kissing his boyfriend. It's wonderful. There's nothing salacious about it," says Scott Seomin, entertainment media director for the Gay and Lesbian Alliance Against Defamation. "*Will & Grace* is a great show, and it has done an amazing amount for our community, but it's a hit because it conforms to the sitcom format to make the majority of this country comfortable. We have seen Grace making lots of passionate noises with her boyfriend. We have not seen that with Will."

6   Unlike the sex-starved Will, Chris and Aneesa date, cuddle, and sleep with their same-sex love interests. And unlike the heated romances of *ER*'s Dr. Kerry Weaver or the "questioning" youth story lines on *Boston Public* and *Once and Again,* their doings can't be dismissed as ratings-driven character development. In a recent episode of *The Real World,* for example, when Aneesa ripped into her game-playing girlfriend for bringing her ex by the apartment, the tears and expletives flowed from immediate emotions, not from a writer's pen.

7   "It was real," recalls Aneesa. "I was upset and I was mad. I wish I wouldn't have cursed as much. I gave [the producers] everything. I kept one or two things private, but everything else is out there. I would be so embarrassed to go home and have people say, 'Aneesa, that is not you.' Aneesa does not hold back one ounce of her personality.

8   "I cried more there than I have in the last five years," she continues. "It was therapy for me. We all make mistakes—and I get to see mine every week." While many will shake their heads at Aneesa's antics, most can relate to her frustration with an unresponsive lover. Such scenes humanize gay relationships to an impressionable audience in a way that fictional shows can't.

9   *Survivor: Africa*'s Brandon Quinton can probably advise Aneesa on living with an over-the-top TV persona. "I knew they were going to play me up to be really flamboyant," Quinton says of his portrayal on the show. "They made us all extreme. I'm a real person. It wasn't Brandon playing someone else. They edited me extremely, but it was still me."

10   But by playing into a gay stereotype, *Survivor*'s producers may have made Quinton an easier target for homophobes. He confesses that he no longer reads the mail forwarded to him from the network since almost

10% of it is hate mail. "I just don't want that 'die-fag-die' stuff in my house," he says.

11   Many gay viewers also bristled at Quinton's campiness. Some even wrote to GLAAD [Gay and Lesbian Alliance Against Defamation] to complain. "I got a lot of E-mail and calls about Brandon," recalls Seomin. "What am I supposed to do, remove him from the show? He's part of the gay community, and we should be embracing him. It was their own internalized homophobia—the fact that he wasn't hypermasculine and had some 'Mary moments,' as I call them. These people E-mailing me are out with their friends calling them 'Mary.' But there is so much shame about who sees that. If we want people to understand our lives, we can't cherry-pick what they see."

12   In its own subversive way, reality TV is challenging the notion that every gay man on ad-supported TV has to be either "straight-acting" or a nonthreatening clown. With each new out reality player, the palette of familiar "gay types" is gradually expanding, whether that means a gay mathematician who gets a Bette Midler question wrong on *Millionaire,* a tough lesbian *Road Rules* contestant who's also one of the show's lookers, or a sensitive gay man on *Big Brother* who loves both his Southern home and his long-term partner.

13   Preferring larger-than-life participants who will quickly stand out, reality TV by its very nature favors more Brandons and fewer Wills. It has been that way since the beginning: Lance Loud's coming-out on the granddaddy of reality TV shows, 1973's *An American Family,* was politically incorrect long before that phrase existed. Loud lived up to his name, and his determination to find his gay self contributed to the messiness that overtook his family during the filming. Nineteen years later, the creators of *The Real World* took that lesson to heart, adding the openly gay Norm to the first season's cast. The show caught the imagination of the MTV generation and became an instant institution, queer characters and all.

14   In the second season, Beth Anthony piqued housemates with her aggressively out manner. Looking back now, Anthony says gay visibility was especially vital during the early '90s, before TV stars like Ellen DeGeneres or Rosie O'Donnell came out. "I've had a lot of people come up to me on the street and say that it changed their lives, that their parents understand a little better, that they were in really shaky places and I helped," she says. "Visibility makes a huge difference. I've had thousands of people tell me that." Anthony, who now lives in Los Angeles with her partner of 10 years, Becks, and their 3-year-old daughter, has put that philosophy into practice with her own T-shirt company, featuring both humorous and earnest gay-related designs.

15   Since Norm and Beth, *The Real World* has presented a parade of warm and colorful out personalities, including person-with-AIDS Pedro Zamora in San Francisco; binge-drinker Ruthie in Hawaii; and, in New Orleans, boy-next-door Danny, who dated an enlisted man during the filming, dramatizing the problems with the Pentagon's "don't ask, don't tell" policy.

16   "The very idea of *The Real World* when we pitched it to MTV in 1992 was putting seven diverse people into a house," observes Jonathan Murray, the show's cocreator. "It almost requires having a gay or lesbian just as it requires having a black or Latino person."

17   The reality genre took a giant step toward the mainstream with the howling success of the first season of *Survivor* on CBS in summer 2000. Unlike broadcast sitcoms and dramas, where network suits psychoanalyze the import of each character's persona down to their haircut, reality TV seems to have dodged a major-network hurdle—execs' fear of risk taking—an advantage guaranteed by the victory of first *Survivor* winner Richard Hatch.

18   With his smirking egotism, bearish build, and preference for nudity, Hatch was no one's idea of a gay role model, much less a network superstar. But his soap-operatic connivings were the best thing for CBS's ratings since J.R. Ewing. "I think that Richard Hatch was so popular because of his scheming," observes Julie Salamon, a TV critic for the *New York Times*. "The fact of his being openly gay became important but incidental. In a lot of ways reality shows have been searching for the next Richard Hatch ever since. Having a gay person in the cast is just part of the formula now."

19   Since the broadcast networks reach a far larger—and more conservative—audience than MTV, the potential social impact of gay people being on major-network shows is profound indeed. After all, reality shows purport to depict reality, so the inclusion of a diverse assortment of gay, lesbian, and bisexual people sends viewers the message that such people are just another variation on who might move in next door. "There's more of a realiza-

Richard Hatch from *Survivor*

tion that this is part of the population, and it's not a monolithic group of people," says Salamon. "Even in the stupidest situations, that's got to be positive. I think that familiarity breeds indifference—which is a good thing, in this case."

20   How the queer folks interact with all the straight players simply becomes part of each show's drama. "What I love about it is you don't control the story lines," says *The Real World*'s Murray. "If you have the courage to put a gay or lesbian person on, then you have to be courageous enough to air wherever it takes you. The audience doesn't have as big a problem with it because they know you haven't made those choices as a network. It's happened and you're just showing it. Reality gives the network a license to go into things that ordinarily they might not go into."

21   With gays popping up all over the cable box, Salamon argues that reality TV has become an easy out for the networks. "Certainly, 10 years ago [having gay people on TV] was something to be commented on," says Salamon. "Now it has become less and less startling. The difference with the people on reality shows [as opposed to fictional series] is that they are there for a short run. On a lot of them, they are kicked off week by week. With something like an *Ellen,* these are characters who are presumably going to be coming into people's homes, in the best case, for years. I don't think this [inclusion] shows a bravery on the part of the reality people. I think it's a different phenomenon."

22   And sometimes it's something a bit stronger. Over the past decade, the gay housemates on *The Real World* have proved to be among the most popular with viewers. "Danny, without a doubt, got more fan mail than anyone else [that season] and just as much from guys as girls," says Murray. "Not long ago I was with the new cast, and when Chris got up, the audience went crazy." Slowly, a new pantheon of demicelebrities is emerging—one with no need for closets, since their lives, including their sex lives, are televised weekly.

23   Many gay reality veterans say they've benefited from a kind of homo affirmative action. Life partners Bill Bartek and Joe Baldassare believed as much when applying for the first installment of *The Amazing Race,* a show that follows 11 two-person teams as they sprint around the world chasing a million-dollar prize and getting eliminated one by one. "We thought that [being gay] was our ticket to fortune if we could promote ourselves as a long-term gay couple," says Bartek.

24   Because the teams consist of people who are already close, *The Amazing Race* "is a relationship show, not just a scavenger hunt," says Bartek, who's been with Baldassare 15 years. "And as far as we knew, there hadn't been a gay couple [on reality TV]. That was the risk we took going into the

whole thing, that it was too groundbreaking. We were told by one of the staff members about halfway through the interview process that we were the most stable relationship he'd seen in about 10 years—gay or straight—and [he said,] 'If CBS decides to have enough courage to put on a gay couple, then essentially you guys are on the program.' " CBS bit, and Bartek and Baldassare—who dubbed themselves Team Guido after their pet Chihuahua—came in third on the show.

25   *Survivor*'s Quinton also played the gay card during auditions. "I talked about [two previous *Survivor* contestants] who were obviously gay but pretended not to be for whatever reason," recalls Quinton. "[CBS president] Les Moonves really enjoyed that. [Series creator] Mark Burnett didn't think I was qualified to be on the show. He didn't think I would last. When I was voted off [after 30 days], he told me he was really impressed. He thought I would have lasted less than 10 days."

26   Another stereotype shattered.

27   Producers also like gay cast members because they are almost certain to rankle their conservative castmates and stir up some drama. On the first *Survivor,* crusty ex-Marine Rudy repeatedly called Hatch "queer." "That's his word, at 72 years old, for two guys who like each other," Hatch says. "Rudy was great. The comments that he made were honest and straightforward. They weren't malicious or hateful or spiteful."

28   Hatch even thinks that being gay gave him a competitive advantage. "It had tons to do with the game, and it is indirectly at least why I won," he explains. "I was much more introspective at a much earlier age than any of my peers, and having done that, I was much more capable in the game *Survivor*—that's what it's about, knowing yourself."

29   But just how *real* are these reality shows? Participants on every program sign extensive agreements giving producers the right to portray them in just about any way they wish. "We are dramatists," says *The Real World*'s Murray. "Every episode is constructed with a beginning, middle, and end. I think we are interested in telling the best stories possible."

30   On the current *Real World,* for instance, editors have focused on Aneesa's conflicts with her mother, who is troubled by her daughter's sexual orientation. "When I see it now, it makes me quite upset," says Aneesa. "I love my mom. I think we could have handled it differently. Now we talk more and listen more. Now I'm more cautious about what I do and how I do it. The show has helped in certain ways. It was hard to watch." In contrast to the emotional rawness of Aneesa's life, the fictional parental struggles of lesbian mom Lindsay on *Queer as Folk* seem muted and artificial at best.

31   Hatch agrees that viewing yourself on national TV can be revelatory. "There was obviously lots that they left out because there were hundreds of hours of tape to fit into 13 one-hour episodes," says Hatch. "I found myself watching at one point and saying, 'Wow! They captured exactly what I was thinking in that facial expression.' " He adds, "But I don't think people understand how the game works enough to respect how bright I was to have pulled it off."

32   Though the reality vets shy away from the term "role model," they understand that having been out on national TV makes their every move noteworthy to our celebrity-crazed press. Both Quinton and *The Real World*'s Beckman have been outspoken about their struggles with substance abuse, for example. On the show, Beckman discusses his decision to quit drinking one year earlier. "All of my peers at that time were going out to clubs," he says now. "I thought that was what being gay was all about—that that was what my identity was. I slowly realized that everything I wanted in life wasn't being achieved because I was so fearful I couldn't ask for help. It came down to the decision that I was going to either keep going down that path and kill myself by the time I got there [or quit]. It was just sickening. I took a look at my life and where it was going—and it was going to the next party."

33   Quinton, who grew up in rural Oklahoma and was tormented by bullies as a kid, also believes he can offer something from his experience. "I changed a couple of people's minds on the show," he says. "I don't think anyone down in Louisiana is going to say, 'Gee, Brandon's gay; I'm going to stop burning crosses.' That's not going to happen. What I hope happens is that some kid in rural Oklahoma—like me—says, 'You know, Brandon is cool with being gay, so maybe I shouldn't be so worried about it.' You know, this sissy fag lasted a long time with no food or water and outlasted a lot of athletes out there."

34   How's that for a role model?

NORAH VINCENT

Listen, Hollywood!

Norah Vincent is a freelance journalist who lives in New York City. Her work frequently appears in The Village Voice *and in the national gay and lesbian newsmagazine* The Advocate. *The essay below first appeared, appropriately enough, in the* Los Angeles Times *on March 18, 2001.*

1   Right now, there's a teenager somewhere in this country standing in his parents' basement holding a homemade noose. He's already tied it to one of the rafters, and he's working up the courage to hang himself. Somewhere else, maybe a mile away, maybe a thousand miles away, another kid is sitting in a closed garage in the driver's seat of her parents' SUV with the windows down and the engine running. Waiting to die. She, like the boy with the noose, is just one of thousands of American teens who will take their lives this year. Almost a third of them are gay and have been driven to this act of desperation because they think this condemns them to a lonely, miserable life on the fringes of respectable society.

2   As the Academy Awards approach, it might be nice to pause for a moment and remember those kids because they, like us, are watching the stars, looking to them as role models. They're looking for a signal from idols that will tell them they aren't doomed to be outcasts all their lives. This alone might give them hope enough to stay alive.

3   For generations, Americans have looked to celluloid celebrities to learn everything from how to fall in love to how to rebel against authority. Naturally, our obsession with the actors we see on-screen spills over into real life, making it almost impossible for Tinseltown's leading ladies and men to have anything resembling a private life. Some celebrities squawk about this, but most of them concede, good-naturedly, that they are in the business of public image-making. In exchange for fabulous wealth, worldwide fame and the public's undying adulation, they've got to put up with the paparazzi following them into the toilet. This seems a fair, if Faustian, bargain.

4   Given this, it's always seemed laughable that some celebrities—when asked about their sexual orientations and why they aren't explicit about them—say that their sex lives are nobody's business. This is a convenient lie. They know all too well that being a public figure makes everything about them everyone's business. Moreover, they know that their celebrity grants them great power in influencing the public on matters of political import.

Hollywood stars often take great pride in being poster people for a good cause, but rarely when it might cost them something personally.

5   Hollywood has been tormented by homophobia for decades. Everyone knows that Ellen DeGeneres is not the only gay person in Hollywood. But most Americans would be amazed to learn just how many of the stars being held up to them as heterosexual icons are really gay. The fact that they would be amazed is exactly why it's so important that the celebrities concerned publicly acknowledge their sexual orientation. Doing so would shatter the prevailing notions of what a gay person looks like, acts like, sounds like, lives and loves like.

6   And there are few things that would make a bigger difference in the lives of young gay people, especially those who are driven to despair by the ingrained prejudices of their families and communities. Imagine what it meant when Rock Hudson was outted, and finally boys whose fathers had ridiculed them as sissies could point to this archetype of masculinity and say, he and I are the same.

7   There are also few things that could do as much to change the public's fears of and distaste for gays, especially now, when activists are pushing so hard for the right to marry, to be open about sexual orientation in the military and to be able to visit their loved ones in the hospital.

8   Bigotry has power only over perceived outsiders. When the myth of gays as the "other" is eradicated and when gays are seen as part of the mainstream, prejudice against them will of necessity abate.

9   And so I challenge any and all conscientious stars to take their same-sex lovers, companions, partners or "friends" to the Oscars this year as an act of solidarity.

10   Will it compromise their box office appeal? Maybe. But wouldn't it be worth it if it saved someone's life? Besides, how rich do you have to be before you'll consider it an acceptable risk to do the right thing and make a powerful statement about something as odious, rampant and downright deadly as homophobia?

11   C'mon Hollywood, show us you're not just limousine liberals. Do something more than wear a ribbon on your lapel. Stand up and be counted.

Immigration

Just about everyone can quote the famous inscription on New York's Statue of Liberty—"Give me your tired, your poor, your huddled masses, yearning to be free. The wretched refuse of your teeming shore, send these, the homeless, tempest-tost to me"—because the United States prides itself on being a nation of immigrants. And recently we have made good on the promise: more than 10 percent of our people, over 30 million in all (and up from 10 million in 1970), were born in other countries. Indeed, according to the 2000 census, one in five U.S. citizens was either born abroad or to foreign-born parents. Steady increases in immigration after World War II developed into a boom during the 1980s and 1990s in part because the 1965 Immigration Act (amended in 1990)

Statue of Liberty

looked favorably on the immigration of relatives of U.S. citizens, repealed quotas on immigrants from certain nations, and therefore encouraged immigration from Asia, Latin America, and Africa. As a result, in 2000 and 2001 over a million people immigrated to the United States. While immigrants in the late nineteenth and early twentieth century mostly came from southern and central Europe, most of today's immigrants come from Mexico, the Caribbean islands, the former Soviet Union, and Asian nations such as China, Vietnam, the Philippines, and India. While those earlier immigrants typically passed by the Statue of Liberty and were processed at Ellis Island before going on to northern cities, more than half of recent immigrants have been attracted to Florida, Texas, and California.

Nevertheless, there has also been a long history of resistance to immigration in the United States, dating at least to those who proudly enrolled in the "Know Nothing" political party of the 1840s and 1850s. Members of that political faction resisted the immigrants from Ireland and Germany who were arriving in waves, and they tended to blame all the nation's ills on immigration—crime, economic problems, social stresses. The questions (and fears) raised by those early critics persist today, except that now they are raised in connection with Asians, Arabs, and Latin Americans. Just what are the social and economic effects of immigration? How quickly and how completely do immigrants become assimilated—learning the majority language, identifying themselves with American cultural values, participating in American political life? What is our national responsibility to support, educate, and help assimilate immigrants? Do immigrants constitute a threat to the nation's economic well-being because they are commonly poor and less educated, because they take jobs away from native workers, and because they require expensive social services—welfare, education, health? Or do immigrants in fact increase the national

Cuban refugees stranded on a makeshift raft float between Key West, Florida, and Cuba, August 24, 1994

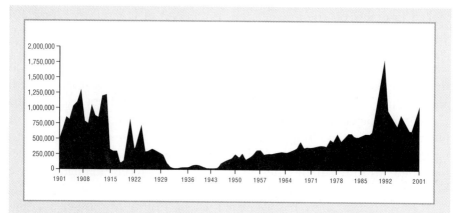

Legal Immigration: 1901–2001
Source: "Legal Immigration, Fiscal Year 2001." Immigration and Naturalization Service, U.S. Department of Justice.

wealth because they are highly motivated and because they supply labor to a perennially labor-hungry economy? Do immigrants endanger our national democracy because they cling to their original national identities, are slow to learn English, and participate only fitfully in political life—or do immigrants enrich the nation with their values and beliefs, ideas and ideals, hopes and hard work? How well do immigrant groups tolerate other minority and majority groups? How does immigration affect political alliances and policies within the United States? Does it threaten to impact our natural environment by leading to overpopulation?

And what should be done about illegal immigration? Experts agree that about 300,000 people enter the country illegally each year, or stay beyond their visa dates. Many others are arrested and deported (or imprisoned) for trying to enter the United States surreptitiously—or even die in the attempt to smuggle themselves across the border. Such facts bother many people who wish to obtain jobs for legal immigrants, to secure our national border and respect for the law, to protect us against criminals, and to make immigration as fair and humane as possible. Illegal immigration and abuses of international student visas have become even more important since the events of September 11, since a number of the terrorists entered the country illegally or on student visas. What should be done about illegal immigrants—an amnesty program that would legitimize as citizens people who have been living here and paying taxes for years? Increased efforts to capture illegals at or near borders? Careful surveillance? What are the rights of illegal aliens and student visitors? Should the Attorney General and the Immigration and

Immigration Web Sites

You can learn more about immigration and read more arguments about it at a number of places on the World Wide Web. Here are a few:

U.S. Department of Justice, Immigration and Naturalization Service, administers and enforces U.S. immigration policy. For information, check the Statistics Division at **<www.ins.usdoj.gov/graphics/aboutins/statistics>**

For information about immigration from the U.S. Census Bureau, see **<www.census.gov/main/www/cen2000.html>**

The CATO Institute offers demographic and economic statistics about immigrants at **<www.cato/org/>**

The Alexis de Tocqueville Institution works to increase public understanding of the cultural and economic benefits of immigration: **<www.adti.net>**

The Center for Immigration Studies conducts research on the impact of immigration: **<www.cis.org>**

The Federation for American Immigration Reform (FAIR) lobbies in favor of placing restrictions on immigration: **<www.fairus.org>**

The National Council of La Raza lobbies on behalf of Latinos in the United States: **<www.nclr.org>**

The National Immigration Forum builds public support for immigration: **<www.immigrationforum.org>**

The Immigration History Research Center, based at the University of Minnesota, is a substantial resource on American immigration and ethnic history: **<www1.umn.edu/ihrc/index.htm>**

Naturalization Service be able to track aliens closely, keep an eye out for possible terrorists who are here on student visas, and try vigorously to identify, locate, prosecute, and deport aliens who are suspected of posing a threat to our security—even if it means violating certain rights that are guaranteed to U. S. citizens? Or do those rights belong to everyone residing in our country by virtue of the Bill of Rights? Would some sort of national identification card be appropriate and useful and practical? Should our nation restrict immigration from nations that have a history of harboring terrorists, even if that would mean denying entry to legitimate dissidents and victims of harsh regimes?

A Time Line on Immigration

1607. First permanent English settlement at Jamestown, Virginia

1607–1776. "Open Door" era: individual colonies encourage immigration, restricting only criminals and "undesirables"

1776–1835. The "First Great Lull" in immigration: immigration numbers are low

1808. Importation of slaves is halted.

1840s. Irish immigration (as a result of famine) initiates an era of mass immigration that lasts until World War I.

1875. Supreme Court decides that immigration policy is the responsibility of the federal government, not the states.

1882–1917. Asian immigration is effectively interdicted. The 1882 Chinese Exclusion Act bars Chinese in particular.

1892. Ellis Island in New York harbor becomes the leading entry point for immigrants.

1890–1920. A wave of immigration from southern and eastern Europe peaks at 1.3 million in 1907.

1921. Quotas are initiated to reduce immigration sharply and to make immigration reflect the established face of the American community (i.e., white and European).

1920–1945. Second "Great Lull" in immigration. More restrictive immigration policies, the effects of the Great Depression, and the Second World War limit the number of immigrants who may settle in the United States.

1940s. Restrictions dropped against Asian immigration.

1954. "Operation Wetback" effectively stops illegal immigration.

1965. Immigration and Nationality Act increases immigration quotas, abolishes the principle of taking into account immigrants' national origins, and emphasizes family unification.

1986. Immigration Reform and Control Act provides amnesty for many illegal immigrants.

1990s. Immigration numbers increase substantially—for both legal and illegal immigrants.

Basic sources: Peter Brimelow, *Alien Nation; CQ Researcher*

Here we reprint several arguments about one or another aspect of immigration. Patrick J. Buchanan articulates the opposition to immigration in a speech that he delivered early in 2000, during his third-party campaign for the presidency. Buchanan is countered by the following item, Richard Rayner's "What Immigration Crisis?" David Cole ("Enemy Nations and American Freedoms") and Michelle Malkin ("The Deportation Abyss: It Ain't Over 'Til the Alien Wins") take opposite sides on the rights of citizens and the responsibilities of the Immigration and Naturalization Service—especially in the wake of the September 11 disaster. Finally, the voices of immigrants themselves are heard: Luz Suarez argues that "My Illegal Status Shouldn't Keep Me from Learning" through participation in our nation's education system; and Kyoko Mori expresses (in "Becoming Midwestern") what it is like for an immigrant from Japan to assimilate into American culture. Elsewhere in *Good Reasons*, on pages 173–179, Leslie Marmon Silko also offers on argument on current immigration policy.

PATRICK J. BUCHANAN

To Reunite a Nation

Patrick J. Buchanan (1939–   ) grew up in Washington, D.C., attended Georgetown University, and received a master's degree in journalism from Columbia. During the 1970s he served as an advisor to Richard Nixon and Gerald Ford, and he was White House Communications Director under Ronald Reagan. He later served as a regular panelist on several national television shows. He made the sharp curtailing of immigration one of the key issues in his bids to secure the Republican Party and Reform Party nominations for the presidency in 1992, 1996, and 2000. Recently he published the incendiary book The Death of the West: How Mass Immigration, Depopulation, and a Dying Faith Are Killing Our Culture and Country. *"To Reunite a Nation" was given as a campaign speech on January 18, 2000, at the Richard Nixon Library in Yorba Linda, California.*

1   Let me begin with a story: In 1979, Deng Xiaoping arrived here on an official visit. China was emerging from the Cultural Revolution, and poised to embark on the capitalist road. When President Carter sat down with Mr. Deng, he told him he was concerned over the right of the Chinese people to emigrate. The Jackson-Vanik Amendment, Mr. Carter said, prohibited granting most favored nation trade status to regimes that did not allow their people to emigrate.

2   "Well, Mr. President," Deng cheerfully replied, "Just how many Chinese do you want? Ten million? Twenty million? Thirty million?" Deng's answer stopped Carter cold. In a few words, the Chinese leader had driven home a point Mr. Carter seemed not to have grasped: Hundreds of millions of people would emigrate to America in a eyelash, far more than we could take in, far more than our existing population of 270 million, if we threw open our borders. And though the U.S. takes in more people than any other nation, it still restricts immigration to about one million a year, with three or four hundred thousand managing to enter every year illegally.

3   There is more to be gleaned from this encounter. Mr. Carter's response was a patriotic, or, if you will, a nationalistic response. Many might even label it xenophobic. The President did not ask whether bringing in ten million Chinese would be good for them. He had suddenly grasped that the real issue was how many would be good for America? Mr. Carter could have asked

another question: Which Chinese immigrants would be best for America? It would make a world of difference whether China sent over ten million college graduates or ten million illiterate peasants, would it not?

4　　Since the Carter-Deng meeting, America has taken in twenty million immigrants, many from China and Asia, many more from Mexico, Central America and the Caribbean, and a few from Europe. Social scientists now know a great deal about the impact of this immigration.

5　　Like all of you, I am awed by the achievements of many recent immigrants. Their contributions to Silicon Valley are extraordinary. The overrepresentation of Asian-born kids in advanced high school math and science classes is awesome, and, to the extent that it is achieved by a superior work ethic, these kids are setting an example for all of us. The contributions that immigrants make in small businesses and hard work in tough jobs that don't pay well merits our admiration and deepest respect. And many new immigrants show a visible love of this country and an appreciation of freedom that makes you proud to be an American.

6　　Northern Virginia, where I live, has experienced a huge and sudden surge in immigration. It has become a better place, in some ways, but nearly unrecognizable in others, and no doubt worse in some realms, a complicated picture overall. But it is clear to anyone living in a state like California or Virginia that the great immigration wave, set in motion by the Immigration Act of 1965, has put an indelible mark upon America.

7　　We are no longer a biracial society; we are now a multiracial society. We no longer struggle simply to end the divisions and close the gaps between black and white Americans; we now grapple, often awkwardly, with an unprecedented ethnic diversity. We also see the troubling signs of a national turning away from the idea that we are one people, and the emergence of a radically different idea, that we are separate ethnic nations within a nation.

8　　Al Gore caught the change in a revealing malapropism. Mr. Gore translated the national slogan, "E Pluribus Unum," which means "Out of many, one," into "Out of one, many." Behind it, an inadvertent truth: America is Balkanizing as never before.

9　　Five years ago, a bipartisan presidential commission, chaired by Barbara Jordan, presented its plans for immigration reform. The commission called for tighter border controls, tougher penalties on businesses that hire illegal aliens, a new system for selecting legal immigrants, and a lowering of the annual number to half a million. President Clinton endorsed the recommendations. But after ethnic groups and corporate lobbies for foreign labor turned up the heat, he backed away.

10   The data that support the Jordan recommendations are more refined today. We have a National Academy of Sciences report on the economic consequences of immigration, a Rand study, and work by Harvard's George Borjas and other scholars. All agree that new immigration to the United States is heavily skewed to admitting the less skilled. Unlike other industrialized democracies, the U.S. allots the vast majority of its visas on the basis of whether new immigrants are related to recent immigrants, rather than whether they have the skills or education America needs. This is why it is so difficult for Western and Eastern Europeans to come here, while almost entire villages from El Salvador have come in.

11   Major consequences flow from having an immigration stream that ignores education or skills. Immigrants are now more likely than native-born Americans to lack a high school education. More than a quarter of our immigrant population receives some kind of welfare, compared to fifteen percent of native-born. Before the 1965 bill, immigrants were less likely to receive welfare. In states with many immigrants, the fiscal impact is dramatic. The National Academy of Sciences contends that immigration has raised the annual taxes of each native household in California by $1,200 a year. But the real burden is felt by native-born workers, for whom mass immigration means stagnant or falling wages, especially for America's least skilled.

12   There are countervailing advantages. Businesses can hire new immigrants at lower pay; and consumers gain because reduced labor costs produce cheaper goods and services. But, generally speaking, the gains from high immigration go to those who use the services provided by new immigrants.

13   If you are likely to employ a gardener or housekeeper, you may be financially better off. If you work as a gardener or housekeeper, or at a factory job in which unskilled immigrants are rapidly joining the labor force, you lose. The last twenty years of immigration have thus brought about a redistribution of wealth in America, from less-skilled workers and toward employers. Mr. Borjas estimates that one half of the relative fall in the wages of high school graduates since the 1980s can be traced directly to mass immigration.

14   At some point, this kind of wealth redistribution, from the less well off to the affluent, becomes malignant. In the 1950s and '60s, Americans with low reading and math scores could aspire to and achieve the American dream of a middle class lifestyle. That is less realistic today. Americans today who do poorly in high school are increasingly condemned to a low-wage existence; and mass immigration is a major reason why.

15   There is another drawback to mass immigration: a delay in the assimilation of immigrants that can deepen our racial and ethnic divisions. As in Al Gore's "Out of one, many."

16   Concerns of this sort are even older than the Republic itself. In 1751, Ben Franklin asked: "Why should Pennsylvania, founded by the English, become a Colony of Aliens, who will shortly be so numerous as to Germanize us instead of our Anglifying them?" Franklin would never find out if his fears were justified. German immigration was halted by the Seven Years' War; then slowed by the Great Lull in immigration that followed the American Revolution. A century and half later, during what is called the Great Wave, the same worries were in the air.

17   In 1915 Theodore Roosevelt told the Knights of Columbus: "There is no room in this country for hyphenated Americanism. . . . The one absolutely certain way of bringing this nation to ruin, of preventing all possibility of its continuing to be a nation at all, would be to permit it to become a tangle of squabbling nationalities." Congress soon responded by enacting an immigration law that brought about a virtual forty-year pause to digest, assimilate, and Americanize the diverse immigrant wave that had rolled in between 1890 and 1920.

18   Today, once again, it is impossible not to notice the conflicts generated by a new "hyphenated Americanism." In Los Angeles, two years ago, there was an anguishing afternoon in the Coliseum where the U.S. soccer team was playing Mexico. The Mexican-American crowd showered the U.S. team with water bombs, beer bottles and trash. The "Star Spangled Banner" was hooted and jeered. A small contingent of fans of the American team had garbage hurled at them. The American players later said that they were better received in Mexico City than in their own country.

19   Last summer, El Cenizo, a small town in south Texas, adopted Spanish as its official language. All town documents are now to be written, and all town business conducted, in Spanish. Any official who cooperates with U.S. immigration authorities was warned he or she would be fired. To this day, Governor Bush is reluctant to speak out on this de facto secession of a tiny Texas town to Mexico.

20   Voting in referendums that play a growing part in the politics of California is now breaking down sharply on ethnic lines. Hispanic voters opposed Proposition 187 to cut off welfare to illegal aliens, and they rallied against it under Mexican flags. They voted heavily in favor of quotas and ethnic preferences in the 1996 California Civil Rights Initiative, and, again, to keep bilingual education in 1998. These votes suggest that in the California of the future, when Mexican-American voting power catches up

with Mexican-American population, any bid to end racial quotas by referendum will fail. A majority of the state's most populous immigrant group now appears to favor set-asides and separate language programs, rather than to be assimilated into the American mainstream.

21   The list of troubling signs can be extended. One may see them in the Wen Ho Lee nuclear secrets case, as many Chinese-Americans immediately concluded the United States was prosecuting Mr. Lee for racist reasons.

22   Regrettably, a cultural Marxism called political correctness is taking root that makes it impossible to discuss immigration in any but the most glowing terms. In New York City billboards that made the simple point that immigration increases crowding and that polls show most Americans want immigration rates reduced were forced down under circumstances that came very close to government-sponsored censorship. The land of the free is becoming intolerant of some kinds of political dissent.

23   Sociologist William Frey had documented an out-migration of black and white Americans from California, some of them seeking better labor market conditions, others in search of a society like the one they grew up in. In California and other high immigration states, one also sees the rise of gated communities where the rich close themselves off from the society their own policies produce.

24   I don't want to overstate the negatives. But in too many cases the American melting pot has been reduced to a simmer. At present rates, mass immigration reinforces ethnic subcultures, reduces the incentives of newcomers to learn English and extends the life of linguistic ghettos that might otherwise be melded into the great American mainstream. If we want to assimilate new immigrants—and we have no choice if we are remain one nation—we must slow down the pace of immigration.

25   Whatever its shortcomings, the United States has done far better at alleviating poverty than most countries. But an America that begins to think of itself as made up of disparate peoples will find social progress far more difficult. It is far easier to look the other way when the person who needs help does not speak the same language, or share a common culture or common history.

26   Americans who feel it natural and right that their taxes support the generation that fought World War II—will they feel the same way about those from Fukien Province or Zanzibar? If America continues on its present course, it could rapidly become a country with no common language, no common culture, no common memory and no common identity. And that country will find itself very short of the social cohesion that makes compassion possible.

27   None of us are true universalists: we feel responsibility for others because we share with them common bonds—common history and a common fate. When these are gone, this country will be a far harsher place.

28   That is why I am proposing immigration reform to make it possible to fully assimilate the thirty million immigrants who have arrived in the last thirty years. As president, I will ask Congress to reduce new entry visas to 300,000 a year, which is enough to admit immediate family members of new citizens, with plenty of room for many thousands with the special talents or skills our society needs. If after several years, it becomes plain that the United States needs more immigrants because of labor shortages, it should implement a point system similar to that of Canada and Australia, and allocate visas on a scale which takes into account education, knowledge of English, job skills, age, and relatives in the United States.

29   I will also make the control of illegal immigration a national priority. Recent reports of thousands of illegals streaming across the border into Arizona, and the sinister and cruel methods used to smuggle people by ship into the United States, demand that we regain control of our borders. For a country that cannot control its borders isn't fully sovereign; indeed, it is not even a country anymore.

30   Without these reforms, America will begin a rapid drift into uncharted waters. We shall become a country with a dying culture and deepening divisions along the lines of race, class, income and language. We shall lose for our children and for the children of the thirty million who have come here since 1970 the last best hope of earth. We will betray them all—by denying them the great and good country we were privileged to grow in. We just can't do that.

31   With immigration at the reduced rate I recommend, America will still be a nation of immigrants. We will still have the benefit of a large, steady stream of people from all over the world whose life dream is to be like us—Americans. But, with this reform, America will become again a country engaged in the mighty work of assimilation, of shaping new Americans, a proud land where newcomers give up their hyphens, the great American melting pot does its work again, and scores of thousands of immigrant families annually ascend from poverty into the bosom of Middle America to live the American dream.

RICHARD RAYNER

What Immigration Crisis?

Richard Rayner, a writer born in England but now living in Los Angeles, contributed the following essay to the New York Times Magazine *on January 7, 1996.*

1   Maria T. bites her nails. At 31, with five children, she's one of the 1.7 million immigrants now estimated to be living in California illegally. She speaks almost no English, even though she has been in America for more than eight years. In her clean and sparsely furnished living room, her kids—Gustavo (11), Mario (7), Maribel (6), Cesar (5) and Joan (4)—are in front of the TV, laughing first at "Home Improvement," then at "The Simpsons."

2   The refrigerator is almost empty; it contains only a gallon of milk, some Kool-Aid, a few tortillas. Her life is frugal, a devotion to the future of her children. Though there are three bedrooms in the apartment, all five sleep with her because she hates to let them out of her sight. Since she has no car and can rarely afford the bus, the family walks everywhere, Maria leading the way like Mother Goose with the kids behind toting Batman and Pocahontas backpacks. On a typical day she walks six miles, shuttling between her apartment and the local school in Van Nuys.

3   In Guadalajara her husband was a thief, a drug addict, a small-time street hustler who with friends jumped some guy and, during the robbery, knocked out his teeth. The man's friends came looking for him with a machete. They chopped off his hands. One was beyond repair, but doctors were able to sew back the other. He also sustained injuries to the head and neck. His brain was damaged, Maria says, and he began to abuse and beat her.

4   For her, as for so many, the decision to make the journey to El Norte was the beginning of an epic. Gustavo was 3 at the time, Mario was 8 months, and she was 5 months pregnant with Maribel. Maria crossed the border with the help of a "coyote," a guide, but when she arrived in San Diego the woman who'd paid for her brothers' crossings didn't have any money this time. Maria was kept a slave in the coyote's house. He beat and raped her until, after three months, her brother raised $300, half the sum agreed for the crossing, and the coyote let her go.

5   She stayed with her brother in Los Angeles, the Pico-Union district, and it was here that Maribel was born. "I'd come out of labor and I was staring at the wall and I said to my sister-in-law, 'Look, she's there.' She said,

'Who?' I said. 'The Virgin Mary.' She said: 'There's nothing there. You're crazy.' But it was true all the same. For eight months the Virgin would appear to me. She made me strong.

6   "At first I had to beg for food. Sometimes I did day work for Latinos, for $10 a day. I'd take off into the city on the bus, not really knowing where I was going, and get off to beg on the streets. I'm ashamed of that."

7   Slowly, she clawed her way up. It is in so many ways a classic immigrant's tale, although she has been the beneficiary not just of her own drive, but also of something equally important—welfare. She's here illegally, with fake ID, and she doesn't work. She receives $723 in cash and $226 in food stamps, and Section 8 takes care of more than two-thirds of her $1,000 rent (high, because landlords know illegals won't complain).

8   It's a myth, however, that anyone can come over the border and start milking the system. Only Medicaid and limited food benefits are available to illegal immigrants, and most don't apply for these because they fear detection by the Immigration and Naturalization Service. Maria T. gets what she does because of those of her children who were born here.

9   Local, state and federal governments spend about $11.8 billion a year educating legal and illegal immigrant children, according to the Urban Institute, a nonpartisan research organization, compared with the $227 billion spent to educate all children. Generally, this is more than offset by the taxes that legal and illegal immigrant families pay—$70.3 billion a year, the Urban Institute says—while receiving $42.9 billion in total services. Illegal immigrants pay $7 billion in taxes.

10   Maria T., however, represents the nightmare scenario—an illegal immigrant who's sucking money from the system and putting nothing back. Even so, it's not clear that she's a villain. She hopes one day to go to work herself. She hopes and believes that her bright children will become outstanding. She believes in America, as the man said at the beginning of *The Godfather*, though it's the government that is helping her out, not Marlon Brando.

11   My wife, from Finland, has a green card; I'm English, in the process of applying for one myself; our son was born an American. When we moved into our house in Venice, California, one of our neighbors, an elderly white woman with whom we're now very friendly, said, "No Americans live on our block anymore."

12   Maybe she had the jitters about new neighbors, or maybe there was something else at play. I knew that her father had been born in Germany and had journeyed to Detroit, where she was born. I wanted to say that logically, therefore, our son is every bit as American as she is. But in any debate about nationality, I know, logic fades fast.

13   My own father once traced our family tree back to 1066, when one Baron de Rainier sailed from Normandy to help conquer England. Since then, give or take the occasional Irish excursion, my progenitors were all born within a hundred or so miles of one another in the north of England. So, when I came to America and found that nearly everyone was from somewhere else if they stepped back a generation or two, I found myself thrilled and oddly at ease. It explained America's drive, its generosity and up-for-anything energy. As Melville wrote, "We are not a nation, so much as a world."

14   Not everyone sees things this way. Many have drawn a line behind which they stand, *true* Americans, fearful and angry about the erosion of their identity. With unintended irony they talk of themselves as "natives." On immigration, they argue that enough is enough, that the borders must be secured and a drastic cutback enforced. Those who are allowed in, they say, must be professionals or skilled workers because the others—mobs of unskilled, third-world peasants—drain resources and take jobs. They cost billions and dilute the gene pool. They are mutating the face of America.

15   California itself, for instance, passed an anti-immigrant measure with scary ease. In last year's state election nearly 60 percent voted for Proposition 187, the so-called Save-Our-State initiative, which sought to deny public education, nonemergency health care and welfare to illegal immigrants. By linking illegal immigration to joblessness and crime, Pete Wilson revived his flagging gubernatorial campaign and was swept back into office, even though, as an exit poll showed, few who voted for 187 actually thought it was going to work.

16   Wilson was avid for votes and a reaction and he got both. Many legal Latinos, fearful of deportation, refused to go near schools and emergency rooms. There was immigrant bashing and hate mail. Since the Republicans took control of the United States House and Senate, moreover, it seems as though all Washington has been grandstanding on the issue. Dozens of immigration-related bills were introduced last term, including two major vehicles, one from Senator Alan Simpson of Wyoming and the other from Representative Lamar Smith of Texas. At some point, the two bills could be rolled into one. Simpson aims to have the new law in force by October 1996. This is all happening at warp speed.

17   Many of the proposals are mean-spirited and, to a lot of observers, wrongheaded. One would impose a tax on employers who hire *legal* aliens. Others would deny citizenship to children born in this country to illegals, or eliminate some categories of family immigration. The anti-immigration forces have done an excellent job of creating an atmosphere of crisis in

which the debate has focused on *how* to slow the "flood" of immigration, legal and illegal. But illegal immigration should not be folded over to scapegoat legals as well. The real point is that there isn't any immigration crisis.

18   Solving the problems we do have will require more than hastily drawn legislation. Demetrios Papademetriou, an immigration expert with the Carnegie Endowment for International Peace, says: "Polls tell us that Americans are worried about illegal immigration. Good. Let's take care of it. Polls say people think some employers are too unscrupulous with immigrants. Let's take care of that, too. But this requires patience and wisdom. Congress has neither at this time."

19   "The perception is that immigration is out of control," says Joel Kotkin, author of *Tribes* and a fellow at the Pepperdine University Institute of Public Policy. "It isn't. If you say to most Americans, 'We have 800,000 legal immigrants a year,' they're going to reply. 'Hey, that's not so bad.' And this is the truth of the situation. But it's somehow been demonized so that people think there are millions coming across the border."

20   The Border Patrol logged 1,094,718 apprehensions in 1994. On page 26 of his *Alien Nation*, a leading restrictionist, Peter Brimelow, writes that legal immigration is "overwhelmed by an estimated 2 to 3 million illegal entries into the country in every recent year." He goes on to note, correctly, that many of these illegal entrants go back home, and that some trundle to and fro across the border every day. By page 33, however, he's writing "a remarkable two to three million illegal immigrants may have succeeded in entering the country in 1993."

21   Within seven pages illegal entrants have mysteriously become illegal immigrants, attached to that hyperbolic 2 to 3 million, a figure vigorously disputed by I.N.S., which regards as preposterous the idea that for every border crosser caught another three get away. Indeed, throughout the 1970s there were some 8 million border apprehensions and during that time, according to the best estimates of I.N.S., about 1 million illegals came to reside—eight apprehensions per illegal immigrant.

22   So how many illegals are coming in and staying each year now? The Urban Institute says 250,000 to 300,000. The Center for Immigration Studies, a conservative research group, says 400,000, while I.N.S. says 300,000. The Census Bureau until recently guessed 200,000 to 400,000; now it agrees with the I.N.S.

23   The 300,000 figure is considered firm because it was based on the years following 1988, when the I.N.S. started to process the genuinely reliable data it amassed following the 1986 amnesty for illegals. Too much of this and the eyes glaze over, but the gist is, the further you get from

1988, the flakier the statistics become. And the argument over the number of illegal immigrants is nothing compared with the furor over how much they cost.

24   The fact is, no one knows for sure; there is simply no up-to-date research. "The issue has caught political fire," Papademetriou says. "But serious academics haven't got out into the field yet. They're reluctant to play into the hands of the politicians."

25   Immigration is in the spotlight not because of money but because it so impinges on issues like race, the role of government, national identity, and change. Name an issue and you can hook it to immigration. One side looks at crime, failing schools, and soaring welfare spending, and sees too many immigrants. The other sees America, the greatest nation on earth, built on the backs of immigrants and still benefiting enormously from the brains, energy, and determination (not to speak of low wages) of the next generation of newcomers. Right now the debate is more emotional than informed. It's all temper tantrums and red-hot sound bites.

26   When people complain about immigration, about the alien "flood," it's Latin Americans they mean, who from their entry points in California and Miami are fanning out through the country. There's concern about the small minority who are criminals, and the seeming reluctance of these people to learn English. Mixed in with this is the prejudice summarized by D. H. Lawrence in "Mornings in Mexico." They are other, he concluded, they are dirty, I don't trust them and they stink. There's also the suggestion that Latinos are lazy, though everywhere you look in Los Angeles you see evidence to the contrary.

27   Until recently the rough understanding was that, though you may have arrived illegally, if you manage to stay you get legal. There's a desire to thwart that now, and an unanticipated effect of Proposition 187 was a record surge in citizenship applications. The Los Angeles district alone receives about 25,000 a month. This scramble for certainty of status prompted the I.N.S. to process 90,000 applications in 1994 and 125,000 in 1995, with 250,000 projected for 1996.

28   On a hot September morning I visit the basement of the Federal Building on Los Angeles Street to sit in on preliminary interviews. Applicants must show that they have been law-abiding, tax-paying residents for at least seven years. They must be able to read, write, and speak English, and correctly answer a substantial proportion of a questionnaire about current affairs, history, and constitutional principles. In a little booth an I.N.S. interviewer asks Maria Elena Ortiz, a Mexican-born resident for 17 years, who the mayor of Los Angeles is.

29 She doesn't know.

  "What is the highest law of the land?"

  "The Ten Amendments," she says.

  "What is the capital of the United States?"

  "Sacramento."

  "No," says the interviewer. "The capital of the *United* States."

  She's unsure.

  "Where does Bill Clinton live?"

  "Washington, D.C.?" she answers, still doubtful.

30 The next day, at the downtown convention center, 3,500 applicants who have successfully negotiated this interview and all the other I.N.S. hurdles attend a ceremony to become citizens. It's a feel-good affair, serious business mixed with Super Bowl hoopla and a celebration of the immigration myth. A guy from I.N.S. in a crisp and collarless white shirt stands up to sing "The Star Spangled Banner." An MTV-style video shows a farmer in the Kansas wheat fields, the Dallas Cowboys, a squadron of F-16's booming out above the Rockies. Federal Judge Dickran Tevrizian talks of the courage it takes to leave one's birthplace and fulfill one's dreams. "We Americans by birth can learn from you Americans by choice," he says. He then requests that these particular new citizens not go out and do graffiti. When the judge finishes, 3,500 fists, 40 percent of them Mexican until just a few moments before, raise high the Stars and Stripes and wave.

31 Maria T. takes me to meet some friends who live in the poor, densely populated, northeast section of the San Fernando Valley. I'm standing on the sidewalk when a skinny white guy comes up, offering a Makita power drill, still in its box, for $20. The street is filled with drug dealers.

32 Behind a locked gate, the building's 32 apartments are cramped around a tiny concrete courtyard where all the young kids play. Two of the kids, maybe four or five years old, get excited when they hear the tinny music of an ice-cream truck and rush out toward the street. Beyond the gate it's gangsters and rap, urban America; inside you could be in Mexico.

33 Agustin C. and Maria V. have four children: Vanessa, Antonio, Alejandro and Catalina. Vanessa, the oldest, seven, is Maria's child by a previous relationship; all were born here. Agustin has a genuine green card valid until 2004, while Maria is here illegally. Her first fake green card, which cost $50, almost got her caught. The second was a much better buy at $150. She shows it to me proudly. "I've already got four jobs with this one."

34 They pay $600 a month for a ground-floor apartment with two bedrooms, one bath and a small living room with kitchen attached. The TV is tuned, as always, to Channel 32, a Spanish-language station. The brown

shag carpet is littered with crayons, empty soda cans and broken tortilla chips. Two fans—one on the floor, the other above the dining table—stir the stagnant air, while flies circle an open trash bin in the center of the room. A cockroach skitters down the wall.

35   "I came to America to work," says Agustin. "Before, I knew only what I was told, that it was easy to earn money. They said you could sweep dollars up from the streets like leaves."

36   With sly humor, Maria says: "And now it's true, he does—in a way. He's a gardener."

37   Agustin's smile shows a shattered top jaw, front teeth victims of a soccer game. He works for a landscape company that tends the lawns, sprinklers and hedges of corporate office buildings throughout the valley. He gets up at 6 in the morning and often doesn't return until 7 at night. For this he receives $300 a week, though his boss has just agreed to a raise to $350. His ultimate goal is citizenship for both him and Maria, though he says, "I'm proud to be Mexican."

38   He came to America in 1986, at age 20. By then he'd worked construction all over Mexico and had unloaded fish at Vera Cruz. He was already married, with two children, when—he's reluctant to admit—he discovered that his wife was cheating on him. His mother-in-law, who now looks after those two children, helped him with money for the journey.

39   Agustin is a hustler, an adventurous survivor. His grandfather died at 132, he says. When I express skepticism he springs out of his chair and hurries into the bedroom, returning with a cheap nylon gym bag, which, he says, contains his grandfather's birth certificate. Rooting around inside, however, he can't find it. Instead, with pride he shows me the stub of the first paycheck he received in America; it's for $105.26, for a forty-hour week. He goes on pulling more and more stuff out of the bag. He has kept not just that first check stub, but every other one since. The bag holds nothing less than the history of his life here—letters and postcards from back home, copies of his tax returns and dealings with I.N.S. and the various fake ID's he used before getting his legal green card. He did all the paperwork himself. He has friends who used lawyers, he says, but they ended up getting cheated.

40   I recall a visit to Room 1001 of the downtown Federal building to pick up my work permit and "advanced parole status" (preliminary green card approval). Room 1001 proved not to be a room at all but a huge induction and inquiry area in which 1,500 people stood in line or waited for their names to be called. More stood outside, around half the block, trying to get in. The crowd was almost entirely Asian, Middle Eastern, and Hispanic. I spotted

only two other whites, one an English hairdresser protesting so loudly at the indignity of being made to wait at all that I moved away and sat next to a middle-aged Mexican with a mustache and a cowboy hat who told me he'd been coming here five years now for his green card.

41   Five years! My heart plunged, but my expensive and very efficient Century City lawyer had provided an immigration specialist, a "facilitator" as he called himself, to walk me through. When, after an hour or so, a list of names mysteriously boomed out over a loudspeaker, mine was at the top. The fellow who had been in the mill all this time shrugged and smiled. It seemed like a miracle, although I knew this was exactly what it was not. Wheels had been oiled, though on this occasion, staring at all those faces dazed with boredom, I felt no guilt, merely gratitude. I waltzed out five minutes later bearing the employment card that made me legal.

42   Agustin doesn't resent his own difficulties. Whites have treated him pretty well, he says. He has no complaints. His mistrust and dislike are reserved for blacks, whom he believes are given all the breaks. "There's a system. You have to learn how to exist within the system."

43   He first heard about Proposition 187 when he came home one night, showered and turned on the TV. "I wasn't comfortable with it. Maria could be deported, with our kids, and it would totally destroy my family. Sure, there are cases of abuse. But nearly all of us want to work. Here in California they hire us happily for low wages. Then they throw immigration at us if we ask for more. I think they're scared that we might become them. We're the people that made California. We built it."

44   By the Treaty of Guadalupe Hidalgo in 1848, Mexico ceded California to the United States. It was just at this time that gold was discovered and lotus-land took on a new importance. Mexicans feel to this day that they were cheated; and that in coming to California they are asserting a historical right; with each payday and welfare check they claim revenge. "It's a scar, not a border," notes the Mexican writer Carlos Fuentes.

45   Sucking at his broken teeth, Agustin says: "Mexico is overshadowed by the U.S., which tends to use smaller countries for its own benefit. Americans buy our oil cheap, refine it and sell it for less. They exploit us and then they get upset when we come here." He goes quiet, and wipes his hands. He seems a little embarrassed. He says sadly, "I agree that the immigration problem is overwhelming."

46   It's true that illegal immigrants put a tremendous burden on the health and education systems. The Los Angeles Unified School District creaks under their influx. Vanessa, a fearless girl with an attention span as long as a rock video, attends a Van Nuys elementary school. She is taken there each

morning and collected each afternoon in a van by "the driver," as he's known in the neighborhood, to whom Maria and other mothers pay $12 a week. Ten years ago there were 750 pupils at the school. Now there are 1,550, and nearly 400 more are bused out. More than 85 percent are Hispanic, most from families like that of Agustin and Maria, for whom getting the kids dressed and out to school is sometimes too much. The school, accordingly, has a high rate of nonattendance and transiency. There's a constant influx of new students throughout the school year.

47   Vanessa's teacher is a chunky young guy with a mustache and a powerful, square jaw. He was born in Los Angeles to Mexican parents with little education. "A lot of people who come to El Norte, they think all their problems disappear," he says. "They know they'll get more money. But the hurricane of getting a job, paying the bills—that soon takes over, and they don't look after their kids' education. I know these people work so hard. But a child can fall behind and behind and behind and then that's it, they're lost."

48   Vanessa, in danger of this, might be sent to special ed. "Maybe she'll make it out," her teacher says. "But most likely she'll marry at a very young age, have kids and depend on the government, welfare."

49   One of the immigrant's implied bargains is this: I'll do your bad jobs for not much money, but you must educate my children. In return, the welcoming country expects that the immigrant and his or her family learn the national language. I remember that in Agustin and Maria's apartment the only reading material of any kind is *Bride's* magazine, from which Maria plots her wedding to Agustin next year. But then I also remember that Agustin and Maria work so hard they haven't time for much else. They're intimidated by the education system, perhaps even by books themselves.

50   Meanwhile, Vanessa, black-haired and beautiful, shoots up her hand to answer all the questions. She's eager, overeager, perhaps because I'm there with the photographer, and gets most of them wrong. Her T-shirt says, "When I Grow Up I Want to Be a Movie Star."

51   By now I think I'm getting to know this family pretty well. I'm doing that writer's thing of congratulating myself on having got out there and actually *met* people. Then one morning out of the blue Maria says: "The other family who live here just had a baby the night before last. They came back from hospital today."

52   I say, "The *other* family?"

53   She gestures back toward the corridor that leads to the bedroom from which Agustin had produced his gym bag, to a shut door behind which I'd supposed the kids slept.

54   Another family lives in there? A whole family?

55   She nods.

56   I'm fascinated. It's not just that I've been naïve. Something has been revealed, one more barrier of mistrust cleared away. Of course, there must be others. And then there's something else: levels of hierarchy don't stop with immigrant and nonimmigrant, legal and illegal. Agustin and Maria have tenants who, it turns out, pay $250 a month for the smaller of the apartment's two bedrooms and use of the bathroom and kitchen. The arrangement doesn't seem to work. Maria is wishing they'd leave so she could bring in one of her sisters who has twin baby girls. Then her sister could baby-sit for her while she worked 13-hour night shifts at a local print shop, a job she had done before and to which she's been asked back.

57   In due course the young couple appear, Ruben and Lena, carrying their new baby in a car seat. Next day, at a wedding party for Maria's sister, Ruben explains that he, like Agustin, was born in a pueblo in the state of Hidalgo and came across when he was 15.

58   Now he's a dayworker, one of the many thousands in Los Angeles who stand on corners waiting to be hired. He takes a 90-minute bus ride each morning to the far southwest side of the valley, because that's where the white people are. "They pay better," he says. "And are less likely to cheat you."

59   At 7:30 in the morning, he stands on a street corner beneath a Bank of America sign that towers above the parking lot of the 7-Eleven. He spoons noodles into his mouth as a flatbed truck pulls in with two workers already in the back. The driver buys a Snapple and the truck heads out again, up into Topanga Canyon. "There's a lot of construction up there," says Ruben. "Many rich people. But they use legal workers. Those guys will get $20 an hour. I'm looking to get $7, $8 an hour." Sometimes, however, he has to take $4.

60   What *patrons* are doing is against the law as well. Negotiations happen in a blink, before the 7-Eleven security guard has a chance to jot down the license of the car, which he passes on to his boss, who'll give it to the police—at least that's the threat. It's a hustling scene. By 8 A.M. there are perhaps a hundred workers, grouped in various spots around the block. The security guard has been instructed to let them stay because, of course, they spend money at the 7-Eleven.

61   Historically, immigration has been tolerated, even encouraged during labor shortages. Labor migration has been going on for centuries and it's hard to see how 300,000 or so illegal immigrants per year will make or break the American economy. Indeed, in Los Angeles they're most likely an asset. The number of illegals in California is thought to be growing by 125,000 a

year—hardly an economic catastrophe in a state of 31 million. In Los Angeles, where 80,000 jobs were created last year, it's a definite plus. The city has a thirst for people who will work for $5 or even $3 an hour.

62   The legal Chinese immigrants who have revitalized the San Gabriel Valley, the Latinos who are opening businesses in depressed areas of South Los Angeles, and the Russians and Iranians who are opening businesses all over are the principal reasons the city is so different from say, Detroit. Despite the fires, the earthquake, the riots, the decimation of the defense and aerospace industries, Los Angeles is very much alive. Says Joel Kotkin: "The only place where American society is evolving is where the immigrant influx is strong. Cities would have no future without them. But if you're sitting in Idaho, it looks different."

63   On Saturday Agustin and Maria and all four kids pile into the family car, a 20-year-old beige Datsun with more than 200,000 miles on it, a type of vehicle so common in Los Angeles that it has a name: Border Brothers' Cadillac. Agustin got it from a man he met through work, in exchange for doing the man's garden each Saturday for a month. Today is the fourth and final Saturday.

64   With Maria at the wheel the Datsun heads out onto Sepulveda Boulevard, and a cop car pulls up alongside. Inside the Datsun there's a sudden alarmed flurry because, it turns out, Maria has no California driver's license; if she's caught, therefore, her fake ID would most likely be discovered and she'd be in all sorts of trouble. But the black-and-white makes a left, and she smiles with nervous relief. I ask why she bothers, if every time she gets behind the wheel she risks deportation and the breakup of her family.

65   "I like to drive," she says.

66   I remember that Elton Gallegly, the Republican Representative for Ventura County, has added a provision to Lamat Smith's bill, to the effect that if you're here for 12 months, undocumented, you'll be prohibited from trying to become legal for 10 years. The motto is seek, bar, deport. He's hoping to make it impossible for illegals to stay.

67   "He's hallucinating," Maria says. "Does he think I'm just going to up and leave? Even if I am found and deported I'm going to crawl back here on my stomach if necessary to be with my children. He'll only push us deeper underground."

68   This is stupid, I say. You should get yourself legal: follow the procedures, marry Agustin, become a citizen—it's not that difficult.

69   "I know," she says, and explains how she dislikes governments telling her what to do. She hated it in Mexico as well. Governments are there to be mistrusted and got around, she says, sounding every bit a member of the

Michigan militia. "I put more into this society than I get out," she says. "I work, I don't claim welfare, my children are Americans."

70 And so, meanwhile, she likes to drive.

71 We head west to a leafier, more prosperous section of the valley and stop outside a big house with a spanking new silver Lincoln in the drive. The electronic garage doors open to reveal two more cars, a new BMW and a new Honda Civic, and Agustin steps inside to heft out the tools. He mows the lawns, front and back, adjusts the sprinklers, wields a buzzing trimmer at the edges.

72 The owner of the house, Antoine, a dapper middle-aged man dressed entirely in white, steps out with sodas for the kids and presents each of them with a crisp dollar bill. "Funny, isn't it?" says Antoine. "How something that means nothing to oneself can mean so much to someone else."

73 Los Angeles has more social gradations than a Henry James novel. People are kept separate by language, by geography, and mostly of course by money, a point Antoine has used $4 to make.

74 Antoine's kindly superiority is without thought or effort. He thinks of himself as a weary and saddened man of the world, not as an American, and certainly not as an immigrant. Yet he's of Armenian descent, born in Lebanon, where he worked in the hotel business. When the civil war really got going back in the 1970s, he was twice kidnapped by Muslim groups, and so he left to come here. His 24-year-old son was killed by shelling in Beirut a month ago, about the time the man decided to give Agustin the car. "I think there are too many immigrants," he says. "But Agustin is a nice guy and a hard worker. I like him."

75 Which pinpoints another problem: too many, but a nice guy and a hard worker. Immigration is typically an area where public pronouncement is at odds with private behavior. The whole debate is an onion. You can go on and on peeling back the layers and incongruities. Governor Wilson himself was embarrassed by the unsurprising revelation that he'd once hired an illegal. In California this is neither remarkable nor unusual, considering the available labor pool. Moreover, the distinction between legal and illegal starts getting fuzzy the moment they decide to stay and try to change their status, a process that—even as I.N.S. struggles manfully—often takes years.

76 South of San Diego I ride out with the Border Patrol, which prides itself on being bigger and much more visible these days. Federal money has boosted the number of agents in the San Diego sector to 1,500, compared with 798 in 1991. At a cost of $46 million, "Operation Gatekeeper" has been put into effect, a clampdown designed to squeeze border runners away from traditional crossing areas, like Imperial Beach, where they can easily hop

onto a bus or train, and into others farther east where the journey is longer and more arduous.

77   The border was once chaotic and violent. Now it's surreal. The "coyotes" occupy the high ground, warning each other with bird calls when agents approach. A Vietnam-vintage Bell chopper, small enough to get into the canyons, whirls with its searchlight blazing. On a hill overlooking the ocean and a former K.G.B. listening station on the Mexican side, a truck looms in the night with a huge, humming infrared periscope sticking out the top. Inside, in the eerie light, an agent stares into a screen on which humans are shown as white blobs, referred to as "glows."

78   Leaning against the hood of another truck, staring up at the ugly 10-foot-high steel wall that now snakes along 24 miles of the border, an agent speaks with regret of the wild days not so long ago when they'd come pouring over 1,000 at a time and he'd nab as many as 50 or even a 100 by himself. All the rest would get away. Now it's more of a cat-and-mouse game, he says, moving toward the fence as a figure clambers on top, spots him and then jumps back. "Do you think you could do this all night?"

79   A big friendship park dedicated by Pat Nixon in 1974 is deserted now, its picnic tables crumbling in the shadow of the wall. "It's a battle, it's a war," says Ed Head, night supervisor at the Imperial Beach station. "It's good to feel that we're winning for a change."

80   Coming up on midnight, an agent takes me on a long and bumpy ride, way out east into the San Ysidro Mountains, where we've heard that two or three groups of illegals, with perhaps as many as 15 or 20 in each group, are being chased by Border Patrol agents. In the end, this is what much of the new game comes down to—guys hoofing it after other guys across rough country in the pitch dark. By the time we arrive the bust has already gone down and 38 glows are sitting in the dirt in the glare of truck headlights.

81   Some have covered their eyes. Others have cuts on their hands and faces. Some have hiked for 12 hours up this 3,000-foot mountain wearing sneakers or toeless sandals. Some are from Central America, and have journeyed for months before that. Their dream to come to America must have been very strong. Within 40 minutes they'll be processed and dumped back over the border in Tijuana, where those who are O.T.M. (another Border Patrol usage: Other Than Mexican) will most likely be treated very unsympathetically indeed by a Mexican government that has its own savage ideas about what to do with aliens.

82   There's one young man with bulging brown eyes and mean, kinky hair. A Border Patrol guy says, "Yo, Prince!"

83   The young man's sad expression doesn't change. He says, "Que?"

84   The next day Arthur Ollman, director of San Diego's Museum of Photographic Arts, walks me through "A Nation of Strangers," an exhibit he has spent four years putting together. It documents the history of immigration in America; indeed, it is a moving and beautiful apologia for the same. "The bottom line is that the stuff we're going through today is not unique. We've been there before. We don't have to panic," he says.

85   One anti-immigration poster, circa 1850, says: "Native Americans! Arouse!" There have been immigrant floods before, at times of economic difficulty, and much the same fears concerning assimilation. Beneath a recent photograph by Don Bartletti of a beefy bleached blonde holding a placard that says, "Control Immigration or Lose America," I read the following, quoted from a 1994 *Utne Reader*: "The rate of immigration relative to the nation's base population is far below historic levels. . . . Moreover the percentage of foreign-born people in the U.S. population has fallen from 8.89 in 1940 to 6.8 today."

86   America's not being overrun after all.

87   "It's true that we're changing to a more international place," says Ollman. "Americans will become more polyglot. The melting-pot metaphor doesn't work anymore. It's a mosaic. But we're not being overrun, and I find it almost offensive this idea that America is no longer strong enough to handle its immigrant influx."

88   I'm reassured.

89   My reactions, that is to say, are predictably liberal. Back home, in Los Angeles, I remind myself how much I like the diversity of the place. And yet we'd just hired a nanny. The only white applicant for the job was a disturbingly energetic 30-something woman with great rifts in her curriculum vitae, a self-confessed graduate of "12 Steps" whose hands were covered in paint and who exclaimed midway through the interview, "And in my spare time I'm a professional clown!"

90   We went the safe route. We hired a 22-year-old legal Mexican immigrant, Christine, who had already worked for three families, came with solid references and has a 2-year-old daughter who is a citizen. With Christine I find myself sympathetic and friendly one moment, a paranoid *patron* the next, questioning her stability, her hygiene, her habits. I can't imagine that Pete Wilson himself would be any crankier than I was when Christine came back with the stroller and told me that while she'd been walking our baby a man on the street had asked her for a date.

91   We've done more than invite Christine into our lives. We're trusting her with our child, our future. She meanwhile looks to me as a way in, a handhold on a society she doesn't understand and can't quite negotiate. She gets me to

write to a lawyer with whom she's in dispute. She asks me to cash a check for her, because, she says, she's in between bank accounts. In a way, I suppose, she's after me to behave like a parent. I feel edgy, threatened. I hate it.

92   Pro-immigration forces have tended to keep their focus tight on the economic issues because they sense that Americans don't want to be told they're racist. Nobody does. Yet, one of the problems with the immigration issue is that it *does* impinge on the race issue, and thus appeals temptingly and dangerously to the worst side of all of us.

93   A central argument of Brimelow's *Alien Nation* is that America has always had an essential nature, an ethnic core, and that it's white. He writes that "the first naturalization law, in 1790, stipulated that an applicant must be a 'free white person.' Blacks became full citizens only after the Civil War."

94   He goes on: "Maybe America should not have been like this. *But it was.*" And now: "Americans are being tricked out of their own identity."

95   Reading this, I'm overcome with a weird looking-glass giddiness. Someone's trying to change the rules here, to wipe a rag over history. America's identity is precisely that of mutation, its power drawn from an energetic and quite fearless ability to adapt and win. Its national book, after all, is *The Adventures of Huckleberry Finn*, about a beautiful and dangerous river that never stops changing.

96   Along with more than 7,000 others, Maria T. and her family stand in line outside the Fred Jordan Mission in downtown Los Angeles, where on a boiling August day they wait for a free handout of clothes and sneakers. They've been huddled in sleeping bags and under blankets all night, during the course of which a man was shot to death outside a Chinese food store on the opposite side of Fifth Street. This is Skid Row, a scary neighborhood.

97   The kids are tired, hot, and hungry, but still excited about getting new Nikes. Television crews from Japan, Spain, and Germany, as well as from local news programs, stand by to record the happy event. People hold umbrellas against the sun, and a man passes up and down the line with a garden hose, drenching upturned faces. Last year, about 8,000 children were helped. In 1995, however, corporate giving has slipped for the first time, and they have only 5,000 pairs of shoes.

98   Only 5,000 pairs of shoes, at least 7,000 children, and so outside, as the hours pass, the huge line gets anxious. Maria is scared because no one helped when a big group came surging up the street and muscled in ahead of them. Now her children are crying, and it looks as if they might not get sneakers after all. The smaller sizes have already run out. Maria talks to one of the mission workers, a man she has met before. Can he help? He's sorry, he says, but there's nothing he can do, and he turns away.

99   Other mission workers walk down the line, quietly inviting families to leave. Maria stands with her arms around her children gathered around her. By now she has waited for almost 24 hours. It's the end of a long and stressful day and her kids feel sick. "This isn't right," she says.

100   America is an immigrant nation; indeed, a nation of strangers. I like it that way, though the arguments in favor of the idea are not merely sentimental and historical. Corporate interests value immigration for something that troubles us—keeping wages lower, and these days not just at the level of busboys and dayworkers.

101   The American economy is in relatively good shape and has pretty much the legal immigration it needs. The system isn't broken, doesn't need fixing—and certainly not in the ways that are now being proposed. Illegal immigration is touchier. Listening to academics makes it easy to forget the racially inflamed brush fire that is the debate in California.

102   Recent polls show a surprising sympathy even for illegal immigrants, provided they otherwise play by the rules: work, get documentation, learn English. Only 20 percent say immigrants take jobs away from citizens, and 69 percent say they do work that citizens don't necessarily want and that needs to be done. Few say that the American-born children of illegals should be deprived of education and welfare, let alone their citizenship. The message here is a sensible one: beef up the Border Patrol; deport criminals; don't break up families; target labor-enforcement at bad-guy sweatshop employers and make an effort to deal with temporary visa overstays, who surprisingly make up as much as 50 percent of all illegals; supply Federal assistance to heavily impacted areas such as Los Angeles, and forget the idea of a national verification system or an identification card.

103   Ultimately, this is a debate about values, not money. This is about how America feels about itself.

104   The last time I meet with Maria T. she has heard of the passing of the new Federal welfare bill, which will cut off welfare payments after five years, a measure that, in some respects, seems like a federalization of Proposition 187. Understanding the vulnerability of her position, she is panicked. I've had a hunch all along that she sends some little portion of the money she gets to her husband in Guadalajara, not so much to support him as to keep him away. "He doesn't understand how much our life has changed," she says. She asks if I know of anyone, an American, who'd be prepared to marry her.

105   I'm not sure this is the solution and, anyway, what about the guy in Guadalajara?

106   "He's not really my husband," she says. "I just call him that," and I re-flect again how fluid human situations slop outside the bucket of any polit-ical oratory.

107   She bites her nails and gathers the kids around her for a walk to the store. Mario, already rebellious, is reluctant to come along. Soon he'll be at the age, Maria knows, where she'll have to start worrying about the danger and lure of the gangs; kids his age, or younger, get slammed in (eerily graphic usage for the youth trap of every poor neighborhood in Los Ange-les). Maria believes in the American dream more than I do, at least to the ex-tent that she trusts the uniquely American promise that her children will have a better life than she does. At the shrine outside a church on Cedros Avenue she lights a candle. She thanks the Virgin for a brand new day and asks for another one. Then she walks to JCPenney, where she buys socks for the kids and then, from another counter, an American flag, for hope.

MICHELLE MALKIN

The Deportation Abyss:
It Ain't Over 'Til the Alien Wins

Michelle Malkin is a nationally syndicated columnist who frequently appears on the Fox News Channel as a commentator on current events. The following essay is drawn from her 2002 book Invasion: How America Still Welcomes Terrorists, Criminals, and Other Menaces to Our Shores.

1   Credibility in immigration policy, as the late Texas congresswoman Barbara Jordan remarked, rests on three simple principles: "People who should get in, get in; people who should not enter are kept out; and people who are deportable should be required to leave."[1]

2   After September 11, the speedy detention of some 1,200 aliens suspected of terrorist ties gave the illusion of competence in this last crucial area of immigration enforcement. Although civil-liberties advocates and Arab-American activists immediately attacked the swift ruthlessness of INS and the Justice Department,[2] the obstacles to actually getting rid of unwanted guests are myriad. The system is clogged by conflicting statutes, incomprehensible administrative regulations, bureaucratic and judicial fiefdoms, selective enforcement, and a feeding frenzy of obstructionist immigration lawyers.

3   It is a climate which continues to favor aliens' rights over citizens' safety.

Cons and Absconders

4   Government watchdogs have found the INS to be habitually lax in its efforts to track down and help boot out the worst criminal offenders among the alien population. A number of federal laws require the agency to initiate deportation actions against aliens convicted of aggravated felonies as quickly as possible and before they are released from federal or state prisons.[3] Congress increased funding and staffing for a Justice Department program to speed up this process. Yet, thousands of criminal aliens have been released into the public after serving their sentences because of the INS's failure to screen and send them into deportation hearings. This failure both endangers the public and is costly. If INS had completed proceedings for all deportable

criminal aliens released from federal and state prisons in 1995 before their release, it could have avoided nearly $63 million in detention costs.[4]

5   Meanwhile, untold hundreds of thousands of "absconders" are roaming the country—illegal alien fugitives who have been ordered deported by immigration judges but who continue to evade the law. In December 2001, INS Commissioner James Ziglar revealed for the first time under oath that the INS did not know the whereabouts of "about 314,000" fugitive deportees. Only then did Justice Department officials move, for the first time ever, to place their names in the FBI's National Crime Information Center database.[5]

6   The absconder statistics remain in dispute after the agency conceded to reporters from Washington, D.C.–based Human Events newspaper that it could not vouch for the accuracy of the number. Some, including Representative George Gekas, a Pennsylvania Republican who chairs the House immigration subcommittee, believe the actual number could run as high as one million.[6] This much remains indisputable: All of these fugitives have been ordered out of the country by an immigration judge. They were either deported in absentia or sentenced in a courtroom and then released on their own recognizance pending final deportation, only to disappear back into the woodwork.

7   In January 2002, the Justice Department unveiled the "Absconder Apprehension Initiative." The government said it would finally begin ejecting fugitive deportees, beginning with about 1,000 immigrants from Middle Eastern countries who had been convicted of felonies in the United States. But after announcing the new campaign to round up these alien evaders, the INS admitted it would take at least a year to enter all their names in the FBI criminal database—and that the new system would probably enable the INS to locate just 10 percent of the missing deportees.[7]

8   Staff shortages also hamper the ambitious absconder apprehension effort. In May 2002, several agents and supervisors told the *New York Times* that the INS office in New York could barely handle the added function. The employees noted "that only fourteen federal immigration agents and 9 police investigators are assigned to find and deport roughly 1,200 illegal immigrants who came from countries where Al Qaeda has been active. . . . After three months, fewer than 150 have been arrested."[8] By the end of May 2002, the Justice Department admitted that only 585 absconders out of 314,000 had been located. Not a single terrorist has been caught.[9]

9   In the meantime, the INS continues to entrust tens of thousands of ordered deportees to leave on an honor system, sending them notices asking them to turn themselves in. Laughed at around the world, the INS notices are known as "run letters" among illegal aliens.[10]

10   Even if the INS tracked down every last one of the absconders, there would be no place to detain them. Detention space has been sorely misallocated and misused. Nearly $30 million earmarked for building new state-of-the-art detention facilities in San Francisco, for example, was diverted to speed up processing of citizenship applications.[11] Currently, the agency has only about 20,000 beds, at a time when as many as 200,000 aliens are ordered deported each year.[12]

Into the Legal Abyss

11   While the INS receives much-deserved flack for the deportation quagmire, a large portion of the blame lies with the independent agency in charge of the nation's immigration courts, the Executive Office for Immigration Review (EOIR), and its appellate body, the Board of Immigration Appeals (BIA), which thrive on making the deportation process as time-consuming and unwieldy as possible. Together, these two independent agencies—separate from the INS, but also housed under the Justice Department—hold the ultimate keys to deportation. While the INS has responsibility for apprehending and bringing immigration charges against aliens, it is the little-known EOIR that has jurisdiction over the nationwide Immigration Courts and their companion appeals system. More than 200 immigration judges preside in fifty-two courts across the country. They oversee removal proceedings, as well as bond redetermination hearings, in which the judges can reduce the bond imposed by the INS for aliens in custody who seek release on their own recognizance before final deportation.[13]

12   The BIA's twenty-odd members, based in Falls Church, Virginia, are politically-appointed bureaucrats who have the power to overturn deportation orders nationwide. The panel—comprised largely of alien-friendly advocates from immigration-law circles—receives more than 30,000 appeals every year, and has a backlog of 56,000 cases, of which 34,000 are more than one year old, 10,000 are more than three years old, and some are more than seven years old.[14] There's even a saying among immigration insiders in Washington about the deportation process: "It ain't over 'til the alien wins."

13   One Justice Department employee who runs an independent Web site on the deportation morass observes:

> Between the incompetence of the INS, the complete lack of alien detention center space, and the bureaucracy of the EOIR, our system for deporting known illegal aliens and criminal alien residents is a sad joke. But no one is laughing. If all of the illegal aliens and deportable resident alien criminals were rounded up

tomorrow, the system would not be capable of handling them. It would be an absolute disaster. The INS and the EOIR wouldn't have the foggiest idea of what to do with them! The aliens would all be released back out on the street on immigration bonds and go back right where they were as if nothing happened, while their cases would grind on through the system of Immigration Court hearings and endless appeals.[15]

14   EOIR director Kevin Rooney summarized the plethora of appeal options available to all aliens—even criminal aliens—in his February 2002 testimony to Congress: "Even if an alien is removable, he or she may file an application for relief from removal, such as asylum, voluntary departure, suspension of deportation, cancellation of removal, adjustment of status, registry or a waiver of inadmissibility."[16] What does all this bureaucratic jargon spell? Delay, delay, delay. Each of the loopholes enumerated by Rooney is written into the Immigration and Nationality Act. If an alien loses a BIA judgment, he can then seek relief in the federal circuit courts of appeal.

15   While most Americans are unaware of these dirty little secrets, the legal tricks for evading the flimsy immigration dragnet are well known among the immigrant population. An Internet search of the phrase "how to avoid deportation" yields thousands of hits, including this one from a Web site called www.GotTrouble.com (which "delivers real-world solutions to people facing serious legal and financial trouble"):

16   **Relief from Deportation**

There may be a way to avoid deportation, even if a person has a criminal record. The law provides relief for:
1. long-term permanent residents who have not been convicted of certain serious felonies;
2. persons who have been in the United States for a long period of time and can show that being forced to leave would cause serious hardship to their family members who are United States citizens or permanent residents;
3. persons who [claim they] would be subject to torture or other physical harm if they were returned to certain countries;
4. persons who [claim they] would be subject to persecution on account of political opinion, race, national origin, or membership in a particular social group; or
5. in some limited situations, persons who are married to United States citizens or can qualify for permanent resident status.

The special circumstances that might allow a person to avoid removal are highly technical. An experienced immigration attorney should be consulted.[17]

17   The Web site provides a helpful directory of immigration lawyers in all
fifty states to assist the troubled alien in need of "relief." These loopholes
have been exploited by countless convicted aliens jailed for crimes ranging
from drunk driving to baby-killing.

18   Here's just a small sample of the criminal aliens let off the deportation
hook:

- Citing "severe emotional hardship" to her family and American-born
  children, a three-member panel of the board halted the deportation of
  Haitian nanny Melanie Beaucejour Jean. She had been convicted in upstate New York of killing an eighteen-month-old baby in her care. "I
  hit him two or three times with my fist on the top of his head. I did this
  to stop him from crying. It did not work," she told Monroe County, New
  York, investigators.[18] "I do not know how long I shook the baby, but I
  did not stop until he was unconscious," her police statement said. At
  the request of the INS, immigration judge Phillip J. Montante, Jr. ordered her deported back to her native land more than two years ago.
  But thanks to a trio of pro-alien, Janet Reno-installed bureaucrats,
  Beaucejour Jean continued to enjoy life in America.[19] Cecilia Espenoza,
  Lory D. Rosenberg, and Gustavo Villageliu—all appointed to the Board
  of Immigration Appeals by Clinton Attorney General Janet Reno—concluded that Jean's crime "does not constitute a crime of violence" and
  is not an aggravated felony subject to deportation guidelines. Legal
  analyst Beverley Lumpkin noted in her ABC News online column that
  Espenoza and Rosenberg are known as "reflexive advocates for aliens
  who just don't care about the facts of a case." Espenoza's left-wing
  roots are so deeply ingrained that she named her son after Marxist
  guerilla Che Guevara.[20]

  In May 2002, Attorney General John Ashcroft announced a rare reversal of the immigration board's decision. "Aliens arriving at our shores
  must understand that residency in the United States is a privilege, not a
  right," Ashcroft wrote. "For those aliens . . . who engage in violent criminal acts during their stay here, this country will not offer its
  embrace."[21] Tough words. But they're not invoked frequently enough.

- Min Song was a Korean national convicted of theft as an 18-year-old in
  1992. He was sentenced to a year in prison for the aggravated felony,

which was a deportable crime. To avoid removal from the country, however, Song persuaded a judge to trim the sentence from a year to 360 days. At less than a year, the suspended sentence was no longer grounds for automatic deportation. The immigration appeals board accepted the sleight of hand and allowed Song to stay in the country.[22] The decision paves the way for convicted aggravated felons of all kinds to pressure sympathetic judges to modify their sentences and avoid deportation.

"It's a great pro-alien, pro-immigrant decision because there's been a lot of setbacks for criminal aliens," crowed John T. Riely, Song's lawyer.[23]

- Fernando Alfonso Torres-Varela, a Mexican national, was convicted of drunk driving three times. He knowingly drove while intoxicated and knew that he was driving with a suspended or revoked license. The INS sought to deport him for committing a crime of moral turpitude. He appealed to the BIA. Despite holding in the past that a crime of moral turpitude involved conduct "that is contrary to the accepted rules of morality and the duties owed between persons or to society in general," the board concluded that Torres-Varela's serial drunk driving did not qualify as such a crime. INS's request to deport Torres-Varela was denied.[24]

- Stephanie Short, a German national, was convicted of encouraging her three-year-old daughter to submit to sexual assault at the hands of her stepfather. He was convicted of sexual offenses; she was convicted of aiding and abetting the assault of a minor with the intent to commit a felony. She served three years of an eight-year sentence and was released on parole. The INS sought Short's deportation based on her conviction for a crime of moral turpitude (in other words, a crime that is inherently base, vile, or depraved). An immigration judge supported the move. Short appealed to the BIA. In a mind-boggling decision, the board determined that it "was inappropriate to consider the husband's conviction record for purposes of determining the underlying crime of which the respondent was convicted of aiding and abetting."[25]

In other words: It was wrong for the judge to consider the fact that Short's husband raped her daughter with her approval. "As the Board no longer holds that an assault with intent to commit any felony necessarily constitutes a crime involving moral turpitude without regard to the nature of the underlying felony," the convoluted decision stated, "the (Immigration) Service has not established that the respondent was in fact convicted of a crime involving moral turpitude where it failed to establish the underlying felony that was intended."[26]

In an outraged column blasting the ruling, the late *Chicago Tribune* columnist Mike Royko wrote: "We actually pay taxes for that kind of gibberish. Here we have a woman who, at one point in the original FBI investigation, confessed to a crime of moral turpitude. She was found guilty of aiding and abetting a crime of moral turpitude. She spent three years in prison for joining in on the moral turpitude. My guess is that even creeps like John Gacy, Richard Speck and Jack the Ripper would agree it was a crime of moral turpitude."[27]

For the word-twisters and definition-stretchers at the BIA, such "gibberish" upholding the rights of baby-killers, burglars, habitual drunk drivers, and accessories to child rape is par for the course. Attorney General Ashcroft shouldn't be forced to spend his time undoing this superfluous board's idiotic—and treacherous—rulings one by one. The board should be abolished. The last thing we need as we wage our war on terrorism are entrenched, unelected sympathizers in the courts who put alien rights over American lives.

Catch and Release

19   The most dangerous loophole exploited by aliens seeking relief from the EOIR and BIA is the voluntary departure option. Intended as a cost-saving measure to streamline the deportation process, voluntary departure allows aliens to enter into an agreement to leave the United States on their own volition and to avoid the consequences of a formal order of removal (such as being barred from reentering the country for ten years). This frees the alien to leave and attempt to reenter legally, leave and enter illegally, or violate the agreement and continue to stay here illegally. Guess which option most aliens are likely to choose?

20   The 1996 Illegal Immigration Reform and Immigrant Responsibility Act passed some new restrictions on the policy, including stricter time limits, increased civil penalties, and added eligibility criteria. Aggravated felons and terrorists are not supposed to be eligible, but in 1999, the Justice Department's Inspector General warned: "INS does not know which illegal aliens granted voluntary departure by immigration judges have left the United States because the process for verifying departures is flawed." There is no tracking system. "Immigration judges and INS trial attorneys are not required to provide information or instructions to aliens about how to verify their departure, nor did we witness them do so in our courtroom observations. In most cases, INS has no further contact with the alien after the im-

migration judge issues the voluntary departure order."[28] Therein lies the recipe for absconders run amok.

21   The Inspector General's report also noted that immigration judges "inappropriately grant voluntary departure to some aggravated felons" because both the courts and the INS fail to conduct adequate criminal history checks on illegal aliens before letting them go.[29] In response to persistent charges that criminal checks were not being done on aliens placed in removal proceedings even after September 11, INS Executive Associate Commissioner for the Field Operations Office Michael Pearson issued a memo on December 20, 2001, to "clarify" that such checks should be done prior to release from INS custody.[30] How reassuring.

22   This "catch and release" process continues to frustrate INS agents on the front lines. Senior Border Patrol agent Mark Hall, whose union represents officers who patrol the United States-Canadian border in Michigan and Ohio, told Congress in November 2001: "When illegal aliens are released, we send a disturbing message. The aliens quickly pass on the word about how easy it is to enter this country illegally and remain here. This practice is devastating to our sound border enforcement strategy."[31]

What to Do

23   The highest-priced, most sophisticated home security system will be ineffective if police don't come and take away the thieves who manage to break in. The same holds true for homeland security. Tight locks and screen doors are important, but the United States must also develop an effective system of detention and deportation to rid our collective home of uninvited guests—and keep them out.

24   Illegal aliens who have been ordered deported must not be allowed to run free. The voluntary departure option is an escape hatch that must be eliminated. This policy benefits no one but the aliens who eagerly volunteer to abuse our deportation system's undeserved trust. Congress should amend the Immigration and Nationality Act to eliminate voluntary departure as an option during removal proceedings before an immigration judge.

25   Moreover, federal law mandates that criminal aliens who reenter the United States after deportation face up to twenty years in jail. Yet, the law is applied only sporadically by United States Attorneys' Offices.

26   Increased enforcement, of course, cannot succeed without greatly expanding the INS's current 20,000-bed detention capacity. Even when deportation absconders are tracked down, they are often let go because there's

nowhere to put them. One official of a bonding company said the INS was freeing 50 percent of the aliens he had been ordered to track down and turn in since September 11.[32] California Representative Elton Gallegly's proposal from 1995 to convert closed military bases to illegal alien detention facilities should be dusted off and put into action immediately.

27   Finally, Attorney General John Ashcroft should abolish the Executive Office for Immigration Review and the Board of Immigration Appeals and transfer their functions to existing law enforcement officers within the immigration bureaucracy. The alien lawyer lobby claims that any streamlining of the deportation bureaucracy poses a "threat to the integrity of the immigration process."[33] Nonsense. Restoring integrity to the immigration process will require closing the loopholes and black holes into which so many fugitive absconders, criminal aliens, and unwelcome guests have disappeared.

28   "Due process" for illegal aliens has for too long resulted in too many endless delays—and too many interminable stays.

Notes

1. Prepared statement of Barbara Jordan, Chairwoman of the United States Commission on Immigration Reform, before the Subcommittee on Immigration and Refugee Affairs, Judiciary Committee, United States Senate, August 3, 1994.
2. Larry Keller, "As United States seeks to root out terrorists, foreign residents who may have run afoul of immigration laws fear they'll fall prey to the hunt." *Palm Beach Daily Business Review,* October 5, 2001: A13.
3. See the Immigration Reform and Control Act (Public Law 99-603); the Anti-Drug Abuse Act of 1988 (Public Law 100-690); the Antiterrorism and Effective Death Penalty Act of 1996 (Public Law 104-132); and the Illegal Immigration Reform and Immigrant Responsibility Act of 1996 (Public Law 104-208).
4. General Accounting Office, Criminal Aliens: INS's Efforts to Identify and Remove Imprisoned Aliens Need to Be Improved. Statement of Norman J. Rankin, Director, Administration of Justice Issues, General Government Division. Available from http://www.gao.gov/archive/1997/gg97154t.pdf.
5. Suzanne Gamboa, "Names of missing foreigners ordered deported to be entered in crime database," Associated Press, December 5, 2001.
6. Joseph D'Agostino, "INS lowballed deportation evaders," *Human Events,* March 18, 2002.
7. Mary Beth Sheridan, "INS seeks law enforcement aid in crackdown; move targets 300,000 foreign nationals living in United States despite deportation orders." *Washington Post,* December 6, 2001: A25.
8. William K. Rashbaum, "I.N.S. agents say staffing shortage is undercutting counterterrorism," *New York Times,* May 20, 2002: B1
9. Dan Eggen, "U.S. search finds 585 deportee 'absconders'," *Washington Post,* May 30, 2002: A7

10. Dan Eggen and Cheryl W. Thompson, "United States seeks thousands of fugitive deportees; Middle Eastern men are focus of search," *Washington Post,* January 8, 2002: A01.
11. Valerie Alvord, "INS unprepared to handle the nation's fastest growing prison population," Copley News Service, February 5, 1999.
12. Greg Gordon, "Borders far from secure," op cit.
13. EOIR Web site available at http://www.usdoj.gov/eoir/; Internet: accessed April 20, 2002; information about BIA available at http://www.usdoj.gov/eoir/biainfo.htm; Internet: accessed April 20, 2002.
14. Kevin Murphy, "United States overhauls immigration court system to speed deportation," *Kansas City Star,* February 7, 2002.
15. Juan Mann, "It's the fraud, stupid!" Available at http://www.geocities.com/deportaliens/fraud.html.
16. Statement of Kevin D. Rooney, Director, Executive Office For Immigration Review, House Committee on the Judiciary, Subcommittee on Immigration and Claims, Oversight Hearing, February 6, 2002. Available at http://www.house.gov/judiciary/rooney020602.htm.
17. Available at http://www.gottrouble.com/legal/immigration/deportation_relief.html.
18. Jerry Seper, "Ashcroft reviews overturned deportation," *Washington Times.* December 19, 2001: A4.
19. Ibid. See also: Seper, Jerry. "Appeals panel, judge differ on fate of nanny; Deportation ordered twice for convicted baby-killer," *Washington Times.* December 10, 2001: A7.
20. Beverley Lumpkin, "Board of Immigration Radicals," abcnews.com. August 24, 2001. Available from http://abcnews.go.com/sections/us/HallsOfJustice/hallsofjustice92.html.
21. Ted Bridis, "Ashcroft orders Haitian mom deported," Associated Press, May 8, 2002. 42. 43.
22. 23 I&N Dec. 173 (BIA 2001). Available from http://www.usdoj.gov/eoir/efoia/bia/Decisions/Revdec/pdfDEC/3455.pdf.
23. Julia Malone, "Federal review board charts new course for criminal aliens," Cox News Service, January 6, 2002.
24. 23 I&N Dec. 78 (BIA 2001). Available from http://www.usdoj.gov/eoir/efoia/bia/Decisions/Revdec/pdfDEC/3449.pdf.
25. Interim Decision: #3125: Matter of Short, A-38827315, Board of Immigration Appeals, 16 November 1989: Volume 20 (page 136). Available from http://www.asylumlaw.org/docs/united_states/BIA/biavol20.pdf.
26. Ibid.
27. Mike Royko, "Legal babble OKs travesty of justice," *Chicago Tribune,* November 22, 1989.
28. United States Department of Justice Office of the Inspector General, Inspections Division, "Voluntary Departure: Ineffective enforcement and lack of sufficient controls hamper the process," Report Number I-99-09, March 1999. Available from http://www.usdoj.gov/oig/i9909/i9909toc.htm.
29. Ibid.
30. Memorandum for Regional Directors from Michael A. Pearson on Criminal Indices Checks, December 20, 2001.

31. Testimony of Mark Hall before the Permanent Investigations Subcommittee, Senate Government Affairs Committee, November 13, 2001.
32. Vincent Smith, President of Capital Bonding Corp., interview with CBS News, May 28, 2002. Available from http://www.cbsnews.com/stories/2002/05/28/eveningnews/main510335.shtml.
33. T. Alexander Aleinikoff and David A. Martin, "Ashcroft's Immigration Threat," *Washington Post,* February 26, 2002: A21

Source: Henry Payne reprinted by permission of United Feature Syndicate, Inc.

DAVID COLE

Enemy Nations and American Freedoms

David Cole, affiliated with the Georgetown University School of Law, is a frequent contributor to The Nation, *where the following essay appeared on September 23, 2002. Based in New York City,* The Nation *has a long history of covering politics, culture, and the arts from a resolutely left-of-center perspective.*

1   From his very first speeches following the horrifying events of September 11, President Bush has maintained that the terrorists attacked us because they hate our freedoms. Hence the war on terrorism's official title "Operation Enduring Freedom." But one year later, it appears that the greatest threat to our freedoms is posed not by the terrorists themselves but by our own government's response.

2   With the exception of the right to bear arms, one would be hard pressed to name a single constitutional liberty that the Bush Administration has not overridden in the name of protecting our freedom. Privacy has given way to Internet tracking and plans to recruit a corps of 11 million private snoopers. Political freedom has been trumped by the effort to stem funding for terrorists. Physical liberty and habeas corpus survive only until the President decides someone is a "bad guy." Property is seized without notice, without a hearing, and on the basis of secret evidence. Equal protection has fallen prey to ethnic profiling. Conversations with a lawyer may be monitored without a warrant or denied altogether when the military finds them inconvenient. And the right to a public hearing upon arrest exists only at the Attorney General's sufferance.

3   Administration supporters argue that the magnitude of the new threat requires a new paradigm. But so far we have seen only a repetition of a very old paradigm-broad incursions on liberties, largely targeted at unpopular noncitizens and minorities, in the name of fighting a war. What is new is that this war has no end in sight, and only a vaguely defined enemy, so its incursions are likely to be permanent. And while many of the most troubling initiatives have initially been targeted at noncitizens, they are likely to pave the way for future measures against citizens. So as we mournfully pass the one-year anniversary of September 11, we should ask whether President Bush's new paradigm is in fact something we want to live with for the rest of our lives.

Targeting Immigrants

4   As is often the case in times of crisis, noncitizens have been hardest hit. In its investigation of September 11, the Administration has detained between 1,500 and 2,000 people, mostly foreigners, under unprecedented secrecy. Attorney General John Ashcroft has justified the use of transparently pretextual charges to hold them by calling them "suspected terrorists," but his grounds for suspicion are apparently so unfounded that not a single one has been charged with involvement in the September 11 attacks, and with the

LUZ SUAREZ

My Illegal Status Shouldn't Keep Me from Learning

The name "Luz Suarez" is a pen name for a student living in Chicago; the writer's real name has been changed to protect his or her identity. The essay appeared in the magazine Black Issues in Higher Education *on September 27, 2001.*

1   I have a secret that I am afraid to share with anyone but my closest friends: I don't have papers; I'm an undocumented immigrant.

2   My father abandoned our family when I was little, and my mother was forced to raise us alone. There was no work in Mexico. So, when I was 10 years old, she left me and my brother in the care of her best friend and went north to see if she could make a better life for us.

3   My mother crawled through sewer pipes full of rats and sludge to cross the border and eventually made her way to Chicago. She sent for us two years later. My brother and I were brought over by a smuggler—known as a coyote—who took us to a remote location where we had to squirm under a fence and then run for dear life.

4   I have never returned. Now I'm 21, and over the years, Chicago has become my home and memories of Mexico have faded. Although I speak Spanish with my mother, my primary language outside of the home is English. Most of my friends were born here and a lot of them don't know anything about my immigration status.

exception of four people indicted on support-for-terrorism charges in late August, no one has been charged with any terrorist act. Those arrested on immigration charges—the vast majority—have been effectively "disappeared." Their cases are not listed on any public docket, their hearings are closed to the public and the presiding judges are instructed to neither confirm nor deny that their cases exist, if asked. Two district courts and a unanimous court of appeals have held this practice unconstitutional, as Judge Damon Keith wrote for the Court of Appeals for the Sixth Circuit, "Democracies die behind closed doors."

5   My mother's sacrifices motivated me to become a hard worker and to do well in school. These days, I attend a community college so I can one day become a teacher. To pay for my education, I spend nights and weekends bagging groceries.

6   Unfortunately, despite my good grades, I may not be able to stay in school much longer because I am undocumented. This is my second community college because the first one kicked me out when I couldn't give them a Social Security number. A woman screamed at me and told me that if I couldn't provide a Social Security number, I would have to leave the school. It was humiliating, and I envisioned myself bagging groceries for the rest of my life.

7   So, I went to another school and started the process all over again. But I fear it won't be long before the same thing happens and I'm forced to leave. In a city that faces a critical teacher shortage, it makes little sense to force someone out of college who wants to become a teacher.

8   I recently learned that there is a bill pending in Congress to help people like me: young, undocumented residents who basically grew up in the United States and are now in high school or college. It would provide us a way to legalize our immigration status by proving that we have lived here for at least five years and that we have shown good moral character during that time. We would be able to get documents that would allow us to go to college and work, and, in turn, contribute to our new home.

9   With legal papers, I could stay in school and become a teacher. Then I could pass my love for education on to the children in my classroom, could use my example to inspire them to overcome life's handicaps and hard knocks, and teach them that in America, every child has an opportunity for a better life.

5   The Administration has repeatedly insisted that it opposes racial or ethnic profiling, but it has simultaneously undertaken numerous measures predicated on little more than a foreign citizen's Arab country of origin. It called 8,000 foreigners in for interviews based solely on the fact that they were recent male immigrants from Arab countries. It has expressly made the deportation of Arabs a priority. And it plans to impose fingerprinting, registration, and reporting requirements selectively on noncitizens from a handful of Arab nations. When the federal government takes such steps, it is hardly surprising that state and local law enforcement officials, airlines, and private companies follow suit and act upon similar stereotypes.

6   The most troubling provisions of the USA Patriot Act, enacted within six weeks of September 11, are similarly reserved for noncitizens. The act permits the Attorney General to detain noncitizens on his own say-so, without a hearing; bars foreign citizens from entering the country, based solely on their speech; and authorizes deportation based on any support to a disfavored group, without any requirement that the support be connected to a terrorist act. Had this law been in place in the 1980s, it would have authorized the government to deny entry to those who publicly endorsed the African National Congress, and would have empowered the Attorney General to detain and deport anyone who contributed to Nelson Mandela's lawful antiapartheid political activities, because until the ANC defeated apartheid in South Africa, our State Department designated it as a terrorist organization.

7   By contrast, security proposals that would directly affect us all, such as national identity cards, airport screening measures, and the Justice Department's Operation TIPS program, have received far more careful scrutiny than initiatives directed at immigrants. Indeed, at House majority leader Dick Armey's insistence, the Republicans' Homeland Security bill expressly prohibited adoption of either a national identity card or Operation TIPS. Where citizens' rights are directly at stake, the political process has proven much more rights-sensitive.

Citizens' Rights

8   But citizens' rights have by no means escaped unscathed. The Patriot Act broadly undermines the rights of all Americans. It reduces judicial oversight of a host of investigative measures, including wiretaps, expands the government's ability to track individuals' Internet use and gives federal officials expansive new powers that are in no way limited to investigating terrorist crimes. It authorizes an end run around the Fourth Amendment by allowing the government to conduct wiretaps and searches in criminal investigations,

without probable cause of a crime, as long as the government claims that it also seeks to gather foreign intelligence—an authority that is particularly questionable in light of recent disclosures from the Foreign Intelligence Surveillance Court that the FBI has repeatedly provided misinformation in seeking such authority in the past.

9   Even property rights, generally sacrosanct among conservatives, have been sharply compromised. Under Patriot Act amendments to preexisting emergency powers laws, the President can designate any organization or individual a terrorist and thereby freeze all their assets and criminalize all transactions with them. He has used it thus far to shut down three of the nation's leading Muslim charities. Two were closed without any charges at all, simply because they are "under investigation." The third, the Holy Land Foundation, was designated a terrorist organization, not based on charges that it had engaged in or even supported terrorist activity but simply on the charge that it is connected to Hamas. The foundation was given no notice or hearing prior to its designation, and when it filed suit after the fact, the district court denied it any opportunity to produce evidence supporting its innocence.

Military Justice

10   All of the above measures implicate the civilian justice system. But the Administration's ultimate trump card is to bypass that system altogether for "military justice," a Bush oxymoron that would have impressed even Orwell. President Bush has asserted the authority to hold people in military custody incommunicado, without any individualized hearing into the basis for their detention, without access to a lawyer, and without judicial review. He has set up military tribunals in which the detainees can be tried, and ultimately executed, without independent judicial review and without anyone outside the military, including the defendant, ever seeing the evidence upon which the conviction rests. And Defense Secretary Donald Rumsfeld has claimed that even if a defendant manages to prevail in such a trial, the military will not release him, but will hold him until there are no longer any terrorist organizations of potentially global reach left in the world, or more simply, for the rest of their lives.

A New Paradigm?

11   This, then, is the state of civil liberties one year after September 11. The Administration's defenders advance three principal arguments to justify what they call the new paradigm required by the war on terrorism. First, they argue that noncitizens, the targets of many of the new measures, are not entitled to the same rights as citizens, especially in time of war. This is hardly a

novel argument. Sacrificing foreign citizens' liberties is always tempting as a political matter. It allows those of us who are citizens to trade someone else's liberties for our security. But doing so is wrong, unlikely to make us more secure and virtually certain to come back to haunt us.

12   As a constitutional matter, basic rights such as due process, equal protection, and the freedoms of speech and association are not limited to citizens but apply to all "persons" within the United States or subject to U.S. authority. The Constitution does restrict the right to vote to citizens, but that restriction only underscores by contrast that the Constitution's other rights apply to all "persons." These are human rights, not privileges of citizenship.

13   Double standards are also unlikely to make us more secure. Even granting that it is rational to assume that Al Qaeda operatives are more likely to be Arab or Muslim, if we are going to identify and capture the few Al Qaeda terrorists among the many millions of law-abiding Arabs and Muslims here and abroad, we need the cooperation of those communities. When we impose on Arabs and Muslims burdens that we would not tolerate for ourselves, we make the targeted communities far less likely to cooperate, and we stoke anti-American sentiments.

14   The double standard is also illusory, for what we do to aliens today provides a precedent for what can and will be done to citizens tomorrow. When the President introduced the concept of military justice with his military tribunal order in November, for example, he reassured Americans that it would not apply to them, but only to "noncitizens." Yet now the Administration has asserted the authority to detain under military custody two U.S. citizens—Yasser Hamdi, a citizen captured in Afghanistan, and Jose Padilla, arrested at O'Hare Airport in May on suspicion that he might be planning to set off a radioactive "dirty bomb." The military claims that simply by attaching the label "enemy combatant," the President can authorize the indefinite, incommunicado incarceration of any U.S. citizen he chooses, without judicial review. Military justice has come home. This proposition is so extreme that even the U.S. Court of Appeals for the Fourth Circuit, by far the most conservative federal circuit in the country, has rejected it. Yet *The Wall Street Journal* reported in August that high-level Administration officials have advocated even broader reliance on this power, and have suggested creating a special camp to house citizen "enemy combatants."

15   The illusory line between alien and citizen has often been crossed before. Two of the most shameful episodes of our nation's history also had their provenance in measures initially targeted at noncitizens. The McCarthy era of the 1940s and '50s, in which thousands of Americans were tarred with guilt by association, was simply an extension to citizens of a similar

campaign using similar techniques against alien radicals in the first Red Scare thirty years earlier. The same is true of the internment of U.S. citizens of Japanese descent during World War II, which treated citizens as we had long treated "enemy aliens"—as suspicious based solely on their group identity, without regard to individual circumstances. So the fact that we have selectively targeted immigrants, far from justifying the new paradigm, condemns it.

Repeating Our Mistakes

16   Administration defenders also contend that the "new paradigm" has avoided the worst mistakes of the past, as if that is the only standard we need to live up to. It is true that dissidents are not facing twenty-year prison terms, as they did during World War I. Individuals have not been penalized for political membership, as they were during the cold war. And we haven't set up internment camps for Arabs—yet. But in another sense, we have simply updated the old mechanisms of control. Where criminalizing speech was the order of the day during World War I, and guilt by association the reigning principle during the cold war, in today's war on terrorism censorship simply takes a new form. In the name of cutting off funds for terrorist activities, the government has made it a deportable offense and a crime to provide virtually any support to a group designated as terrorist, irrespective of whether the support has any connection to violence, much less terrorism. Because these laws require no showing that an individual's support was intended to aid terrorism, they would permit the government to prosecute or deport as a terrorist even a Quaker who sent Al Qaeda a book by Gandhi on the virtues of nonviolence in an attempt to persuade it to disavow violence.

17   In defending such laws, the Administration argues that money is fungible, so support of a group's lawful activities will free up resources that can be spent on terrorism. But that argument proves too much, for it would authorize guilt by association whenever any organization engages in some illegal activity. Donations to the Democratic Party, if could be argued, "free up" resources that are used to violate campaign finance laws, yet surely we could not criminalize all support to the Democratic Party simply because it sometimes violates campaign finance laws. And the fungibility argument assumes that every marginal dollar provided to a designated group will in fact be spent on violence, but in many cases that assumption is not warranted. No one would seriously contend, for example, that every dollar given to the African National Congress in the 1980s for its lawful antiapartheid work in South Africa freed up a dollar that was spent on terrorist attacks.

18   So while we have steered clear of directly criminalizing speech and association—action that in any event is clearly prohibited by Supreme Court precedent—we have achieved much the same ends through the new rubric of cutting off funds for terrorism.

19   Similarly, while we have not yet interned Arabs simply because of their ethnic identity, virtually all those caught up in the Justice Department's preventive detention campaign appear to have been Arab or Muslim. The government's veil of secrecy has impeded a full airing of the facts, but when they are ultimately revealed, it is likely that many of these detentions will be explicable by little more than ethnic identity. Here, too, the government has avoided explicit reliance on ethnicity for detention, but has used indirect means to accomplish a similar end—the detention of 1,500–2,000 Arabs and Muslims as "suspected terrorists," nearly all of whom ultimately had no connection to terrorism whatsoever.

Now Threats?

20   The Administration's final line of defense maintains that unprecedented risks warrant an unprecedented response. The availability of weapons of mass destruction, the relative ease of worldwide travel, communication and financial transfers, the willingness of our enemies to give their own lives for their cause and the existence of a conspiracy that would go to the previously unthinkable lengths illustrated on September 11 require a recalibration of the balance between liberty and security. It is hard to dispute that the world grows more dangerous every day. But that could also be said during World War II, where modern weapons inflicted far more severe damage than those employed in World War I, including a devastating surprise attack on U.S. soil. It also appeared to be true during the cold war, when we were locked in battle not with a small band of terrorists but with the world's other superpower, armed with an enormous stockpile of nuclear, chemical, and biological weapons.

21   Our experiences during World War II and the cold war teach us that whatever the magnitude of the threat, certain principles remain sacrosanct. First, we should hold people responsible for their own actions, not treat them as culpable based on their ethnic, political, or religious identity. Insisting on individual culpability not only serves basic interests of fair play but focuses government investigators on the true perpetrators, avoiding the wasteful expenditure of resources on people who are guilty only by reason of their skin color or political ideology.

22   Second, the government should not be able to imprison people without a public accounting, reviewable in court, establishing that it has a sound

legal basis for doing so. The mutually reinforcing checks of judicial review and public scrutiny, reflected in the ancient writ of habeas corpus, and the constitutional right to a public trial, are essential to insuring that the innocent are not caught up as John Ashcroft's "suspected terrorists" or President Bush's "bad guys."

23   Third, we must insist on public accountability and oversight of law enforcement powers. Past abuses have often been shrouded in secrecy, only to be discovered and condemned years later, as when the Church Committee in 1975 revealed the excesses of the CIA and the FBI in the 1950s and '60s. The Bush Administration has sought to pursue this war under unprecedented secrecy, even refusing to divulge basic facts about its employment of new legislative measures to Congress.

24   Fourth, we should adopt only those measures that we are willing to have imposed on ourselves. Where everyone has an interest at stake, the political process is much more likely to strike an appropriate balance between liberty and security. Where we sacrifice the rights of some for the purported security of the majority, we violate our most basic constitutional commitments.

25   Finally, we must avoid repeating past mistakes. After a terrorist bomb exploded at the home of Attorney General A. Mitchell Palmer in 1919, the Justice Department responded by launching the Palmer Raids, in which thousands of immigrants across the country were rounded up and hundreds deported, not for their involvement in the bombing but for their political associations. Eighty years later, the Ashcroft Raids similarly arrested 1,500–2,000 people and deported hundreds—again, without netting anyone charged with the crime under investigation.

26   None of these principles are new. But the fact that they are old and that they have been forged over the course of many prior crises that also appeared to call for "new paradigms" should count in their favor, not against them. The attacks of September 11 were indeed unthinkable, and the anthrax scare that followed vividly underscored our postmodern vulnerability. But the Administration has yet to make the case that these threats justify compromising our fundamental principles of liberty and justice. In the area of human rights and civil liberties, what is needed is not a "new paradigm" but true conservatism. Only then will freedom endure this operation.

K Y O K O   M O R I

Becoming Midwestern

Born and raised in Japan, Kyoko Mori came to the United States to attend college. She has published two novels, a book of poetry, and a memoir about her life as an immigrant entitled The Dream of Water: On Being a Woman Caught Between Cultures. *She is currently a lecturer in creative nonfiction at Harvard. The following essay appeared in a book edited by Meri Nana-Ama Danquah,* Becoming American, *which collects the stories of immigrant women who have come to the United States from a variety of countries.*

1   A few months ago in Lake Geneva, Wisconsin, a librarian asked me if I felt "more and more American these days." *I've lived here for twenty-two years,* I thought. The question was particularly disappointing because we were at an annual convention of the Wisconsin Library Association, where I had been invited to read my work as a Wisconsin author—my graduate degrees are from the University of Wisconsin, Milwaukee—and I now live and write in Green Bay. The material I read made many references to these facts. The librarian who asked the question, however, assumed that after all these years I was still slowly adjusting myself to "being in America," that living here every day was not something I took for granted, the way she must take it for granted. Even though all of my writing life has taken place in the American Midwest, I was still considered to be a foreigner whose identity and allegiance were at some formative stage—more and more but not fully American.

2   I felt defensive enough to give a snide answer. "I don't know what it means for anyone to feel *American* or *un-American.* I'm not sure if *feeling American* is something that happens to people in degrees, as in *more and more.*" The question made me defensive for the same reason that another often-asked question does: "When you first came to this country from Japan, what was the hardest thing for you to adjust to?" When people ask these questions, there is something they want and expect to hear. The stories they are waiting for—of a brave but disadvantaged immigrant woman trying to understand an unfamiliar language, missing the customs and the foods of the homeland, overcoming one "culture shock" after another—have nothing to do with me. I resent being expected to tell such stories because I have none to tell and also because, even when they are the true stories for many

first-generation immigrant women, there is something self-congratulatory or condescending in most listeners' attitudes. The stories of immigration are often heard by nonimmigrants in the spirit of "I am so lucky that I was always an American." They are the adult, quality-of-life versions of "those poor starving children in China" for whom we were supposed to eat all the food on our plates.

3   The city where I spent my first two years in the Midwest—Rockford, Illinois—is not far from Lake Geneva. It's a medium-sized, industrial town an hour and a half north of Chicago. When I went there, I was twenty; I had decided to transfer from the college I was attending in Kobe, Japan, to its sister college, Rockford College. The day I left Japan, I knew that I would never go back there to live. There was no future in Japan for a woman from my upper-middle-class milieu who wanted to be a writer more than she wanted to be a nice suburban homemaker. Even though I only had a student visa at the time, I was determined to live my adult life in the States. I had been bilingual since I was a child. Many of my friends in Japan were Americans. I had already spent a year in Mesa, Arizona, attending high school as an AFS student. I was prepared for being in America. Being in a small town was another matter.

4   All the way from Chicago's O'Hare Airport to Rockford, the bus went through flat stretches of cornfields. Sitting in the back with my two suitcases, I began to cry. I had grown up in a big city among tall buildings, busy storefronts, and crowded residential neighborhoods. The vast, flat landscape outside the bus window inspired an almost existential fear: I imagined giant hawks coming to carry me off. Things didn't look much better when the bus arrived in Rockford. The college was on the edge of town, in the middle of cornfields. Nearby, there were a few gas stations, a Stop-and-Go, a Dutch Pantry where you could get weak coffee and greasy doughnuts, and a motel that was supposed to look like a Swiss chalet. For the first two weeks, the girl from the Bronx and I marveled at squirrels crossing the road right in front of cars. I walked two miles to the nearest magazine stand, looking for the magazines I was used to reading in Kobe—*New Yorker, Atlantic Monthly, National Geographic.* They only had *Good Housekeeping* and some car and hunting magazines. This is what I have to tell people who ask me about my hardest adjustment when I came to America. There was more American culture in my Japanese city than in a medium-sized Midwestern city like Rockford; I missed the magazines, movies, paintings. Back home, I hopped on the train and went to museums if I had a few hours in the afternoon. From Rockford, it was a two-hour bus ride through the cornfields back to Chicago, where I stood in front of paintings by Georgia O'Keeffe and Mark

Rothko in the Art Institute on weekends and cried—relieved, finally, to see something familiar.

5   But I did not mourn the life of going to museums, coffee shops, bookstores, and concerts in the big city I had left behind. It was a life I would have lost, had I stayed. One by one, my friends in Kobe got engaged to the sons of their fathers' business associates. Soon, they sent me their wedding pictures—their faces painted white with rice powder, their heads covered with the traditional lacquered wigs, my friends scarcely looked like themselves. Their elaborate weddings involved three, four changes of clothing. The last pictures showed them leaving the reception in prim dresses and pillbox hats that were oddly *retro,* making my friends look like Japanese Jackie Kennedys. They seemed not only an ocean away but also decades away, stuck in some time warp. Their days of going to museums and concerts with girlfriends were long over now. If I had stayed, I'd have been alone anyway.

6   At Rockford, I found a home in books. I continued to read the writers I had been reading since high school: Jane Austen, the Brontës, Edith Wharton, Sylvia Plath, Emily Dickinson, Walt Whitman, J. D. Salinger, Ernest Hemingway. In what might be called "the life of the mind," I had been an immigrant long before I left the country and went to Rockford. My reading and thinking self had immigrated to the world of English and American literature during high school because the Japanese authors we read seemed so very cerebral and authoritarian. Even the people who were considered to be eccentrics and nonconformists—Mishima, for instance, or Tanizaki—wrote books that were ponderous with big ideas and dark, heavy symbolism. In their work, I did not find the moments that rang true to me—as when Holden Caulfield is upset to see an obscenity scrawled on the wall, or when Emma Woodhouse offers Jane Fairfax her carriage because she is ashamed of the selfish and stuck-up way she's been behaving. Though I didn't feel completely at home in the city of Rockford, I felt rooted in the books I read in my classes at the college.

7   In Rockford and Milwaukee, I studied creative writing as well as literature. In my writing, too, my immigration had been long under way. Back in Japan, I had attended a private junior and senior high school where we studied English with American teachers, whose teaching method emphasized giving detailed and specific feedback on our writing, instead of the vague words of wisdom that their Japanese counterparts tended to give. As a result, by the time I was eighteen, I knew more about writing in English than I knew about writing in Japanese. One of the reasons I left Japan at twenty was that I wanted to study creative writing, which is not taught in

Japan, in Japanese or in English. Because all of my formal training as a writer took place in an American setting, and because I only write in English, I always thought of myself as an American writer—a writer who has learned much from contemporary American literature and expects to be measured by its tradition. I could not think of myself as a Japanese writer because I don't identify with the Japanese literary tradition and I don't write in Japanese.

8   The story of my immigration is also a story of becoming an adult. I've spent the last twenty-two years in the American Midwest: two years in Rockford, five years in Milwaukee, fifteen years in Green Bay. In that time, I've experienced the big events that make up the lives of many American adults: pursuing and completing advanced studies, finding employment, getting married and divorced, buying a car, buying a house. I have been an American citizen since 1984: I've voted, paid taxes, signed petitions, volunteered in a local election campaign. I have only experienced these events— events which are marks of full adulthood—in the American Midwest. Maybe that's why I'm miffed by people asking me if I feel American. As an adult, I have never been or felt anything else.

9   Another important fact of my immigrant life is that except for my five years in Milwaukee, I have lived in small Midwestern towns where people think that some store or someone's house is "clear across town" if the trip there takes more than twenty minutes by car. Most people in Green Bay come from Green Bay—they did not grow up somewhere else and move here. It's a big event for someone to relocate from the east side of town to the west side. There have never been many people of color in any part of Green Bay. Most people are third- or fourth-generation European immigrants— their grandparents or great-grandparents came from Holland, Sweden, Norway, Germany, Poland, Belgium, Czechoslovakia. This is Willa Cather country, though the people themselves may not be very aware of their own ethnic heritage. Many families started as farm families and then became working class people in the paper mills, and now, in what is called "the service industry." Along the way, they came to think of themselves as having always been "American." I don't fit into these people's preconceived notions about Asian women as war brides or refugees. I am forced to confront the gap between the stereotypes people have about me, on one hand, and who I think I am, on the other. My neighbors might not remember which country their grandmother came from, but if I had children and grandchildren, they would always be asked if they thought of themselves as American.

10   So I don't think of myself as American in the unquestioning way that people around me think of themselves. No one of color can do that, living in Willa Cather country. But certainly, I don't identify myself as a citizen of any other place. I'm not one of those people who argues that countries don't matter, that we are all citizens of the world at large, fellow residents in the international global community. Undoubtedly, that is true on some level, but most of us want to classify and identify ourselves in a more *micro* sort of way, and I am no exception. Reading a newspaper is a good test. I go through the international news with a sense of intellectual and civil duty. As an educated person, I ought to stay informed. An article about whether the city council is likely to give a go-ahead to the new bike trail in my town or one about some altercations in a bar between two country board members who have always hated each other—now, that is real news. My eyes skip everything else and go to those headlines.

11   A further way I can identify my American citizenship is to say that I am an Asian-American or a Japanese-American. These are classifications that are important to me. Several years ago, I was part of a group in Madison called Asian and Pacific American Women's Alliance. We got together once or twice a month to have dinner, organize presentations and readings, raise money for special events. I felt a sense of belonging with women whose backgrounds were similar but also varied: Some of us were first-generation immigrants, others were third or even fourth; many of us taught at colleges; all of us had other issues we were deeply committed to, such as reproductive choice, environmental protection, or gay rights. We were a good community because we were similar and different. I was sorry when many of the women moved away and the group dispersed. Being with these women gave me a stronger, more immediate sense of being Asian-American. Maybe that's how an identity based on who we are differs from an identity based on what we do. If I were to live in a town where no one else runs, my sense of being a runner would be just as strong and immediate as when I belonged to a running club in Milwaukee. But my sense of being Asian-American feels a little more abstract when I don't have an Asian-American community to belong to.

12   The Japanese part of the Japanese-American is important because I discovered Japan by being an American as an adult. When I lived in Japan as a child, being Japanese was something I took for granted at times and rebelled against at other times. In the very Westernized big city where I grew up, what remained Japanese were the male-dominated expectations and attitudes that underlay every marriage, family, and other personal relation-

ships. These were the very things I wanted to reject because they threatened my ambition to become a writer instead of someone's wife and mother. But when I left Japan and was not threatened every day by these oppressive aspects of Japanese culture, I began to remember the things I loved and was nourished by: the flowers my mother and grandmother grew in their gardens, the Buddhist altar where my maternal grandparents burned incense for the souls of their ancestors, the mountains and the sea of my hometown. Sometimes, we have to leave a place to realize the impact it had on us. We make a place our own by the act of leaving it. Living in the Midwest and thinking/writing about Japan has done that for me.

13   Now, I am on the verge of another departure. I have just accepted a five-year teaching appointment at Harvard. After twenty-two years in Illinois and Wisconsin, I will be moving to Boston. I already know that I will miss the corn and hay fields where I've learned to identify the various kinds of sparrows. My existential fear of open spaces is long gone. I have come to love the landscape of the Midwest and its various natural elements. I've learned the names of the wildflowers that grow in ditches near cornfields. If a hawk comes swooping down, I can tell if it's a red-tailed or a Cooper's. Walking through the woods on the bluff of Lake Michigan, I know this isn't my native country—but neither is it for most people who now live in Wisconsin, so the land seems as much mine as anyone else's. Maybe in Boston, I'll walk along the Charles River with my binoculars, hoping to see the same blue herons and killdeer and pintails I'm used to seeing here.

14   The Midwest has left an imprint on my work. Many of my poems were inspired by walking, running, bicycling, bird-watching, and gardening in various parts of Wisconsin. Although my first two novels were set in Japan, many of the characters and events actually originated in my experiences as an adult here; the novel I'm currently working on is set in Milwaukee. My last book of essays has a subtitle: *On Being a Woman Caught Between Two Cultures.* The two cultures I refer to are the Japanese culture of my childhood and the Midwestern American culture of my adulthood. As a reader, too, I've come to appreciate the portrayal of small-town Midwestern characters by authors like Garrison Keillor and Jon Hassler. Though I don't share their ethnic and religious backgrounds, I understand their characters' complete acceptance of their own and other people's eccentricity. In the small towns in the Midwest, people are not obsessively driven to psychoanalyze themselves or each other. If someone behaves in an odd way, people around him or her would politely accommodate that behavior so long as it's not malicious. This polite but ironic acceptance of human frailties is at the heart

of these authors' comic gift. It's something I've come to identify with both in life and literature and will surely miss.

15   A move across five states at forty-two feels just as large—perhaps even larger—than a move across the ocean at twenty. When I left Japan, I was only leaving a place I had been born to. I didn't have a sense of ownership or attachment that comes from having chosen a place. This time, I'll be leaving a place I chose a long time ago, for a place I am choosing now. I'd like to think of the upcoming move as Part Two of my immigration. An immigrant is a person who is able to move on and be nourished by the place she has left as well as by the place she has arrived in. Just as I needed to become American to also become Japanese, moving out east will complete my settlement in the Midwest. As an immigrant, I'll know how to let go and hold on at the same time.

Body Language

The U.S. Capitol building in Washington, D.C.

In the "Controlling Substances" section, on page 585, you will encounter Adbusters's mock ad for "Absolut Impotence," which is meant to counteract some of the print ads we see every day that encourage us to consume alcoholic beverages. It is clear from that ad—and from the hundreds of other ads we see every day—that argument is not confined to words; plenty of other things besides written or oral statements make arguments. One of the central premises of this textbook is that you must learn to manage other aspects of argument in addition to the verbal ones.

But it is not just pictures and words that persuade. If you think about it for a minute, you will agree that many objects also make arguments of a sort. Objects can embody certain values, and they can attempt to convince us to adhere to those values. Take the U.S. Capitol building in Washington, D.C., for instance. As you can see from the photo on the previous page, it embodies in its architecture all sorts of values: Its size suggests a kind of grandeur associated with our nation's aspirations; its symmetrical shape suggests order and orderliness, which are associated with the law that is constructed inside the building; its Greek revival architecture associates our government with ancient Athens, the site of the original, if partial, Western democracy; and so forth. Or take the famous AIDS quilt that circulated around the country in the mid-1990s: It physically argued for the humanity of AIDS victims, furthering the cause of toleration and increasing funding for AIDS research.

If human constructs can make arguments, so can human bodies themselves. Think for a moment about the bodies of the Hare Krishnas, whom you might have seen on your campus or in other public places—shaven-headed men dressed in white or saffron robes, women in multicolored saris, in the act of chanting "Hare Krishna, Hare Krishna, Krishna Krishna, Hare Hare" to the accompaniment of drums and hand cymbals. Can you see that the Hare Krishna physically embody a criticism of Western institutional religion and a radical devotion to bodily cleanliness and sexual abstinence that is contrary to traditional American norms about sexuality and diet—and that is reminiscent of the

Hare Krishnas chanting near a college campus

antimaterialist, antitechnology values of the 1960s counterculture? Or maybe you have seen the famous documentary by Marton Riggs titled *Ethnic Notions*, a film that shows how stereotypes of the Black Sambo, the Mammy, and the Pickaninny carry the message that black Americans are ugly, savage, lazy, and stupid. Or think of the pictures of Jenny Thompson, Steve Austin, James Dean, and Kate Moss on pages 72, 75, 157 and 525 of this book: Can you see in those bodies arguments about sexuality, nonconformity, and the value of thinness in our culture?

In this section of *Good Reasons with Contemporary Arguments*, we present a section on the arguments embodied in nonverbal items. In one sense, the discussion of these items offers more examples of traditional arguments because they are interpretations argued for in words by means of ethos, pathos, and logos. But in another sense, each encourages you to become more aware of the nonverbal arguments we see every day—the nonverbal persuaders that have explicit designs on our actions and beliefs. We have anticipated this section by including in our book not only the photos just mentioned but also other arguments: about whether or not a photo of a seminude female athlete is demeaning or invigorating (see Rick Reilly's essay "Bare in Mind" on pages 71–74); about how female bodies are disciplined into eating disorders in Natasha Potek's "The Diet Zone" (pages 162–66); about how the culture of thinness might be resisted in Klein's *Eat Fat* (pages 78–80); and still another about how cheerleading embodies athleticism in Meghan O'Connor's "Cheerleading" (pages 122–25). Here we present additional arguments along the same lines. The first is a 1930s poster developed by the Nazis that associates and condemns Jews, African Americans, and jazz all at once. Then comes a study of "body painting": Emily Jenkins's argument on cosmetics. Next are a study of constructions of the male body in Malcolm Gladwell's "Listening to Khakis" and Terrence Rafferty's plea for more rounded female role models in film, "Kate Winslet, Please Save Us!" Then come two pieces by minority writers—Richard Rodriguez's account of the meanings of skin color and bell hooks's "Straightening Our Hair"—along with two ads that together try to influence students to adopt safer sex practices. We also include Ynestra King's argument about the meanings that disabled bodies carry in our culture and Evan Wright's account of how female bodies are disciplined in certain directions by the sorority system.

Not everyone will agree with Wright's indictment of sororities. Some of the other items in this section will raise questions too, as much as they answer them. But that only opens the way for additional arguments on those subjects—and on other subjects related to rhetorical bodies: bodies that argue.

How the Nazis Interpreted Jazz

The Entartete Musik poster advertises a 1938 Nazi exhibition on "degenerate" art. The words can be translated as follows: "'Degenerate Music': A presentation by Dr. H. S. Ziegler of the State Council. Admission—40 cents." (The poster is now in the holdings of the Los Angeles Museum of Art's Robert Gore Rivkind Center for German Expressionist Studies.)

EMILY JENKINS

Inkmarks

Emily Jenkins's book Tongue First: Adventures in Physical Culture, *published in 1998, is an irreverent, entertaining, first-person discussion of the meanings associated with various bodily practices—clothing, tattooing, sexuality, fetishes, go-go dancing, nude beachgoing, tongue piercing, yoga, acupuncture, and so on. The following piece is a selection from that book. Jenkins (1967–) is a doctoral student in English at Columbia University in New York City.*

1   When I was nineteen, and still imagined my innocence would be a good thing to shed, I spent the summer working with a woman named Rebecca at a bead shop. She was a soft, generous spirit and at thirty-four or so seemed very old to me. She worked weekends as a masseuse, and spoke with the soothing affect of a new-age service provider. I used to lounge around reading Charlotte Brontë novels while she sorted beads and rang up sales. One morning, a man came into the store with his wife—he a burly dockworker type, she a stout blonde holding a baby who was sucking hard on a pink rubber hedgehog. On the man's red, fleshy bicep was a tattoo, faded by years in the sun to a barely legible smudge of blue: SUSAN. They bought several sacks of beads and his wife paid with a check. Her name was Joan.

2   "That guy's tattoo was sickening," growled Rebecca as they walked out the door. I expected a speech on the sacrilege of permanent body modification. Thorny roses on the breasts of biker girls bared in naughty magazines, blurry anchors on the forearms of ancient sailors—the tattoos I had seen were all violations of the nurturing attitude Rebecca took toward her body. Even the process seemed angry to me—dark ink and sharp needles, a fat man with stained blue arms wiping blood off the pimply back of a frat boy, buzz-cut hair and friends drinking beer in the waiting room. What are the three traits common to serial killers? They are white, male, and possess a tattoo. Rebecca was the antithesis of what tattoos were about; she was all comfortable shoes, no meat, no caffeine, sweet-smelling massages.

3   But she surprised me: "A tattoo can bring your spirit to the surface." She spoke low so the customers wouldn't hear. "It should make your body reflect your mind."

4   "*You* have one?" I asked her. We ducked behind the canvas curtain that led to the storage area, and Rebecca lifted up her dress. Covering her torso

was a blazing phoenix, red-orange and violet. Its head was in profile just under one breast, its wings soared up across her shoulder blades and down her belly. The tail feathers stretched through dumpy white underpants to trail along her thigh.

5   This phoenix transformed Rebecca from a meek woman living alone with a cat and six pairs of Birkenstocks into a mysterious person who underwent voluntary pain and indulged in secret moments of self-display. She had defined her body as a site for decoration, even celebration. It didn't make her pretty. Not at all. It made her visible in a way I had never imagined possible.

6   A few months later I was living in New York City on my own for the first time and I started drawing on myself. I was learning photography and earnestly reading all of Jane Austen. I didn't have many friends, and late at night I'd indulge in fantasies of a life more intensely lived. I had some idea about doing justice to Greenwich Village. There is a portrait I took of myself where my hands are covered in ballpoint pen. My fingers are crisscrossed with lines and sad-looking fish swim across my knuckles. I am wearing fake nails and smoking a cigarette. My face is the round moon of a nineteen-year-old who's barely outgrown *Little Women,* but my hands appear strangely savage and artificial. I would also draw false tattoos on my torso, blue lines coiling around my waist. A tattoo would give me depth, I thought, and I felt myself in need. It would be proof of something, of experience. There was a scary man with a tattooed face named Spider Webb whom I saw on public access television. You could find his phone number on the back page of *The Village Voice.* Maybe I'd have him do it.

7   It is ten years later and I still don't have a tattoo. What I have instead is lipstick. Lots of it, every day. My lipstick, in its little phallic tube, goes up when I want it to, down when I want it to, at my command. It can go with me anywhere; it's always in my pocket. Just like men who pat their pants to make sure their equipment is all in place, I pat my jeans to reassure myself my tube of Desire is there. Really, that's what it's called. If it's not in my pocket, I'm unprepared. Like a condom, it's a covering for one of my most sexual parts. I wouldn't go on a date without it. Carrying it is a sign of adulthood, but of course I don't take it out in public. I decorate myself with it in the privacy of the restaurant bathroom, and come out ready for action.

8   My favorite color before Desire was Media. It was practically a black, very leather bar. Now it's out of fashion, and the names rolling around my top dresser drawer are less overt. Soft, cheerful titles like Cherries Jubilee or Spicy Rose make it seem like fruits and flowers are the images we think of

when we draw attention to our lips. Hah. I say let's call 'em what they really mean: Postcoital Flush, Bloody Valentine, Costly Bordeaux, Vampire Sex Goddess, Adulterous Heat, Shark Bite. Names that imply the mouth is bloody with meat juice or murder, or that appetites for wine and sex have been recklessly indulged—because lipstick is about voracious consumption, in the marketplace and on the body. I always need another one, a matte, a gloss, a frost, a lighter or heavier, paler or darker version of my usual shade. I can never have just one. I need one for my purse and one for my jacket pocket and one for the bathroom and one at the office. At the very least. And when I carry them around so much, they get lost; Tawny Lust rolls out under the seat in the movie theater. Scarlet Indiscretion succumbs to a clumsy pick-pocket. The dog eats most of Steak Tartare. My favorite, Manischewitz, got left in the bathroom of a dive bar in Lansing, Michigan. I have to buy more. The consumption process is in motion again.

9   My friend Roxy steals her lipsticks from the drugstore. She must have a hundred tubes. She says she read *The Beauty Myth* and decided that the true oppression of women by the patriarchy occurs when we pay too much for cosmetics.

10   Red lips require constant upkeep. Women eat lipstick off, kiss it off, dab it off with a napkin, talk it off. We reapply. We consume it literally, licking it from our lips. It has a chemical, waxy taste. As we age, lipstick bleeds into the wrinkles around our mouths, literalizing the blurred physicality that characterizes later life, when steps become more hesitant and the body shows signs of its tenure in the world. Ancient ladies with piles of half-used tubes in their bathrooms collect lipsticks like past loves, flavors they have tasted. Each color may have made only a temporary mark but still is not to be thrown out. Their present shades ooze into cracked old lips with something more like permanence.

11   I wander through the glitzed-out cosmetics floor of a major department store in search of the perfect lipstick. A clique of adolescent girls bounces from counter to counter. They try on lip gloss at the table next to me.

12   "I like this one, I like pale colors," says the ringleader. "I like, I like, I like." She puts two smears of color on one hand and shows them to her friend. "Which is better?"

13   "That one," the friend says pointing, "for your skin."

14   "Eeeew!" cries the leader. "That's disgusting. Am I that ugly? Ohmygod, you're so mean!"

15   Looking through a glistening rack of oily shades, I find myself sharing a mirror with a tall, freckled woman who has just had her lips injected with a prodigious amount of collagen. I can tell because they look like they're

about to split open, especially the top one. She is very beautiful, and her dress shows a lot of tit. Her shoes are cheap.

16   "Are you buying *another* lipstick?" the saleswoman asks nasally, and walks away.

17   "Yeah," she says, a little challenge in her voice, as if to say, *so what if I am?* A California drawl. She leans in to me and whispers, "I hate shopping here. The people are so rude. They never help you at all."

18   "Not until you pull out your credit card," I say.

19   "They're always mean to you," she goes on, smearing her swollen mouth with a brownish color. "Last time I was here, one of them made me cry."

20   "What happened?"

21   "It was at Shiseido," she says. "And the lady was just so mean. I was all tired from jobbing and everything. I'll tell you, I am never shopping Shiseido again."

22   Two Indian women in cardigan sweaters have joined us, pushing in to reach the rack of lipsticks. They, like me, are in search of a phantom color, the red they picture and cannot find. One of them writes down notes on an index card, and complains to her companion about her Pekinese, who swallowed a lipstick she had just bought. "Now why would he do that?" the companion wonders.

23   "It smells nice," I offer, by way of explanation.

24   "Oh no," the Peke owner says. "I don't think it was the smell. I think the tube reminded him of the little canisters from the pharmacy that he likes."

25   "Look at this one!" cries the collagen woman. "It looks like I threw up." I wonder if she is a prostitute, and that is why the salesladies are so cruel.

26   Lipstick brings me, a grad student in a college sweatshirt, together with this possible call girl and the suburban Indian lady on prescription drugs. We share a miniature, frivolous passion. The Bonne Bell lipsmackers that shined on girls' lips at the roller rink in seventh grade have been replaced by dark slashes of adult color, but the special nature of the cosmetic remains the same. Women hide in the bathroom together at parties and share shades, confiding our secrets through lips heavy with the same pigment. Lipstick is an affirmation of sexual potency. It is a collector's item to be hoarded because it is perpetually in need of replenishing. Self-perpetuating material consumption and fleeting erotic appetites are fused in the moist moment of its application.

27   I think of lipstick as such a girlie decoration, such a badge of shared femininity, that I'm surprised to encounter two men shopping for themselves. A pale white European wearing a jeans outfit is pressing a series of tan lipsticks to his mouth without the usual American antigerm precaution

of wiping the product with a tissue. He is being helped by a tiny Asian-American woman in angora. She has shaved off her eyebrows and her eye shadow is the color of egg yolks. The European man is rather uncertain, and she tries to make him buy a clear gloss. His English is not very good, but I can see he wants a color.

28   One counter over, a buff salesman wearing lots of eye makeup and a name tag that reads MONTANA is helping a tall, dapper man in a pinstripe suit. Montana is bustling about, confirming the sale of two sparkly eye shadows. The dapper man is round, with long fingernails and a sleek mustache. He asks for lipstick to match the shadows, and shows me a hand covered with purple streaks of cosmetic. "I'm not sure this doesn't look bruised," he chuckles, "like somebody has been in a bad accident." I smile at him. Is he a drag queen? Will he shave his mustache, then? Or is he decorating himself at home, alone? Or for someone in particular?

29   "I need it for tonight!" he calls to Montana, who has gone in search of a less violent color. When he comes back, the dapper man hands over his plastic.

30   I am coaxed toward another counter by a woman of terrifying drama whose devotion to cosmetics nearly obscures her humanity. Her weighted eyelashes are thickly fused together, much darker than her almost nonexistent brows, and she wears black lipstick interrupted by a blob of rust in the center of her bottom lip. She must be nearly seventy, and her dyed, red-brown hair is pulled tightly back from her face into an enormous bun that threatens to topple her backward. She wants to make me over. I offer excuses and escape with relief, as if the taint of her longing for a lost youth might rub off on me. The woman's face conveyed a kind of painful gullibility that's at the core of my worst fears about using makeup. She had, I suspect, a completely different image of herself than the one I saw. Her gullibility is the essence of mascara.

31   Mascara users have faith. They believe the lashes in the ads are real. They trust that the complex process of application looks natural, when heavy mascara is one of the most obvious cosmetics. That wide-open eye suggests youth and charming stupidity. When I was in junior high, a makeup expert told *Seventeen* magazine that of all cosmetics, black mascara (top and bottom lashes) was the most indispensable. I took this as gospel.

32   Mascara's trusting, unblinking gaze was Twiggy's great achievement, allowing her to embody an age when the nude beach and free love signaled people's wide-eyed faith in a universal oneness. The look has a true-believing, incorruptible optimism that was the ultimate goal behind Tammy Faye Bakker's weighted lashes. How could those open eyes be up

to anything naughty? It is the "Oh, Mr. Grant!" face that Mary Tyler Moore can no longer sustain now that her years belie the girlish innocence her mascara tries to uphold. It is the face that Bette Davis as Baby Jane, angelic child star turned decaying alcoholic bat, was trying to hold on to.

33   Perhaps it is this apparent faith in what makeup can do for you that makes me uncomfortable around the nearly surreal excesses of ardent mascara users. They seem to have lost control over their looks, to be ashamed of their loss of innocence, to trust that they are creating an illusion even when they are making fools of themselves.

34   If mascara is about gullibility and lipstick is about the pleasures of consumption and self-decoration, then nail polish is about denial. And abjection. And power. And self-discipline. The person with long, beautifully polished nails says to the world, "I don't type. I don't do dishes. I don't finger-fuck. I don't garden. I don't change diapers. I don't pick my nose. Hell, I don't even dial my own phone." Even if she does do all these things with her two-inch red talons, it doesn't look like she can. If she did, her polish would chip or someone's soft flesh would get ruptured.

35   The perfect scarlet shine declares both a removal from traditional women's work such as typing and cleaning, and a dissociation from the grittier aspects of living in a human body filled with fluids and wastes. The woman with those perfect nails has transformed the hands that might get dirty with work and physical contact into decorative objects with little function—that is, traditional symbols of femininity. Nails are a contradiction. They emphasize femininity at the same time as they deny participation in the activities associated with women. The woman with perfectly groomed hands lives life on a pedestal—or else she's a CEO, so powerful she's never bothered with chores and diapers and letters to type. She's got a housekeeper, a nanny, and a secretary, or at least an obedient husband. Her hands declare her freedom from such low-paying, undervalued work. Barbra Streisand is famous for her nails. So is Imelda Marcos.

36   Four of the fourteen customers at my local nail salon last weekend were men. Two were tall and good-looking, brothers on their way to a family event. One was a corporate white guy in a suit, and one an enormous farmhand type (I swear to God) with a military haircut. Why were they there? Maybe their mommies never taught them how to trim their own cuticles. Maybe they, like the men at the lipstick counter, are pursuing the small pleasures of self-decoration that so many women indulge in every day. Or maybe they want access to the kind of strength conveyed by the manicured hand, a pristine power removed from the harsh reality of menial chores and the daily grime of physical existence.

37   The ladies who work in the salon know all about the meaning of nails, though their own are short and stained yellow with chemicals. They snicker at my chewed-on stubs and say gently, "Clear polish, right?" They can see I will never be one of the nail elite. I don't have denial nails at all. I have nails that confess all my sins—dirty, bitten, hangnailed. It's pathetic.

38   I ask for pink, just a pale one, but my manicurist will not let me have it. She makes me go with one that is all but clear, assuring me that my choice is no good. There are rules to nail beauty that I don't understand. I let her have her way. When I leave, my nails look fantastic, little pearly nuggets of cleanliness. Three days later, they are a cry for help. Color number 14 is bubbling up from the sides, loosened by several showers and a sink full of dishes. The hangnail on my thumb has come back from its temporary banishment, and I chewed one nail down several layers before I tasted polish and stopped myself. My denial isn't very effective, I guess. My bad habits and household chores will out.

39   By wearing makeup a person goes into dialogue with commonly held ideas about femininity. This is true of the thirteen-year-old with her mom's old blue eye shadow, of the executive applying blush behind the closed door of her office, of the man standing nervously at the cosmetics counter, of the ballerina lining her eyes for a performance as the dying swan. Makeup is a kind of self-decoration that's easy to be comfortable with because, unlike a tattoo, it accommodates a mind that isn't sure of itself. Its essence is to be temporary. It can be applied differently every day, and for all its claims to be long-lasting, can always be removed with the swipe of a tissue. Usually, makeup helps keep our social roles straight. Men don't wear it unless they're challenging convention. Women do. In painting my face, I actively bring myself more in line with the convention of what a woman is, here and now.

40   I paint my face only within certain unspoken limits, and only with the qualities it supposedly has from nature: rosy cheeks, red lips, shadowed lids, thick lashes. Lipstick is almost never blue. Eyebrows are almost never red. People in our culture rarely put representational drawings or even decorative designs on their faces. Socially acceptable makeup tries to be an enhancement, not a separate work of art with the body as its canvas.

41   This has been the easy thing to say about cosmetics. I think it is true, but something else is also going on when people wear makeup. Something about play that would begin to explain why I saw those two men at the lipstick counter. Something about sex that goes beyond just the way we construct our femininity or masculinity. Something about reinventing the self, about the freedom of having a changeable appearance. About products and purchases, the sensual pleasures of shining pots of gloss and sparkling

powders. About artifice, and about art, about challenging the limitations of *beautification* in order to celebrate the body as a site for *decoration*. There is an intense pleasure in the reinvention of the self that makeup allows, and it is anything but trivial.

42   Makeup is a tool by which we shame, flaunt, and mold our inner landscapes along with our exteriors. It is full of meanings that can always be suspended or reimagined. It is sinful and deviant. It is normal, necessary for social acceptance. It is overt. It is secretive. The pleasure lies in the illusion that it isn't there, and isn't needed. The pleasure lies in its blatancy. It is sexually attractive because it is fake. It is sexually repulsive for the same reason. And because it is temporary, makeup triggers only fleetingly the shame or pride that more permanent or powerful tools might make more dramatically. Clothes. Haircuts. Surgeries.

MALCOLM GLADWELL

Listening to Khakis

Born in 1963, Malcolm Gladwell has been writing for some time about fascinating cultural developments of one kind or another—why crime can drop suddenly, how a particular book becomes a best-seller, the rise of hair coloring products for women and suicide rates in Micronesia, the fascination for Ritalin, the spread of coffee. In 2000 he published The Tipping Point, *a book that investigates a number of cultural phenomena as if they were "social epidemics" that spread in the same way that infectious diseases do. Gladwell was a reporter, often on science, for the* Washington Post *from 1987 to 1996; since then his work has often appeared in* The New Yorker, *as did the following piece (in July 1997). (For another example of his work, see his essay on steroids on page 588.)*

1.

1   In the fall of 1987, Levi Strauss & Co. began running a series of national television commercials to promote Dockers, its new brand of men's khakis. All the spots—and there were twenty-eight—had the same basic structure. A handheld camera would follow a group of men as they sat around a living room or office or bar. The men were in their late thirties, but it was hard to tell, because the camera caught faces only fleetingly. It was trained instead on the men from the waist down—on the seats of their pants, on the pleats of their khakis, on their hands going in and out of their pockets. As the camera jumped in quick cuts from Docker to Docker, the men chatted in loose, overlapping non sequiturs—guy-talk fragments that, when they are rendered on the page, achieve a certain Dadaist poetry. Here is the entire transcript of "Poolman," one of the first—and, perhaps, best—ads in the series:

2   "She was a redhead about five foot six inches tall."

3   "And all of a sudden this thing starts spinning, and it's going round and round."

4   "Is that Nelson?"

5   "And that makes me safe, because with my wife, I'll never be that way."

6   "It's like your career, and you're frustrated. I mean that-that's-what you want."

7   "Of course, that's just my opinion."

8   "So money's no object."

9   "Yeah, money's no object."

10   "What are we going to do with our lives, now?"

11   "Well . . ."

12   "Best of all . . ."

13   [Voice-over] "Levi's one-hundred-per-cent-cotton Dockers. If you're not wearing Dockers, you're just wearing pants."

14   "And I'm still paying the loans off."

15   "You've got all the money in the world."

16   "I'd like to at least be your poolman."

17   By the time the campaign was over, at the beginning of the nineties, Dockers had grown into a $600 million business—a brand that if it had spun off from Levi's would have been (and would still be) the fourth-largest clothing brand in the world. Today, seventy per cent of American men between the ages of twenty-five and forty-five own a pair of Dockers, and khakis are expected to be as popular as blue jeans by the beginning of the next century. It is no exaggeration to call the original Dockers ads one of the most successful fashion-advertising campaigns in history.

18   This is a remarkable fact for a number of reasons, not the least of which is that the Dockers campaign was aimed at men, and no one had ever thought you could hit a home run like that by trying to sell fashion to the American male. Not long ago, two psychologists at York University, in Toronto—Irwin Silverman and Marion Eais—conducted an experiment in which they had men and women sit in an office for two minutes, without any reading material or distraction, while they ostensibly waited to take part in some kind of academic study. Then they were taken from the office and given the real reason for the experiment: to find out how many of the objects in the office they could remember. This was not a test of memory so much as it was a test of awareness—of the kind and quality of unconscious attention that people pay to the particulars of their environment. If you think about it, it was really a test of fashion sense, because, at its root, this is what fashion sense really is—the ability to register and appreciate and remember the details of the way those around you look and dress, and then reinterpret those details and memories yourself.

19   When the results of the experiment were tabulated, it was found that the women were able to recall the name and the placement of seventy per cent more objects than the men, which makes perfect sense. Women's fashion, after all, consists of an endless number of subtle combinations and variations—of skirt, dress, pants, blouse, T-shirt, hose, pumps, flats, heels, necklace, bracelet, cleavage, collar, curl, and on and on—all driven by the fact that when a woman walks down the street she knows that other women, consciously or otherwise, will notice the name and the placement of what

she is wearing. Fashion works for women because women can appreciate its complexity. But when it comes to men what's the point? How on earth do you sell fashion to someone who has no appreciation for detail whatsoever?

20   The Dockers campaign, however, proved that you could sell fashion to men. But that was only the first of its remarkable implications. The second—which remains as weird and mysterious and relevant to the fashion business today as it was ten years ago—was that you could do this by training a camera on a man's butt and having him talk in yuppie gibberish.

2.

21   I watched "Poolman" with three members of the new team handling the Dockers account at Foote, Cone & Belding (F.C.B.), Levi's ad agency. We were in a conference room at Levi's Plaza, in downtown San Francisco, a redbrick building decorated (appropriately enough) in khaki like earth tones, with the team members—Chris Shipman, Iwan Thomis, and Tanyia Kandohla—forming an impromptu critical panel. Shipman, who had thick black glasses and spoke in an almost inaudible laid-back drawl, put a videocassette of the first campaign into a VCR—stopping, starting, and rewinding—as the group analyzed what made the spots so special.

22   "Remember, this is from 1987," he said, pointing to the screen, as the camera began its jerky dance. "Although this style of film making looks everyday now, that kind of handheld stuff was very fresh when these were made."

23   "They taped real conversations," Kandohla chimed in. "Then the footage was cut together afterward. They were thrown areas to talk about. It was very natural, not at all scripted. People were encouraged to go off on tangents."

24   After "Poolman," we watched several of the other spots in the original group—"Scorekeeper" and "Dad's Chair," "Flag Football," and "The Meaning of Life"—and I asked about the headlessness of the commercials, because if you watch too many in a row all those anonymous body parts begin to get annoying. But Thomis maintained that the headlessness was crucial, because it was the absence of faces that gave the dialogue its freedom. "They didn't show anyone's head because if they did the message would have too much weight," he said. "It would be too pretentious. You know, people talking about their hopes and dreams. It seems more genuine, as opposed to something stylized."

25   The most striking aspect of the spots is how different they are from typical fashion advertising. If you look at men's fashion magazines, for example, at the advertisements for the suits of Ralph Lauren or Valentino or Hugo Boss, they almost always consist of a beautiful man, with something

interesting done to his hair, wearing a gorgeous outfit. At the most, the man may be gesturing discreetly, or smiling in the demure way that a man like that might smile after, say, telling the supermodel at the next table no thanks he has to catch an early-morning flight to Milan. But that's all. The beautiful face and the clothes tell the whole story. The Dockers ads, though, are almost exactly the opposite. There's no face. The camera is jumping around so much that it's tough to concentrate on the clothes. And instead of stark simplicity, the fashion image is overlaid with a constant, confusing patter. It's almost as if the Dockers ads weren't primarily concerned with clothes at all—and in fact that's exactly what Levi's intended. What the company had discovered in its research, was that baby boomer men felt that the chief thing missing from their lives was male friendship. Caught between the demands of the families that many of them had started in the eighties and career considerations that had grown more onerous, they felt they had lost touch with other men. The purpose of the ads—the chatter, the lounging around, the quick cuts—was simply to conjure up a place where men could put on one-hundred-per-cent-cotton khakis and reconnect with one another. In the original advertising brief, that imaginary place was dubbed Dockers World.

26   This may seem like an awfully roundabout way to sell a man a pair of pants. But that was the genius of the campaign. One of the truisms of advertising is that it's always easier to sell at the extremes than in the middle, which is why the advertisements for Valentino and Hugo Boss are so simple. The man in the market for a thousand-dollar suit doesn't need to be convinced of the value of nice clothes. The man in the middle, though—the man in the market for a forty-dollar pair of khakis—does. In fact, he probably isn't comfortable buying clothes at all. To sell him a pair of pants you have to take him somewhere he is comfortable, and that was the point of Dockers World. Even the apparent gibberish of lines like. "'She was a redhead about five foot six inches tall.' / 'And all of a sudden this thing starts spinning, and it's going round and round.' / 'Is that Nelson?'" have, if you listen closely enough, a certain quintessentially guy-friendly feel. It's the narrative equivalent of the sports-highlight reel—the sequence of five-second film clips of the best plays from the day's basketball or football or baseball games, which millions of American men watch every night on television. This nifty couplet from "Scorekeeper," for instance—"'Who remembers their actual first girlfriend?' / 'I would have done better, but I was bald then, too'"—is not nonsense but a twenty-minute conversation edited down to two lines. A man schooled in the highlight reel no more needs the other nineteen minutes and fifty-eight seconds of that exchange than he needs

to see the intervening catch and throw to make sense of a sinking liner to left and a close play at the plate.

27   "Men connected to the underpinnings of what was being said," Robert Hanson, the vice-president of marketing for Dockers, told me. "These guys were really being honest and genuine and real with each other, and talking about their lives. It may not have been the truth, but it was the fantasy of what a lot of customers wanted, which was not just to be work-focussed but to have the opportunity to express how you feel about your family and friends and lives. The content was very important. The thing that built this brand was that we absolutely nailed the emotional underpinnings of what motivates baby boomers."

28   Hanson is a tall, striking man in his early thirties. He's what Jeff Bridges would look like if he had gone to finishing school. Hanson said that when he goes out on research trips to the focus groups that the Dockers holds around the country he often deliberately stays in the background, because if the men in the group see him they won't necessarily respond as positively or as openly. When he said this, he was wearing a pair of stone-white Dockers, a deep-blue shirt, a navy blazer, and a brilliant-orange patterned tie, and these worked so well together that it was obvious what he meant. When someone like Hanson dresses up that fabulously in Dockers, he makes it clear just how many variations and combinations are possible with a pair of khakis—but that, of course, defeats the purpose of the care-

World message, which is to appeal to the man who wants nothing to do with fashion's variations and combinations. It's no coincidence that every man in every one of the group settings profiled in each commercial is wearing—albeit in different shades—exactly the same kind of pants. Most fashion advertising sells distinctiveness. (Can you imagine, say, an Ann Taylor commercial where a bunch of thirtyish girlfriends are lounging around chatting, all decked out in matching sweater sets?) Dockers was selling conformity.

29   "We would never do anything with our pants that would frighten anyone away," Gareth Morris, a senior designer for the brand, told me. "We'd never do too many belt loops, or an unusual base cloth. Our customers like

one-hundred-per-cent-cotton fabrics. We would never do a synthetic. That's definitely in the market, but it's not where we need to be. Styling-wise, we would never do a wide, wide leg. We would never do a peg-legged style. Our customers seem to have a definite idea of what they want. They don't like tricky openings or zips or a lot of pocket flaps and details on the back. We've done button-through flaps, to push it a little bit. But we usually do a welt pocket—that's a pocket with a button-through. It's funny. We have focus groups in New York, Chicago, and San Francisco, and whenever we show them a pocket with a flap—it's a simple thing—they hate it. They won't buy the pants. They complain, 'How do I get my wallet?' So we compromise and do a welt. That's as far as they'll go. And there's another thing. They go, 'My butt's big enough. I don't want flaps hanging off of it, too.' They like inseam pockets. They like to know where they put their hands." He gestured to the pair of experimental prototype Dockers he was wearing, which had pockets that ran almost parallel to the waistband of the pants. "This is a stretch for us," he said. "If you start putting more stuff on than we have on our product, you're asking for trouble."

30   The apotheosis of the notion of khakis as nonfashion-guy fashion came several years after the original Dockers campaign, when Haggar Clothing Co. hired the Goodby, Silverstein & Partners ad agency, in San Francisco, to challenge Dockers' khaki dominance. In retrospect, it was an inspired choice, since Goodby, Silverstein is Guy Central. It does Porsche ("Kills Bugs Fast") and Isuzu and the recent "Got Milk?" campaign and a big chunk of the Nike business, and it operates out of a gutted turn-of-the-century building downtown, refurbished in what is best described as neo-Erector set. The campaign that it came up with featured voice-overs by Roseanne's television husband, John Goodman. In the best of the ads, entitled "I Am," a thirtyish man wakes up, his hair all mussed, pulls on a pair of white khakis, and half-sleepwalks outside to get the paper. "I am not what I wear, I'm not a pair of pants, or a shirt," Goodman intones. The man walks by his wife, handing her the front sections of the paper. "I'm not in touch with my inner child. I don't read poetry, and I'm not politically correct." He heads away from the kitchen, down a hallway, and his kid grabs the comics from him. "I'm just a guy, and I don't have time to think about what I wear, because I've got a lot of important guy things to do." All he has left now is the sports section and, gripping it purposefully, he heads for the bathroom. "One-hundred-per-cent-cotton wrinkle-free khaki pants that don't require a lot of thought. Haggar. Stuff you can wear."

31   "We softened it," Richard Silverstein told me as we chatted in his office, perched on chairs in the midst of—among other things—a lacrosse stick,

a bike stand, a gym bag full of yesterday's clothing, three toy Porsches, and a giant model of a Second World War Spitfire hanging from the ceiling. "We didn't say 'Haggar Apparel' or 'Haggar Clothing.' We said, 'Hey, listen, guys, don't worry. It's just stuff. Don't worry about it.' The concept was 'Make it approachable.'" The difference between this and the Dockers ad is humor. F.C.B. assiduously documented men's inner lives. Goodby, Silverstein made fun of them. But it's essentially the same message. It's instructive, in this light, to think about the Casual Friday phenomenon of the past decade, the loosening of corporate dress codes that was spawned by the rise of khakis. Casual Fridays are commonly thought to be about men rejecting the uniform of the suit. But surely that's backward. Men started wearing khakis to work because Dockers and Haggar made it sound as if khakis were going to be even easier than a suit. The khaki-makers realized that men didn't want to get rid of uniforms; they just wanted a better uniform.

32   The irony, of course, is that this idea of nonfashion—of khakis as the choice that diminishes, rather than enhances, the demands of fashion—turned out to be a white lie. Once you buy even the plainest pair of khakis, you invariably also buy a sports jacket and a belt and a whole series of shirts to go with it—maybe a polo knit for the weekends, something in plaid for casual, and a button-down for a dressier look—and before long your closet is thick with just the kinds of details and options that you thought you were avoiding. You may not add these details as brilliantly or as consciously as, say, Hanson does, but you end up doing it nonetheless. In the past seven years, sales of men's clothing in the United States have risen an astonishing twenty-one per cent, in large part because of this very fact—that khakis, even as they have simplified the bottom half of the male wardrobe, have forced a steady revision of the top. At the same time, even khakis themselves—within the narrow constraints of khakidom—have quietly expanded their range. When Dockers were launched, in the fall of 1986, there were just three basic styles: the double-pleated Docker in khaki, olive, navy, and black; the Steamer, in cotton canvas; and the more casual flat-fronted Docker. Now there are twenty-four. Dockers and Haggar and everyone else has been playing a game of bait and switch: lure men in with the promise of a uniform and then slip them, bit by bit, fashion. Put them in an empty room and then, ever so slowly, so as not to scare them, fill the room with objects.

3.

33   There is a puzzle in psychology known as the canned-laughter problem, which has a deeper and more complex set of implications about men and women and fashion and why the Dockers ads were so successful. Over the

years, several studies have been devoted to this problem, but perhaps the most instructive was done by two psychologists at the University of Wisconsin, Gerald Cupchik and Howard Leventhal. Cupchik and Leventhal took a stack of cartoons (including many from *The New Yorker*), half of which an independent panel had rated as very funny and half of which it had rated as mediocre. They put the cartoons on slides, had a voice-over read the captions, and presented the slide show to groups of men and women. As you might expect, both sexes reacted pretty much the same way. Then Cupchik and Leventhal added a laugh track to the voice-over—the subjects were told that it was actual laughter from people who were in the room during the taping—and repeated the experiment. This time, however, things got strange. The canned laughter made the women laugh a little harder and rate the cartoons as a little funnier than they had before. But not the men. They laughed a bit more at the good cartoons but much more at the bad cartoons. The canned laughter also made them rate the bad cartoons as much funnier than they had rated them before, but it had little or no effect on their ratings of the good cartoons. In fact, the men found a bad cartoon with a laugh track to be almost as funny as a good cartoon without one. What was going on?

34   The guru of male-female differences in the ad world is Joan Meyers-Levy, a professor at the University of Chicago business school. In a ground-breaking series of articles written over the past decade, Meyers-Levy has explained the canned-laughter problem and other gender anomalies by arguing that men and women use fundamentally different methods of processing information. Given two pieces of evidence about how funny something is—their own opinion and the opinion of others (the laugh track)—the women came up with a higher score than before because they added the two clues together: they integrated the information before them. The men, on the other hand, picked one piece of evidence and ignored the other. For the bad cartoons, they got carried away by the laugh track and gave out hugely generous scores for funniness. For the good cartoons, however, they were so wedded to their own opinion that suddenly the laugh track didn't matter at all.

35   This idea—that men eliminate and women integrate—is called by Meyers-Levy the "selectivity hypothesis." Men are looking for a way to simplify the route to a conclusion, so they seize on the most obvious evidence and ignore the rest, while women, by contrast, try to process information comprehensively. So-called bandwidth research, for example, has consistently shown that if you ask a group of people to sort a series of objects or ideas into categories, the men will create fewer and larger categories than

the women will. They use bigger mental bandwidths. Why? Because the bigger the bandwidth the less time and attention you have to pay to each individual object. Or consider what is called the invisibility question. If a woman is being asked a series of personal questions by another woman, she'll say more if she's facing the woman she's talking to than she will if her listener is invisible. With men, it's the opposite. When they can't see the person who's asking them questions, they suddenly and substantially open up. This, of course, is a condition of male communication which has been remarked on by women for millennia. But the selectivity hypothesis suggests that the cause of it has been misdiagnosed. It's not that men necessarily have trouble expressing their feelings; it's that in a face-to-face conversation they experience emotional overload. A man can't process nonverbal information (the expression and body language of the person asking him questions) and verbal information (the personal question being asked) at the same time any better than he can process other people's laughter and his own laughter at the same time. He has to select, and it is Meyers-Levy's contention that this pattern of behavior suggests significant differences in the way men and women respond to advertising.

36   Joan Meyers-Levy is a petite woman in her late thirties, with a dark pageboy haircut and a soft voice. She met me in the downtown office of the University of Chicago with three large folders full of magazine advertisements under one arm, and after chatting about the origins and the implications of her research she handed me an ad from several years ago for Evian bottled water. It has a beautiful picture of the French Alps and, below that, in large type, "Our factory." The text ran for several paragraphs, beginning:

37   You're not just looking at the French Alps. You're looking at one of the most pristine places on earth. And the origin of Evian Natural Spring Water.

38   Here, it takes no less than 15 years for nature to purify every drop of Evian as it flows through mineral-rich glacial formations deep within the mountains. And it is here that Evian acquires its unique balance of minerals.

39   "Now, is that a male or a female ad?" she asked. I looked at it again. The picture baffled me. But the word "factory" seemed masculine, so I guessed male.

40   She shook her head. "It's female. Look at the picture. It's just the Alps, and then they label it 'Our factory.' They're using a metaphor. To understand this, you're going to have to engage in a fair amount of processing. And look at all the imagery they're encouraging you to build up. You're not just looking at the French Alps. It's 'one of the most pristine places on earth' and it will take nature 'no less than fifteen years' to purify." Her point was that this is an ad that works only if the viewer appreciates all its elements—if the

viewer integrates, not selects. A man, for example, glancing at the ad for a fraction of a second, might focus only on the words "Our factory" and screen out the picture of the Alps entirely, the same way he might have screened out the canned laughter. Then he wouldn't get the visual metaphor. In fact, he might end up equating Evian with a factory, and that would be a disaster. Anyway, why bother going into such detail about the glaciers if it's just going to get lost in the big male bandwidth?

41   Meyers-Levy handed me another Evian advertisement. It showed a man—the Olympic Gold Medal swimmer Matt Biondi—by a pool drinking Evian, with the caption "Revival of the fittest." The women's ad had a hundred and nineteen words of text. This ad had just twenty-nine words: "No other water has the unique, natural balance of minerals that Evian achieves during its 15-year journey deep within the French Alps. To be the best takes time." Needless to say, it came from a men's magazine. "With men, you don't want the fluff," she said. "Women, though, participate a lot more in whatever they are processing. By giving them more cues, you give them something to work with. You don't have to be so literal. With women you can be more allusive, so you can draw them in. They will engage in elaboration, and the more associations they make the easier it is to remember and retrieve later on."

42   Meyers-Levy took a third ad from her pile, this one for the 1997 Mercury Mountaineer four-wheel-drive sport-utility vehicle. It covers two pages, has the heading "Take the Rough with the Smooth," and shows four pictures—one of the vehicle itself, one of a mother and her child, one of a city skyline, and a large one of the interior of the car, over which the ad's text is superimposed. Around the border of the ad are forty-four separate, tiny photographs of roadways and buildings and construction sites and manhole covers. Female. Next to it on the table she put another ad—this one a single page, with a picture of the Mountaineer's interior, fifteen lines of text, a picture of the car's exterior, and, at the top, the heading: "When the Going Gets Tough, the Tough Get Comfortable." Male. "It's details, details. They're saying lots of different stuff," she said, pointing to the female version. "With men, instead of trying to cover everything in a single execution, you'd probably want to have a whole series of ads, each making a different point."

43   After a while, the game got very easy—if a bit humiliating. Meyers-Levy said that her observations were not antimale—that both the male and the female strategies have their strengths and their weaknesses—and, of course, she's right. On the other hand, reading the gender of ads makes it painfully obvious how much the advertising world—consciously or not—talks

down to men. Before I met Meyers-Levy, I thought that the genius of the famous first set of Dockers ads was their psychological complexity, their ability to capture the many layers of eighties guyness. But when I thought about them again after meeting Meyers-Levy, I began to think that their real genius lay in their heroic simplicity—in the fact that F.C.B. had the self-discipline to fill the allotted thirty seconds with as little as possible. Why no heads? The invisibility rule. Guys would never listen to that Dadaist extem-porizing if they had to process nonverbal cues, too. Why were the ads set in people's living rooms and at the office? Bandwidth. The message was that khakis were wide-bandwidth pants. And why were all the ads shot in almost exactly the same way, and why did all the dialogue run together in one ge-nial, faux-philosophical stretch of highlight reel? Because of canned laugh-ter. Because if there were more than one message to be extracted men would get confused.

4.

44   In the early nineties, Dockers began to falter. In 1992, the company sold sixty-six million pairs of khakis, but in 1993, as competition from Haggar and the Gap and other brands grew fiercer, that number slipped to fifty-nine million six hundred thousand, and by 1994 it had fallen to forty-seven mil-lion. In marketing-speak, user reality was encroaching on brand personality; that is, Dockers were being defined by the kind of middle-aged men who wore them, and not by the hipper, younger men in the original advertise-ments. The brand needed a fresh image, and the result was the "Nice Pants" campaign currently being shown on national television—a campaign widely credited with the resurgence of Dockers' fortunes. In one of the spots, "Vive la France," a scruffy young man in his early twenties, wearing Dockers, is sit-ting in a café in Paris. He's obviously a tourist. He glances up and sees a beautiful woman (actually, the supermodel Tatjana Patitz) looking right at him. He's in heaven. She starts walking directly toward him, and as she passes by she says, "Beau pantalon." As he looks frantically through his French phrase book for a translation, the waiter comes by and cuffs him on the head: "Hey, she says, 'Nice pants.'" Another spot in the series, "Subway Love," takes place on a subway car in Chicago. He (a nice young man wear-ing Dockers) spots her (a total babe), and their eyes lock. Romantic music swells. He moves toward her, but somehow, in a sudden burst of pushing and shoving, they get separated. Last shot: she's inside the car, her face pushed up against the glass. He's outside the car, his face pushed up against the glass. As the train slowly pulls away, she mouths two words: "Nice pants."

45   It may not seem like it, but "Nice Pants" is as radical a campaign as the original Dockers series. If you look back at the way that Sansabelt pants, say, were sold in the sixties, each ad was what advertisers would call a pure "head" message: the pants were comfortable, durable, good value. The genius of the first Dockers campaign was the way it combined head and heart: these were all-purpose, no-nonsense pants that connected to the emotional needs of baby boomers. What happened to Dockers in the nineties, though, was that everyone started to do head and heart for khakis. Haggar pants were wrinkle-free (head) and John Goodman—guy (heart). The Gap, with its brilliant billboard campaign of the early nineties—"James Dean wore khakis," "Frank Lloyd Wright wore khakis"—perfected the heart message by forging an emotional connection between khakis and a particular nostalgic, glamorous all-Americanness. To reassert itself, Dockers needed to go an extra step. Hence "Nice Pants," a campaign that for the first time in Dockers history raises the subject of sex.

46   "It's always been acceptable for a man to be a success in business," Hanson said, explaining the rationale behind "Nice Pants." "It's always been expected of a man to be a good provider. The new thing that men are dealing with is that it's O.K. for men to have a sense of personal style, and that it's O.K. to be seen as sexy. It's less about the head than about the combination of the head, the heart, and the groin. It's those three things. That's the complete man."

47   The radical part about this, about adding the groin to the list, is that almost no other subject for men is as perilous as the issue of sexuality and fashion. What "Nice Pants" had to do was talk about sex the same way that "Poolman" talked about fashion, which was to talk about it by not talking about it—or, at least, to talk about it in such a coded, cautious way that no man would ever think Dockers was suggesting that he wear khakis in order to look pretty. When I took a videotape of the "Nice Pants" campaign to several of the top agencies in New York and Los Angeles, virtually everyone agreed that the spots were superb, meaning that somehow F.C.B. had managed to pull off this balancing act.

48   What David Altschiller, at Hill, Holliday/Altschiller, in Manhattan, liked about the spots, for example, was that the hero was naïve: in neither case did he know that he had on nice pants until a gorgeous woman told him so. Naïveté, Altschiller stressed, is critical. Several years ago, he did a spot for Claiborne for Men cologne in which a great-looking guy in a bar, wearing a gorgeous suit, was obsessing neurotically about a beautiful woman at the other end of the room: "I see this woman. She's perfect. She's looking at me. She's smiling. But wait. Is she smiling at me? Or laughing at me? . . . Or look-

ing at someone else?" You'd never do this in an ad for women's cologne. Can you imagine? "I see this guy. He's perfect. Ohmigod. Is he looking at me?" In women's advertising, self-confidence is sexy. But if a man is self-confident—if he knows he is attractive and is beautifully dressed—then he's not a man anymore. He's a fop. He's effeminate. The cologne guy had to be neurotic or the ad wouldn't work. "Men are still abashed about acknowledging that clothing is important," Altschiller said. "Fashion can't be important to me as a man. Even when, in the first commercial, the waiter says 'Nice pants,' it doesn't compute to the guy wearing the nice pants. He's thinking, What do you mean, 'Nice pants'?" Altschiller was looking at a videotape of the Dockers ad as he talked—standing at a forty-five-degree angle to the screen, with one hand on the top of the monitor, one hand on his hip, and a small, bemused smile on his lips. "The world may think they are nice, but so long as he doesn't think so he doesn't have to be self-conscious about it, and the lack of self-consciousness is very important to men. Because 'I don't care.' Or 'Maybe I care, but I can't be seen to care.' " For the same reason, Altschiller liked the relative understatement of the phrase "nice pants," as opposed to something like "great pants," since somewhere between "nice" and "great" a guy goes from just happening to look good to the unacceptable position of actually trying to look good. "In focus groups, men said that to be told you had 'nice pants' was one of the highest compliments a man could wish for," Tanyia Kandohla told me later, when I asked about the slogan. "They wouldn't want more attention drawn to them than that."

49   In many ways, the "Nice Pants" campaign is a direct descendant of the hugely successful campaign that Rubin-Postaer & Associates, in Santa Monica, did for Bugle Boy Jeans in the early nineties. In the most famous of those spots, the camera opens on an attractive but slightly goofy-looking man in a pair of jeans who is hitchhiking by the side of a desert highway. Then a black Ferrari with a fabulous babe at the wheel drives by, stops, and backs up. The babe rolls down the window and says, "Excuse me. Are those Bugle Boy Jeans that you're wearing?" The goofy guy leans over and pokes his head in the window, a surprised half smile on his face: "Why, yes, they are Bugle Boy Jeans."

50   "Thank you," the babe says, and she rolls up the window and drives away.

51   This is really the same ad as "Nice Pants"—the babe, the naïve hero, the punch line. The two ads have something else in common. In the Bugle Boy spot, the hero wasn't some stunning male model. "I think he was actually a box boy at Vons in Huntington Beach," Larry Postaer, the creative director of Rubin-Postaer & Associates, told me. "I guess someone"—at Bugle Boy—

"liked him." He's O.K.-looking, but not nearly in the same class as the babe in the Ferrari. In "Subway Love," by the same token, the Dockers man is medium-sized, almost small, and gets pushed around by much tougher people in the tussle on the train. He's cute, but he's a little bit of a wimp. Kandohla says that F.C.B. tried very hard to find someone with that look—someone who was, in her words, "aspirational real," not some "buff, muscle-bound jock." In a fashion ad for women, you can use Claudia Schiffer to sell a cheap pair of pants. But not in a fashion ad for men. The guy has to be believable. "A woman cannot be too gorgeous," Postaer explained. "A man, however, can be too gorgeous, because then he's not a man anymore. It's pretty rudimentary. Yet there are people who don't buy that, and have gorgeous men in their ads. I don't get it. Talk to Barneys about how well that's working. It couldn't stay in business trying to sell that high-end swagger to a mass market. The general public wouldn't accept it. Look at beer commercials. They always have these gorgeous girls—even now, after all the heat—and the guys are always just guys. That's the way it is. We only reflect what's happening out there, we're not creating it. Those guys who run the real high-end fashion ads—they don't understand that. They're trying to remold how people think about gender. I can't explain it, though I have my theories. It's like a Grecian ideal. But you can't be successful at advertising by trying to re-create the human condition. You can't alter men's minds, particularly on subjects like sexuality. It'll never happen."

52   Postaer is a gruff, rangy guy, with a Midwestern accent and a gravelly voice, who did Budweiser commercials in Chicago before moving West fifteen years ago. When he wasn't making fun of the pretentious style of East Coast fashion advertising, he was making fun of the pretentious questions of East Coast writers. When, for example, I earnestly asked him to explain the logic behind having the goofy guy screw up his face in such a—well, goofy—way when he says, "Why, yes, they are Bugle Boy Jeans," Postaer took his tennis shoes off his desk, leaned forward bemusedly in his chair, and looked at me as if my head came to a small point. "Because that's the only way he could say it," he said. "I suppose we might have had him say it a little differently if he could actually act."

53   Incredibly, Postaer said, the people at Bugle Boy wanted the babe to invite the goofy guy into the car, despite the fact that this would have violated the most important rule that governs this new style of groin messages in men's-fashion advertising, which is that the guy absolutely cannot ever get the girl. It's not just that if he got the girl the joke wouldn't work anymore; it's that if he got the girl it might look as if he had deliberately dressed to get the girl, and although at the back of every man's mind as he's

dressing in the morning there is the thought of getting the girl, any open admission that that's what he's actually trying to do would undermine the whole unself-conscious, antifashion statement that men's advertising is about. If Tatjana Patitz were to say "Beau garçon" to the guy in "Vive la France," or the babe on the subway were to give the wimp her number, Dockers would suddenly become terrifyingly conspicuous—the long-pants equivalent of wearing a tight little Speedo to the beach. And if the Vons box boy should actually get a ride from the Ferrari babe, the ad would suddenly become believable only to that thin stratum of manhood which thinks that women in Ferraris find twenty-four-dollar jeans irresistible. "We fought that tooth and nail," Postaer said. "And it more or less cost us the account, even though the ad was wildly successful." He put his tennis shoes back up on the desk. "But that's what makes this business fun—trying to prove to clients how wrong they are."

5.

54 The one ad in the "Nice Pants" campaign which isn't like the Bugle Boy spots is called "Motorcycle." In it a nice young man happens upon a gleaming Harley on a dark back street of what looks like downtown Manhattan. He strokes the seat and then, unable to contain himself, climbs aboard the bike and bounces up and down, showing off his Dockers (the "product shot") but accidentally breaking a mirror on the handlebar. He looks up. The Harley's owner—a huge, leather-clad biker—is looking down at him. The biker glowers, looking him up and down, and says, "Nice pants." Last shot: the biker rides away, leaving the guy standing on the sidewalk in just his underwear.

55 What's surprising about this ad is that, unlike "Vive la France" and "Subway Love," it does seem to cross the boundaries of acceptable sex talk. The rules of guy advertising so carefully observed in those spots—the fact that the hero has to be naïve, that he can't be too good-looking, that he can't get the girl, and that he can't be told anything stronger than "Nice pants"—are all, in some sense, reactions to the male fear of appearing too concerned with fashion, of being too pretty, of not being masculine. But what is "Motorcycle"? It's an ad about a sweet-looking guy down in the Village somewhere who loses his pants to a butch-looking biker in leather. "I got so much feedback at the time of 'Well, God, that's kind of gay, don't you think?'" Robert Hanson said. "People were saying, 'This buff guy comes along and he rides off with the guy's pants. I mean, what the hell were they doing?' It came from so many different people within the industry. It came from some of our most conservative retailers. But do you know what? If you

put these three spots up—'Vive la France,' 'Subway Love,' and 'Motorcycle'— which one do you think men will talk about ad nauseam? 'Motorcycle.' It's No. 1. It's because he's really cool. He's in a really cool environment, and it's every guy's fantasy to have a really cool, tricked-out fancy motorcycle."

56   Hanson paused, as if he recognized that what he was saying was quite sensitive. He didn't want to say that men failed to pick up the gay implications of the ad because they're stupid, because they aren't stupid. And he didn't want to sound condescending, because Dockers didn't build a $600 million business in five years by sounding condescending. All he was trying to do was point out the fundamental exegetical error in calling this a gay ad, because the only way for a Dockers man to be offended by "Motorcycle" would be if he thought about it with a little imagination, if he picked up on some fairly subtle cues, if he integrated an awful lot of detail. In other words, a Dockers man could only be offended if he did precisely what, according to Meyers-Levy, men don't do. It's not a gay ad because it's a guy ad. "The fact is," Hanson said, "that most men's interpretation of that spot is: You know what? Those pants must be really cool, because they prevented him from getting the shit kicked out of him."

TERRENCE RAFFERTY

Kate Winslet, Please Save Us!

Brooklyn native Terrence Rafferty has a special interest in film, and his articles have appeared in The Atlantic, The Village Voice, Film Quarterly, the *New York Times, and many other places. Since 1997 he has been the "critic-at-large" for* GQ *(short for* Gentleman's Quarterly*), a fashion-and-culture magazine geared to young professional men that carried the following argument in May 2001. Do the think the argument would have been constructed differently if it had been published elsewhere?*

1 When I go to the movies these days, I sometimes find myself gripped by a very peculiar sort of nostalgia: I miss flesh. I see skin, I see bones, I see many rocklike outcroppings of muscle, but I rarely see, in the angular bodies up there on the screen—either the hard, sculpted ones or the brittle, anorexic ones—anything *extra,* not even a hint of the soft layer of fatty tissue that was once an essential component of the movies' romantic fantasy, the cushion that made encounters between the sexes seem like pleasant, sensual experiences rather than teeth-rattling head-on collisions. The sleek form-follows-function physiques of today's film stars suggest a world in which power and brutal effi-ciency are all that matter, in the bed-room no less than in the pitiless, sun-seared arena of *Gladiator.* This may well be an accurate reflection of our anxious time, but it's also mighty de-pressing. When I come out of the multiplex now, I often feel like the ar-chetypal ninety-eight-pound weak-ling in the old Charles Atlas ads—like big bullies have been kicking sand in my face for two hours. And that's just the women.

2 This is a touchy area, I realize. Where body type is concerned, an amazingly high percentage of social and cultural commentary is fueled by simple envy, resentment of the young and the buff. A few years ago, when Calvin Klein ads featuring the stunning, waiflike Kate Moss

Kate Moss, waiflike

appeared on the sides of New York City buses, they were routinely defaced with bitter-sounding graffiti—FEED ME was the most popular—which was, you had to suspect, largely the product of women who were enraged by her distinctive beauty. (Men, to my knowledge, had few complaints about having to see Moss in her underwear whiz past them on Madison Avenue.) Protesters insisted that images such as those in the Klein ads promote eating disorders in impressionable teenage girls. Maybe that's so—I don't have the statistics—but the sheer violence of the attacks on Moss, along with the fact that they seemed to be directed more at the model herself than at the marketing wizards who exploited her, strongly suggested another, less virtuous agenda. The taste of sour grapes was unmistakable.

3   I happened to think Moss looked great—small, but well-proportioned, and mercifully lacking the ropy musculature that had begun to creep into pop-culture images of femininity, in the cunning guise of "empowerment." The Bionic Woman could only dream of the bulging biceps sported by Linda Hamilton in *Terminator 2: Judgment Day* (1991); and Ginger Rogers, even when she was struggling to match steps with Astaire, never had the calf muscles of the mighty Madonna. (Nor would she have wanted them: She was a dancer and not, like Mrs. Ritchie or any of her brood of MTV chicks, a kinky aerobics instructor.) It's understandable, I suppose, that women might have felt the impulse to bulk up during the might-makes-right regimes of Ronald Reagan and George Herbert Walker Bush, when the rippling behemoths of machismo, Arnold and Sly, ruled the screen; in that context, working on one's abs and pecs could be considered a prudent strategy of self-defense. But the arms buildup in the Cold War between the sexes was not a pretty sight. Applied to sex, the doctrine of Mutually Assured Destruction is kind of a bummer. The wages of sinew is the death of romance.

4   At least that's how it looks to people of my generation, whose formative years were the '60s, and to many of Moss's generation (the one commonly designated "X"), who in their youth embraced, for a while, the antipower aesthetic of grunge. What we oversaturated pop-culture consumers consider attractive—i.e., what's sexy in the opposite gender and worth aspiring to in one's own—usually develops in adolescence, as the relevant body parts do, and doesn't change much thereafter. For men older than I am, the perfect woman might have been Sophia Loren or Elizabeth Taylor or Marilyn Monroe or Rita Hayworth or the wartime pinup Betty Grable or (reaching back to the hugely eroticized flapper era) the original It girl, Clara Bow. And for them, the image of the ideal masculine self might have been Cary Grant or Clark Gable or Henry Fonda or Gary Cooper or even, for the less physically prepossessing—OK, shorter—guys, Cagney or Bogart or Tracy. By the time the

'60s rocked and rolled into history, some subtle transformations had occurred, primarily in female sexual iconography. While the male stars of that decade remained more or less within the range of body types of their predecessors—Steve McQueen and Sean Connery might have looked a bit more athletic than the old norms demanded, but they wouldn't qualify as hardbodies by today's standards—the shape of desirability in women distinctly altered, to something less voluptuous and more elongated. The fashions of the era tended to shift the erotic focus southward, from the breasts and the hips down to the legs, which, in a miniskirt, did rather overwhelm all other possible indicators of a woman's sexual allure. Although smaller-chested, leaner-hipped women, such as Julie Christie, stole some thunder from the conspicuously curvaceous, a certain amount of flesh was still required. Minis didn't flatter skinny legs any more than they did chubby ones.

5   So there was, to the avid eyes of teenage boys like me, a fine balance struck in the body aesthetic of the '60s, between, so to speak, length and width, Giacometti and Rubens. And muscles weren't part of the equation. He-men such as Steve Reeves—whose 1959 *Hercules,* a cheap Italian import, initiated a spate of "sword and sandal" epics—seemed, to both sexes, ridiculous, vain rather than truly manly. (It's worth noting that in those days it was widely perceived that the primary market for body-building magazines was gay men.) And women? Forget it. The epitome of the muscular gal was the Russian or East German Olympic athlete, an Olga or a Helga, whose gender identity was frequently, and often justly, a matter of some dispute. There's an echo of that attitude in Ridley Scott's 1997 *G.I. Jane,* in which a feminist senator played by Anne Bancroft, trying to select a candidate for the first woman to undergo Navy SEAL training, summarily dismisses several of the beefier applicants on the grounds of ambiguous sexuality. She settles on Demi Moore, who is slender and pretty and, on the evidence of a spectacularly obvious boob job, unquestionably straight.

6   But bodies like Moore's puzzle me. What, exactly, is the empowering element here—the iron she's pumped or the silicone that's been pumped into her chest? My number one teenage crush, Diana Rigg, didn't need either in order to be wholly convincing as kick-ass secret agent Emma Peel in the TV series *The Avengers.* Paired with a dapper male partner, John Steed (played by Patrick Macnee), Mrs. Peel was not only fully empowered but was also by far the more physically active of the two. In her mod pantsuits and go-go boots, she did most of the actual fighting in the kung fu-ish battles that climaxed virtually every episode, while Steed, perhaps mindful of potential damage to his impeccably cut Pierre Cardin suits, generally limited his martial activity to an occasional deft thrust with the umbrella.

7   Maybe if I'd come of age with visions of Madonna dancing in my head, I might find GI Demi devastatingly sexy rather than grotesque, but, objectively, I think the idea that women's power depends on either sculpted muscles or gigantic, orblike breasts (much less both) smacks of desperation. Mrs. Peel wielded her power so coolly, so confidently, and clearly never felt the need to enhance it by strenuous training or expensive medical procedures. Comfort in one's own skin is always appealing, which is probably why, in this sweating, striving, aggressively self-improving era, I find bodies as diverse as Kate Moss's and Kate Winslet's mighty attractive. It's not the body type per se—neither the frail Kate nor the ampler one precisely conforms to my Riggian ideal—but a woman's attitude toward her body that makes her sexy.

Kate Winslet from *Titanic* days

8   What's unnerving about today's pop-culture images of women is how extreme they are—and how much emphasis they place on the *effort* required to correct nature, to retard the aging process, to be all that you can be (and not, God forbid, simply what you are). The ethic of progress through hard work and technology is deeply ingrained in our society, as is the democratic notion that everyone should be whatever he or she wants to be—a noble idea that gets a tad problematic when what everyone wants to be is a star. And every star wants to be a bigger star. As a result, we're seeing, in the movies and on television and in the pages of fashion magazines, increasingly bizarre manifestations of our paradoxical collective need to feel unique and, more, admired. Being really fat, for example, can confer on a person a certain distinction, but not the kind most of us yearn for. (In the old days, for men, a degree of heft often indicated prosperity; the movies embodied their image of financial success in portly figures such as Eugene Pallette and Edward Arnold. No more.) To stand out on the runway these days, a model has to be significantly gaunter—and younger—than even the FEED ME–era Moss. And to make her mark on the screen, an actress has several equally grueling options: starve herself skeletal, go to the gym and get muscular, or—sometimes in perverse combination with one of the previous—have her breasts inflated surgically. In each case, the result is a wild exaggeration of what would be, in moderation, a desirable quality: slimness, fitness or voluptuousness. When I look at

women in the movies now, I often feel as if I were gazing not at real people but at cartoon characters—Olive Oyl, Popeye (in drag) and Jessica Rabbit.

9   Of course, there are exceptions: the spectacular Winslet; the cherubic and blissfully unself-conscious Drew Barrymore; the graceful, athletic Asian stars Michelle Yeoh and Maggie Cheung; and (no epithet necessary) Julia Roberts. But too many of the screen's great beauties have been developing a lean and hungry look in recent years. They've felt the burn, and something more than body fat appears to have been eliminated—a certain amount of joy seems to have melted away at the same time. Clearly, we live in extraordinarily ruthless and competitive times, and popular culture is bound to reflect that condition, but I can't think of another age in which the competitive anxieties of the performers themselves were so mercilessly exposed to the public's view. When tough, chunky guys like Cagney squared off against one another in a boxing ring or on the mean streets of New York or Chicago, you sensed that the survival of an entire community of immigrants was at stake; you could see it in every movement of their squat brawler's bodies. And when the Depression was over, those fierce small men just about vanished from the movies, giving way to their larger, better-nourished children, who left the field, in turn, to generations who would be conscious of their bodies without having nearly as much use for them as their ancestors had had. What's at stake for today's action heroes and heroines, all pumped up with no place to go except to the "explosive" climax of a fanciful plot? The steroidal action pictures of the '80s and '90s created a race of pointless Supermen. Everyone in the audience was in on the joke: Bruce Willis and Tom Cruise and Nicolas Cage and Keanu Reeves didn't bulk up to save the world or any recognizable part of it; they did it because starring in an action franchise was, and remains, a surefire means of moving up the Hollywood ladder.

10   As the historian Lynne Luciano points out in her useful new book, *Looking Good: Male Body Image in America,* in a white-collar, service economy all most of us do with our bodies is compare them with everybody else's. We look, we admire, we envy, we check the mirror, we get dissatisfied, we go back to the old drawing board (the gym, the plastic surgeon, Jenny Craig, whatever). And this strikes many as perfectly reasonable and natural: You have to keep an edge, and you have to *work* on it. Constant vigilance is required for both men and women, and folks are starting to look a little haggard. This applies even to the beautiful people of the silver screen. We can see the strain as they try to hang on to their precarious positions, like Tom Cruise at the beginning of *M.I.2.* And who, aside from the stars themselves, their families and their agents, could possibly care?

11   I haven't used the word *narcissism* yet, and it's long overdue. The unseemly vanity once ascribed to poor Steve Reeves has become the norm in Hollywood, which, kind of hilariously, apparently believes that we're so vain we probably think their movies are about us. I can't come up with another explanation for berserk pictures like David Fincher's *Fight Club* (1999), in which Edward Norton, as a harried white collar Everyman, takes as his guru and alter ego an alarmingly buff *Übermensch* played by Brad Pitt. If the weak box-office returns are any indication, *Fight Club* did not strike the deep chord in the hearts of American men that its makers evidently thought it would, and, to add insult to injury, the picture didn't even provoke the "controversy" that might have validated the artists' sense of their own fearlessness and edginess. The whole spectacle was simply self-important and silly—as silly as *Hercules* and, because no one involved seemed to recognize it, then some.

12   It's time to stop the madness. Sure, we viewers are stressed-out and perhaps slightly self-absorbed, but more of us than Hollywood thinks have some perspective on the absurdities of our lives and the inanities of our culture. Fewer of us than the studios imagine actually believe that a diet or a set of weights or silicone implants will change our lives, even if every movie star worth his or her (pardon the expression) salt apparently does believe it. That's their business, and, as we know—though Hollywood has obviously forgotten—there's *no* business like show business. The feral, predatory creatures prowling across the screen for our amusement are in a world of their own. And although they carry themselves as if they were wolves, magnificent in their power, they're really just coyotes, roaming the hills restlessly for scraps and deluding themselves even more doggedly than Chuck Jones's indefatigable Wile E. At least he knew what he was.

13   In a sense, body image represents the final frontier of postmodernism, the only area as yet untouched by our culture's pervasive irony. It would be useful, I think, for moviemakers to drop the pretense that entertainment is a life-and-death struggle, which only the strong survive. The stars of earlier eras, with their variety of unapologetically eccentric physiques, understood it was all a lovely con, a game played for pleasure: That's what those discreet little layers of flesh ultimately meant. But what would it take, I wonder, to make today's hardbodies lighten up and laugh at their own desperate exertions or, failing that, merely stop gazing out at us cowed viewers as if they were dying to beat the crap out of us? I don't know, but I suspect that cranky magazine columns won't do the job. A higher power will have to be invoked. Mrs. Peel, you're needed.

RICHARD RODRIGUEZ

Complexion

Richard Rodriguez (1944–), born into a Spanish-speaking Mexican American family in California, was educated at Stanford, Columbia, and Berkeley. Many of his eloquent essays, like "Complexion," mix memoir and argument.

1   Complexion. My first conscious experience of sexual excitement concerns my complexion. One summer weekend, when I was around seven years old, I was at a public swimming pool with the whole family. I remember sitting on the damp pavement next to the pool and seeing my mother, in the spectators' bleachers, holding my younger sister on her lap. My mother, I noticed, was watching my father as he stood on a diving board, waving to her. I watched her wave back. Then saw her radiant, bashful, astonishing smile. In that second I sensed that my mother and father had a relationship I knew nothing about. A nervous excitement encircled my stomach as I saw my mother's eyes follow my father's figure curving into the water. A second or two later, he emerged. I heard him call out. Smiling, his voice sounded, buoyant, calling me to swim to him. But turning to see him, I caught my mother's eye. I heard her shout over to me. In Spanish she called through the crowd: "Put a towel on over your shoulders." In public, she didn't want to say why. I knew.

2   That incident anticipates the shame and sexual inferiority I was to feel in later years because of my dark complexion. I was to grow up an ugly child. Or one who thought himself ugly. (*Feo.*) One night when I was eleven or twelve years old, I locked myself in the bathroom and carefully regarded my reflection in the mirror over the sink. Without any pleasure I studied my skin. I turned on the faucet. (In my mind I heard the swirling voices of aunts, and even my mother's voice, whispering, whispering incessantly about lemon juice solutions and dark, *feo* children.) With a bar of soap, I fashioned a thick ball of lather. I began soaping my arms. I took my father's straight razor out of the medicine cabinet. Slowly, with steady deliberateness, I put the blade against my flesh, pressed it as close as I could without cutting, and moved it up and down across my skin to see if I could get out, somehow lessen, the dark. All I succeeded in doing, however, was in shaving my arms bare of their hair. For as I noted with disappointment, the dark would not come out. It remained. Trapped. Deep in the cells of my skin.

3   Throughout adolescence, I felt myself mysteriously marked. Nothing else about my appearance would concern me so much as the fact that my complexion was dark. My mother would say how sorry she was that there was not money enough to get braces to straighten my teeth. But I never bothered about my teeth. In three-way mirrors at department stores, I'd see my profile dramatically defined by a long nose, but it was really only the color of my skin that caught my attention.

4   I wasn't afraid that I would become a menial laborer because of my skin. Nor did my complexion make me feel especially vulnerable to racial abuse. (I didn't really consider my dark skin to be a racial characteristic. I would have been only too happy to look as Mexican as my light-skinned older brother.) Simply, I judged myself ugly. And, since the women in my family had been the ones who discussed it in such worried tones, I felt my dark skin made me unattractive to women.

5   Thirteen years old. Fourteen. In a grammar school art class, when the assignment was to draw a self-portrait, I tried and I tried but could not bring myself to shade in the face on the paper to anything like my actual tone. With disgust then I would come face to face with myself in mirrors. With disappointment I located myself in class photographs—my dark face undefined by the camera which had clearly described the white faces of classmates. Or I'd see my dark wrist against my long-sleeved white shirt.

6   I grew divorced from my body. Insecure, overweight, listless. On hot summer days when my rubber-soled shoes soaked up the heat from the sidewalk, I kept my head down. Or walked in the shade. My mother didn't need anymore to tell me to watch out for the sun. I denied myself a sensational life. The normal, extraordinary, animal excitement of feeling my body alive—riding shirtless on a bicycle in the warm wind created by furious self-propelled motion—the sensations that first had excited in me a sense of my maleness, I denied. I was too ashamed of my body. I wanted to forget that I had a body because I had a brown body. I was grateful that none of my classmates ever mentioned the fact.

7   I continued to see the *braceros*, those men I resembled in one way and, in another way, didn't resemble at all. On the watery horizon of a Valley afternoon, I'd see them. And though I feared looking like them, it was with silent envy that I regarded them still. I envied them their physical lives, their freedom to violate the taboo of the sun. Closer to home I would notice the shirtless construction workers, the roofers, the sweating men tarring the street in front of the house. And I'd see the Mexican gardeners. I was unwilling to admit the attraction of their lives. I tried to deny it by looking away. But what was denied became strongly desired.

8   In high school physical education classes, I withdrew, in the regular company of five or six classmates, to a distant corner of a football field where we smoked and talked. Our company was composed of bodies too short or too tall, all graceless and all—except mine—pale. Our conversation was usually witty. (In fact we were intelligent.) If we referred to the athletic contests around us, it was with sarcasm. With savage scorn I'd refer to the "animals" playing football or baseball. It would have been important for me to have joined them. Or for me to have taken off my shirt, to have let the sun burn dark on my skin, and to have run barefoot on the warm wet grass. It would have been very important. Too important. It would have been too telling a gesture—to admit the desire for sensation, the body, my body.

9   Fifteen, sixteen. I was a teenager shy in the presence of girls. Never dated. Barely could talk to a girl without stammering. In high school I went to several dances, but I never managed to ask a girl to dance. So I stopped going. I cannot remember high school years now with the parade of typical images: bright drive-ins or gliding blue shadows of a Junior Prom. At home most weekend nights, I would pass evenings reading. Like those hidden, precocious adolescents who have no real-life sexual experiences, I read a great deal of romantic fiction. "You won't find it in your books," my brother would playfully taunt me as he prepared to go to a party by freezing the crest of the wave in his hair with sticky pomade. Through my reading, however, I developed a fabulous and sophisticated sexual imagination. At seventeen, I may not have known how to engage a girl in small talk, but I had read *Lady Chatterley's Lover.*

10   It annoyed me to hear my father's teasing: that I would never know what "real work" is; that my hands were so soft. I think I knew it was his way of admitting pleasure and pride in my academic success. But I didn't smile. My mother said she was glad her children were getting their educations and would not be pushed around like *los pobres*. I heard the remark ironically as a reminder of my separation from *los braceros*. At such times I suspected that education was making me effeminate. The odd thing, however, was that I did not judge my classmates so harshly. Nor did I consider my male teachers in high school effeminate. It was only myself I judged against some shadowy, mythical Mexican laborer—dark like me, yet very different.

BELL HOOKS

Straightening Our Hair

bell hooks (1955–   ; real name: Gloria Watkins) is a prolific writer and educator who has taught at Oberlin College and City University of New York. Here she recollects and meditates on the practice of hair-straightening in the African American community. The essay originally appeared in 1988 in the avant-garde Z magazine, which frequently carries articles by hooks.

1   On Saturday mornings we would gather in the kitchen to get our hair fixed, that is straightened. Smells of burning grease and hair, mingled with the scent of our freshly washed bodies, with collard greens cooking on the stove, with fried fish. We did not go to the hairdresser. Mama fixed our hair. Six daughters—there was no way we could have afforded hairdressers. In those days, this process of straightening black women's hair with a hot comb (invented by Madame C. J. Walker) was not connected in my mind with the effort to look white, to live out standards of beauty set by white

bell hooks

supremacy. It was connected solely with rites of initiation into womanhood. To arrive at that point where one's hair could be straightened was to move from being perceived as child (whose hair could be neatly combed and braided) to being almost a woman. It was this moment of transition my sisters and I longed for.

2   Hair pressing was a ritual of black women's culture—of intimacy. It was an exclusive moment when black women (even those who did not know one another well) might meet at home or in the beauty parlor to talk with one another, to listen to the talk. It was as important a world as that of the male barber shop—mysterious, secret. It was a world where the images constructed as barriers between one's self and the world were briefly let go, before they were made again. It was a moment of creativity, a moment of change.

3   I wanted this change even though I had been told all my life that I was one of the "lucky" ones because I had been born with "good hair"—hair that was fine, almost straight—not good enough but still good. Hair that had no nappy edges, no "kitchen," that area close to the neck that the hot comb

could not reach. This "good hair" meant nothing to me when it stood as a barrier to my entering this secret black woman world. I was overjoyed when mama finally agreed that I could join the Saturday ritual, no longer looking on but patiently waiting my turn. I have written of this ritual: "For each of us getting our hair pressed is an important ritual. It is not a sign of our longing to be white. There are no white people in our intimate world. It is a sign of our desire to be women. It is a gesture that says we are approaching womanhood. . . . Before we reach the appropriate age we wear braids, plaits that are symbols of our innocence, our youth, our childhood. Then, we are comforted by the parting hands that comb and braid, comforted by the intimacy and bliss. There is a deeper intimacy in the kitchen on Saturdays when hair is pressed, when fish is fried, when sodas are passed around, when soul music drifts over the talk. It is a time without men. It is a time when we work as women to meet each other's needs, to make each other feel good inside, a time of laughter and outrageous talk."

4   Since the world we lived in was racially segregated, it was easy to overlook the relationship between white supremacy and our obsession with hair. Even though black women with straight hair were perceived to be more beautiful than those with thick, frizzy hair, it was not overtly related to a notion that white women were a more appealing female group or that their straight hair set a beauty standard black women were struggling to live out. While this was probably the ideological framework from which the process of straightening black women's hair emerged, it was expanded so that it became a real space of black women bonding through ritualized, shared experience. The beauty parlor was a space of consciousness raising, a space where black women shared life stories—hardship, trials, gossip; a place where one could be comforted and one's spirit renewed. It was for some women a place of rest where one did not need to meet the demands of children or men. It was the one hour some folk would spend "off their feet," a soothing, restful time of meditation and silence. These positive empowering implications of the ritual of hair pressing mediate but do not change negative implications. They exist alongside all that is negative.

5   Within white supremacist capitalist patriarchy, the social and political context in which the custom of black folks straightening our hair emerges, it represents an imitation of the dominant white group's appearance and often indicates internalized racism, self-hatred, and/or low self-esteem. During the 1960s black people who actively worked to critique, challenge, and change white racism pointed to the way in which black people's obsession with straight hair reflected a colonized mentality. It was at this time that the natural hairdo, the "afro," became fashionable as a

sign of cultural resistance to racist oppression and as a celebration of blackness. Naturals were equated with political militancy. Many young black folks found just how much political value was placed on straightened hair as a sign of respectability and conformity to societal expectations when they ceased to straighten their hair. When black liberation struggles did not lead to revolutionary change in society the focus on the political relationship between appearance and complicity with white racism ceased and folks who had once sported afros began to straighten their hair.

6   In keeping with the move to suppress black consciousness and efforts to be self-defining, white corporations began to acknowledge black people and most especially black women as potential consumers of products they could provide, including hair-care products. Permanents specially designed for black women eliminated the need for hair pressing and the hot comb. They not only cost more but they also took much of the economy and profit out of black communities, out of the pockets of black women who had previously reaped the material benefits (see Manning Marable's *How Capitalism Underdeveloped Black America,* South End Press). Gone was the context of ritual, of black woman bonding. Seated under noisy hair dryers black women lost a space for dialogue, for creative talk.

7   Stripped of the positive binding rituals that traditionally surrounded the experience, black women straightening our hair seemed more and more to be exclusively a signifier of white supremacist oppression and exploitation. It was clearly a process that was about black women changing their appearance to imitate white people's looks. This need to look as much like white people as possible, to look safe, is related to a desire to succeed in the white world. Before desegregation black people could worry less about what white folks thought about their hair. In a discussion with black women about beauty at Spelman College, students talked about the importance of wearing straight hair when seeking jobs. They were convinced and probably rightly so that their chances of finding good jobs would be enhanced if they had straight hair. When asked to elaborate they focused on the connection between radical politics and natural hairdos, whether natural or braided. One woman wearing a short natural told of purchasing a straight wig for her job search. No one in the discussion felt black women were free to wear our hair in natural styles without reflecting on the possible negative consequences. Often older black adults, especially parents, respond quite negatively to natural hairdos. I shared with the group that when I arrived home with my hair in braids shortly after accepting my job at Yale my parents told me I looked disgusting.

8   Despite many changes in racial politics, black women continue to ob-
sess about their hair, and straightening hair continues to be serious business.
It continues to tap into the insecurity black women feel about our value in
this white supremacist society. Talking with groups of women at various college campuses and with black women in our communities there seems to be
general consensus that our obsession with hair in general reflects continued
struggles with self-esteem and self-actualization. We talk about the extent
to which black women perceive our hair as the enemy, as a problem we must
solve, a territory we must conquer. Above all it is a part of our black female
body that must be controlled. Most of us were not raised in environments
where we learned to regard our hair as sensual or beautiful in an unprocessed
state. Many of us talk about situations where white people ask to touch our
hair when it is unprocessed then show surprise that the texture is soft or feels
good. In the eyes of many white folks and other non-black folks, the natural
afro looks like steel wool or a helmet. Responses to natural hairstyles worn
by black women usually reveal the extent to which our natural hair is perceived in white supremacist culture as not only ugly but frightening. We also
internalize that fear. The extent to which we are comfortable with our hair
usually reflects on our overall feelings about our bodies. In our black
women's support group, *Sisters of the Yam,* we talk about the ways we don't
like our bodies, especially our hair. I suggested to the group that we regard
our hair as though it is not part of our body but something quite separate—
again a territory to be controlled. To me it was important for us to link this
need to control with sexuality, with sexual repression. Curious about what
black women who had hot-combed or had permanents felt about the relationship between straightened hair and sexual practice I asked whether people worried about their hairdo, whether they feared partners touching their
hair. Straightened hair has always seemed to me to call attention to the desire for hair to stay in place. Not surprisingly many black women responded
that they felt uncomfortable if too much attention was focused on their hair,
if it seemed to be too messy. Those of us who have liberated our hair and let
it go in whatever direction it seems fit often receive negative comments.

9   Looking at photographs of myself and my sisters when we had
straightened hair in high school I noticed how much older we looked than
when our hair was not processed. It is ironic that we live in a culture that
places so much emphasis on women looking young, yet black women are
encouraged to change our hair in ways that make us appear older. This past
semester we read Toni Morrison's *The Bluest Eye* in a black women's fiction
class. I asked students to write autobiographical statements which reflect
their thoughts about the connection between race and physical beauty. A

vast majority of black women wrote about their hair. When I asked individual women outside class why they continued to straighten their hair, many asserted that naturals don't look good on them, or that they required too much work. Emily, a favorite student with very short hair, always straightened it and I would tease and challenge her. She explained to me convincingly that a natural hairdo would look horrible with her face, that she did not have the appropriate forehead or bone structure. Later she shared that during spring break she had gone to the beauty parlor to have her perm and as she sat there waiting, thinking about class reading and discussion, it came to her that she was really frightened that no one else would think she was attractive if she did not straighten her hair. She acknowledged that this fear was rooted in feelings of low self-esteem. She decided to make a change. Her new look surprised her because it was so appealing. We talked afterwards about her earlier denial and justification for wearing straightened hair. We talked about the way it hurts to realize connection between racist oppression and the arguments we use to convince ourselves and others that we are not beautiful or acceptable as we are.

10   In numerous discussions with black women about hair one of the strongest factors that prevents black women from wearing unprocessed hairstyles is the fear of losing other people's approval and regard. Heterosexual black women talked about the extent to which black men respond more favorably to women with straight or straightened hair. Lesbian women point to the fact that many of them do not straighten their hair, raising the question of whether or not this gesture is fundamentally linked to heterosexism and a longing for male approval. I recall visiting a woman friend and her black male companion in New York years ago and having an intense discussion about hair. He took it upon himself to share with me that I could be a fine sister if I would do something about my hair (secretly I thought mama must have hired him). What I remember is his shock when I calmly and happily asserted that I like the touch and feel of unprocessed hair.

11   When students read about race and physical beauty, several black women describe periods of childhood when they were overcome with longing for straight hair as it was so associated with desirability, with being loved. Few women had received affirmation from family, friends, or lovers when choosing not to straighten their hair and we have many stories to tell about advice we receive from everyone, including total strangers, urging [us] to understand how much more attractive we would be if we would fix (straighten) our hair. When I interviewed for my job at Yale, white female advisers who had never before commented on my hair encouraged me not

to wear braids or a large natural to the interview. Although they did not say straighten your hair, they were suggesting that I change my hairstyle so that it would most resemble theirs, so that it would indicate a certain conformity. I wore braids and no one seemed to notice. When I was offered the job I did not ask if it mattered whether or not I wore braids. I tell this story to my students so that they will know by this one experience that we do not always need to surrender our power to be self-defining to succeed in an endeavor. Yet I have found the issue of hairstyle comes up again and again with students when I give lectures. At one conference on black women and leadership I walked into a packed auditorium, my hair unprocessed wild and all over the place. The vast majority of black women seated there had straightened hair. Many of them looked at me with hostile contemptuous stares. I felt as though I was being judged on the spot as someone out on the fringe, an undesirable. Such judgments are made particularly about black women in the United States who choose to wear dreadlocks. They are seen and rightly so as the total antithesis of straightening one's hair, as a political statement. Often black women express contempt for those of us who choose this look.

12   Ironically, just as the natural unprocessed hair of black women is the subject of disregard and disdain we are witnessing return of the long dyed, blonde look. In their writing, my black women students described wearing yellow mops on their heads as children to pretend they had long blonde hair. Recently black women singers who are working to appeal to white audiences, to be seen as crossovers, use hair implanting and hair weaving to have long straight hair. There seems to be a definite connection between a black female entertainer's popularity with white audiences and the degree to which she works to appear white, or to embody aspects of white style. Tina Turner and Aretha Franklin were trend setters; both dyed their hair blonde. In everyday life we see more and more black women using chemicals to be blonde. At one of my talks focusing on the social construction of black female identity within a sexist and racist society, a black woman came to me at the end of the discussion and shared that her seven-year-old daughter was obsessed with blonde hair, so much so that she had made a wig to imitate long blonde curls. This mother wanted to know what she was doing wrong in her parenting. She asserted that their home was a place where blackness was affirmed and celebrated. Yet she had not considered that her processed straightened hair was a message to her daughter that black women are not acceptable unless we alter our appearance or hair texture. Recently I talked with one of my younger sisters about her hair. She

uses bright colored dyes, various shades of red. Her skin is very dark. She has a broad nose and short hair. For her these choices of straightened dyed hair were directly related to feelings of low self-esteem. She does not like her features and feels that the hairstyle transforms her. My perception was that her choice of red straightened hair actually called attention to the features she was trying to mask. When she commented that this look receives more attention and compliments, I suggested that the positive feedback might be a direct response to her own projection of a higher level of self-satisfaction. Folk may be responding to that and not her altered looks. We talked about the messages she is sending her dark-skinned daughters—that they will be most attractive if they straighten their hair.

13   A number of black women have argued that straightened hair is not necessarily a signifier of low self-esteem. They argue that it is a survival strategy; it is easier to function in this society with straightened hair. There are fewer hassles. Or as some folk stated, straightened hair is easier to manage, takes less time. I responded to this argument in our discussion at Spelman by suggesting that perhaps the unwillingness to spend time on ourselves, caring for our bodies, is also a reflection of a sense that this is not important or that we do not deserve such care. In this group and others, black women talked about being raised in households where spending too much time on appearance was ridiculed or considered vanity. Irrespective of the way individual black women choose to do their hair, it is evident that the extent to which we suffer from racist and sexist oppression and exploitation affects the degree to which we feel capable of both self-love and asserting an autonomous presence that is acceptable and pleasing to ourselves. Individual preferences (whether rooted in self-hate or not) cannot negate the reality that our collective obsession with straightening black hair reflects the psychology of oppression and the impact of racist colonization. Together racism and sexism daily reinforce to all black females via the media, advertising, etc. that we will not be considered beautiful or desirable if we do not change ourselves, especially our hair. We cannot resist this socialization if we deny that white supremacy informs our efforts to construct self and identity.

14   Without organized struggles like the ones that happened in the 1960s and early 1970s, individual black women must struggle alone to acquire the critical consciousness that would enable us to examine issues of race and beauty, our personal choices, from a political standpoint. There are times when I think of straightening my hair just to change my style, just for fun. Then I remind myself that even though such a gesture could be simply playful on my part, an individual expression of desire, I know that such a gesture would carry other implications beyond my control. The reality is: straight-

ened hair is linked historically and currently to a system of racial domination that impresses upon black people, and especially black women, that we are not acceptable as we are, that we are not beautiful. To make such a gesture as an expression of individual freedom and choice would make me complicit with a politic of domination that hurts us. It is easy to surrender this freedom. It is more important that black women resist racism and sexism in every way; that every aspect of our self-representation be a fierce resistance, a radical celebration of our care and respect for ourselves.

15   Even though I have not had straightened hair for a long time, this did not mean that I am able to really enjoy or appreciate my hair in its natural state. For years I still considered it a problem. (It wasn't naturally nappy enough to make a decent interesting afro. It was too thin.) These complaints expressed my continued dissatisfaction. True liberation of my hair came when I stopped trying to control it in any state and just accepted it as it is. It has been only in recent years that I have ceased to worry about what other people would say about my hair. It has been only in recent years that I could feel consistent pleasure washing, combing, and caring for my hair. These feelings remind me of the pleasure and comfort I felt as a child sitting between my mother's legs feeling the warmth of her body and being as she combed and braided my hair. In a culture of domination, one that is essentially anti-intimacy, we must struggle daily to remain in touch with ourselves and our bodies, with one another. Especially black women and men, as it is our bodies that have been so often devalued, burdened, wounded in alienated labor. Celebrating our bodies, we participate in a liberatory struggle that frees mind and heart.

Advertising Safer Sex Practices

These two ads were published in several Pennsylvania newspapers in the spring of 1999. The ads were created by members of a Penn State class titled Communications and Community; designed to resemble "real" ads, each one actually features fictitious people and scenarios.

Don't sleep with this Jerk!

Hey Mark,
Now do I have your attention?

Since, you haven't returned my calls this was the only way I could get a hold of you. I wasn't trying to go out with you again, **I just wanted to tell you I have a freakin' STD and I got it from you.** So hey girls, don't sleep with him and don't let this happen to you.

STDs—the Risk is Real.

For more information call 237-7371   Brought to you by: **Family Health Services, Inc.**

"Brainchild" is the name the students gave to the imaginary corporation that developed the ads. But though the ads are fictional, in another sense they are very real: Their aim was to encourage safer sex practices.

JENN,
I thought I was your first.

Yeah, right. The first to get your genital warts! Don't wear a condom you said. Don't worry, huh? **Well you better start worrying 'cause your secret's out.** Be careful, the people you sleep with are not always honest about their sexual past.

STDs—the Risk is Real.

For more information call 237-7371

Brought to you by: **Family Health Services, Inc.**

YNESTRA KING

The Other Body: Disability and Identity Politics

Ynestra King (1957–   ) is a social activist who lives, works, teaches, and writes in New York City. Her books include Ecofeminism and the Reenchantment of Nature *(1993). King published the following argument in* Ms. *magazine in the spring of 1993.*

1   Disabled people rarely appear in popular culture. When they do, their disability must be a continuous preoccupation overshadowing all other areas of their character. Disabled people are disabled. That is what they "do." That is what they "are."

2   My own experience with a mobility impairment that is only minorly disfiguring is that one must either be a creature of the disability, or have transcended it entirely. For me, like most disabled people (and this of course depends on relative severity), neither extreme is true. It is an organic, literally embodied fact that will not change—like being a woman. While it may be possible to "do gender," one does not "do disability." But there is an organic base to both conditions that extends far into culture, and the meaning that "nature" has. Unlike being a woman, being disabled is not a socially constructed condition. It is a tragedy of nature, of a kind that will always exist. The very condition of disability provides a vantage point of a certain lived experience in the body, a lifetime of opportunity for the observation of reaction to bodily deviance, a testing ground for reactions to persons who are readily perceived as having something wrong or being different. It is fascinating, maddening, and disorienting. It defies categories of "sickness" and "health," "broken" and "whole." It is in between.

3   Meeting people has an overlay: I know what they notice first is that I am different. And there is the experience of the difference in another person's reaction who meets me sitting down (when the disability is not apparent), and standing up and walking (when the infirmity is obvious). It is especially noticeable when another individual is flirting and flattering, and has an abrupt change in affect when I stand up. I always make sure that I walk around in front of someone before I accept a date, just to save face for both of us. Once the other person perceives the disability, the switch on the sexual circuit breaker often pops off—the connection is broken. "Chemistry" is

over. I have a lifetime of such experiences, and so does every other disabled woman I know.

4   White middle-class people—especially white men—in the so-called First World have the most negative reactions. And I always recognize studied politeness, the attempt to pretend that there's nothing to notice (this is the liberal response—Oh, you're black? I hadn't noticed). Then there's the do-gooder response, where the person falls all over her/himself, insisting on doing everything for you; later they hate you; it's a form of objectification. It conveys to you that that is all they see, rather like a man who can't quit talking with a woman about sex.

5   In the era of identity politics in feminism, disability has not only been an added cross to bear, but an added "identity" to take on—with politically correct positions, presumed instant alliances, caucuses to join, and closets to come out of. For example, I was once dragged across a room to meet someone. My friend, a very politically correct lesbian feminist, said, "She's disabled, too. I thought you'd like to meet her." Rather than argue— what would I say? "I'm not interested in other disabled people," or "This is my night off"? (The truth in that moment was like the truth of this experience in every other moment, complicated and difficult to explain)—I went along to find myself standing before someone strapped in a wheelchair she propels by blowing into a tube with a respirator permanently fastened to the back of the chair. To suggest that our relative experience of disability is something we could casually compare (as other people stand by!) demonstrates the crudity of perception about the complex nature of bodily experience.

6   My infirmity is partial leg paralysis. I can walk anywhere, climb stairs, drive a car, ride a horse, swim, hang-glide, fly a plane, hike in the wilderness, go to jail for my political convictions, travel alone, and operate heavy equipment. I can earn a living, shop, cook, eat as I please, dress myself, wash and iron my own clothes, clean my house. The woman in that wheelchair can do none of these fundamental things, much less the more exotic ones. On a more basic human level I can spontaneously get my clothes off if I decide to make love. Once in bed my lover and I can forget my disability. None of this is true of the woman in the wheelchair. There is no bodily human activity that does not have to be specially negotiated, none in which she is not absolutely "different." It would take a very long time, and a highly nuanced conversation, for us to be able to share experiences as if they were common. The experience of disability for the two of us was more different than my experience is from the daily experience of people who are not considered disabled. So much for disability solidarity.

7   With disability, one is somewhere on a continuum between total bodily dysfunction—or death—and complete physical wholeness. In some way,
this probably applies to every living person. So when is it that we call a person "disabled"? When do they become "other"? There are "minor" disabilities
that are nonetheless significant for a person's life. Color blindness is one example. But in our culture, color blindness is considered an inconvenience
rather than a disability.

8   The ostracization, marginalization, and distortion response to disability are not simply issues of prejudice and denial of civil rights. They reflect
attitudes toward bodily life, an unease in the human skin, and an inability
to cope with contingency, ambiguity, flux, finitude, and death.

9   Visibly disabled people (like women) in this culture are the scapegoats
for resentments of the limitations of organic life. I had polio when I was
seven, finishing second grade. I had excelled in everything, and rarely missed
school. I had one bad conduct notation—for stomping on the boys' blocks
when they wouldn't let me play with them. Although I had leg braces and
crutches when I was ready to start school the next year, I wanted desperately to go back and resume as much of the same life as I could. What I was
not prepared for was the response of the school system. They insisted that I
was now "handicapped" and should go into what they called "special education." This was a program aimed primarily at multiply disabled children,
virtually all of whom were mentally retarded as well as physically disabled.
It was in a separate wing of another school, and the children were completely segregated from the "normal" children in every aspect of the school
day, including lunch and recreational activities. I was fortunate enough to
have educated, articulate parents and an especially aggressive mother; she
went to the school board and waged a tireless campaign to allow me to
come back to my old school on a trial basis—the understanding being that
the school could send me to special education if things "didn't work out" in
the regular classroom.

10   And so began my career as an "exceptional" disabled person, not like
the *other* "others." And I was glad. I didn't want to be associated with those
others either. Apart from the objective limitations caused by the polio, the
transformation in identity—the difference in worldly reception—was terrifying and embarrassing, and it went far beyond the necessary considerations
my limitations required.

11   My experience as "other" is much greater and more painful as a disabled person than as a woman. Maybe the most telling dimension of this
knowledge is my observation of the reactions of others over the years, of
how deeply afraid people are of being outside the normative appearance

(which is getting narrower as capitalism exaggerates patriarchy). It is no longer enough to be thin; one must have ubiquitous muscle definition, nothing loose, flabby, or ill defined, no fuzzy boundaries. And of course, there's the importance of control. Control over aging, bodily processes, weight, fertility, muscle tone, skin quality, and movement. Disabled women, regardless of how thin, are without full bodily control.

12   I see disabled women fight these normative standards in different ways, but never get free of negotiating and renegotiating them. I did it by constructing my life around other values and, to the extent possible, developing erotic attachments to people who had similar values, and for whom my compensations were more than adequate. But at one point, after two disastrous but steamy liaisons with a champion athlete and a dancer (during which my friends pointed out the obvious unkind truth and predicted painful endings), I discovered the worlds I had tried to protect myself from: the disastrous attraction to "others" to complete oneself. I have seen disabled women endure unspeakably horrible relationships because they were so flattered to have such a conventionally attractive individual in tow.

13   And then there's the weight issue. I got fat by refusing to pay attention to my body. Now that I'm slimming down again, my old vanities and insecurities are surfacing. The battle of dieting can be especially fraught for disabled women. It is more difficult because exercising is more difficult, as is traveling around to get the proper foods, and then preparing them. But the underlying rage at the system that makes you feel as if you *are* your body (female, infirm) and that everything else is window dressing—this also undermines the requisite discipline. A tempting response is to resort to an ideal of self as bodiless essence in which the body is completely incidental, and irrelevant.

14   The wish that the body should be irrelevant has been one of my most fervent lifelong wishes. The knowledge that it isn't is my most intense lifelong experience.

15   I have seen other disabled women wear intentionally provocative clothes, like the woman in a wheelchair on my bus route to work. She can barely move. She has a pretty face, and tiny legs she could not possibly walk on. Yet she wears black lace stockings and spike high heels. The other bus occupants smile condescendingly, or pretend not to notice, or whisper in appalled disbelief that this woman could represent herself as having a sexual self. That she could "flaunt" her sexual being violates the code of acceptable appearance for a disabled woman. This woman's apparel is no more far out than that of many other women on our bus—but she refuses to fold up and be a good little asexual handicapped person.

16   The well-intentioned liberal new campaigns around "hire the handicapped" are oppressive in related ways. The Other does not only have to demonstrate her competence on insider terms; she must be better, by way of apologizing for being different and rewarding the insiders for letting her in. And the happy handicapped person, who has had faith placed in her/him, must vindicate "the race" because the politics of tokenism assumes that there are in fact other qualifications than doing the job.

17   This is especially prejudicial in a recession, where there are few social services, where it is "every man for himself." Disabled people inevitably have greater expenses, since assistance must often be paid for privately. In the U.S., public construction of the disabled body is that one either is fully disabled and dysfunctional/unemployable (and therefore eligible for public welfare) or totally on one's own. There is no in-between—the possibility of a little assistance, or exceptions in certain areas. Disabled people on public assistance cannot work or they will lose their benefits. (In the U.S. ideology that shapes public attitudes and public policy, one is either fully dependent or fully autonomous.) But the reality of human and organic life is that everyone is different in some way; there is no such thing as a totally autonomous individual. Yet the mythology of autonomy perpetuates in terrible ways the oppression of the disabled. It also perpetuates misogyny—and the destruction of the planet.

18   It may be that this clear lack of autonomy—this reminder of mortal finitude and contingency and embeddedness of nature and the body—is at the root of the hatred of the disabled. On the continuum of autonomy and dependence, disabled people need help. To need help is to feel humiliated, to have failed. I think this "help" issue must be even harder for men than women. But any disabled person is always negotiating both the provisionality of autonomy and the rigidity of physical norms.

19   From the vantage point of disability, there are some objective and desirable aspects of autonomy. But they have to do with independence. The preferred protocol is that the attendant or friend perform the task that the disabled person needs done in the way the disabled person *asks it to be done*. Assistance from friends and family is a negotiated process, and often maddening. For that reason most disabled people prefer to live in situations where they can do all the basic functions themselves, with whatever special equipment or built-ins are required.

20   It's a dreadful business, this needing help. And it's more dreadful in the U.S. than in any place in the world, because our heroes are dynamic overcomers of adversity, and there is an inevitable cultural contempt for weakness.

21   Autonomy is on a continuum toward dependency and death. And the idea that dependency could come at any time, that one could die at any time, or be dismembered or disfigured, and still have to live (maybe even *want to live*) is unbearable in a context that understands and values autonomy in the way we moderns do.

22   I don't want to depict this experience of unbearability as strictly cultural. The compromising of the human body before its natural time is tragic. It forces terrible hardship on the individual to whom it occurs. But the added overlay of oppression on the disabled is intimately related to the fear of death, and the acknowledgement of our embeddedness in organic nature. We are finite, contingent, dependent creatures by our very nature; we will all eventually die. We will all experience compromises to our physical integrity. The aspiration to human wholeness is an oppressive idealism. Socially, it is deeply infantilizing.

23   It promotes a simplistic view of the human person, a static notion of human life that prevents the maturity and social wisdom that might allow human beings to more fully apprehend the human condition. It marginalizes the "different," those perceived as hopelessly wedded to organic existence—women and the disabled. The New Age "human potential movement"—in the name of maximizing human growth—is one of the worst offenders in obscuring the kind of human growth I am suggesting.

24   I too believe that the potential for human growth and creativity is infinite—but it is not groundless. The common ground for the person—the human body—is a place of shifting sand that can fail us at any time. It can change shape and properties without warning; this is an essential truth of embodied existence.

25   Of all the ways of becoming "other" in our society, disability is the only one that can happen to anyone, in an instant, transforming that person's life and identity forever.

Sister Act

Evan Wright's condemnation of the Greek system—in particular, an exposé of how the sorority system disciplines female bodies in certain ways—appeared in Rolling Stone *in October 1999. You are no doubt aware of* Rolling Stone: *It covers contemporary pop culture, especially music, for a hip audience of under-thirties.*

1   The dogwoods are in bloom here at Ohio State in Columbus, the second-largest university in the United States. Stark residential towers rise to the north and south. A collection of 1950s and 1960s aluminum-and-glass buildings facing the main thoroughfare have the look of Stalinist architecture. They lend the campus that air of impersonality that many large universities seem to strive for.

2   With more than 35,000 undergrads, including more than 7,000 minority students, OSU can be overwhelming to the sheltered incoming teenager. Still, it is shocking that flocks of OSU's young women are joining sororities, the cornier the better. They are embracing honor badges, sacred oaths and archaic codes of feminine virtue. Seventeen sororities—many housed in expansive mansions along Indianola Avenue and Fifteenth Street—claim a membership of nearly 2,000, and pledge classes have doubled over the past two years.

3   Sorority members say that their organizations make strong female role models and promote ideals of service, sisterhood and leadership. Their success at teaching these values can be judged during OSU's Greek week, the oldest celebration of college fraternal organizations in the land. "Greek week," its organizers say, "is a chance for the Greek community to come together and shine on campus."

4   A solemn event on the Greek-week calendar is Alcohol Awareness Day. For twenty-four hours, all sorority sisters and fraternity brothers pledge to abstain from liquor. To help get them through it, organizers have planned a night of Survival Bingo in Raney Commons, a hall that will seat about 300 ostensibly sober bingo players.

5   Seven sorority presidents gather at a table half an hour prior to the event. Six are blond. All wear beige khaki shorts and white blouses or T-shirts adorned with either Greek letters or Gap and Abercrombie & Fitch logos. Their hair is pulled back straight behind their ears with either hair bands or sunglasses. Each wears silver hoop earrings.

6   Raney Commons fills to capacity with sober, white, clean-cut young people and begins to resemble a fantasy from deep inside the brain of Ronald Reagan, during whose presidency most of these Greeks were born. Black students congregate elsewhere: There are eleven African-American Greek organizations, known as the "black Greeks." The black Greeks evince little interest in joining in with the white Greeks. Leon Coleman, president of all of OSU's black Greeks, says, "In a struggle, sometimes you have to have your own, be around your own."

7   The monotony of the ensuing bingo game is broken only when the number sixty-nine is called. Cheers grow louder when sixty-nine is again called. At last, a hooting fraternity boy is driven over the brink when sixty-nine sounds yet again. He hurls a bingo prize, a bag of Capri-Sun Coolers, at a table packed with sorority sisters. They throw it back, and flocks of the silvery bags arc across the Commons.

8   Preparing to leave, two sorority sisters berate a pledge who has forgotten to carry out their winnings, a case of Sprite.

9   "It's your job to carry it back to the house," one of the elder sisters scolds.

10   "Can't one of you help?" the pledge asks plaintively.

11   "That's your job," explains the other sister. As the pledge trudges back into Raney Commons, the two sisters confer about her performance and leadership potential.

12   "Dude, she is such a whore."

13   "Totally."

14   At 3 A.M., two wobbly-legged sorority girls stand in an alley off Fifteenth Street. A third girl kneels between them on her hands and knees and throws up. Her two friends yank her backward. "Don't get it on you," one of them says. "A sober monitor will smell it."

15   All sororities have a zero tolerance alcohol policy. Many do not even allow a single can of beer in a twenty-one-year-old girl's personal refrigerator.

16   Fraternities, however, are allowed to serve beer in bottles under an elaborate system of ID bracelets, drink cards and monitoring by student sober patrols. They offer the only Greek parties that sorority girls can go to in order to get drunk. Everyone swears that the system works beautifully, and it does, insofar as it allows all Greeks, whatever their ages, to get drunk at pretty much any time of the day or night.

17   Two young women hang out by the main pedestrian crossroads, called the Oval. One has hair dyed lightbulb yellow; the other has dark purple hair

braided in strands around alphabet beads. They are both first-year students, and neither would dream of joining a sorority.

18 "Girls in sororities are so conformist," says the yellow-haired one. "They're like Gap clones or something."

19 "I don't know if that's really true or fair," her friend interjects. "Like, I read a survey about sorority girls. It said sorority girls have, like, the highest percentage of pierced clits."

20 She cannot recall in which magazine or scholarly journal she found this fact.

21 The first girl volunteers that her friend from across the hall in her dorm recently pledged with a sorority: "She'll still talk about it now, because she hasn't moved into her house yet. Once they move in, it's kind of like a cult, and they stop speaking to their friends outside the sorority."

22 Yellow hair leads the way to a residential tower on north campus, where her roommate Heather, 18, slouches on a metal cot. Heather is soon to be a resident of Chi Omega's sandstone-and-brick mansion. Her chestnut hair falls to her jaw line. She smiles frequently and smokes a Marlboro red.

23 Heather says she feels "truly blessed" to have been accepted by her sorority. She was intimidated by the size of OSU, and being a sorority sister makes the university feel like a small college.

24 At the same time, Heather criticizes the cruelty of the rush process, in which some sorority girls rate the appearance of potential pledges down to the straightness of their teeth and the number of zits on their faces. (Other girls have spoken of secret sorority guidebooks that subtract points for frizzy hair and cheese thighs.)

25 Heather alleges that at least one sorority at OSU practices a form of hazing known as the "fat table." She describes it: "You have to strip down to your underwear and bra. You sit on a table, and all your sorority sisters circle the fat and ugly parts of your body with magic markers."

26 Heather says her own sorority is cruelty-free. Even if it weren't, she has little to worry about since her teeth are straight, her body is slim and her skin is as pure as a cold glass of milk.

27 "Some sororities you have to dress definitely a certain way," she elaborates. "You have to have your nails done, your hair perfect. You have to dress up all the time in very nice clothes from Express, the Limited, Gap. Anything with heels for shoes. And for going out, all the girls must have tight, hot-bod sex pants."

28 Heather produces a pair of black Lycra pants and models them, holding them in front of her waist.

29   "My particular brand is called Hot Kiss. Tight, hot sex pants are always black. They flare out at the bottom, and they're tight. They're hip-huggers. You wear these with a tight shirt. Maybe a bare midriff. It depends how much you want to show when you go out at night. Some girls wear these to class. I don't."

30   One of the chief benefits of joining a sorority, she says, is having a brimming social calendar.

31   "We have TGs practically every week. This is just a party at a fraternity house. TGs are a group of fraternity guys and a group of sorority girls getting as drunk as they can and dancing.

32   "A crush party is when you have a crush on someone and you send this little note to them. It says, 'You've been crushed, and if you come to this party, you'll find out who has a crush on you.' Usually, we have this at a bar, so everyone can drink a lot.

33   "The formal is, we have to get all dressed up and go in limos somewhere and dance and drink.

34   "My sorority does a lot of philanthropies. We have parties that raise money for them. We usually go to parks. It has to be somewhere we can drink. Because drinking's a big part of philanthropy.

35   "Sororities are almost like an intense version of Girl Scouts, but with lots of alcohol," she observes.

36   According to Heather, a sorority girl reaches the pinnacle of social achievement when she is lavaliered. "Being lavaliered is when a guy gives you his fraternity pin. It's like a pre-engagement to be engaged.

37   "To wear a guy's fraternity pin is a big thing. And for him to give you his fraternity pin is a big thing, because he'll get the crap beat out of him by his fraternity brothers for doing it. First [the young man and his fraternity brothers] all come to the house and sing a serenade for the girl being lavaliered. Then his brothers have to beat the crap out of him. That way, he only gives his pin to a very special girl."

38   Heather beams; a recent lavaliering party comes to mind.

39   "It goes like this: After a sister is lavaliered, the president calls a meeting. We all get in a big circle and pass a candle around. We sing a song. It's about something in the spring, and in all the seasons, how we'll always be sisters. And whoever has been lavaliered will hold the candle and blow it out.

40   "Sometimes a girl will go up to a boy's bedroom at a TG. The big thing in that type of situation is to get his shirt. She'll come down wearing it, but that's not like being lavaliered at all."

41   Some people say that the Greek system is a sort of apartheid, enabling children from predominately white, upper-middle-class enclaves to safely

attend a messily diverse university such as OSU without having to mix with those who are different. Presumably, a sorority is a place where a young white woman can be lavaliered by a fraternity boy, and they can move on to form their own family in a predominately white, upper-middle-class enclave, preferably one that is gated.

42   This theory seems at first to be affirmed when Andrea, a twenty-year-old Alpha Delta Pi, leads the way into her sorority house. She opens the door and enters the all-clear code on the house's burglar alarm. "We have to be safe," she says, pointing south toward a black area of Columbus. "It's total ghetto a few blocks from here. Serious."

43   Andrea is a former cheerleader with scars on her knees from injuries sustained while building a high school homecoming float. As if these credentials weren't enough, she is a straight-A computer-engineering major.

44   She goes into the large, institutional kitchen: "Our cook is a black guy named Bob. He says his wife is a queen in Africa or something." She rolls her eyes with exaggerated disbelief. But later she laughs. "Personally, I'm down with the brown," she says. "Serious. My boyfriend's black."

45   Andrea then describes how, contrary to the apartheid theory, joining a sorority broadened her cultural horizons. She grew up in a rural Ohio town. There were no blacks in her neighborhood, and her high school had a small but active White Knights association, which she describes as a "mini-Ku Klux Klan."

46   "When I got into my sorority," she says, "I found out five of my sisters here were dating black guys. I couldn't believe it. I was like, 'Oh, my God.' I had no idea that went on. And they're, like, marrying these guys, who were really cool.

47   "It was instant attraction when I met my boyfriend. Almost instant. At first, he chased me for a while, because I was, like, scared of the fact that he was black.

48   "I started sleeping with him after we'd been dating not very long. Usually, the rule is I don't sleep with a guy until, like, after two or three months—at least, and a major exchange of gifts at a holiday. Serious. Meet the family, the whole thing. It only took him a month."

49   In the grass outside the student union, a campus lesbian leader and "theoretical feminist" named Mary deconstructs sorority mating rituals. Mary is Hispanic and on full financial aid. She says, "I could never get in. A sorority is a class thing. It's a breeding ground for the next conservative America."

50   Mary lights a cigarette: "I like to look at the power constructs of their rituals, like lavaliering, where the guy gives the girl his pin. Like, he goes to the girl and says, 'I'm going to marry you.'

51   "So then his fraternity brothers beat the crap out of him because he's negating his power as a single male by making that commitment with the girl. He's compromised his male power.

52   "Then she gets to blow out the candle, and that's ending her power in the sorority. She's saying, 'I'm leaving my sisters because I'm going to go live with this dude, and I'm going let him govern my life.'

53   "I look at sororities as whorehouses."

54   Mary tamps out her cigarette and enters the student union. A third-floor meeting room has been reserved for the planners of OSU's fourth annual Take Back the Night Rally, billed as a "march and candlelight vigil to protest rape and other forms of violence against women."

55   The meeting, organized largely by radical feminists, is also being supported by two Delta Phi Epsilons, Rachel Glass and Hallie Fleisch. Hallie and Rachel enter wearing khaki Gap sorority uniforms. Rachel, with her short dark hair in a bob, smiles warmly and sits near Mary. Hallie looks around the room with muted horror, as if she is about to undergo a weird hazing ritual. She peeps a barely audible "hi" and drops into a corner.

56   The other women wear an eclectic mix of combat fatigues, Guatemalan peasant dresses and biker leather gear, such as spiked wrist cuffs and dog collars. As they sprawl out on the floor, vast swaths of armpit and leg hair are exposed.

57   The lesbians are chatting about the Live Homosexual Acts event they are planning to stage on the Oval.

58   "We'll have a lesbian and gay volleyball game."

59   "We should have people bring coat hangers and wire cutters to, like, symbolize putting an end to illegal abortions."

60   Mary brings the meeting to order. A blonde in combat boots suggests that everyone should go around, introduce herself and describe her "first crime." It's intended as a humorous icebreaker.

61   Everyone except Hallie laughs.

62   "My first crime," begins the first person up. "When I was little, I used to go under the porch and pee."

63   "I don't know if porn is a crime in Ohio," says a girl in glasses that resemble welding goggles, "but when I was in elementary school, I used to write porno stories for my girlfriends and write dirty things about the guys they had crushes on."

64   Rachel relates a story about getting a speeding ticket when she was seventeen.

65   It is now Hallie's turn. She looks up with a pained expression. She struggles to say something, then blurts out, "I can't think of anything I've done wrong."

66   Sensing Hallie's discomfort, the others rush to put her at ease. There is a murmur of "That's OK, Hallie."

67   The first order of business is raised by a woman who would like to exclude men from marching. She argues that men shouldn't participate because they are the principal perpetrators of violence against women.

68   Across the room, a young woman begins to cry. "You all know how I feel," she says. "There's a lot of pain."

69   Somebody else begins to cry, and soon everyone is either sniffling or rubbing somebody's back in a comforting, supportive way—except for Hallie, who looks up with a somewhat annoyed expression and asks, "Shouldn't we have a vote or something?"

70   Rachel raises her hand. "I have something to say. Didn't we already put out a press release saying men were invited? Wouldn't we look dumb if we changed our minds now?"

71   "I guess we have to let them march," someone says.

72   "How about if we have them march, like, forty feet behind us?" suggests somebody else.

73   "It's OK if they march," says the leader who originally wanted to ban men altogether, "but they have to make the posters."

74   When the meeting ends, Rachel Glass discusses the balance between being a sorority girl and a feminist. "I'm probably one of the only self-defined, outspoken feminists in my sorority," Rachel says. A senior who is graduating at the end of the summer with a degree in women's studies, Rachel describes herself as coming from an affluent background, "a completely shallow, materialistic culture which pushed me into sorority life."

75   She takes issue with fraternity men, whom she feels view sorority sisters merely as "bodies," but cherishes the sorority's sisterhood and opportunities for leadership, which she feels have made her a strong woman. Her sorority experience was complemented by her exposure to feminism. Both influences have made her stronger and more capable of dealing with a sometimes confusing and hostile male-dominated world. Rachel cites an experience in which she drew on her strength as a feminist.

76   "A [sorority] friend and I were walking home from a party junior year and we got sexually assaulted," she says. "We were walking down the street and this guy totally grabbed my friend's ass. She stopped in her tracks, and

she was like, 'Oh, my God! That guy just touched me.' We were like, 'Oh, my God; oh, my God.' We started walking away really fast. He just, like, unzipped his pants, whipped it out and started jerking off. We both felt violated.

77   "But I coped with it a lot better than she did, and I think that was due to being a feminist and being a women's-studies major and understanding, like, the system of patriarchy and how women are oppressed. I just got angry.

78   "My friend very much internalized it. She blamed herself and was like, 'I shouldn't have worn these tight black pants tonight.' "

79   Reggaefest falls on the day after Greek week ends, but the Kappa Sigma frat brothers who host the event see it as the last big Greek blowout of the year before exams and the farewell of another graduating class.

80   Reggaefest is open to the public and offers four bands performing on the grassy slope in front of the Kappa Sig house, the former governor's mansion. Up to 8,000 people are expected to show.

81   Orange cyclone fencing cordons off the streets surrounding the Kappa Sig grounds. It is drizzling. Columbus police in white caps and shirts that make them resemble sinister ice-cream men with guns mill around beneath a canopy by the stage.

82   Nearby, a campus administrator is having a heated discussion with Jeff, a Kappa Sig organizer of the event. The administrator has smelled alcohol on the breath of Kappa Sigs and their sorority "goddesses" (sorority sisters invited to the private, VIP Kappa Sig house party in exchange for selling tickets) manning the front entrances. Reggaefest is a designated alcohol-free event.

83   Jeff is a lanky, twenty-three-year-old senior political-science major. His attempt to mollify the administrator is hampered by the fact that his own breath reeks of beer, and he is slurring.

84   Jeff finally walks away shouting, "Reggaefest has been voted the Number Two party in America! Now the administration won't even let us serve alcohol! The American people need to know what's happening."

85   Jeff enters the Kappa Sig house. A long-neck Bud appears in his hand as he climbs the stairs. The frat house bears all the signs of wear and tear from heavy partying. Carpets are crusty, walls scuffed and punched in. The halls smell like a truck-stop men's room. A sign tacked to the wall from two nights ago says, "Tonight is May Fifth, Cinco de Mayo. Dress Like Mexicans!"

86   The unofficial, private VIP Kappa Sig party is being held on the third floor. Woozy sorority goddesses stumble through the narrow halls.

87   Two of them, Jenn and Tricia, raise beers and drunken grins. "They try to come down on us," says Jenn. "But we still set it off!"

88   Jenn turns to Tricia: "You know what less alcohol means."

89   "More drugs!" they scream in unison, clinking bottles and guzzling.

90   "Do I have beer on my pants?" Jenn pulls up the tail of the men's shirt she's wearing. A dark stain runs down her pants' butt seam and disappears between her legs. Could be beer; could be pee.

91   Another girl comes by and waves a ruby-red drink under Jeff's nose. "This is a Terry Special. Rum, gin and six different kinds of fruit drinks. It's tasty!"

92   Jeff ignores her. He does an about-face. He clambers down four flights of stairs, leading the way into the basement TG (party) room. There is a mirrored disco ball overhead. The tile floor is so sticky with beer, it's like fly paper. Jeff shoves open a steel fire door leading into a dank cement chamber.

93   "You want to know about sorority girls?" asks Jeff. He sits on a loose foundation stone. "This fraternity taught me how to be a gentleman. You know what they call us [the Kappa Sigs]? The Gentlemen on the Hill.

94   "Here's the secret: We learn how to treat girls like ladies."

95   Jeff begins to sing what he calls the "sweetheart song": "You're as pretty as a picture/You're as sweet as you can be/I love you most sincerely/You're all this world to me."

96   He stops. "That's it. When a girl is really special, that's what we do. You serenade her, you pin her, give her a ring, give her a rose."

97   At ten o'clock the Itals are playing, but the lawn in front of the Kappa Sig house is mostly empty. There are just a few hundred dancers, not the expected 8,000.

98   The sorority goddess who had been drinking the Terry Special on the third floor is outside talking excitedly to someone in the darkness. "I want to marry a rich man," she declares. "I want to go to an Ivy League grad school, find a brilliant professor and follow him!"

99   Jeff surveys the dismal turnout. "This party sucks. It's a disgrace. I'm ashamed," he states. "Let's go fuck some sorority girls. It can be arranged. Anyone you want."

100   He stumbles across the lawn. "Fuck a sorority girl," he repeats, apparently forgetting the bull session of twenty minutes ago in which he declared his chivalrous ideals, learned through fraternity life.

101   Jeff climbs under a section of plastic cyclone fence along the driveway. In the darkness there appears to be a row of cinder blocks, perhaps the top of a wall. Jeff steps forward, then disappears. There is a dull thump, like a cantaloupe dropping onto the floor in a supermarket.

102   Jeff lies on the asphalt at the bottom of a five foot drop. He springs up, unfazed by his fall. "Anybody see?" he asks.

103   There is an apartment block thirty feet across the yard. Partyers spill out from the yellow light of a sliding porch door.

104   "You want to fuck a sorority girl?" Jeff babbles, leading the way into the apartment. "My Kappa Sig brothers can arrange everything."

105   Inside, girls are piled two and three deep on the couches of a small TV room. They stare ahead, smiling and laughing dully at nothing in particular.

106   There is a large guy in sunglasses. Someone identifies him as a recently graduated Kappa Sig. He reaches into his pocket and pulls out a handful of triangle-shaped, blue-green pills. Ecstasy.

107   "Let's double team one of these babes tonight!" he shouts, handing out tabs to all takers.

108   Jeff leans against a sliding door in the entrance. The flesh around his mouth is slack. His forehead looks chalky and damp. His eyes are dull. First-aid manuals commonly describe these symptoms as the initial signs of shock.

109   Jeff's collar is flecked with blood. Partially coagulated blood runs down the back of his neck in the shape of a slug. It is suggested he go back to the Kappa Sig house and seek medical attention, or at least lie down.

110   Jeff weaves back to the Kappa Sig house, cutting a wide swath around the wall that felled him minutes ago. The gentleman on the hill vanishes inside the former governor's mansion.

111   The sorority goddess who had been drinking Terry Specials, then plotting to find a brilliant Ivy League professor, stands on the steps. She is being supported by two fraternity brothers. "I never drink," she babbles. "I'm a good girl. I'm a good girl. I'm really a good girl."

Controlling Substances

The U.S. prison population—now at 1.8 million—has nearly quadrupled since the early 1980s, which means that our nation now has the highest rate of incarceration in the world. A great many of those in prison are nonviolent drug offenders, usually small-timers who need help with their own addictions. In the late 1980s, in the face of a crack cocaine epidemic that was then ravaging the nation's cities and claiming the lives of citizens as prominent as Boston Celtics star Len Bias, legislators and law enforcement agents cracked down by instituting mandatory minimum sentences. Because those who inform on others can often win reduced sentences, small-time drug violators often get stiffer sentences than major dealers. According to *Newsweek*, 6 percent of those in state prisons in 1980 were there for drug violations; in 1996 the figure was 23 percent. In 1980, 25 percent of those in federal prisons were drug violators, while in 2000 the figure had risen to over 60 percent.

Should we be so hard on drug dealers and abusers? Is the "war on drugs" that has been conducted by the federal government (and by the states) in the 1990s going so poorly that it should be abandoned? Many people think so. Often they call attention not only to the figures on in-

An estimated 70 million Americans have tried marijuana.

> **Of every one hundred people who have smoked marijuana, only twenty-eight have tried cocaine—and only one uses cocaine weekly.**

carceration but also to the other social costs associated with strict drug laws. For example, many addicts resist treatment because they fear punishment; instead, they commit crimes to support their bad habits. Widespread urine testing and seizures of drug-related property have threatened basic civil rights and undermined respect for police. Extensions of the drug war have led to conflicts with other nations where drugs are produced. Moreover, if drugs were considered a medical and social problem rather than a criminal one, citizens could be helped rather than sent to prison. Needle-exchange programs could help check the spread of AIDS by reducing the incidence of shared needles. Recognizing that illegal drugs often are no worse and no better than alcohol (legal since the disastrous 1920s experiment known as Prohibition), Californians voted to legalize marijuana use for cancer and AIDS patients. Many people, drawing from the experiences of other nations, are now calling for moves to decriminalize some kinds of drug use, or at least to reduce penalties and increase treatment. In other words, the war on drugs might be maintained—but without quite so much prison warehousing.

On the other hand, many people argue for a continuing hard line on drugs because of the damage that illegal drugs do. They point to the health risks

Reformer Carry Nation holding the weapons of her trade: a hatchet for destroying liquor containers and a copy of the Bible

and social costs—to early deaths, lost work days, and broken lives attributable to substance abuse. In the tradition of Carry Nation and other temperance warriors who successfully lobbied for prohibition of alcohol in the 1920s, they have evidence that drug use (especially cocaine use) has decreased during the years of the war on drugs, that marijuana may be a "gateway drug" to more dangerous substances (because marijuana smokers are far more likely to try other drugs, such as cocaine), and that the war on drugs is worth waging for all sorts of other reasons.

Advocates of a hard line on drugs sometimes take on not only drug kingpins but also others—alcohol producers, Big Tobacco, performance-enhancing drug users. For example, they promote stiff taxes on cigarettes and alcohol on the grounds that making harmful sub-stances expensive discourages use and pays for the social costs involved. And they are often proponents of testing athletes for the use of unfair and danger-ous performance-enhancing new substances, such as steroids (which promote muscle growth but have harmful side effects), androstenedione (which base-ball slugger Mark McGwire used during his pursuit of home-run records), and creatine (a "dietary supplement" that many athletes feel helps their training). They point to the popularity of such substances among youngsters. They also work to combat binge drinking on campuses, regarding it as a frightening epi-demic that encourages date rape, promotes vandalism, and otherwise ruins or undermines the lives of countless college students.

Should certain substances be tightly regulated—and which ones? Is sub-stance abuse a victimless crime we have to live with in order to preserve a free society? Is education the only proper approach to the problem? If not, what exactly should be done about various drugs, alcohol, tobacco, and other con-troversial substances? Just how should we weigh the risks of drug use against the social costs of overzealous law enforcement? We offer here in *Good Reasons with Contemporary Arguments* a number of arguments related to these ques-tions. You might begin by looking again at the exchange on pages 187–190 be-tween Milton Friedman and William Bennett on the issue of legalizing drugs—and then consider the similar debate below among Joseph Kane, Gerald Lynch, and Joseph Califano. Then follow spirited arguments by Robert Samuelson and others (on tobacco), a cartoon and an ad that ridicule the pos-sibility of restrictions on junk food, and two other visual arguments, directed toward students, on the dangers of alcohol. The final two arguments have to do with performance-enhancing drugs used by athletes—an evaluation of major league base-ball's anti-steroid legisla-tion by Tom Verducci and a proposal for creat-ing fairer conditions for Olympic-caliber athletes by Malcolm Gladwell.

> **Androstenedione (aka "andro") is now being marketed in a chewing gum by a California company. The product is expected to be available on the market soon. Andro supposedly increased the libido in German athletes in the 1980s to levels that "bordered on nymphomania."**
>
> **—*www.healthcentral.com***

J O S E P H   P.   K A N E

The Challenge of Legalizing Drugs

*Joseph P. Kane, a Jesuit priest, has worked in a low-income area of the
Bronx, New York, and served as chaplain at Rikers Island prison for over
two decades. He has edited* Who Is the Prisoner, *a collection of articles
on possible reforms in the U.S. justice system. The following essay
appeared in 1992 in* America, *a weekly magazine for Catholics that has a
middle-of-the-road editorial position. The article is answered in the
selection by Gerald W. Lynch that follows.*

1   Why are many responsible people proposing that the manufacture and
distribution of drugs should be legally regulated just as alcohol is? Has
legalization effectively controlled alcohol use? Alcohol consumption, we
know, actually increased with the repeal of Prohibition. Given the devastating harm that addictive drugs cause, and the heartache, broken homes and
carnage on U.S. highways caused by alcohol, why would intelligent and
well-intentioned people like Milton Friedman and many other conservatives
want to legalize drugs? In this article, I want to examine attitudes toward
drug users, evaluate some positive and harmful effects of present drug policies and discuss what America needs to deal effectively with drugs. Finally, I
will argue, legalizing drugs is only part of the solution.

How Prohibition Fosters Crime and Abuse

2   How does legalization affect drug users and addicts? America's history with
addictive drugs suggests that policy for drug users is more effectively developed by a Surgeon General than by an Attorney General. During Prohibition,
society often abused moonshiners and drunks. When a drunkard violated the
law, we often saw only a criminal and forgot the person. Prohibition surely
did not create the proper attitudes within America to treat alcoholism effectively. Today, however, precisely because alcohol consumption is legal, alcoholics can be treated compassionately as sick people. The same result
would obtain, I suggest, if we legalized addictive drugs.

3   Even if legalization could increase opportunities for compassionate
treatment toward users/abusers, would not legalizing drugs increase crime?
I doubt it. In fact, present drug policies actually foster crime in four ways.

4   First, because the price of illegal drugs is very high, poor addicts rob
and burglarize. Wealthy users/abusers can afford not to steal. As a prison

chaplain, I do not see addicted movie stars, sports figures or Wall Street bro-kers, because their money buys expensive drugs without the need to steal and obtains drug therapy without months of waiting. Pricing drugs reason-ably by legalization would virtually eliminate the crimes that terrify us. How many Americans rob or kill, I ask you, for a six-pack of beer?

5   Second, illegal drugs net astronomical profits for which people are will-ing to kill. Drug-related homicide rates are soaring, and innocent bystanders are caught in the cross fire. The same thing happened during the Prohibition era. *The Untouchables* and similar film portrayals of the roaring 20's depict the ruthless violence among alcohol pushers that afflicted mainstream soci-ety. Today's slaughter mirrors those Prohibition homicide rates, which dropped immediately upon repeal. Homicides did not rise to the same rates until 1979. Such figures invite reflection on lessons painfully learned during Prohibition.

6   Third, present drug policies foster crime by overwhelming our criminal justice system with drug arrests. Police resources, courts and prisons are mired in drug arrests and consequently unable to deal effectively with other serious threats to our safety.

7   Fourth, by subjecting addicts to imprisonment instead of offering therapy, we further debase and alienate them. Such treatment confirms their belief that they are bad people and makes awareness of their sickness and possible treatment less probable. Ex-convicts return to our streets as angry and desperate addicts more likely to rob for a fix.

Abusing the Poor

8   Besides fostering crime, present drug policies abuse our society in many ways. Illegal drugs foster irresponsible attitudes about work. On my block, for example, kids who work in supermarkets or McDonald's are considered "chumps." Who would work for $120 a week when they can earn $300 per evening? This fast money buys fancy clothing and may even earn respect at home for young dealers paying their families' bills. A local Boy Scout leader surprised me by insisting that drug legalization is the only way to save his friends from the lucrative and dangerous drug world. These illegal dealers are not evil. They say, "Good evening, Father," and I respond warmly with the same respect that I give to bartenders.

9   Our war on drugs, furthermore, teaches that some people are "better dead than drugged." Heroin users/abusers are dying from AIDS, and still we refuse to legalize the dispensation of clean syringe needles to them. In ef-fect, our drug policies deliberately endanger any person who wants to use a drug that may be lethal, just as "hooch" and "moonshine" endangered another generation—because these drugs are produced by outlaws.

10   Then, by not providing adequate detoxification and therapy programs, we systematically abuse addicted people who want to stop their drug use. New York City incarcerates one drug user/abuser at a cost of more than $150 per day—whereas therapy programs that actually deal with the problem of addiction cost half that. Drug-war money hires police, Federal agents, judges, court personnel, prison contractors, correctional officers and parole officers—and for all practical purposes ignores the needs of people who use/abuse drugs. Addicts without money face at least a four-month waiting period for therapy. Without access to drug programs upon request, they cannot break the bonds of addiction.

11   Indeed, the so-called drug war grievously abuses minorities with grossly higher rates of incarceration. New York City, for example, warehouses about 20,000 prisoners on any given day; over 14,000 are incarcerated for drug-related crimes. They are the city's poor and over 90 percent are young blacks and Hispanics. Percentages vary throughout the country, but statistics clearly indicate that America disproportionately imprisons minorities with the highest incarceration rate in the world. Illegal drugs are sold to these prisoners even in maximum security prisons—with much higher profits for illegal distributors. What does this say about stopping drugs at our borders?

12   In addition, America's drug war abuses poor people in other countries. Can we honestly expect Peruvians to grow their nation's food when coca increases their earnings astronomically? All the violence over drug turf that we experience in the United States has become a tragic reality in some very poor areas of South America. Our Government's use of military operations against the coca industry exposes nothing so much as the futility of drug policies that must battle uphill against the power of sheer economics. Worse yet, desperately poor foreigners become "mules." They swallow balloon bags of cocaine or conceal drug packages in terrifying attempts to pass through U.S. Customs and earn $3,000. After they are arrested, our justice system destroys them. "Three years to life" is the usual minimum sentence that I hear; often they receive eight years to life. Unfortunately, selling lucrative illegal drugs is also a sore temptation for many poor Americans when their legal income is inadequate for basic needs.

Changing Attitudes

13   Merely legalizing dangerous drugs, of course, does not solve drug problems. Our attitudes toward even legal drugs must change. As educated, middle-class Americans cut down on drinking and stop smoking cigarettes, tobacco and liquor companies focus their advertising upon third-world people within and outside the United States. This was recently dramatized by a

clergyman in Harlem. He and some parishioners whitewashed billboards advertising alcohol and cigarettes. The pastor's message was clear: "Don't seduce my people with death-dealing drugs." In effect, they were protesting against America's tendency to lose interest in issues that do not affect mainstream people—and our lack of commitment to those who are least able to protect themselves from exploitative advertising.

14 In order to deal effectively with addictive drugs, our perceptions need to include the broader and disturbing reality of America's use and abuse of medicinal drugs. Many average Americans use such drugs irresponsibly. Bathroom medicine chests of the 1930's contained aspirin, band-aids, cotton, mercurochrome, peroxide; open a medicine chest today and you discover a whole pharmacy. Indigestion must be relieved so that we can return immediately to eating irresponsibly. Bloodshot eyes, nasal congestion, insomnia, heartburn or headaches—all require drugs. Unfortunately, we and our doctors often turn to drugs before determining whether a change of behavior might be more appropriate. This "quick-fix" mentality, I say, provides the context for America's abuse of more menacing drugs.

15 There has always been, is now and will always be abuse/addiction. Some who seek escape from too much pressure or too little meaning in their lives will become alcoholics, addicted gamblers or "crack heads." But the normal way to limit the damage is to ban 100 percent alcohol, to crack down on loan sharks and to legalize lotteries—and we could do the same with cocaine. Unless we see drug users/abusers in this context, we will remain unable to respond to them humanely and effectively. The law is misused if it aspires to make saints.

16 In addition, we need to realize, first, that seductive advertising for alcohol and nicotine, although legal, is immoral and should become a serious issue for everyone. Given America's present concern for the danger of cocaine, heroin and marijuana, we have a unique opportunity to restrict all dishonest advertising that irresponsibly tempts people to use any addictive substances. We can enact regulations that foster responsible advertising and distribution of tobacco or alcohol. Such controls will be appropriate, as well, for advertising and distributing other dangerous drugs that Americans seek for a buzz even at the risk of addiction.

17 Second, Americans need to learn more about the sickness called addiction. Drug-rehabilitation centers show us proven methods for treating drug addicts and helping their families. The highly effective 12-step programs for various addictions are based on spiritual healing, which is diametrically opposed to our present drug laws based on coercion and violence that can never heal.

18   Despite the adamant rejection of legalization by many ex-addicts and drug-program personnel, we need to face the fact that today's drug policies incarcerate and debase people just for using drugs, whereas addicts need drug programs. Is there not something dishonest about drug policies in which lower-class drug users, labeled criminals, go to prison while middle-class addicts, labeled alcoholics, go to therapy?

Effective Policy

19   The legalization of hard drugs does not mean that we don't need law enforcement to help protect us from dangerous drug users. Everyone who wants to operate cars, trains and buses should be monitored for alcohol or other drug consumption that would impede his or her performance. We also require protection from abusive drug and alcohol users who constitute a menace to other citizens. But why arrest people just for using addictive drugs?

20   What we need instead are "statutory abuse" laws similar to statutory rape laws that protect minors. Anyone arrested for selling drugs to a minor would have no excuse based on ignorance of the purchaser's age: Seller beware!

21   We also need to empower young people to deal responsibly with seductive invitations to drug use. Adults can help to protect children by showing them the fantasy and intent of captivating commercials. Responsible concern for honest advertising entails more than minuscule skull-and-bones warnings on cigarette packs. Laws do not remove our obligation to educate others about the danger surrounding us—and laws that lull America into complacency are no substitute for that education.

22   Mothers Against Drunk Drivers (MADD) provides a good model. Instead of lobbying to restore Prohibition, this group educates us about the danger of mixing alcohol and driving. The mothers lobby for the enforcement of strict laws against driving while under the influence of a drug, and thus they show us that education and intelligent law enforcement—not prohibition—are the effective approaches to addictive and potentially dangerous drugs.

23   Education about drugs is essential; otherwise, drugs—legal or not—will remain a grave problem. The elementary and middle schools in the town of Islip, N.Y., recently published a booklet of students' articles and drawings to educate youngsters about the dangers of drugs. The approach showed concern for alcohol and tobacco use and abuse. There was no mention of jails. Powerful drugs were treated as substances dangerous to one's health and well-being. The message was positive: We are concerned for you. Love yourself and treat yourself well. This should be America's attitude to all drug users.

Legalization: Part of a First Step

24   Legalizing addictive drugs would probably increase their use. At least we know that the repeal of alcohol prohibition had that effect. So, how can we responsibly legalize them? For the same reasons that we keep alcohol legal! Just as we do not choose to return to Prohibition because we do not want gang wars, a growing disrespect for law, astronomical illegal profits, corrupted law enforcement personnel or the sickness and even deaths from impure substances, so we do not want our loved ones—whether addicts or social users who want a buzz from a drug or a drink—to become involved with outlaws.

25   A responsible approach to addictive drugs requires control of production with safe dosages, accountable advertising and restricted distribution through state-managed "drug stores." Distribution centers should offer drug education, counseling and treatment referrals to adequately funded programs. This responsible tone is absent in today's liquor stores, off-track betting parlors and gambling casinos. Offering these addictive drugs and activities in a responsible manner might show the way for using them in a saner manner. Our present policies are unable to fulfill these requirements.

26   What could we expect from a new drug policy that promoted respect, education and therapy? Drug dealers would be licensed and supervised in a market controlled by laws—not, as now, by outlaws. Eliminating inflated prices would reduce the crimes perpetrated by people desperate for a fix. Law enforcement personnel would be freed to protect us from crime. The release of Drug War prisoners convicted of drug use, possession and sales would save vast sums of money. Taxes on all legalized drugs should fund the education and treatment programs that a responsible society would create as a sane response to addictive drugs.

27   Changing present drug laws makes sense. Americans wisely rejected the prohibition of alcohol and we are not considering it for tobacco because we realize the waste of money involved. Instead of prisons for people who use or abuse drugs, the United States needs legal control, education and therapy programs.

GERALD W. LYNCH

Legalizing Drugs Is Not the Solution

Gerald W. Lynch responds to the previous argument in the following piece, which was originally published in the same magazine, America, *in 1993. Lynch is president of the John Jay College of Criminal Justice in New York City.*

1   In "The Challenge of Legalizing Drugs" (*America,* August 8, 1992), Joseph P. Kane, S. J., presents a compelling description of the devastation wreaked on our society by drug abuse, but draws some troubling conclusions supporting the legalization of drugs. Father Kane argues that illegal drugs promote the proliferation of crime because of the huge profits associated with their import and sales. Violence and murder have increased dramatically as dealers and gangs compete for turf and drug profits. Youngsters are attracted to selling drugs in order to earn more money than they could ever hope to earn in legitimate jobs. Addicts steal to pay for their drugs. The criminal justice system is overwhelmed by the increasing number of drug arrests.

2   He further argues that because drugs are illegal, addicts are treated as criminals rather than as sick people in need of help. Addicts are often arrested and processed through the criminal justice system rather than offered legitimate rehabilitation or treatment. Finally, he states that illegal drugs exploit the poor, whose struggle to survive makes drug dealing a sometimes necessary alternative.

3   The solution to the problem, he concludes, is to legalize drugs while at the same time (1) changing attitudes within our society about drugs; (2) changing laws and public policy; (3) and providing drug education and treatment to all those who want it. While Father Kane's description of the toll drugs are taking on our society and our citizens is poignant, the solution to this problem is not legalization.

4   Legalizing drugs will almost certainly increase their use. This has been well documented in a number of studies. J. F. Mosher points out that alcohol usage and rates of liver disease declined significantly during Prohibition ("Drug Availability in a Public Health Perspective" in *Youth and Drugs: Society's Mixed Messages* [1990]). Moreover, following repeal of the 18th Amendment, the number of drinkers in the United States increased by 60 percent.

5   The most widely abused drugs in our society are tobacco, alcohol and prescription drugs—the legal drugs and those which are most widely available.

A recent report issued by the Federal Government states that approximately 57 million people in this country are addicted to cigarettes, 18 million are addicted to alcohol and 10 million are abusing psychotherapeutic drugs. By comparison, crack, heroin and hallucinogens each accounts for one million addicts. Further, the report states that every day in this country 1,000 people die of smoking-related illnesses, 550 die of alcohol-related accidents and diseases, while 20 die of drug overdoses and drug-related homicides. In addition, the annual costs of health care and lost productivity to employers are estimated at $600 billion for alcoholism and $60 billion for tobacco-related ailments. For all illegal drugs, however, the comparable cost is an estimated $40 billion (see "Making America Drug Free: A New Vision of What Works," *Carnegie Quarterly* [Summer 1992]). These data clearly demonstrate that the drugs which are most available are the most abused, the most dangerous and the most costly.

6   As the number of people using drugs increases, babies born to addicted mothers will increase as well. According to a report issued by the New York City Public Schools in 1991, during the preceding 10 years babies born to substance-abusing mothers increased 3,000 percent. It is estimated that each year approximately 10,000 babies are born exposed to drugs. With greater availability of drugs, it is inevitable that more babies will be born to substance-abusing mothers. According to guidelines offered by the Children Prenatally Exposed to Drugs Program of the Los Angeles Unified School District, the following are among the characteristics of the child prenatally exposed to drugs: neurological problems, affective disorders, poor concentration, delayed language development, impaired social skills, difficulty in play. The extent to which children of addicted fathers may be impaired is not yet known. Legalizing drugs will surely compound the tragedy to our society of these most innocent victims.

7   Drug legalization would not eliminate crime. Although crimes associated with obtaining drugs might decrease with legalization, other crimes, especially violent crimes, would increase. As many as 80 percent of violent crimes involve alcohol and drugs. A number of studies have demonstrated the relationship between drugs and homicides, automobile deaths, child abuse and sexual abuse. It is estimated that drugs and alcohol are involved in 50 percent to 75 percent of cases of suicidal behavior. According to recent pharmacological research, certain drugs, especially cocaine, have the tendency to elicit violent behavior because of changes that take place in the neurotransmitter systems of the brain.

8   Many experts think that unless there were free access to unlimited quantities of drugs, there would be a black market even after legalization.

Drugs, even if legal, would still cost money. Since many addicts cannot maintain jobs, they would continue to engage in stealing and prostitution to pay for drugs and would continue to subject their families and friends to abuse.

9   Experiments with the decriminalization of drugs have failed. A case in point is Zurich, Switzerland. There the city set aside a park, the Platzpitz, in which drugs were decriminalized and were available with no legal consequences. Health care was made accessible and clean syringes were supplied. It was hoped that there would be a reduction in crime, better health care for addicts and containment of the problem to a defined area of the city. The experiment failed dramatically.

10   As reported in the *New York Times* on February 11, 1992, and London's *Financial Times* on January 4, 1992, Zurich's drug-related crime and violence actually increased. Drug users and dealers converged on the Swiss city from other countries throughout Europe. The health-care system was overwhelmed as drug users had to be resuscitated. As drug dealers began to compete for business, the cost of drugs decreased. One addict was quoted as saying, "Too many kids were getting hooked too easily." The Platzpitz, a garden spot in the center of Zurich, was devastated. Statues were marred with graffiti. The ground was littered with used syringes and soaked with urine. Citizens avoided the area and the city finally ended its experiment. The park was closed and surrounded by a high fence to keep out the drug addicts and dealers. Plans are now being implemented to renovate the park and restore its original beauty. Zurich has served as a real-life experiment that proves the failure of decriminalization.

11   We believe that we must change public attitudes toward drugs and focus on prevention and treatment, but we must also maintain the laws making drugs illegal. A goal of prevention is to create an environment that rejects drug use and dealing. Effective prevention involves a comprehensive approach that includes the following components: education, including information about drugs; helping children understand the pressures from friends, family and school that may promote the use of drugs; social-competency skills to assist them in resisting the temptations of drugs; making available intervention (counseling, treatment) to those who have begun to use drugs; promoting positive alternatives to drug use; providing training to those who relate to children and influencing social policies (see *An Assessment of Substance Abuse Prevention,* New York State Division of Substance Abuse Services, October 1989).

12   Effective prevention efforts also attempt to promote negative attitudes toward drug use by communicating clear, consistent anti-substance-abuse messages through the mass media, within communities and in educational

settings. A final important prevention strategy is to enforce stringently the laws against illegal drugs in order to control their availability.

13   When community prevention efforts are coupled with strong and decisive national leadership, the chances for change are greatly enhanced. Perhaps the most dramatic examples of the effectiveness of these partnerships are the anti-drunk driving and anti-smoking campaigns. These campaigns grew out of public intolerance of problems that not only plagued their communities, but decimated their children. Volunteers, community activists, parents and youth groups organized, developed community prevention strategies and applied unrelenting pressure on public officials, the private sector and the media. These activists were influential in shifting public attitudes. At the same time, Federal as well as state and local officials passed laws and changed public policies to regulate smoking in public areas, limit advertising and increase drunk-driving penalties. The result has been fewer traffic fatalities and a decrease in the social acceptability of drunk driving and smoking.

14   A study conducted by the New York State Division of Substance Abuse Services in 1990 found that during the preceding 12 years marijuana, cocaine and alcohol use had declined among school-age children. National data show similar trends. Studies of high school seniors conducted over the past decade have shown a dramatic decline in drug use as well. Legalizing drugs now would only send a confused message that could be interpreted as implying that the Government condones their use.

15   While legalization may appear to be a realistic solution to a very difficult problem, it would be a tremendous mistake. With legalization would come an increase in availability of drugs and an increase in the problems associated with their abuse: the suffering of addicts and their loved ones; the death and loss of thousands of innocent lives; great costs to society, to the health-care system, to employers, and, above all, social, economic and emotional costs to our children.

16   Instead of legalizing drugs, we must devote massive resources to education and treatment. We must communicate the clear and consistent message that drugs are destructive and will not be tolerated. We must so change public policy and attitudes that every addict who wants treatment can receive it. We must continue to use our resources to enforce the laws against drugs in order to keep drugs out of our communities. Rather than giving up the fight and legalizing drugs, it is crucial that we redouble our efforts to solve the problem.

JOSEPH CALIFANO, JR.

It's Drugs, Stupid

Joseph Califano, Jr. (1931–   ) served as Secretary of Health, Education, and Welfare in the Carter administration, during which he promoted antismoking campaigns—and quit smoking four packs a day himself in 1975. He is now president of a nonprofit research center dealing with all forms of drug abuse: the National Center on Addiction and Substance Abuse at Columbia University in New York. His argument reprinted here appeared in the New York Times Magazine *on January 29, 1995.*

1   Despite all the Republican preening and Democratic pouting since November 8, neither political party gets it. If Speaker Newt Gingrich is serious about delivering results from his party's "Contract With America" and if President Clinton means to revive his Presidency, each can start by recognizing how fundamentally drugs have changed society's problems and that together they can transform Government's response.

Joseph Califano, Jr.

2   For 30 years, America has tried to curb crime with more judges, tougher punishments and bigger prisons. We have tried to rein in health costs by manipulating payments to doctors and hospitals. We've fought poverty with welfare systems that offer little incentive to work. All the while, we have undermined these efforts with our personal and national denial about the sinister dimension drug abuse and addiction have added to our society. If Gingrich and Clinton want to prove to us that they can make a difference in what really ails America, they should "get real" about how drugs have recast three of the nation's biggest challenges.

3   LAW, ORDER AND JUSTICE   In 1960 there were fewer than 30,000 arrests for drug offenses; in 30 years, that number soared beyond one million. Since 1989, more individuals have been incarcerated for drug offenses than for *all violent crimes*—and most violent crimes are committed by drug (including alcohol) abusers.

4   Probation and parole are sick jokes in most cities. As essential first steps to rehabilitation, many parolees need drug treatment and after-care,

which means far more monitoring than their drug-free predecessors of a generation ago required, not less. Yet in Los Angeles, for example, probation officers are expected to handle as many as 1,000 cases at a time. With most offenders committing drug- or alcohol-related crimes, it's no wonder so many parolees go right back to jail: 80 percent of prisoners have prior convictions and more than 60 percent have served time before.

5   Congress and state legislatures keep passing laws more relevant to the celluloid gangsters and inmates of classic 1930's movies than 1990's reality. Today's prisons are wall to wall with drug dealers, addicts, alcohol abusers and the mentally ill (often related to drug abuse). The prison population shot past a million in 1994 and is likely to double soon after the year 2000. Among industrialized nations, the United States is second only to Russia in the number of its citizens it imprisons: 519 per 100,000, compared with 368 for next-place South Africa, 116 for Canada and 36 for Japan.

6   Judges and prosecutors are demoralized as they juggle caseloads of more than twice the recommended maximum. In 1991 eight states had to close their civil jury trial systems for all or part of the year to comply with speedy trial requirements of criminal cases involving drug abusers. Even where civil courts remain open, the rush of drug-related cases has created intolerable delays—4 years in Newark, 5 in Philadelphia and up to 10 in Cook County, Ill. In our impersonal, bureaucratic world, if society keeps denying citizens timely, individual hearings for their grievances, they may blow off angry steam in destructive ways.

7   HEALTH CARE COST CONTAINMENT   Emergency rooms from Boston to Baton Rouge are piled high with the debris of drug use on city streets—victims of gunshot wounds, drug-prompted child and spouse abuse, and drug-related medical conditions like cardiac complications and sexually transmitted diseases. AIDS and tuberculosis have spread rapidly in large part because of drug use. Beyond dirty needles, studies show that teenagers high on pot, alcohol or other drugs are far more likely to have sex, and to have it without a condom.

8   Each year drugs and alcohol trigger up to $75 billion in health care costs. The cruelest impact afflicts the half-million newborns exposed to drugs during pregnancy. Crack babies, a rarity a decade ago, crowd $2,000-a-day neonatal wards. Many die. It can cost $1 million to bring each survivor to adulthood.

9   Even where prenatal care is available—as it is for most Medicaid beneficiaries—women on drugs tend not to take advantage of it. And as for drug treatment, only a relatively small percentage of drug-abusing pregnant

mothers seek it, and they must often wait in line for scarce slots. Pregnant mothers' failure to seek prenatal care and stop abusing drugs accounts for much of the almost $3 billion that Medicaid spent in 1994 on inpatient hospital care related to drug use.

10 THE FIGHT AGAINST POVERTY   Drugs have changed the nature of poverty. Nowhere is this more glaring than in the welfare systems and the persistent problem of teenage pregnancy.

11   Speaker Gingrich and President Clinton are hell-bent to put welfare mothers to work. But all the financial lures and prods and all the job training in the world will do precious little to make employable the hundreds of thousands of welfare recipients who are addicts and abusers.

12   For too long, reformers have had their heads in the sand about this unpleasant reality. Liberals fear that admitting the extent of alcohol and drug abuse among welfare recipients will incite even more punitive reactions than those now fashionable. Conservatives don't want to face up to the cost of drug treatment. This political denial assures failure of any effort to put these welfare recipients to work.

13   The future is not legalization. Legalizing drug use would write off millions of minority Americans, especially children and drug-exposed babies, whose communities are most under siege by drugs. It has not worked in any nation where it's been tried, and our own experience with alcohol and cigarettes shows how unlikely we are to keep legalized drugs away from children.

14   Drugs are the greatest threat to family stability, decent housing, public schools and even minimal social amenities in urban ghettos. Contrary to the claim of pot proponents, marijuana is dangerous. It devastates short-term memory and the ability to concentrate precisely when our children need them most—when they are in school. And a child 12 to 17 years old who smokes pot is 85 times as likely to use cocaine as a child who does not. Cocaine is much more addictive than alcohol, which has already hooked more than 18 million Americans. Dr. Herbert D. Kleber, a top drug expert, estimates that legalizing cocaine would give us at least 20 million addicts, more than 10 times the number today.

15   It's especially reckless to promote legalization when we have not committed research funds and energies to addiction prevention and treatment on a scale commensurate with the epidemic. The National Institutes of Health spend some $4 billion for research on cancer, cardiovascular disease and AIDS, but less than 15 percent of that amount for research on substance abuse and addiction, the largest single cause and exacerbator of those diseases.

16   Treatment varies widely, from inpatient to outpatient, from quick-fix acupuncture to residential programs ranging a few weeks to more than a year, from methadone dependence to drug-free therapeutic communities. Fewer than 25 percent of the individuals who need drug or alcohol treatment enter a program. On average, a quarter complete treatment; half of them are drug- or alcohol-free a year later. In other words, with wide variations depending on individual circumstances, those entering programs have a one-in-eight chance of being free of drugs or alcohol a year later. Those odds beat many for long-shot cancer chemotherapies, and research should significantly improve them. But a recent study in California found that even at current rates of success, $1 invested in treatment saves $7 in crime, health care and welfare costs.

17   Here are a few suggestions for immediate action to attack the dimension drugs have added to these three problems:

- Grant Federal funds to state and Federal prison systems only if they provide drug and alcohol treatment and after-care for all inmates who need it.

- Instead of across-the-board mandatory sentences, keep inmates with drug and alcohol problems in jails, boot camps or halfway houses until they experience a year of sobriety after treatment.

- Require drug and alcohol addicts to go regularly to treatment and after-care programs like Alcoholics Anonymous while on parole or probation.

- Provide Federal funds for police only to cities that enforce drug laws throughout their jurisdiction. End the acceptance of drug bazaars in Harlem and southeast Washington that would not be tolerated on Manhattan's Upper East Side or in Georgetown.

- Encourage judges with lots of drug cases to employ public health professionals, just as they hire economists to assist with antitrust cases.

- Cut off welfare payments to drug addicts and alcoholics who refuse to seek treatment and pursue after-care. As employers and health professionals know, addicts need lots of carrots and sticks, including the threat of loss of job and income, to get the monkey off their back.

- Put children of drug- or alcohol-addicted welfare mothers who refuse treatment into foster care or orphanages. Speaker Gingrich and First Lady Hillary Rodham Clinton have done the nation a disservice by playing all-or-nothing politics with this issue. The compassionate and cost-effective middle ground is to identify those parents who abuse their children by their own drug and alcohol abuse and place those children in decent orphanages and foster care until the parents shape up.

- Subject inmates, parolees and welfare recipients with a history of substance abuse to random drug tests, and fund the treatment they need. Liberals must recognize that getting off drugs is the only chance these individuals (and their babies) have to enjoy their civil rights. Conservatives who preach an end to criminal recidivism and welfare dependency must recognize that reincarceration and removal from the welfare rolls for those who test positive is a cruel Catch-22 unless treatment is available.

18   Fortunately, the new Congress and the new Clinton are certain not to legalize drugs. Unfortunately, it is less clear whether they will recognize the nasty new strain of intractability that drugs have added to crime, health costs and welfare dependency, and go on to tap the potential of research, prevention and treatment to save billions of dollars and millions of lives.

19   If a mainstream disease like diabetes or cancer affected as many individuals and families as drug and alcohol abuse and addiction do, this nation would mount an effort on the scale of the Manhattan Project to deal with it.

ROBERT SAMUELSON

The Amazing Smoke Screen

The following attack by Robert Samuelson on the antismoking crusade appeared in Newsweek *on November 30, 1998.*

1   We may have closure—at least temporarily—to the anti-smoking crusade of the 1990s. The agreement between state attorneys general and the tobacco companies for the industry to pay the states roughly $200 billion over 25 years may quiet the controversy. If so, this will be the agreement's main benefit, because otherwise it is a parody of good government policy. It imposes a steep tax on a heavily poor part of the population; it offers only modest health benefits; and it deepens popular confusion about the public consequences of smoking.

2   Let's concede the small possible health gains. The agreement will raise cigarette prices; tobacco analyst Martin Feldman of Salomon Smith Barney figures that retail prices will go from an average $2.07 a pack now to $2.90 in the year 2000. Higher prices might reduce the number of smokers by a few percentage points of the population. However, it seems unlikely that the restrictions on advertising (banning billboards and promotional giveaways) will lower teen smoking. In the 1990s, the country has been awash in anti-smoking news stories and TV programs that are worth billions of dollars in counter-advertising. Meanwhile, some surveys show teen smoking has risen. This seems to confirm the industry's contention that advertising mainly determines which brands people smoke, not whether they smoke.

3   Let's also note that the agreement aids the tobacco industry. By reducing the threat of lawsuits, it bolsters companies' stock prices. Still, the great myth of this struggle is that, just because cigarettes are unhealthy and the tobacco industry is often dishonest, the people on the other side must be morally superior. In truth, they—meaning plaintiffs' lawyers, politicians and public-health advocates—also frequently pursue their goals with a single-minded dishonesty and hypocrisy. And their motives are often selfish: personal enrichment (the lawyers); power and popularity (the politicians); and ego gratification (the public-health advocates).

4   Little wonder the results are disheartening. Almost everyone has long known that smoking is dangerous, as a review of surveys by Lydia Saad for the Roper Center for Public Opinion Research at the University of Connecticut reveals: in 1954, 70 percent of the public thought smoking "harmful"

and 42 percent thought it "one of the causes of lung cancer"; by 1990, these responses were 96 percent and 94 percent. Most Americans also think that smokers decide for themselves whether to smoke. A 1997 poll asked who is "more responsible for . . . smoking-related illnesses," smokers or tobacco companies. By 76 percent to 17 percent, respondents said smokers.

5   The debate's central issue ought to be: how much is society entitled to penalize smokers for their decisions, because—in society's view—those decisions are unhealthy? Should present smokers be punished (via higher taxes) to deter future smokers? Should Congress order the Food and Drug Administration to mandate safer, and maybe less satisfying, cigarettes? These hard questions pit Americans' belief in personal freedom against the desire to protect public health. Precisely because the questions are hard, anti-smoking advocates diverted the debate to three other ideas, all dubious.

6   First, smokers aren't responsible for their behavior. As teens, they're seduced by industry ads; then they can't stop because smoking is addictive.

7   Second, smoking creates huge social costs—mainly higher health spending—that nonsmokers pay through higher taxes.

8   Finally, the tobacco industry should be punished and forced to compensate nonsmokers for smoking's social costs.

9   Well. Even if smoking is addictive, people can—often with much pain and hard work—break addictions. There are now more ex-smokers than smokers. As for higher government costs, studies have shown that—because smokers die earlier than nonsmokers—they create savings for government through lower lifetime health and pension costs. The states' anti-tobacco suits alleged that smokers raised states' health costs under the Medicaid program. This, too, is unproven; the industry's analysis disputed it.

10   But suppose smokers lack free will and raise government's costs. Still, the industry could not pay those costs directly without going bankrupt. The money always has had to come from smokers through higher cigarette prices—the equivalent of a tax increase. Anti-smoking advocates rarely discuss this, because the implications are devastating. Smokers have low incomes. Only 20 percent of cigarette taxes are paid by those with incomes over $50,000; 34 percent are paid by those with incomes under $20,000 and 19 percent by those with incomes between $20,000 and $30,000. Moreover, smokers already pay steep federal and state cigarette taxes (now averaging about 58 cents a pack) that more than cover any possible public costs they create.

11   As a result, the anti-smoking crusade becomes a reverse Robin Hood arrangement: it sanctifies soak-the-poor taxes and robs the poor to pay the rich. The attorneys general's agreement now enshrines this. The rich, of

course, are the private lawyers who represent the states in their tobacco suits. The agreement allows up to $500 million in annual fees for perhaps a few hundred and at most a few thousand lawyers. For how long? Arbitrators will decide; these payments come atop fees to be paid in four existing state settlements that will almost certainly total billions. The cigarette dispute has evolved into a welfare program that may create some instant billionaires and many multimillionaires.

12   Because none of this can be defended, it is camouflaged. For self-interested reasons, the anti-smoking advocates never openly described public choices. Beyond taxing smokers to cut smoking, politicians want to keep the taxes—and not to rebate them. Public-health advocates covet extra money for pet programs; and lawyers crave their fees. All this has involved an adept manipulation of courts and legislatures. A gullible public—aided by a pliant press—embraced the anti-smoking hysteria. Because the campaign succeeded, it will inspire assaults against other industries. We can't tell the target (whether alcohol, or autos or fatty foods) or the tactics. But it's just a matter of time.

The American Legacy Foundation, based in Washington, D.C., is dedicated to "building a world where young people reject tobacco and where anyone can quit," according to its Web site (www.americanlegacy.org). Among other things, the foundation places antismoking ads in the mass media. The one published here appeared in The New Yorker *in September 2002.*

Garry Trudeau (1948–   ) won the Pulitzer Prize for his comic strip "Doonesbury" in 1975. A graduate of Yale University, Trudeau began making fun of bigwigs while in college, and his widely syndicated cartoons continue to satirize prominent figures and address current controversies. The strip published here appeared in January 2002.

Source: DOONESBURY © 2002 G. B. Trudeau. Reprinted with permission of UNIVERSAL PRESS SYNDICATE. All rights reserved.

The two visual arguments on this page ridicule the idea that American corporations might be held responsible for obesity. Do you agree that obesity is simply a matter of personal responsibility?

© 1998 John Trever, *Albuquerque Journal*. Reprinted by permission.

Binge Drinking on College Campuses

Faced with what they viewed as an epidemic of alcohol abuse on college campuses (and, more specifically, an epidemic of binge drinking), college presidents at over 100 major universities in 1999 sponsored an antibinge-drinking ad campaign. The presidents placed ads, like the one on this page, in college newspapers all over the United States.

Hitting

college campuses

this fall.

It's tough to be a college kid today. That's why we've developed Binge Beer.® At Binge, we understand that sometimes you just need five or six drinks the night before that big test. And there's nothing quite like a couple of quarts of liquid courage before going out to make new friends. We understand what it's like. Who says falling off a balcony is such a bad thing? And what's an occasional riot? Or even a little assault between friends? Thousands of college students across the country have already discovered Binge. And this year, thousands more will try it. Don't think that's a good idea? Neither do we, but we need your help in convincing our students of the dangers. Talk to your kids about binge drinking, or visit our website at www.nasulgc.org/bingedrink.

An Argument about Alcohol

*Ads promoting Absolut vodka are among the most recognizable ones
that appear in mass circulation magazines. These ads cleverly show
Absolut vodka bottles that mimic the shape of common objects in
order to indicate the pervasiveness—and social acceptance—of alcohol
consumption in general and the consumption of Absolut vodka in
particular. Recently an organization called Adbusters has been trying
to make people more critical of the ads they consume each day. The
ad reprinted here, parodying Absolut ads, represents one of the ways
that Adbusters is attempting to educate the public.*

TOM VERDUCCI

A Dopey Policy

Tom Verducci joined the staff of Sports Illustrated *in 1993, and he remains one of the magazine's top baseball writers. He also contributes regular commentary to CNN and to CNNSI.com. Born in 1969 in East Orange, New Jersey, where he was a star athlete, he received his journalism degree from Penn State in 1982. The following analysis appeared in* Sports Illustrated *in the summer of 2002.*

1   Major League Baseball and the players' association made sure to pat themselves on the back for including a steroid-testing program in the labor agreement they announced on August 30. Yeah. And Communist Russia once boasted of holding free elections. If there is anything in baseball easier to beat than the Tampa Bay Devil Rays, it's the steroid-testing plan. "It's not a drug test. It's an IQ test," said Gary Wadler, a New York University School of Medicine professor and a member of the World Anti-Doping Agency research committee. "You would have to flunk an IQ test to flunk it."

2   The testing program is the laughingstock of drug experts. The American Swimming Coaches Association is so outraged at the policy that it is seeking to have players' union head Donald Fehr removed from the United States Olympic Committee, calling his position on the board of directors "anathema to the USOC antidoping efforts" and saying that he "continues to give the USA an international black eye." Fehr declined to comment.

3   Baseball's plan amounts to nothing more than a public relations attempt to quell fan distrust after an SI investigation into rampant use of steroids and other performance-enhancing drugs in baseball. Said Wadler, "They're trying in escape the bullet by coming out with a sound bite."

4   One veteran player who was close to the negotiations admitted that the owners "came to us and basically said, 'Come up with something to make this [image problem] go away.'

5   "Let's face it," the player went on, "they like all the home runs. This policy is a small step forward, but it's not going to change a whole lot."

6   Baseball will test only for Schedule III steroids, which are illegal without a prescription. Players can continue to freely take muscle enhancers such as human growth hormone, which is clinically used to treat dwarfism, and androstenedione, an over-the-counter supplement that has the proper-

ties of a steroid because the body converts it into testosterone. Both of those are banned by the IOC and the NFL.

7   Unlike those organizations, baseball will not conduct off-season testing, giving players the green light to juice up for four months before competition. Testing next year will be conducted for survey purposes only. Half the players will be tested in spring training and half in the regular season. Most of the steroids used by players leave the body a couple of weeks after use. "You get off the stuff right before spring training, and then your only risk is which batch of players you're in," the veteran player said. "Then, once you take your test, you're home free [to use again]." The NFL tests seven or eight players per team every week of its season.

8   "Baseball players will learn to pick and choose when to use, when to start and stop," said Wadler. "It's really not that hard."

9   If more than 5 percent of next year's tests return positive, all players will then be subject to random testing for each of the next two years. If fewer than 5 percent of the tests are positive, only survey testing will remain in place. Because the union represents 40-man rosters, that means baseball allows up to 60 players to use steroids before it even considers it has a problem. That's the equivalent of two major league teams.

10   Mets catcher Vance Wilson, the team's assistant player representative, said even one unannounced test "is going to deter people from using—definitely." More likely, it will simply force them to work their steroid cycles around the test. And next spring, when the usual passel of players reports to camp having added 20 pounds of bulk over the winter, you'll have every right to raise an eyebrow when they credit their weight room dedication for the increased strength.

MALCOLM GLADWELL

Drugstore Athlete

*Malcolm Gladwell (1963–   ) has been writing for some time about
fascinating cultural developments of one kind or another—why crime
can drop suddenly, how a particular book becomes a best seller, the rise
of hair coloring products for women and suicide rates in Micronesia, the
fascination for Ritalin, the spread of coffee. In 2000 he published* The
Tipping Point, *a book that investigates a number of cultural phenomena
as if they were "social epidemics" that spread in the same way that
infectious diseases do. Gladwell was a reporter, often on science, for the*
Washington Post *from 1987 to 1996; since then his work has often
appeared in* The New Yorker, *as did the following piece (September 10,
2001). (For another example of his work, see his essay "Listening to
Khakis" on page 509.)*

1.

1   At the age of twelve, Christiane Knacke-Sommer was plucked from a small
town in Saxony to train with the elite SC Dynamo swim club, in East Berlin.
After two years of steady progress, she was given regular injections and
daily doses of small baby-blue pills, which she was required to take in the
presence of a trainer. Within weeks, her arms and shoulders began to
thicken. She developed severe acne. Her pubic hair began to spread over her
abdomen. Her libido soared out of control. Her voice turned gruff. And her
performance in the pool began to improve dramatically, culminating in a
bronze medal in the hundred-metre butterfly at the 1980 Moscow Olympics.
But then the Wall fell and the truth emerged about those little blue pills. In
a new book about the East German sports establishment, *Faust's Gold*,
Steven Ungerleider recounts the moment in 1998 when Knacke-Sommer
testified in Berlin at the trial of her former coaches and doctors:

2   "Did defendant Gläser or defendant Binus ever tell you that the blue
pills were the anabolic steroid known as Oral-Turinabol?" the prosecutor
asked. "They told us they were vitamin tablets," Christiane said, "just like
they served all the girls with meals." "Did defendant Binus ever tell you the
injection he gave was Depot-Turinabol?" "Never," Christiane said, staring at
Binus until the slight, middle-aged man looked away. "He said the shots
were another kind of vitamin." "He never said he was injecting you with the
male hormone testosterone?" the prosecutor persisted. "Neither he nor Herr

Gläser ever mentioned Oral-Turinabol or Depot-Turinabol," Christiane said firmly. "Did you take these drugs voluntarily?" the prosecutor asked in a kindly tone. "I was fifteen years old when the pills started," she replied, beginning to lose her composure. "The training motto at the pool was, 'You eat the pills, or you die.' It was forbidden to refuse."

3   As her testimony ended, Knacke-Sommer pointed at the two defendants and shouted, "They destroyed my body and my mind!" Then she rose and threw her Olympic medal to the floor.

4   Anabolic steroids have been used to enhance athletic performance since the early sixties, when an American physician gave the drugs to three weight lifters, who promptly jumped from mediocrity to world records. But no one ever took the use of illegal drugs quite so far as the East Germans. In a military hospital outside the former East Berlin, in 1991, investigators discovered a ten-volume archive meticulously detailing every national athletic achievement from the mid-sixties to the fall of the Berlin Wall, each entry annotated with the name of the drug and the dosage given to the athlete. An average teenage girl naturally produces somewhere around half a milligram of testosterone a day. The East German sports authorities routinely prescribed steroids to young adolescent girls in doses of up to thirty-five milligrams a day. As the investigation progressed, former female athletes, who still had masculinized physiques and voices, came forward with tales of deformed babies, inexplicable tumors, liver dysfunction, internal bleeding, and depression. German prosecutors handed down hundreds of indictments of former coaches, doctors, and sports officials, and won numerous convictions. It was the kind of spectacle that one would have thought would shock the sporting world. Yet it didn't. In a measure of how much the use of drugs in competitive sports has changed in the past quarter century, the trials caused barely a ripple.

5   Today, coaches no longer have to coerce athletes into taking drugs. Athletes take them willingly. The drugs themselves are used in smaller doses and in creative combinations, leaving few telltale physical signs, and drug testers concede that it is virtually impossible to catch all the cheaters, or even, at times, to do much more than guess when cheating is taking place. Among the athletes, meanwhile, there is growing uncertainty about what exactly is wrong with doping. When the cyclist Lance Armstrong asserted last year, after his second consecutive Tour de France victory, that he was drug-free, some doubters wondered whether he was lying, and others simply assumed he was, and wondered why he had to. The moral clarity of the East German scandal—with its coercive coaches, damaged athletes, and corrupted competitions—has given way to shades of gray. In today's climate,

the most telling moment of the East German scandal was not Knacke-Sommer's outburst. It was when one of the system's former top officials, at the beginning of his trial, shrugged and quoted Brecht: "Competitive sport begins where healthy sport ends."

2.

6   Perhaps the best example of how murky the drug issue has become is the case of Ben Johnson, the Canadian sprinter who won the one hundred metres at the Seoul Olympics, in 1988. Johnson set a new world record, then failed a post-race drug test and was promptly stripped of his gold medal and suspended from international competition. No athlete of Johnson's calibre has ever been exposed so dramatically, but his disgrace was not quite the victory for clean competition that it appeared to be.

7   Johnson was part of a group of world-class sprinters based in Toronto in the nineteen-seventies and eighties and trained by a brilliant coach named Charlie Francis. Francis was driven and ambitious, eager to give his athletes the same opportunities as their competitors from the United States and Eastern Europe; and in 1979 he began discussing steroids with one of his prize sprinters, Angella Taylor. Francis felt that Taylor had the potential that year to run the two hundred metres in close to 22.90 seconds, a time that would put her within striking distance of the two best sprinters in the world, Evelyn Ashford, of the United States, and Marita Koch, of East Germany. But, seemingly out of nowhere, Ashford suddenly improved her two-hundred-metre time by six-tenths of a second. Then Koch ran what Francis calls, in his autobiography, *Speed Trap*, a "science fictional" 21.71. In the sprints, individual improvements are usually measured in hundredths of a second; athletes, once they have reached their early twenties, typically improve their performance in small, steady increments, as experience and strength increase. But these were quantum leaps, and to Francis the explanation was obvious. "Angella wasn't losing ground because of a talent gap," he writes; "she was losing because of a drug gap, and it was widening by the day." (In the case of Koch, at least, he was right. In the East German archives, investigators found a letter from Koch to the director of research at VEB Jenapharm, an East German pharmaceutical house, in which she complained, "My drugs were not as potent as the ones that were given to my opponent Brbel Eckert, who kept beating me." In East Germany, Ungerleider writes, this particular complaint was known as "dope-envy.") Later, Francis says, he was confronted at a track meet by Brian Oldfield, then one of the world's best shot-putters:

8   "When are you going to start getting serious?" he demanded. "When are you going to tell your guys the facts of life?" I asked him how he could tell they weren't already using steroids. He replied that the muscle density just wasn't there. "Your guys will never be able to compete against the Americans—their careers will be over," he persisted.

9   Among world-class athletes, the lure of steroids is not that they magically transform performance—no drug can do that—but that they make it possible to train harder. An aging baseball star, for instance, may realize that what he needs to hit a lot more home runs is to double the intensity of his weight training. Ordinarily, this might actually hurt his performance. "When you're under that kind of physical stress," Charles Yesalis, an epidemiologist at Pennsylvania State University, says, "your body releases corticosteroids, and when your body starts making those hormones at inappropriate times it blocks testosterone. And instead of being anabolic—instead of building muscle—corticosteroids are catabolic. They break down muscle. That's clearly something an athlete doesn't want." Taking steroids counteracts the impact of corticosteroids and helps the body bounce back faster. If that home-run hitter was taking testosterone or an anabolic steroid, he'd have a better chance of handling the extra weight training.

10   It was this extra training that Francis and his sprinters felt they needed to reach the top. Angella Taylor was the first to start taking steroids. Ben Johnson followed in 1981, when he was twenty years old, beginning with a daily dose of five milligrams of the steroid Dianabol, in three-week on-and-off cycles. Over time, that protocol grew more complex. In 1984, Taylor visited a Los Angeles doctor, Robert Kerr, who was famous for his willingness to provide athletes with pharmacological assistance. He suggested that the Canadians use human growth hormone, the pituitary extract that promotes lean muscle and that had become, in Francis's words, "the rage in elite track circles." Kerr also recommended three additional substances, all of which were believed to promote the body's production of growth hormone: the amino acids arginine and ornithine and the dopamine precursor L-dopa. "I would later learn," Francis writes, "that one group of American women was using three times as much growth hormone as Kerr had suggested, in addition to 15 milligrams per day of Dianabol, another 15 milligrams of Anavar, large amounts of testosterone, and thyroxine, the synthetic thyroid hormone used by athletes to speed the metabolism and keep people lean." But the Canadians stuck to their initial regimen, making only a few changes: Vitamin B_{12}, a non-steroidal muscle builder called inosine, and occasional shots of testosterone were added; Dianabol was dropped in favor of a newer steroid

called Furazabol; and L-dopa, which turned out to cause stiffness, was re-placed with the blood-pressure drug Dixarit.

11   Going into the Seoul Olympics, then, Johnson was a walking phar-macy. But—and this is the great irony of his case—none of the drugs that were part of his formal pharmaceutical protocol resulted in his failed drug test. He had already reaped the benefit of the steroids in intense workouts leading up to the games, and had stopped Furazabol and testosterone long enough in advance that all traces of both supplements should have disap-peared from his system by the time of his race—a process he sped up by tak-ing the diuretic Moduret. Human growth hormone wasn't—and still isn't—detectable by a drug test, and arginine, ornithine, and Dixarit were legal. Johnson should have been clean. The most striking (and unintentionally hi-larious) moment in *Speed Trap* comes when Francis describes his bewilder-ment at being informed that his star runner had failed a drug test—for the anabolic steroid stanozolol. "I was floored," Francis writes:

12   To my knowledge, Ben had never injected stanozolol. He occa-sionally used Winstrol, an oral version of the drug, but for no more than a few days at a time, since it tended to make him stiff. He'd always discontinued the tablets at least six weeks be-fore a meet, well beyond the accepted "clearance time." . . . After seven years of using steroids, Ben knew what he was doing. It was inconceivable to me that he might take stanozolol on his own and jeopardize the most important race of his life.

13   Francis suggests that Johnson's urine sample might have been deliber-ately contaminated by a rival, a charge that is less preposterous than it sounds. Documents from the East German archive show, for example, that in international competitions security was so lax that urine samples were sometimes switched, stolen from a "clean" athlete, or simply "borrowed" from a noncompetitor. "The pure urine would either be infused by a catheter into the competitor's bladder (a rather painful procedure) or be held in con-doms until it was time to give a specimen to the drug control lab," Ungerlei-der writes. (The top East German sports official Manfred Höppner was once in charge of urine samples at an international weight-lifting competition. When he realized that several of his weight lifters would not pass the test, he broke open the seal of their specimens, poured out the contents, and, Ungerleider notes, "took a nice long leak of pure urine into them.") It is also possible that Johnson's test was simply botched. Two years later, in 1990, track and field's governing body claimed that Butch Reynolds, the world's four-hundred-metre record holder, had tested positive for the steroid nan-

drolone, and suspended him for two years. It did so despite the fact that half of his urine-sample data had been misplaced, that the testing equipment had failed during analysis of the other half of his sample, and that the lab technician who did the test identified Sample H6 as positive—and Reynolds's sample was numbered H5. Reynolds lost the prime years of his career.

14   We may never know what really happened with Johnson's assay, and perhaps it doesn't much matter. He was a doper. But clearly this was something less than a victory for drug enforcement. Here was a man using human growth hormone, Dixarit, inosine, testosterone, and Furazabol, and the only substance that the testers could find in him was stanozolol—which may have been the only illegal drug that he hadn't used. Nor is it encouraging that Johnson was the only prominent athlete caught for drug use in Seoul. It is hard to believe, for instance, that the sprinter Florence Griffith Joyner, the star of the Seoul games, was clean. Before 1988, her best times in the hundred metres and the two hundred metres were, respectively, 10.96 and 21.96. In 1988, a suddenly huskier FloJo ran 10.49 and 21.34, times that no runner since has even come close to equalling. In other words, at the age of twenty-eight—when most athletes are beginning their decline—Griffith Joyner transformed herself in one season from a career-long better-than-average sprinter to the fastest female sprinter in history. Of course, FloJo never failed a drug test. But what does that prove? FloJo went on to make a fortune as a corporate spokeswoman. Johnson's suspension cost him an estimated $25 million in lost endorsements. The real lesson of the Seoul Olympics may simply have been that Johnson was a very unlucky man.

3.

15   The basic problem with drug testing is that testers are always one step behind athletes. It can take years for sports authorities to figure out what drugs athletes are using, and even longer to devise effective means of detecting them. Anabolic steroids weren't banned by the International Olympic Committee until 1975, almost a decade after the East Germans started using them. In 1996, at the Atlanta Olympics, five athletes tested positive for what we now know to be the drug Bromantan, but they weren't suspended, because no one knew at the time what Bromantan was. (It turned out to be a Russian-made psycho-stimulant.) Human growth hormone, meanwhile, has been around for twenty years, and testers still haven't figured out how to detect it.

16   Perhaps the best example of the difficulties of drug testing is testosterone. It has been used by athletes to enhance performance since the fifties,

and the International Olympic Committee announced that it would crack down on testosterone supplements in the early eighties. This didn't mean that the I.O.C. was going to test for testosterone directly, though, because the testosterone that athletes were getting from a needle or a pill was largely indistinguishable from the testosterone they produce naturally. What was proposed, instead, was to compare the level of testosterone in urine with the level of another hormone, epitestosterone, to determine what's called the T/E ratio. For most people, under normal circumstances, that ratio is 1:1, and so the theory was that if testers found a lot more testosterone than epitestosterone it would be a sign that the athlete was cheating. Since a small number of people have naturally high levels of testosterone, the I.O.C. avoided the risk of falsely accusing anyone by setting the legal limit at 6:1.

17   Did this stop testosterone use? Not at all. Through much of the eighties and nineties, most sports organizations conducted their drug testing only at major competitions. Athletes taking testosterone would simply do what Johnson did, and taper off their use in the days or weeks prior to those events. So sports authorities began randomly showing up at athletes' houses or training sites and demanding urine samples. To this, dopers responded by taking extra doses of epitestosterone with their testosterone, so their T/E would remain in balance. Testers, in turn, began treating elevated epitestosterone levels as suspicious, too. But that still left athletes with the claim that they were among the few with naturally elevated testosterone. Testers, then, were forced to take multiple urine samples, measuring an athlete's T/E ratio over several weeks. Someone with a naturally elevated T/E ratio will have fairly consistent ratios from week to week. Someone who is doping will have telltale spikes—times immediately after taking shots or pills when the level of the hormone in his blood soars. Did all these precautions mean that cheating stopped? Of course not. Athletes have now switched from injection to transdermal testosterone patches, which administer a continuous low-level dose of the hormone, smoothing over the old, incriminating spikes. The patch has another advantage: once you take it off, your testosterone level will drop rapidly, returning to normal, depending on the dose and the person, in as little as an hour. "It's the peaks that get you caught," says Don Catlin, who runs the U.C.L.A. Olympic Analytical Laboratory. "If you took a pill this morning and an unannounced test comes this afternoon, you'd better have a bottle of epitestosterone handy. But, if you are on the patch and you know your own pharmacokinetics, all you have to do is pull it off." In other words, if you know how long it takes for you to get back under the legal limit and successfully stall the test for that period, you can probably pass the test. And if you don't want to take that chance, you can

just keep your testosterone below 6:1, which, by the way, still provides a whopping performance benefit. "The bottom line is that only careless and stupid people ever get caught in drug tests," Charles Yesalis says. "The elite athletes can hire top medical and scientific people to make sure nothing bad happens, and you can't catch them."

4.

18   But here is where the doping issue starts to get complicated, for there's a case to be made that what looks like failure really isn't—that regulating aggressive doping, the way the 6:1 standard does, is a better idea than trying to prohibit drug use. Take the example of erythropoietin, or EPO. EPO is a hormone released by your kidneys that stimulates the production of red blood cells, the body's oxygen carriers. A man-made version of the hormone is given to those with suppressed red-blood-cell counts, like patients undergoing kidney dialysis or chemotherapy. But over the past decade it has also become the drug of choice for endurance athletes, because its ability to increase the amount of oxygen that the blood can carry to the muscles has the effect of postponing fatigue. "The studies that have attempted to estimate EPO's importance say it's worth about a three-, four-, or five-per-cent advantage, which is huge," Catlin says. EPO also has the advantage of being a copy of a naturally occurring substance, so it's very hard to tell if someone has been injecting it. (A cynic would say that this had something to do with the spate of remarkable times in endurance races during that period.)

19   So how should we test for EPO? One approach, which was used in the late nineties by the International Cycling Union, is a test much like the T/E ratio for testosterone. The percentage of your total blood volume which is taken up by red blood cells is known as your hematocrit. The average adult male has a hematocrit of between thirty-eight and forty-four per cent. Since 1995, the cycling authorities have declared that any rider who had a hematocrit above fifty per cent would be suspended—a deliberately generous standard (like the T/E ratio) meant to avoid falsely accusing someone with a naturally high hematocrit. The hematocrit rule also had the benefit of protecting athletes' health. If you take too much EPO, the profusion of red blood cells makes the blood sluggish and heavy, placing enormous stress on the heart. In the late eighties, at least fifteen professional cyclists died from suspected EPO overdoses. A fifty-per-cent hematocrit limit is below the point at which EPO becomes dangerous.

20   But, like the T/E standard, the hematocrit standard had a perverse effect: it set the legal limit so high that it actually encouraged cyclists to titrate

their drug use up to the legal limit. After all, if you are riding for three weeks through the mountains of France and Spain, there's a big difference between a hematocrit of forty-four per cent and one of 49.9 per cent. This is why Lance Armstrong faced so many hostile questions about EPO from the European press—and why eyebrows were raised at his five-year relationship with an Italian doctor who was thought to be an expert on performance enhancing drugs. If Armstrong had, say, a hematocrit of forty-four per cent, the thinking went, why wouldn't he have raised it to 49.9, particularly since the rules (at least, in 2000) implicitly allowed him to do so. And, if he didn't, how on earth did he win?

21   The problems with hematocrit testing have inspired a second strategy, which was used on a limited basis at the Sydney Olympics and this summer's World Track and Field Championships. This test measures a number of physiological markers of EPO use, including the presence of reticulocytes, which are the immature red blood cells produced in large numbers by EPO injections. If you have a lot more reticulocytes than normal, then there's a good chance you've used EPO recently. The blood work is followed by a confirmatory urinalysis. The test has its weaknesses. It's really only useful in picking up EPO used in the previous week or so, whereas the benefits of taking the substance persist for a month. But there's no question that, if random EPO testing were done aggressively in the weeks leading to a major competition, it would substantially reduce cheating.

22   On paper, this second strategy sounds like a better system. But there's a perverse effect here as well. By discouraging EPO use, the test is simply pushing savvy athletes toward synthetic compounds called hemoglobin-based oxygen carriers, which serve much the same purpose as EPO but for which there is no test at the moment. "I recently read off a list of these new blood-oxygen expanders to a group of toxicologists, and none had heard of any of them," Yesalis says. "That's how fast things are moving." The attempt to prevent EPO use actually promotes inequity: it gives an enormous advantage to those athletes with the means to keep up with the next wave of pharmacology. By contrast, the hematocrit limit, though more permissive, creates a kind of pharmaceutical parity. The same is true of the T/E limit. At the 1986 world swimming championships, the East German Kristin Otto set a world record in the hundred-metre freestyle, with an extraordinary display of power in the final leg of the race. According to East German records, on the day of her race Otto had a T/E ratio of 18:1. Testing can prevent that kind of aggressive doping; it can insure no one goes above 6:1. That is a less than perfect outcome, of course, but international sports is not a perfect world. It is a place where Ben Johnson is disgraced and FloJo runs free,

where Butch Reynolds is barred for two years and East German coaches pee into cups—and where athletes without access to the cutting edge of medicine are condemned to second place. Since drug testers cannot protect the purity of sport, the very least they can do is to make sure that no athlete can cheat more than any other.

5.

23 The first man to break the four-minute mile was the Englishman Roger Bannister, on a windswept cinder track at Oxford, nearly fifty years ago. Bannister is in his early seventies now, and one day last summer he returned to the site of his historic race along with the current world-record holder in the mile, Morocco's Hicham El Guerrouj. The two men chatted and compared notes and posed for photographs. "I feel as if I am looking at my mirror image," Bannister said, indicating El Guerrouj's similarly tall, high-waisted frame. It was a polite gesture, an attempt to suggest that he and El Guerrouj were part of the same athletic lineage. But, as both men surely knew, nothing could be further from the truth.

24 Bannister was a medical student when he broke the four-minute mile in 1954. He did not have time to train every day, and when he did he squeezed in his running on his hour-long midday break at the hospital. He had no coach or trainer or entourage, only a group of running partners who called themselves "the Paddington lunch time club." In a typical workout, they might run ten consecutive quarter miles—ten laps—with perhaps two minutes of recovery between each repetition, then gobble down lunch and hurry back to work. Today, that training session would be considered barely adequate for a high-school miler. A month or so before his historic mile, Bannister took a few days off to go hiking in Scotland. Five days before he broke the four-minute barrier, he stopped running entirely, in order to rest. The day before the race, he slipped and fell on his hip while working in the hospital. Then he ran the most famous race in the history of track and field. Bannister was what runners admiringly call an "animal," a natural.

25 El Guerrouj, by contrast, trains five hours a day, in two two-and-a-half-hour sessions. He probably has a team of half a dozen people working with him: at the very least, a masseur, a doctor, a coach, an agent, and a nutritionist. He is not in medical school. He does not go hiking in rocky terrain before major track meets. When Bannister told him, last summer, how he had prepared for his four-minute mile, El Guerrouj was stunned. "For me, a rest day is perhaps when I train in the morning and spend the afternoon at the cinema," he said. El Guerrouj certainly has more than his share of natural ability,

but his achievements are a reflection of much more than that: of the fact that he is better coached and better prepared than his opponents, that he trains harder and more intelligently, that he has found a way to stay injury free, and that he can recover so quickly from one day of five-hour workouts that he can follow it, the next day, with another five-hour workout.

26   Of these two paradigms, we have always been much more comfortable with the first: we want the relation between talent and achievement to be transparent, and we worry about the way ability is now so aggressively managed and augmented. Steroids bother us because they violate the honesty of effort: they permit an athlete to train too hard, beyond what seems reasonable. EPO fails the same test. For years, athletes underwent high-altitude training sessions, which had the same effect as EPO—promoting the manufacture of additional red blood cells. This was considered acceptable, while EPO is not, because we like to distinguish between those advantages which are natural or earned and those which come out of a vial.

27   Even as we assert this distinction on the playing field, though, we defy it in our own lives. We have come to prefer a world where the distractable take Ritalin, the depressed take Prozac, and the unattractive get cosmetic surgery to a world ruled, arbitrarily, by those fortunate few who were born focused, happy, and beautiful. Cosmetic surgery is not "earned" beauty, but then natural beauty isn't earned, either. One of the principal contributions of the late twentieth century was the moral deregulation of social competition—the insistence that advantages derived from artificial and extraordinary intervention are no less legitimate than the advantages of nature. All that athletes want, for better or worse, is the chance to play by those same rules.

On Censorship

In 1967 Congress established the National Commission on Pornography that concluded, in a 1970 report, that it is not pornography but puritanical attitudes toward sexuality that contribute to sexual deviancy in the United States. But this conclusion hardly resolved the issue: A minority of the commission members released its own final report condemning the conclusions of the majority and attempting to establish links between pornography and crime that would justify restrictions on pornography. Since then the war of words has continued unabated, with censors attempting to restrict the kind of art supported by the

Larry Flint

National Endowment for the Arts and free speech advocates uneasily defending the likes of Larry Flint and his *Hustler* magazine.

When pornographic depictions seemed to grow more explicit and sadistic after the commission's reports, attorney Catharine MacKinnon in the 1980s opposed pornography on feminist grounds. MacKinnon and writer Andrea Dworkin, regarding pornography (especially visual pornography in magazines and film) as a form of prostitution, as a matter of power and powerlessness,

> The harm of pornography is the harm of male supremacy made difficult to see because of its pervasiveness, potency, and success in making the world a pornographic place. . . . To the extent that pornography succeeds in constructing social reality, it becomes invisible as harm.
>
> —*Catharine MacKinnon, 1989*

and as a de facto humiliation that degrades women in the service of male supremacy, advocated civil rights laws restricting pornography that were subsequently passed in Minneapolis, Indianapolis, and other cities (but overturned in the courts). MacKinnon and Dworkin have been both widely supported and widely opposed in their efforts by people—feminists and nonfeminists alike—who feel that they have overstated the incidence and the negative effects of pornography in the United States.

Censorship is not directed at pornography alone. Some citizens have been more concerned about suppressing violence in the media. In the wake of stubborn and sensational violence that seems endemic to American life, many have blamed depictions of violence on television and in films for desensitizing people, especially children, to violence, or for glamorizing violence so that young people are more likely to engage in violent behaviors themselves. Still other people have been concerned with restricting certain books and other materials from being available in schools. Lists of the Ten Commandments and the flag of the Confederate States of America have been "censored" in certain places. And you have probably also witnessed arguments by those who would restrict "free" expression in other ways as well. The arguments offered on both sides indicate why censorship issues can make for strange bedfellows: It is not easy to predict what a "liberal" or a "conservative" position on a given censorship issue might be.

In recent years, concern has shifted to the Internet. Shocked by the prevalence of pornography on the Internet (sometimes including the dissemination of sexually explicit photographs without the permission of the person photographed), by Web sites created by extremist militia groups and hate groups, or by individuals who offer guns—

> Congress shall make no law . . . abridging the freedom of speech, or of the press.
>
> —*First Amendment to the U.S. Constitution*
>
> If the First Amendment means anything, it means that a state has no business telling a [person], sitting alone in his own house, what books he may read or what films he may watch.
>
> —*Supreme Court Justice Thurgood Marshall, 1969*

or advice on bomb construction—on the Internet, many have called for schools and libraries to install censorware on computers. Some libraries are being sued by parents for not keeping indecent electronic materials away from children, and some universities have disciplined students for posting hate messages on the Internet. In 1996 Congress passed the Communications Decency Act in an effort to regulate pornography on line; when it was declared unconstitutional, Congress then responded in 1998 with the Child Online Protection Act, which prohibits the publication of materials on line that could be harmful to children. And America Online (AOL) now requires each of its subscribers to agree "to use the AOL service only for lawful purposes. Member is prohibited from posting or transmitting through the AOL service any unlawful, harmful, threatening, abusive, harassing, defamatory, vulgar, obscene, profane, hateful, racially, ethnically or otherwise objectionable material of any kind."

Is such a policy bad? Do laws designed to restrict speech, writing, and images violate the Constitution? AOL supporters note that some restrictions

A protester (flanked by TV cameras) outside the Capitol building in Washington, D.C., testing a law that banned flag burning

The most stringent protection of free speech would not protect a man in falsely shouting "Fire!" in a crowded theater and causing a panic. The question in every case is whether the words used are used in such circumstances and are of such a nature as to create a clear and present danger that they will bring about the substantive evils that Congress has a right to prevent.

—*Supreme Court Justice*
Oliver Wendell Holmes, 1919

There is no such thing as a moral or immoral book. Books are well written or badly written. That is all.

—*Oscar Wilde*

Some Internet Links to the Censorship Issue and Usenet Groups

alt.censorship	alt.society.civil-liberties
alt.comp.acad-freedom.talk	clari.news.issues.censorship
alt.freedom.of.information.act	news.admin.censorship
alt.politics.correct	eff.org
alt.primenet.censorship	safesurf.com
alt.privacy.clipper	

---

on speech have been recognized as legal ever since Supreme Court Justice Oliver Wendell Holmes decided that restrictions were appropriate in the face of a "clear and present danger" to citizens; because subscribers know about such restrictions when they sign up, perhaps AOL is not censoring members any more than Blockbuster Video is censoring its customers by not carrying pornographic movies for rent. Do we really want children—or anyone, for that matter—exploring www.erotica.bestiality or www.pictures.erotica.children or www.alt.pictures.masturbation.necrophilia.female.teen? Should we be more vigilant when *Newsweek* can report that more than half of all current requests on search engines are for sexually explicit sites and that over 25 percent of teens report that they have visited X-rated sites?

The arguments in this segment take up issues related to First Amendment protections of free speech and writing. Is pornography harmful? Should it be censored? Does violence on television and in movies teach violence to children, and should it therefore be restricted in some way? Is it a good idea to regulate so-called hate speech on campuses or to keep people from placing pornography, or hate speech, or other destructive messages on the Internet?

IRVING KRISTOL

Pornography, Obscenity, and the Case for Censorship

Irving Kristol (1920–1999) wrote the following essay for the New York Times Magazine *in 1971, just after the National Commission on Pornography had issued its minority and majority reports. He later included it in his 1983* Reflections of a Neoconservative. *Kristol wrote on conservative causes during the last half century. The father of William Kristol, a leading conservative Republican advisor, he began his writing career in New York as a fervent leftist in the 1930s, but he grew increasingly disaffected with communism and increasingly conservative after World War II. After serving in World War II, he worked as a journalist and professor in New York and Washington, D.C.*

1   Being frustrated is disagreeable, but the real disasters in life begin when you get what you want. For almost a century now, a great many intelligent, well-meaning and articulate people have argued eloquently against any kind of censorship of art and entertainment. Within the past ten years, courts and legislatures have found these arguments so persuasive that censorship is now a relative rarity in most states.

2   Is there triumphant exhilaration in the land? Hardly. Somehow, things have not worked out as they were supposed to, and many civil-libertarians have said this was not what they meant. They wanted a world in which Eugene O'Neill's *Desire under the Elms* could be produced, or James Joyce's *Ulysses* published, without interference. They got that, of course; but they also got a world in which homosexual rape is simulated on the stage, in which the public flocks to witness professional fornication, in which New York's Times Square has become a hideous marketplace for printed filth. But does this really matter? Might not our disquiet be merely a cultural hangover? Was anyone ever corrupted by a book?

3   This last question, oddly enough, is asked by the same people who seem convinced that advertisements in magazines or displays of violence on television do have the power to corrupt. It is also asked, incredibly enough and in all sincerity, by university professors and teachers whose very lives provide the answer. After all, if you believe that no one was ever corrupted by a book, you have also to believe that no one was ever improved by a

book. You have to believe, in other words, that art is morally trivial and that education is morally irrelevant.

4   To be sure, it is extremely difficult to trace the effects of any single book (or play or movie) on any reader. But we all know that the ways in which we use our minds and imaginations do shape our characters and help define us as persons. That those who certainly know this are moved to deny it merely indicates how a dogmatic resistance to the idea of censorship can result in a mindless insistence on the absurd.

5   For the plain fact is that we all believe that there is a point at which the public authorities ought to step in to limit the "self-expression" of an individual or a group. A theatrical director might find someone willing to commit suicide on the stage. We would not allow that. And I know of no one who argues that we ought to permit public gladiatorial contests, even between consenting adults.

6   No society can be utterly indifferent to the ways its citizens publicly entertain themselves. Bearbaiting and cockfighting are prohibited only in part out of compassion for the animals; the main reason is that such spectacles were felt to debase and brutalize the citizenry who flocked to witness them. The question with regard to pornography and obscenity is whether they will brutalize and debase our citizenry. We are, after all, not dealing with one book or one movie. We are dealing with a general tendency that is suffusing our entire culture.

7   Pornography's whole purpose, it seems to me, is to treat human beings obscenely, to deprive them of their specifically human dimension. Imagine a well-known man in a hospital ward, dying an agonizing death. His bladder and bowels empty themselves of their own accord. His consciousness is overwhelmed by pain, so that he cannot communicate with us, nor we with him. Now, it would be technically easy to put a television camera in his room and let the whole world witness this spectacle. We don't do it—at least not yet—because we regard this as an obscene invasion of privacy. And what would make the spectacle obscene is that we would be witnessing the extinguishing of humanity in a human animal.

8   Sex—like death—is an activity that is both animal and human. There are human sentiments and human ideals involved in this animal activity. But when sex is public, I do not believe the viewer can see the sentiments and the ideals, but sees only the animal coupling. And that is why when most men and women make love, they prefer to be alone—because it is only when you are alone that you can make love, as distinct from merely copulating. When sex is a public spectacle, a human relationship has been debased into a mere animal connection.

9   But even if all this is granted, it doubtless will be said that we ought not to be unduly concerned. Free competition in the cultural marketplace, it is argued by those who have never otherwise had a kind word to say for laissez-faire, will dispose of the problem; in the course of time, people will get bored with pornography and obscenity.

10   I would like to be able to go along with this reasoning, but I think it is false, and for two reasons. The first reason is psychological, the second, political.

11   In my opinion, pornography and obscenity appeal to and provoke a kind of sexual regression. The pleasure one gets from pornography and obscenity is infantile and autoerotic; put bluntly, it is a masturbatory exercise of the imagination. Now, people who masturbate do not get bored with masturbation, just as sadists don't get bored with sadism, and voyeurs don't get bored with voyeurism. In other words, like all infantile sexuality, it can quite easily become a permanent self-reinforcing neurosis. And such a neurosis, on a mass scale, is a threat to our civilization and humanity, nothing less.

12   I am already touching upon a political aspect of pornography when I suggest that it is inherently subversive of civilization. But there is another political aspect, which has to do with the relationship of pornography and obscenity to democracy, and especially to the quality of public life on which democratic government ultimately rests.

13   Today a "managerial" conception of democracy prevails, wherein democracy is seen as a set of rules and procedures, and nothing but a set of rules and procedures, by which majority rule and minority rights are reconciled into a state of equilibrium. Thus, the political system can be fully reduced to its mechanical arrangements.

14   There is, however, an older idea of democracy—fairly common until about the beginning of this century—for which the conception of the quality of public life is absolutely crucial. This idea starts from the proposition that democracy is a form of self-government, and that you are entitled to it only if that "self" is worthy of governing. Because the desirability of self-government depends on the character of the people who govern, the older idea of democracy was very solicitous of the condition of this character. This older democracy had no problem in principle with pornography and obscenity; it censored them; it was not about to permit people to corrupt themselves. But can a liberal—today—be for censorship? Yes, but he ought to favor a liberal form of censorship.

15   I don't think this is a contradiction.

16   I therefore see no reason why we should not be able to distinguish repressive censorship from liberal censorship of the written and spoken word. In

Britain, until a few years ago, you could perform almost any play you wished, but certain plays, judged to be obscene, had to be performed in private theatrical clubs. In the United States, all of us who grew up using public libraries are familiar with the circumstances under which certain books could be circulated only to adults, while still other books had to be read in the library. In both cases, a small minority that was willing to make a serious effort to see an obscene play or book could do so. But the impact of obscenity was circumscribed, and the quality of public life was only marginally affected.

17   It is a distressing fact that any system of censorship is bound, upon occasion, to treat unjustly a particular work of art—to find pornography where there is only gentle eroticism, to find obscenity where none really exists, or to find both where the work's existence ought to be tolerated because it serves a larger moral purpose. That is the price one has to be prepared to pay for censorship, even liberal censorship.

18   But if you look at the history of American or English literature, there is precious little damage you can point to as a consequence of the censorship that prevailed throughout most of that history. I doubt that many works of real literary merit ever were suppressed. Nor did I notice that hitherto suppressed masterpieces flooded the market when censorship was eased. I should say, to the contrary, that literature has lost quite a bit now that so much is permitted. It seems to me that the cultural market in the United States today is awash in dirty books, dirty movies, dirty theater. Our cultural condition has not improved as a result of the new freedom.

19   I'll put it bluntly: if you care for the quality of life in our American democracy, then you have to be for censorship.

NADINE STROSSEN

The Perils of Pornophobia

The following essay, which appeared in The Humanist *in 1995, is a version of a chapter in a book published that same year,* Defending Pornography: Free Speech, Sex, and the Fight for Women's Rights. *Strossen (1950–) is president of the American Civil Liberties Union, an organization famous for defending the First Amendment rights of U.S. citizens.*

Nadine Strossen

1   In 1992, in response to a complaint, officials at Pennsylvania State University unceremoniously removed Francisco de Goya's masterpiece, *The Nude Maja,* from a classroom wall. The complaint had not been lodged by Jesse Helms or some irate member of the Christian Coalition. Instead, the complainant was a feminist English professor who protested that the eighteenth-century painting of a recumbent nude woman made her and her female students "uncomfortable."

2   This was not an isolated incident. At the University of Arizona at Tucson, feminist students physically attacked a graduate student's exhibit of photographic self-portraits. Why? The artist had photographed *herself* in her *underwear.* And at the University of Michigan Law School feminist students who had organized a conference on "Prostitution: From Academia to Activism" removed a feminist-curated art exhibition held in conjunction with the conference. Their reason? Conference speakers had complained that a composite videotape containing interviews of working prostitutes was "pornographic" and therefore unacceptable.

3   What is wrong with this picture? Where have they come from—these feminists who behave like religious conservatives, who censor works of art because they deal with sexual themes? Have not feminists long known that censorship is a dangerous weapon which, if permitted, would inevitably be turned against them? Certainly that was the irrefutable lesson of the early women's rights movement, when Margaret Sanger, Mary Ware Dennett, and other activists were arrested, charged with "obscenity" and prosecuted for distributing educational pamphlets about sex and birth control. Theirs was a

struggle for freedom of sexual expression and full gender equality, which they understood to be mutually reinforcing.

4   Theirs was also a lesson well understood by the second wave of feminism in the 1970s, when writers such as Germaine Greer, Betty Friedan, and Betty Dodson boldly asserted that women had the right to be free from discrimination not only in the workplace and in the classroom but in the bedroom as well. Freedom from limiting, conventional stereotypes concerning female sexuality was an essential aspect of what we then called "women's liberation." Women should not be seen as victims in their sexual relations with men but as equally assertive partners, just as capable of experiencing sexual pleasure.

5   But it is a lesson that, alas, many feminists have now forgotten. Today, an increasingly influential feminist pro-censorship movement threatens to impair the very women's rights movement it professes to serve. Led by law professor Catharine MacKinnon and writer Andrea Dworkin, this faction of the feminist movement maintains that sexually oriented *expression*—not sex-segregated labor markets, sexist concepts of marriage and family, or pent-up rage—is the preeminent cause of discrimination and violence against women. Their solution is seemingly simple: suppress all "pornography."

6   Censorship, however, is never a simple matter. First, the offense must be described. And how does one define something so infinitely variable, so deeply personal, so uniquely individualized as the image, the word, and the fantasy that cause sexual arousal? For decades, the U.S. Supreme Court has engaged in a Sisyphean struggle to craft a definition of *obscenity* that the lower courts can apply with some fairness and consistency. Their dilemma was best summed up in former Justice Potter Stewart's now famous statement: "I shall not today attempt further to define [obscenity]; and perhaps I could never succeed in intelligibly doing so. But I know it when I see it."

7   The censorious feminists are not so modest as Justice Stewart. They have fashioned an elaborate definition of *pornography* that encompasses vastly more material than does the currently recognized law of *obscenity*. As set out in their model law (which has been considered in more than a dozen jurisdictions in the United States and overseas, and which has been substantially adopted in Canada), pornography is "the sexually explicit subordination of women through pictures and/or words." The model law lists eight different criteria that attempt to illustrate their concept of "subordination," such as depictions in which "women are presented in postures or positions of sexual submission, servility, or display" or "women are presented in scenarios of degradation, humiliation, injury, torture . . . in a context that makes these conditions sexual." This linguistic driftnet can ensnare anything

from religious imagery and documentary footage about the mass rapes in the Balkans to self-help books about women's health. Indeed, the Boston Women's Health Book Collective, publisher of the now-classic book on women's health and sexuality, *Our Bodies, Ourselves,* actively campaigned against the MacKinnon-Dworkin model law when it was proposed in Cambridge, Massachusetts, in 1985, recognizing that the book's explicit text and pictures could be targeted as pornographic under the law.

8   Although the "MacDworkinite" approach to pornography has an intuitive appeal to many feminists, it is *itself* based on subordinating and demeaning stereotypes about women. Central to the pornophobic feminists—and to many traditional conservatives and right-wing fundamentalists, as well—is the notion that *sex* is inherently degrading to women (although not to men). Not just sexual expression but sex itself—even consensual, nonviolent sex—is an evil from which women, like children, must be protected.

9   MacKinnon puts it this way: "Compare victims' reports of rape with women's reports of sex. They look a lot alike. . . . The major distinction between intercourse (normal) and rape (abnormal) is that the normal happens so often that one cannot get anyone to see anything wrong with it." And from Dworkin: "Intercourse remains a means or the means of physiologically making a woman inferior." Given society's pervasive sexism, she believes, women cannot freely consent to sexual relations with men; those who do consent are, in Dworkin's words, "collaborators . . . experiencing pleasure in their own inferiority."

10   These ideas are hardly radical. Rather, they are a reincarnation of disempowering puritanical, Victorian notions that feminists have long tried to consign to the dustbin of history: woman as sexual victim; man as voracious satyr. The MacDworkinite approach to sexual expression is a throwback to the archaic stereotypes that formed the basis for nineteenth-century laws which prohibited "vulgar" or sexually suggestive language from being used in the presence of women and girls.

11   In those days, women were barred from practicing law and serving as jurors lest they be exposed to such language. Such "protective" laws have historically functioned to bar women from full legal equality. Paternalism always leads to exclusion, discrimination, and the loss of freedom and autonomy. And in its most extreme form, it leads to purdah, in which women are completely shrouded from public view.

12   The pro-censorship feminists are not fighting alone. Although they try to distance themselves from such traditional "family-values" conservatives as Jesse Helms, Phyllis Schlafly, and Donald Wildmon, who are less interested

in protecting women than in preserving male dominance, a common hatred of sexual expression and fondness for censorship unite the two camps. For example, the Indianapolis City Council adopted the MacKinnon-Dworkin model law in 1984 thanks to the hard work of former council member Beulah Coughenour, a leader of the Indiana Stop ERA movement. (Federal courts later declared the law unconstitutional.) And when Phyllis Schlafly's Eagle Forum and Beverly LaHaye's Concerned Women for America launched their "Enough Is Enough" anti-pornography campaign, they trumpeted the words of Andrea Dworkin in promotional materials.

13   This mutually reinforcing relationship does a serious disservice to the fight for women's equality. It lends credibility to and strengthens the right wing and its anti-feminist, anti-choice, homophobic agenda. This is particularly damaging in light of the growing influence of the religious right in the Republican Party and the recent Republican sweep of both Congress and many state governments. If anyone doubts that the newly empowered GOP intends to forge ahead with anti-woman agendas, they need only read the party's "Contract with America" which, among other things, reintroduces the recently repealed "gag rule" forbidding government-funded family-planning clinics from even discussing abortion with their patients.

14   The pro-censorship feminists base their efforts on the largely unexamined assumption that ridding society of pornography would reduce sexism and violence against women. If there were any evidence that this were true, anti-censorship feminists—myself included—would be compelled at least to reexamine our opposition to censorship. But there is no such evidence to be found.

15   A causal connection between exposure to pornography and the commission of sexual violence has never been established. The National Research Council's Panel on Understanding and Preventing Violence concluded in a 1993 survey of laboratory studies that "demonstrated empirical links between pornography and sex crimes in general are weak or absent." Even according to another research literature survey that former U.S. Surgeon General C. Everett Koop conducted at the behest of the staunchly anti-pornography Meese Commission, only two reliable generalizations could be made about the impact of "degrading" sexual material on its viewers: it caused them to think that a variety of sexual practices was more common than they had previously believed, and to more accurately estimate the prevalence of varied sexual practices.

16   Correlational studies are similarly unsupportive of the pro-censorship cause. There are no consistent correlations between the availability of pornography in various communities, states, and countries and their rates of sexual offenses. If anything, studies suggest an inverse relationship: a

greater availability of sexually explicit material seems to correlate not with higher rates of sexual violence but, rather, with higher indices of gender equality. For example, Singapore, with its tight restrictions on pornography, has experienced a much greater increase in rape rates than has Sweden, with its liberalized obscenity laws.

17   There *is* mounting evidence, however, that MacDworkinite-type laws will be used against the very people they are supposed to protect—namely, women. In 1992, for example, the Canadian Supreme Court incorporated the MacKinnon-Dworkin concept of pornography into Canadian obscenity law. Since that ruling, in *Butler* v. *The Queen*—which MacKinnon enthusiastically hailed as "a stunning victory for women"—well over half of all feminist bookstores in Canada have had materials confiscated or detained by customs. According to the *Feminist Bookstore News,* a Canadian publication, "The *Butler* decision has been used . . . only to seize lesbian, gay, and feminist material."

18   Ironically but predictably, one of the victims of Canada's new law is Andrea Dworkin herself. Two of her books, *Pornography: Men Possessing Women* and *Women Hating,* were seized, customs officials said, because they "illegally eroticized pain and bondage." Like the MacKinnon-Dworkin model law, the *Butler* decision makes no exceptions for material that is part of a feminist critique of pornography or other feminist presentation. And this inevitably overbroad sweep is precisely why censorship is antithetical to the fight for women's rights.

19   The pornophobia that grips MacKinnon, Dworkin, and their followers has had further counterproductive impacts on the fight for women's rights. Censorship factionalism within the feminist movement has led to an enormously wasteful diversion of energy from the real cause of and solutions to the ongoing problems of discrimination and violence against women. Moreover, the "porn-made-me-do-it" defense, whereby convicted rapists cite MacKinnon and Dworkin in seeking to reduce their sentences, actually impedes the aggressive enforcement of criminal laws against sexual violence.

20   A return to the basic principles of women's liberation would put the feminist movement back on course. We women are entitled to freedom of expression—to read, think, speak, sing, write, paint, dance, dream, photograph, film, and fantasize as we wish. We are also entitled to our dignity, autonomy, and equality. Fortunately, we can—and will—have both.

DIANA E. H. RUSSELL

Nadine Strossen: The Pornography Industry's Wet Dream

A native of South Africa who came to the United States for graduate study in social psychology, Diana E. H. Russell taught sociology for many years at Mills College in Oakland, California. In her retirement she has become outspoken about sexual violence against women, and she has appeared often on Oprah Winfrey, Donahue, Geraldo, *and NPR. Her articles and books on rape, other violence against women, and pornography (including* The Secret Trauma: Incest in the Lives of Girls and Women *and* Against Pornography) *are widely cited and admired. The following review-essay on Nadine Strossen, written in 1995, appears on her Web site, www.dianarussell.com.*

1   Nadine Strossen's objective in *Defending Pornography* is to destroy the reputation and achievements of the feminist movement against pornography. To this end, she dishes up the same tired old caricature of us as anti-sex prudes, pro-censorship, and in collusion with the right wing.

2   Not until the very last chapter does Strossen address the scientific evidence on the harmful effects of pornography, and her discussion of that evidence is a sham. Most of the key researchers on the relationship between pornography and violence against women (Neil Malamuth, James Check, Dolf Zillman, Bryant Jennings, myself) do not rate a single mention in her book.

3   I confronted Strossen on National Public Radio in February about the gaping holes in her review of the scientific literature. Her disinguous defense was that she had relied on a short book—which she described as the best source on the subject—by her nonacademic pal, anti-censorship advocate Marcia Pally, founder and president of Feminists for Free Expression and a columnist for *Penthouse.* Pally concluded that (surprise! surprise!) "no credible evidence substantiates a clear causal connection between any type of sexually explicit material and any sexist or violent behavior."

4   Strossen's book was enthusiastically feted by the media not because it's so brilliant but because she's president of the American Civil Liberties Union (an organization that has increasingly become a watchdog for the interests of pornographers). The fact that Strossen professes to be a feminist gives her a lot more clout than a man would have doing the same dirty work for a dirty industry. Men can sit back and applaud the cat fight. Pornogra-

phers can breathe a sigh of relief and get on with their lucrative business of exploiting women to facilitate men's ejaculations.

5   Strossen makes no distinction between erotica and pornography. Her failure makes it so much easier to identify anti-porn feminists (who have no objection to nondegrading images that turn people on—unless the woman in the image was abused in its production) with the right wing (many of whom do oppose all sexually explicit images).

6   Over the last twenty years I have been engaged in considerable research and writing on pornography—which I define as *material that combines sex and/or genital exposure with abuse or degradation in a manner that appears to endorse, condone, or encourage such behavior.* My most recent works include *Making Violence Sexy: Feminist Views on Pornography* (Teachers College Press, 1993) and *Against Pornography: The Evidence of Harm* (Russell Publications, 1994). I have been an anti-porn activist for the same length of time. The high point in my activist career was discovering the thrill in tearing up porn magazines. Doing this in private is no fun. It has to be a public act executed with other women, preferably in front of the porn store owner and his male customers. The catharsis I felt was definitely worth the night I spent in jail.

7   In *Against Pornography* I reprinted over 100 examples of pornography because I was bored to death by talking about its effects with people who haven't seen it, or whose exposure to it has been so minimal that they equate it with pictures of nude people in sexual encounters. I had also repeatedly found that many women are more convinced of the harmful effects of pornography by seeing examples of it than by reading about the scientific evidence.

8   Some critics of *Against Pornography* accused me of including more negative images than they believe is typical of pornography. Similarly, Strossen charges anti-porn feminists with selecting "overtly violent, sexist samples" of porn for our educational slide presentations. This is analogous to a neo-Nazi arguing that the horror and devastation of anti-Semitism in Nazi Germany cannot be judged from photographs of the concentration camps, because a lot of Jews weren't incarcerated in them.

9   Strossen devotes a hefty chunk of her book to a vehement and demonizing attack on Catharine MacKinnon and Andrea Dworkin. Assuming that all the rest of us agree with everything MacKinnon or Dworkin has ever said, done, or written, Strossen both scapegoats those two and makes invisible many other prominent feminists who have also opposed pornography. Besides me, for instance, she does not mention Gloria Steinem, Alice Walker, Susan Brownmiller, Susan Griffin, Nikki Craft, Kathleen Barry, Florence Rush,

Ann Simonton, Melissa Farley, Jane Caputi, Catherine Itzin—all of whose commitment to this issue is public knowledge.

10   Strossen spends most of the book arguing against censorship, claiming that MacKinnon and Dworkin and the rest of us unmentionable clones are virulent advocates of it. Although censorship appears to be Strossen's favorite word, she never even attempts to define it. From the examples she cites, though, her definition appears indistinguishable from what most people would consider the exercise of their free speech and civil rights.

11   Strossen accuses Dworkin, for example, of censorship for organizing a protest campaign against *A Woman's Book of Choices.* A particular passage included advice on how women could qualify to get an abortion by falsely claiming to have been raped. The passage explained how women could increase the credibility of such a false rape claim "by wearing torn clothes and borrowing semen from a friend or lover to spread on their clothes or bodies." When the publisher and the authors claimed it was impossible to revise this passage, Dworkin organized a successful campaign to get them to change their minds.

12   This incident inspired Strossen to criticize "the censorial impact of such coercive tactics as boycotts." To call any protest censorship is utter nonsense. In the context of the First Amendment, censorship involves *state-based action to prohibit the publication of literature before it reaches the stands.* There is a vital distinction between state action and acts of individuals. Dworkin's campaign involved individuals, myself included, exercising our First Amendment rights to exert pressure on the authors and publisher to change an appallingly misogynist paragraph.

13   Strossen insists that anti-porn feminists are the darlings of the media. Nothing could be further from the truth. Strossen, like other female feminist-bashers (Camille Paglia, Christina Hoff Sommers, and Katie Roiphe, for example) had the media falling over themselves to publicize her pro-porn views.

14   And Strossen doesn't just defend pornography; she enthusiastically celebrates it. In her chapter on "positive aspects of pornographic imagery," she includes testimonials by other women. One is Sally Tisdale (author of *Talk Dirty to Me*): "Pornography tells me . . . that anything goes." Another is Ann Snitow (an editor of *Powers of Desire*):

> Think, for example, of all the pornography about servants fucking mistresses, old men fucking young girls, guardians fucking wards. Class, age, custom—all are deliciously sacrificed, dissolved by sex.

15   Whether some women get off on what Strossen approvingly calls "rape scenes and scenes dramatizing the so-called rape myth," that does not mitigate the fact that many other women feel violated by such images, that some are violated by acts inspired by those images, and that some who were used to make those images are exploited or abused in the process. In her myopic individualism, Strossen repeatedly fails to address the consequences of pornography for women or for male consumers in general.

16   Here is another Strossen gem to delight pornographers: "The more unconventional the sexual expression is, the more revolutionary its social and political implications become." I suppose rape doesn't qualify as unconventional sexual expression anymore—but would child porn qualify as revolutionary? Or images of sexual mutilation and woman-killing?

17   I know what *would* be revolutionary: Strossen keeps telling us how much women love pornography, so why not pictures of gangs of women raping men, sticking broomsticks up their asses as they smile and ejaculate and say, "Encore," snipping their balls off with pliers, sticking wire up their penile openings? Why haven't pornographers saturated the market with these kinds of images to match what they've done to women? Isn't this evidence that porn is discriminatory?

18   But Strossen denies there is any inequality in pornography. She even contests that "women have historically and consistently been subjugated in the realm of sexuality." She thinks the conditions for women in the porn industry are just dandy, and that there is no reason "to believe that force or violence are endemic in the sex industry, or more prevalent there than in other sectors of our society." In the event that the odd problem emerges, says Strossen, there are a "panoply of criminal and civil remedies for women who have been physically or psychologically abused in the production of sexual materials." What a bunch of fatuous Pollyanaisms.

19   Many anti-porn feminists today reject the concepts of obscenity and censorship as appropriate frameworks for judging pornography. Dworkin and MacKinnon have proposed a law enabling women who have been damaged by pornography to sue the pornographer(s) responsible. The trial court would decide whether or not the evidence is convincing. The rationale for this law is similar to the rationale for laws against sexual harassment: it can cause harm, and it is disproportionately harmful to women, and therefore discriminatory. People who support the laws against sexual harassment would, if consistent, approve similar laws against pornography.

20   But Strossen complains sexual harassment laws are having a chilling effect on the joys of finding sexual affirmation in the workplace. She calls sexual harassment (a concept referring to *unwanted* sexual advances, not

those that are welcome) a "stigmatizing epithet." She can't seem to get the difference between sex and sexual abuse.

21   No wonder Strossen fails to reckon with my theoretical work on pornography as a causal factor in rape. I believe there are many different causes of rape, and the significance of pornography varies depending on its availability, its content, and the degree of its acceptability in a particular country. In nations saturated with porn, as the United States is, scientific evidence shows

> 1. Pornography predisposes some men to want to rape women, and intensifies the predisposition in some other men already so predisposed.

22   For example, research has shown that porn combining sex and violence against women teaches some male viewers to be turned on by such violence.

> 2. Pornography undermines some men's internal inhibitions against acting out their desire to rape.

23   Research shows that by promoting rape myths, beliefs in interpersonal violence, and callous attitudes toward women, porn undermines the internal inhibitions that restrain many men from raping. The more convinced men who would like to rape a woman are that women enjoy rape, the more likely they are to do it. And a very high proportion of men would like to rape women. Neil Malamuth and colleagues have shown that 30 to 60 percent of male college students report some likelihood that they would rape or force sex acts on a woman if they could get away with it.

> 3. Pornography undermines some men's social inhibitions against acting out their desire to rape.

24   By rewarding men in porn for objectifying, dominating, violating, and raping women, the social message conveyed to consumers is just as Tisdale said: "Anything goes." Moreover, "It's easy to get away with."

25   Many people share Strossen's opinion that men who consume porn but who have never raped a woman disprove the theory that porn can cause rape. This is comparable to arguing that because some cigarette smokers don't die of lung disease, there cannot be a causal relationship between smoking and lung cancer. Only members of the tobacco industry and some seriously addicted smokers consider this a valid argument today.

26   Although the scientific evidence that porn can cause rape is at least as strong as the evidence that smoking can cause lung cancer, many people are

so ideologically committed to the view that porn is harmless that they find a multitude of excuses to disregard it. Strossen and the ACLU's strategy seems to be to ignore information, arguments, and theories that they find too difficult to tackle, no matter how much dishonesty and misrepresentation it takes.

CATHLEEN CLEAVER

The Internet: A Clear and Present Danger?

Cathleen Cleaver was working in Washington, D.C., at the Family Research Council (a research and advocacy organization) as director of legal education when, in October 1997, she delivered the following speech at Boston University. The argument was later posted on a Web site. Outspoken in support of efforts to regulate the Internet, Cleaver often contributes op-ed articles on subjects related to the protection of children and families. She now works as counsel to the U.S. House of Representatives subcommittee on the Constitution.

1
- Someone breaks through your firewall and steals proprietary information from your computer systems. You find out and contact a lawyer who says, "Man, you shouldn't have had your stuff online." The thief becomes a millionaire using your ideas, and you go broke, if laws against copyright violation don't protect material on the Internet.

- You visit the Antiques Anonymous Web site and decide to pay their hefty subscription fee for a year's worth of exclusive estate sale previews in their private online monthly magazine. They never deliver, and, in fact, never intended to—they don't even have a magazine. You have no recourse, if laws against fraud don't apply to online transactions.

- Bob Guccione decides to branch out into the lucrative child porn market, and creates a Teen Hustler Web site featuring nude adolescents and preteens. You find out and complain, but nothing can be done, if child pornography distribution laws don't apply to computer transmissions.

- A major computer software vendor who dominates the market develops his popular office software so that it works only with his browser. You're a small browser manufacturer who is completely squeezed out of the market, but you have to find a new line of work, if antitrust laws don't apply online.

- Finally, a pedophile e-mails your son, misrepresenting himself as a twelve-year-old named Jenny. They develop an online relationship and one day arrange to meet after school, where he intends to rape your son. Thankfully, you learn in advance about the meeting and go there yourself, where you find a forty-year-old man instead of Jenny. You flee to the police, who'll tell you there's nothing they can do, if child-stalking laws don't apply to the Internet.

The Issue

2   The awesome advances in interactive telecommunication that we've witnessed in just the last few years have changed the way in which many Americans communicate and interact. No one can doubt that the Internet is a technological revolution of enormous proportion, with outstanding possibilities for human advancement.

3   As lead speaker for the affirmative, I'm asked to argue that the Internet poses a "clear and present danger," but the Internet, as a whole, isn't dangerous. In fact, it continues to be a positive and highly beneficial tool, which will undoubtedly improve education, information exchange, and commerce in years to come. In other words, the Internet will enrich many aspects of our daily life. Thus, instead of defending this rather apocalyptic view of the Internet, I'll attempt to explain why some industry and government regulation of certain aspects of the Internet is necessary—or, stated another way, why people who use the Internet should not be exempt from many of the laws and regulations that govern their conduct elsewhere. My opening illustrations were meant to give examples of some illegal conduct which should not become legal simply because someone uses the Internet. In looking at whether Internet regulation is a good idea, I believe we should consider whether regulation is in the public interest. In order to do that, we have to ask the question: Who is the public? More specifically, does the "public" whose interests we care about tonight include children?

Children and the Internet

4   Dave Barry describes the Internet as a "worldwide network of university, government, business, and private computer systems, run by a thirteen-year-old named Jason." This description draws a smile precisely because we acknowledge the highly advanced computer literacy of our children. Most children demonstrate computer proficiency that far surpasses that of their parents, and many parents know only what their children have taught them about the Internet, which gives new relevance to Wordsworth's insight: "The child is father of the man." In fact, one could go so far as to say that the Internet is as accessible to many children as it is inaccessible to many adults. This technological evolution is new in many ways, not the least of which is its accessibility to children, wholly independent of their parents.

5   When considering what's in the public interest, we must consider the whole public, including children, as individual participants in this new medium.

Pornography and the Internet

6   This new medium is unique in another way. It provides, through a single avenue, the full spectrum of pornographic depictions, from the more familiar convenience store fare to pornography of such violence and depravity that it surpasses the worst excesses of the normal human imagination. Sites displaying this material are easily accessible, making pornography far more freely available via the Internet than from any other communications medium in the United States. Pornography is the third largest sector of sales on the Internet, generating $1 billion annually. There are an estimated seventy-two thousand pornographic sites on the World Wide Web alone, with approximately thirty-nine new explicit sex sites every day. Indeed, the *Washington Post* has called the Internet the largest pornography store in the history of mankind.

7   There is little restriction of pornography-related activity in cyberspace. While there are some porn-related laws, the specter of those laws does not loom large in cyberspace. There's an implicit license there that exists nowhere else with regard to pornography—an environment where people

---

J O H N   P E R R Y   B A R L O W

A Declaration of the Independence of Cyberspace

After seventeen years as a Wyoming rancher who, on the side, wrote songs for the Grateful Dead, John Perry Barlow (1947–   ) in the late 1980s began writing about computer-mediated communications. He serves on the board of directors of WELL—the Whole Earth 'Lectronic Link—and he is a co-founder of the Electronic Frontier Foundation, which advocates keeping government regulations out of the Internet.

John Perry Barlow

1   Governments of the Industrial World, you weary giants of flesh and steel, I come from Cyberspace, the new home of Mind. On behalf of the future, I ask you of the past to leave us alone. You are not welcome among us. You have no sovereignty where we gather.

are free to exploit others for profit and be virtually untroubled by legal deterrent. Indeed, if we consider cyberspace to be a little world of its own, it's the type of world for which groups like the ACLU have long fought, but, so far, fought in vain.

8   I believe it will not remain this way, but until it changes, we should take the opportunity to see what this world looks like, if for no other reason than to reassure ourselves that our decades-old decisions to control pornography were good ones.

9   With a few clicks of the mouse, anyone, any child, can get graphic and often violent sexual images—the kind of stuff it used to be difficult to find without exceptional effort and some significant personal risk. Anyone with a computer and a modem can set up public sites featuring the perversion of their choice, whether it's mutilation of female genitals, eroticized urination and defecation, bestiality, or sites featuring depictions of incest. These pictures can be sold for profit, they can be sent to harass others, or posted to shock people. Anyone can describe the fantasy rape and murder of a specific person and display it for all to read. Anyone can meet children in chat rooms

2   We have no elected government, nor are we likely to have one, so I address you with no greater authority than that with which liberty itself always speaks. I declare the global social space we are building to be naturally independent of the tyrannies you seek to impose on us. You have no moral right to rule us nor do you possess any methods of enforcement we have true reason to fear.

3   Governments derive their just powers from the consent of the governed. You have neither solicited nor received ours. We did not invite you. You do not know us, nor do you know our world. Cyberspace does not lie within your borders. Do not think that you can build it, as though it were a public construction project. You cannot. It is an act of nature and it grows itself through our collective actions.

4   You have not engaged in our great and gathering conversation, nor did you create the wealth of our marketplaces. You do not know our culture, our ethics, or the unwritten codes that already provide our society more order than could be obtained by any of your impositions.

5   You claim there are problems among us that you need to solve. You use this claim as an excuse to invade our precincts. Many of these problems don't exist. Where there are real conflicts, where there are wrongs, we will identify them and address them by our means. We are forming our own So-

or via e-mail and send them pornography and find out where they live. An adult who signs onto an AOL chat room as a thirteen-year-old girl is hit on thirty times within the first half hour.

10 All this can be done from the seclusion of the home, with the feeling of near anonymity and with the comfort of knowing that there's little risk of legal sanction.

11 The phenomenon of this kind of pornography finding such a welcome home in this new medium presents abundant opportunities for social commentary. What does Internet pornography tell us about human sexuality? Photographs, videos, and virtual games that depict rape and the dehumanization of women in sexual scenes send powerful messages about human dignity and equality. Much of the pornography freely available without restriction on the Internet celebrates unhealthy and antisocial kinds of sexual

cial Contract. This governance will arise according to the conditions of our world, not yours. Our world is different.

6 Cyberspace consists of transactions, relationships, and thought itself, arrayed like a standing wave in the web of our communications. Ours is a world that is both everywhere and nowhere, but it is not where bodies live.

7 We are creating a world that all may enter without privilege or prejudice accorded by race, economic power, military force, or station of birth.

8 We are creating a world where anyone, anywhere may express his or her beliefs, no matter how singular, without fear of being coerced into silence or conformity.

9 Your legal concepts of property, expression, identity, movement, and context do not apply to us. They are based on matter. There is no matter here.

10 Our identities have no bodies, so, unlike you, we cannot obtain order by physical coercion. We believe that from ethics, enlightened self-interest, and the commonweal, our governance will emerge. Our identities may be distributed across many of your jurisdictions. The only law that all our constituent cultures would generally recognize is the Golden Rule. We hope we will be able to build our particular solutions on that basis. But we cannot accept the solutions you are attempting to impose.

11 In the United States, you have today created a law, the Telecommunications Reform Act, which repudiates your own Constitution and insults the dreams of Jefferson, Washington, Mill, Madison, deToqueville, and Brandeis. These dreams must now be born anew in us.

12 You are terrified of your own children, since they are natives in a world where you will always be immigrants. Because you fear them, you entrust

activity, such as sadomasochism, abuse, and degradation. Of course, by its very nature, pornography encourages voyeurism.

12   Beyond the troubling social aspects of unrestricted porn, we face the reality that children are accessing it and that predators are accessing children. We have got to start considering what kind of society we'll have when the next generation learns about human sexuality from what the Internet teaches. What does unrestricted Internet pornography teach children about relationships, about the equality of women? What does it teach little girls about themselves and their worth?

13   Opponents of restrictions are fond of saying that it's up to the parents to deal with the issue of children's exposure. Well, of course it is, but placing the burden solely on parents is illogical and ineffective. It's far easier for a distributor of pornography to control his material than it is for parents, who

your bureaucracies with the parental responsibilities you are too cowardly to confront yourselves. In our world, all the sentiments and expressions of humanity, from the debasing to the angelic, are parts of a seamless whole, the global conversation of bits. We cannot separate the air that chokes from the air upon which wings beat.

13   In China, Germany, France, Russia, Singapore, Italy, and the United States, you are trying to ward off the virus of liberty by erecting guard posts at the frontiers of Cyberspace. These may keep out the contagion for a small time, but they will not work in a world that will soon be blanketed in bit-bearing media.

14   Your increasingly obsolete information industries would perpetuate themselves by proposing laws, in America and elsewhere, that claim to own speech itself throughout the world. These laws would declare ideas to be another industrial product, no more noble than pig iron. In our world, whatever the human mind may create can be reproduced and distributed infinitely at no cost. The global conveyance of thought no longer requires your factories to accomplish.

15   These increasingly hostile and colonial measures place us in the same position as those previous lovers of freedom and self-determination who had to reject the authorities of distant, uninformed powers. We must declare our virtual selves immune to your sovereignty, even as we continue to consent to your rule over our bodies. We will spread ourselves across the Planet so that no one can arrest our thoughts.

16   We will create a civilization of the Mind in Cyberspace. May it be more humane and fair than the world your governments have made before.

must, with the help of software, search for and find the pornographic sites, which change daily, and then attempt to block them. Any pornographer who wants to can easily subvert these efforts, and a recent Internet posting from a teenager wanting to know how to disable the filtering software on his computer received several effective answers. Moreover, it goes without saying that the most sophisticated software can only be effective where it's installed, and children will have access to many computers that don't have filtering software, such as those in libraries, schools, and at neighbors' houses.

Internet Transactions Should Not Be Exempt

14   Opponents of legal restrictions often argue simply that the laws just cannot apply in this new medium, but the argument that old laws can't apply to changing technology just doesn't hold. We saw this argument last in the early '80s with the advent of the videotape. Then, certain groups tried to argue that, since you can't view videotapes without a VCR, you can't make the sale of child porn videos illegal, because, after all, they're just plastic boxes with magnetic tape inside. Technological change mandates legal change only insofar as it affects the justification for a law. It just doesn't make sense that the government may take steps to restrict illegal material in *every* medium—video, television, radio, the private telephone, *and* print—but that it may do *nothing* where people distribute the material by the Internet. While old laws might need redefinition, the old principles generally stand firm.

15   The question of enforcement usually is raised here, and it often comes in the form of: "How are you going to stop people from doing it?" Well, no law stops people from doing things—a red light at an intersection doesn't force you to stop but tells you that you should stop and that there could be legal consequences if you don't. Not everyone who runs a red light is caught, but that doesn't mean the law is futile. The same concept holds true for Internet laws. Government efforts to temper harmful conduct online will never be perfect, but that doesn't mean they shouldn't undertake the effort at all.

16   There's clearly a role for industry to play here. Search engines don't have to run ads for porn sites or prioritize search results to highlight porn. One new search engine even has *sex* as the default search term. Internet service providers can do something about unsolicited e-mail with hotlinks to porn, and they can and should carefully monitor any chat rooms designed for kids.

17   Some charge that industry standards or regulations that restrict explicit pornography will hinder the development of Internet technology. But that is to say that its advancement *depends upon* unrestricted exhibition of

this material, and this cannot be true. The Internet does not belong to pornographers, and it's clearly in the public interest to see that they don't usurp this great new technology. We don't live in a perfect society, and the Internet is merely a reflection of the larger social community. Without some mitigating influences, the strong will exploit the weak, whether a Bill Gates or a child predator.

Conclusion: Technology Must Serve Man

18 To argue that the strength of the Internet is chaos or that our liberty depends upon chaos is to misunderstand not only the Internet but also the fundamental nature of our liberty. It's an illusion to claim social or moral neutrality in the application of technology, even if its development may be neutral. It can be a valuable resource only when placed at the service of humanity and when it promotes our integral development for the benefit of all.

19   Guiding principles simply cannot be inferred from mere technical efficiency or from the usefulness accruing to some at the expense of others. Technology by its very nature requires unconditional respect for the fundamental interests of society.

20   Internet technology must be at the service of humanity and of our inalienable rights. It must respect the prerogatives of a civil society, among which is the protection of children.

Fahrenheit 451.2:
Is Cyberspace Burning?

The American Civil Liberties Union is famous for its advocacy on a whole range of civil liberties issues. Among other things, it is resolute in its support of First-Amendment freedoms, particularly the rights of free speech and assembly: see www.aclu.org. The following argument about restrictions on the Internet, written mostly by ACLU staff members Ann Beeson, Chris Hansen, and Barry Steinhardt, appeared on the ACLU Web site on March 17, 2002.

Introduction

1   In his chilling (and prescient) novel about censorship, *Fahrenheit 451*, author Ray Bradbury describes a futuristic society where books are outlawed. "Fahrenheit 451" is, of course, the temperature at which books burn.

2   In Bradbury's novel and in the physical world people censor the printed word by burning books. But in the virtual world, one can just as easily censor controversial speech by banishing it to the farthest corners of cyberspace using rating and blocking programs. Today, will Fahrenheit, version 451.2, a new kind of virtual censorship, be the temperature at which cyberspace goes up in smoke?

3   The first flames of Internet censorship appeared two years ago, with the introduction of the Federal Communications Decency Act (CDA), outlawing "indecent" online speech. But in the landmark case *Reno v. ACLU*, the Supreme Court overturned the CDA, declaring that the Internet is entitled to the highest level of free speech protection. In other words, the Court said that online speech deserved the protection afforded to books and other printed matter.

4   Today, all that we have achieved may now be lost, if not in the bright flames of censorship then in the dense smoke of the many ratings and blocking schemes promoted by some of the very people who fought for freedom. And in the end, we may find that the censors have indeed succeeded in "burning down the house to roast the pig."

Is Cyberspace Burning?

5   The ashes of the CDA were barely smoldering when the White House called a summit meeting to encourage Internet users to self-rate their speech and to urge industry leaders to develop and deploy the tools for blocking

"inappropriate" speech. The meeting was "voluntary," of course: the White House claimed it wasn't holding anyone's feet to the fire.

6   The ACLU and others in the cyber-liberties community were genuinely alarmed by the tenor of the White House summit and the unabashed enthusiasm for technological fixes that will make it easier to block or render invisible controversial speech. (*Note:* see appendix for detailed explanations of the various technologies.)

7   Industry leaders responded to the White House call with a barrage of announcements:

- Netscape announced plans to join Microsoft; together the two giants have 90 percent or more of the Web browser market in adopting PICS (Platform for Internet Content Selection), the rating standard that establishes a consistent way to rate and block online content;

- IBM announced it was making a $100,000 grant to RSAC (Recreational Software Advisory Council) to encourage the use of its RSACi rating system. Microsoft Explorer already employs the RSACi ratings system, Compuserve encourages its use and it is fast becoming the de facto industry standard rating system;

- Four of the major search engines, the services which allow users to conduct searches of the Internet for relevant sites, announced a plan to cooperate in the promotion of "self-regulation" of the Internet. The president of one, Lycos, was quoted in a news account as having "thrown down the gauntlet" to the other three, challenging them to agree to exclude unrated sites from search results;

- Following announcement of proposed legislation by Sen. Patty Murray (D-Wash.), which would impose civil and ultimately criminal penalties on those who mis-rate a site, the makers of the blocking program Safe Surf proposed similar legislation, the "Online Cooperative Publishing Act."

8   But it was not any one proposal or announcement that caused our alarm; rather, it was the failure to examine the longer-term implications for the Internet of rating and blocking schemes.

9   What may be the result? The Internet will become bland and homogenized. The major commercial sites will still be readily available, they will have the resources and inclination to self-rate, and third-party rating services will be inclined to give them acceptable ratings. People who disseminate quirky and idiosyncratic speech, create individual home pages, or post to controversial news groups, will be among the first Internet users blocked by filters and made invisible by the search engines. Controversial speech will

still exist, but will only be visible to those with the tools and know-how to penetrate the dense smokescreen of industry "self-regulation."

10   As bad as this very real prospect is, it can get worse. Faced with the reality that, although harder to reach, sex, hate speech, and other controversial matter is still available on the Internet, how long will it be before governments begin to make use of an Internet already configured to accommodate massive censorship? If you look at these various proposals in a larger context, a very plausible scenario emerges. It is a scenario which in some respects has already been set in motion:

- First, the use of PICS becomes universal; providing a uniform method for content rating.

- Next, one or two rating systems dominate the market and become the de facto standard for the Internet.

- PICS and the dominant rating(s) system are built into Internet software as an automatic default.

RAY BRADBURY

Afterword to *Fahrenheit 451*

Ray Bradbury (1920–   ) established his reputation as a leading writer of science fiction with the publication of The Martian Chronicles *in 1950. Bradbury's* Fahrenheit 451 *(1953), a classic of science fiction that has been reissued many times, is set in a future in which the written word has been forbidden and books are burned when they are discovered. In 1979, Bradbury added the following comments to his afterword to that novel.*

1   About two years ago, a letter arrived from a solemn young Vassar lady telling me how much she enjoyed reading my experiment in space mythology, *The Martian Chronicles.*

2   But, she added, wouldn't it be a good idea, this late in time, to rewrite the book inserting more women's characters and roles?

3   A few years before that I got a certain amount of mail concerning the same Martian book complaining that the blacks in the book were Uncle Toms and why didn't I "do them over"?

- Unrated speech on the Internet is effectively blocked by these defaults.

- Search engines refuse to report on the existence of unrated or "unacceptably" rated sites.

- Governments frustrated by "indecency" still on the Internet make self-rating mandatory and mis-rating a crime.

11   The scenario is, for now, theoretical but inevitable. It is clear that any scheme that allows access to unrated speech will fall afoul of the government-coerced push for a "family-friendly" Internet. We are moving inexorably toward a system that blocks speech simply because it is unrated and makes criminals of those who mis-rate.

12   The White House meeting was clearly the first step in that direction and away from the principle that protection of the electronic word is analogous to protection of the printed word. Despite the Supreme Court's strong rejection of a broadcast analogy for the Internet, government and

4   Along about then came a note from a Southern white suggesting that I was prejudiced in favor of the blacks and the entire story should be dropped.

5   Two weeks ago, my mountain of mail delivered forth a pipsqueak mouse of a letter from a well-known publishing house that wanted to reprint my story "The Fog Horn" in a high school reader.

6   In my story, I had described a lighthouse as having, late at night, an illumination coming from it that was a "God-Light." Looking up at it from the viewpoint of any sea-creature one would have felt that one was in "the Presence."

7   The editors had deleted "God-Light" and "in the Presence."

8   Some five years back, the editors of yet another anthology for school readers put together a volume with some 400 (count 'em) short stories in it. How do you cram 400 short stories by Twain, Irving, Poe, Maupassant and Bierce into one book?

9   Simplicity itself. Skin, debone, demarrow, scarify, melt, render down and destroy. Every adjective that counted, every verb that moved, every metaphor that weighed more than a mosquito—out! Every simile that would have made a sub-moron's mouth twitch—gone! Any aside that explained the two-bit philosophy of a first-rate writer—lost!

10   Every story, slenderized, starved, bluepenciled, leeched and bled white, resembled every other story. Twain read like Poe read like Shakespeare read

industry leaders alike are now inching toward the dangerous and incorrect position that the Internet is like television, and should be rated and censored accordingly.

13   Is cyberspace burning? Not yet, perhaps. But where there's smoke, there's fire.

Free Speech Online: A Victory Under Siege

14   On June 26, 1997, the Supreme Court held in *Reno* v. *ACLU* that the Communications Decency Act, which would have made it a crime to communicate anything "indecent" on the Internet, violated the First Amendment. It was the nature of the Internet itself, and the quality of speech on the Internet, that led the Court to declare that the Internet is entitled to the same broad free speech protections given to books, magazines, and casual conversation.

15   The ACLU argued, and the Supreme Court agreed, that the CDA was unconstitutional because, although aimed at protecting minors, it effectively banned speech among adults. Similarly, many of the rating and block-

like Dostoevsky read like—in the finale—Edgar Guest. Every word of more than three syllables had been razored. Every image that demanded so much as one instant's attention—shot dead.

11   Do you begin to get the damned and incredible picture?

12   How do I react to all of the above?

13   By "firing" the whole lot.

14   By sending rejection slips to each and every one.

15   By ticketing the assembly of idiots to the far reaches of hell.

16   The point is obvious. There is more than one way to burn a book. And the world is full of people running about with lit matches. Every minority, be it Baptist/Unitarian, Irish/Italian/Octogenarian/Zen Buddhist, Zionist/Seventh-Day Adventist, Women's Lib/Republican, Mattachine/Four Square Gospel feels it has the will, the right, the duty to douse the kerosene, light the fuse. Every dimwit editor who sees himself as the source of all dreary blanc-mange plain porridge unleavened literature, licks his guillotine and eyes the neck of any author who dares to speak above a whisper or write above a nursery rhyme.

17   Fire-Captain Beatty, in my novel *Fahrenheit 451*, described how the books were burned first by the minorities, each ripping a page or a paragraph from this book, then that, until the day came when the books were empty and the minds shut and the libraries closed forever.

ing proposals, though designed to limit minors' access, will inevitably restrict the ability of adults to communicate on the Internet. In addition, such proposals will restrict the rights of older minors to gain access to material that clearly has value for them.

Rethinking the Rush to Rate

16 This paper examines the free speech implications of the various proposals for Internet blocking and rating. Individually, each of the proposals poses some threat to open and robust speech on the Internet; some pose a considerably greater threat than others.

17 Even more ominous is the fact that the various schemes for rating and blocking, taken together, could create a black cloud of private "voluntary" censorship that is every bit as threatening as the CDA itself to what the Supreme Court called "the most participatory form of mass speech yet developed."

18 "Shut the door, they're coming through the window, shut the window, they're coming through the door," are the words to an old song. They fit my life-style with newly arriving butcher/censors every month. Only six weeks ago, I discovered that, over the years, some cubbyhole editors at Ballantine Books, fearful of contaminating the young, had, bit by bit, censored some 75 separate sections from the novel. Students, reading the novel which, after all, deals with censorship and book-burning in the future, wrote to tell me of this exquisite irony. Judy-Lynn Del Rey, one of the new Ballantine editors, is having the entire book reset and republished this summer with all the damns and hells back in place.

19 A final test for old Job II here: I sent a play, *Leviathan 99* [later titled *That Ghost, That Bride of Time: Excerpts from a Play in Progress*], off to a university theater a month ago. My play is [dedicated to] Melville, and concerns a rocket crew and a blind space captain who venture forth to encounter a Great White Comet and destroy the destroyer. My drama premieres as an opera in Paris this autumn. But, for now, the university wrote back that they hardly dared do my play—it had no women in it! And the ERA ladies on campus would descend with ballbats if the drama department even tried!

20 Grinding my bicuspids into powder, I suggested that would mean, from now on, no more productions of *Boys in the Band* (no women), or *The*

18   We call on industry leaders, Internet users, policy makers, and parents groups to engage in a genuine debate about the free speech ramifications of the rating and blocking schemes being proposed.

19   To open the door to a meaningful discussion, we offer the following recommendations and principles:

Recommendations and Principles

- Internet users know best. The primary responsibility for determining what speech to access should remain with the individual Internet user: parents should take primary responsibility for determining what their children should access.

- Default setting on free speech. Industry should not develop products that require speakers to rate their own speech or be blocked by default.

- Buyers beware. The producers of user-based software programs should make their lists of blocked speech available to consumers. The industry should develop products that provide maximum user control.

- No government coercion or censorship. The First Amendment prevents the government from imposing, or from coercing industry into imposing, a mandatory Internet ratings scheme.

Women (no men). Or, counting heads, male and female, a good lot of Shakespeare that would never be seen again, especially if you count lines and find that all the good stuff went to the males!

21   I wrote back maybe they should do my play one week, and *The Women* the next. They probably thought I was joking, and I'm not sure that I wasn't.

22   For it is a mad world and it will get madder if we allow the minorities, be they dwarf or giant, orangutan or dolphin, nuclear-head or water conservationist, pro-computerologist or Neo-Luddite, simpleton or sage, to interfere with aesthetics. The real world is the playing ground for each and every group, to make or unmake laws. But the tip of the nose of my book or stories or poems is where their rights end and my territorial imperatives begin, run and rule. If Mormons do not like my plays, let them write their own. If the Irish hate my Dublin stories, let them rent typewriters. If the teachers and grammar school editors find my jawbreaker sentences shatter their mushmilk teeth, let them eat stale cake dunked in weak tea of their own ungodly manufacture. If the Chicano intellectuals wish to re-cut my "Wonderful Ice Cream Suit" so it shapes "Zoot," may the belt unravel and the pants fall.

- Libraries are free speech zones. The First Amendment prevents the government, including public libraries, from mandating the use of user-based blocking software.

Six Reasons Why Self-Rating Schemes Are Wrong for the Internet

20　To begin with, the notion that citizens should "self-rate" their speech is contrary to the entire history of free speech in America. A proposal that we rate our online speech is no less offensive to the First Amendment than a proposal that publishers of books and magazines rate each and every article or story, or a proposal that everyone engaged in a street corner conversation rate his or her comments. But that is exactly what will happen to books, magazines, and any kind of speech that appears online under a self-rating scheme.

21　　In order to illustrate the very practical consequences of these schemes, consider the following six reasons, and their accompanying examples, illustrating why the ACLU is against self-rating:

Reason #1: Self-Rating Schemes Will Cause Controversial
Speech to Be Censored.

22　Kiyoshi Kuromiya, founder and sole operator of Critical Path Aids Project, has a Web site that includes safer sex information written in street language with

23　　For, let's face it, digression is the soul of the wit. Take philosophic asides away from Dante, Milton or Hamlet's father's ghost and what stays is dry bones. Laurence Sterne said it once: Digressions, incontestably, are the sunshine, the life, the soul of the reader! Take them out and one cold eternal winter would reign in every page. Restore them to the writer—he steps forth like a bridegroom, bids all-hail, brings in variety and forbids the appetite to fail.

24　　In sum, do not insult me with the beheadings, finger-choppings or the lung-deflations you plan for my work. I need my head to shake or not, my hand to wave or make a fist, my lungs to shout or whisper with. I will not go gently onto a shelf, degutted, to become a non-book.

25　　All you umpires, back to the bleachers. Referees, hit the showers. It's my game. I pitch, I hit, I catch. I run the bases. At sunset I've won or lost. At sunrise, I'm out again, giving it the old try.

26　　And no one can help me. Not even you.

explicit diagrams, in order to reach the widest possible audience. Kuromiya doesn't want to apply the rating "crude" or "explicit" to his speech, but if he doesn't, his site will be blocked as an unrated site. If he does rate, his speech will be lumped in with "pornography" and blocked from view. Under either choice, Kuromiya has been effectively blocked from reaching a large portion of his intended audience—teenage Internet users as well as adults.

23   As this example shows, the consequences of rating are far from neutral. The ratings themselves are all pejorative by definition, and they result in certain speech being blocked.

24   The White House has compared Internet ratings to "food labels" but that analogy is simply wrong. Food labels provide objective, scientifically verifiable information to help the consumer make choices about what to buy, e.g., the percentage of fat in a food product like milk. Internet ratings are subjective value judgments that result in certain speech being blocked to many viewers. Further, food labels are placed on products that are readily available to consumers unlike Internet labels, which would place certain kinds of speech out of reach of Internet users.

25   What is most critical to this issue is that speech like Kuromiya's is entitled to the highest degree of constitutional protection. This is why ratings requirements have never been imposed on those who speak via the printed word. Kuromiya could distribute the same material in print form on any street corner or in any bookstore without worrying about having to rate it. In fact, a number of Supreme Court cases have established that the First Amendment does not allow government to compel speakers to say something they don't want to say and that includes pejorative ratings. There is simply no justification for treating the Internet any differently.

Reason #2: Self-Rating Is Burdensome, Unwieldy, and Costly.
26   Art on the Net is a large, nonprofit Web site that hosts online "studios" where hundreds of artists display their work. The vast majority of the artwork has no sexual content, although there's an occasional Rubenesque painting. The ratings systems don't make sense when applied to art. Yet Art on the Net would still have to review and apply a rating to the more than 26,000 pages on its site, which would require time and staff that they just don't have. Or, they would have to require the artists themselves to self-rate, an option they find objectionable. If they decline to rate, they will be blocked as an unrated site even though most Internet users would hardly object to the art reaching minors, let alone adults.

27   As the Supreme Court noted in *Reno* v. *ACLU*, one of the virtues of the Internet is that it provides "relatively unlimited, low-cost capacity for communication of all kinds." In striking down the CDA, the Court held that im-

posing age-verification costs on Internet speakers would be "prohibitively expensive for noncommercial as well as some commercial speakers." Similarly, the burdensome requirement of self-rating thousands of pages of information would effectively shut most noncommercial speakers out of the Internet marketplace.

28   The technology of embedding the rating is also far from trivial. In a winning ACLU case that challenged a New York state online censorship statute, *ALA* v. *Pataki,* one long-time Internet expert testified that he tried to embed an RSACi label in his online newsletter site but finally gave up after several hours.

29   In addition, the ratings systems are simply unequipped to deal with the diversity of content now available on the Internet. There is perhaps nothing as subjective as a viewer's reaction to art. As history has shown again and again, one woman's masterpiece is another woman's pornography. How can ratings such as "explicit" or "crude" be used to categorize art? Even ratings systems that try to take artistic value into account will be inherently subjective, especially when applied by artists themselves, who will naturally consider their own work to have merit.

30   The variety of news-related sites on the Web will be equally difficult to rate. Should explicit war footage be labeled "violent" and blocked from view to teenagers? If a long news article has one curse word, is the curse word rated individually, or is the entire story rated and then blocked?

31   Even those who propose that "legitimate" news organizations should not be required to rate their sites stumble over the question of who will decide what is legitimate news.

Reason #3: Conversation Can't Be Rated.

32   You are in a chat room or a discussion group, one of the thousands of conversational areas of the Net. A victim of sexual abuse has posted a plea for help, and you want to respond. You've heard about a variety of ratings systems, but you've never used one. You read the RSACi Web page, but you can't figure out how to rate the discussion of sex and violence in your response. Aware of the penalties for mislabeling, you decide not to send your message after all.

33   The burdens of self-rating really hit home when applied to the vibrant, conversational areas of the Internet. Most Internet users don't run Web pages, but millions of people around the world send messages, short and long, every day, to chat rooms, news groups and mailing lists. A rating requirement for these areas of the Internet would be analogous to requiring all of us to rate our telephone or street corner or dinner party or water cooler conversations.

34   The only other way to rate these areas of cyberspace would be to rate entire chat rooms or news groups rather than individual messages. But most discussion groups aren't controlled by a specific person, so who would be responsible for rating them? In addition, discussion groups that contain some objectionable material would likely also have a wide variety of speech totally appropriate and valuable for minors; but the entire forum would be blocked from view for everyone.

Reason #4: Self-Rating Will Create "Fortress America" on the Internet.

35 You are a native of Papua, New Guinea, and as an anthropologist you have published several papers about your native culture. You create a Web site and post electronic versions of your papers, in order to share them with colleagues and other interested people around the world. You haven't heard about the move in America to rate Internet content. You don't know it, but since your site is unrated none of your colleagues in America will be able to access it.

36   People from all corners of the globe—people who might otherwise never connect because of their vast geographical differences—can now communicate on the Internet both easily and cheaply. One of the most dangerous aspects of ratings systems is their potential to build borders around American- and foreign-created speech. It is important to remember that today, nearly half of all Internet speech originates from outside the United States.

37   Even if powerful American industry leaders coerced other countries into adopting American ratings systems, how would these ratings make any sense to a New Guinean? Imagine that one of the anthropology papers explicitly describes a ritual in which teenage boys engage in self-mutilation as part of a rite of passage in achieving manhood. Would you look at it through the eyes of an American and rate it "torture," or would you rate it "appropriate for minors" for the New Guinea audience?

Reason #5: Self-Ratings Will Only Encourage, Not Prevent, Government Regulation.

38 The webmaster for Betty's Smut Shack, a Web site that sells sexually explicit photos, learns that many people won't get to his site if he either rates his site "sexually explicit" or fails to rate it at all. He rates his entire Web site "okay for minors." A powerful congressman from the Midwest learns that the site is now available to minors. He is outraged, and quickly introduces a bill imposing criminal penalties for mis-rated sites.

39   Without a penalty system for mis-rating, the entire concept of a self-ratings system breaks down. The Supreme Court that decided *Reno* v. *ACLU* would probably agree that the statute theorized above would violate the

First Amendment, but as we saw with the CDA, that won't necessarily prevent lawmakers from passing it.

40   In fact, as noted earlier, a senator from Washington state—home of Industry giant Microsoft, among others—has already proposed a law that creates criminal penalties for mis-rating. Not to be outdone, the filtering software company Safe Surf has proposed the introduction of a virtually identical federal law, including a provision that allows parents to sue speakers for damages if they "negligently" mis-rate their speech.

41   The example above shows that, despite all good intentions, the application of ratings systems is likely to lead to heavy-handed government censorship. Moreover, the targets of that censorship are likely to be just the sort of relatively powerless and controversial speakers, like the groups Critical Path Aids Project, Stop Prisoner Rape, Planned Parenthood, Human Rights Watch, and the various gay and lesbian organizations we represented in *Reno* v. *ACLU.*

Reason #6: Self-Ratings Schemes Will Turn the Internet into a Homogenized Medium Dominated by Commercial Speakers.

42   Huge entertainment conglomerates, such as the Disney Corporation or Time Warner, consult their platoons of lawyers who advise that their Web sites must be rated to reach the widest possible audience. They then hire and train staff to rate all of their Web pages. Everybody in the world will have access to their speech.

43   There is no question that there may be some speakers on the Internet for whom the ratings systems will impose only minimal burdens: the large, powerful corporate speakers with the money to hire legal counsel and staff to apply the necessary ratings. The commercial side of the Net continues to grow, but so far the democratic nature of the Internet has put commercial speakers on equal footing with all of the other noncommercial and individual speakers.

44   Today, it is just as easy to find the Critical Path AIDS Web site as it is to find the Disney site. Both speakers are able to reach a worldwide audience. But mandatory Internet self-rating could easily turn the most participatory communications medium the world has yet seen into a bland, homogenized, medium dominated by powerful American corporate speakers.

Is Third-Party Rating the Answer?

45   Third-party ratings systems, designed to work in tandem with PICS labeling, have been held out by some as the answer to the free speech problems posed by self-rating schemes. On the plus side, some argue, ratings by an independent third party could minimize the burden of self-rating on speakers

and could reduce the inaccuracy and mis-rating problems of self-rating. In fact, one of the touted strengths of the original PICS proposal was that a variety of third-party ratings systems would develop and users could pick and choose from the system that best fit their values. But third-party ratings systems still pose serious free speech concerns.

46   First, a multiplicity of ratings systems has not yet emerged on the market, probably due to the difficulty of any one company or organization trying to rate over a million Web sites, with hundreds of new sites, not to mention discussion groups and chat rooms springing up daily.

47   Second, under third-party rating systems, unrated sites still may be blocked.

48   When choosing which sites to rate first, it is likely that third-party raters will rate the most popular Web sites first, marginalizing individual and noncommercial sites. And like the self-rating systems, third-party ratings will apply subjective and value-laden ratings that could result in valuable material being blocked to adults and older minors. In addition, available third-party rating systems have no notification procedure so speakers have no way of knowing whether their speech has received a negative rating.

49   The fewer the third-party ratings products available, the greater the potential for arbitrary censorship. Powerful industry forces may lead one product to dominate the marketplace. If, for example, virtually all households use Microsoft Internet Explorer and Netscape, and the browsers, in turn, use RSACi as their system, RSACi could become the default censorship system for the Internet. In addition, federal and state governments could pass laws mandating use of a particular ratings system in schools or libraries. Either of these scenarios could devastate the diversity of the Internet marketplace.

50   Pro-censorship groups have argued that a third-party rating system for the Internet is no different from the voluntary Motion Picture Association of America ratings for movies that we've all lived with for years. But there is an important distinction: only a finite number of movies are produced in a given year. In contrast, the amount of content on the Internet is infinite. Movies are a static, definable product created by a small number of producers; speech on the Internet is seamless, interactive, and conversational. MPAA ratings also don't come with automatic blocking mechanisms.

The Problems with User-Based Blocking Software in the Home

51   With the explosive growth of the Internet, and in the wake of the recent censorship battles, the marketplace has responded with a wide variety of user-based blocking programs. Each company touts the speed and efficiency of its

staff members in blocking speech that they have determined is inappropriate for minors. The programs also often block speech based on keywords. (This can result in sites such as www.middlesex.gov or www.SuperBowlXXX.com being blocked because they contain the keywords "sex" and "XXX.")

52   In *Reno* v. *ACLU,* the ACLU successfully argued that the CDA violated the First Amendment because it was not the least restrictive means of addressing the government's asserted interest in protecting children from inappropriate material. In supporting this argument, we suggested that a less restrictive alternative was the availability of user-based blocking programs, e.g., Net Nanny, that parents could use in the home if they wished to limit their child's Internet access.

53   While user-based blocking programs present troubling free speech concerns, we still believe today that they are far preferable to any statute that imposes criminal penalties on online speech. In contrast, many of the new ratings schemes pose far greater free speech concerns than do user-based software programs.

54   Each user installs the program on her home computer and turns the blocking mechanism on or off at will. The programs do not generally block sites that they haven't rated, which means that they are not 100 percent effective.

55   Unlike the third-party ratings or self-rating schemes, these products usually do not work in concert with browsers and search engines, so the home user rather than an outside company sets the defaults. (However, it should be noted that this "stand-alone" feature could theoretically work against free speech principles, since here, too, it would be relatively easy to draft a law mandating the use of the products, under threat of criminal penalties.)

56   While the use of these products avoids some of the larger control issues with ratings systems, the blocking programs are far from problem-free. A number of products have been shown to block access to a wide variety of information that many would consider appropriate for minors. For example, some block access to safer sex information, although the Supreme Court has held that teenagers have the right to obtain access to such information even without their parents' consent. Other products block access to information of interest to the gay and lesbian community. Some products even block speech simply because it criticizes their product.

57   Some products allow home users to add or subtract particular sites from a list of blocked sites. For example, a parent can decide to allow access to "playboy.com" by removing it from the blocked sites list, and can deny access to "powerrangers.com" by adding it to the list. However most products

consider their lists of blocked speech to be proprietary information which they will not disclose.

58   Despite these problems, the use of blocking programs has been enthusiastically and uncritically endorsed by government and industry leaders alike. At the recent White House summit, Vice President Gore, along with industry and nonprofit groups, announced the creation of www.netparents.org, a site that provides direct links to a variety of blocking programs.

59   The ACLU urges the producers of all of these products to put real power in users' hands and provide full disclosure of their list of blocked speech and the criteria for blocking.

60   In addition, the ACLU urges the industry to develop products that provide maximum user control. For example, all users should be able to adjust the products to account for the varying maturity level of minors, and to adjust the list of blocked sites to reflect their own values.

61   It should go without saying that under no set of circumstances can governments constitutionally require anyone whether individual users or Internet Service Providers to run user-based blocking programs when accessing or providing access to the Internet.

Why Blocking Software Should Not Be Used by Public Libraries

62   The "never-ending, worldwide conversation" of the Internet, as one lower court judge called it, is a conversation in which all citizens should be entitled to participate whether they access the Internet from the library or from the home. Just as government cannot require home users or Internet Service Providers (ISPs) to use blocking programs or self-rating programs, libraries should not require patrons to use blocking software when accessing the Internet at the library. The ACLU, like the American Library Association (ALA), opposes use of blocking software in public libraries.

63   Libraries have traditionally promoted free speech values by providing free books and information resources to people regardless of their age or income. Today, more than 20 percent of libraries in the United States offer free access to the Internet, and that number is growing daily. Libraries are critical to realizing the dream of universal access to the Internet, a dream that would be drastically altered if they were forced to become Internet censors.

64   In a recent announcement stating its policy, the ALA said:

> Libraries are places of inclusion rather than exclusion. Current blocking/filtering software prevents not only access to what some may consider "objectionable" material, but also blocks in-

formation protected by the First Amendment. The result is that legal and useful material will inevitably be blocked.

65   Librarians have never been in the business of determining what their patrons should read or see, and the fact that the material is now found on Internet is no different. By installing inaccurate and unreliable blocking programs on library Internet terminals, public libraries, which are almost always governmental entities, would inevitably censor speech that patrons are constitutionally entitled to access.

66   It has been suggested that a library's decision to install blocking software is like other legitimate selection decisions that libraries routinely make when they add particular books to their collections. But in fact, blocking programs take selection decisions totally out of the hands of the librarian and place them in the hands of a company with no experience in library science. As the ALA noted, "(F)ilters can impose the producer's viewpoint on the community."

67   Because, as noted above, most filtering programs don't provide a list of the sites they block, libraries won't even know what resources are blocked. In addition, Internet speakers won't know which libraries have blocked access to their speech and won't be able to protest.

68   Installing blocking software in libraries to prevent adults as well as minors from accessing legally protected material raises severe First Amendment questions. Indeed, that principle that governments can't block adult access to speech in the name of protecting children was one of the key reasons for the Supreme Court's decision in *Reno* v. *ACLU.*

69   If adults are allowed full access, but minors are forced to use blocking programs, constitutional problems remain. Minors, especially older minors, have a constitutional right to access many of the resources that have been shown to be blocked by user-based blocking programs.

70   One of the virtues of the Internet is that it allows an isolated gay teenager in Des Moines, Iowa, to talk to other teenagers around the globe who are also struggling with issues relating to their sexuality. It allows teens to find out how to avoid AIDS and other sexually transmitted diseases even if they are too embarrassed to ask an adult in person or even too embarrassed to check out a book.

71   When the ACLU made this argument in *Reno* v. *ACLU,* it was considered controversial, even among our allies. But the Supreme Court agreed that minors have rights too. Library blocking proposals that allow minors full access to the Internet only with parental permission are unacceptable.

72   Libraries can and should take other actions that are more protective of online free speech principles. First, libraries can publicize and provide links to particular sites that have been recommended for children. Second, to avoid

unwanted viewing by passersby (and to protect the confidentiality of users), libraries can install Internet access terminals in ways that minimize public view. Third, libraries can impose "content-neutral" time limits on Internet use.

Conclusion

73   The ACLU has always favored providing Internet users, especially parents, with more information. We welcomed, for example, the American Library Association's announcement at the White House summit of *The Librarian's Guide to Cyberspace for Parents and Kids*, a "comprehensive brochure and Web site combining Internet terminology, safety tips, site selection advice, and more than fifty of the most educational and entertaining sites available for children on the Internet."

74   In *Reno* v. *ACLU,* we noted that federal and state governments are already vigorously enforcing existing obscenity, child pornography, and child solicitation laws on the Internet. In addition, Internet users must affirmatively seek out speech on the Internet; no one is caught by surprise.

75   In fact, many speakers on the Net provide preliminary information about the nature of their speech. The ACLU's site on America Online, for example, has a message on its home page announcing that the site is a "free speech zone." Many sites offering commercial transactions on the Net contain warnings concerning the security of Net information. Sites containing sexually explicit material often begin with a statement describing the adult nature of the material. Chat rooms and newsgroups have names that describe the subject being discussed. Even individual e-mail messages contain a subject line.

76   The preliminary information available on the Internet has several important components that distinguish it from all the ratings systems discussed above: (1) it is created and provided by the speaker; (2) it helps the user decide whether to read any further; (3) speakers who choose not to provide such information are not penalized; (4) it does not result in the automatic blocking of speech by an entity other than the speaker or reader before the speech has ever been viewed. Thus, the very nature of the Internet reveals why more speech is always a better solution than censorship for dealing with speech that someone may find objectionable.

77   It is not too late for the Internet community to slowly and carefully examine these proposals and to reject those that will transform the Internet from a true marketplace of ideas into just another mainstream, lifeless medium with content no more exciting or diverse than that of television.

78   Civil libertarians, human rights organizations, librarians and Internet users, speakers and providers, all joined together to defeat the CDA. We achieved a stunning victory, establishing a legal framework that affords the

Internet the highest constitutional protection. We put a quick end to a fire that was all but visible and threatening. The fire next time may be more difficult to detect and extinguish.

Appendix: Internet Ratings Systems—How Do They Work?

The Technology: PICS, Browsers, Search Engines, and Ratings

The rating and blocking proposals discussed below all rely on a few key components of current Internet technology. While none of this technology will by itself censor speech, some of it may well enable censorship to occur.

PICS: * The Platform for Internet Content Selection (PICS) is a rating standard that establishes a consistent way to rate and block online content. PICS was created by a large consortium of Internet industry leaders, and became operational last year. In theory, PICS does not incorporate or endorse any particular rating system; the technology is an empty vessel into which different rating systems can be poured. In reality, only three third-party rating systems have been developed for PICS: SafeSurf, Net Shepherd, and the de facto industry standard RSACi.

Browsers: Browsers are the software tool that Internet users need in order to access information on the World Wide Web. Two products—Microsoft's Internet Explorer and Netscape—currently control 90 percent of the browser market. Microsoft's Internet Explorer is now compatible with PICS. That is, the Internet Explorer can now be configured to block speech that has been rated with PICS-compatible ratings. Netscape has announced that it will soon offer the same capability. When the blocking feature on the browser is activated, speech with negative ratings is blocked. In addition, because a vast majority of Internet sites remain unrated, the blocking feature can be configured to block all unrated sites.

Search Engines: Search engines are software programs that allow Internet users to conduct searches for content on a particular subject, using a string of words or phrases. The search result typically provides a list of links to sites on the relevant topic. Four of the major search engines have announced a

---

*While PICS could be put to legitimate use with adequate free speech safeguards, there is a very real fear that governments, especially authoritarian governments, will use the technology to impose severe content controls.

plan to cooperate in the move towards Internet ratings. For example, they may decide not to list sites that have negative ratings or that are unrated.

Ratings Systems: There are a few PICS-compatible ratings systems already in use. Two self-rating systems include RSACi and Safe Surf. RSACi, developed by the same group that rates video games, attempts to rate certain kinds of speech, like sex and violence, according to objective criteria describing the content. For example, it rates levels of violence from "harmless conflict; some damage to objects" to "creatures injured or killed." Levels of sexual content are rated from "passionate kissing" to "clothed sexual touching" to "explicit sexual activity; sex crimes." The context in which the material is presented is not considered under the RSACi system; for example, it doesn't distinguish educational materials from other materials.

Safe Surf applies a complicated ratings system on a variety of types of speech, from profanity to gambling. The ratings are more contextual, but they are also more subjective and value-laden. For example, Safe Surf rates sexual content from "artistic" to "erotic" to "explicit and crude pornographic."

Net Shepherd, a third-party rating system that has rated 300,000 sites, rates only for "maturity" and "quality."

GREGG EASTERBROOK

Watch and Learn

The following argument appeared in the May 17, 1997, issue of The New Republic—*a New York City weekly magazine that is considered middle of the road in its editorial outlook. Gregg Easterbrook writes frequently for* The New Republic *and for other publications.*

1   Millions of teens have seen the 1996 movie *Scream,* a box-office and home-rental hit. Critics adored the film. The *Washington Post* declared that it "deftly mixes irony, self-reference, and social wry commentary." The *Los Angeles Times* hailed it as "a bravura, provocative send-up." *Scream* opens with a scene in which a teenage girl is forced to watch her jock boyfriend tortured and then disemboweled by two fellow students who, it will eventually be learned, want revenge on anyone from high school who crossed them. After jock boy's stomach is shown cut open and he dies screaming, the killers stab and torture the girl, then cut her throat and hang her body from a tree so that Mom can discover it when she drives up. A dozen students and teachers are graphically butchered in the film, while the characters make running jokes about murder. At one point, a boy tells a big-breasted friend she'd better be careful because the stacked girls always get it in horror films; in the next scene, she's grabbed, stabbed through the breasts, and murdered. Some provocative send-up, huh? The movie builds to a finale in which one of the killers announces that he and his accomplice started off by murdering strangers but then realized it was a lot more fun to kill their friends.

2   Now that two Colorado high schoolers have murdered twelve class-mates and a teacher—often, it appears, first taunting their pleading victims, just like celebrity stars do in the movies!—some commentators have dismissed the role of violence in the images shown to the young, pointing out that horrific acts by children existed before celluloid or the phosphor screen. That is true—the Leopold-Loeb murder of 1924, for example. But mass murders by the young, once phenomenally rare, are suddenly on the increase. Can it be coincidence that this increase is happening at the same time that Hollywood has begun to market the notion that mass murder is fun?

3   For, in cinema's never-ending quest to up the ante on violence, murder as sport is the latest frontier. Slasher flicks began this trend; most portray carnage from the killer's point of view, showing the victim cowering,

begging, screaming as the blade goes in, treating each death as a moment of festivity for the killer. (Many killers seek feelings of power over their victims, criminology finds; by reveling in the pleas of victims, slasher movies promote this base emotion.) The 1994 movie *Natural Born Killers* depicted slaying the helpless not only as a way to have a grand time but also as a way to become a celebrity; several dozen onscreen murders are shown in that film, along with a discussion of how great it makes you feel to just pick people out at random and kill them. The 1994 movie *Pulp Fiction* presented hit men as glamour figures having loads of interesting fun; the actors were mainstream stars like John Travolta. The 1995 movie *Seven,* starring Brad Pitt, portrayed a sort of contest to murder in unusually grotesque ways. (Screenwriters now actually discuss, and critics comment on, which film's killings are most amusing.) The 1995 movie *The Basketball Diaries* contains an extended dream sequence in which the title character, played by teen heartthrob Leonardo DiCaprio, methodically guns down whimpering, pleading classmates at his high school. A rock soundtrack pulses, and the character smiles as he kills.

4   The new Hollywood tack of portraying random murder as a form of recreation does not come from schlock-houses. Disney's Miramax division, the same mainstream studio that produced *Shakespeare in Love,* is responsible for *Scream* and *Pulp Fiction.* Time-Warner is to blame for *Natural Born Killers* and actually ran television ads promoting this film as "delirious, daredevil fun." (After it was criticized for calling murder "fun," Time-Warner tried to justify *Killers* as social commentary; if you believe that, you believe *Godzilla* was really about biodiversity protection.) Praise and publicity for gratuitously violent movies come from the big media conglomerates, including the newspapers and networks that profit from advertising for films that glorify murder. Disney, now one of the leading promoters of violent images in American culture, even feels that what little kids need is more violence. Its Christmas 1998 children's movie *Mighty Joe Young* begins with an eight-year-old girl watching her mother being murdered. By the movie's end, it is 20 years later, and the killer has returned to stalk the grown daughter, pointing a gun in her face and announcing, "Now join your mother in hell." A Disney movie.

5   One reason Hollywood keeps reaching for ever-more-obscene levels of killing is that it must compete with television, which today routinely airs the kind of violence once considered shocking in theaters. According to studies conducted at Temple University, prime-time network (non-news) shows now average up to five violent acts per hour. In February, NBC ran in prime time the movie *Eraser,* not editing out an extremely graphic scene in which a

killer pulls a gun on a bystander and blasts away. The latest TV movie based on *The Rockford Files,* which aired on CBS the night of the Colorado murders, opened with a scene of an eleven-year-old girl in short-shorts being stalked by a man in a black hood, grabbed, and dragged off, screaming. *The Rockford Files* is a *comedy.* Combining television and movies, the typical American boy or girl, studies find, will observe a stunning 40,000 dramatizations of killing by age 18.

6   In the days after the Colorado slaughter, discussion of violent images in American culture was dominated by the canned positions of the anti-Hollywood right and the mammon-is-our-God film lobby. The debate missed three vital points: the distinction between what adults should be allowed to see (anything) and what the inchoate minds of children and adolescents should see; the way in which important liberal battles to win free expression in art and literature have been perverted into an excuse for antisocial video brutality produced by cynical capitalists; and the difference between censorship and voluntary acts of responsibility.

7   The day after the Colorado shooting, Mike De Luca, an executive of New Line Cinema, maker of *The Basketball Diaries,* told *USA Today* that, when kids kill, "bad home life, bad parenting, having guns in the home" are "more of a factor than what we put out there for entertainment." Setting aside the disclosure that Hollywood now categorizes scenes of movie stars gunning down the innocent as "entertainment," De Luca is correct: studies do show that upbringing is more determinant of violent behavior than any other factor. But research also clearly shows that the viewing of violence can cause aggression and crime. So the question is, in a society already plagued by poor parenting and unlimited gun sales, why does the entertainment industry feel privileged to make violence even more prevalent?

8   Even when researchers factor out other influences such as parental attention, many peer-reviewed studies have found causal links between viewing phony violence and engaging in actual violence. A 1971 surgeon general's report asserted a broad relationship between the two. Studies by Brandon Centerwall, an epidemiologist at the University of Wisconsin, have shown that the postwar murder rise in the United States began roughly a decade after TV viewing became common. Centerwall also found that, in South Africa, where television was not generally available until 1975, national murder rates started rising about a decade later. Violent computer games have not existed long enough to be the subject of many controlled studies, but experts expect it will be shown that playing such games in youth also correlates with destructive behavior. There's an eerie likelihood

that violent movies and violent games amplify one another, the film and television images placing thoughts of carnage into the psyche while the games condition the trigger finger to act on those impulses.

9   Leonard Eron, a psychologist at the University of Michigan, has been tracking video violence and actual violence for almost four decades. His initial studies, in 1960, found that even the occasional violence depicted in 1950s television—to which every parent would gladly return today—caused increased aggression among eight-year-olds. By the adult years, Eron's studies find, those who watched the most TV and movies in childhood were much more likely to have been arrested for, or convicted of, violent felonies. Eron believes that ten percent of U.S. violent crime is caused by exposure to images of violence, meaning that 90 percent is not but that a ten percent national reduction in violence might be achieved merely by moderating the content of television and movies. "Kids learn by observation," Eron says. "If what they observe is violent, that's what they learn." To cite a minor but telling example, the introduction of vulgar language into American public discourse traces, Eron thinks, largely to the point at which stars like Clark Gable began to swear onscreen, and kids then imitated swearing as normative.

10   Defenders of bloodshed in film, television, and writing often argue that depictions of killing don't incite real violence because no one is really affected by what they see or read; it's all just water off a duck's back. At heart, this is an argument against free expression. The whole reason to have a First Amendment is that people *are* influenced by what they see and hear: words and images do change minds, so there must be free competition among them. If what we say, write, or show has no consequences, why bother to have free speech?

11   Defenders of Hollywood bloodshed also employ the argument that, since millions of people watch screen mayhem and shrug, feigned violence has no causal relation to actual violence. After a horrific 1992 case in which a British gang acted out a scene from the slasher movie *Child's Play 3*, torturing a girl to death as the movie had shown, the novelist Martin Amis wrote dismissively in *The New Yorker* that he had rented *Child's Play 3* and watched the film, and it hadn't made him want to kill anyone, so what was the problem? But Amis isn't homicidal or unbalanced. For those on the psychological borderline, the calculus is different. There have, for example, been at least two instances of real-world shootings in which the guilty imitated scenes in *Natural Born Killers*.

12   Most telling, Amis wasn't affected by watching a slasher movie because Amis is not young. Except for the unbalanced, exposure to violence in

video "is not so important for adults; adults can watch anything they want," Eron says. Younger minds are a different story. Children who don't yet understand the difference between illusion and reality may be highly affected by video violence. Between the ages of two and eight, hours of viewing violent TV programs and movies correlates closely to felonies later in life; the child comes to see hitting, stabbing, and shooting as normative acts. The link between watching violence and engaging in violence continues up to about the age of 19, Eron finds, after which most people's characters have been formed, and video mayhem no longer correlates to destructive behavior.

13   Trends in gun availability do not appear to explain the murder rise that has coincided with television and violent films. Research by John Lott Jr., of the University of Chicago Law School, shows that the percentage of homes with guns has changed little throughout the postwar era. What appears to have changed is the willingness of people to fire their guns at one another. Are adolescents now willing to use guns because violent images make killing seem acceptable or even cool? Following the Colorado slaughter, The *New York Times* ran a recounting of other postwar mass murders staged by the young, such as the 1966 Texas tower killings, and noted that they all happened before the advent of the Internet or shock rock, which seemed to the *Times* to absolve the modern media. But all the mass killings by the young occurred after 1950—after it became common to watch violence on television.

14   When horrific murders occur, the film and television industries routinely attempt to transfer criticism to the weapons used. Just after the Colorado shootings, for instance, TV talk-show host Rosie O'Donnell called for a constitutional amendment banning all firearms. How strange that O'Donnell didn't call instead for a boycott of Sony or its production company, Columbia Tristar—a film studio from which she has received generous paychecks and whose current offerings include *8MM*, which glamorizes the sexual murder of young women, and *The Replacement Killers*, whose hero is a hit man and which depicts dozens of gun murders. Handguns should be licensed, but that hardly excuses the convenient sanctimony of blaming the crime on the weapon, rather than on what resides in the human mind.

15   And, when it comes to promoting adoration of guns, Hollywood might as well be the NRA's marketing arm. An ever-increasing share of film and television depicts the firearm as something the virile must have and use, if not an outright sexual aid. Check the theater section of any newspaper, and you will find an ever-higher percentage of movie ads in which the stars are prominently holding guns. Keanu Reeves, Uma Thurman, Laurence Fishburne, Geena Davis, Woody Harrelson, and Mark Wahlberg are just a few of the hip stars who have posed with guns for movie advertising. Hollywood endlessly

congratulates itself for reducing the depiction of cigarettes in movies and movie ads. Cigarettes had to go, the film industry admitted, because glamorizing them gives the wrong idea to kids. But the glamorization of firearms, which is far more dangerous, continues. Today, even female stars who otherwise consider themselves politically aware will model in sexualized poses with guns. Ads for the new movie *Goodbye Lover* show star Patricia Arquette nearly nude, with very little between her and the viewer but her handgun.

16   But doesn't video violence merely depict a stark reality against which the young need be warned? American society is far too violent, yet the forms of brutality highlighted in the movies and on television—prominently "thrill" killings and serial murders—are pure distortion. Nearly 99 percent of real murders result from robberies, drug deals, and domestic disputes; figures from research affiliated with the FBI's behavioral sciences division show an average of only about 30 serial or "thrill" murders nationally per year. Thirty is plenty horrifying enough, but, at this point, each of the major networks and movie studios alone depicts more "thrill" and serial murders annually than that. By endlessly exploiting the notion of the "thrill" murder, Hollywood and television present to the young an entirely imaginary image of a society in which killing for pleasure is a common event. The publishing industry, including some TNR advertisers, also distorts for profit the frequency of "thrill" murders.

17   The profitability of violent cinema is broadly dependent on the "downrating" of films—movies containing extreme violence being rated only R instead of NC-17 (the new name for X)—and the lax enforcement of age restrictions regarding movies. Teens are the best market segment for Hollywood; when moviemakers claim their violent movies are not meant to appeal to teens, they are simply lying. The millionaire status of actors, directors, and studio heads—and the returns of the mutual funds that invest in movie companies—depends on not restricting teen access to theaters or film rentals. Studios in effect control the movie ratings board and endlessly lobby it not to label extreme violence with an NC-17, the only form of rating that is actually enforced. *Natural Born Killers,* for example, received an R following Time-Warner lobbying, despite its repeated close-up murders and one charming scene in which the stars kidnap a high school girl and argue about whether it would be more fun to kill her before or after raping her. Since its inception, the movie ratings board has put its most restrictive rating on any realistic representation of lovemaking, while sanctioning ever-more-graphic depictions of murder and torture. In economic terms, the

board's pro-violence bias gives studios an incentive to present more death and mayhem, confident that ratings officials will smile with approval.

18   When R-and-X battles were first fought, intellectual sentiment regarded the ratings system as a way of blocking the young from seeing films with political content, such as *Easy Rider,* or discouraging depictions of sexuality; ratings were perceived as the rubes' counterattack against cinematic sophistication. But, in the 1960s, murder after murder after murder was not standard cinema fare. The most controversial violent film of that era, *A Clockwork Orange,* depicted a total of one killing, which was heard but not on-camera. (*Clockwork Orange* also had genuine political content, unlike most of today's big-studio movies.) In an era of runaway screen violence, the '60s ideal that the young should be allowed to see what they want has been corrupted. In this, trends in video mirror the misuse of liberal ideals generally.

19   Anti-censorship battles of this century were fought on firm ground, advocating the right of films to tackle social and sexual issues (the 1930s Hays office forbade among other things cinematic mention of cohabitation) and free access to works of literature such as *Ulysses, Story of O,* and the original version of Norman Mailer's *The Naked and the Dead.* Struggles against censors established that suppression of film or writing is wrong.

20   But to say that nothing should be censored is very different from saying that everything should be shown. Today, Hollywood and television have twisted the First Amendment concept that occasional repulsive or worthless expression must be protected, so as to guarantee freedom for works of genuine political content or artistic merit, into a new standard in which constitutional freedoms are employed mainly to safeguard works that make no pretense of merit. In the new standard, the bulk of what's being protected is repulsive or worthless, with the meritorious work the rare exception.

21   Not only is there profit for the performers, producers, management, and shareholders of firms that glorify violence, so, too, is there profit for politicians. Many conservative or Republican politicians who denounce Hollywood eagerly accept its lucre. Bob Dole's 1995 anti-Hollywood speech was not followed up by any anti-Hollywood legislation or campaign-funds strategy. After the Colorado murders, President Clinton declared, "Parents should take this moment to ask what else they can do to shield children from violent images and experiences that warp young perceptions." But Clinton was careful to avoid criticizing Hollywood, one of the top sources of public backing and campaign contributions for him and his would-be successor,

Vice President Al Gore. The president had nothing specific to propose on film violence—only that parents should try to figure out what to do.

22   When television producers say it is the parents' obligation to keep children away from the tube, they reach the self-satire point of warning that their own product is unsuitable for consumption. The situation will improve somewhat beginning in 2000, by which time all new TVs must be sold with the "V chip"—supported by Clinton and Gore—which will allow parents to block violent shows. But it will be at least a decade before the majority of the nation's sets include the chip, and who knows how adept young minds will prove at defeating it? Rather than relying on a technical fix that will take many years to achieve an effect, TV producers could simply stop churning out the gratuitous violence. Television could dramatically reduce its output of scenes of killing and still depict violence in news broadcasts, documentaries, and the occasional show in which the horrible is genuinely relevant. Reduction in violence is not censorship; it is placing social responsibility before profit.

23   The movie industry could practice the same kind of restraint without sacrificing profitability. In this regard, the big Hollywood studios, including Disney, look craven and exploitative compared to, of all things, the porn-video industry. Repulsive material occurs in underground porn, but, in the products sold by the mainstream triple-X distributors such as Vivid Video (the MGM of the erotica business), violence is never, ever, ever depicted—because that would be irresponsible. Women and men perform every conceivable explicit act in today's mainstream porn, but what is shown is always consensual and almost sunnily friendly. Scenes of rape or sexual menace never occur, and scenes of sexual murder are an absolute taboo.

24   It is beyond irony that today Sony and Time-Warner eagerly market explicit depictions of women being raped, sexually assaulted, and sexually murdered, while the mainstream porn industry would never dream of doing so. But, if money is all that matters, the point here is that mainstream porn is violence-free and yet risqué and highly profitable. Surely this shows that Hollywood could voluntarily step back from the abyss of glorifying violence and still retain its edge and its income.

25   Following the Colorado massacre, Republican presidential candidate Gary Bauer declared to a campaign audience, "In the America I want, all of these producers and directors, they would not be able to show their faces in public" because fingers "would be pointing at them and saying, 'Shame, shame.' " The statement sent chills through anyone fearing right-wing thought-control. But Bauer's final clause is correct—Hollywood and televi-

sion do need to hear the words "shame, shame." The cause of the shame should be removed voluntarily, not to stave off censorship, but because it is the responsible thing to do.

26   Put it this way. The day after a teenager guns down the sons and daughters of studio executives in a high school in Bel Air or Westwood, Disney and Time-Warner will stop glamorizing murder. Do we have to wait until that day?

By permission of Chuck Asay and Creators Syndicate, Inc.

HENRY LOUIS GATES, JR.

Truth or Consequences: Putting Limits on Limits

Henry Louis Gates, Jr. (1950-   ), a leading public intellectual, is chair of Harvard's Afro-American Studies Program. He writes prodigiously—columns in The New Yorker *and elsewhere, influential books such as* The Signifying Monkey *(1988),* Colored People—A Memoir *(1994), and an edition of the* Norton Anthology of African-American Literature—*and he frequently shows up in the media when important public issues are under discussion. The following essay appeared in* Academe *in January 1994.*

> *It is by the goodness of God that in our country we have those three unspeakably precious things: freedom of speech, freedom of conscience, and the prudence never to practice either of them.*
>
> —Mark Twain

1   These are challenging times for First Amendment sentimentalists. After decades in which the limits of expression were steadily pushed back, the pendulum, to switch metaphors, is beginning to swing the other way. Legal scholars on the left are busily proposing tort approaches toward hate speech. Senator Jesse Helms attaches a rider to a bill funding the National Endowment for the Arts that would prevent it from supporting offensive art—the terms of offense being largely imported from a Wisconsin hate speech ordinance. What Robin West calls the feminist-conservative alliance has made significant inroads in municipalities across the country, while the Canadian Supreme Court has promulgated Catharine MacKinnon's approach toward pornography as law of the land. And the currently fashionable communitarian movement has given the impression that it believes that excessive deference has been given to the creed of free speech. In short, over the past few years, a new suppressionist alliance seemed to betoken the declining significance of liberalism.

2   First Amendment absolutism has never entailed absolute devotion to free expression; the question has always been where to draw the line. The salient exceptions to First Amendment protection do, however, all involve the concrete prospect of significant—and involuntary—exposure to harm. For example: speech posing imminent and irreparable threat to public order or the

nation; libel and the invasion of privacy; and the regulated domain of "commercial speech," encompassing, for instance, "blue sky" laws governing truth in advertising. (Obscenity is the notable deviation from this norm.) I like to describe myself as a First Amendment sentimentalist, because I believe that the First Amendment should be given a generous benefit of the doubt in contested cases; but I also know that there are no absolutes in our fallen state.

3   Let me admit, at the onset, that I believe some figures on the academic/cultural left have too quickly adopted the strategies of the political right. Here, I'm thinking principally of that somewhat shopworn debate over "hate speech" as a variance from protected expression, and it may be a topic worth reviewing briefly.

4   As Michael Kinsley has pointed out, most college statutes restricting freedom of expression were implemented by conservative forces in the early 1970s. Under the banner of "civility," their hope was to control campus radicals who seized on free speech as a shield for their own activities. (Remember the Free Speech Movement? Dates you, doesn't it?) Ironically, however, the very ascent of liberal jurisprudence in the 1960s finally made the free speech banner less appealing for left and oppositional intellectuals, who viewed such formal civil liberties as a subterfuge and rationale for larger social inequities. The sort of intellectual contrarians and vanguardists who would have rallied behind the ideology of freedom of expression in the days before its (at least partial) ascendance are now, understandably enough, more disposed to explore its limits and failings. And so the rubric of "free speech," in the 1960s an empowering rubric of campus radicals, has today been ceded to their conservative opponents as an ironic instrument of requital. As a result, the existence of speech ordinances introduced by conservatives in the early 1970s can today be cited as evidence of a marauding threat from the thought police on the left. Well, at the very least, I think the convergence of tactics from one era to another ought to give us pause.

5   Let me be clear on one point. I am very sensitive to the issues raised in the arguments for hate speech bans. Growing up in a segregated mill-town in Appalachia, I thought there was a sign on my back saying "nigger," because that's what some white folk seemed to think my name was. So I don't deny that the language of racial prejudice can inflict harm. At the same time—as the Sondheim song has it—I'm still here.

6   The strongest arguments for speech bans are, when you examine them more closely, arguments *against* arguments against speech bans. They are often very clever; often persuasive. But what they don't establish is that a ban on hate speech is so indispensable, so essential to avoid some present danger, that it justifies handing their opponents on the right a gift-wrapped,

bow-tied, and beribboned rallying point. In the current environment of symbolic politics, the speech ban is a powerful thing: it can turn a garden-variety bigot into a First Amendment martyr.

7   So my concern is, first and foremost, a practical one. The problem with speech codes is that they make it impossible to challenge bigotry without creating a debate over the right to speak. And that is too great a price to pay. If someone calls me a nigger, I don't want to have to spend the next five hours debating the fine points of John Stuart Mill. Speech codes kill critique: For me, that's what it comes down to.

8   Given the fact that verbal harassment is already, and pretty uncontroversially, prohibited; given the fact, too, that campus speech bans are rarely enforced, the question arises: do we need them? Their proponents say yes—but they almost always offer *expressive* rather than *consequentialist* arguments for them. That is, they do not say, for instance, that the statute will spare vulnerable students some foreseeable amount of psychic trauma. They say, rather, that by adopting such a statute, the university *expresses* its opposition to hate speech and bigotry. The statute symbolizes our commitment to tolerance, to the creation of an educational environment where mutual colloquy and comity are preserved. (The conservative sociologist James Q. Wilson has made the argument for the case of obscenity when he writes of his "belief that human character is, in the long run, affected not by occasional furtive experiences [but] by whether society does or does not state that there is an important distinction between the loathsome and the decent.")

9   Well, yes, tolerance and mutual respect sound like nice things to symbolize. What we forget is that once we have retreated to the level of symbolic, gestural politics, you have to take into account all the other symbolic considerations. So even if you think that the free speech position contains logical holes and inconsistencies, you need to register *its* symbolic force. And it is this level of scrutiny that tips the balance in the other direction.

10   But there's a larger issue involved: Is the regulation of verbal expression among the laity the right place to begin, if your concern is to redress broad-gauged injustice? Can social inequity be censored out of existence?

11   As an English professor, I can report that our more powerful "discourse theories"—focussing on the political dimension of the most innocent seeming texts—can encourage this dream. But social critique allies itself with its natural antagonist, the state apparatus of law enforcement, at its own peril. There are states—and Islamic ones are the most obvious in their vigilance—that do engage in the widespread censorship of public representations, including imagery in advertisement, television, and entertainment. Their task

is not to censor misogyny and perpetuate sexual equality, but to cover the elbows and ankles of females and discourage blasphemy, prurience, and other such illicit thoughts.

12   A reluctance to embark on any such exercise of massive state coercion does not wed one to the *status quo*. To defend the free speech right (or even, as *Miller* v. *California* requires, the cultural "value") of racist or misogynistic material is not to defend racism or misogyny—nor is it to shun, silence, or downgrade social critique of these things. To insist that expression should be free of state censorship is not to exempt it from critical censure. This is a point that both Kimberlè Crenshaw and I have argued elsewhere in connection with the Broward County prosecution of Luther Campbell and company.

13   To be sure, the distinction would mean little to some critics of First Amendment expansionism. On the one hand, Catharine MacKinnon would observe that we do not find it sufficient to "critique" rape; we punish it. Since, for her, expression degrading or hostile to women is as much an act of violence as other crimes of violence against women, such expression should be the subject of criminal and civil sanctions aimed at its abolition. On the other hand, the conservative legal philosopher Alexander Bickel has told us, "To listen to something on the assumption of the speaker's right to say it is to legitimate it. . . . Where nothing is unspeakable, nothing is undoable."

14   And I think there's an important point of convergence there: Bickel's precept, that to "listen to something on the assumption of the speaker's right to say it is to legitimate it," underlies much of the contemporary resistance to unfettered expression in the academic setting.

15   Nor has the literary or cultural realm been held to be exempt from these strictures. Suzanne Kappeler has argued that there are "no sanctuaries from political reality, no aesthetic or fantastic enclaves, no islands for the play of desire." It's a charge that Federal Circuit Judge Richard Posner (a former Brennan clerk) has neatly turned on its head. If so, Posner rejoins, "the vilest pornographic trash is protected." After all, "ideological representations are at the center of the expression that the First Amendment protects." (This also highlights the contradiction between modern obscenity law and MacKinnonism: according to liberal jurisprudence, the obscene has, by stipulation, no significant political content according to MacKinnonite jurisprudence; it's precisely the significant political content of obscenity that *makes* it obscene.)

16   Content-based restrictions abound in other countries. In Britain, it is illegal to foment racial hatred; literature propagating such attitudes is subject to prosecution and suppression. (By custom, only egregious examples are subject to scrutiny.) In this country, I can buy scores of racist tracts. And

yet, granted the unhappy condition of our society, perhaps we shouldn't have it any other way: the possibilities of abuse are too clear and present.

17   As the political philosopher Josh Cohen writes: "In a society in which there are relatively poor and powerless groups, members of those groups are especially likely to do badly when the regulation of expression proceeds on the basis of vague standards whose implementation depends on the discretion of powerful actors."

18   A tort approach toward hate speech, which would allow the recovery of damages in the event of hurtful expression, would be difficult to reign in. Tort approaches toward hurtful expression propose to allocate costs of communications in a way that assigns the risk to the producer instead of the consumer. How you feel about this depends on your feelings about freedom of expression *per se* as a moral value, or a social good; in general, I would find unattractive the degree of paternalism involved in restricting speech on the basis of a few unreasonable even if foreseeable reactions, when these do not constitute a significant threat to the social order. Moreover, while these approaches would compel actors to internalize costs of "risky" speech, we do not allow it to reap the equally fortuitous benefits. The net result of this asymmetry would be to discourage speech.

19   There's also the possible model of "hostile environment." Thus (to choose a fairly recent example) a student walks into a classroom at the University of Michigan and reads, chalked anonymously on the blackboard, the motto "A mind is a terrible thing to waste . . . especially on a nigger." Arguably, remarks of this sort create what civil rights law has called, with respect to sexual harassment, a "hostile environment"—an environment inimical to the aims and objectives of university education. Similarly, a professor who seems to promulgate racist or anti-Semitic doctrines in the classroom might appear to contravene the education mission of the university in important ways.

20   So I want to take the issue of offense seriously. But it is only one of many considerations that must weigh in the balance. One recalls justice William O. Douglas's 1973 remarks, "One of the most offensive experiences in my life was a visit to a nation where bookstalls were filled only with books on mathematics and books on religion."

21   Another plane of analysis would recognize not simply formal equity and formal freedom, but also imbalances and inequities of access. In an old slogan, freedom of the press belongs to those who own the press. So there are issues about freedom of expression that subtend issues of democracy. Some of these surfaced in the debates over the NEA in the years of Republican control of the White House. The legal scholar Geoffrey Stone has argued

to the effect that the disbursement of government funding to the arts, though not constitutionally required, does involve constitutional questions (to do with "government neutrality in the field of ideas") once implemented. I admit I find Stone's argument more ingenious than persuasive. At the end of the day, there's a distinction worth preserving between not supporting and suppressing. And, as many have pointed out, there's something bathetic about the avowed dependence of oppositional art upon subsidy from the executive branch. "My dance exposes your greed, your hypocrisy, your bigotry, your philistinism, your crass vulgarity," says one of Jules Feiffer's cartoon monologists. "Fund me!"

22   Was the NEA "politicized"? Of course. But the charge of "politics" isn't one we can fling with good conscience, save in the spirit of *tu quoque*. If art is political, how can judgment not be? The fig leaf of formalities fools no one, and the tidy distinction between the "artistic" and "political" ought to be left for the genteel likes of former NEA chair John Frohnmayer. For art that robustly challenges the distinction is poorly served by stealthy recourse to it.

23   I said just now that there's a useful distinction between not supporting and suppressing. Of course, there is a sense in which the distinction counts for little: if I can't make my film, what does it matter whether I was prevented by poverty or prohibition? But in that impact-oriented sense, we have no free speech anyway, since access to a mass audience is hardly democratically distributed. In that sense, we should worry more about NBC than NEA. More important than our unendowed National Endowment would be to have governmental agencies only, the Public Broadcasting System or Voice of America.

24   No effective defense of relatively unfettered colloquy can presume the inertness of speech. Speech is not impotent, but listeners are not impotent either: they are not tempest-tossed rag dolls blown about by every evil wind. Any unconscious assumption of the passivity of reception neglects the fact that resistance begins with reaction. That the attempt to filter the environment of offense itself reeks of condescension and paternalism. As the legal scholar David Richard has written, "It is a contempt of human rationality for any other putative sovereign, democratic or otherwise, to decide to what communications mature people can be exposed."

25   The limits of intellectual expression may turn out to limit intellectual expression. But freedom of expression is too important a value to sacrifice to the vainglory of a professor Tony Martin or Leonard Jeffries or William Shockley. So it's important to remember that obscenity and hate speech alike only *become* free speech issues when their foes turn from censure to censorship. When we decided to let a thousand flowers bloom, we always knew that some of them would be weeds.

Affirmative Action

A central document of the Civil Rights movement, the Civil Rights Act of 1964 outlaws discrimination from a number of public institutions in the United States. Part of that act prohibits discrimination on the job: "It shall be an unlawful employment practice for an employer . . . to fail or refuse to hire or to discharge any individual, or otherwise to discriminate against any individual with respect to his compensation, terms, conditions, or privileges of employment, because of such individual's race, color, religion, sex, or national origin. . . . If the court finds that the respondent has intentionally engaged in an unlawful employment practice . . . the court may enjoin the respondent from engaging in such unlawful employment practice, and order such affirmative action as may be appropriate."

And so "affirmative action" was born. But what does affirmative action mean in practical terms? Should it be a means of commanding employers and educators not to discriminate so that everyone has equal opportunity for jobs and education? Or should it mean more active measures—goals, timetables, and quotas designed to promote balanced results? Has the need for affirmative action expired in the thirty-five years since the Civil Rights Act? Can we now justify passing over someone or favoring someone because of the group that person is born into? Is affirmative action inefficient in that it favors racial and gender factors over performance? Or has affirmative action been responsible for much of our recent national prosperity by giving all citizens the opportunity to develop to their fullest potential? Does affirmative action damage self-esteem or promote it? Should colleges and universities eliminate racial and gender considerations in admissions decisions—or act affirmatively to enforce a richly diverse student population?

The Supreme Court in 1978 ruled (in the Allen Bakke case) that universities and other institutions could indeed use race as one of many factors that determine whether someone gets hired or admitted to a particular college. But

The History of Affirmative Action Policies

1961. President John F. Kennedy's Executive Order (E.O.) 10925 used affirmative action for the first time by instructing federal contractors to take "affirmative action to ensure that applicants are treated equally without regard to race, color, religion, sex, or national origin." Created the Committee on Equal Employment Opportunity.

1964. Civil Rights Act of 1964 was signed into law. This landmark legislation prohibited employment discrimination by large employers (over 15 employees), whether or not they have government contracts. Established the Equal Employment Opportunity Commission (EEOC).

1965. President Lyndon B. Johnson issued E.O. 11246, requiring all government contractors and subcontractors to take affirmative action to expand job opportunities for minorities. Established Office of Federal Contract Compliance (OFCC) in the Department of Labor to administer the order.

1967. President Johnson amended E.O. 11246 to include affirmative action for women.

1970. The Labor Department, under President Richard M. Nixon, issued Order No. 4, authorizing flexible goals and timetables to correct "underutilization" of minorities by federal contractors.

1971. Order No. 4 was revised to include women.

1973. The Nixon administration issued "Memorandum-Permissible Goals and Timetables in State and Local Government Employment Practices," distinguishing between proper goals and timetables and impermissible quotas.

1978. The U.S. Supreme Court, in *Regents of the University of California* v. *Bakke*, upheld the use of race as one factor in choosing among qualified applicants for admission. At the same time, it also ruled unlawful the University Medical School's practice of reserving 18 seats in each entering class of 100 for disadvantaged minority students.

1979. The Supreme Court ruled in *United Steel Workers of America, AFL-CIO* v. *Weber*, that race-conscious affirmative action efforts designed to eliminate a conspicuous racial imbalance in an employer's workforce resulting from past discrimination are permissible if they are temporary and do not violate the rights of white employees.

1983. President Ronald Reagan issued E.O. 12432, which directed each federal agency with substantial procurement or grant-making authority to develop a Minority Business Enterprise (MBE) development plan.

(continued)

in 1995 the Board of Regents of the University of California decided to bar racial and gender considerations from admissions decisions, and soon after California citizens also passed Proposition 209 banning the use of race and ethnicity in admissions decisions. As a result, the proportion of African-American students abruptly dropped at most University of California campuses. The best way to build diverse institutions, wrote California's then-Governor Pete Wilson in the January 18, 1996 *San Francisco Chronicle*, "isn't to grant special preferences in admissions to some students at the expense of others, it's to ensure that every student receives the elementary and secondary education that will allow them to compete . . . regardless of the color of their skin, their race, ethnicity, or gender." A year later, when a federal judge ordered an end to affirmative action admission policies in Texas, the University of Texas and state legislators in Austin decided to decrease the importance of standardized test scores in determining admissions: students in the top 10 per-

The History of Affirmative Action Policies *(continued)*

1985. Efforts by some in the Reagan administration to repeal Executive Order 11246 were thwarted by defenders of affirmative action, including other Reagan administration officials, members of Congress from both parties, civil rights organizations, and corporate leaders.

1989. The Supreme Court, in *City of Richmond* v. *J. A. Croson Co.*, struck down Richmond's minority contracting program as unconstitutional, requiring that a state or local affirmative action program be supported by a "compelling interest" and be narrowly tailored to ensure that the program furthers that interest.

1994. In *Adarand Constructors, Inc.* v. *Pena*, the Supreme Court held that a federal affirmative action program remains constitu-

tional when narrowly tailored to accomplish a compelling government interest such as remedying discrimination.

1995. The Regents of the University of California voted to end affirmative action programs at all University of California campuses.

1996. California's Proposition 209 passed by a narrow margin in the November election. It abolished all public-sector affirmative action programs in the state in employment, education, and contracting. Clause (C) permits gender discrimination that is "reasonably necessary" to the "normal operation" of public education, employment, and contracting.

1996. In *Texas* v. *Hopwood*, the U.S. Court of Appeals for the Fifth Circuit ruled against the University of

Texas, deciding that its law school's policy of considering race in the admissions process was a violation of the Constitution's equal-protection guarantee. In response to Hopwood, the Texas legislature passed the Texas Ten Percent Plan, which ensures that the top 10 percent of students at all high schools in Texas have guaranteed admission to the University of Texas and Texas A&M system.

1997. Voters in Houston supported affirmative action programs in city contracting and hiring by rejecting an initiative that would banish such efforts. Houston proved that the wording on an initiative is a critical factor in influencing the voters' response. Instead of deceptively focusing attention on "preferential treatment," voters were asked directly if they

cent of their high school graduating classes are now admitted automatically to the university. This decision, supported by then-Governor (later President) George W. Bush, has maintained the diversity of the student body.

The issue of affirmative action in higher education and in employment has continued to be debated passionately by people across the country, as Chris Thomas's overview essay on affirmative action (see pages 310–320) indicates all too clearly. The issue is perennially and profoundly troubling. While affirmative action has vociferous champions and opponents, most Americans seem to be internally conflicted over the matter: they appreciate both the attractions and disadvantages of affirmative action. Thus it is certain that the issue will continue to generate much thoughtful argument—some of it represented in the selections reprinted in this section. In addition to the essay by Chris Thomas, read carefully the arguments presented below—and then decide what you think.

The History of Affirmative Action Policies *(continued)*

wanted to "end affirmative action programs." They said no.

1997. Lawsuits were filed against the University of Michigan and the University of Washington School of Law regarding their use of affirmative action policies in admissions standards.

1998. Ban on use of affirmative action in admissions at the University of California went into effect. UC Berkeley experiences a 61 percent drop in admissions of African American, Latino/a and Native American students.

2000. The Florida legislature passed "One Florida" Plan, banning affirmative action. The program also included the Talented 20 Percent Plan that guarantees the top 20 percent admission to the University of Florida system.

2000. In an effort to promote equal pay, the U.S. Department of Labor promulgated new affirmative action regulations including an Equal Opportunity Survey, which requires federal contractors to report hiring, termination, promotions, and compensation

data by minority status and gender.

2001. California enacted a new plan allowing the top 12.5 percent of high school students' admission to the UC system, either for all four years or after two years outside the system.

2002. The Sixth Circuit, in *Grutter* v. *Bollinger*, upheld as constitutional the use of race as one of many factors in making admissions decisions at the University of Michigan's Law School.

Source: Americans for a Fair Choice

An Affirmative Action Case

Diane Joyce had been working for four years as an account clerk at the Santa Clara County Transportation Agency, whose mission is to maintain county roads. When a higher-paying position as a road dispatcher opened up, Joyce applied for it. Dispatchers assign road crews, equipment, and materials, and maintain records on the road maintenance work to be done. The dispatcher job was one of 238 positions in the agency classified as "skilled crafts worker." Not a single one of those positions had ever been held by a woman. The Santa Clara County Transportation Agency had an affirmative action plan, but up to that point not much had been done to desegregate a workplace that was highly segregated by sex.

Joyce was told that she was ineligible for the dispatcher position because she had not served as a road maintenance worker. There were 110 road maintenance jobs in the agency, and none of them had ever been held by a woman either. Joyce was allowed to take a job in the road maintenance crew, but her experience there was not easy. Her first supervisor was apparently not inclined to welcome her. Male workers were routinely provided with coveralls to protect their clothing, but none were given to her. After ruining one set of clothes, she complained to the supervisor, but nothing was done. After her clothing was ruined three more times, she filed a formal grievance. The next day, before the grievance could be formally processed, Joyce was issued the four pairs of coveralls that the men were routinely given.

Joyce worked on road maintenance crews for almost five years and during that period filled in temporarily as a road dispatcher on a number of occasions. She also served as chair of the Roads Operations Safety Committee. When a regular job as a road dispatcher again opened up, she applied for it. Joyce was one of nine applicants for the position who were deemed "well qualified." Another applicant was a man named Paul

An Affirmative Action Case *(continued)*

Johnson; his career with the agency had been similar to Diane Joyce's. He had joined the agency three years before Joyce did and had had some previous dispatcher experience, although he had worked only two years on road maintenance crews, compared with her five years.

The candidates were called to an interview with a two-person board. The board gave the candidates numerical scores, all of them between 70 and 80. Paul Johnson was tied for second with a 75, while Diane Joyce was next with a score of 73. The last and decisive interview was with a three-person board of agency supervisors. One of the members of that board was the supervisor who had behaved antagonistically toward Joyce when she joined the road maintenance crew and against whom she had been forced to file a grievance. A second was a man with whom she had had a disagreement in her capacity as chair of the safety committee. He had called her a "rebel-rousing [*sic*], skirt-wearing person." The three supervisors recommended that Paul Johnson be promoted to the dispatcher's job.

Diane Joyce sought the help of the agency's affirmative action officer. He recommended to the top management that the job go to her, and she was placed in the job. Paul Johnson sued the agency, charging that he had been kept out of the job on account of his sex, and that what had occurred should be viewed as sex discrimination. The case eventually reached the Supreme Court. The Court upheld the agency in placing Joyce instead of Johnson in the job.

The case illustrates the difficulties in breaking down occupational segregation even in a public agency with an affirmative action plan. It also exemplifies the merit issue: in all likelihood, the assessment of merit in this case produced fuzzy results.

Source: From Barbara R. Bergmann, *In Defense of Affirmative Action*, 113–115.

LINDA CHAVEZ

Promoting Racial Harmony

An intellectual whose interests center about education, Linda Chavez (1947–) is outspoken in the service of contemporary conservatism: witness her latest book, An Unlikely Conservative: The Transformation of an Ex-Liberal *(2002). She is particularly interested in issues relevant to the Hispanic community—e.g., immigration, affirmative action, bilingual education, voting rights—and she offered a personal commentary on those matters in her 1991 book,* Out of the Barrio: Toward a New Politics of Hispanic Assimilation. *Currently the long-time president of the Center for Equal Opportunity in Washington, D.C., she wrote the following essay for a book called* The Affirmative Action Debate *in 1996.*

1   Senator Hubert Humphrey took the floor of the Senate in 1964 to defend the landmark Civil Rights Act. Humphrey, the bill's chief sponsor, had to respond to conservatives who said that the bill would violate individual rights. He declared that the Civil Rights Act would make it a crime to classify human beings into racial groups and give preference to some groups but not others. He denied assertions that the bill would force employers to hire less

Linda Chavez

qualified people because of their race. The goal, he said, was to ensure race-neutral treatment for all individuals. "Title VII [of the bill]," he noted, "does not require an employer to achieve any sort of racial balance in his work force by giving preferential treatment to any individual or group." Sure of his principles, Humphrey promised to eat the pages of the Civil Rights Act if it ever came to require racial preferences.

2   Today, of course, the Civil Rights Act of 1964 is interpreted by many civil rights advocates as requiring all sorts of racial preference programs. Assistant attorney general for civil rights Deval Patrick cited that law in court to defend race-based layoffs being used in a New Jersey school district to maintain racial balance. A law that was intended to replace racial rights with individual rights is being used to install a new system of racial rights.

3   The very words "affirmative action" have also been bent to new purposes. Originally, that phrase referred only to outreach and training programs to help minorities compete equally with whites. Today it designates

programs that exclude whites from participation altogether (such as minority scholarships and government contract "set-asides") or enforce artificially low standards for minorities.

Playing the Game by the Rules

4 My recent exchange with William Raspberry shows the difference. At a National Press Club panel discussion and in his syndicated *Washington Post* column, Mr. Raspberry drew an analogy he thought would put the issue in focus. Suppose, he said, that during halftime at a basketball game it is discovered that the referees cheated during the first half of the game. The crooked referees allowed one team to rack up sixteen undeserved points. The referees are expelled from the game, but that doesn't fix the score. What to do?

5 My response to Mr. Raspberry was simple: Compensate the victims of discrimination. Give sixteen points to the team that was discriminated against. Wherever we can, in basketball or in society, we should apply specific remedies to specific victims of discrimination. The antidiscrimination laws of this country already allow us to do just that. Courts are empowered to force employers to hire or promote victims of discrimination and award the back pay and seniority those employees would have had. Similar tools are available to redress discrimination in housing, schools, and contracting. It's not even necessary for every person who is discriminated against to file a complaint; courts routinely provide relief to whole groups of people when they find that an individual or company has discriminated against more than one person.

6 Let's return to the basketball analogy. If a particular team in a particular game has been unfairly deprived of sixteen points, it would certainly be foolish and unfair to award sixteen extra points to that team in every game it plays from that time forward. It would be even more perverse to extend this preferential treatment to the children of the players on that team, awarding them extra points in their playground games because their parents suffered. Yet government-sponsored racial preference programs, which disregard individual cases of discrimination, are considered by some to be the only reasonable solution to discrimination.

7 Now, the analogy between a basketball game and American society may not be perfect, but it certainly is instructive. In sports, all participants are treated in a race-neutral manner. Team colors, not skin colors, are the basis of group affiliation. It may be true that the rules are often broken, but specific remedies and punishments for specific violations are available when this happens. Everybody is expected to play by the same rules—in fact, fans are never angrier than when they think the referees favor one team. Isn't that the model we should strive toward in our society?

8   The alternative to that model is to continue classifying our citizens by race, attaching an official government label "black," "white," "Asian," "Hispanic," and so on to each individual. Then the all-wise federal bureaucracy can decide how much special privilege each group deserves and spoon out benefits based on the labels: five portions to this group, three to that one, seven and a half to the next.

The Race Box Problem

9   Any attempt to systematically classify human beings according to race will fail, because race is an arbitrary concept. There will always be people—lots of them—who disagree with the way the labels are dispensed. An ugly power struggle among racial groups competing to establish their claims to victimhood is the inevitable result.

10   Native Hawaiians, for example, are currently classified as Native Americans. But many of them want their own racial classification in the next census in the year 2000. The National Congress of American Indians, however, insists that Native Hawaiians are really just Native Americans. The classification of 250,000 Native Hawaiians is at stake, and being able to claim a quarter-million people in your racial group makes a big difference when it's time to dole out federal benefits.

11   Other groups make similar claims. Many Americans of eastern European ancestry complain about being lumped into the "white" box. Five different Asian groups have petitioned for sub-boxes. The U.S. Department of Housing and Urban Development has gone so far as to establish preference for "Hasidic Jewish Americans." Before he changed his mind about racial preferences, California governor Pete Wilson approved a law that gives special protections to Portuguese-Americans.

12   For years, the government of Puerto Rico has forbidden the Census Bureau from asking any question about race on forms distributed on the island, so vexing is the issue among Puerto Ricans. Now the national council of La Raza demands that "Hispanics," currently an ethnic group, be declared a separate race. When the Census Bureau created a special racial category for Mexicans in the 1930 census, the government of Mexico lodged an official protest that the move was racist. The bureau quickly abandoned the practice. My, how times change.

13   Black leaders who demand "race-conscious" remedies are discovering that race consciousness cuts both ways. A proposal to add a "multiracial" box to census forms brought outrage from those leaders. The most recent study, done in 1980, found that 70% of multiracial Americans checked "black" on the census—meaning that a multiracial box would reduce the

number of people defined as black, and hence the power base of black leaders, because a significant number of people who now check "black" would check "multiracial" instead. Roderick Harrison, head of the Census Bureau's Racial Statistics division, estimated that a multiracial box would reduce the "black" population by 10%.

14   Aware of this possibility, Billy Tidwell of the National Urban League complained in a hearing before the House Census Subcommittee in June 1993 that a multiracial box would "turn the clock back on the well-being" of African-Americans because it would be divisive, splitting light-skinned blacks from dark-skinned ones. Perhaps it has not occurred to him that any kind of racial classification is arbitrarily divisive in the same way—splitting light-skinned Americans from dark-skinned ones and, to the extent that they are treated differently, turning them against each other. Is it divisive for the government to group black people and treat them differently on the basis of their skin color, but acceptable—even necessary—for it to group other Americans and treat them differently on the basis of skin color?

15   Racial categories are never permanent anyway. Earlier this century, "whites" were not considered a single race. Nativists like Madison Grant, writing in his book *The Passing of the Great Race,* worried about the dilution of "Nordic" bloodlines by immigrants from eastern and southern Europe. Alarmists cried out that within fifty years "Nordic" Americans, a false category if there ever was one, would sink into the minority. By the time that actually occurred, nobody noticed. Nobody cared about the purity of "Nordic" blood anymore. The definition of race had changed.

16   Today, alarmists cry out that within fifty years whites will be in the minority in the United States. But today's young people, raised in a society where racism is no longer acceptable, marry between races at record rates. Half of all Mexican-Americans in California now marry non-Hispanic spouses. Half of Japanese-Americans now marry non-Japanese spouses, and similarly high rates prevail among other Asian groups. More and more children defy racial classification. In fifty years, our racial categories will no longer exist as such. Should we write those categories into our laws today, and count on the government to update them constantly to reflect the changing population? Better we should acknowledge the simple fact that categorizing people by race is not just divisive and degrading. It is impossible.

Who Really Needs Help?

17   Just as it's impossible to classify people by race, it's impossible to say that one race or ethnic group is clearly lagging behind whites socially and economically. Minorities are not clearly lagging behind anybody.

18   Hispanics, as I have said for years, are doing quite well. The category of "Hispanics" seems to trail others because it includes a large number of immigrants—nearly half of the adult Hispanic population is foreign-born. These immigrants often come to this country with practically nothing and therefore skew the economic numbers downward. Unfortunately, most statistics do not distinguish between native-born and foreign-born Hispanics. Those that do, however, indicate that native-born Hispanics earn wages commensurate to their educational level. Mexican-American men with thirteen years of education, for example, earn 93% of the earnings of non-Hispanic whites with comparable education. Other statistics indicate that even immigrants do just fine if they work hard and learn English. Despite all this, people who claim to represent the interests of Hispanics continue to deny their record of success, painting them as a failed underclass in order to persuade government bureaucrats to give them special treatment. Rather than treat them as a downtrodden minority, we should see Hispanics for what they are—an upwardly mobile immigrant group.

19   Asian-Americans are also doing well. By many measures, they are doing better than whites. In fact, they are doing so well that racial preference programs sometimes discriminate against them in order to make room for other races. For years, the University of California has, as a matter of official policy, denied bright young Asian-American students admission to college, law school, medical school, and the rest of the university system because they are Asian-American. They have "too many" qualified Asian-American applicants, so discrimination against them is necessary to uphold the system of racial rights.

20   According to Michael Lynch of the Pacific Research Institute, Asian-American applicants to the University of California qualify for admission based on merit at more than six times the rate of blacks and Hispanics, and more than two and a half times the rate of whites. "These inconvenient facts create problems for UC administrators seeking ethnic proportionality," says Lynch. "Without bending the rules for some groups, there is no hope of achieving proportionality." According to a report released by the UC, Asian-American admissions would increase by 15 to 25% if the university based its decisions on academics and socioeconomic status but not race. That means countless Asian-Americans have been shut out of UC by racial preferences.

21   In a very recent case, two grade-schoolers in Montgomery County, Maryland, were initially denied permission to transfer to a new school in order to participate in a French language immersion program. The two girls are half Asian-American, and county bureaucrats decided that their departure would disrupt the delicate racial balance of the school they are currently attending. The school system denied these students an extraordinary educational opportunity solely because they are of the wrong race. If they were white, county

policy would have favored them. The *Washington Post*, hardly a right-wing newspaper, denounced this discrimination in an editorial titled "Asians Need Not Apply." Under public pressure, the girls were allowed to transfer.

22   Blacks, too, are moving up in society. There is a healthy, thriving black middle class in America. There are blacks at the top levels of society. A recent *New York Times* story, for example, reported that 18% of working, non-Hispanic blacks in New York City between the ages of twenty-five and sixty-five held managerial or professional jobs, and that another 28% held technical, sales, and administrative support positions. Furthermore, 30% were living in households with incomes of $50,000 or more. Statistics that seem to show lingering effects of racism often hide other explanations. For example, household income among blacks is lower than household income among whites, but to a large extent this is caused by the fact that black households are much more likely than white households to include only one adult, usually a single woman, and therefore only one income.

23   I am the first to say that some minorities are wrestling with enormous problems, racial discrimination among them. Significant groups of minorities, especially blacks, are living in poverty. The condition of our inner cities is a disgrace, and that is a special problem that deserves special attention. But we have to ask: Do all minorities face these problems?

24   Clearly, the answer to the first part of that question is no. People from ethnic minorities have been successful in climbing into the middle class. If we are going to help minorities who are still struggling, we have to find programs that target those minorities and not the broad spectrum of blacks, Hispanics, and other minorities in the middle class. But racial preferences are irrelevant to minorities who are truly in need. Richard Rodriguez writes in the *Baltimore Sun:* "I was talking to a roomful of black teenagers, most of them street kids or kids from the projects. Only one of them in a room of 13 had ever heard of anything called affirmative action." Racial preferences, he says, don't reach the people who need help because they depend on a trickle-down effect that never actually occurs. "Many leftists today have [a] domino theory," he writes. "They insist that by creating a female or a non-white leadership class at Harvard or Citibank, people at the bottom will be changed."

25   The time is past when every member of a racial minority is truly "disadvantaged." It is illogical, even cynical, to cite statistics about minority inner-city poverty in defense of preferences for minority bankers, CEOs, contractors, and investors, but this is what happens all the time. The federal government has nineteen separate regulations giving preferential treatment to rich, but "economically disadvantaged," bank owners. It has innumerable "minority set-asides" for its public contracts, which go to corporations owned by minorities who are rich enough to own corporations. It allows rich

minorities to buy broadcasting licenses and facilities far below market values—in one famous case, the then mayor of Charlotte, North Carolina, Harvey Gantt, who is black, and his partners made $3 million by buying a TV station under minority-preference rules and then selling it to whites four months later at full price. This didn't advance the status of blacks in society, but it did boost Gantt's bank account. Ironically, anyone who is already in a position to benefit from racial preference programs in these fields does not need special help in the first place.

26   The same can be said of racial preference policies at universities. Contrary to what many big universities say, racial preference programs in university admissions generally help people who don't really need the help. The vast majority of minority applicants to top universities come from comfortable, middle-class homes. Some of them come from affluent families. The University of California at Berkeley says that the average Hispanic student admitted through its racial preference program comes from a middle-class family; many, if not most, attended integrated schools, often in the suburbs. In fact, 17% of Hispanic entering freshmen in 1989, along with 14% of black freshmen, were truly well off, coming from families with incomes over $75,000. That's about twice the median family income in the United States. Yet these comfortable middle- and upper-middle-class students were admitted under reduced standards because of their race. Why should a university lower its expectations of affluent students who are minorities?

Racial Preferences Don't Help Minorities

27   The answer to the further question of whether racial preferences are effective in solving the problems some minorities face is also no. Not only do racial preference programs generally help people who don't need help, but more important, racial preferences create a surface appearance of progress while destroying the substance of minority achievement. Holding people to lower standards or giving them special help will make them look as if they are succeeding, but it can't make them succeed. B students who are admitted to top universities because of their race are still B students.

28   The Pacific Research Institute's Michael Lynch cites graduation rates at UCLA of 50% for blacks and 62% for Hispanics. By comparison, whites and Asians graduate at rates of 80% and 77%, respectively. UCLA admits blacks and Hispanics based on drastically lower standards. Forty-one percent of Hispanic students and over half of black students at UCLA gained admission on a special "minority track," where the standards are significantly lower than they are for other students. These students could have gone to any of California's less competitive colleges and received their degrees, but instead they were placed in California's most rigorous colleges by racial preference programs.

29   Companies that aren't efficient enough to survive in the marketplace but which get government contracts anyway because they are owned by minorities are still inefficient businesses. "The prospect of getting government contracts as a result of belonging to a protected group is sometimes a false inducement for people to go into business without being adequately prepared," wrote successful black businessman and University of California regent Ward Connerly in *Policy Review*. "They often are undercapitalized and lack the business acumen to remain in business without government contracts." Ultimately, success depends on ability. No preference program can protect minorities from that fact forever. In the meantime, the beneficiaries of such programs *are* protected from having to learn the skills and habits they need to become truly successful.

30   Furthermore, racial preferences rob minorities of the credit they deserve. How many times have people assumed that a particular member of a minority got a job, a promotion, a college admission, a scholarship, or any other achievement because of racial preference? The hard work of minority executives, employees, and students can easily be brushed off if there is even a small chance that their honors and accolades were awarded because of their skin color. "It is time for America to acknowledge that affirmative action doesn't work," writes black businessman Daniel Colimon, head of a litigation support firm with over two hundred clients, in *Policy Review*. "Affirmative-action programs have established an extremely damaging stereotype that places African-Americans and other racial minorities in a very precarious position. We are now perceived as a group of people who regardless of how hard we work, how educated we become, or what we achieve, would not be where we are without the preferential treatment afforded by affirmative-action programs."

31   Remember Rutgers president Francis Lawrence? A strong supporter of racial preferences throughout his career, he let the cat out of the bag last year when he told a faculty group that minorities need admissions preferences because they are a "disadvantaged population that doesn't have the genetic hereditary background" to do as well as whites on the SAT. Racial preferences encourage that kind of belief, and they will continue to do so as long as they exist.

32   Along with that is the racial antagonism caused by racial preferences. More and more whites are getting angry and resentful about perceived reverse discrimination. No doubt many whites exaggerate the extent to which they have been discriminated against, but that's beside the point. Any time groups are treated differently because of their race, the group that is treated worse has a legitimate complaint. This makes it all the more difficult to get whites to feel sympathy across racial lines. "If anything, the white 'backlash' to affirmative action has perpetuated the polarization of America's various

ethnic groups," writes Colimon. When whites complain about racial preference programs, many minority supporters of these programs become all the more antagonistic toward whites. It's a vicious circle that can't be broken as long as racial preference programs are in force.

33   Racial preferences may not cause whites to hate minorities when they would not otherwise do so, but they undeniably stir up negative feelings. Paul Sniderman, a political science professor at Stanford University, and Thomas Piazza, a survey researcher at the University of California at Berkeley, authors of the 1993 book *The Scar of Race,* found that "merely asking whites to respond to the issue of affirmative action increases significantly the likelihood that they will perceive blacks as irresponsible and lazy." In a poll, they asked one group of whites to evaluate certain images of black people in general. They asked another group of whites the same questions, but this group was first asked to give an opinion on a racial preference program in a nearby state. Forty-three percent of whites who were first asked about racial preferences said that blacks in general were "irresponsible," compared with 26% of whites who were not asked about racial preferences. "No effort was made to whip up feelings about affirmative action," wrote the authors. But one neutral question about racial preferences "was sufficient to excite a statistically significant response, demonstrating that dislike of particular racial policies can provoke dislike of blacks, as well as the other way around."

34   That is why racial preferences cannot be justified by the desire for "diversity." Some say employers and college administrators should seek to promote diversity by hiring more minorities than they otherwise would. But racial harmony and integration are much more important goals than diversity—the purpose of seeking diversity is to promote racial harmony and the integration of different races into one society. Racial preferences produce a diversity of skin colors but a division of sentiments. They put people of many different races together in a way that makes each racial group see other racial groups as competitors for arbitrary advantage. That's not the way to produce an integrated, harmonious society.

35   Racial preferences have divided us for too long. We are all for equal opportunity. We all agree that antidiscrimination laws should be vigorously enforced. We have the legal tools and the consensus we need to go after people who discriminate against minorities. We should be getting on with that job instead of arguing over how much privilege the government should dispense to which racial groups. Nobody should be entitled to something just for being born with a certain color of skin.

JESSE JACKSON

Save the Dream

Born in 1941 in Greenville, South Carolina, Jesse Jackson became involved as a college student in the movement for civil rights that was animating the nation early in the 1960s. Inspired by the example of Martin Luther King, Jr., he was ordained a Baptist minister in 1968. In 1971 he founded PUSH (People United to Save Humanity), an effort to improve material conditions for African-American citizens and to inspire young people to improve their lives through their own efforts. Jackson's charismatic ability to connect with young people helped to revive pride and discipline within public schools during the 1970s. During the 1980s, Jackson ran for president under the banner of his Rainbow Coalition, an umbrella organization, and finished a strong second in the Democratic primaries of 1988. Since then Jackson moved his Rainbow Coalition to Chicago and then to Washington, D.C.; he has remained active in the Civil Rights movement and on behalf of related causes such as crime, drug use, health care, teen pregnancy, and voting rights. He has also been active in foreign affairs, sometimes as a special U.S. envoy to Africa, and has traveled to Iraq, Cuba, Syria, Yugoslavia, South Africa, and Nigeria on specific missions to encourage peace and to free political prisoners. In the speech reprinted below, delivered on October 27, 1997, Jackson was addressing citizens at a march on the Capitol in Sacramento, California, to rally opposition to voter initiatives (Proposition 209) that would have limited affirmative action. Proposition 209 was later passed by the voters.

1   To God be the glory. I congratulate you, the people of faith and hope, who have come to insist on the highest moral and ethical standards of our nation, with an insistence on the American dream being fulfilled. It is a joy to look into your faces, the great American Rainbow Coalition. Here you stand representing the breadth and depth and power of the American experience. Your dreaming, your will to dignity, your will to inclusion, your will to a one big tent America has transforming and healing power. That will, will not be denied.

Jesse Jackson

2   Today, we gather at the state capitol—a state which was founded as an official bilingual state, a new state of inclusion and sharing. Today we march for fairness, inclusion, public policy, humane

priorities. When we march, we affirm our resolve to dignity. When we march, we exercise one of our great freedoms, the right to protest for the right. When we march, we motivate. We educate. We expand the public debate. We alter the environment. When we march, we inspire. We raise hope to new levels. When we march together in coalition, with determination, driven by the moral imperative, we almost always win. Marching is always in contrast to surrendering, cynicism, loss of confidence and doing nothing. Dr. King warned that we had to move beyond a paralysis of analysis, to direct action.

3   We march in a great tradition. When Moses marched across the Red Sea, the moral imperative could not be ignored. It altered the course of human history. The marchers changed public policy. When Joshua marched around the walls, steadfastly and with determination, seven days and seven nights, nobody could get in and nobody could get out. It was a boycott. The walls of division and oppression came tumbling down.

4   When Jesus marched with a rugged cross of redemption and reconciliation and selfless suffering, it had healing power. When Gandhi marched to the sea, it led to the freedom of a great, but beleaguered nation. When Dr. King marched in Washington projecting the dream, and marched across the Edmund Pettus bridge in Selma for the right to vote, with the willingness to die so that others might live, those marches generated hope and strength and a renewal of faith.

5   Today, we march on Sacramento honoring the tradition of the martyrs and the marchers who led the world to high plateaus of civility and freedom. In the face of a trail of abusive states' rights propositions committed against America's people, diminishing the gains for inclusion and equality, it is time to rise up in dignity and fight back! There is no moral imperative to cooperate with unjust, oppressive laws. Elected officials, students, people of conscience, must defy, challenge, resist, any law or set of laws, that diminishes equal opportunity and federal civil rights afforded by many years of struggle.

Dreamers and Dream Busters

6   Thirty-four years ago, I remember the march on Washington as if it were yesterday. As students, we gathered in Washington for a multiracial, multicultural coalition of the faithful and the hopeful. We stood there looking for a brighter future. We stood there dreaming. We stood full of anxiety bearing the scars of apartheid and segregation, experiencing the violence of exclusion and marginalization, and yet driven by a vibrant sense of hope. We marched on.

7   Dr. King called America's highest and best self a dream. The American dream is a dream of hope and new possibilities. Then, as now, learning to live together under one big tent remains the moral imperative and the great op-

portunity of our times. For this dream, we challenged closed-door policies. We faced dogs, jails, untimely deaths. I had already been to jail twice for trying to use a library and other public facilities. Then, as today, there was a struggle at the crossroads, a struggle, a tug of war defining America and determining its destiny. There was a struggle by the dreamers versus the dream busters. There were the dream busters who were demagogues of racial and gender fears, division, hatred and violence. But the dreamers of hope and faith and inclusion remained insistent.

8   Dream-busting governors standing at schoolhouse doors is not new. They, too, have a tradition. Today, there is a generation of dream busters who did not march with Dr. King. They were not at Montgomery. They did not march in Washington. They were not bloodied at Selma. They did not support the poor people's campaign. These propagandists invoke Dr. King's dream of an America where one day all of God's children would be judged by the content of their character and not by the color of their skin to justify an attack on civil rights laws. They suggest that Dr. King would support measures that would reduce opportunities of the historically excluded. They suggest he would not support a plan to repair and remedy past and present acts of exclusion. Dr. King had compassion on those who were left behind, or locked out, and a vision that realized that building bridges was the key to a future of shared security and greater prosperity. In Orwellian fashion, they rip King's text from its content and turn his truth into a lie.

9   What did Dr. King actually believe? He gloried in the progress made against segregation and racism in America, but he was no idle dreamer. He warned that America remained poisoned by racism, "which is as native to our soil as pine trees, sagebrush, and buffalo grass." America must recognize "that justice for black people cannot be achieved without radical changes in the structures of our society."

10   In essence, Dr. King's dream was a nation that practiced equal protection under the law, and equal opportunity. He supported a Marshall Plan for America, some plan to offset structural inequality, some bridge to let more across who had been left behind or locked out. He said it didn't cost anything to grant public accommodations or the right to vote, but it would cost to offset years of denial and structural inequality. He knew that building bridges would be a sound investment and he supported a plan for repair and inclusion. His last great effort, the poor people's campaign, was a testimony to his commitment to offer a rope of hope for those who were down, an access bridge to those who have been locked out.

11   Today, thirty-four years after the death of the dreamer, Dr. King, and a host of martyrs—Medgar Evars, the four babies at the Birmingham church,

Viola Liuzzo, Rev. James Reed, Schwerner, Goodman, and Chaney, the violent death of Vincent Chin, the beloved Cesar Chavez who gave every measure of his body, his mind, his breath and his being to lift the lot of the common people—we gather again asserting the dream, revisiting the chilly winds and viruses of fear and hostility let loose by the dream busters.

Trail of Abuses

12   It is shameful that thirty-four years after the dream of hope and inclusion was projected that Proposition 209, which makes it illegal to consider gender or race as factors in opportunity, is under consideration, as is Proposition 187, which subjects Hispanic citizens to suspicion and marginalization, antibilingual schemes, encroachment on Indian sovereignty, guest worker and sweatshop labor schemes, unwired and structurally unsound schools and first-class architecturally award-winning jails. This trail of abuses and moral contradictions has been unleashed like scud missiles with the effect of bludgeoning the dreams of this generation.

13   These are divisive, painful propositions that leave us asking why. At a time of such abounding prosperity, why is there this virus of cynicism and division enticing our body politic? It leaves us asking, why California, a state that has held so much promise for so many for so long?

14   In the face of awesome odds, we will not surrender our spirits. We have never been neutralized by fear in the face of governors blocking doors of opportunity in the past, nor retarded by the cynicism that they projected. We have always gone forward by hope and healing. Dr. King projected the dream. We must preserve the dream. Our children must realize the dream. It is a reasonable expectation.

What Is the Dream?

15   What is the dream? The invitation to America will give you a hint. "Give me your tired, your poor, your huddled masses who yearn to breathe free." Test scores and literacy tests were not used to exclude dreamers but, rather, a will to contribute, a yearning for freedom, was the ticket price of admission.

16   The dream: one big tent America with five basic tenets under the tent: 1) equal protection under the law; 2) equal opportunity; 3) equal access; 4) fair share; 5) an extended hand for the least of these who languish in the margins who are trying to make it to shore.

17   The dream that Dr. King projected was of new laws for security under one tent, shared public facilities, shared voting rights, shared economic opportunities, shared risks, shared responsibilities. Our mission in Washington was a public accommodations bill, a voting rights act. His children could not

use the theme park at Stone Mountain, Georgia, as white children did because of states' rights laws and culture.

18   He dreamed one day that the walls of legal structure that separated races would be replaced by a bridge and that under one big tent we could be judged by the content of our character and not by the color of our skin. The dream is not to be color-blind nor gender blind, but to be color and gender sensitive and caring and inclusive.

19   We choose vision over blindness. We do not need to pray for cataracts over our eyes for clarity. That is confusing, contradictory, and unnecessary. The dream: e pluribus unum—of the many we are one. The dream: liken unto the quilt, made up of many patches, many colors and textures and sizes, bound by a common thread. Each patch has integrity. Each patch has made contributions. But only bound together can they make a quilt of beauty and art and security.

20   Today, that dream is under attack in California. The violence of exclusion and elimination has resounded with fierce determination and the resurrection of walls that divide.

21   This is a strange development at a time in American history. We are experiencing an unprecedented opportunity for hope, healing, and inclusion. We are experiencing growth, expanded wealth, and prosperity. Our collective efforts made it all possible. When we remove walls, we create opportunities and development and growth. And then we are all winners. In the South, when the walls came down the cotton curtain was removed, the South could host the Olympics, professional athletic teams, international investment and growth. The Florida Marlins could not have been in the World Series until the cotton curtain came down. The Civil Rights movement made the Florida Marlins and the new South growth possible.

22   In South Africa, when the walls came down the stage was set for unprecedented growth. In Berlin, when the wall came down a new world order was in the making. When women and people of color are excluded from opportunity and development, growth is limited.

23   What is driving the fear? For the wealthy, the ceiling has been removed, but for the poor, there is no floor. The middle class is experiencing downsizing, part-time workers, stagnant wages, subcontracting, more work, less security—a sinking feeling. The middle class is not sharing in the great boom of prosperity, growth, and wealth. Anxiety leads to fear and then hatred and then violence. The violence of exclusion often leads to physical violence unless we chart a clearer and higher course.

24   Dr. King's dream is in danger of becoming a modern American nightmare. Your governor has left a trail of abuses in his wake.

25   Three strikes: a new jail industrial complex, locking up our youth for sport. Excess jails and deficient schools. In Sacramento alone, there are 77 schools, but only four of them are wired for the computer. All are technically deficient. They stand in stark contrast to state-of-the-art jails. First-class jails and second-class schools is a nightmare.

Resegregating Our Schools and Society

26   What is the impact of this latest scud missile, Proposition 209, which makes it illegal to consider women and people of color? Women are beginning to lose contracts. People of color are losing access to schools, jobs, contracts. Four hundred African-American and Latino students applied to medical school at UC San Diego, UC Davis: all four hundred were rejected. Eric Brooks, the sole African-American student in UC Berkeley's freshman class, is a holdover from last year. At UCLA, an 80 percent drop in Black, Hispanic, and Native American enrollment at the law school. A radical resegregation of our schools and reduction of opportunity is not good for America.

27   I am convinced that if the battleground were Alabama or Mississippi or Arkansas in the South, the national media and politicians from both parties would be jumping on the issue to establish their national reputation by demanding that these southern states not be allowed to resegregate, that states' rights would not prevail. The federal government would not hesitate to move. In the South, fighting Prop 209 or 187 would be a proving ground, proving ground that people are for social justice.

28   But California has been protected from the same standards applied to southern states because it is big, because it is the financial source of many campaigns. This atmosphere of intimidation and double standards is real campaign finance corruption. In the face of the trail of attacks on civil rights and retreats from both side of the aisle, there has been silence and a conspicuous absence of dissent. It is as if we have one party with two names. Or two parties with one assumption. All eating from the same trough. The American people deserve clarity. They deserve choices. They should expect leadership that will champion the American dream.

29   The radical resegregation of these schools and reduction of opportunity for women and people of color is even more dangerous than 100 years ago when the court ruled "separate but equal" under *Plessy* v. *Ferguson*. The assumption 100 years ago was, inasmuch as there is a race problem, solve it through separation and the building of parallel institutions. Thus, Howard University and other universities for people of color. Under the apartheid scheme, at least there was an acknowledgment of a problem.

30   Proposition 209 is driven by an assumption that inasmuch as there is no longer a race or a gender problem, therefore make it illegal to consider a remedy. In the face of blatant discrimination, such indifference to reality is a sin.

31   The reality is that affirmative action is a majority issue that benefits everybody:

- California Department of Fair Employment and Housing reports since July 1, 1985, 150,000 discrimination cases have been filed.

- In education, whites possess 75 percent of all BA degrees. The remaining 25 percent are held by all other ethnic groups. This is projected as a race gap, but in reality this is an opportunity gap.

- In labor, the California manufacturing industry, white males hold 77 percent of the middle- and upper-level managerial positions. African Americans 4.2 percent. Mexican Americans 1.5 percent. In all industries, the mean income for white males is $60,000; for Mexican Americans and African Americans it is $35,000, meaning that black and brown males make 55 cents for every dollar that every white male is making.

- When comparing average income by education, ethnicity, gender, and age, studies show that white men and women earn more than their minority counterparts of the same age and educational level.

- African-American men graduating from college and entering the California workforce at the managerial and executive level can expect to get paid an average of 12 percent less than their white former classmates.

- Since 1985 more than 9,000 housing discrimination complaints have been filed.

32   Affirmative action benefits everybody. It results in increased productivity and strengthens the economy. For instance, at the UC Davis medical school, 94 percent of the special admissions students graduated, compared with 98 percent of the students admitted through regular admissions. In addition, there was no difference in the groups in completed residency training in their residency performance or in obtaining board certification.

33   The American democracy does not guarantee equal results, it must guarantee equal opportunity. The evidence is that when there is equal opportunity, results are amazingly similar.

States' Rights versus Federal Civil Rights

34   Mayors, city county officials: These facts are the case for keeping the bridges and extending the hands of support. We urge you not to honor

these Proposition 187/209 unjust decrees. You must resist allowing these states' rights initiatives to undermine federal civil rights. This is not just a civil rights question. This is a Civil War question. No state has the right through popular sovereignty to undermine federal civil rights securities. Well, they say, the people of California voted for Propositions 187 and 209; based upon states' rights, slavery would have prevailed. But thank God the Union won. The American flag flies higher than a state flag.

35   Based upon states' rights, the children of Little Rock, the Little Rock 9, would have been denied entrance by a dream-busting governor. Eisenhower said the American flag and the Union had to prevail. On this basis, Wallace in Alabama blocking school doors would have blocked public accommodations. Johnson reminded him that the American flag flies higher. And now as Governor Wilson blocks school doors, we the people are marching. The Department of Justice, Department of Education, President Clinton must remind California and Governor Wilson that, as a member of the Union, no proposition which undermines federal civil rights can prevail.

36   Title IX for women and Title VII are gender and race sensitive. Proposition 209 makes it illegal to consider either. There is a collision course between Proposition 209 and Title IX, and the American flag must fly higher.

37   There are those who say affirmative action is hurting whites. Let's look at that reasoning. The primary beneficiaries are the white family. The majority of beneficiaries under Title IX are white women who, with education, as they join the workforce, and get contracts, help stabilize the white family and expand the economy. Plus women of other hues. Plus people of color. Plus persons with disabilities.

38   Affirmative action is a majority issue. No ethnic group should have to bear the burden of this remedy and be seen in a pejorative way. When more people are educated, they add to expansion and growth. When there is growth, they are all winners. If we did not educate women and people of color, we would have two choices: slow down productivity, or import labor. With affirmative action, we have turned tax consumers into taxpayers, 35 percent of our workforce is white male. Expanding the education and job and contracts basis is morally right and key to our economic growth. Rational people, caring people, must rise up for dignity and fight back.

Why Do We March—Where Do We Go from Here?

39   There is power in our marching feet. Today, Dr. King would say we face the fierce urgency of now. We cannot wait and we cannot go backwards now, for the time to coalesce and build an ark is as the floodwaters rise. We will

survive the flood. We can get better and not bitter. If we are determined and not distracted, we will save the dream, and sustain hope.

40   We march in the tradition of the prophets, the martyrs, and the children who sacrificed to raise the level of stability and public ethics in the world community from South Carolina to South Africa, from Tiananmen Square to Gdansk, Poland.

41   Our march will set a climate for inclusion. The marching in the South allowed Kennedy and Johnson to emerge as leaders of lasting credibility. It made Presidents Carter and Clinton possible. How President Clinton handles this matter of a states' rights attack and radical reduction of opportunity, could very well define his presidency. The gender, race, and class dialogue is taking place in California in school admissions, jobs, and contracts.

42   In a greater measure America of the next century is being defined right here today in Sacramento.

43   Where do we go from here? Let us have a massive voter registration drive in every city, field, campus, hamlet, and mountainside. We must vote for dignity with a passion.

44   Where do we go from here? We must set forth a process of signing more than a quarter million signatures of registered voters. We are determined to go forward by hope and participation.

45   Where do we go from here? At a date to be determined in February, a Save the Dream Part III March in Los Angeles. Where do we go from here? A resistance at the city, campus, and county levels to these unjust decrees. Where do we go from here? Calling upon our senators to conduct hearings on the impact of these decrees on school admissions, jobs and contracts, bank lending, housing, and health.

46   Where do we go from here? The mobilization of national leadership to stop the scud missile attacks on the dream, state by state. Where do we go from here? Urge our youth to not despair, and stop the self-destructive behavior of consuming drugs and alcohol, engaging in violence and making babies that they cannot raise.

47   Where do we go from here? A determination to raise our moral and ethical expectations of ourselves and our nation. When I look at the despair and the inaction around the country, I'm clear that it is easier to tell Pharaoh to let my people go than to convince my people to let Pharaoh go. People are so bound by Pharaoh's antics of intimidation and so mesmerized by media distraction.

48   They have developed such a comfort level, yet this generation must sing with the Lord a new song of hope. The writer and the 137th Psalm described it best when he said they carried us away captive and we hung our

harps on the trees. They actually surrendered. They hung their talents, their dreams, their religion, their convictions, their hopes, on the trees. They developed spiritual deficit disorder. They lost confidence in themselves and in their God.

49   That's why they ask how could they sing the Lord's song in a strange land? The fact is, you can't sing anywhere unless there's a restoration of confidence and hope and high expectations.

50   And so we march until mountains are made low and until valleys are exalted. Until crooked ways are made straight. Until the least of these have their right to the tree of life. We march for all of us to say with assurance that this land is our land. It was made for you and me. We will march until the song of hope resounds from every valley and mountainside. In many languages there will be a common message that says, yes we can!

51   I would say in Spanish, "Sí se puede!"

52   Whatever language, the message is hope over fear. Inclusion over exclusion.

53   This land is our land. It was made for you and me.

54   "Esta tierra es nuestra tierra."

55   Thank you very much. God bless you.

JUDY LICHTMAN, JOCELYN FRYE,
AND HELEN NORTON

Why Women Need Affirmative Action

Judy Lichtman, Jocelyn Frye, and Helen Norton were all associated with the National Partnership for Women and Families (NPWF) when they wrote the following essay in 1996 for a book titled The Affirmative Action Debate. *Lichtman is now the organization's president, Frye is director of legal and public policy, and Norton recently left NPWF to become special counsel to the assistant attorney general for civil rights in the Justice Department. NPWF, founded in 1971 as the Women's Legal Defense Fund, is a nonprofit organization that promotes fairness in the workplace, quality health care, and policies that help women and men meet the dual demand of work and family.*

1   Throughout our nation's history, qualified women have been shut out of employment, education, and business opportunities solely because of their sex. Affirmative action has countered this discrimination by opening doors for women previously denied opportunities regardless of their merit. Despite significant progress in recent years, however, women remain far short of reaching equality. Without affirmative action, discrimination will continue to thwart efforts to make our national dream of equal opportunity a reality.

2   Unfortunately, some opponents of affirmative action have deliberately distorted the public policy debate into a series of false choices, seeking to pit blacks against whites, men against women, Americans against immigrants. These opponents have often purposefully centered their attacks on race-based affirmative action programs to capitalize on racial fears and divisions. Their failure to address women's stake in this debate demonstrates their ignorance of or indifference to women's ongoing quest for equality.

Limited Choices, Limited Income

3   Recognizing our long national history of sex discrimination—and our nation's comparatively short commitment to antidiscrimination efforts—is key to understanding affirmative action's continuing relevance to the lives of American women.

4   Sex discrimination has long limited women's choices. Women have too often been cut off from educational opportunities and tracked into lower-paying, sex-segregated jobs—discouraged, for example, from pursuing fields

like medicine, business, or the skilled trades. As late as 1968, for instance, newspapers and employers segregated help-wanted ads by gender, with one section advertising the better-paying jobs only for men and a separate section listing "women's jobs"—thus systematically excluding women from choice opportunities without regard to their qualifications.

5   Though some of the most blatant forms of discrimination have grown rare with time and aggressive law enforcement, sex discrimination remains all too prevalent. Indeed, it's important to note that, despite centuries of discrimination, Title VII of the Civil Rights Act, the federal law barring job discrimination, is barely thirty years old.[1] Federal laws banning sex discrimination in education date only to 1972, and less than twenty-five years have passed since the Supreme Court first recognized that governmental sex discrimination was indeed unconstitutional.[2]

6   Given this short history of efforts to realize equal opportunity in our society, the ongoing force of sex discrimination should surprise no one. A few examples make clear how discrimination continues to limit women's opportunities. For instance, a federal judge in California recently found that Lucky's Stores, a major grocery chain, routinely segregated women in low-wage, dead-end jobs while hiring men for jobs that led to management opportunities. Women were denied access to critical training programs and were steered, against their wishes, into part-time rather than full-time jobs.

7   In yet another recent example, a District of Columbia federal court found that Price Waterhouse, the major accounting firm, refused to promote a woman to partnership because she wasn't considered sufficiently "feminine"—even though she had generated millions of dollars more revenue than any other candidate.

8   Social science studies further document the continued vitality of sex discrimination. A National Bureau of Economic Research project sent equally qualified pairs of male and female applicants to seek jobs at a range of Philadelphia restaurants. This "audit" found that high-priced restaurants offering good pay and tips were twice as likely to offer jobs to the male applicants over their equally qualified female counterparts.[3]

9   The not-so-surprising result of ongoing discrimination is that white men still dominate most upper-level, managerial jobs. For example, women and people of color make up fewer than 5% of senior managers (vice president and above) in *Fortune* 1000 companies, even though women constitute 46% and people of color 21% of the overall workforce.[4] Women also continue to face significant barriers when seeking the higher-paying nontraditional jobs offered in the skilled and construction trades. In 1993, fewer

than 1% of American auto mechanics, carpenters, and plumbers were women; only 1.1% of electricians and 3.5% of welders were women.[5]

10   Not surprisingly, men are much more likely to be high wage earners than women. For example, 16.4% of white men were high wage earners (earning $52,364 or more annually) in 1992, compared to only 3.8% of white women, 1.6% of black women, and 1.8% of Hispanic women. In contrast, only 11.6% of white men were low wage earners (earning $13,091 or less a year), compared to 21.1% of white women, 26.9% of black women, and 36.6% of Hispanic women.[6]

11   Women are painfully aware that merit still too often takes a back seat to discrimination. Qualified women consistently earn less than their male counterparts. For example:

- College-educated Hispanic women annually earn $1,600 less than white male high school graduates and nearly $16,000 less than college-educated white men.[7]

- College-educated black women annually earn only $1,500 more than white male high school graduates and almost $13,000 less than college-educated white men.[8]

- College-educated white women earn only $3,000 more a year than white male high school graduates and $11,500 less than white men with college degrees.[9]

How Affirmative Action Corrects Discrimination

12   Affirmative action seeks to prevent the sort of discrimination described above *before* it happens by urging institutions to scrutinize their decision-making practices for sex-based stereotyping and other discriminatory actions. Affirmative action also enables institutions to correct discrimination once it is identified. Here are examples of the sorts of programs that have greatly improved women's access to key opportunities:

- Procter & Gamble's affirmative action program includes aggressive outreach of women and people of color to ensure a substantial and diverse pool of candidates for promotion to leadership positions. Over the last five years, 40% of new management hires have been women and 26% people of color.[10]

- In the aftermath of the Lucky's Stores case discussed above, Lucky's created an affirmative action program to identify and groom women candidates for promotion that has doubled the percentage of women managers.[11]

- A number of universities and employers have developed initiatives to provide specialized counseling and training to encourage women to enter engineering and other technical programs.

- The Department of Labor's Office of Federal Contract Compliance Programs, which enforces federal contractors' affirmative action responsibilities, has opened doors for women through targeted enforcement. It created thousands of new opportunities for women in the coal mining industry in the 1970s and in the banking industry in the 1980s. In the 1990s, the OFCCP's Glass Ceiling Initiative, which reviews contractors' efforts to create leadership opportunities for women and people of color, has generated promising changes in corporate attitudes and actions.

13   These programs counter the sex discrimination that too often taints decisions about education, business, and job opportunities. Largely because of programs like these, women have made significant progress in recent years:

- Women earn more—in 1963, women earned fifty-nine cents for every dollar earned by men; today, women earn on average seventy-one cents for every dollar earned by men.

- More women are in the pipeline for top jobs—in 1980, white women were 27.1% of all managers (middle and upper level) and women of color 3.2%; by 1990, white women were 35.3% of managers and women of color 6.9%.[12]

- Women have moved into professional jobs previously occupied almost entirely by men—in 1993, 18.6% of architects were women compared to only 4.3% in 1975, 47.6% of economists were women compared to only 13.1% in 1975, and 22.8% of lawyers and judges were women compared to only 7.1% in 1975.[13]

Affirmative action has proven successful in opening doors for qualified women. Rolling back these programs would prematurely abandon our long-standing national commitment to women's equality.

14   Indeed, affirmative action is critically important to women because it strives to create an environment where merit can thrive and succeed, allowing qualified women to compete fairly on a level playing field, free from sex and race discrimination. To paraphrase Professor Roger Wilkins of George Mason University, affirmative action encourages institutions to develop fair and realistic criteria for assessing merit, and then to recruit a diverse mix of individuals qualified to take advantage of the available opportunities.[14]

15　　　　　However, affirmative action's opponents too often mischaracterize such programs as the enemy of merit. Yet in a string of cases spanning nearly two decades and most recently reaffirmed in June 1995 in *Adarand Constructors, Inc.* v. *Pena,* the Supreme Court has made clear that lawful affirmative action in no way permits or requires quotas, reverse discrimination, or favorable treatment of unqualified women and minorities. The Supreme Court thus developed principles to ensure that affirmative action expands opportunities in a way that is fair to all Americans; it and other courts have consistently struck down programs that abuse or disregard these safeguards. In this manner, affirmative action creates a climate where qualified women—and men—can compete and excel.

16　　　　　Indeed, affirmative action programs have opened doors for qualified white men, too. For example, women-owned businesses currently create more jobs than all of the *Fortune* 500 companies combined, employing millions of women, people of color—and white men.[15] Similarly, the affirmative action programs developed to respond to severe underrepresentation of minorities often create new training slots for black and white workers, thus generating opportunities for white workers that would not have existed without a commitment to affirmative action.

Affirmative Action and the Bottom Line

17　Affirmative action also improves businesses' bottom line—again, creating an environment where excellence can prevail. A growing number of businesses recognize that affirmative action policies boost productivity and increase profits by creating a diverse workforce drawn from a larger talent pool, generating new ideas, targeting new markets, and improving workplace morale.

18　　　　　Recent studies document how diversity boosts a company's performance. For example, a 1993 University of North Texas study pitted ethnically diverse teams of business students against all-white teams in solving business-related problems. The researchers found that the ethnically diverse teams viewed business situations from a broader range of perspectives and produced more innovative solutions to problems. Moreover, a recent study of stock market leaders by Covenant Investment Management found that the market performance of companies with good records of hiring and promoting women and people of color was 2.4 times higher than the performance of companies with poor records. Indeed, the one hundred companies with the best records of hiring women and people of color earned an 18.3% average return of investment, while the one hundred lowest ranked companies earned an average return of only 7.9%.[16]

19   Tools like affirmative action have enabled women to make significant progress. Women today are professors, corporate executives, police officers, road dispatchers, and pilots. Yet they are still far, far short of reaching equality. As discussed above, women with college degrees earn only slightly more than men with high school diplomas—and substantially less than their male counterparts with college degrees.

20   The need for affirmative action remains. Because the law establishes clear safeguards against abuses, thus allowing affirmative action to create a climate where excellence can prevail, any concerns about unfairness can be answered simply by *enforcing the law* rather than scuttling it and its promise of equal opportunity for all. Unfortunately, however, too many opponents of affirmative action prefer to blame such programs for continuing racial and gender divisions, instead of confronting the root problems of sexism and racism. The sad truth is that our country's long history of discrimination lingers today in sex- and race-based stereotyping and other stigmatizing assumptions. Affirmative action seeks to help break down these barriers by bringing together diverse individuals at school and on the job.

Notes

1. In fact, Title VII's inclusion of protections against sex discrimination came about only by accident—the result of southern segregationists' political miscalculation. Seeking to break Congress's resolve to enact groundbreaking laws against race discrimination, the segregationists gambled that even the most ardent civil rights advocates would balk at passing Title VII if it meant opening up employment opportunities not just for people of color but for women, too. Thus, on the last day of House debate on the Civil Rights Act in 1964, the segregationist Howard Smith (D-Va.) offered an amendment adding sex to the types of discrimination barred by Title VII. Happily for women and people of color, this attempt to sabotage the Civil Rights Act backfired, and the bill was enacted into law as amended.
2. *Reed v. Reed,* 404 U.S. 71 (1971).
3. David Neumark, Roy J. Bank, and Kyle D. Van Nort, "Sex Discrimination in Restaurant Hiring: An Audit Study," National Bureau of Economic Research, Working Paper no. 5024 (1995).
4. U.S. Department of Labor, Office of Federal Contract Compliance Programs, Glass Ceiling Commission, *Good for Business: Making Full Use of the Nation's Human Capital/The Environmental Scar* (Washington, D.C.: GPO, 1995), 11–12.
5. U.S. Bureau of Labor Statistics, *Employment and Earnings* (January 1994), table 22.
6. U.S. Bureau of the Census, "The Earnings Ladder: Who's at the Bottom? Who's at the Top?" *Statistical Brief* (June 1994).
7. U.S. Bureau of the Census, Current Population Survey, March 1994, table 15 (unpublished data for 1993).
8. Ibid.
9. Ibid.

10. U.S. Bureau of National Affairs, *Affirmative Action After* Adarand: *A Legal, Regulatory, Legislative Outlook,* Fair Employment Practices Cases 68 (special supplement) (Aug. 7, 1995), S-33.
11. Kara Swisher, "At the Checkout Counter: Winning Women's Rights," *Washington Post,* June 12, 1994, A-16.
12. Institute for Women's Policy Research, "Restructuring Work: How Have Women and Minorities Fared?" *Research in Brief* (January 1995), fig. 2.
13. Cynthia Costello and Anne J. Stone, *The American Woman 1994–95: Where We Stand* (New York: Norton, 1994), table 3-10; U.S. Bureau of Labor Statistics, *Employment and Earnings* (January 1994), table 22.
14. Roger Wilkins, "The Case for Affirmative Action," *The Nation,* Mar. 27, 1995, 409.
15. National Foundation of Women Business Owners Fact Sheet (June 1995).
16. U.S. Department of Labor, Federal Glass Ceiling Commission, *Good for Business,* 14, 61. Any honest critic of affirmative action must also acknowledge that factors other than pure merit often influence decisions about opportunities. For example, in 1994, 40% of the children of Harvard alumni who applied to Harvard were admitted, compared to a 14% admission rate for students whose parents were not alumni. A Department of Education report also found that the SAT scores of alumni children admitted to Harvard averaged thirty-five points *lower* than those of other Harvard students (Jonathan Tilove, "Affirmative Action Networks for Insiders," *Sunday Oregonian,* Apr. 2, 1995). Indeed, another recent research report on higher education concluded that far more whites have entered the gates of the ten most elite American academic institutions through "alumni preference" than the combined numbers of all the blacks and Latinos entering through affirmative action (Institute for the Study of Social Change, *The Diversity Project Final Report* [November 1991], 5).

ROGER WILKINS

Racism Has Its Privileges

Roger Wilkins (1932–   ) is a professor of history at George Mason University in northern Virginia. He wrote the following argument for The Nation *(a politically liberal magazine) in 1995.*

1   The storm that has been gathering over affirmative action for the past few years has burst. Two conservative California professors are leading a drive to place an initiative on the state ballot in 1996 that will ask Californians to vote affirmative action up or down. Since the state is beloved in political circles for its electoral votes, advance talk of the initiative has put the issue high on the national agenda. Three Republican presidential contenders—Bob Dole, Phil Gramm and Lamar Alexander—have already begun taking shots at various equal opportunity programs. Congressional review of the Clinton Administration's enforcement of these programs has begun. The President has started his own review, promising adherence to principles of nondiscrimination and full opportunity while asserting the need to prune those programs that are unfair or malfunctioning.

2   It is almost an article of political faith that one of the major influences in last November's election was the backlash against affirmative action among "angry white men," who are convinced it has stacked the deck against them. Their attitudes are shaped and their anger heightened by unquestioned and virtually uncheckable anecdotes about victimized whites flooding the culture. For example, *Washington Post* columnist Richard Cohen recently began what purported to be a serious analysis and attack on affirmative action by recounting that he had once missed out on a job someplace because they "needed a woman."

3   Well, I have an anecdote too, and it, together with Cohen's, offers some important insights about the debate that has flared recently around the issues of race, gender and justice. Some years ago, after watching me teach as a visiting professor for two semesters, members of the history department at George Mason University invited me to compete for a full professorship and endowed chair. Mason, like other institutions in Virginia's higher education system, was under a court order to desegregate. I went through the appropriate application and review process and, in due course, was appointed. A few years later, not long after I had been honored as one of the university's distinguished professors, I was shown an article by a white historian assert-

ing that he had been a candidate for that chair but that at the last moment the job had been whisked away and handed to an unqualified black. I checked the story and discovered that this fellow had, in fact, applied but had not even passed the first threshold. But his "reverse discrimination" story is out there polluting the atmosphere in which this debate is taking place.

4   Affirmative action, as I understand it, was not designed to punish anyone; it was, rather—as a result of a clear-eyed look at how America actually works—an attempt to enlarge opportunity for *everybody*. As amply documented in the 1968 Kerner Commission report on racial disorders, when left to their own devices, American institutions in such areas as college admissions, hiring decisions and loan approvals had been making choices that discriminated against blacks. That discrimination, which flowed from doing what came naturally, hurt more than blacks: It hurt the entire nation, as the riots of the late 1960s demonstrated. Though the Kerner report focused on blacks, similar findings could have been made about other minorities and women.

5   Affirmative action required institutions to develop plans enabling them to go beyond business as usual and search for qualified people in places where they did not ordinarily conduct their searches or their business. Affirmative action programs generally require some proof that there has been a good-faith effort to follow the plan and numerical guidelines against which to judge the sincerity and the success of the effort. The idea of affirmative action is *not* to force people into positions for which they are unqualified but to encourage institutions to develop realistic criteria for the enterprise at hand and then to find a reasonably diverse mix of people qualified to be engaged in it. Without the requirements calling for plans, good-faith efforts and the setting of broad numerical goals, many institutions would do what they had always done: assert that they had looked but "couldn't find anyone qualified," and then go out and hire the white man they wanted to hire in the first place.

6   Affirmative action has done wonderful things for the United States by enlarging opportunity and developing and utilizing a far broader array of the skills available in the American population than in the past. It has not outlived its usefulness. It was never designed to be a program to eliminate poverty. It has not always been used wisely, and some of its permutations do have to be reconsidered, refined or, in some cases, abandoned. It is not a quota program, and those cases where rigid numbers are used (except under a court or administrative order after a specific finding of discrimination) are a bastardization of an otherwise highly beneficial set of public policies.

7   President Clinton is right to review what is being done under present laws and to express a willingness to eliminate activities that either don't

work or are unfair. Any program that has been in place for thirty years should be reviewed. Getting rid of what doesn't work is both good government and good politics. Gross abuses of affirmative action provide ammunition for its opponents and undercut the moral authority of the entire effort. But the President should retain—and strengthen where required—those programs necessary to enlarge social justice.

8   What makes the affirmative action issue so difficult is that it engages blacks and whites exactly at those points where they differ the most. There are some areas, such as rooting for the local football team, where their experiences and views are virtually identical. There are others—sometimes including work and school—where their experiences and views both overlap and diverge. And finally, there are areas such as affirmative action and inextricably related notions about the presence of racism in society where the divergences draw out almost all the points of difference between the races.

This Land Is My Land

9   Blacks and whites experience America very differently. Though we often inhabit the same space, we operate in very disparate psychic spheres.

10   Whites have an easy sense of ownership of the country; they feel they are entitled to receive all that is best in it. Many of them believe that their country—though it may have some faults—is superior to all others and that, as Americans, they are superior as well. Many of them think of this as a white country and some of them even experience it that way. They think of it as a land of opportunity—a good place with a lot of good people in it. Some suspect (others *know*) that the presence of blacks messes everything up.

11   To blacks there's nothing very easy about life in America, and any sense of ownership comes hard because we encounter so much resistance in making our way through the ordinary occurrences of life. And I'm not even talking here about overt acts of discrimination but simply about the way whites intrude on and disturb our psychic space without even thinking about it.

12   A telling example of this was given to me by a black college student in Oklahoma. He said whites give him looks that say: "What are *you* doing here?"

13   "When do they give you that look?" I asked.

14   "Every time I walk in a door," he replied.

15   When he said that, every black person in the room nodded, and smiled in a way that indicated recognition based on thousands of such moments in their own lives.

16   For most blacks, America is either a land of denied opportunity or one in which the opportunities are still grudgingly extended and extremely limited. For some—that one-third who are mired in poverty, many of them iso-

lated in dangerous ghettos—America is a land of desperadoes and desperation. In places where whites see a lot of idealism, blacks see, at best, idealism mixed heavily with hypocrisy. Blacks accept America's greatness but are unable to ignore ugly warts that many whites seem to need not to see. I am reminded here of James Baldwin's searing observation from *The Fire Next Time:*

> The American Negro has the great advantage of having never believed that collection of myths to which white Americans cling: that their ancestors were all freedom-loving heroes, that they were born in the greatest country the world has ever seen, or that Americans are invincible in battle and wise in peace, that Americans have always dealt honorably with Mexicans and Indians and all other neighbors or inferiors, that American men are the world's most direct and virile, that American women are pure.

17   It goes without saying, then, that blacks and whites remember America differently. The past is hugely important since we argue a lot about who we are on the basis of who we think we have been, and we derive much of our sense of the future from how we think we've done in the past. In a nation in which few people know much history these are perilous arguments, because in such a vacuum, people tend to weave historical fables tailored to their political or psychic needs.

18   Blacks are still recovering the story of their role in America, which so many white historians simply ignored or told in ways that made black people ashamed. But in a culture that batters us, learning the real history is vital in helping blacks feel fully human. It also helps us understand just how deeply American we are, how richly we have given, how much has been taken from us and how much has yet to be restored. Supporters of affirmative action believe that broad and deep damage has been done to American culture by racism and sexism over the whole course of American history and that they are still powerful forces today. We believe that minorities and women are still disadvantaged in our highly competitive society and that affirmative action is absolutely necessary to level the playing field.

19   Not all white Americans oppose this view and not all black Americans support it. There are a substantial number of whites in this country who have been able to escape our racist and sexist past and to enter fully into the quest for equal justice. There are other white Americans who are not racists but who more or less passively accept the powerful suggestions coming at them from all points in the culture that whites are entitled to privilege and to freedom from competition with blacks. And then there are racists who just don't like blacks or who actively despise us. There are still others who may or may not feel deep antipathy, but who know how to manipulate racism and white

anxiety for their own ends. Virtually all the people in the last category oppose affirmative action and some of them make a practice of preying upon
those in the second category who are not paying attention or who, like the
Post's Richard Cohen, are simply confused.

The Politics of Denial

20 One of these political predators is Senate majority leader Bob Dole. In his
offhandedly lethal way, Dole delivered a benediction of "let me now forgive
us" on *Meet the Press* recently. After crediting affirmative action for the 62
percent of the white male vote garnered by the Republicans, he remarked
that slavery was "before we were born" and wondered whether future generations ought to have to continue "paying a price" for those ancient wrongs.

21 Such a view holds that whatever racial problems we once may have
had have been solved over the course of the past thirty years and that most
of our current racial friction is caused by racial and gender preferences that
almost invariably work to displace some "qualified" white male. Words and
phrases like "punish" or "preference" or "reverse discrimination" or "quota"
are dropped into the discourse to buttress this view, as are those anecdotes
about injustice to whites. Proponents of affirmative action see these arguments as disingenuous but ingenious because they reduce serious and complex social, political, economic, historical and psychological issues to
bumper-sticker slogans designed to elicit Pavlovian responses.

22 The fact is that the successful public relations assault on affirmative
action flows on a river of racism that is as broad, powerful and American as
the Mississippi. And, like the Mississippi, racism can be violent and deadly
and is a permanent feature of American life. But while nobody who is sane
denies the reality of the Mississippi, millions of Americans who are deemed
sane—some of whom are powerful and some even thought wise—deny,
wholly or in part, that racism exists.

23 It is critical to understand the workings of denial in this debate because it is used to obliterate the facts that created the need for the remedy
in the first place. One of the best examples of denial was provided recently
by the nation's most famous former history professor, House Speaker Newt
Gingrich. According to *The Washington Post*, "Gingrich dismissed the argument that the beneficiaries of affirmative action, commonly African Americans, have been subjected to discrimination over a period of centuries. 'That
is true of virtually every American,' Gingrich said, noting that the Irish were
discriminated against by the English, for example."

24 That is breathtaking stuff coming from somebody who should know
that blacks have been on this North American continent for 375 years and

that for 245 the country permitted slavery. Gingrich should also know that for the next hundred years we had legalized subordination of blacks, under a suffocating blanket of condescension and frequently enforced by nightriding terrorists. We've had only thirty years of something else.

25   That something else is a nation trying to lift its ideals out of a thick, often impenetrable slough of racism. Racism is a hard word for what over the centuries became second nature in America—preferences across the board for white men and, following in their wake, white women. Many of these men seem to feel that it is un-American to ask them to share anything with blacks—particularly their work, their neighborhoods or "their" women. To protect these things—apparently essential to their identity—they engage in all forms of denial. For a historian to assert that "virtually every American" shares the history I have just outlined comes very close to lying.

26   Denial of racism is much like the denials that accompany addictions to alcohol, drugs or gambling. It is probably not stretching the analogy too much to suggest that many racist whites are so addicted to their unwarranted privileges and so threatened by the prospect of losing them that all kinds of defenses become acceptable, including insistent distortions of reality in the form of hypocrisy, lying or the most outrageous political demagogy.

"Those People" Don't Deserve Help

27   The demagogues have reverted to a new version of quite an old trick. Before the 1950s, whites who were busy denying that the nation was unfair to blacks would simply assert that we didn't deserve equal treatment because we were *inferior.* These days it is not permissible in most public circles to say that blacks are inferior, but it is perfectly acceptable to target the *behavior* of blacks, specifically poor blacks. The argument then follows a fairly predictable line: The behavior of poor blacks requires a severe rethinking of national social policy, it is said. Advantaged blacks really don't need affirmative action anymore, and when they are the objects of such programs, some qualified white person (unqualified white people don't show up in these arguments) is (as Dole might put it) "punished." While it is possible that color-blind affirmative action programs benefiting all disadvantaged Americans are needed, those (i.e., blacks) whose behavior is so distressing must be punished by restricting welfare, shriveling the safety net and expanding the prison opportunity. All of that would presumably give us, in William Bennett's words, "what we want—a color-blind society," for which the white American psyche is presumably fully prepared.

28   There are at least three layers of unreality in these precepts. The first is that the United States is not now and probably never will be a color-blind

society. It is the most color-conscious society on earth. Over the course of 375 years, whites have given blacks absolutely no reason to believe that they can behave in a color-blind manner. In many areas of our lives—particularly in employment, housing and education—affirmative action is required to counter deeply ingrained racist patterns of behavior.

29   Second, while I don't hold the view that all blacks who behave badly are blameless victims of a brutal system, I do believe that many poor blacks have, indeed, been brutalized by our culture, and I know of *no* blacks, rich or poor, who haven't been hurt in some measure by the racism in this country. The current mood (and, in some cases like the Speaker's, the cultivated ignorance) completely ignores the fact that some blacks never escaped the straight line of oppression that ran from slavery through the semislavery of sharecropping to the late mid-century migration from Southern farms into isolated pockets of urban poverty. Their families have always been excluded, poor and without skills, and so they were utterly defenseless when the enormous American economic dislocations that began in the mid-1970s slammed into their communities, followed closely by deadly waves of crack cocaine. One would think that the double-digit unemployment suffered consistently over the past two decades by blacks who were *looking for work* would be a permanent feature of the discussions about race, responsibility, welfare and rights.

30   But a discussion of the huge numbers of black workers who are becoming economically redundant would raise difficult questions about the efficiency of the economy at a time when millions of white men feel insecure. Any honest appraisal of unemployment would reveal that millions of low-skilled white men were being severely damaged by corporate and Federal Reserve decisions; it might also refocus the anger of those whites in the middle ranks whose careers have been shattered by the corporate downsizing fad.

31   But people's attention is kept trained on the behavior of some poor blacks by politicians and television news shows, reinforcing the stereotypes of blacks as dangerous, as threats, as unqualified. Frightened whites direct their rage at pushy blacks rather than at the corporations that export manufacturing operations to low-wage countries, or at the Federal Reserve, which imposes interest rate hikes that slow down the economy.

Who Benefits? We All Do

32   There is one final denial that blankets all the rest. It is that only society's "victims"—blacks, other minorities and women (who should, for God's sake, renounce their victimological outlooks)—have been injured by white male supremacy. Viewed in this light, affirmative action remedies are a kind of

zero-sum game in which only the "victims" benefit. But racist and sexist whites who are not able to accept the full humanity of other people are themselves badly damaged—morally stunted—people. The principal product of a racist and sexist society is damaged people and institutions—victims and victimizers alike. Journalism and education, two enterprises with which I am familiar, provide two good examples.

33   Journalistic institutions often view the nation through a lens that bonds reality to support white privilege. A recent issue of *U.S. News & World Report* introduced a package of articles on these issues with a question on its cover: "Does affirmative action mean NO WHITE MEN NEED APPLY?" The words "No white men need apply" were printed in red against a white background and were at least four times larger than the other words in the question. Inside, the lead story was illustrated by a painting that carries out the cover theme, with a wan white man separated from the opportunity ladders eagerly being scaled by women and dark men. And the story yielded up the following sentence: "Affirmative action poses a conflict between two cherished American principles: the belief that all Americans deserve equal opportunities and the idea that hard work and merit, not race or religion or gender or birthright, should determine who prospers and who does not."

34   Whoever wrote that sentence was in the thrall of one of the myths that Baldwin was talking about. The sentence suggests—as many people do when talking about affirmative action—that America is a meritocratic society. But what kind of meritocracy excludes women and blacks and other minorities from all meaningful competition? And even in the competition among white men, money, family and connections often count for much more than merit, test results (for whatever they're worth) and hard work.

35   The *U.S. News* story perpetuates and strengthens the view that many of my white students absorb from their parents: that white men now have few chances in this society. The fact is that white men still control virtually everything in America except the wealth held by widows. According to the Urban Institute, 53 percent of black men aged 25–34 are either unemployed or earn too little to lift a family of four from poverty.

36   Educational institutions that don't teach accurately about why America looks the way it does and why the distribution of winners and losers is as it is also injure our society. Here is another anecdote.

37   A warm, brilliant young white male student of mine came in just before he was to graduate and said that my course in race, law and culture, which he had just finished, had been the most valuable and the most disturbing he had ever taken. I asked how it had been disturbing.

38   "I learned that my two heroes are racists," he said.

39   "Who are your heroes and how are they racists?" I asked.

40   "My mom and dad," he said. "After thinking about what I was learning, I understood that they had spent all my life making me into the same kind of racists they were."

41   Affirmative action had brought me together with him when he was 22. Affirmative action puts people together in ways that make that kind of revelation possible. Nobody is a loser when that happens. The country gains.

42   And that, in the end, is the case for affirmative action. The arguments supporting it should be made on the basis of its broad contributions to the entire American community. It is insufficient to vilify white males and to skewer them as the whiners that journalism of the kind practiced by *U.S. News* invites us to do. These are people who, from the beginning of the Republic, have been taught that skin color is destiny and that whiteness is to be revered. Listen to Jefferson, writing in the year the Constitution was drafted:

> The first difference that strikes us is that of colour. . . . And is the difference of no importance? Is it not the foundation of a greater or less share of beauty in the two races? Are not the fine mixtures of red and white . . . in the one, preferable to that eternal monotony, which reigns in the countenances, that immoveable veil of black which covers all the emotions of the other race? Add to these, flowing hair, a more elegant symmetry of form, their own judgment in favor of the whites, declared by their preference for them, as uniformly as is the preference of the Oran-ootan for the black women over those of his own species. The circumstance of superior beauty, is thought worthy attention in the propagation of our horses, dogs, and other domestic animals; why not in that of man?

In a society so conceived and so dedicated, it is understandable that white males would take their preferences as a matter of natural right and consider any alteration of that a primal offense. But a nation that operates in that way abandons its soul and its economic strength, and will remain mired in ugliness and moral squalor because so many people are excluded from the possibility of decent lives and from forming any sense of community with the rest of society.

43   Seen only as a corrective for ancient wrongs, affirmative action may be dismissed by the likes of Gingrich, Gramm and Dole, just as attempts to federalize decent treatment of the freed slaves were dismissed after Reconstruction more than a century ago. Then, striking down the Civil Rights Act of 1875, Justice Joseph Bradley wrote of blacks that "there must be some

stage in the progress of his elevation when he takes the rank of a mere citizen, and ceases to be the special favorite of the laws, and when his rights, as a citizen or a man, are to be protected in the ordinary modes by which other men's rights are protected."

44   But white skin has made some citizens—particularly white males—*the special favorites of the culture.* It may be that we will need affirmative action until most white males are really ready for a color-blind society—that is, when they are ready to assume "the rank of a mere citizen." As a nation we took a hard look at that special favoritism thirty years ago. Though the centuries of cultural preference enjoyed by white males still overwhelmingly skew power and wealth their way, we have in fact achieved a more meritocratic society as a result of affirmative action than we have ever previously enjoyed in this country.

45   If we want to continue making things better in this society, we'd better figure out ways to protect and defend affirmative action against the confused, the frightened, the manipulators and, yes, the liars in politics, journalism, education and wherever else they may be found. In the name of longstanding American prejudice and myths and in the service of their own narrow interests, power-lusts or blindness, they are truly victimizing the rest of us, perverting the ideals they claim to stand for and destroying the nation they pretend to serve.

DINESH D'SOUZA

Sins of Admission

Dinesh D'Souza (1961–   ) made his reputation in conservative circles with the publication of Illiberal Education *(1991), a scathing attack on political correctness and on various other "liberal" features associated with modern universities. Since then he has written a biography of Ronald Reagan, and he appears frequently on* Nightline, Crossfire, *and similar TV shows. The following essay appeared in* The New Republic *in February 1991.*

1   When Michael Williams, head of the civil rights division of the Department of Education, sought to prevent American universities from granting minority-only scholarships, he blundered across the tripwire of affirmative action, the issue that is central to understanding racial tensions on campus and the furor over politically correct speech and the curriculum.

2   Nearly all American universities currently seek to achieve an ethnically diverse student body in order to prepare young people to live in an increasingly multiracial and multicultural society. Diversity is usually pursued through "proportional representation," a policy that attempts to shape each university class to approximate the proportion of blacks, Hispanics, whites, Asian Americans, and other groups in the general population. At the University of California, Berkeley, where such race balancing is official policy, an admissions report argues that proportional representation is the only just allocation of privileges for a state school in a democratic society, and moreover, "a broad diversity of backgrounds, values, and viewpoints is an integral part of a stimulating intellectual and cultural environment in which students educate one another."

3   The lofty goals of proportional representation are frustrated, however, by the fact that different racial groups perform very differently on academic indicators used by admissions officials, such as grades and standardized test scores. For example, on a scale of 400 to 1600, white and Asian-American students on average score nearly 200 points higher than black students on the Scholastic Aptitude Test (SAT). Consequently, the only way for colleges to achieve ethnic proportionalism is to downplay or abandon merit criteria, and to accept students from typically underrepresented groups, such as blacks, Hispanics, and American Indians, over better-qualified students from among whites and Asian Americans.

4   At Ivy League colleges, for instance, where the median high school grade average of applicants approaches 4.0 and SAT scores are around 1300, many black, Hispanic, and American Indian students are granted admission with grade scores below 3.0 and SATs lower than 1000. Each year state schools such as Berkeley and the University of Virginia turn away hundreds of white and Asian-American applicants with straight As and impressive extracurriculars, while accepting students from underrepresented groups with poor to mediocre academic and other credentials. John Bunzel, former president of San Jose State University, argues that since the pool of qualified minority students is small, selective colleges "soon realize they have to make big academic allowances" if they are going to meet affirmative action targets.

5   Although universities strenuously deny the existence of quota ceilings for Asians, it is mathematically impossible to raise the percentage of students from underrepresented groups without simultaneously reducing the percentage of students from overrepresented groups. Former Berkeley chancellor Ira Heyman has admitted and apologized for his university's discriminatory treatment of Asians, and this year the Department of Education found the University of California, Los Angeles, guilty of illegal anti-Asian policies. Stanford, Brown, and Yale are among the dozen or so prestigious institutions under close scrutiny by Asian groups.

6   For Asian Americans, the cruel irony is that preferential admissions policies, which are set up to atone for discrimination, seem to have institutionalized and legitimized discrimination against a minority group that is itself the victim of continuing prejudice in America. Moreover, for Asians, minority quotas that were intended as instruments of inclusion have become instruments of exclusion.

7   The second major consequence of proportional representation is not an overall increase in the number of blacks and other preferred minorities in American universities, but rather the *misplacement* of such students throughout higher education. In other words, a student who might be qualified for admission to a community college now finds himself at the University of Wisconsin. The student whose grades and extracurriculars are good enough for Wisconsin is offered admission to Bowdoin or Berkeley. The student who meets Bowdoin's or Berkeley's more demanding standards is accepted through affirmative action to Yale or Princeton. Somewhat cynically, one Ivy League official terms this phenomenon "the Peter Principle of university admissions."

8   Aware of the fact that many affirmative action students are simply not competitive with their peers, many colleges offer special programs in remedial reading, composition, and basic mathematics to enable disadvantaged

students to keep pace. But enrollment in such programs is generally poor: students who are already experiencing difficulties with their regular course load often do not have the time or energy to take on additional classes. Consequently, the dropout rate of affirmative action students is extremely high. Figures from the Department of Education show that blacks and Hispanics are twice as likely as whites and Asians to drop out for academic reasons. A recent study of 1980 high school graduates who entered four-year colleges found that only 26 percent of black and Hispanic students had graduated by 1986.

9   Even taking into account other factors for leaving college, such as financial hardship, the data leave little doubt that preferential admissions seriously exacerbate what universities euphemistically term "the retention problem." An internal report that Berkeley won't release to the public shows that, of students admitted through affirmative action who enrolled in 1982, only 22 percent of Hispanics and 18 percent of blacks had graduated by 1987. Blacks and Hispanics not admitted through preferential programs graduated at the rates of 42 and 55 percent respectively.

10   Although most universities do everything they can to conceal the data about preferential admissions and dropout rates, administrators will acknowledge the fact that a large number of minority students who stay in college experience severe academic difficulties. These classroom pressures, compounded by the social dislocation that many black and Hispanic students feel in the new campus environment, are at the root of the serious racial troubles on the American campus.

11   It is precisely these pressures that thwart the high expectations of affirmative action students, who have been repeatedly assured by college recruiters that standards have not been abridged to let them in, that they belong at the university, indeed, that they provide a special perspective that the school could not hope to obtain elsewhere. Bewildered at the realities of college life, many minority students seek support and solace from others like them, especially older students who have traveled the unfamiliar paths. Thus begins the process of minority separatism and self-segregation on campus, which is now fairly advanced and which has come as such a surprise to universities whose catalogs celebrate integration and the close interaction of diverse ethnic groups.

12   Distinctive minority organizations, such as Afro-American societies and Hispanic student organizations, provide needed camaraderie, but they do not provide academic assistance to disadvantaged students. Instead, they offer an attractive explanation: classroom difficulties of minorities are attributed not to insufficient academic preparation, but to the pervasive atmosphere of

bigotry on campus. In particular, both the curriculum and testing systems are said to embody a white male ethos that is inaccessible to minorities.

13   Through the political agitation of minority organizations, many black and Hispanic students seek to recover a confident identity and sense of place on campuses where they otherwise feel alienated and even inadequate. Consequently, minority activists at several universities now have elaborate campaigns to identify and extirpate bigotry, such as racism hotlines and mandatory consciousness-raising sessions directed at white students. In addition, activists demand that "institutional racism" be remedied through greater representation of blacks and Hispanics among administrators and faculty. The logical extreme of this trend is a bill that Assemblyman Tom Hayden has introduced in the California legislature that mandates not just proportional admissions but equal pass rates for racial groups in state universities.

14   Both survey data and interviews with students published in *The Chronicle of Higher Education* over the past few years show that many white students who are generally sympathetic to the minority cause become weary and irritated by the extent of preferential treatment and double standards involving minority groups on campus. Indeed, racial incidents frequently suggest such embitterment; at the University of Michigan, for example, the affirmative action office has been sent a slew of posters, letters, poems—many racist—objecting specifically to special treatment for blacks and deriding the competence of minority students at the university. An increasing number of students are coming to believe what undergraduate Jake Shapiro recently told the *MacNeil-Lehrer NewsHour:* "The reason why we have racial tensions at Rutgers is they have a very strong minority recruitment program, and this means that many of my friends from my hometown were not accepted even though they are more qualified."

15   Other students have complained that universities routinely recognize and subsidize minority separatist organizations, black and Hispanic fraternities, and even racially segregated residence quarters while they would never permit a club or fraternity to restrict membership to whites. A couple of American campuses have witnessed the disturbing rise of white student unions in bellicose resistance to perceived minority favoritism on campus.

16   A new generation of university leaders, weaned on the protest politics of the 1960s, such as Nannerl Keohane of Wellesley, James Freedman of Dartmouth, and Donna Shalala of the University of Wisconsin-Madison, are quite happy to attribute all opposition to resurgent bigotry. Some of this may be true, but as thoughtful university leaders and observers are now starting to recognize, administration policies may also be playing a

tragic, counterproductive role. A redoubling of those policies, which is the usual response to racial tension, is not likely to solve the problem and might make it worse.

17   If universities wish to eliminate race as a factor in their students' decision-making, they might consider eliminating it as a factor in their own. It may be time for college leaders to consider basing affirmative action programs on socioeconomic disadvantage rather than ethnicity. This strategy would help reach those disadvantaged blacks who desperately need the education our colleges provide, but without the deleterious effects of racial head-counting. And it would set a color-blind standard of civilized behavior, which inspired the civil rights movement in the first place.

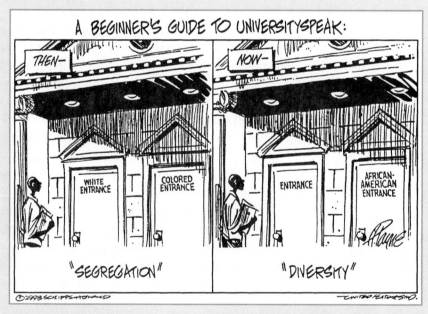

© Henry Payne. Reprinted by permission of United Feature Syndicate, Inc.

Title IX: Women in College Sports

> No person in the United States shall, on the basis of sex, be excluded from participation in, be denied the benefits of, or be subjected to discrimination under any educational program or activity receiving Federal financial assistance.
>
> —*Title IX, Educational Amendments Act, 1972*

When the U.S. women's soccer team won the World Cup in 1999, many of the players called themselves "the Title IX team" because all of them were products of college women's athletic teams that had benefited from Title IX. "We all know that there was a time when girls didn't have equal opportunities that men had," midfielder Tiffany Milbrett said. Goaltender Briana Scurry, who played college soccer at UMass, added in the same spirit "We never really went through what girls did years ago, when there was no Title IX and they had no place to play."

The triumph of the World Cup team offered a moment of national euphoria and reinforced national pride in the athletic accomplishments of other U.S. women—Sheryl Swoopes, Sue Bird, and Lisa Leslie in basketball, for example. But that euphoria has not ended the controversy that has accompanied Title IX since its inception in 1972. Indeed, as you know from Donna Lopiano's essay earlier in this book, Title IX—the federal statute that prohibits sex discrimination at college and universities that receive federal aid—is one of the most heated issues being discussed on campuses today. Often the issue divides people in strange ways—both men and women are found on both sides, and liberals and conservatives can line up in unusual ways.

We summarized the main sources of controversy on pages 200–203. On the one hand, advocates of Title IX note that 75 percent of athletic funds currently go to men, that women receive only 38 percent of scholarship dollars (on average) even though they make up 53 percent of the typical student body, and that coaches of women's teams receive lower pay than coaches of men's teams. Furthermore, they feel that equalizing opportunities will encourage more women to take up a serious interest in sports, to the long-term benefit of women who will enjoy short- and long-term benefits of sports such as assertiveness, physical health, self-confidence, and just plain fun. Supporters of a strict interpretation of Title IX, which was upheld in a 1997 Supreme Court ruling involving Brown University, feel that it is simple justice to provide equal funds for men and women, even if it means that in the short run some men's sports must be discontinued. While conceding that Title IX might undermine some men's sports to the greater good of equal opportunity for women, they also contend that there is actually quite a bit of money in the budgets for men's sports—for training tables, expensive travel, and other perks (especially for football players)—that could be diverted to women without hurting men's sports very much at all. And they press relentlessly for social advances for women in sports at a time when, let's face it, *Sports Illustrated* is still publishing a swimsuit issue and when other women athletes are being marketed as sex objects. Even the heroic U.S. women's soccer team was regarded "affectionately" as "booters with hooters."

On the other hand, many critics contend that many of the imbalances in the expenditures for men's and women's sports can be attributed to the fact that only men play college football, a sport which sometimes generates the money that supports the entire athletic department; a football squad with one hundred members and eighty-five scholarship athletes can throw figures out of balance rather quickly even as they generate funds that everyone else can use. Others feel that because far more men are interested in sports than women are in the United States (and on college campuses), it is appropriate for men to receive a preponderance of the funding for sports, just as women sometimes receive more support for participating in musical groups or majoring in the arts, and men receive more support for majoring in engineering in disproportionate numbers. To them, "separate but equal" athletic programs sounds as retro as "separate but equal" educational facilities for various racial groups. On the basis of those criticisms, several members of Congress have periodically offered amendments to the Title IX statute (so far without success) that would exempt athletic teams, and a commission appointed by the administration of George W. Bush (but condemned by Donna Lopiano) proposed changes in Title IX provisions early in 2003. Many people especially object when men's sports are discontinued (or "sacrificed") by universities in order to even up the raw proportions between funded male and female athletes. Feeling that such a move does nothing to increase opportunities for women and simply hurts men, they argue that figures should be equalized only by the addition of women's sports, not by the discontinuation of men's programs.

In 1972, 1 in 27 high school girls participated in varsity sports. In 2002, the number was 1 in 2.5.

More than 170 men's wrestling programs have been disbanded in the past twenty years.

In 1999, women received 33% of the sports budgets in NCAA institutions, 41% of the sports scholarships, and 30% of the recruiting dollars.

In 1995, UCLA dropped men's swimming and men's gymnastics to save money. The swim team has produced 16 Olympic gold medal winners.

Source: Sports Illustrated, *June 24, 2002*

But where would the money come to make such additions to the budget? Why should women be expected to participate in sports at the same proportion as men? Does Title IX actually benefit majority women at the expense of minorities, particularly when the sports funded tend to be things like soccer, swimming, golf, and tennis? Should women be given preference in the selection of coaches for women's teams? (Currently it is common to see male coaches of female teams, but still quite rare to see a woman coaching a men's sport.) Should salaries for women coaches approximate the salaries of men— or would that be futile when coaches for football and men's basketball routinely earn more than college presidents? Will Title IX be the death blow to football—or has football for no good reason become a sacred cow that deserves no special protection? Would we be better off and avoid the whole mess by ending the practice of supporting intercollegiate athletics with scholarships and other support? And what about the implications of Title IX for high schools: should the same principles that guide practices for higher education also guide the conduct of high schools?

In short, what is fair? That question, and the other questions that Title IX is generating, will continue to animate college campuses for years to come. Donna Lopiano's argument on pages 203–207 is a good starting point for study, so you might begin with that essay if you have not already read it. Her arguments are seconded in the selections by Alisa Solomon and Christine Brennan, who testify to the personal benefits that Title IX has brought to many women. We also present two arguments that are highly critical of Title IX, one by Michael Lynch and the other by Ira Berkow.

Key Court Cases Related to Title IX

Grove City College v. Bell In 1984, the Supreme Court ruled that if an athletic program receives federal funds directly, the institution should not have to comply with Title IX mandates. This ruling was then negated by the Civil Rights Restoration Act of 1988, which required all educational institutions receiving federal aid to be in compliance with Title IX.

Franklin v. Gwinnett County In 1992, the Supreme Court found that compensatory and punitive damages may be awarded when an institution has taken intentional action to avoid complying with Title IX.

Brown University v. Amy Cohen Brown University, arguing that in general women are less interested in sports than men and that the direct proportionality rule implied in Title IX amounts to an illegal quota system, wished to fund more male than female athletes. In 1997 the Supreme Court decided against Brown; the court in effect ruled that the total number of varsity positions for men and women must reflect their overall percentages in the student body.

Getting Pinned

While colleges eliminated 1,464 varsity spots for wrestlers between 1981 and 1998, both men and women have seen gains in their opportunities to participate in National Collegiate Athletic Association sports.

Source: National Collegiate Athletic Association and *Chronicle of Higher Education*

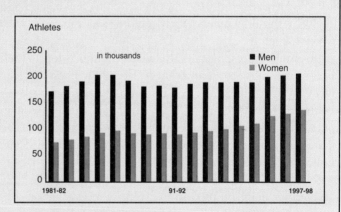

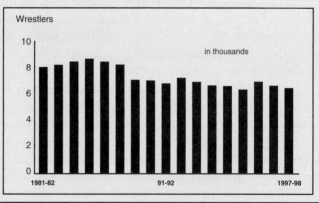

MICHAEL LYNCH

Title IX's Pyrrhic Victory

Michael Lynch serves as a writer and editor for Reason *magazine, based in Washington, D.C.* Reason *bills itself as "the monthly print magazine of free minds and free markets," covering politics, culture, and the news. It proposes to offer an alternative to right-wing and left-wing opinion magazines by making a case for liberty and free choice whenever possible. The piece below was published in April 2001 in* Reason Online, *an ezine that is updated daily.*

1   Former National Wrestling Champion Stephen Neal is grappling with his toughest opponent yet. The 6 foot 5 inch 270-pounder racked up numerous awards during his four-year wrestling career at California State University at Bakersfield (CSUB). He was a four-time All American and an Academic All American, and he took home the Heisman Trophy of wrestling, the Dan Hodge Award. Yet the heavyweight, who graduated in 1999, burns for one more win—not on a wrestling mat but in a court of law.

2   Neal's longest match started in 1996, when officials at CSUB announced plans to cut the wrestling team. It's not that the team wasn't performing. The only Division I sport at CSUB, the program had distinguished itself over the years, winning two PAC 10 championships and finishing in the top ten in the NCAA finals three out of the previous four years. The problem had to do with "gender equity," the proportion of male to female athletes. Critics charged that CSUB, like many other colleges and universities, had too many men playing sports and was discriminating against women.

3   In 1993, when Neal was a junior wrestling at a San Diego high school, the California chapter of the National Organization for Women (CAL-NOW) was completing litigation against the California State University System, of which CSUB is a part. CAL-NOW claimed that the Cal State System discriminated against women in its athletics programs. A state superior court judge crafted a consent decree that gave individual CSU campuses five years to bring the gender breakdown of their student athletes and scholarships to within five percentage points of the breakdown in the student body. If a school's student body consisted of 55 percent women, then at least 50 percent of intercollegiate athletes needed to be women. On the financial front, total expenditures for men's and women's programs were to be within 10 percentage points of each other.

4   When he learned of the consent decree, CSUB wrestling coach T. J. Kerr knew he had a problem. CSUB's student body is dominated by women, 63 percent. And even though the school had seven women's teams and only six men's teams, men accounted for 61 percent of its varsity athletes. Kerr studied the issue and developed a plan, figuring that the way to comply with the court order was to expand opportunities. He took the initiative to start a women's wrestling team. "I started looking at the participation number of women wrestlers in high school—it had doubled over five years," says Kerr. "I was thinking if I could get women on my team, I could leverage this thing." School administrators denied his request for women's wrestling, but Kerr went around them and started it as a club sport. Soon he had 17 women on his team. Two even competed for the varsity squad.

5   The cuts came anyway. In late 1995, CSUB's athletic director capped Kerr's squad at 27 men, and the coach was forced to cut 10 male athletes. Five former wrestlers filed grievances with the school, alleging sex discrimination. Then Kerr was told he could carry a total of only 34 wrestlers, forcing him to cut seven women. In 1996, on the eve of the PAC 10 finals and the Division I championships, the Intercollegiate Athletics Advisory Committee, which advises CSUB's president on athletic policy, announced plans to cut the wrestling program to meet the consent decree.

6   Enough was enough, thought Stephen Neal, who'd experienced the damage on a personal level. His roommate, a freshman walk-on, was cut from the squad. "He didn't know what to do. He was in shock," says Neal, adding that the roommate ultimately quit school. Neal, along with 21 male wrestlers and eight female ones, filed suit against CSUB in the U.S. District Court for the Eastern District of California for sex discrimination.

7   The root of Neal's problem—and that of thousands of male athletes across the country—lies in the widespread push for gender equity in scholastic and collegiate sports. In California, Neal and hundreds of other male athletes have been affected by state law. Elsewhere, it's a federal law that's at issue: Title IX of the 1972 Amendments to the Education Act. Title IX sought to give women equal access to educational programs, including athletics. Now it's evicting men from the locker room.

Struck Out

8   There's no arguing that women didn't face a shortage of athletic opportunities in the 1950s, '60s, and early '70s. A year before Title IX's passage, only 294,015 girls played high school sports, compared to 3.7 million boys. "I was the classic tomboy growing up in middle America who played football, bas-

ketball, and baseball with my brothers and the neighborhood guys," recalls 50-year-old Mary Jo Kane, who teaches sports sociology at the University of Minnesota and directs the Tucker Center for Research on Women and Girls in Sport. "I lived to play those sports. But when I got to high school, there weren't teams available for me in those sports. So I did what a lot of girls in my generation did and started playing a more 'appropriate' sport, golf."

9   In the three decades since Title IX's passage, women's participation in school athletics has increased impressively. During the 1999–2000 school year, 2.7 million girls played high school sports, compared to 3.8 million boys, according to the National Federation of State High School Associations. In 1998–99, 148,803 women played NCAA sports, up from 80,040 16 years earlier.

10   "In one generation, young girls have gone from hoping there is a team to hoping they can make the team. That's an incredible difference," says Kane, who credits Title IX and the hard work of women's sports activists for this change—and who jokingly declares that she's never been a communist and still loves football. Women can now earn a living playing basketball in America. In 1999, the U.S. women's soccer team filled the Rose Bowl and captivated the country, beating China for a World Cup victory.

11   Still, Kane is frustrated with the pace of change. "Only 9 percent of Division I schools are in compliance," she says. "And that's 30 years after passage." Women still account for only about 35 percent of college athletes and garner less than a quarter of annual athletic operating and recruiting budgets.

12   Yet while the intent of Title IX was to provide opportunity for girls and women, today it is often applied in ways that do nothing but kill athletic opportunities for boys and men, an outcome no one claims to want. In the gender-equity debate, few people blame Title IX itself, which, after all, seeks only to ensure equal opportunity for both men and women. Most women's sports advocates recognize there's a problem with cutting men's teams to equalize participation rates. But they blame the choices made by administrators who they say refused to restrain football programs. For their part, male coaches and athletes say they agree with the spirit behind Title IX. It's the rules promulgated by bureaucrats dictating hard gender-based quotas that are the problem.

13   Rhode Island's Providence College provides a vivid example of how Title IX often plays out. In the late '90s, Providence found itself in a familiar bind. Women accounted for 59 percent of its students, yet they were only 43 percent of student athletes. The school was facing a peer review by the NCAA, and it needed to show quick "progress" toward gender equity. Providence simply had too many male athletes, and the easiest course of action

was to cut some men's programs to bring its numbers into line. In the fall of 1998, the administration announced that the 1999 season would be the last for the school's 78-year-old baseball team. After 2002, Providence would no longer support men's golf or tennis. Not one new women's team would be created, but the male-female ratio would still be greatly improved.

14   "Baseball, tennis, and golf were the three sports that, when you combine their resources together, delete them from the male side of the picture, [and] add those resources to the women's side of the picture, put . . . us in compliance with Title IX's proportionality mandate," explained Providence Athletic Director John Marinatto to the PBS special *National Desk*. School administrators had watched neighboring Brown University get sued and lose for not having its numbers right; they feared a similar lawsuit. "We just couldn't risk that kind of litigation," the Rev. Terence J. Keegan, Providence's executive vice president, told the *New York Times*. "We felt we were backed into a corner."

15   "I was trying to figure out if it was a dream or not," recalls former Providence baseball coach Charlie Hickey, who started as an assistant in 1991 and took over the program in 1996. "A lot of wild thoughts came to mind, a lot of hatred, bitterness. Then I had to tell 29 kids."

16   Providence outfielder Jason Hairston recalls the October day when the coach interrupted practice to deliver the news. "It was like someone had taken your heart out of you," he says. Hairston had good reason to be upset. Like others on the squad, he had chosen Providence because of its baseball team. As a high school senior in Connecticut, he'd made all-state teams in soccer and baseball and was heavily recruited in both sports by such schools as the Naval Academy, West Point, and Boston College. He decided to pursue his options in baseball because he found it more challenging. "People say I was better at soccer," says Hairston. "But I played baseball for the love of the game." He chose Providence because he liked its atmosphere, its location, its academic reputation, its standing in the prestigious Big East sports conference, and the relative largess of its scholarship offer.

17   The unexpected demise of Providence's baseball team forced Hairston to make a tough decision. He'd already completed two years of academics at Providence. If he played his junior year at Providence, the team's last season, it was unlikely that he'd be able to transfer and play his last year of eligibility at another school. Even if he was able to play his final year of eligibility, it would cost him academically. Most schools will not accept three years of academic work, so transferring would delay his graduation for at least a year. Hairston decided to stay and play at Providence. It's a decision he doesn't regret but one that came at a steep price for a young man who planned to play four years of Division I baseball, with the goal of getting

drafted into the pros. "It made me give up my dream," says Hairston, who graduated last year and now works for KPMG Consulting. "I could have worked here, played Division I baseball, and showcased myself. Now I can't."

18   The same qualities that convinced Hairston to choose Providence—the school's size, familial atmosphere, and Big East schedule—were helping Coach Hickey produce the best baseball teams in Providence College's history. In 1995 and 1996 the team was the Big East season champion. Hairston's dream of playing Major League Baseball was hardly a pie in the sky. Two of Providence's recent graduates have made it, if only briefly, to the big leagues. Six or seven Providence alumni are sprinkled through the minor leagues.

The Biggest Quota

19   Title IX itself says nothing about athletics. It simply prohibits discrimination based on sex in federally funded education programs. "No person in the United States, shall, on the basis of sex, be excluded from participation in, be denied the benefits of, or be subjected to discrimination under any education program or activity receiving federal financial assistance," states the relevant part of the law.

20   Title IX also says nothing about quotas based on population proportions. In fact, the law's creators emphatically argued against such things. "The thrust of the amendment is to do away with every quota," explained its chief Senate sponsor, Birch Bayh (D-Ind.). House sponsor Albert Quie (R-Minn.) similarly underscored that Title IX "would provide that there shall be no quotas in the sex antidiscrimination title."

21   Despite such intentions, Title IX has become, in the approving words of Rep. Maxine Waters (D-Calif.), "the biggest quota you've ever seen." Speaking at a 1997 House Constitution Subcommittee hearing, Waters emphasized that point, calling Title IX, "a quota—[a] big, round quota."

22   What happened? In 1979, following standard operating procedure, the federal Department of Health, Education, and Welfare issued a policy interpretation for athletics. Schools would be in compliance with Title IX, HEW decreed, if they met any one prong of a three-prong test: They could provide sporting opportunities to the sexes in "numbers substantially proportionate to their respective enrollments"; they could show a "history of continuing program expansion"; or they could show they were already meeting the "interests and abilities" of women.

23   In the 1990s, federal courts elevated this interpretation to the level of law. At the same time, they focused on the proportionality test as the only definitive means to prove compliance. A 1992 court decision further established

that plaintiffs could collect attorneys' fees and damages, which substantially raised the stakes for colleges and universities. Once compensatory and punitive damages could be awarded in Title IX cases, the lawsuits effectively became self-financing. Even when damages aren't awarded, public interest attorneys can bill the court at several times their actual costs. In fact, enterprising lawyers don't even need aggrieved plaintiffs; suits can be filed by anyone based on aggregate numerical disparities.

24   In 1996 Norma Cantu, assistant secretary for civil rights at the Department of Education, made it clear that while a school could theoretically meet Title IX requirements in any one of the three ways outlined by HEW, the only true "safe harbor" for a school was to offer "proportional opportunity." At the same time, Cantu redefined *opportunity* to mean the number of women playing sports, not the number of spots available on a school's teams. On this reading, explains Mark Martel, attorney for former CSUB wrestler Stephen Neal, "an *opportunity* equals an actual participant. So if a woman's team could have had 25 athletes but only 20 go out for the team, there are only 20 opportunities. If a men's team has 25 opportunities and 25 men go out, then there is unequal opportunity."

25   In short, what happened to Title IX is a classic Washington story. Ideological activists take words that appeal to a general sense of fair play, such as *opportunity,* and then redefine them. While they argue for their new definition in court, they simultaneously justify their actions to the public based on the old, common-sense understanding.

26   The redefinition of opportunity turns out to be critical to the new wave of Title IX enforcement, because men go out for sports in greater numbers than women do. Women's sports activists claim that in the absence of discrimination, women would play sports in equal numbers to men. "You treat sports the same way, and girls are just as interested in playing as boys," Donna Lopiano, executive director of the Women's Sports Foundation, told ABC's John Stossel on *20/20* in 1998. She said there was "no doubt in [her] mind" that discrimination is the reason girls and boys don't play in equal number. "If you build it," she told Stossel, "they will come."

27   There's some evidence for Lopiano's claim. Recall that in 1970 12 boys played high school sports for every girl. As the number of girls' teams grew, so did the number of female participants. In 1970 just one out of every 27 high school girls played varsity sports, according to Lopiano. Today that figure is about one in three. If women with athletic aspirations had simply accepted the status quo in the 1960s, we'd likely think the 12-to-1 disparity was "natural," simply the result of girls' preferences. Yet over the past three decades, millions of girls have filled up soccer fields, softball diamonds, lacrosse fields, and basketball courts.

Paying for Parity

28   Yet there is ample reason to believe that there is more to gender disparity in college sports than lack of opportunity—however that term is defined. If Lopiano is right, compliance with Title IX shouldn't be too difficult for schools: All they would have to do is offer the same number of teams for women, and the problem would go away. But this doesn't always work. Schools have indeed built sports opportunities for girls, but boys continue to turn out in greater numbers. Hence, as of 1998–99, there are more male college athletes (211,273 men versus 148,803 women, according to the NCAA), even though there are more female teams (8,374 women's versus 8,004 men's). In other words, women have more chances to play sports, but they don't take advantage of them as often. College-level intramural sports, which are purely voluntary, are dominated by men, with nearly eight in 10 athletes being male, according to a 1994 study by consulting firm Pacey Economics.

29   What might explain those numbers, if not discrimination? "Girls are interested in more things," says Kimberly Schuld, who works on gender-equity issues for the Independent Women's Forum, a conservative, D.C.-based organization that is critical of Title IX. "They are more likely than boys to participate in multiple extracurricular activities, not just sports. If we applied a gender quota to other activities, it would destroy opportunities for girls in fields such as journalism, law, and science. Who would stand for that?"

30   Coaches and other investigators also challenge the idea that discrimination is at the root of numerical disparities. "Interest in sports has gone up tremendously among women," says Janet Sherman, head coach of the women's softball team at California State University at Northridge. "But is it as high as on the men's side? I don't think so."

31   "There's no question in my mind that women are less interested in playing sports than men," says Lamar Daniel, a former investigator at the Department of Education's Office for Civil Rights who conducted the very first Title IX investigation, back in 1978. Daniel went on to conduct over 20 reviews before retiring in 1995 to become a consultant. "But logically, in my experience, you can't prove that," he adds. "It's just not provable." In practice, Daniel says, this means schools must seek proportionality, either by adding women athletes, cutting or capping men's teams, or doing a little of both.

32   The University of Louisville opted for that last option. In 1997 the school brought in Daniel as a consultant to review its sports program. The new athletic director, Tom Jurich, had been forced to deal with the aftermath of a Title IX investigation at Colorado State, and he knew Louisville was legally vulnerable. At that time, women accounted for 52 percent of its students but only 33 percent of its athletes.

Before Title IX

- Many schools and universities had separate entrances for male and female students.
- Female students were not allowed to take certain courses, such as auto mechanics or criminal justice; male students could not take home economics.
- Most medical and law schools limited the number of women admitted to 15 or fewer per school.
- Many colleges and universities required women to have higher test scores and better grades than male applicants to gain admission.
- Women living on campus were not allowed to stay out past midnight.
- Women faculty members were excluded from faculty clubs and encouraged to join faculty wives' clubs instead.
- After winning two gold medals in the 1964 Olympics, swimmer Donna de Varona could not obtain a college swimming scholarship. For women they did not exist.

Source: Report Card on Gender Equity, National Coalition for Women and Girls in Education

33   Jurich wanted Louisville to enjoy the safe harbor of proportionality, but he didn't want to have to cut men's teams to get there. He planned to build Louisville's program into compliance. He added three women's teams (softball, rowing, and golf) while cutting one men's team (indoor track). He went into a fund-raising frenzy to reach his goal.

34   In the early 1990s, Louisville built a new $70 million football stadium and made its first-class training facilities available to all student athletes. In 1998 it refurbished the old football facility to accommodate baseball, women's field hockey, rowing, and men's and women's golf. It spent $13 million building Cardinal Park, which houses a new softball stadium, a track and field stadium, and a soccer field for both men and women. Jurich is currently raising money for a new $18 million swimming facility that he expects to complete in 2002.

35   The price tag for such efforts is not small: Louisville's sports program costs about $25 million annually. (Since 1983, it has paid for itself through gate receipts, TV contracts, and fund-raising.) But such efforts paid off in terms of proportionality. By fall 1999, Louisville had increased its women's sports participation to 45 percent; there are now a total of 200 female and 245 male athletes. It expects to achieve parity within three years.

36   Washington State University took a different, though equally successful, route to proportionality. In the early 1990s, the state legislature passed a bill providing tuition waivers for female athletes, which allowed its state-supported colleges and universities to beef up their squads for less direct

After Title IX

- In 1973, 43% of female high school graduates were enrolled in college. This grew to 63% in 1997. Fifty-four percent of all college students are currently female.
- In 1971, 18% of young women and 26% of young men had completed four years or more of college; in 1998, 27% of both men and women had earned bachelor's degrees.
- In 1972, women received 9% of medical degrees but by 1998 that number had moved up to 38%; 1% of dental degrees grew to 38%; and the percentage of law degrees earned by women had moved from 7% in 1971 to 43%.
- Today, more than 100,000 women participate in intercollegiate athletics, a four-fold increase from 1971. That same year 300,000 women (7.5%) were high school athletes; in 1996, that figure had increased to 2.4 million (39%).
- Title IX prohibits schools from suspending, expelling, or discriminating against pregnant high school students in educational programs and activities. From 1980 to 2000, dropout rates for pregnant students declined 30%, increasing the chances the mothers will be able to support and care for their children.
- Eighty percent of female managers of *Fortune* 500 companies have a sports background.
- High school girls who participate in team sports are less likely to drop out of school, smoke, drink, or become pregnant.

Source: Title IX, 25 Years of Progress, U.S. Department of Education

money. "Washington State is at parity, and the University of Washington is close," says the Independent Women's Forum's Schuld, who points out that this option shifts costs to taxpayers and is unavailable for private schools.

37   Proportionality can be achieved, as Louisville and Washington State demonstrate. But they are the exception: Most schools can't fund expansions through massive fund-raising campaigns or use state-granted tuition waivers. For the great majority of schools, being safe from a Title IX investigation or private lawsuit means cutting men's programs.

Swimming Upstream

38   While no one denies that many men's programs have been cut in the pursuit of gender parity, there's disagreement about the overall numbers. On the high end, Leo Kocher, the University of Chicago's wrestling coach, says there have been massive cuts. Analyzing one set of NCAA numbers (the group is notoriously slow to release easy-to-use data related to Title IX issues), Kocher claims that between 1992 and 1997 more than 200 men's teams were cut, a loss of more than 20,000 men's roster spots. Only 5,800 women's spots were added, for a male-pain-to-female-gain ratio of 3.4 to 1. Donna

Lopiano disputes Kocher's tally. She points to other NCAA data which show that total men's sports participation in the NCAA has actually increased by more than 13,000 in recent years. The problem with this is that new schools were added to the NCAA over the period, so overall numbers could go up even if many schools were cutting men's teams.

39   The General Accounting Office took a crack at the issue in 1999. In an attempt to hold the pool of schools constant, it found that from the 1985–86 academic year to the 1996–97 academic year 21,000 male athletic spots disappeared, a 12 percent drop overall. On the female side, 14,500 spots appeared, for a jump of 16 percent.

40   Regardless of the exact numbers, it's clear that men's programs get dropped on a regular basis. This is especially true for teams that generate little revenue and small crowds. In 1999, for instance, Miami University of Ohio announced it was cutting its wrestling, men's soccer, and men's tennis teams to comply with Title IX. That same year the University of New Mexico shut down wrestling, men's gymnastics, and men's swimming. Brigham Young University axed wrestling and men's gymnastics. In 2000 the University of Miami announced plans to cut its award-winning men's swimming and diving programs as well as men's crew. Wrestling, track, cross-country, swimming, and tennis have been hit particularly hard, each losing more than 20 programs in the past seven years. With the possible exception of basketball, every men's sport is vulnerable.

41   Even programs that can fund themselves through alumni donations aren't safe. Winning traditions similarly count for little. In 1994 UCLA cut men's swimming and gymnastics, programs that consistently produced Olympic medalists. In exchange, it added women's soccer and water polo.

42   "I think it's great that the women have those two sports," says former UCLA swimming coach Ron Ballatore. "It's too bad they had to drop two great men's sports. It's a terrible blow. Here's a place that has had swimming since the 1920s. It was one of the top programs in the country. It would be like Notre Dame or Nebraska cutting its football team." In the 16 years Ballatore coached UCLA, the school produced 26 NCAA champions and 10 Olympic gold medalists. It won the NCAA championship in 1982 and finished out of the top five just a handful of times. The only season it finished out of the top 10 was its last, lame-duck season.

43   Ballatore's swimmers fought hard to save the program. With the exception of one swimmer, his entire team elected to swim the 1994 season and work to save the team instead of transferring. "The day it happened, Coach Ballatore called me and gave me the choice of transferring right

there or coming back for another year and trying to fight," recalls backstroker Michael Andrews. "I decided to stay and fight."

44   The swimmers raised money from alumni. They filed a lawsuit. In the end, though, nothing helped. "It didn't matter about success or the fact that your program was good," says Ballatore, who went on to coach at Brown and then the University of Florida, where he is currently an administrator. "It boiled down to money and Title IX. But money really wasn't an issue. We had raised enough money. We had an alumnus who was going to give us a bunch of money."

45   UCLA's gymnasts were cut loose as well, although they stayed on to train at the school's facility. Peter Vidmar, a UCLA alumnus who won two gold medals and a silver in the 1984 Olympics, says the school's chancellor told him it was due to Title IX. Jim Foody, who had hoped to make the 2000 Olympic team, is blunt. "In 1984 we had half the men's Olympic team," he told *The Daily Bruin.* "In 1992 we had the No. 1 and No. 2 ranked guys. . . . For them to drop that team after what they did for the school, it's definitely shitty."

46   Even these cuts didn't protect UCLA from charges of discrimination. In December 1998 CAL-NOW filed a Title IX complaint with the federal Office for Civil Rights, which is still under investigation. Betsy Stephenson, associate athletic director and senior women's administrator, told *The Daily Bruin,* "I would hope that we wouldn't have gotten this complaint because I don't believe women athletes are being mistreated, but we can't control complaints from coming." Says Ballatore, "UCLA got rid of us, but they are still faced with the same problem."

Title IX versus Quotas

47   The tragedy of Title IX is that virtually nobody is pleased with its current results. The day after Providence announced it was killing its baseball team, the college gym filled up with angry students trying to make sense of what had happened. The women's soccer team threatened to boycott their game that day in solidarity with their fellow athletes. The girl's volleyball team warmed up in the baseball team's jerseys. Alexa Ricardo, a senior soccer player recalls that nobody agreed with axing baseball and nobody thought it was necessary. Swimmer Michelle Hackmer told the *New York Times:* "When the announcement was made about eliminating baseball, the women athletes were as mad about it as anyone else. . . . Sure we want women athletes to be treated fairly, but at this expense? I don't think this is what Title IX was supposed to be about."

48   Hackmer is right. Without policy changes, Title IX is likely to keep killing men's teams. The Independent Women's Forum and other critics hope that the Bush administration will return to the original intention of the provision. Since the problem is with the bureaucratic regulations and enforcement policies, not the statute itself, they are optimistic about the prospects for change. "I think [Bush] will have a huge effect," enthuses the IWF's Schuld, who notes that a clause concerning Title IX made it into the 2000 Republican platform. "This whole issue can be solved in 12 months by rewriting policy. It was created by policy, it can be undone by policy."

49   That's a rosy scenario. While the Bush administration may reinterpret Title IX, it will face staunch opposition from the industry that has grown up around the college sports issue. There's no reason to believe that groups invested in Title IX lawsuits will simply admit defeat and leave the legal playing field. Consider Deborah Brake, an attorney with the National Women's Law Center. Brake believes that the only problem with Title IX is that it hasn't been enforced comprehensively enough. She once told a reporter she'd like "to bring immediate lawsuits against as many universities as possible to force them to comply with the law." In June 1997 Brake's group filed 25 complaints with the Office for Civil Rights to celebrate the 25th anniversary of Title IX's passage and hasn't slowed down since.

50   In the meantime, Stephen Neal, the wrestler from California State University at Bakersfield, continues his own legal grudge match against Title IX. The law, he says, shouldn't have to hurt men to help women. In fact, he thinks cutting men's teams simply to get to proportional numbers—to meet a quota—is expressly forbidden by Title IX, which is about ending real, not just statistical, discrimination.

51   Neal is attempting a bit of legal jujitsu: He's using the text of Title IX to argue against the CAL-NOW consent decree. In February 1999 U.S. District Court Judge Robert E. Coyle agreed with Neal and enjoined CSUB from further cutting the men's wrestling team. But Neal lost round two in December 1999, when a three-judge panel of the U.S. Court of Appeals for the Ninth Circuit reversed the injunction. Neal, who sees the larger context of his struggle, will be back in federal court in February, pressing his case.

52   "We feel we are the last stand for wrestling," says Neal. "We're going to keep fighting."

IRA BERKOW

The Other Side of Title IX

Ira Berkow (1940–) became a sportswriter for the New York Times *in 1981, and since then he has covered baseball, hockey, basketball, and other sports. He has also written fiction and biography, as well as the HBO documentary* Champions of American Sports. *The following article appeared in the* Times *on May 19, 1999.*

1   It was a glorious spring day for baseball in Providence, R.I., last Saturday, in which the home team, the Providence College Friars, was about to play the Villanova Wildcats.

2   The well-occupied metal bleachers sparkled under the noon sun; fans had set up beach chairs behind the screen and spread out blankets on the grass beyond the left-field line at Hendricken Field. The dust from the tan infield had been hosed down by some of the players themselves in their white uniforms.

3   So why the sadness? Why the anger? Why the passion? And where was Father Smith?

4   "After what happened," said Barry Sullivan, an all-America baseball player for Providence in the 1970's, referring to the college president, "you'd think he'd have the guts to show his face."

5   This was the 78th season of Providence College baseball, making it the school's oldest athletic team.

6   This season, the Friars are rated best in the Northeast and 26th in the nation in a poll of coaches. They came into Saturday's game with a 42-13 record, two victories short of the school record, and were assured of being seeded in the Big East tournament, which begins today in Trenton.

7   It is one of the best baseball seasons in school history, and it will be its last.

8   Last October, the Rev. Philip A. Smith, the school president, announced that baseball, along with men's golf and tennis, would be eliminated from the varsity athletic program.

9   He said the cuts were made in order to comply with gender equity and proportionality strictures set down by the National Collegiate Athletic Association, driven by the Federal Office of Civil Rights.

10   "I'm still so upset that I can hardly express it," said Angelo Ciminiello, the senior third baseman, an academic all-American for four years who will soon be going to medical school.

11   Shortly after the announcement was made, three players transferred to other schools. But the rest of the team decided to stay, to play, perhaps with a commitment that they never had before. At one stage, they won a school-record 15 straight games.

12   Before the game against Villanova, each player and coach was introduced, their team contributions briefly noted by a young announcer on the crackling p.a. system. The team heard and saw the fans standing and clapping for this last home game.

13   "It was so emotional," Mike Scott, the freshman right-fielder, said later. "I had tingles all up and down my body."

14   The Friars fell behind by 1-0 in the fourth, tied the score in the bottom of the inning, only to fall behind in the fifth, 2-1. Again, they mounted a rally in the bottom half of the inning and took a 3-2 lead.

15   "It's amazing what this team has done," said Lou Merloni, a former Providence infielder who was with the Boston Red Sox early this season, before having been sent to the Pawtucket farm team the other day. He had come to lend his support on this last home game. "And it's so sad. I feel like something has been ripped out of my insides. But this team has never quit, even when the school quit on them."

16   Smith sees his decision differently.

17   "I do not feel good about the decision to drop baseball, but in the end we had to have our academic priorities come first," he said on Monday. "We tried other ways, but nothing else worked. It seemed we'd be taking from Peter to pay Paul, and still falling short. Ultimately I had to make this unfortunate decision."

18   The baseball team also has the support of female athletes at Providence, who were angered by the decision.

19   "When the announcement was made about eliminating baseball, the women athletes were as mad about it as anyone else," said Michelle Hackmer, a junior on the swimming team, who attended the game. "Sure, we want women athletes to be treated fairly, but at this expense? I don't think this is what Title IX was supposed to be about.

20   "The day after the announcement, the women's volleyball team had a game at home, and threatened to boycott the game. They didn't, but to show their support to the men they warmed up in the baseball team's jerseys."

21   The Women's Sports Foundation has issued a position paper on Title IX and the elimination of men's varsity sports in that regard. "Most schools cite, as the reason for their decision, the need to reduce expenditures in order to provide opportunities for women," it reads. "Title IX requires no such reduc-

tion in opportunities for men. The Foundation is not in favor of reducing athletic opportunities for men as the preferred method of achieving Title IX compliance."

22   Enrollment at Providence is 59 percent women, and 41 percent men. But 57 percent of the athletes are men, with the men receiving the majority of athletic scholarships. At Providence, there will soon be 11 women's varsity teams to go along with 9 men's varsity teams. The N.C.A.A. insisted on 1 percent gender equity proportionality, meaning that the percentage of female students and the money spent on their sports must be within 1 percent of each other. Participation of women in sports continues to trail enrollment rates of women at many colleges, according to the *Chronicle of Higher Education*. Nationally, women constitute 53 percent of the undergraduates on Division I campuses, but only 40 percent of their athletes.

23   The Rev. Terence J. Keegan, the school's executive vice president and designated spokesman, said Providence was fearful of dragging on Title IX compliance, especially after Brown, the Ivy League school across town, fought it in court and lost the case, which cost the school almost $7 million.

24   "We just couldn't risk that kind of litigation," said Keegan, who met with reporters on Saturday, away from the field. "We felt we were backed into a corner."

25   As the game at Hendricken Field continued, Smith was noticeably absent.

26   "We had commencement exercises the following day," Smith later said. "I had three speaking engagements on Saturday, and didn't have a minute's time for anything else."

27   On Saturday, Keegan had offered this explanation: "He was advised that it might be a hostile environment. And we wanted this day and this team not to be mired in ugliness but to go out in a blaze of glory. They deserve that."

28   In the game now, the Friars went ahead by 7-3, with Ciminiello leading the attack with a home run and first baseman Mike O'Keefe adding three hits. In the bottom of the ninth, Villanova scored one run and had runners on first and third with one out.

29   The fans were standing, quiet with expectation. Villanova's Pat King hit a high chopper to Ciminiello at third.

30   "It was an easy ball," recalled Ciminiello, "but my thought was, 'God, just make a good throw to second.' "

31   He did, to start a double play and end the game. Friends and family and parents streamed onto the field, hugging each other and crying. "There wasn't a dry eye among us," Ciminiello said later.

32   "I love it here," said Scott, the right fielder, who went 2 for 5 in the game, and leads the nation with 105 hits. "I love the school. I love the guys. We're a family. I wish I didn't have to leave." But he wants to play college baseball, and he has accepted a partial scholarship to the University of Connecticut.

33   "Strangely enough," said Ciminiello, "the school's decision has been the ultimate motivation for us. We're looking forward to the Big East tournament. And then, we hope, the N.C.A.A. regionals."

34   The Friars' coach, Charlie Hickey, was milling around the field, congratulating people, being congratulated. "This was a special day," he said. "This will be a year that none of us will ever forget."

35   He added, evenly, about Title IX: "It wasn't meant to have this kind of negative impact. We all want fairness. There just has to be another way."

36   The sun had sunk behind trees, and players and fans and family, talking softly, began to drift out of Hendricken Field, for the last time.

ALISA SOLOMON

Twisting and Tainting Title IX

The Village Voice, *an irreverent and influential weekly paper that emphasizes the arts, popular culture, and current events, published the following argument in its Jockbeat column in June 1999. Note that its first line refers to the essay by Ira Berkow included in this section. Alisa Solomon, who played field hockey as a University of Michigan under-graduate before earning a Ph.D. at Yale, is a staff writer at* The Village Voice *who also teaches English and theater courses at Baruch College, City University of New York (CUNY), and at CUNY Graduate Center.*

1   The *Times* runs an Ira Berkow story headlined "The Other Side of Title IX." PBS airs a program called, "Title IX and Women in Sports: What's Wrong with This Picture?" And in a CNN/SI Web site piece, *Sports Illustrated* columnist David Fleming cries, "It's time to deep-six Title IX." And all within just the last few weeks. Look back a little further, and you'll find men moaning in media all over the country that males, poor creatures, have become victims of the 1972 law that outlawed sex discrimination in federally funded educational programs. Jockbeat smells a conspiracy. And it's stinkier than a postgame locker room.

2   Several right-wing public policy groups have seized on Title IX as the latest target of their campaign to undo civil rights legislation. Now that the anti-affirmative action brushfires they set in Texas and California are spreading across the land, they are tossing Title IX into the flames, remembering perhaps better than the rest of us that Title IX had as much to do with creating opportunities for women in science labs as on playing fields. The rhetoric is familiar. As a document from the anti-feminist Independent Women's Forum (one of the leaders of this crusade) puts it: "It is apparent that this law [Title IX] . . . has degenerated into an ever-expanding gender quota system."

3   Why are mainstream media pairing them? First, because IWF and one of its comrades, the Center for Individual Rights, famed for bringing some of the most significant lawsuits challenging affirmative action, aren't exactly making up the facts—they're just twisting them. And the facts are compelling: Men's "minor" sports, such as wrestling, golf, and gymnastics, are being dropped by schools at accelerating rates, and athletic directors often blame Title IX, specifically the requirement that the percentage of women athletes at a school parallel the percentage of female students. Journalists are, unconscionably, taking these athletic directors at their word, and thus repeating the

Big Lie that conservative organizations are pushing. In reality, proportionality is only one of three ways in which a school can comply with Title IX. It may opt, instead, for demonstrating a continuing history of expanding opportunities for women, or show that it is fully accommodating the demand for athletic opportunity from its student body. Title IX is not forcing anybody to eliminate men's programs, and supporters of Title IX, such as the Women's Sports Foundation, do not support that method of compliance.

4   Of course it's the outrageous spending on football and basketball that is gobbling up the men's teams at the bottom of the food chain. Do Division I football teams need 100 players, 85 on scholarship? It doesn't take much shaving of those numbers to save a wrestling squad. Is it really necessary for the whole roster to stay in a hotel the night before a home game? Women's programs could be increased substantially with some judicious cuts that would do no damage to opportunities for football players. But no one—least of all coaches of threatened male teams—has the courage to take the behemoths to the mat. So they're going for the easy takedown: scapegoating the women. Instead, they should be joining forces with women's teams to develop more sensible and equitable programs for all.

5   Meanwhile, the right-wing ideologues are having a field day, adding unabashed manipulation of the press to their efforts. In a recent letter to leaders of top wrestling associations, the full-time director of IWF's Title IX campaign, Kimberly Schuld, brags that IWF was instrumental in getting *U.S. News & World Report, The Wall Street Journal,* and other publications to cover the issue from their point of view. She takes credit for an anti-"quota" *20/20* episode last May, noting how "the show's producer was on the phone several times a week" with her and her colleagues, "who directed the tone of the show." As for the segment on PBS last month, Schuld crows, "I was a key player with the production staff," assisting them on "how to write the story line."

6   But why should facts get in the way of the heart-wrenching drama in Berkow's story of men having to hang up their baseball cleats, or of such teary copy from Fleming, who wonders whether the varsity letter he earned for wrestling at Ohio's Miami U., which just announced eliminating the program, "would look better in the bottom of my trash can"?

7   No such emotion from these guys on the annual stats from Division I schools, published in the *Chronicle of Higher Education* last week: In 1997–98, 40 percent of Division I athletes, but 53 percent of undergraduates, were women. Women received 40 percent of the athletics scholarship budgets, 32 percent of recruiting budgets, 36 percent of total team operating budgets, and only 28 percent of salary expenditures on coaches. Run it by us again, fellas. Who's getting shafted?

Title IX and Scholarship Funds, 2000–2001

Here are the 45 institutions that are in compliance with Title IX rules covering scholarship funds allocated to female athletes. The rules specify that, absent nondiscriminatory circumstances, colleges must award the same proportion of aid (within one percentage point) to female athletes as there are women participating in varsity sports. Athletes who compete in more than one sport are counted only once.

Alabama State University
American University
Appalachian State University
Arkansas State University
Bowling Green State University
College of Charleston
College of the Holy Cross
College of William and Mary
Duke University
East Carolina University
Furman University
George Washington University
Georgia Institute of Technology
Georgia Southern University
Howard University
Illinois State University
Jackson State University
Lafayette College
Mississippi Valley State University
Montana State University at Bozeman
Norfolk State University
Northeastern University
Ohio State University at Columbus

Rutgers University at New Brunswick
South Carolina State University
Southwest Texas State University
Syracuse University
Texas Tech University
University of Akron
University of Alabama at Birmingham
University of Arkansas at Pine Bluff
University of Central Florida
University of Connecticut
University of Iowa
University of Kansas
University of Maine
University of Maryland at College Park
University of North Carolina at Asheville
University of North Carolina at Chapel Hill
University of Richmond
University of Tulsa
University of Virginia
University of Wisconsin at Green Bay
Vanderbilt University
Wofford College

These are the 10 institutions that award the lowest proportion of their scholarships to women:

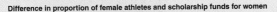

Difference in proportion of female athletes and scholarship funds for women

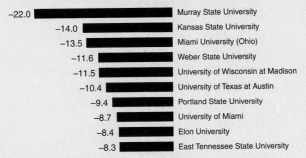

−22.0	Murray State University
−14.0	Kansas State University
−13.5	Miami University (Ohio)
−11.6	Weber State University
−11.5	University of Wisconsin at Madison
−10.4	University of Texas at Austin
−9.4	Portland State University
−8.7	University of Miami
−8.4	Elon University
−8.3	East Tennessee State University

Source: *Chronicle of Higher Education*

CHRISTINE BRENNAN

Colleges Should Kick Off the Excesses of Football

Christine Brennan, a sports columnist for USA Today, *specializes in the Olympics, international sports, and women in sports. She has served as a television commentator for the Olympics since 1984, appears regularly on National Public Radio, ESPN SportsCenter, Nightline, and the* Today *show; and she has written several books. The argument below appeared in her regular* USA Today *column on March 9, 2000.*

1   The news item was jarring in its simplicity: The University of Miami (Florida), which has produced 26 Olympic swimmers and divers, including four-time gold medalist Greg Louganis, is dropping its men's swimming and diving programs to comply with Title IX gender-equity laws.

2   The decision, difficult as it was, put the Hurricanes in good company. In the past 18 years, 30 NCAA Division I schools have dropped men's swimming and diving programs, including UCLA, Illinois, and Arkansas.

3   And it's not just swimming and diving. Men's gymnastics is slowly becoming extinct. There were more than 140 college programs in the 1970s. Now there are 24.

4   What's the problem?

5   College football.

6   I can hear the football coaches screaming already. They'll tell you football isn't the problem, those darn women are. Women and that Title IX, the law signed by President Nixon in 1972 that requires high schools and colleges to give women and girls the same opportunities to participate in sports as men and boys, proportional to the gender enrollment in the student body.

7   To obey this law, colleges either have to add women's programs or cut men's programs or, sometimes, do both. When they don't obey the law—and indeed quite a few of our institutions of higher learning amazingly have treated this law as if it's some kind of half-baked recommendation—they sometimes get sued. And when they get sued, they lose.

8   Equal rights? Proportional opportunity? And a judge and a courtroom in the good ol' USA?

9   You do the math.

10   Which brings us back to football, which, by the way, is a sport I have adored since childhood. Nonetheless, it has become too big and greedy for

today's new collegiate dynamic. With its 85 scholarships and top-heavy budget, football is slowly killing off minor men's sports in America, college programs that often serve as a feeder system for the nation's Olympic teams.

11   Why is this happening? Don't blame Title IX. It's here to stay, as it should be.

12   No, blame the conferences and athletic directors who can't or won't stand up to their football coaches and say, simply, it's time to cut back. It's time to scale down to, say, 70 scholarships. Coaches won't admit it, because they've been spoiled, but a football game can actually be played without 120 kids standing on the sideline in uniform.

13   If football scholarships were decreased, there would be two fascinating results: More of college football's have-nots would get a chance to compete with the behemoths in Division I-A, which would make for more interesting games. And of course, freeing up 15 scholarships on the men's side could save a men's swimming program or two.

14   Instead, colleges are getting into messes like this: Faced with an imbalanced scale tipped too far in favor of its men's sports, Miami nuked a program that brought nothing but respect and honor to the school. That's because swimmers and divers almost always graduate and go on to bigger and better things, which is not necessarily the case with football players.

15   To feel better about scenarios like this, we tell ourselves that football is sacred because it not only pays for itself, it pays for many other sports on campus. That would be fine, except for this:

16   Most college football programs lose money.

17   It's true, according to various surveys. More than 50 percent of Division I-A and I-AA football programs don't pay for themselves, much less any other sport.

18   So explain this to me: Are we really going to wait until there's nothing left but football and women's sports before we wake up and wonder why?

Credits

607: Photo, Courtesy of Nadine Strossen, American Civil Liberties Union

612–617: Diana E. H. Russell, "Nadine Strossen: The Pornography Industry's Wet Dream," December 2, 2002. www.dianarussell.com. Copyright © Diana E. H. Russell.

618–625: Cathleen Cleaver, "The Internet: A Clear and Present Danger?" [speech given at Boston University, October 29, 1997]. Reprinted with permission of the author.

620–623: John Perry Barlow, "A Declaration of the Independence of Cyberspace." Reprinted with the permission of the author.

620: Photo, Courtesy of John Perry Barlow, Electronic Frontier Foundation

626–644: American Civil Liberties Union, "Fahrenheit 451.2: Is Cyberspace Burning?" (March 17, 2002). www.aclu.org. Reprinted by permission of the American Civil Liberties Union.

628–633: Ray Bradbury, Author's Afterword from *Fahrenheit 451*. Reprinted by permission of Don Congdon Associates, Inc. Copyright © 1979 by Ray Bradbury.

645–653: Gregg Easterbrook, "Watch and Learn" from *The New Republic* (May 17, 1999). Reprinted by permission of *The New Republic*. Copyright © 1999 by The New Republic, Inc.

654–659: Henry Louis Gates, Jr., "Truth or Consequences: Putting Limits on Limits" from *Academe* (January/February 1994). Copyright © 1994 by Henry Louis Gates, Jr. Reprinted with the permission of the author.

664–665: From *In Defense of Affirmative Action* by Barbara R. Bergmann. Copyright © 1996 by Basic Books. Reprinted by permission of Basic Books, a member of Perseus Books, LLC.

666–674: Linda Chavez, "Promoting Racial Harmony" from *The Affirmative Action Debate*, edited by George Curry (Reading, Mass.: Addison-Wesley, 1996). Reprinted with the permission of the author.

666: Photo, Courtesy Linda Chavez, Center for Equal Opportunity

675–684: Jesse Jackson, "Save the Dream" speech on October 27, 1997, Sacramento, California. Copyright © Jesse Jackson.

675: Michael S. Green/AP/Wide World Photos

685–691: Judy Lichtman, Jocelyn Frye, and Helen Norton, "Why Women Need Affirmative Action" from *The Affirmative Action Debate*, edited by George Curry (Reading, Mass.: Addison-Wesley, 1996). Reprinted with the permission of National Partnership for Women and Families.

692–701: Roger Wilkins, "Racism Has Its Privileges" from *The Nation* (March 27, 1995). Copyright © 1995 by *The Nation*. Reprinted with permission from the March 27, 1995 issue of *The Nation*.

702–706: Dinesh D'Souza, "Sins of Admission" from *The New Republic* (February 1991). Reprinted with the permission of the author and *The New Republic*. Copyright © 1991 by The New Republic, Inc.

711–722: Michael Lynch, "Title IX's Pyrrhic Victory" from *Reason Online*. Reprinted, with permission, from April 2001 issue of *Reason* magazine. Copyright 2003 by Reason Foundation, 3415 S. Sepulveda Blvd., Suite 400, Los Angeles, CA 90034. www.reason.com.

723–726: Ira Berkow, "The Other Side of Title IX" from *The New York Times* (May 19, 1999). Copyright © 1999 by The New York Times Co. Reprinted by permission.

727–728: Alisa Solomon, "Twisting and Tainting Title IX" from *The Village Voice* (May 26–June 1, 1999). Reprinted with the permission of the author.

729: From the *Chronicle of Higher Education*, May 21, 1999. Copyright © 1999, the *Chronicle of Higher Education*. Reprinted with permission.

730–731: Christine Brennan, "Colleges Should Kick Off the Excesses of Football" from *USA Today* (March 9, 2000). Copyright 2000, USA TODAY. Reprinted with permission.

Other credits appear onpage.

Index